ΙΕΡΟΤΕΛΕΣΤΙΚΟΝ

Fr. Alkiviadis C. Calivas

ΙΕΡΟΤΕΛΕΣΤΙΚΟΝ

A Handbook on
Orthodox Liturgical Practice:
History, Meanings, Challenges

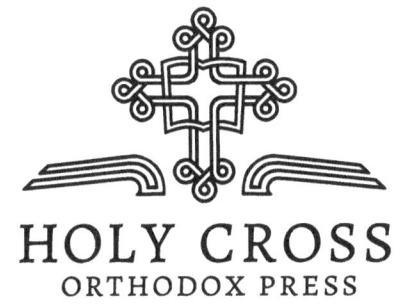

Brookline, Massachusetts

© 2023 Alkiviadis C. Calivas

Published by Holy Cross Orthodox Press
Hellenic College, Inc.
50 Goddard Avenue
Brookline, MA 02445

ISBN: 978-1-935317-96-8

1-935317-96-2

All rights reserved. No part of this publication may be reproduced stored in a retrieval system, or transmitted, in any form or by any means, electronic, mechanical, photocopying, recording or otherwise without the prior permission of Holy Cross Orthodox Press.

Cover art: With thanks to Romfea.gr, Aimilios Polygenis

Interior: page xx courtesy of Romfea.gr, Aimilios Polygenis

Line drawings: pp. 212, Drawing vested clergy by Nicholas, now V. Rev. Maximos Constas; pp. 226 Drawing of Prothesis by Fr. Iakovos Bakos of Simonopetras Monastery.

Publisher's Cataloging-in-Publication

(Provided by Cassidy Cataloguing Services, Inc.)

Names: Calivas, Alkiviadis C., author. | Demetrios, Archbishop of America, 1928- writer of prologue. | Orthodox Eastern Church. Typicon. English

Title: ΙΕΡΟΤΕΛΕΣΤΙΚΟΝ : a handbook on Orthodox liturgical practice: history, meanings, challenges / Fr. Alkiviadis C. Calivas ; prologue by Archbishop Demetrios Trakatellis.

Other titles: Ierotelestikon.

Description: Brookline, Massachusetts : Holy Cross Orthodox Press, [2023] | Revision of the author's "Hierotelestikon: a handbook of rubrics" (Brookline, MA : Holy Cross Greek Orthodox School of Theology, 1984). | Includes bibliographical references.

Identifiers: ISBN: 978-1-935317-96-8 (paperback)

Subjects: LCSH: Orthodox Eastern Church--Liturgy--Texts. | Orthodox Eastern Church--Prayers and devotions--Texts. | Divine office--Orthodox Eastern Church--Texts. | Sacraments--Orthodox Eastern Church--Texts. | Baptism--Orthodox Eastern Church--Texts.

Classification: LCC: BX375.T9 C35 2023 |

Dedicated to

The Seminarians of Holy Cross Greek Orthodox School of Theology
and to all
Who love the beauty of the Lord's house and serve in it

CONTENTS

Prologue 9
Preface 13
Introduction 21
Prelude to the Liturgy: The Byzantine Rite 29

Part One: The Daily Prayer of the Church

An Introduction to the Daily Cycle of Worship 55
  1. The Service of Vespers: its forms, elements, and order ... 67
    A Note on Church Doors 70
    Order of Vespers When a Hierarch Presides 87
    The Service of Artoklasia 90
  2. The Orthros Service: its forms and the elements
    and orderof its two distinct parts,
    one nocturnal the other a morning office 95
    The Morning Gospel 109
    The Ninth Ode and the Censing 116
    The Concluding Elements of the Orthros 120
    A Note on Byzantine Music 128

Part Two: The Holy Sacraments

A Note on the Holy Sacraments 119
The Sacrament of Holy Baptism 122
  The Pre-baptismal Rites for Infants 124
  Celebrating the Service of the Fortieth Day 127
  Infants and Baptism 131
  The Received Rite or Service of Baptism 133
  The Reality of Evil – Guarding Heart 143
  The Catechesis 156
  The Service of Baptism – Proper 161
  Adult Baptism, Clinical Baptism, Reception of Converts ... 177

Part Three: The Divine Liturgy

A Brief Introduction 185
The Preparatory Rites:
Kairos, Vestments and Vesting, and the Lavabo 198
The Proskomide at the Prothesis 217
Celebrating the Divine Liturgy:
Enarxis, Antiphons, and Entrance 240
The Trisagion, its Prayer and Hymn; and the Cathedra 252
The Scripture Readings and Homily 263

Fervent Litany, Catechumens,
Prayers of the Faithful, and Antimension 272
The Great Entrance: Cherubic Hymn,
Prayer of the Cherubikon, Censing, Procession. 278
The Proanaphoral Rites:
Supplications, Prayer, Kiss, Creed 288
The Anaphora or Great Eucharistic Prayer. 306
The Gifts of Holy Communion 320
The Intercessions and the Diptychs 326
The Pre-Communion Rites:
Litany, Communion Prayer, Lord's Prayer,
Peace, and Prayer of Inclination 329
The Communion Rites: Prayer of Elevation, the Elevation
and showing of the Amnos, One is Holy, Communion Hymn,
Who can receive Communion? 338
The Manual Acts: the Fraction, Zeon, and Comminution 348
The Forgotten Practice. 356
Devotional Communion Prayers. 359
Reception of Communion by the Clergy 363
Communion of the People 365
Post-Communion Rites 372
Dismissal Rites:
Payer Behind the Ambon, Prayer of the Skeuophylakion,
the Blessing, Apolysis, Greetings and Acclamations 382
A note on the Antidoron 397
Consuming the Gifts at the Prothesis and a Final Note 398

APPENDICES

A note on the anteri, rason, and kalemaukion 402
On the Color of Vestments 406
A Note on the Kingdom of God 409
What and Where Is Heaven 415
A Word on the Liturgical Homily 419
On the Catechumenate. 422
The Eiliton and Antimension 424
Regarding the Command, "the doors, the doors." 428
The Phrase, "κατά παντα και δια παντα" –
What does it mean?. 431
The Meaning of Sacrifice 433
The Communion Spoon 435
What does God's Inheritance mean 443

PROLOGUE

The academic field of Liturgical Studies constitutes one of the most fascinating fields within the body of theological research and study. It so happens that liturgical studies focused on Orthodox liturgical texts and practices, involve extensive work with texts covering both the Old Testament and the New Testament, early Christian literature, Patristic literature, and the texts published after the fall of Constantinople and up to our days.

At the same time, liturgical studies deal not only with texts but also with liturgical practices, starting with the apostolic and early period of the Church and reaching the twenty-first century, studying everything from the initial worshipping community in Jerusalem to the liturgical practices of the myriads of Orthodox parishes spread today all over the world.

Such an amazing trajectory of the history of Orthodox worship both in terms of relevant texts and concurring applied practices, opens a huge field for promising theological research and contemplation. This explains the impressive scholarly work on liturgical issues related to the Orthodox Church. This also explains the publication in a second more extensive edition of the present important contribution to the Orthodox Liturgical Studies under the title ΙΕΡΟΤΕΛΕΣΤΙΚΟΝ.

The author of this volume, the Reverend Father Dr. Alkiviadis Calivas, had the necessary qualifications to write such a book. He spent many years as the presiding priest of a large parish in New York City with the opportunity of innumerable liturgical activities (Divine Liturgies, sacraments, and various Ἀκολουθίες). He dedicated plenty of his time to his doctoral liturgical studies at the Aristotle University of Thessalonike, where because of his command of the Greek language and the assistance of prominent liturgical scholars there, he had the advantage of reaching and studying significant original liturgical and patristic texts. Perhaps more importantly, he had a most valuable experience of serving for 26 years as the Dean of Holy Cross Greek Orthodox School of Theology in Brookline, Massachusetts and of teaching as Professor of Liturgics at the same School. His multifaceted liturgical practice, worshipping experience, methodical research and dedicated teaching led Protopresbyter Alkiviadis Calivas to produce the present volume as an enlarged and revised edition of his original book on liturgical issues.

The present book under the title ΙΕΡΟΤΕΛΕΣΤΙΚΟΝ, A Handbook on Orthodox Practice: History, Meaning, Challenges, even by its title suggests its importance since it points directly to major areas of Liturgics. Its contents correspond exactly and fully to its title.

More specifically the ΙΕΡΟΤΕΛΕΣΤΙΚΟΝ deals methodically and extensively with the various liturgical services, namely the Divine Liturgies of Saint Basil, Saint John Chrysostom, and the Presanctified Liturgy, the Sacraments (Μυστήρια), and the basic services (Ἀκολουθίαι) of day and night (e.g., Matins, Vespers, etc.). The presentation includes the corresponding texts, the indispensable rubrics, and the history and practice of each service. A thorough discussion accompanies each presentation. In addition, the book offers an impressive footnoting in which the reader will find references to innumerable liturgical texts and studies connected with ancient authors and Fathers of the Church as well as with contemporary prominent scholars in the fertile field of Liturgics. Equally impressive is the lengthy Introduction in which under the sub-titles, The Importance of Rubrics, The Role of the Presiding Celebrant, and Liturgy at its Best, the author offers rich insightful liturgical information.

Furthermore, this second edition of ΙΕΡΟΤΕΛΕΣΤΙΚΟΝ contains a number of special discussions on challenges related to contemporary liturgical practices by the Orthodox Churches, showing always the decisive importance and authoritative nature of the relevant texts and directives originating in the Ecumenical Patriarchate of Constantinople.

The ΙΕΡΟΤΕΛΕΣΤΙΚΟΝ is a book displaying an impeccable and impressive scholarship. At the same time the book displays a strong spirituality and an emphasis on the worshipping of God as the ultimate purpose of any studies in the field of Liturgics. Such a combination of pure scholarship and genuine spirituality is a remarkable achievement which in addition to other elements establishes the truly great value of the book.

Certainly, the ΙΕΡΟΤΕΛΕΣΤΙΚΟΝ is a book that should be in the personal library of all clergy of our Greek Orthodox Archdiocese of America. And beyond that its author the Reverend Protopresbyter Dr. Alkiviadis Calivas, deserves our sincere thanks and our warmest congratulations for his precious offering to the Church and to theology especially the branch of Liturgics.

+Archbishop Demetrios Trakatellis,Ph.D.,Th.D.

Formerly of America

PREFACE

The first humble version of the Ἱεροτελεστικόν was prepared hurriedly in 1984 to meet the immediate needs of the students of Holy Cross Greek Orthodox School of Theology who were preparing for ordination. My intention at the time was to review, revise, and expand the original text, which was in the form of class notes, within five years of its initial distribution. For a variety of reasons, however, in spite of good intentions and three attempts, the goal was never met or completed until now with the publication of this volume, Book One of the revised *Ierotelestikon*.

I remember fondly with gratitude my faculty assistant, Br. Charles-Kyriakos S. Anthony, now Director of the Panagia Center at the Convent of the Annunciation in Ormylia, Greece, who helped me in the production of the original text, and the two students who graciously provided me with the art work: V. Rev. Dr. Maximos Constas, now Director of the Pappas Patristic Institute and Professor of Patristics and Orthodox Spirituality at Holy Cross, and Fr. Iakovos Bakos, a priest-monk at the Holy Monastery of Simonopetra on Mt. Athos.

With equal fondness and gratitude, I remember three other beloved faculty assistants who sequentially offered me their kind assistance in my failed attempts to revise and expand the original text: Fr. Theodore Barbas, the longtime Chancellor of the Metropolis of Boston, Rev. Dr. Perry Hamalis and Rev. Dr. Stefanos Alexopoulos, now distinguished academicians. I am also grateful to my beloved colleague, Rev. Dr. Philip Zymaris, Professor of Liturgics at Holy Cross, who used the original text as a student and continues to share it with his students in his liturgics and teleturgics courses. At his urging I decided to finally undertake the revision of the original text. I am indebted also to my former student, friend, and concelebrant Fr. Luke Kontgas who offered to scan the original version and provide me with a computer-ready text from which to produce the present revised and expanded version. Thanks are also due to my beloved son-in-law Fr. Thomas Chininis, for his technical assistance and pastoral insights.

Special thanks are due to Fr. Peter A. Chamberas, a valued friend and respected colleague. A distinguished pastor, theologian, writer, and translator, Fr. Peter graciously reviewed the entire manuscript and the Greek texts, offering valuable comments and advice. I am deeply appreciative of his efforts and indebted to him for his many acts of kindness.

I wish also to express my deep appreciation to several of my beloved colleagues and friends who graciously agreed to read portions of the text and offer their valued and constructive suggestions: His Eminence Metropolitan Savas of Pittsburgh, Rev. Dr. Romanos Karanos, Rev. Dr. Eugen Pentiuc, Rev. Dr. Theodore Stylianopoulos, and Dr. Lewis Patsavos.

I am indebted to Sister Nectaria McLees, an accomplished author, translator, and editor of the journal, *Road to Emmaus*, who meticulously read the entire manuscript and improved it with her keen editorial eye. Thanks are also due to Mr. Michael Hostetler, the copy editor, and Fr. David Eynon, the graphic designer, for their methodical work.

I am grateful also for the support provided by the Holy Cross Greek Orthodox School of Theology, which I thank in the person of its President, Mr. George M. Cantonis, and its Dean, Rev. Dr. George Parsenios. I especially acknowledge and thank the publisher, Holy Cross Orthodox Press, its Director, Archimandrite Anton Vrame, Ph.D., and the Editorial Committee of the press for accepting my manuscript and guiding it into print. The suggestions of Fr. Vrame were particularly helpful.

Most especially, I am indebted and deeply grateful to His Eminence DEMETRIOS, the highly esteemed Former Archbishop of America, the eminent biblical scholar, insightful theologian, and gifted teacher, a beloved friend and valued colleague on the Holy Cross Faculty—a cultured man of diverse gifts and an exemplar of Christian virtue—for contributing the Foreword to this book, an honor of the highest degree.

With profound appreciation for his generosity and support of the priestly ministry, I remember in prayer the late George J. Tatakis, a devout Orthodox Christian, whose devotion to family, heritage, and church was exemplary. His espousal of noble causes and endeavors in support of the Church's mission in the world is worthy of praise, gratitude, and emulation. May he, together with his beloved wife Lola, a church musician, be remembered in prayer by everyone who reads and uses this book. May George and Lola rest in peace among the Just in the Kingdom of Heaven.

The Introduction, which follows this Preface, highlights the importance of rubrics, the role of the presider-celebrant, and the need for orderly worship – which is to say, liturgy at its best.[1] The Prelude to the Liturgy that follows the Introduction provides the reader with an introduction to the Byzantine rite, the development of the Typikon, and a brief account of the liturgical books of the Church. This is followed by Part One, which contains a survey of the daily prayer of the Church and the divine services that comprise it, including a detailed outline of each service as it is conducted and practiced in the Greek Orthodox Archdiocese of America. Comments both in the text and in the footnotes offer the reader extensive explanations and clarifications on the various components and rubrical directives of the services under discussion. Part Two deals with the pre-baptismal and baptismal rites of the Church. Part Three focuses on the Divine Liturgy. All these together constitute Book One of the revised Ierotelestikon—*A Handbook on Orthodox Liturgical Practice*. The Books that will follow, should the Lord allow it, will deal with the other sacraments and divine services of the Church for which a parish priest is essentially responsible.

Much of what is written in the present volume is drawn largely from my lectures in the courses on liturgics, teleturgics, and sacramental theology which I was privileged to teach at Holy Cross and from the published materials that I was able to produce through the years.

With paternal love and affection I dedicate the new and expanded edition of the Ierotelestikon to the seminarians of Holy Cross Greek Orthodox School of Theology and to my former students, now ordained deacons, priests, and bishops—beloved and respected concelebrants—serving here and abroad, whom I was privileged to teach during my years at Holy Cross.

I am filled with great admiration for four of the alumni of our school who have excelled in advanced liturgical studies and are now teaching in prestigious universities or major seminaries and are contributing to the understanding of liturgical theology and practice as they mine the riches of our Orthodox liturgical tradition and explain its inner meanings through their research, writings, and teaching: Rev. Dr. Stefanos Alexopoulos, Dr. John Klentos, Rev. Dr. Stelyios Muksuris, and Rev. Dr. Philip Zymaris.

In addition to the seminarians of Holy Cross, I dedicate this volume to the unsung heroes of our parishes who love the beauty of the Lord's house and serve in it, enriching parish worship through their God-given talents and

---

1 The words worship (λατρεία) and liturgy (λειτουργία) are used interchangeably and denote the whole range of the Church's divine services and sacred rites. The term Divine Liturgy (Θεία Λειτουργία) is used to denote the sacred service by which the Orthodox Church celebrates the sacrament of the Holy Eucharist.

devoted service: the chanters, choir members, readers, catechists, sextons, and altar servers together with the countless *φιλακόλουθοι* – the devout worshippers who love and find solace and meaning in the divine services of our Church.

It is my hope that the new and revised Ierotelestikon will help the reader – clergy as well as laypeople – understand better the sacred rites of the Church, come to love them more deeply, appreciate and rejoice in their beauty, and draw strength and courage from them on their pilgrimage of faith. *"So I will go about your altar, O Lord, singing aloud a song of thanksgiving and telling all your wondrous deeds. O Lord, I love the habitation of your house, and the place where your glory dwells"* (Ps. 25/26:7-8).[2]

A special word to our beloved seminarians: I urge you to study the Church's superb liturgical texts in the original or in translation with great care and unremitting attention so that you may come to appreciate their theological depth and beauty. Learn from everything the liturgy offers you and be inspired by it. Be mindful of the fact that the Church is primarily a worshipping community and that authentic worship is a window into the mind and ethos of the Orthodox Church. Should the liturgical life of your parish become devoid of energy—opaque, uninspiring, or trivial—the parish's witness and mission to the world will suffer greatly. Therefore, every priest is obliged to maintain the liturgical life of the community in a mode of constant valuation and regeneration. The work begins with you. As priests (ἱερεῖς) and ministers (λειτουργοί) of the sacred mysteries, the people under your care will expect you to preside at and celebrate the sacred rites with joy, faith, and deep reverence; preach the word of God with power; teach the truths of the faith with conviction; and pastor the faithful under your care with an all-embracing love and concern. Be vigilant, therefore, and take care. *"Do not neglect the gift you have, which was given you by prophetic utterance when the council of elders laid their hands upon you. Practice these duties, devote yourself to them, so that all men may see your progress"* (1 Tim. 4:14-15).

I pray the Ἱεροτελεστικόν, in some small way, will contribute to your priestly formation and prepare you for the awesome responsibilities that you will be called to undertake. Keep the words of our Lord Jesus Christ which he spoke to his disciples at the Last Supper deep in your hearts: *"You did not choose me, but I chose you and appointed you that you should go and bear fruit and that your fruit should abide."* (John 15:16).

Let me also address a note of gratitude to the devoted ministers of song, word, and service—the lovers of the beauty of Lord's house—the *singers* who sing

---

2 An alternative reading from the Septuagint text: "I will go about your altar, O Lord, that I may hear the sound of your praise and declare all your wondrous deeds. Lord, I love the beauty of your house and the dwelling place of your glory" (Ps. 25: 6-8).

and make melody to the Lord and give voice to the joy of the worshippers; the *readers* who communicate the word of God with grace and conviction and warm the worshippers' hearts; the *catechists* who instruct the young with great devotion and help edify them in the faith; the *servers* who delight in preserving the good order of the Lord's house; and the devout *Council members* who are attentive to the needs of the congregants and the temple. Each of you, both personally and collectively, in your specific role and service reflects the sense of correctness and excellence concerning the rituals which God's people enact in faith in the Lord's House.

Let us all, clergy and laypeople alike, remember the words of St. Hesychios the Priest (ca. 8th-9th century), "*Light is the property of a star, as simplicity and humility are the property of a holy and God-fearing people. Nothing distinguishes more clearly the disciples of Christ than a humble spirit and a simple way of life.*"

Fr. Alkiviadis C. Calivas,

Professor Emeritus of Liturgics,
Holy Cross Greek Orthodox School of Theology, Brookline, MA
Feast of St. Mary Magdalene – July 22, 2020

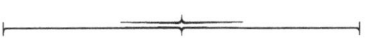

Historical Note

The final draft of this study was completed in mid-July of 2020, during the unprecedented period of the global pandemic, the Corona Virus—COVID-19, a contagion with lethal force which first appeared in 2019 and upended all social, economic, political, cultural, and religious norms worldwide. The pandemic was, in large measure, also the reason for the delay in the publication of this text. By the winter of 2019—2020 the pandemic was already wreaking havoc throughout the world, marked daily by thousands of deaths. From mid-March of 2020 throughout the country all divine services were conducted within closed doors by only the priest(s), chanter, and altar server of each community. The services were live-streamed to the faithful wherever the technology was available. Baptisms and weddings were postponed, except for emergencies. Funerals were conducted in the presence of close family members only. All parish activities were suspended, except for those that could be conducted via Zoom or other similar forms of contact. Quarantines or "Stay in Place" requirements, and mandates for the use of face masks in public areas were strictly observed. Access to public buildings was severely limited. Churches, schools, work places, government offices, restaurants, gymnasiums, and arenas were closed. Professional sports were played in empty stadiums. Remote learning and work became the new norm. Hospitals and nursing homes were overwhelmed and admitted only the seriously ill and the dying. Visitors, including close family members, were not permitted. Early in the pandemic, the availability of medical equipment was limited. In large urban areas, temporary hospital units were made available as were temporary morgues to house the dead. All forms of social intercourse were disrupted. Even the 2020 Clergy-Laity Congress of the Greek Orthodox Archdiocese was conducted virtually. Gradually, the churches, workplaces, and other public institutions were opened under the strict protocols and guidelines issued by federal, state and local governments. These guidelines were operative in most States through the winter of 2021-2022 and beyond.

Early in 2021, a variant of COVID-19, Delta, raised new alarms worldwide. In November and December of 2021, a new and more contagious variant, Omicron, also made its appearance, to be followed shortly thereafter by a subvariant of Omicron, raising new fears and concerns among government officials and medical experts. The development of new vaccines and booster shots helped to stem the tide but the dangers remain and so the orderly life of peoples and their institutions remains tenuous. Even now in mid-2022, concerns have been expressed for a possible new surge of other new variants of the demonic COVID-19 virus. May the Lord God deliver us from the perils of the dreadful pandemic. And may the Lord shed his grace upon the doctors, nurses, and medical staffs, the scientists and researchers, and the first-responders and essential workers who have served and continue to serve the people of the world in these troubling times of anguish and distress.

Another Note

After the completion of the final draft of this text and its submission for publication several important articles and books have been published, which warrant the reader's attention. Of these, let me cite the following: Evangelist, Shepherd, and Teacher: Studies in Honor of Archbishop Demetrios of America, James Skedros, Archimandrite Maximos Constas, and Vasiliki M. Limberis, editors (HCOP, Brookline, MA 2020); For the Life of the World: Toward a Social Ethos of the Orthodox Church, David Bentley Hart and John Chryssavgis, editors (HCOP Brookline, MA 2020). Archbishop Job Getcha, The Euchologion Unveiled: An Explanation of Byzantine Liturgical Practice II (Yonkers, NY 2021); Introduction to Eastern Christian Liturgies, Stefanos Alexopoulos and Maxwell E. Johnson, editors (); and the new Ieratikon published by the Ecumenical Patriarchate (Piraeus, 2020). These volumes and other important works not mentioned here contain valuable information and references to the Orthodox liturgical tradition and practice.

INTRODUCTION

1. The Importance of Rubrics

> *Since all these things are clear to us, and we have looked into the depths of divine knowledge, we ought in proper order to do all things which the Lord has commanded us to perform at appointed times. He has commanded offerings and ministrations to be carried out, and not carelessly or disorderly, but at fixed seasons and times/hours. He has himself fixed according to his surpassing counsel where and by whom he desires them to be performed, in order that all things may be done in holy fashion according to his good pleasure and acceptable to his will. Those who make their offerings at the appointed times, therefore, are acceptable and blessed, for they err not, following ordinances of the Lord. For the high-priest [bishop] has been allotted his proper ministrations, and to the priests their proper place has been assigned, and on the Levites [deacons] their own duties are laid. The layman is bound by lay ordinances.*
>
> St. Clement of Rome,
First Letter to the Corinthians: 40 – ca. 96 AD.

This text is important for several reasons. It tells us that the Church in the first century had already developed a rule of prayer that consisted of different services that may be classified as eucharistic and non-eucharistic. The text also refers to fixed prayer times and to a rudimentary festal calendar. In addition, it speaks about liturgical space and a variety of liturgical ministries and roles – where and by whom. Moreover, the text claims without hesitation that the liturgical practices championed by the author are based on a received tradition that comes from the Lord; and that these customs and ritual activities are appropriate to the Church and should be observed with due cáre and conducted in proper order. One may, therefore, reach the conclusion that the text provides us with the foundational elements that in time would constitute a liturgical tradition and rite and a written or printed manual of directives – rubrics (the *Typikon*).[1]

From all that is said about prayer and worship in the New Testament (Acts 2:42, 46; 1 Cor. 14:26, 40; 2 Thess. 2:15; Ephes. 5:19) and in early Christian literature, we can safely assume that the Church favored orderly prayer and developed a well-organized system of worship from the start. As liturgical rites grew through the centuries, rubrics were also developed to protect their orderly practice.

At the beginning, the directives for the performance of the various ceremonials and rituals of the divine services were conveyed, for the most part, orally. Even now, when the rubrics of a given ritual are spelled out, an oral tradition is presupposed, as no rubric is in and of itself complete or capable of transmitting all the nuances of a particular liturgical act, gesture, or movement.

Parenthetically, the same could be said about this volume: its incompleteness. The liturgy is like a deep treasure chest, whose riches and complexities cannot be adequately explored and set forth in one or two volumes. One question, one fact, one insight leads to another and another.[2]

Manuals of rubrics, as I have noted elsewhere, began to appear after the tenth century. These directives (διατάξεις) – called rubrics in English from the Latin word *rubrica*, meaning red – were written in red ink to distinguish them from the text of the prayers and litanies. The practice continues to the present. Rubrical manuals as separate liturgical books fell into disuse centuries ago. The need for such resources was obviated when the ceremonial directives

---

1 *The Didache of the Twelve Apostles*, the earliest of the Church Orders, which some scholars believe to be a composite document that developed in stages (beginning as early 50-70 AD), consists of two parts. The first deals with Christian morals and the second with liturgical practices, including valuable directives related to baptism, the Eucharist, penance, ministry, fasting, and the Lord's Prayer. It also gives the text of the Prayer, which is to be prayed three times a day. *The Didache* like the Letter of Clement of Rome provides further evidence that the early Church had an orderly rule of prayer.

2 I use the word liturgy to denote the full range of the Church's services, and I apply the term Divine Liturgy to designate the sacrament of the Holy Eucharist. The liturgy includes all the sacred rites of the Orthodox Church that comprise its rule of prayer.

were placed initially at the beginning of the service books and, later, when the rubrics were interpolated at the appropriate places in the texts.

Of the many manuals that appeared between the twelfth and fourteenth centuries, none proved to be more influential than the two written by Philotheos Kokkinos, twice patriarch of Constantinople (1353 - 1355 and 1364 - 1376).[3] His rubrics gained universal recognition as part of the liturgical reforms that took place in the wake of the hesychastic controversy and were gradually incorporated into the divine services of the Greek Church. In fact, the rubrics were incorporated into the first printed edition (*editio princeps*) of the Divine Liturgies published by Demetrios Doukas the Cretan in 1526.[4] Though changes have been made through the centuries, the rubrics of Philotheos retain their vitality to this day.

Rubrics are not an end unto themselves, to be used blindly, arbitrarily, or in isolation. They are best understood in terms of language and grammatical rules, a metaphor suggested by the noted liturgical scholar, Aidan Kavanagh. "The adequacy of liturgical celebration," he writes, "rests upon [rubrics] as adequacy of language rests upon rules of grammar. And while grammatical rules alone will not produce a great speech any more than liturgical rubrics alone will result in a great act of celebration, neither great speech nor great liturgy can afford to ignore the rules basic to each without risking the collapse of both."[5]

Fr. Alexander Schmemann likens rubrics to canons: "the relationship of the written rubrics to worship is analogous to the relationship of the canons to the structure of the Church. The canons did not create the Church or determine her structure; they arose for the defense, clarification, and definition of that structure, which already existed...The written ordo does not so much determine the law of worship as it adapts this law to this or that need."[6]

Rubrics are meant to provide continuity in liturgical practice and ethos, secure recognizable standards and good liturgical order, and maintain a balanced

---

3 The two manuals of Philotheos Kokkinos are *The Diataxis of the Diaconate* with rubrics for the daily office and the *Diataxis of the Divine Liturgy*.

4 Demetrios Doukas, Αἱ θεῖαι Λειτουργίαι τοῦ ἁγίου Ἰωάννου τοῦ Χρυσοστόμου, Βασιλείου τοῦ Μεγάλου, καὶ ἡ τῶν Προηγιασμένων (Rome 1526). By 1800 the volume was published sixty times. Significantly, the eighth-century commentary on the Divine Liturgy by Patriarch Germanos of Constantinople (+733) was included in Doukas' volume. On the commentary of St. Germanos, see Paul Meyendorff, *St. Germanus of Constantinople on the Divine Liturgy* (Crestwood, NY 1984).

5 Aidan Kavanagh, Elements of Rite (New York 1982) 3.

6 Alexander Schmemann, *Introduction to Liturgical Theology* (Crestwood, NY 1996) 39-40.

and healthy tension between tradition and life. The *Typikon*, the book which contains liturgical rubrics – or the order of liturgical celebration – underscores an essential fact: the liturgy is an act of the whole Church, clergy and laity, not of a particular individual or group.[7]

Good liturgical order requires vigilance. The received rites must not become prey to those who would impose their subjective antiquarianisms or arbitrary experimentations upon the liturgy. Subjective liturgical experiments usually produce trivial liturgy and result in making trivial Christians. While qualified persons may propose changes and work diligently to achieve them, in the end, when all is said and done, the local Church acting judiciously is the final arbiter and the responsible agent of liturgical change and not an individual priest or community. Otherwise, chaos would prevail, and the liturgy would not only lose its authenticity and catholicity, but also be robbed of its dignity and vitality.

2. The Role of the Presider Celebrant

The clergy are set apart by ordination. They are ordained to lead, teach, and guide the people, to preside over the divine services, and to sanctify the lives of the faithful through the holy sacraments. The clergy draw their authority from Christ. In the execution of their duties and tasks, the clergy act as ministers of Christ. The clergy, however, do not possess any *individual* power apart from and independent of the ministry of the laity. No one order or person stands apart from and/or above the Church. The clergy and the people together constitute the Body of Christ and partake equally of the same salvation wrought by our Lord Jesus Christ.[8] At the liturgy, no one is a mere spectator, as the liturgy is the work of all the people.

The liturgy is, first of all, an act of God. The Triune God draws us unto himself through the liturgy to renew our spirit and sanctify our lives. Thus, the prayer of the Church is primarily a response – an offering in return for God's abundant mercy and love and a praise of thanksgiving for his mighty acts in creation and salvation history.

---

[7] For a comprehensive study of the typikon and Orthodox liturgical practice, see the excellent work of Archbishop Job Getcha, *The Typikon Decoded: An Explanation of Byzantine Liturgical Practice*, Paul Meyendorff, trans. (Yonkers, NY 2012) and Konstantinos Papayiannis, Σύστημα Τυπικοῦ τῶν Ἱερῶν Ἀκολουθιῶν τοῦ ὅλου Ἐνιαυτοῦ (Athens, 2006). See also Calivas, *Aspects of Orthodox Worship*, 63-101.

[8] On the diverse but interdependent gifts, responsibilities, roles, and duties of the clergy and the laity, see Alkiviadis Calivas, *Church, Clergy, Laity, and the Spiritual Life* (Brookline, MA 2013), 1-63.

Of the many activities the Church enacts in the world, four are constitutive of her nature, or being, and are thus indispensable: worship, evangelization, catechesis, and philanthropy.[9] Indeed, the effectiveness of the Church's mission in the world is measured against her ability to perform these four fundamental activities or ministries with due diligence, competence, vigor, faithfulness, confidence, and boldness. And the responsibility for doing these things faithfully, effectively, and dynamically rests chiefly with the clergy, and specifically with hierarchs and priests.

The Church is, first and foremost, a worshipping community and Christians are, above all else, liturgical or worshipping beings. Hence, worship, the gathering of the people humbly and joyfully before God in prayer and solemn feast, is the Church's primary activity. The liturgy is the matrix by which the other essential activities of the Church are formed, informed, taught, and enacted. The evangelization of the world, i.e., the proclamation of the Good News of salvation, always starts at the liturgy with the preaching of the Word with power and conviction. Catechesis, the 'doing of theology', is accomplished primarily through the liturgy, the unique setting in which the Church remembers, imparts, and celebrates her faith – the revealed truths about the Triune God and the created order – through word, song, symbol, and ritual. The liturgy is the Church's faith in motion, conveying, recommending, and instilling in the worshipper a particular vision and way of life centered on God's righteousness and self-giving love. The liturgy also inspires and calls upon both the individual worshipper and the worshipping community to imitate God's goodness and mercy, so that both individually and collectively, they can initiate and accomplish works of love or philanthropy.

For the liturgy to be an educative, formative, evocative, restorative, and transformative experience, all of God's people – clergy and laity alike – must acquire a liturgical mind, meaning that they are willing to pursue and accomplish, according to the desire and capacity of each, the following: harvest, grasp, and apply the doctrinal, ethical, and devotional riches of the liturgy to everyday life so that the truths of the faith are not barren abstractions but hymns of exulting praise and bright guideposts that direct worshippers toward the depths of divine wisdom so that they may learn to live by the Spirit (Gal. 5:25) and thereby "do justice, love kindness, and walk humbly with God" (Micah 6:8).

Hence a priest is obliged to make every liturgical service *liturgy at its best*, which is to say, an aesthetically, intellectually, emotionally, and spiritually enriching experience so that both he and the worshippers may move beyond

---

9 Ibid., 65-87.

the ordinary, beyond the confines of naïve religiosity. Spiritual worship, clothed in form and language, must be performed in faith with sober splendor, devotion, earnestness, passion, and joyfulness.

Consequently, every celebrant who presides at the sacred mysteries should be genuine, faithful, humble, and true to his calling, ever mindful of the gift of priesthood bestowed upon him. He is obliged to cultivate a prayerful spirit and a serene bearing; acquire a deep love for the liturgy by studying, understanding, and embracing it; be respectful of tradition;[10] and value good order. Above all, he must be in awe of the holy place in which he stands (Exod. 3:5), humbly offering gifts and spiritual sacrifices to the Triune God on behalf of, for, and with the people entrusted to his loving care. Especially, he must be a man whose soul is aflame with divine passion in his love for Christ.

3. Liturgy at Its Best

Through the liturgy, we live and breathe our Orthodox faith and reaffirm our ultimate identity, purpose, and destiny, both as persons and as the Church. Hence, the liturgy in all its varied components must be loved, studied, analyzed, learned, and, above all, lived. The liturgy is more than texts, words, songs, gestures, ceremonials, and rubrics. It is the meeting ground of heaven and earth, the place where faithful people meet the self-giving of God and where, through this encounter, they meet their own human lives in unexpected form.

As I have noted elsewhere, the liturgy is an act of God, as indicated by the deacon's address to the presiding celebrant before the start of the Divine Liturgy, "It is time for the Lord to act" (Psalm 118/119:126).[11] In worship, the eternal God, who is described as "ineffable, beyond comprehension, invisible, beyond understanding, existing forever and always the same,"[12] brings us to himself as a child their father and admits us to an area of non-death. In the liturgy, the Word and Son of God, our Lord Jesus Christ, is present to his people, fulfilling his promise to be in their midst when they gather together in his name (Matt. 18:20).

For this reason, every priest is obliged to pay special attention to the essential elements that constitute the liturgical experience of the faith community, namely, time, space, action, speech, art, and song. Worship operates best

---

10 Tradition is not only a protective and conserving principle; it is also a principle of regeneration and growth. The Church is always in a mode of creative continuity. Authentic worship is changeless and changing, ageless but also adaptable. It is traditional but also relevant, in a mode of continuous renewal. See Alkiviadis Calivas, *The Liturgy in Dialogue: Exploring and Renewing the Tradition* (Brookline, MA 2018).

11 Calivas, *Aspects of Orthodox Worship*, 5-7.

12 From the Anaphora of the Divine Liturgy of St. John Chrysostom.

when it stirs the hearts and minds of the worshippers and engages the people actively in the liturgical action.

Worship becomes most attractive and effective when performed with faith and characterized by simplicity, beauty, clarity, directness, solemnity, and joyful dignity. Many factors contribute to a healthy liturgical environment and a meaningful liturgical experience. An inspired priestly celebration and a coherent and persuasive homily are basic crucial elements. The performance of liturgical actions with grace and dignity as well as the reading of Scripture lessons and other texts with care and conviction are also important. The quality of liturgical music and singing is crucial. The prayerful attentiveness of the congregation and its ability to respond gracefully with voice and posture equally crucial.

Every priest must know that the parish he serves is, above all else, a fundamental eucharistic cell of the Church, in which the saving work of the Church is actively pursued and enacted. The parish exists for one essential purpose, namely, to bring salvation to the world through the celebration of the sacraments, the preaching of the Word, the teaching the Orthodox faith, and the caring for the least of the brethren. Everything the parish is and does emanates from these four activities, and especially from the weekly celebration of the Divine Liturgy.[13]

---

13 Calivas, *Aspects of Orthodox Worship*, 235-48.

A PRELUDE TO THE LITURGY: THE BYZANTINE RITE

1. The Byzantine Rite: A Synthesis of Liturgical Riches

It is well known that the Byzantine liturgical rite (Βυζαντινὸς λειτουργικὸς τύπος), also known as the Constantinopolitan rite, constitutes the final unification of liturgical practice in the Orthodox Church.[14] As the primary ecclesial see of the Christian East, Constantinople, the great imperial city, became the receptacle of the liturgical traditions of the leading liturgical centers of the East: Antioch (Syria), Jerusalem (Palestine), Caesarea in Cappadocia (Pontus), and Heraclea (Thrace). In addition to the reception, assimilation, and synthesis of the liturgical riches of these centers, the Byzantine rite also represents the intermingling of cathedral and monastic practices. The rite passed through various stages of development and, as Fr. Robert Taft notes, is "renowned for the sumptuousness of its ceremonial and liturgical symbolism, and the heritage of the imperial splendors of Constantinople before the eighth century. [It] gradually synthesized during the ninth to the fourteenth centuries in the monasteries of the Orthodox world, beginning in the period of the struggle with Iconoclasm."[15]

---

14 For more on the Byzantine Rite, see Robert F. Taft, *The Byzantine Rite: A Short History* (Collegeville, MN 1992). See also Calivas, *Aspects of Orthodox Worship,* 54-101.

15 Robert Taft, *The Byzantine Rite* (Collegeville, MN 1992), 16.

The Byzantine rite spread steadily far and wide and became the common inheritance of all the Orthodox Churches, albeit with minor local variations, having supplanted the native rites of the other ancient patriarchates of the East. This happened not by any imposition, force, or synodical decree but simply by practice. For Theodore Balsamon, the noted canonist and patriarch of Antioch (d. 1214), the Byzantine rite was the established liturgical practice of his day, as evidenced by his response to Mark, patriarch of Alexandria, concerning the correctness of celebrating the ancient liturgies attributed to the holy Apostles James the Brother of the Lord and Mark the Evangelist. "All the Churches of God," Balsamon wrote, "must follow the custom of the New Rome, which is Constantinople, and celebrate the liturgy according to the tradition of those great Church Fathers and beacons of piety, St. John Chrysostom and St. Basil."

As with all classical rites, the Byzantine rite is composed of several basic components and by certain characteristic theological and ritual attributes. The rite has a wide range of liturgical services, including three eucharistic liturgies, sacramental rites, and other occasional services. It also has a daily office, a lectionary system, and a calendar of feasts and fasts. In addition, it has distinctive and highly developed forms of the liturgical arts, i.e., architecture, iconography, hymnography, music, and textiles.

The history of the Byzantine rite is intimately related to the history of the *cathedral rite* and the rise and subsequent domination of the *monastic rite*.[16] Monasticism defined as a community of persons committed to personal sanctification living apart from the Christian community in the world originated in the third century, long after the Church's establishment. Thus, the early Church's parochial forms of communal worship, which would eventually evolve into the cathedral rite, predate the monastic.

2. A Note on the Cathedral Rite

The term *cathedral rite* comes from the hierarch's church, known as the cathedral, which was from the earliest times the center of the Church's liturgical life.[17] During the first two centuries, the people gathered at one Eucharist united under the leadership of one hierarch.[18] When individual parishes began to emerge under the leadership of priests in the mid-to-late

---

16 For a brief account on the development of the cathedral and monastic offices, see Calivas, *Aspects*, 63-101.

17 For a representative list of sources on the cathedral rite of Constantinople see Calivas, *Aspects of Orthodox Worship*, 259-60.

18 See John D. Zizioulas, *Eucharist, Bishop, Church* (Brookline, MA 2001).

third century,[19] the liturgical usages of the cathedral were emulated by the parishes. Simply stated, what was done in the cathedral was done in the parishes, although on a smaller scale.

In the East, the Cathedral of Hagia Sophia in Constantinople emerged as the single most significant church and its usages played a decisive role in the formation of the liturgical rites of the imperial city and eventually the Orthodox Church as a whole. The Cathedral rite of Constantinople was also known as the Secular Office (Κοσμικὴ Ἀκολουθία) in contrast to the monastic and as the Sung Office (Ἀσματικὴ Ἀκολουθία) because everything was either sung or intoned. The Cathedral rite included the whole array of services that constituted a rite, all of which have survived to the present day in one form or another. A major exception was its daily office, which consisted of four services: Vespers, Pannychis (a type of vigil), Orthros, and Trithekte (a service for the late morning hours). The cathedral daily office differed from its monastic counterpart in the number, content, structure, order, spirit, and purpose of its services. For example, the cathedral daily office was usually celebrated only twice daily, once in the evening (Vespers) and once in the morning (Orthros).[20] When a nocturnal vigil was indicated for a given feast, the Pannychis followed the Vespers. On fast days, when the Divine Liturgy was not celebrated, the service of Trithekte was celebrated in the late morning, between the Third (τρίτη) and Sixth (ἕκτη) Hours.

Although the daily services of the Cathedral Office gradually fell into disuse, many of their elements were incorporated into the monastic daily office.

3. A Note on the Monastic Rite

All monastic communities are governed by certain rules that are codified in the community's typikon. The typikon of a monastery usually includes three parts: the community's rule of life, rule of governance, and rule of prayer (the order and type of its divine services). In the early monastic typika, the rule of prayer was fairly simple, reflecting the sober contemplative ethos of early monastic prayer. However, as the daily office became more elaborate, the later typika began to contain an ever-greater amount of liturgical material and detail. The monastic liturgical tradition of the Orthodox Church originates from the typikon of the Great Lavra (a community of anchorites) founded by

---

19 On the development of the parish see Ibid., 197-246.

20 In 530, Emperor Justinian issued a decree ordering the daily celebration of Vespers and Orthros in the churches to which clergy were assigned.

St. Savas (+532) in the Judean desert southeast of Jerusalem in 484.[21] Because of its prestige, the usages of this great monastic center became an authoritative model for large segments of Eastern monasticism.

Desert monasticism, however, would eventually compete with an emerging urban monastic movement which would also play a significant role in the development of the style and structures of ecclesial governance and on the shape of the Church's liturgy. One such important urban community was the Monastery of Studios founded in Constantinople in 454. The monastery prospered until 765, but thereafter fell into decline due to attacks from iconoclasts. In 798 or 799, a learned monk, Theodore, who was to be called "the Studite," arrived in Constantinople with a company of monks and took up residence in the Monastery of Stoudios and laid the foundations for a new cenobitic community. To invigorate the life and mission of his newly founded community, St. Theodore invited monks from the Lavra of St. Savas to join as he began a program of reforms that would greatly influence the development of Orthodox monasticism and have lasting effects on Orthodox worship.

At Studios, St. Theodore created a new order of services, often referred to as the Studite synthesis, which was essentially the combination of elements from the monastic office of St. Savas with the cathedral or sung office of Constantinople. He grafted the prayers and litanies of the *Euchologion of the Great Church* to the Palestinian daily office with its hymns and psalmody. In other words (and of crucial importance), the Byzantine rite is a hybrid rite: its daily office derives mostly from the monastic tradition, while the Divine Liturgies, sacramental rites, and other services come from the *Euchologion of the Cathedral Office*.

Eventually, the Studite Typikon found its way back to Palestine and the Great Lavra of St. Savas, where it would undergo yet another transformation, which would later be identified as the Neo-Sabaitic synthesis. In essence, this synthesis constitutes and represents the extant Byzantine rite. In its final form, the monastic daily office has seven prayer times with eight services and includes an all-night vigil (ἀγρυπνία) on the eve of Sundays and major feast days. The vigil was eliminated by the Studites but reintroduced again

---

21 See the comprehensive introduction by Abbot Dositheos in the handsome edition of the *Typikon of St. Savas* recently published by the Monastery of Panagia Tatarne of Evrytania, Τυπικὸν τοῦ Ὁσίου καὶ Θεοφόρου Πατρὸς ἡμῶν Σάββα τοῦ Ἡγιασμένου – Διορθωθὲν μεθ' ὅσης ἐπιμελείας καὶ ὑπομνηματισθὲν τὸ κατὰ δύναμιν ὑπὸ Ἀρχιμ. Δοσιθέου Ἡγουμένου τῆς Ἱερᾶς Σταυροπηγιακῆς Μονῆς Παναγίας Ταταρνῆς (Athens 2009). In addition to the Introduction, Dositheos provides the reader with comprehensive explanatory notes at the end of each chapter. The first edition of the *Typikon of St. Savas* was published in 1545 under the title, Τυπικὸν τῆς Ἐκκλησιαστικῆς Ἀκολουθίας τῆς ἐν Ἱεροσολύμοις Ἁγίας Λαύρας τοῦ Ὁσίου καὶ Θεοφόρου Πατρὸς ἡμῶν Σάββα + αὕτη δὲ ἡ ἀκολουθία γίνεται καὶ ἐν ταῖς λοιπαῖς τῶν ἐν Ἱεροσολύμοις Μονῶν, ἔτι δὲ καὶ ἐν ταῖς κατὰ τόπον ἁγίαις τοῦ Θεοῦ Ἐκκλησίαις.

in the monastic communities of Palestine. Their penchant for long services was evidenced in other ways as well. For example, the Psalter was read in its entirety each week, the Orthros was expanded, and a growing collection of hymns was incorporated into the divine services.

The monks of Studios and St. Savas were dedicated to the cultivation of hymnography. Together with other eminent hymnographers they produced a large repertoire of ecclesial poetry that was codified between the eighth and tenth centuries in the collection of liturgical books that we now know as the Psalter, *Horologion, Octoechos* (or *Paracletike*), *Triodion, Pentekostarion,* and the twelve *Menaia*, which contain both the fixed and variable elements of the daily office.

The newly revised *Sabaitic Typikon,* with its intense rule of prayer and strict fasting discipline, began to find its way back to the monasteries of Constantinople, from there to Mount Athos, and from there to the entire Orthodox world. By the fifteenth century, the sung office of Constantinople and the Studite synthesis had fallen into disuse and had been supplanted by the *Neo-Sabaitic Typikon.* The publication of the new typicon in 1545 further solidified its ascendancy. This, the first print edition of the new typikon, was, in fact, the fourteenth-century Athonite codification of the new Sabaitic usage, authorized and sanctioned by Philotheos Kokkinos, the celebrated hesychast and abbot of the Great Lavra of Mt. Athos and later patriarch of Constantinople.

From the fifteenth century until 1838, except for minor local variations and rubrical details, the Orthodox Churches throughout the world followed the same typikon, the Neo-Sabaitic synthesis.

4. The Typikon of the Great Church of Christ (1838 and 1888)

By the beginning of the nineteenth century, it had become obvious to many leaders of the Greek Church that the daily office, with its long and complex monastic services, could not be sustained at the parish level. Already, numerous abbreviations and omissions were taking place. To forestall further arbitrary changes and sanction new practices, the Ecumenical Patriarchate took steps toward revising the monastic typikon in order to accommodate parish needs.[22] In 1838, the Ecumenical Patriarchate authorized the publication of a new typikon prepared and edited by Konstantinos the Protopsaltis (precentor) under the title, *The Ecclesiastical Typikon according to the Style of the Great Church of Christ* ("Great Church of Christ" refers to the Ecumenical Patriarchate). This new typikon was published for parish use under the supervision of the patriarchate. Monastic communities, however, were expected to retain the *Typikon of St. Savas.*

---

22 See Calivas, *Aspects of Orthodox Worship,* 89-101.

The patriarchate initiated another review of the typikon in 1878, and these efforts resulted in the creation of yet another typikon, which survives today. In 1888, the Ecumenical Patriarchate authorized the publication of the *Typikon of the Great Church of Christ,* edited by the Protopsaltis Georgios Violakis.

As with its immediate forerunner, the *Typikon of Violakis* did not create a new body of material. The services of the daily office remain mostly the same and still bear the marks of their monastic origins and identity. This typikon, however, created a new liturgical practice that can be described as an abbreviated form of the monastic office adapted to parochial needs. Essentially, the *Typikon* of Violakis sought to correct the inaccuracies in the *Typikon* of 1838 and, more importantly, to introduce additional revisions based on the received oral and written traditions of the Ecumenical Patriarchate and on the established liturgical practices of the late nineteenth century.

The *Typikon* of 1888 was adopted by all the local churches under the immediate jurisdiction of the Ecumenical Patriarchate and gradually by other Churches to varying degrees.[23] The liturgical practice of the Greek Orthodox Archdiocese of America, as an eparchy of the Ecumenical Patriarchate, is governed by the 1888 *Typikon of the Great Church of Christ.* Hence, to the degree possible after taking into consideration local circumstances, conditions, and needs, we follow the liturgical traditions of the patriarchate as outlined in the annual *Epetiris.*

The Epetiris (formerly known as the *Hemerologion* – an almanac or calendar) is a digest of the typikon. It is published annually by the patriarchate under the title, *The Epetiris of the Ecumenical Patriarchate.*[24] It is made available to all the dioceses and eparchies of the patriarchate and their respective parishes and institutions. The purpose of the Epitiris is to assist those responsible for the execution and performance of the divine services: clergy, chanters, readers, choirs, and others.

The patriarchate also issues annually a much shorter digest, the *Kanonion,* which is sent to all the parishes and is especially helpful to the clergy. The Kanonion provides on a single page the following information for each Sunday of a given year: the tone of the week (ἦχος), the Gospel lesson of the Orthros

---

[23] The *Typikon of St. Savas* continues to be used by most, if not all, monastic communities and by the Churches of Jerusalem, Russia, Georgia, and Serbia as well as several jurisdictions in the United States.

[24] In addition to the comprehensive summary of the typikon for the given year, the *Epetiris* contains general information about the patriarchate, its dioceses, eparchies, and institutions throughout the world and information on the other autocephalous and autonomous Orthodox Churches. In fact, all the Autocephalous and Autonomous Orthodox Churches publish a similar digest of their own for use by their local bishoprics and parishes.

('Εωθινόν), and the Epistle and Gospel lessons for the Divine Liturgy. It also lists other information related to fasting periods and the *Paschalia* (Paschal Tables).

Similar digests are prepared and published by individuals and groups with or without formal ecclesial authorization. For example, the National Forum of Greek Orthodox Musicians (under the auspices of the Greek Orthodox Archdiocese of America) publishes a helpful annual guide for choirs and chanters.

5. The Liturgical Books of the Church

The various elements of the liturgical rites are codified in the liturgical books.[25] The mind and faith of the Church is expressed in these books in doxological, poetical, and rhetorical language. As previously noted, the liturgical books are considered authoritative.[26]

With a combined doctrinal, ethical, and devotional purpose, these books consist mainly of prayers, litanies, hymns, biblical texts, and rubrics. The prayers and hymns represent and interpret the central truths and core values of the Orthodox faith, conveying the fundamental vision of the Church in a given rite. By proclaiming the promise of salvation, the prayers and hymns evoke devotional responses of the mind and heart and provide the faithful, clergy and laypeople alike, with direction for their continued edification and growth in the life of faith and guidance and inspiration for their life and mission in the world.

Professor Stefano Parenti, the noted liturgist, reminds us that each liturgical book expresses only part of the history of Orthodox worship. "Every liturgical book," he notes, "reveals and describes the act of worship from the perspective of its intended recipient. It follows that no book taken on its own can give us a complete and reliable state of the liturgical tradition in the period it

---

25 For more on the liturgical books see Getcha, *The Typikon Decoded*, 15-66 and Ioannis M. Fountoulis, Λειτουργικὰ Θέματα, vol. 2 (Thessaloniki 1977) and vol. 5 (Thessaloniki 1986), 61-78. See also the introductory chapters in the books published by the Holy Transfiguration Monastery, Boston, MA: *The Psalter* (1974), *The Great Horologion* (1977), and *Pentecostarion* (1990); and the two volumes by Mother Mary and Archimandrite Kallistos Ware, *The Festal Menaion* (London, 1969 & South Canaan, PA, 1990) and *The Lenten Triodion* (London and Boston 1978). Also see Calivas, *Aspects of Orthodox Worship*, 61-3 and 102-16.The articles of Basil Studer, "Liturgical Documents of the First Four Centuries" and Elena Velkova Velkovska, "Byzantine Liturgical Books" in *Handbook for Liturgical Studies*, volume I, Anscar J. Chupungco, editor (Collegeville MN. 1997) 199-224, 225-40.

26 Calivas, *Aspects of Orthodox Worship*, 61.

was written."²⁷ For this reason, priests – to the degree possible for each – are obliged to be familiar with all the liturgical books, their history, content, and substance.

The liturgical books fall into four major categories. In the **first category** are the books that contain the prayers and petitions of the various divine services used by the clergy. These are the *Euchologion* and its derivatives, the *Small Euchologion*, the *Archieratikon* (hierarch's book or pontifical), the *Ieratikon* (priest's book), the *Diakonikon* (deacon's book), and the *Compendium* (lector's book).

The **second category** includes the books that contain the fixed and variable elements of the daily office that are used primarily by chanters, readers, and choirs. These are the Horologion, Octoechos, Triodion, Pentecostarion, and the twelve Menaia, one for each month of the year. The Menaia contain the services of the fixed feasts of the liturgical year.

The **third category** includes the books of the received lectionary system. They are the *Evangelion (Gospel Book)*, the *Apostolos (Epistle Book)*, the *Prophetologion*, and the *Psalter*. Of these four books, the Evangelion alone is enthroned on the Holy Table and its lections are read by the clergy. The other books are used mainly by chanters and readers.

The **fourth category** contains the *Typikon* and the *Diataxeis*, the books of directives and rubrics.

Much of the history and formation of the typikon have already been discussed in the preceding chapter. Nonetheless, some additional things must be noted about the typikon.

1. The Typikon. From the beginning the Church has favored orderly prayer and developed a well-organized system of worship.²⁸ Authentic worship requires faithfulness and constancy. The typikon, as previously mentioned, secures recognizable standards of usage.²⁹ A repertoire of authoritative texts, music, and ceremonies as well as intelligent rules and directives are essential characteristics of authentic liturgy. This does not mean that liturgical texts and rubrics are absolute and immutable, as some would have us believe. Such

---

27 Stefano Parenti, "The Cathedral Rite of Constantinople: Evolution of a Local Tradition," a paper given at the Third International Congress of the Society of Oriental Liturgy, Volos, Greece, May 26-30, 2010. See also the paper delivered at the same Congress by Elena Velkovska, "Byzantine Liturgical Books between Jerusalem and Constantinople: Toward a Taxonomy of the Sources of Byzantine Liturgical Books."

28 See 1 Cor. 14:40; 2 Thess. 2: 15; the *Didache*; and Clement of Rome, *First Epistle to the Corinthians* (chapter 40).

29 Calivas, *Aspects of Orthodox Worship*, 63-9, 100-1.

an attitude denies historical realities and contradicts the pastoral dimensions of the liturgy. Nonetheless, authentic texts and rubrics are indispensable. Without them, Orthodox worship would lose its objectivity, integrity, continuity, coherency, and communal character. The liturgy is traditional but not formalistic. Significantly, one must always keep in mind that the typikon does not create the liturgy; it presupposes its existence. The function of rubrics is to adapt the liturgy – in an orderly, intelligent, and respectful fashion – to one or another pastoral need in a given situation, time, and place without causing a radical break from tradition or the loss of the liturgy's objectivity, dignity and beauty. The liturgy expresses the mind of the Church, not that of an individual cleric.

2. The Euchologion is the official service book of the Church. It contains the priestly prayers, diaconal petitions, rubrics, and ceremonials of the holy sacraments and other divine services, together with many other prayers and blessings for special needs and circumstances. The Euchologion was formed over the course of many centuries. Hence its contents vary according to time and place. However, with the appearance of the first printed editions in the sixteenth century, the arrangement and contents of the Euchologion (and for that matter of all the liturgical texts) were more or less standardized.[30] Significantly, as previously noted, the priestly prayers and diaconal petitions in the Euchologion come mostly from the defunct cathedral office of Constantinople.

Over time, the prayer of the Church was augmented and refined to assure and reflect doctrinal accuracy. Composed by many persons both known and unknown, the prayers and hymns of the Church were collected to form distinct volumes. The collections of formularies (prescribed forms of prayers) differed in content since they were intended for the use of particular orders. These collections were generally called *Euchologia* (prayer books or service books). When an Euchologion was designed for a particular order, it generally bore the name of the order, as for example the Ieratikon, which contains the prayers and ceremonials of the rites performed by a presbyter or priest (ἱερεύς).

The earliest extant collection of priestly prayers, thirty in all, is the *Prayer Book of Serapion*, Bishop of Thmuis in Egypt, which he composed or compiled around 350 AD. The earliest extant manuscript of a Constantinopolitan Euchologion is the eighth-century *Barberini Codex – S. Marci III. 55*, now referred to as *Barberini 336* or *Vat. Gr. 336*. The codex was discovered among the famous collection of manuscripts in the library of the noble Barberini family of Rome. Remarkably,

---

30 On the history, spirit, and ethos of the Euchologion see Calivas *Aspects of Orthodox Worship*, 102-24. Also see Getcha, *Typikon Decoded*, 47-51.

a comparison of the essential elements of the *Great Euchologion* in current usage and the contents of the *Barberini Codex* reveals that significant portions of the divine services have remained the same over time.

The first printed edition of the Greek Euchologion appeared in 1526. In 1647, the Dominican monk Jacques Goar published his now famous Εὐχολόγιον *Sive Rituale Graecorum*, based on ancient manuscripts and the early printed editions of the Euchologion.[31] In 1901, Aleksej Dmitrievskij published in Kiev a large collection of manuscripts, *Opisanie Liturgitsekich Rukopsej*, vol. II, Εὐχολόγια. Panayiotis Trembelas published three critical editions of parts of the Euchologion: the three Divine Liturgies (1935); on marriage, unction, ordination, baptism, and chrismation (1950); and on the divine services of the *hagiasmos*, the consecration of churches, the Orthros, and Vespers (1955).

The recent editions of the Greek Euchologion are based chiefly on two editions. The first is the *Great Euchologion*, edited by the priest Spyridon Zervos, an archimandrite of the Ecumenical Patriarchate. It was first published in Venice in 1851, and a second edition appeared in 1862. The other is the *Great Euchologion* edited by the priest Nikolaos Papadopoulos, which was published in Athens in 1927. This latter edition was an improvement over other earlier publications.

Each autocephalous Church has its own official version of the Euchologion in the liturgical language of the local Church. These are based largely on ancient manuscripts and on earlier printed editions of the Greek Euchologion. They also reflect liturgical traditions, practices, and reforms of the local Church. These differences, however, are not substantive in nature.

The first English translation of parts of the Euchologion was produced and published in 1772 by John Glen King, a Fellow of the Royal and Antiquarian Society and Anglican chaplain to the British Factory at St. Petersburg. The book was reproduced in 1970 by the AMS Press of New York. In recent years numerous English translations of the sacramental rites and other divine services of the Euchologion have appeared both here and abroad.

There are several abridged versions of the Euchologion, which are intended for particular orders of the clergy. One such abridged version or derivative of the Euchologion is the *Small Euchologion* (Μικρὸν Εὐχολόγιον), published specifically for parish clergy.[32] Other derivatives include the *Archieratikon, Ieratikon,*

---

31 An improved edition of Goar's Euchologion appeared in 1730 and a facsimile of the same edition in 1960. It should not escape notice that Goar's endeavors were directed at proselytism.

32 For the contents of the Great and Small *Euchologion* see Calivas, *Aspects of Orthodox Worship*, 108-10.

Diakonikon, and *Sylleitourgikon* or *Egkolpion tou Anagnostou* (Compendium of the Reader).[33] For our purposes we will focus briefly on the Ieratikon.

The earliest printed version of an Ieratikon was the *edition principes* of the three Divine Liturgies published by Demetrios Doukas in 1526.[34] Although many printed editions of the Greek Ieratikon began to appear in subsequent centuries, the first to receive the official approval of the Church appeared in 1895. It was edited and published by the priest Makarios Tantalides with the consent of the Ecumenical Patriarchate. Later editions include the *Divine Liturgy* (Θεία Λειτουργία) edited by the priest Nikolaos Papadopoulos (1927). This book enjoyed wide use among the Greek clergy until it was displaced by the Ieratikon, which was first published in 1956 by the Apostolike Diakonia of the Church of Greece. This second work became the preferred text of the Greek clergy both here and abroad. In 2002 the Church of Greece authorized the publication of a new edition prepared under the auspices of the Synodical Committee and edited by the learned priest Konstantinos Papayiannis. The new edition contains a seventeen-page addendum in which the editor offers comments, explains the changes, and lists the reference works used in its preparation. Various monolingual and bilingual forms of the Ieratikon have been published by the Orthodox Churches in the Americas.[35]

3. The Horologion contains the fixed elements of the daily office and is used primarily by readers, chanters, choirs, and the people. The priestly prayers and diaconal petitions are either omitted or given in an abbreviated form. Of course, priests and deacons often consult and use the Horologion for various services and private devotions. It is, in fact, a basic prayer book used by clergy and laypeople alike for its rich collection of prayers, psalms, hymns, and other material for daily devotions.

As noted above, the gradual demise of the cathedral office resulted in the establishment of a single form of the daily office: the monastic, following the Neo-Sabaitic typikon. This form is reflected in the Horologion and in other liturgical books required for the celebration of the daily office. The early manuscripts and printed editions of the Horologion contained only the fixed elements of the daily office. Gradually, the primitive model was expanded to include other useful material for readers and chanters. This expanded, comprehensive form is called the *Great Horologion* (Ὡρολόγιον τὸ Μέγα). As with other liturgical books, the form and content of the book has varied in its

---

33 Ibid., 111, 113-4, regarding the Archieratikon, Diakonikon, and Sylleitourgikon.

34 Ibid., 111-3, regarding the Ieratikon and its contents. See also Getcha, *The Typikon Decoded*, 51-2.

35 See Calivas, *Aspects of Orthodox Worship*, 114-6, regarding the emerging ecclesial realities in America and the liturgy. See also Calivas, "Liturgy and Language," in his *Liturgy in Dialogue*, 243-59.

various manifestations or editions. The differences, however, are minor, and relate more to form than essence.

The first printed edition of the Great Horologion appeared in Venice in 1509. The initial printing was followed by many other Greek and Slavic versions. In 1832, with the blessings of the Ecumenical Patriarchate, the learned Hieromonk Bartholomaios of the Monastery of Koutloumousios on Mt. Athos produced a new three-part version of the Great Horologion. In 1857, he published a second augmented and corrected edition. This text became the standard for all subsequent Greek editions, including the excellent English translation of the Great Horologion produced and published by the Holy Transfiguration Monastery in Boston.[36] Editors and publishers, as in the case of the English edition, have occasionally added helpful supplementary materials and amplified rubrics.[37]

The Great Horologion is divided into three major parts and includes an addendum. The first of the three parts bears the title, "Prayer of the Entire Daily Office – Προσευχὴ τῆς Ὅλης Ἡμερονυκτίου Ἀκολουθίας," and constitutes the primitive form of the Horologion. It contains the order and the fixed elements (psalms, prayers, and hymns) of the eight services that comprise the daily office beginning with the *Mesonyktikon* or Nocturns (for weekdays, Saturdays, and Sundays), followed by the Orthros (with rubrics for its several forms), the four Hours (First, Third, Sixth, and Ninth), the Service of Typika, the Prayers at Table, Vespers (with rubrics for its several forms), and the *Apodeipnon* or Compline (in its two forms, Great and Small). The daily cycle of services is preceded by a set of "Prayers upon Awakening" for private devotions. In addition, the service of each mid-hour follows immediately after its proper hour.

The order of the services in the Great Horologion differs from the order in all other liturgical books used for the daily office. Whereas, these books begin with the service of Vespers, the *Horologion* starts with the service of the Mesonyktikon. Monastics awaken from sleep in the pre-dawn hours to start their workday in communal prayer with the office of Mesonyktikon and end their day with the reading of the Apodeipnon, the last service before sleep.

---

[36] For an introduction see *The Great Horologion* (Holy Transfiguration Monastery, Boston, MA 1997), 9-12.

[37] In 1973 the Publishing House, Ἀστήρ – Παπαδημητρίου, in Athens published a *Great Horologion* with a valuable supplement (ἐπίμετρον) containing a body of new hymns for the *menologion* (festal *apolytikia, kontakia*, and *megalynaria*) which are found only here. Most, if not all, of these hymns are the creations of the hymnographer of the Ecumenical Patriarchate, the late hieromonk Gerasimos of *Mikra Agia Anna* (Little Anne's Skete) a hermitage on Mt. Athos. For a critical study of the Horologion see Nilo Borgia, Ὡρολόγιον – *Diurno delle Chiesa di rito Bizantino* (Rome 1929).

The second part of the *Great Horologion* contains material related to the *Menologion* or calendar with its cycle of fixed and movable feasts. The calendar of the fixed feasts and commemorations for each day of the calendar year starts on September 1, which marks the beginning of the new ecclesiastical year. Appropriate apolytikia and kontakia are provided for most of the days of the year together with a brief synaxarion.

The third part contains a series of services: the Akathist Hymn, two Supplicatory Canons (Small and Great) to the Theotokos, a Service for Holy Communion, a Supplicatory Canon to our Lord Jesus Christ, a Supplicatory canon to the Guardian Angel, another Supplicatory Canon to the Heavenly Powers and to all the saints, and an Akathist for the Life-giving Cross.

The addendum includes various materials, the most useful of which is an alphabetical listing of the names of the saints with the feast day of each.

The 1973 edition of the Horologion published by the house of Aster and Papademetriou in Athens contains an additional section, which contains new apolytikia, kontakia, and megalynaria that complement those in the received text of the Horologion. These hymns were composed by the late elder Gerasimos, the official hymnographer of the Ecumenical Patriarchate and a Monk of *Mikra Agia Anna* (St. Anne's Skete) of Mt. Athos.

4. The Octoechos (Ὀκτώηχος) or Parakletike (Παρακλητική) is the book of the festal cycle of the week, centered on the Lord's Day (Sunday), the first day of the week when the Church celebrates weekly the resurrection of our Lord.[38] The book is structured on a recurring cycle of eight weeks (fifty-six days) and the eight tones of Byzantine music. One of the eight tones is assigned to each week in rotation. The name of the book, Octoechos – Book of the Eight Tones is derived from this system. The book is divided into eight sections or periods (περιόδους), one for each of the eight tones. The first period contains hymns composed in the first tone (περίοδος τοῦ πρώτου ἤχου). The seven subsequent periods contain hymns in the three other authentic or fundamental tones (the second, third, and fourth), followed by hymns in the four derivative or plagal tones (plagal first, plagal second, grave, and plagal fourth). Each period contains hymns for the Vespers and Orthros services of each day of the week, beginning with Sunday, or more precisely, with Vespers of Saturday evening.[39]

---

38 On the festal cycle or calendar of the week, see below.

39 In addition to these services, the Octoechos contains the hymns in each tone for the Saturday Small Vespers, which are sung in monastic communities prior to Great Vespers and the Vigil. It also has the hymns for the Beatitudes for the daily celebration of the Divine Liturgy and a canon in honor of the Holy Trinity for the Midnight Service of each Sunday.

Initially, liturgical hymns were gathered into various collections by type, such as the *Irmologion*, *Kontakarion*, *Sticherarion*, *Sticherokathismatarion*, *Theotokarion*, and *Tropologion*. This last book appeared around the sixth century and survived through at least the ninth century, perhaps even as late as the twelfth century.[40] Around the eighth century (possibly earlier), the ever-increasing number of hymns began to be arranged differently, no longer according to genre but according to liturgical cycles. This resulted in the formation of the current liturgical books, including the Octoechos.[41] Additionally, the number of hymns for a given service was no longer optional.

According to contemporary scholarship, the Octoechos is older than many of the exceptional hymnographers, who contributed to its formation, including Germanos of Constantinople, John of Damascus, Cosmas of Maiouma, Andrew of Crete, Theophanes Graptos, Theodore the Studite and his brother Joseph Archbishop of Thessaloniki, Joseph the Hymnographer, Metrophanes of Smyrna, and the emperors Leo VI the Wise and his son Constantine VII Porphyrogenitos. The book was initially shaped by the hymnographers of the Palestinian school (cathedral and monastic) and was later supplemented by the Constantinopolitan School (cathedral and monastic).

The core of the Octoechos is the Sunday hymn cycle (starting with Saturday evening Vespers), which is often attributed to St. John of Damascus (+780), but has been shown to predate him. However, there is no doubt that he contributed to the collection and was likely one of its early editors.[42]

The core was gradually expanded to include a weekday series of hymns in each of the eight tones based on the cycle of feasts of the week. This series was called Parakletike (from the verb παρακαλέω, to entreat, supplicate, console). Thus was born the second title, which is often used currently in parentheses to identify the book.

A distinctive feature of many weekday hymns is their personal, ascetical characteristics. Many of these hymns bear the title, "Hymns of Compunction" (κατανυκτικά), and are written in the first person singular, giving voice to a

---

40 See Svetlana Kujumdzieva, *The Hymnographic Book of Tropologion* (Routledge 2018).

41 See Getcha, *Typikon Decoded*, 25-30.

42 Ibid., 28-9

repentant sinner in their struggles for perfection and holiness. These hymns aim to make the worshipper aware of personal failings and iniquities, of one's need for constant vigilance, and of God's tender mercies, which heal the wounds of a contrite heart (Ps. 50/51:17).[43]

By contrast, the Sunday cycle's hymns are mostly communal in nature. The people, with one voice and one heart, sing joyful praises of thanksgiving to the Triune God for his mighty deeds, centering chiefly on the Christ event and the gifts of redemption that flow from it.[44]

The Octoechos is used throughout the year, except on Palm Sunday, the Sunday of Pascha, the Sunday of Thomas, and the Sunday of Pentecost. Its use is also interrupted during the ordinary days of Lent, during Holy Week, and when a dominical feast (e.g., Christmas, Theophany) falls on a Sunday. The recurring cycle of the eight periods begins annually on the first Sunday after Pentecost, the Sunday of All Saints, with the plagal fourth tone.

Each day of Renewal Week (Διακαινησίμος Ἑβδομάς or Bright Week) is identified with Paschal Sunday and is considered an extension of it. Hence, hymns from seven of the eight periods of the Sunday cycle in the Octoechos are allocated to each day of the week beginning with the first tone, which is assigned to the Paschal Vigil and the Paschal Orthros (Matins). The hymns of the second tone are assigned to the Vespers of Pascha Sunday and the Orthros of Monday. Similarly, the hymns of the third tone are assigned to Tuesday (starting with Monday Vespers); the fourth tone is assigned to Wednesday; the plagal first to Thursday; the plagal second to Friday; and the plagal fourth to Saturday. The grave tone is omitted from the cycle. On the Sunday of Thomas, only the hymns of the feast in the Pentecostarion are sung. Many hymns of the Octoechos are incorporated in the Pentecostarion.

The form and content of the Octoechos developed gradually. The first strata

---

43 See, for example, the kathisma troparion in the Orthros of Monday of the third period in the Octoechos: "Παροικοῦσα ἐν τῇ γῇ ψυχῇ μου…While you sojourn upon the earth, repent, O my soul; dust in the grave does not give praise and is not redeemed from offences. Thus, cry out unto Christ God: O Knower of hearts, I have sinned; before you condemn me, have mercy on me." When writing these hymns, the hymnographers were inspired by the psalmist in his pleas to God for help, forgiveness, and deliverance, as with these words: "Be mindful of your mercy, O Lord, and of your steadfast love…Remember not the sins of my youth, or my transgressions…Turn to me and be gracious to me; for I am lonely and afflicted. Relieve the troubles of my heart and bring me out of my distress" (Ps. 24/25:6-7, 16-17). On the formation and understanding of the self through the liturgy, see Derek Krueger, *Liturgical Subjects: Christian Ritual, Biblical Narrative, and the Formation of the Self in Byzantium* (Philadelphia 2014).

44 See the Hymn of the Praises (Αἶνοι) in the Octoechos, Sunday of the third tone: "Δεῦτε πάντα τὰ ἔθνη… Come all you nations, learn the power of this awesome mystery; for Christ our Savior, the Word who was in the beginning, was crucified for us, and was buried of his own will, and arose from the dead, that he might save all things. Let us worship him."

of hymns included stichera, troparia and canons. Other types of hymns (kathismata, hypakoai, kontakia-oikoi, prokeimena, anavathmoi) were added in stages.

In a further development, an added addendum includes several sets of hymns and canons. These include a set of eleven resurrectional exaposteilaria and eothina idiomela; hymns to the Holy Trinity (Triadika) and hymns of light (photagogika) in each of the eight tones; exaposteilaria for weekdays; and sets of theotokia in each of the eight tones. It also has three supplicatory canons to the Theotokos: *The Small Paraklesis*, attributed to the Monk Theostiriktos (by others to Theophanes); *The Great Paraklesis,* composed by Emperor (of Nicaea) Theodore II Laskaris (+1258); and the *Canon of the Akathist Hymn*, written by Joseph the Hymnographer (+883). The kontakion and the twenty-four oikoi (stanzas) of the akathist are attributed to St. Romanos the Melodist.

The contents of the book began to stabilize in the twelfth century and became set in the sixteenth century with the first printed edition published in Venice in 1521.[45]

5. The Triodion (Τριώδιον) contains the hymns and biblical texts for the services of pre-Lent, Lent, and Holy Week, covering a period of ten weeks (the three preparatory weeks with four Sundays, the six weeks of Lent, and Holy Week).[46] This ten-week span is often referred to as the Triodion. Although the

---

45 The first Greek edition was preceded by two Slavic editions in 1492 and 1494. For more on the Triodion, see Evangelos Theodorou, Ἡ Μορφωτικὴ Ἀξία τοῦ Ἰσχύοντος Τριωδίου (Athens 1958) and Alexander Schmemann, *Great Lent* (Crestwood, NY 1974).

46 While the Triodion covers a period of ten weeks, it contains hymnic material for only fifty-nine days. The services for the first two weeks of the Triodion – the Sunday of the Publican and Pharisee and the Sunday of the Prodigal Son – contain only the Sunday cycle of hymns, starting with Saturday evening Vespers. During the week before Lent, the consumption of meat is forbidden. Thus, the forty-day Lenten fast is extended by a week. Together with the fast of Holy Week, which is separate from Lent, the entire fast covers a period of eight weeks. According to the nun Egeria, (an Iberian pilgrim to the Holy Land, 381-384) the extra week was added before the start of Lent to compensate for the softening of the rules for Saturdays and Sundays during Lent. In her account of the liturgical practices of the East and most notably of Jerusalem, she makes the following interesting observations in her *Diary* (chapter 27 and 41). "When the season of the Lent is at hand, it is observed in the following manner. Now whereas with us [in the West] the forty days preceding Easter are observed, here they observe eight weeks before Easter. This is the reason they observe eight weeks: On Sundays and Saturdays they do not fast, except on the one Saturday [Holy Saturday] which is the vigil of Easter, when it is necessary to fast...From Easter to the fiftieth day, that is, to Pentecost, absolutely no one fasts here..." See George E. Gingras, *Egeria: Diary of a Pilgrimage* (New York 1970), 97 and 117. The fasting rules of the Church, like all liturgical practices, have evolved over the course of centuries. They have been affected by monastic practices and the cultural milieu in which they were first generated. It is fair to say that the received fasting discipline of the Church should be revisited. See Nathaniel Symeonides, ed., *Toward the Holy and Great Council: Theological Reflections* (New York, 2016), 57-73.

Triodion is used in conjunction with the Octoechos and the Menaia according to its own set of directives, it does not contain any hymnic material from either of these.

As with all liturgical books, the Triodion went through several stages of development. Originally, the Triodion and Pentecostarion were a single volume containing the texts of the services of the entire movable cycle of feasts based on the annual celebration of Pascha (the date of which changes yearly).[47] The single volume was divided into two sections: the Κατανυκτικόν –*Compunctious (or Penitential) Triodion* and the Χαρμόσυνον – *Joyful Triodion* (also known as the Τριώδιον τῶν ἀνθέων – *Triodion of the Flowers*). The second section became the Pentecostarion.[48]

The decision to create two separate volumes is of little consequence. What is significant, however, is the point at which the book was divided into two. The oldest Russian books, for example, began the Pentecostarion with the Saturday of Lazarus.[49] The received Triodion, on the other hand, ends with Holy Saturday and includes the Vesperal Liturgy of the Pascal Vigil, while the Pentecostarion begins with the Intermediate Service and the Orthros of Pascha Sunday.[50] The division of the single volume at this point dramatically alters the liturgical unity of the Paschal celebration and blurs the meaning of Holy Saturday, the only day of the year on which the celebration of a eucharistic liturgy is strictly prohibited.[51]

The hymns of the Triodion have been authored by many hymnographers, both known and unknown.[52] The early versions of the Triodion contained sets of canons for all the days of the week. According to the earliest tradition, only three biblical odes with their corresponding canons were assigned to weekdays. Of the nine odes, the eighth and ninth were stable, sung each day. In addition to the two stable odes, each day was assigned an additional ode.

---

47 See Alkiviadis Calivas, *Great Week and Pascha in the Greek Orthodox Church* (Brookline, MA 1992), 6. See also Getcha, *Typikon Decoded*, 35.

48 For more on the *Triodion*, see Evangelos Theodorou, Ἡ Μορφωτικὴ Ἀξία τοῦ Ἰσχύοντος Τριωδίου (Athens 1958) and Alexander Schmemann, *Great Lent* (Crestwood, NY 1974).

49 Getcha, *Typikon Decoded*, 35.

50 The Intermediate Service is conducted after the *Pannychis* and before the Paschal Orthros. It contains two elements: the ceremony of the Paschal light and the proclamation of the Resurrection (Gospel pericope). See Calivas, *Great Week*, 108-11.

51 Calivas, *Great Week*, 6, 97-112. The return of the Paschal Vigil to its proper place and the restoration of the unity the Paschal celebration is a topic worthy of attention in any process of liturgical renewal and reform.

52 Among the known contributors are Sts. Andrew of Crete, John of Damascus, Kosmas of Maiouma, Theodore and Joseph the Studites, and Kassiane the Nun.

Monday, for example, is assigned the first ode and Friday the fifth. Saturday was assigned four odes, the sixth and seventh in addition to the eighth and ninth.[53] From the beginning, Sunday had the full complement of nine odes. In later times, the tradition of nine odes prevailed. The Triodion, however, maintains the earlier tradition, from which its name is derived, i.e., *Triodion* or the *Book of Three Odes* (τρεῖς + ᾠδαί).

The Triodion was gradually expanded to include a variety of troparia (kathismata, sticheta, aposticha), The Great Canon of St. Andrew of Crete, The Akathist Hymn,[54] Synaxaria for the special festal commemorations of the period,[55] the Synodikon of the Sunday of Orthodoxy, various prokeimena, rubrical directives, and several biblical lections (including Old Testament readings, Epistle lessons, and the psalms and biblical lessons of the Great Hours of Holy Friday).[56]

In addition to these, the Triodion contains an addendum consisting of two series of hymns: a set of triadika and photagogika troparia, and a set of stichera and kathismata troparia (for each of the eight tones). The format of the Triodion is similar to that of the Octoechos with hymns for the services of Vespers and Orthros. Significantly, the Triodion does not contain any priestly or diaconal petitions and prayers. It is strictly a book for the laity and their representatives, the chanters, readers, and choirs.

In time, the Triodion was expanded through the addition of new material, several of which gradually replaced more primitive elements. In many instances, traces of the earlier strata can be found in the text. For instance, the present commemoration on the first Sunday of Lent (the Sunday of Orthodoxy) is related to the restoration of the icons and the final defeat of iconoclasm. The event was first celebrated in the ninth century (843). Previously, on the

---

53 See Fountoulis, Λειτουργικὰ Θέματα, Ε, 77-81.

54 The *Akathist* is attributed by many to St. Romanos the Melodist; his kontakion for the feast of the Annunciation, based on the infant narratives of Jesus in the Gospels.

55 The *Synaxaria* were composed by Nikephoros Kallistos Xanthopoulos (+ca. 1335), a renowned cleric, church historian, and rhetorician.

56 The Old Testament lections of Lent include two readings at Vespers (Monday through Friday) one from the Book of Genesis and the other from the Book of Proverbs; and one reading at the Orthros (Monday through Friday) from the Prophecy of Isaiah. These lessons form (an almost) continuous reading (*lectio continua*) of the three books. The lessons from Isaiah together with their prokeimena are taken from the Orthros of the cathedral rite of Constantinople and appended to the monastic Orthros. During Holy Week these lessons are replaced with select readings from the Book of Exodus, the Book of Job, and the Prophecy of Ezekiel respectively. The services of Holy Week contain additional readings from these and other Old Testament books.

first Sunday of Lent, the Church remembered Moses and the Prophets, which the doxastikon of the Orthros and the Epistle and Gospel readings of the Divine Liturgy bear out. The remembrance of St. Gregory Palamas (+1359) on the second Sunday of Lent was adopted in the fifteenth century.[57] The earlier celebration, according to local custom, was devoted to the saint of the day or to one of two Parables, the Prodigal Son (Luke 15:11-32) or the Publican and Pharisee (Luke 18:10-14). Traces of these commemorations are found in the hymns of the week. The Third Sunday of Lent, the Veneration of the Cross, is the oldest of the Sunday commemorations. It was celebrated at least from the sixth century (if not earlier) in Constantinople.[58] The current commemoration of St. John Climacus (+649) on the Fourth Sunday of Lent was adopted in the fifteenth century. The more primitive commemoration was centered on the Parable of the Good Samaritan (Luke 10:25-37) as indicated by the hymnography of the week. The same is true of the fifth Sunday. The present commemoration of St. Mary of Egypt entered the Triodion in the twelfth century or later. Earlier, the commemoration was focused on the Parable of the Rich Man and Lazarus (Luke 16:19-31). The earlier commemorations appear to have been the work of the Jerusalem School. The latter revisions were introduced by the Constantinopolitan School.[59]

For the most part, the contents of the Triodion reflect the period and are essentially penitential in nature. They constitute a joyful call to repentance – a conscious opening of the mind and heart to the ways of the Lord in preparation for the celebration of the Paschal mystery: the crucifixion, burial, resurrection, and glorification of Christ.

Repentance, however, as the hymns and readings in the Triodion tell us, involves more than a contrite heart and a change of mind with respect to a specific sin or sins. It implies an inner crisis that leads to a reversal of values, to a different view of life, and to another, ecclesial way of existence, mindful of the fact that salvation comes through a community, the Church. As the Church prepares to celebrate the Paschal mystery, she calls the faithful to reinvigorate their prayer-life and vigorously engage the spiritual warfare through fasting and ascesis – the disciplines through which one acquires dispassion or the state

---

57 The commemoration of St. Gregory Palamas on the second Sunday of Lent is considered an extension of the Sunday of Orthodoxy for his role in the Hesychastic Controversy.

58 According to others, the third Sunday also had an earlier commemoration, centered on the Parable of the Publican and Pharisee. See Getcha, *Typikon Decoded*, 38.

59 See ibid. and Fountoulis, Λειτουργικὰ Θέματα, 2, 64-70.

of reintegration and spiritual freedom, in which the virtue of watchfulness and the practice of forgiveness, compassion, and almsgiving blossom.[60]

By the fourteenth century the Triodion began to appear in its present form, and the first printed edition was published in 1525.

6. The Pentecostarion (Πεντηκοστάριον), as noted above, is the book of the Paschal season, starting with the Orthros of the Sunday of Pasha and ending with the Sunday after Pentecost, the Sunday of All Saints. It covers a period of eight weeks marked by joyfulness and spiritual exhilaration. Originally, the Pentecostarion, as previously noted, comprised a single volume with the Triodion – the second part of which bore the title, *Joyful Triodion* or *Triodion of the Flowers* or simply the *Floral Triodion*.[61]

The title, Pentecostarion, was bestowed on the book when it was separated from the Triodion and became a separate volume. The name is derived from the Greek adjective for fifty, Πεντηκοστή or *Pentecost*. In the Old Testament the title, "Pentecost," was applied to the fiftieth day after Passover. It was a day of holy convocation and one of the three appointed feasts of the Old Testament, known as the feast of weeks or the feast of the first-fruits of the harvest (Lev. 23:10-21; Cf. 2 Macc. 12:31-32; Tobit 2:1).

In the Christian tradition, the title Pentecost is applied to the wondrous event described in the Book of Acts related to the descent of the Holy Spirit upon the Apostles, which happened fifty days after the resurrection of Christ: "When the day of Pentecost had come, they were all together in one place...and there appeared to them tongues as of fire, distributed and resting on each one of them. And they were all filled with the Holy Spirit..." (Acts 2:1-4). Gradually, the name Pentecost came to define not only the day or feast of Pentecost, but also the entire Paschal season, i.e., the period of the fifty days from Pascha to Pentecost and the week after, ending with the Sunday of All Saints. The name was also applied to the hymns of the period and to the book that contained them, the Pentecostarion.

The early manuscript versions of the Pentecostarion were not identical in content or title. Some included the services of Holy Week starting with the Saturday of Lazarus. Uniformity came about gradually and became fixed by the sixteenth century with the first printed editions. The earliest edition appeared

---

60 Note the words of one hymn, "Let us observe a fast acceptable and pleasing to the Lord. True fasting [*ascesis*] is to put away all evil, to control the tongue, to forbear from anger, to abstain from lust, slander, falsehood, and perjury. If we renounce these things, then is our fasting true and acceptable to God." (An apostichon, Monday Vespers, first week of Lent.)

61 This latter title continues to be used in the Slavic tradition.

in 1568 in Venice. Most of the known hymnographers who contributed to the development of the Pentecostarion lived before the tenth century.[62]

The Pentecostarion is organized in much the same way as the Octoechos and the Triodion with hymns for the daily cycle of worship centered on Vespers and Orthros. Because the book starts with the Paschal Orthros, the services for the days of the week begin with Orthros, in stark contrast with the order in the other books, which start with Vespers, or the Horologion, which starts with the Mesonyktikon. The Pentecostarion also contains the texts for the Compline and Mesonyktikon of Pascha and Renewal Week, Canons for the other offices of Mesonyktikon, sets of antiphons for the Divine Liturgy, and biblical lessons for the several feasts of the period, including the feasts of Mid-Pentecost and the Ascension of the Lord, the latter of which occurred forty days after the Resurrection (Acts 1:2-4).[63] Many of the hymns in the Pentecostarion are borrowed from the Octoechos and are so identified.

7. The Menaia (from the Greek word μήν–μηναῖον = month–monthly) are a collection of twelve volumes, one for each of the twelve months of the year. The Menaia contain the texts of the services of the fixed feasts of the year. The basis of the Menaia were the Synaxaria – the lists of saints, which were kept by local churches. In time, the lists were embellished with the addition of hymns extolling the virtues and contributions of the local and regional saints, including founders, hierarchs, martyrs, confessors, ascetics, and righteous men, women, and children, some of whom gained universal recognition. At first, generic hymns were created for the various categories of saints together with sets of biblical readings. It was customary to commemorate the saints annually on the day of their respective deaths.[64]

---

62 For more on the history of the Pentecostarion, its authors and published editions see *The Pentecostarion*, translated and published by Holy Transfiguration Monastery (Boston 1990), 12-16.

63 It has been argued that the feast of Mid-Pentecost, the dominant theme of which is the Wisdom of God, who is Christ the Lord, was celebrated annually as the festival of the Church of the Holy Wisdom (*Hagia Sophia*), the cathedral church of Constantinople.

64 The first recorded instance of a feast in honor of a saint is the letter written in 156 by the church of Smyrna. The letter recounts the martyrdom of Smyrna's venerable and revered Bishop Polycarp, the honor paid to his relics and to his memory annually. "For him [Christ] being the Son of God we adore, but the martyrs as disciples and imitators of the Lord we venerate, as they deserve, for their matchless affection towards their own King and Master... We later took up his [Polycarp's] bones, more precious than costly stones and more valuable than gold, and laid them away in a suitable place. There the Lord will permit us so far as possible to gather together in joy and gladness to celebrate the day of his martyrdom as a birthday, in memory of those that have already fought in the contest and for the training and preparation of those that shall do so hereafter." (*Martyrdom of Polycarp*).

The synaxaria also contained memorable events in the life of the local and/or universal Church.[65] Gradually, the commemorations began to include events in the life of our Lord, the Theotokos, St. John the Baptist, and the Holy Apostles. Commemorations of the patriarchs and prophets of the Old Testament were also added to the synaxaria.

In due course, the synaxaria together with the hymns for the fixed feasts were gathered into special books, the precursors of the Menaia.[66] Two such collections, representing the ancient Jerusalem festal tradition, are the *Armenian Lectionary*, a fifth-century Armenian version of the ancient Jerusalem calendar, and the *Old Iadgari*, the Georgian version of the Jerusalem hymnal, also of the fifth century. The fixed festal calendar received its final form in Constantinople, where the *synaxarion* of the Imperial City prevailed. Significantly, the Menaia are open ended. Their content is continually expanding with the addition of new hymns honoring newly canonized saints.

According to Archbishop Job Getcha, the earliest Constantinopolitan manuscripts, the *Studite Menaia*, date to the eleventh century, while the earliest printed edition dates to 1551. A corrected version of the Greek Menaia was published in 1843.[67] Getcha also notes correctly that Menaia bear a distinctly local character. Therefore, they cannot always meet the actual needs of the Church and often require the publication of individual booklets containing the services written for newly canonized saints not contained in the printed Menaia.[68]

---

65 Such events include the commemoration of Ecumenical Synods and various dreadful calamities. For instance, on October 26, the day on which we commemorate the Great Martyr Demetrios of Thessaloniki, the service also includes a remembrance of the devastating earthquake that occurred in 740 during the reign of Leo III the Isaurian.

66 While the twelve Menaia share the same basic structure and form a single collection, each volume is independent. Liturgically, each volume is used only during its corresponding month of the year.

67 Getcha, *Typikon Decoded*, 33.

68 Slavic Menaia, for example, contain material not found in the Greek Menaia. Someday, in the not too distant future, the Church in America will have to carefully develop its own *Synaxarion*, bringing together the *synaxaria* of the churches. This process has already started. For example, the *Great Horologion* published by the Holy Transfiguration Monastery commemorates saints that have not been formerly listed in the Greek *synaxaria*.

8. The Psalter is the preeminent prayer book of the Church.[69] Entire psalms or parts of psalms are found in every service.[70] The faithful also use psalms in their private or personal prayers.

The Psalter contains the 150 psalms attributed to David as well as nine biblical odes, eight of which are from the Old Testament and one from the New Testament, which is comprised by two different odes, the *Magnificat* or the Song of Mary and the *Benedictus*, the Prayer of Zacharias, the father of St. John the Baptist, both of which are recorded in the Gospel of Luke. In fact, the psalms and the Nine Odes are the basic parts upon which the services of the daily office have been structured and fashioned.

The Orthodox Church recognizes the Septuagint (Greek) translation as the official liturgical version of the Old Testament. Hence, the psalms in all the liturgical books are numbered according to the Septuagint. The Septuagint is the third century BC Greek translation of the Old Testament (Ἡ Παλαιὰ Διαθήκη κατὰ τοὺς Ἑβδομήκοντα). The numbering of the Book of Psalms in the Septuagint is different from the numbering in the Hebrew version – the *Masoretic text* – on which most English translations are based. In the present volume (*Ierotelestikon*), the first number of a given psalm is the Septuagint number found in all the official liturgical books of the Church. The second number, after the slash or in parenthesis, indicates the number in the English translations, as for example Psalm 50/51 or 50 (51).[71]

The received Psalter represents the Palestinian monastic tradition, according to which the psalms are divided into twenty sections (sessions or sittings) called *kathismata* (κάθισμα, καθίσματα), each of which is divided into three sub-sections called *stasis* (στάσις, στάσεις). Each stasis has one, two, or three psalms depending on the length of each. Psalm 118 (119), the longest of the psalms, which contains 176 verses, is divided into three staseis and constitutes a single kathisma, the seventeenth.

---

69 For more on the Psalter and how it is used liturgically see *The Psalter* (Holy Transfiguration Monastery-Boston, MA, 1974); Getcha, *Typikon Decoded*, 15-23; Fountoulis, Λειτουργική, 78-80; and Velkovska, "Byzantine Liturgical Books," in *Liturgische Bücher in der Kulturgeschichte Europas*, 225 and 229.

70 On the psalms see J.A. Lamb, *The Psalms in Christian Worship* (London 1962), and more recently, Archbishop Demetrios Trakatelis, "The Book of Psalms: The Ecumenical and Universal Prayer," in his collection of essays, *The Seeds of Spirituality* (Brookline, MA 2019), 141-59.

71 Care is needed in reading some psalms in English translation. The Septuagint version may differ not only in the psalm's assigned number, but also in its verse order and count. For example, Psalm 113 in the Septuagint includes Psalms 114 and 115 of the Hebrew version. Psalm 114 in the Septuagint is Psalm 116:1-9 of the Hebrew. And Psalm 115 of the Septuagint is Psalm 116:10-19 of the Hebrew.

The Psalter of the cathedral office of Constantinople was divided into sixty-eight units called antiphons, each with its own number of psalms. The cathedral Psalter also contained fifteen odes of the Old and New Testament. The psalms in each antiphon were grouped together not in numerical order, but for their content, i.e., for their appropriateness for a particular service or feast. Traces of the cathedral Psalter can be found in a number of services. For example, the Orthros of Great and Holy Friday (Service of the Twelve Gospels), now celebrated on Holy Thursday evening, is partially structured on fifteen antiphons. In time, the appointed psalms of the antiphons were suppressed, but the troparia sung after the psalm's verses have remained.

9. The Byzantine Lectionary System was codified in three separate liturgical books beginning in the eighth century: the *Evangelion* (Εὐαγγέλιον), the *Apostolos* (Ἀπόστολος), and the *Anagnostikon* (Ἀναγνωστικόν), also known as the *Prophetologion* – (Προφητολόγιον).[72] Of the three books, the Evangelion (or Gospel lectionary) is the object of special honor. It is venerated as the icon of Christ par excellence. It is kissed, carried in processions, placed on the Holy Table, and reverenced with other honorific acts. The Evangelion is also fitted with special front and back covers, usually made of metal, which are engraved with the icons of the Crucifixion and Resurrection respectively.

The lectionary system is based on four cycles: the Sunday, Saturday, weekday, and festal cycles, each of which is at once both independent of and dependent on the others. Of the four, the Sunday system of readings (ἀναγνώσματα) was developed first, having received its basic form by the end of the fifth century. It was followed closely by the Saturday system, which is regarded as a liturgical day in the East from at least the fourth century, if not earlier. The weekday series of readings was the last to emerge and came about as a result of the daily celebration of the Divine Liturgy, especially in monasteries. The festal cycle is both old and new; it is in continuous development as new feasts are added to the calendar.

With few exceptions, the received system of readings was established in Constantinople well before the tenth century. It is important to note that before the seventh century, the Eucharistic liturgies of Constantinople had three readings, one each from the Prophetologion, Apostolos, and Evangelion. By the eighth century, the Old Testament pericope (lection or reading) had already disappeared from the Eucharistic liturgies.

---

72 For a concise bibliography on the development of the lectionary and the use of Scripture in the Orthodox Church see Calivas, "The Sunday Lucan Pericopes in the Byzantine Lectionary," in *The Liturgy in Dialogue: Exploring and Renewing the Tradition* (Brookline, MA 2018), 225-42. See also Fountoulis, Ἀπαντήσεις εἰς Λειτουργικὰς Ἀπορίας, vol. 2 (Thessaloniki 1975), 156-70.

Old Testament pericopes are read only during certain seasons, on a select number of feasts, and from a limited number of books. The Old Testament lessons were codified in the Anagnostikon or Prophetologion, which was last printed in 1595. From then on, its contents were incorporated into the Triodion, Pentecostarion, and Menaia. More recently the Church of Greece has published a version of the Prophetologion in the original Greek Septuagint with a modern Greek translation. Father Ephrem Lash and Bishop Demetri Khoury have compiled and edited a version of Prophetologion in English.

Both the Evangelion and Apostolos contain two large collections of readings totaling several hundred pericopes. The first, and by far the largest, collection is based on the movable cycle of feasts centered on Pascha. In earlier times this collection was called the *Synaxarion* (συναξάριον) and referred to the lessons read at the Divine Liturgy on Sundays, Saturdays, and weekdays. The second collection in both books is based on the fixed feasts, beginning with the month of September and is called the *Menologion* (μηνολόγιον). This section contains a set of two pericopes, one from each of the two books, which are read at the Divine Liturgy on a given feast. Some feasts also have a Gospel lesson assigned to the Orthros. Other feasts have three Old Testament readings, which are assigned to Vespers. The Vespers of Christmas, Theophany, and Pascha have multiple Old Testament readings but are limited to three in the established parish practice as per the rubrics in the *Typikon of the Great Church*.

In addition to these two collections, the Evangelion contains two smaller sets. The first is comprised of the eleven Morning (Ἑωθινά) Gospels assigned to the Sunday Orthros. The second set consists of Gospel lessons assigned to sacramental rites and other services. The Apostolos also contains a similar set for various rites and services.

The synaxarion collection in both the Evangelion and the Apostolos begins on the Sunday of Pascha with readings from the Gospel of John and the Book of the Acts of the Apostles respectively, a pairing that dates to the formative years of the lectionary system. In fact, the pairing of the two lessons – Epistle and Gospel – is not accidental. The two pericopes are meant to complement and reinforce one another.

From Monday after the Sunday of Pentecost the lessons in the Apostolos are organized in five periods covering a span of thirty-five weeks, that is, from the day after Pentecost in one year to the Palm Sunday of the following year. The sequence of readings begins with the Epistles of St. Paul, which are followed by the other epistles in the order in which they are found in the New Testament. Significantly, the Sunday-Saturday pericopes are taken exclusively from the Epistles of St. Paul.

In the course of a liturgical year, the lectionary offers the New Testament almost in its entirety through the prescribed pericopes in the Apostolos and Evangelion. Conspicuously, the Book of Revelation is not part of the lectionary system. Nonetheless, the clergy and the people are encouraged to read and study it.

The Gospel lessons in the Evangelion are organized in four periods, starting with the Gospel of John, as initially noted. Lessons from the Gospel of Matthew follow and cover a period of seventeen weeks or less, depending on the date of Pascha. The Matthean pericopes start on the day after Pentecost and end on the Friday after the Elevation of the Cross in mid-September. The pericopes from the Gospel of Luke begin on the Monday immediately following the Sunday after the Elevation of the Cross and end at the beginning of the Pre-Lenten season. The Gospel of Mark is associated with Great Lent and is read on the Saturdays and Sundays of the Lenten period (except for the first Sunday). The Gospel of Mark is also read on the weekdays from the twelfth to the sixteenth weeks of Matthew and on the weekdays from the thirteenth to the seventeenth week of Luke. As with the other Gospels, the missing passages in the continuous reading – *lectio continua* – of Mark are found in the services of Holy Week, Pascha, and the Menologion.

As elsewhere noted, it is difficult to know precisely when, how, and by whom the Byzantine lectionary system was devised. We know that it was never discussed or approved by an Ecumenical Synod. Hence it is both proper and right for the Church in her collective wisdom to initiate a review of it. Not only the times, but also the limitations within the inherited system require that one studies it prayerfully, critique it reverently, and revise prudently what needs revision.[73]

---

73 See Calivas, "Sunday Lucan Pericopes."

PART ONE
THE DAILY PRAYER OF THE CHURCH

"It is good to give thanks to the Lord, to sing praises to your name, O Most High; to declare your steadfast love in the morning and your faithfulness by night" (Psalm 91/92:1-2).

"Seven times a day I praise you for your righteous ordinances" (Psalm 118/119:164).

"But I call upon God; and the Lord will save me. Evening and morning and at noon I utter my complaint and moan and he will hear my voice" (Psalm 54/55:16-17).

"And they shall stand every morning, thanking and praising the Lord, and likewise at evening" (1 Chron. 23:30).

An Introduction to the Daily Cycle of Worship

Daily Worship

Although it is difficult to draw definitive conclusions about the forms of daily prayer in the early church, it is safe to assume that the practice of daily worship goes back to apostolic times, as evidenced by the many references to prayer in the New Testament.[74] The early Christians, like the Jews before them, adopted the custom of praying at certain fixed times during the day and night.[75] Clear evidence of a pattern of daily prayer-times emerges during the course of the second century. By the middle of the fourth century the Church had in place several public communal services that comprised the daily office.

As already noted in the Introduction, the daily office developed chiefly along two lines, the cathedral and the monastic.[76] The cathedral rite represents the form of services that were developed and practiced in the parochial or secular churches. The monastic rite originated in monastic communities in two forms: the *desert monastic* (which originated in Egypt and Palestine) and the *urban monastic* (which began in Cappadocia and Syria and flourished in Jerusalem and Constantinople).

The cathedral and monastic offices, each with its own distinctive characteristics and features, coexisted for many centuries. This early distinction, however, came to a gradual end in the post-iconoclastic period with the eventual demise of the cathedral office. The "monasticization" of ecclesial and liturgical life in the Eastern Church began with the Penthekte Synod (691-692), which introduced celibacy as a requirement for the episcopacy.[77] It was reinforced during the iconoclastic controversy and grew progressively in the ensuing centuries through today.

The daily office is intimately related to time and more specifically to fixed hours and periods of the day and night. In fact, the Church has organized her worship – the liturgy – around time and the sacraments or, put another way, around a calendar (day, week, month, and year) and a set of ritual acts

---

74 On the daily prayer of the Church, see Robert F. Taft, *The Liturgy of the Hours in East and West* (Collegeville, MN 1986). Paul F. Bradshaw, *Daily Prayer in the Early Church* (London and New York 1981); *Early Christian Worship* (Collegeville, MN 1996); and *The Search for the Origins of Christian Worship* (Oxford and New York 2002). See also Alkiviadis Calivas, *Come Before God in Prayer and Solemn Feast* (Brookline, MA 1986) and *Aspects of Orthodox Worship*, 66-9.

75 See, for example, *The Didache* (1st/2nd century) – chapter 8: "Thus shall you pray: Our Father...Three times in the day pray thus."); and Hippolytus, *On the Apostolic Tradition* (Crestwood, NY 2001), 164-6. The *Apostolic Tradition* (c. 215) is perhaps the first document to refer to a daily cycle of prayer found in later centuries, with evening and morning prayers supplemented by prayers at the third, sixth, and ninth hours and at midnight.

76 See Paul Fr. Bradshaw, *Two Ways of Praying* (Maryville, TN 2008). W. Jardine Grisbrooke, "The Formative Period – Cathedral and Monastic Offices," in *The Study of Liturgy*, C. Jones, G. Wainwright, E. Yarnold, and P. Bradshaw, eds. (London and New York 1992), 403-20.

77 The term *monasticization* was introduced by Taft to describe the significant influence of monasticism on the life and worship of the Church.

that make Christ and his saving work of the past and future a present reality especially through the sacraments. The Liturgy of the Hours sanctifies time and space while the sacraments sanctify life.[78]

Our common, everyday experiences of time have been integrated into liturgical time. Key events of salvation history have been tied to certain times of the day and periods of the year, filling them with meanings and sanctifying them with the memory of God's transforming presence in the unfolding history of the world.

Reckoning the Beginning of the Day and the Week

The Church has inherited two important notions concerning the measurement of time from Judaism. First, Orthodox Christians reckon the liturgical beginning of the day at sunset, a concept based on the Genesis account of creation: "God called the light Day, and the darkness he called Night. And there was evening and there was morning, one day" (Gen. 1:5). Accordingly, the liturgical day begins with the service of Vespers at sunset. The last service of the daily cycle in a given day is the Ninth Hour (late afternoon).

The Church additionally adopted the seven-day week from Judaism and embraced the Jewish tradition of assigning numerical names to the days of the week also based on the creation narrative in the book of Genesis. The tradition of the early Church lives in the native languages of the people in whose lands Orthodox Christianity took root, prospered, and flourished. The ecclesial and civil calendars in these lands have numerical names for some days of the week (second, third, fourth, fifth – Δευτέρα, Τρίτη, Τετάρτη, Πέμπτη) and proper names for the other days, which are also rooted in Jewish tradition. The seventh day is called Sabbath (Σάββατον) while the sixth day is named *Paraskevi* (Παρασκευή) or Day of Preparation. The first day of the week (πρώτη – ἡ μία τῶν Σαββάτων) is known by its distinctly Christian name Κυριακὴ Ἡμέρα or the Lord's Day.[79]

While the Semitic or Judaic method of reckoning the day is dominant in the Orthodox liturgical tradition, the Church also inherited another method, the Roman-Byzantine, according to which the day begins at midnight. This reckoning was part of Roman law and passed into the civil law of the Byzantine Empire and, in fact, is the method used today throughout the world in civil

---

78 See Alexander Schmemann, *Introduction to Liturgical Theology* (Crestwood, NY 1996).

79 It was customary in ancient cultures to assign the names of planet-gods to each day of the week. In fact, in the prevailing civil calendar, the days of the week in English are the Teutonic equivalents of the ancient Roman planetary names. See Alkiviadis Calivas, "The Lord's Day in Orthodox Liturgical Practice and Spirituality," in *Sunday, Sabbath, and the Weekend: Managing Time in Global Culture*, Edward O'Flaherty and Rodney Peterson with Timothy A. Norton, eds. (Grand Rapids, MI/Cambridge, UK 2010) 67-84; and in Calivas, *The Liturgy in Dialogue*, 202-24.

law. A striking example which points to the co-existence of the two methods in the liturgical practices of the Church is the rule on fasting. All days begin liturgically at sunset with Vespers, whether they are ordinary, feast, or fast days. The proscribed fast, however, on a fast day begins at midnight. For example, the weekly fast on Wednesdays and Fridays starts at midnight. The same is true for the Eucharistic fast: it begins at midnight and ends with the reception of Holy Communion at the morning Divine Liturgy.

The Services of the Daily Office

The received daily office of the Orthodox Church, as already noted, is monastic in origin and contains seven fixed prayer intervals or hours with eight services: Vespers, Apodeipnon (Compline), Mesonyktikon (Midnight Service or Nocturns), Orthros (Matins) with the First Hour, followed by the Third, Sixth, and Ninth Hours.[80] The priestly prayers and diaconal petitions of Vespers and Orthros are borrowed from the cathedral office of Constantinople.

The entire daily office is celebrated routinely in all monastic communities throughout the world.[81] Parishes, however, are required to serve Vespers and Orthros daily to the degree that this is feasible. All Orthodox Christians are encouraged to develop a rule of prayer that allows for communal worship and for personal devotions at different intervals of the day and night using elements of the daily office.

The fixed elements of the services of the daily office are contained in the Horologion. The variable festal hymns are contained in the Octoechos, which is structured on a recurring cycle of eight weeks, one for each of the eight tones of the ecclesiastical (Byzantine) music. The sequence of the weeks and tones begins on the Sunday after Pascha and ends on the final day of the Great Fast or Lent in the following year. The Octoechos also reflects the festal cycle of the week (more on this later).

The Octoechos is used together with the Triodion at the start of the Pre-Lenten season (Sunday of the Publican and Pharisee) until the Friday of *Apokreo* and on all Sundays of Lent. The Triodion is used through Great and Holy Week, ending with the Paschal Vigil. It is replaced by the Pentecostarion starting with the Intermediate Service and the Orthros of Pascha Sunday. The Octoechos is also used with the Pentecostarion on all the Sundays of the Paschal season, except for Palm Sunday, Pascha Sunday, the Sunday of Thomas, and Pentecost.

---

80 For more on these services see Ioannis M. Fountoulis, Λογικὴ Λατρεία (Thessaloniki 1971).

81 In many monasteries, to facilitate the activities of the community, the services of the daily office are clustered into several groups. The Midnight Office is followed immediately by the Orthros and First Hour. The Third and Sixth Hours are recited in the late morning. The Ninth Hour precedes Vespers. The Apodeipnon is said before the community prepares to retire.

The Pentecostarion is set aside after the Sunday of All Saints, whereupon the use of the Octoechos is resumed. The Menaion of each month is used daily in combination with the Octoechos, Triodion or Pentecostarion and the Horologion.[82]

The order of Vespers and Orthros on a given day is determined by the Typikon. The Epetiris produced annually by the Ecumenical Patriarchate provides a concise yearly summary of the rubrics contained in the Typikon.

The Daily Office Incorporates Us into the Mystery of Christ

The daily office through its cycle of services at different intervals of the day and night incorporates us into the mystery of Christ, in order to transform our ordinary time into the time of salvation – into a decisive moment, into a day of grace. In other words, in worship, our time acquires a new significance through the *anamnesis* or remembrance of the Christ event. Each day holds the possibility of sharing existence with eternity, with the Risen Christ, the Word and Son of God made flesh, the Author of life, and the Lord of history.

Of all natural phenomena, none is more conspicuous and central to human life than the setting and the rising of the sun. For devout Christians, the disappearance and appearance of light are more than natural occurrences. They are reminders of the death and resurrection of Christ. They are also a sign that reflects the way by which the only, truly existing, personal God relates to his creation: he is absent yet present, transcendent but immanent, inaccessible and at the same time accessible. Unknowable in his essence, the Triune God – Father, Son, and Holy Spirit – is known through his energies or acts – his voluntary self-revelation in the economy of salvation. Paradoxically and incomprehensibly, our God is a transcendent and immanent Trinity.[83]

We experience God and his saving power as immaterial, indescribable, unapproachable, inaccessible light – "God is light and in him there is no darkness at all...but if we walk in the light as he is in the light we have fellowship with one another, and the blood of Jesus his Son cleanses us from all sin" (1 Jn. 1:5, 7). The inaccessible light becomes accessible to those in whom it rises, in those who keep the commandments. Thus, the rising and the setting of the sun are the most propitious time for prayer and the remembrance

---

[82] For the sake of brevity, the Octoechos is seldom used on weekdays in parishes. As is generally known, the Orthodox liturgical year contains a succession of feasts and fasts divided into two large categories: immovable and movable. The immovable feasts occur on the same date each year. The texts for these feasts, as already noted, are contained in the Menaia. The movable feasts cover a period of eighteen consecutive weeks based on the feast of Pascha, the date of which changes from year to year.

[83] See John Meyendorff, *Byzantine Theology* (New York 1979), 180-90.

and celebration of Jesus Christ, the true Light of the world, who dispels the darkness and grants us grace to overcome our fears, limitations, and failures (Jn. 1:4-5; 8:12; 12:35-36, 46).[84]

Three basic themes are diffused in the psalms, prayers and hymns of Vespers and Orthros. The first theme is light, and more specifically the coming of Jesus Christ, who is "the true light that enlightens every man was coming into the world" (Jn. 1:9). He is the light that shines in darkness and dispels it by overcoming sin, corruption, and death (Jn. 1:5, 12:46; Matt. 4:16). He is also the Light that reveals the Father (Matt. 11:27; Jn. 14:6-11). The second theme is repentance. The psalms, prayers, and hymns seek to draw worshippers to the mystery of repentance by making them aware of not only the destructive effects of sin, but also the transforming power, goodness, love, and mercy of God, who alone forgives all iniquities and heals all infirmities. The two services also contain a variety of festal elements that concentrate on the memorable events of sacred history and the lives of saints. Through these festal elements, the liturgy draws the worshippers' attention to the third theme: God's transforming and sanctifying presence in history, in the world, in the Church, and in the lives of individual persons.

In addition, the Orthros provides us with the opportunity to thank God for the coming of a new day with all its challenges and opportunities and ask that it may be spent wisely by keeping the commandments. Vespers, in contrast, allow us to give thanks for the day that has passed, make amends for mistakes, and offer prayers for our safe-keeping during the night. Some also say that, in broad terms, the structure of Vespers and Orthros speak to the four great themes of Orthodox theology: creation, God's continuing providential care, salvation, and eschatology.

The Apodeipnon or Compline is recited after supper and before retiring. It focuses on three things: thanksgiving for the day that has passed; forgiveness of wrongs committed during the day; and protection during the ensuing night when sleep overtakes us – the time at which we are the most vulnerable. The Apodeipnon has two forms, the Small and the Great. The Great Apodeipnon originated in monastic communities. It is a long service comprised of psalms, hymns, and prayers. When the monastic typikon supplanted the parochial typikon, this lengthy service could not be sustained nightly in personal or communal devotions whether in private dwellings or parish settings. Hence, sometime between the fourteenth and fifteenth centuries, a new form of the Apodeipnon, the Small, was introduced. The new service quickly gained

---

84 1 John 1:5: "*God is light* and in him is no darkness at all." 1 Tim. 6:11-16: "But as for you, man of God... I charge you keep the commandment unstained...and this will be made manifest... by the King of kings and Lord of lords, *who alone has immortality and dwells in unapproachable light...*"

popular support. Eventually, the Great Apodeipnon was assigned to the weekdays (Monday through Thursday) of Great Lent. On the Fridays of Lent, the Small Apodeipnon is said in conjunction with the Salutations to the Theotokos.

Midnight Office: The "middle" of the night is an important hour in the Bible. The resurrection of Christ is among the significant events that have occurred in the deep of night (Luke 24:1, John 20:1). Scripture also implies that the Parousia or the Second Coming of Christ will occur in the middle of the night (Matt. 25:1-13; 1 Thess. 5:2; 2 Peter 3:10). The Midnight Office is structured on these two themes. Closely connected to the Parousia is the call for spiritual vigilance and watchfulness (Matt. 25: 13; cf. Matt. 26:41 and 1 Peter 5:8). The Midnight Office includes an additional element: the remembrance of the dead. Also, in the deep of night, the clatter of human activity is at its lowest ebb. In these moments of profound silence, an attentive ear is able to hear the hum of creation glorifying the Creator of all things, both visible and invisible. In these moments of silence, an awakened, vigilant, and grateful soul can also break into songs of praise and thanksgiving: "At midnight I will rise to give thanks to you, because of your righteous judgments" (Psalm 118/119:62). Indeed, in ancient times, it was not uncommon for households to awaken in the middle of the night and return to sleep again after a period of social interaction. Prayer at the midnight hour served to remind and draw the members of the household into the mystery of Christ and specifically to his Second glorious Coming, when he will come to judge the living and the dead, when "he will wipe away every tear...and death shall be no more, neither shall there be mourning nor crying nor pain any more, for the former things have passed away" (Rev. 21:4).

Each of the four Hours has a particular theme and sometimes a sub-theme, and in the case of the Great Hours a specific festal theme.[85] The general theme of each Hour is as follows: at the First Hour, which constitutes an extension of the Orthros, the Church celebrates the coming of the true Light, our Lord Jesus Christ; at the Third Hour (mid-morning), we celebrate the descent of the Holy Spirit on the day of Pentecost (Acts 2:15); at the Sixth Hour (noontime),

---

85 The Great Hours of Christmas celebrate the Nativity of our Lord and Savior Jesus Christ; those of Theophany the Baptism of our Lord by St. John the Forerunner in the Jordan; and those of Great and Holy Friday commemorate the passion and burial of the Lord. Two of the three psalms in each of the Hours differ from those in the ordinary Hours. These psalms were selected for their suitability for the particular feast. Also, each of the Great Hours contains festal troparia and three Scripture lessons. For more on the Hours, see Stefanos Alexopoulos, "Οἱ Ἀκολουθίες τῆς Πρώτης, Τρίτης, Ἕκτης καὶ Ἐνάτης Ὥρας" and "Οἱ Ἀκολουθίες τῶν Μεγάλων Ὡρῶν" in Ἐκκλησία, 92 (2015), 480-96 and 686-701 respectively. Also see his "Anamnesis, Epiclesis, and Mimesis in the Minor Hours of the Byzantine Rite," in *Worship*, vol. 94 (July 2020), 228-45.

we remember the passion and crucifixion of our Lord (Luke 23:44); and at the Ninth Hour (mid-afternoon), we commemorate the death and burial of the Lord (Matt. 27:46-50).[86]

Notably, the festal elements of a given day are incorporated in the Vespers and Orthros. The other services of the daily office are largely unaffected by the festal calendar. The Great Hours of Christmas, Theophany, and Holy and Great Friday constitute the exception.[87]

Saint Paul admonishes us to "rejoice always, pray without ceasing, in everything give thanks; for this is the will of God in Christ Jesus for you" (1 Thess. 5:16-18). He also said, "Continue earnestly in prayer, being vigilant in it with thanksgiving" (Col. 4:2) and "Pray at all times in the Spirit, with all prayer and supplication. To that end keep alert with all perseverance, making supplication for all the saints" (Eph. 6:18; cf. Luke 18:1-7 and 21:36).

Daily devotions, whether private or communal, at frequent intervals of the day have salutary effects on the lives of Christians. The remembrance of Christ through prayer and meditation permeates and sanctifies one's whole life. It energizes the soul, softens and warms the heart, illumines thoughts, strengthens the will for the good, and leads to works of righteousness. The continuous remembrance of God transforms one's very life, allowing everyday occupations and pursuits to become an act of ceaseless prayer. Put another way, a life lived in Christ becomes an act of prayer as whoever holds the Lord Jesus within one's heart will not tire in following him. As Origin noted:

> He prays without ceasing who combines his prayer with necessary works, and suitable activities with his prayer, for his virtuous deeds or the precepts he has fulfilled are taken up as part of his prayer. Only in this way can we take the saying, "Pray without ceasing," as being possible, if we can say that the whole life of the [person] is one mighty integrated prayer (On Prayer, 12).

---

86 The Horologion also contains an Inter-hour, in Greek Μεσώριον, for each of the four Hours. The inter-hours are usually read in monastic communities during certain fasting periods.

87 See Calivas, *Come Before God*, 7-11.

Basic Structure of the Services of the Daily Office

The basic structure of each service of the daily office is formed around the psalms and odes (songs or canticles) of the Bible. Indeed, the daily office points to the centrality of the Psalter in Orthodox worship. For example, Vespers begins with Psalm 103/104. Following the Great *Synapte*, ordinarily the appointed kathisma from the Psalter is read.[88] This is followed by the four evening psalms (140/141; 141/142; 120/130; and 116/117) with the accompanying hymns (stichera troparia), which are interpolated between the last few verses of the final two psalms in the series. The ancient hymn, "O joyous Light," is followed by the evening prokeimenon, which consists of select verses of a specific psalm. Following the diaconal petitions, we sing the aposticha troparia together with verses from a select psalm. The service draws to its conclusion with the recitation or singing of the Song (or Prayer) of St. Symeon the God-Receiver (Luke 2:29-32).

Also, by way of example, each of the four Hours contains three psalms, one of which is a stable or fixed element of the service.[89] Each Hour also shares a common prayer, "You who are at all times and at every hour, in heaven and on earth…" In addition, each Hour ends with a distinct prayer that reflects the central theme of the Hour.

---

88 In parish worship, the *kathisma* of the Psalter is usually omitted for the sake of brevity.

89 The fixed psalm of the First Hour is Ps. 5; of the Third Hour, Ps. 50/51; of the Sixth Hour, Ps. 90/91; and of the Ninth Hour, Ps. 85/86.

The Annual and Weekly Festal Calendar

The festal calendar is a result of continuous development. Through the passage of time each local Church adds to the calendar its own martyrs and holy persons and its own significant ecclesial events. Some saints are honored only locally whereas others are recognized universally.[90]

The feasts and fasts of the liturgical year, which begins on the first day of September, vary in importance and are usually divided into two large categories, fixed and movable. The movable feasts are related to the Great and Holy Pascha, the date of which changes from year to year. The fixed feasts occur on the same date each year. The texts for the various feasts are contained in the several liturgical books of the Church. The festal calendar includes feasts dedicated to our Lord and Savior Jesus Christ, the Theotokos, St. John the Forerunner and Baptist, and the holy Apostles. The Church also honors in feast the holy angels, patriarchs, prophets, martyrs, confessors, ascetics, and every righteous spirit made perfect in faith, i.e., men, women and children from all stations of life who achieved holiness. Also remembered are significant events in the life of the Church, such as ecumenical synods.

---

90 In the last several centuries a host of neomartyrs have been added to the *synaxaria* of local Churches as a result of the persecutions perpetrated by the Ottomans and, more recently, by the Communist rulers of Eastern Europe. We refer to these men and women of faith, who gave their lives for Christ, as neomartyrs. Newly proclaimed saints throughout the Orthodox world have also been added to the *synaxaria*. For example, St. Nektarios of Aegina (feast day November 9) was canonized by the Ecumenical Patriarchate on April 20, 1961. On August 9, 1970, the Orthodox Church in America (OCA) canonized St. Herman of Alaska (feast day December 13) and the Holy Neomartyrs Juvenaly the Heiromonk and Peter the Aleut (feast day September 24). More recently, on January 16, 2004, the Ecumenical Patriarchate canonized St. Maria Skobtsova of Paris (feast day July 20); on November 27, 2013, St. Porphyrios (feast day December 2); and on January 13, 2015, the Venerable Elder Paisios (feast day July 12). In his challenging reflection on sainthood, "Men, Monks, and Making Saints," which appeared on the website *Public Orthodoxy* (December 2019), which is the online publication of the Orthodox Christian Studies Center of Fordham University, Fr. John Chryssavgis writes, "Saints are completely and consistently human – neither superhuman nor semi-divine." When synods act to recognize holiness, they do so based on how the clergy and the people, the conscience of the Church, refer to the holy. On the process by which saints are recognized in the Orthodox Church, see Peter Chamberas and John Chryssavgis, *The Recognition of Saints in the Orthodox Church: Past and Present* (Newfound Publishing: Hebron, NH, 2021); K. Papadopoulos, "Γιὰ τὴν διακήρυξη τῶν Ἁγίων" in Σύναξη, vol. 102 (2007); George Tsetsis, "Ἡ διαδικασία ἐντάξεως Ἁγίων στὸ ἑορτολόγιο κατὰ τὴν πρᾶξη τοῦ Οἰκουμενικοῦ Πατριαρχείου," in Ὀρθοδοξία (2001); Stylianos Papadopoulos, Διαπίστωση καὶ Διακήρυξη τῆς Ἁγιότητας τῶν Ἁγίων (Katerini 1990); P. Papageorgiou, "Ἀνακήρυξις Ἁγίων ἐν τῇ Ὀρθοδόξῳ Ἐκκλησίᾳ" in Γρηγόριος Παλαμᾶς, vol. 43 (1960); Amilka Alivizatos, "Ἡ Ἀναγνώρισις τῶν Ἁγίων ἐν τῇ Ὀρθοδόξῳ Ἐκκλησίᾳ," in Θεολογία, vol. 19 (1941-1948), 18-52; Also see the brief yet informative article, "The Saints of the Orthodox Church," on the website of the Greek Orthodox Archdiocese of America.

In addition to the annual calendar of feasts, the Church has also assigned a specific observance to each day of the week. The festal cycle of the week summarizes succinctly and ingeniously the entire annual festal cycle of feasts and fasts. Each day has a special commemoration. The cycle begins on Sunday, the Lord's Day (Κυριακὴ Ἡμέρα) and first day of the week, which marks the Church's joyous weekly celebration of the Paschal mystery – Christ's crucifixion, burial, resurrection, and glorification. The Lord's Day is a Christian institution, a Christian festival founded on the event and fact of Christ's resurrection. It is a day for rejoicing and for holy convocation. It is, thus, the preeminent day for the celebration of the Divine Liturgy. On Monday, the second day of the week (Δευτέρα), we commemorate the Holy Angels; on Tuesday, St. John the Forerunner and Baptist; on Wednesday, the Theotokos and the betrayal of Jesus; on Thursday, the Holy Apostles and St. Nicholas the Wonder-worker; on Friday, the Crucifixion, death and burial of our Savior; and on Saturday, we remember the holy martyrs and ascetics, and the dead who have fallen asleep in the hope of resurrection.

Except for certain times of the year, every Wednesday and Friday, from the earliest days of the Church, have been observed with a fast, because the Lord was betrayed on a Wednesday and he was crucified on a Friday.[91] In addition to these two days, the Church has established a number of other fast days and fast periods of varying length, among which are Great Lent and Holy Week.[92]

---

91 See the *Didache or Teaching of the Twelve Apostles*, chapter 8.

92 For example, September 14 and August 29 are fast days. On September 14 we celebrate the Feast of the Exaltation of the Life-giving Cross and on August 29 we commemorate the Beheading of St. John the Baptist. In addition to Great Lent and Holy Week, the Church also observes three other fasting periods: the feast of the Nativity of Christ (November 15-December 24), the feast of the Holy Apostles (the number of days varies from year to year), the feasts of the Transfiguration of our Lord and the Dormition of the Theotokos (August 1-August 14). For more on the practice and significance of fasting see *The Lenten Triodion*, Mother Mary and Kallistos Ware, trans. (London & Boston, 1978), 13-28, 35-37; and Calivas, *Come Before God*, 22-25 and 29-32. See also *Toward the Holy and Great Council: Theological Reflections*, Nathaniel Symeonides, ed. (Greek Orthodox Archdiocese, NY, 2016), 57-73, and the final document on fasting promulgated by the Holy and Great Council (June 17-26, 2016) on the website of the Ecumenical Patriarchate of Constantinople under Holy and Great Council-2016.

1. THE SERVICE OF VESPERS (ΕΣΠΕΡΙΝΟΣ)

Introduction

The Church has several forms of Vespers: The Saturday and Feast-day Vespers (also known as Great Vespers); the Small Vespers (related to Vigils);[93] the Daily Vespers (without an entrance), the Sunday Vespers of Lent; the daily Vespers of Lent; and the Vespers of Pascha and Renewal or Bright Week. One can also include the festal Vespers of Christmas and Theophany as well as of Pentecost Sunday, which is also known as the Service of Kneeling.

The priestly prayers, petitions, and prokeimena of these services are found in the Ieratikon. The fixed elements (psalms, prayers, prokeimena) are contained in the Horologion and in the *Reader's Compendium or Manual* ('Εγκόλπιον

---

[93] According to the monastic typikon every Sunday and major feast is celebrated with an All-Night Vigil (at least in theory if not always in practice). Hence, in the Octoechos and other liturgical books, there exist two services of Vespers for Saturday night and on the eve of major feast days. The first of these is called Small Vespers and the second, Great Vespers. Small Vespers is simpler in form and content and is conducted in monasteries at the appointed time, sunset. Following the Apodeipnon, the Vigil commences with the celebration of Great Vespers followed by the Orthros, the Hours, and the Divine Liturgy. For more on the Monastic Vespers and Monastic Orthros see Ioannis Fountoulis, Κείμενα Λειτουργικῆς, Nos. 6 and 10 (Thessaloniki, 1978) respectively; In Greek parish usage, only the service of Great Vespers is celebrated on Saturday evenings and on the eve of major feast days. The Orthros is celebrated in the morning and is followed by the Divine Liturgy. In keeping with the monastic typikon, many Slavic churches celebrate a 'mini-vigil' on Saturday evenings, which consists of Great Vespers followed by the Orthros (full or modified). In the morning, the Third and Sixth Hours are read before the Divine Liturgy.

Ἀναγνώστου).[94] The festal hymns are found in the Octoechos, Triodion, or Pentecostarion (according to the liturgical season) and in the Menaia. Other festal elements, such as Scripture readings, are contained in the Menaia, Triodion, and Pentecostarion.[95]

The service of Great Vespers is conducted every Saturday evening and on the eve of important feast days. Thanks to the efforts of some enterprising people, the celebration of these and other services has been greatly simplified for the clergy as well as for readers and chanters or choirs. I am referring especially to the works produced in recent years by Fr. Spencer Kezios of Narthex Press; Fr. Seraphim Dedes through his online Digital Chant Stand (formerly, the Ages Initiative); and the Divine Music Project of the Monastery of St. Anthony.

A. Saturday Evening and Feast Day Vespers – Great Vespers

As celebrated by one priest with a deacon. (If there is no deacon, the priest, within the sanctuary, says the petitions and biddings assigned to the deacon).

The Priest begins the service wearing the exorasson and epitrachilion (stole). The **Deacon** wears the sticharion and orarion. (In some traditions, the deacon also wears the epimanika).

The Initial Blessing or Doxology and Introductory Psalm

Deacon

Receives the blessing of the priest to vest. When he is vested, he comes and stands to the right of the priest and slightly behind him. (He reverences together with the priest and then kisses the Holy Table).

Priest

Stands before the Holy Table and reverences three times, repeating each time the words, "God, be merciful to me a sinner" (Luke 18:13). He kisses the Evangelion and the Holy Table. Then he intones the opening doxology: *"Blessed is our God* – Εὐλογητὸς ὁ Θεὸς ἡμῶν..."

---

[94] The *Reader's Compendium* contains material extracted from the Horologion and other liturgical books to assist readers and chanters in the performance of their duties.

[95] On the use of the Bible in the liturgy, see Calivas, *The Liturgy in Dialogue*. (Brookline 2018), 225-42.

Reader

Recites the call to worship (*Come let us worship and bow down...*) and the Introductory Psalm 103/104 (Ὁ Προοιμιακὸς Ψαλμός).⁹⁶

Priest

While the psalm is being read, the priest stands in front of the Holy Table and recites the seven evening prayers in a low voice.

The Introductory Psalm was sung originally in its entirety with a short melodic refrain after each verse sung by the choir and the people. Short refrains included one word, phrase, or single verse from the psalm, as, for example, "Alleluia;" "Glory to you, O God, glory to you"; "O Lord, how manifold are your works! In wisdom you have made them all" (24a). In fact, this verse is repeated at the end of the psalm, an indication that it was likely a popular refrain as it summarizes the content of the psalm, a hymn of thanksgiving and praise of the Creator of all things, both visible and invisible.

The Seven Evening Prayers originated in the cathedral office of Constantinople. In current practice they are said in a low voice one after the other. Initially, however, they were recited aloud at different intervals of the service. For example, the first prayer was read at the conclusion of the Great Litany; the second after the kathisma of the Psalter; and the seventh at the conclusion of the Dismissal Litany or Litany of Completion ("Let us complete our evening prayer to the Lord"). A return to the original practice would be a welcome and meaningful change. From a liturgical and theological perspective, the current practice is pointless and ineffective.

---

96 Note the following important details regarding the Introductory Psalm 103/104. (a) When a hierarch presides, he will read both the call to worship and the psalm. (b) On the Sunday of Pascha and throughout Renewal or Bright Week and on the *Apodosis* of Pascha, the call to worship and the introductory psalm are omitted. Instead, we sing the hymn "*Christ is risen from the dead*" ten times with the designated verses. (c) During the Paschal season, the call to worship is eliminated and the hymn, "*Christ is risen*," is sung three times, first by the priest and then twice by the chanters/choirs. (d) If the *Anoixantaria* are chanted at Vespers of a major feast, the reader ends the recitation of the introductory psalm at verse 28a, "What you give them they gather in." The remaining verses (28b–35) are sung melodically by the choir together with short melodic hymns (refrains) in praise of the Holy Trinity. The hymns are interpolated between the verses of the psalm according to the prescribed order. The earliest version of these hymns is attributed to Ioannis Koukouzelis (twelfth century), the famous melodist. The word, *Anoixantaria*, comes from the first word of verse 28b: "Ἀνοίξαντός σου τὴν χεῖρα...When you *open* your hand."

A Note on Church Doors

Of the many doors through which the clergy and the people had access to the galleries; the outer and inner narthex; the nave; and the sanctuary of the Great Church of St. Sophia, two were especially significant: the central door of the inner narthex leading into the nave and the central door of the bema or the iconostasis leading into the sanctuary. Both doors acquired distinct names or titles. These names became established and were used to identify the same doors in every other cathedral and temple. In time, however, after the Fall of Constantinople, some names were forgotten, and others misapplied.

The central door of the narthex leading into the nave was called Beautiful Gate, Great Doors, or Royal Doors, among other names. The name, Beautiful Gate (Ὡραία Πύλη), comes from one of the gates of the Temple of Solomon in Jerusalem, which is mentioned by St. Luke in Acts 3:2, 10. At that gate, St. Peter healed a lame beggar. The central door was also called the Great Gates or Doors (Πύλαι Μεγάλαι) because of their imposing size and exquisite beauty. The central door was also known as the Royal or Imperial Gates or Door (Πύλαι Βασιλικαί or Βασιλική Πύλη) because the emperor and his entourage together with the patriarch and senior clerics entered into the nave through them. To emphasize this fact, above the Royal Doors of St. Sophia is a mosaic depicting a prostrate emperor at the feet of an enthroned Christ, on either side of whom are two busts in a circular frame of the Theotokos and the Archangel Gabriel. The Doors are called Royal for another, symbolic reason as well. Through them, God's faithful people, the royal priesthood, enter into his presence, who is the "King of Kings and Lord of Lords" (Rev. 19:16).

The central door of the bema or the iconostasis is called Door or Doors of the Bema (Βημόθυρα) or, simply, Holy Doors (Ἅγίαι Θύραι). Only hierarchs, priests, and deacons may enter through them. By the fourteenth century the Holy Doors had acquired an established iconographic theme: the Annunciation with the Archangel Gabriel depicted on one leaf of the door and the Virgin Theotokos standing on the other leaf. Symbolically, the Holy Doors have come to represent the doors to Paradise. The two other smaller doors on either side of the bema also leading into the sanctuary are called side doors (πλαγίαι θύραι, παραπόρτια). The two side doors are also referred to as the north door (βορεία πύλη) and south door (νοτία πύλη), because, at least in theory, they are on the north and south sides of the sanctuary, respectively. (The Greek language has two basic words for door and gate: θύρα (door) and πύλη (gate and secondarily door).

Today, in many books, documents, and liturgical texts, the names once applied to the central door of the narthex have been transferred to the Holy Door of the iconostasis. In this text, I have maintained the original name, Holy Door(s).[97]

The Great Synapte or Great Litany

Deacon

While the doxology of the Introductory Psalm is being sung, the deacon receives the priest's blessing and exits the sanctuary from the north door (close to the *prothesis* – the table of preparation). He proceeds to the middle of the solea and, facing the sanctuary, he intones the Great Synapte or Great Litany. He holds the front end of the orarion in his right hand, which he raises slightly as he intones each petition. When he concludes the petitions, he bows reverently toward the Holy Doors, proceeds to the south door, and enters the sanctuary. He stands in his usual place facing the Holy Table.

Priest

At the conclusion of the Great Litany, the priest intones the *ekfonesis* (the concluding doxology of a given prayer).

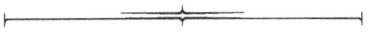

> **The Great Synapte or Great Litany** *is found in most, if not all, the sacramental rites and other corporate services of the Church. It consists of a series of eleven petitions, which are followed by a plea for God's help and mercy, a commemoration of the Theotokos and the saints, and a call for the people's personal and communal commitment to Christ. The Synapte ends with a priestly prayer. Special petitions are added to the eleven core petitions of the litany in other rites and celebrations, including baptism, marriage, ordination, holy unction, the Great Blessing of the Waters, Vespers of Pentecost, etc. The Great Synapte, as with all diaconal litanies, is a form of intercession. The Synapte is a diaconal invitation addressed to the people indicating the intentions to be prayed for. The people respond to each petition, addressing God with the plea, "Lord, have mercy ... (Κύριε, ἐλέησον)." To the bidding, "let us commit ourselves and one another," the people respond, "To you, O Lord ... Σοί, Κύριε."*

---

97 On church doors see, among others, Konstantinos Kallinikos, Ὁ Χριστιανικός Ναός καὶ τὰ Τελούμενα ἐν αὐτῷ (Athens 1958), 100-1; 126-7; and the specific references in Thomas F. Mathews, *The Early Churches of Constantinople: Architecture and Liturgy* (Pennsylvania State University Press and London, 1977); Rowland J. Mainstone, *Hagia Sophia: Architecture, Structure, and Liturgy of Justinian's Great Church* (New York, 1988).

Other diaconal invitations, admonitions, and litanies have their own special responses. The appearance of the Great Synapte at the beginning of the Divine Liturgy (and other services) began around the tenth century. Previously, as will be examined below, it was said after the readings. In some texts we find the petition, "For all pious and Orthodox Christians, let us pray to the Lord" inserted before the petition for the local hierarch. This particular petition began to appear in texts after the fall of Constantinople in place of the petition for the Imperial family. The petition, however, is both unnecessary and redundant. The people are prayed for in two of the fixed petitions that follow. Interestingly, early sources tell us that the people knelt during the Great Synapte. Of course, this happened only on weekdays as kneeling is prohibited on Sundays and the entire Paschal period from Pascha to Pentecost. [98]

[*At this point the reader recites the appointed* Kathisma of the Psalter. **However, in parish usage the Kathisma of the Psalter is omitted, according to long-standing practice.** *Hence, the chanter/choir immediately begins singing the Evening Psalms*].

---

98 See Canons 20 of the First Ecumenical Synod and 90 of the Penthekte; also St. Basil, *On the Holy Spirit*, 27:66. The prohibition on kneeling, however, is not absolute as evidenced by the rites of ordination, which require the ordinand to kneel (Canons of St. Nikephoros, can. 10).

The Evening Psalms and Stichera Troparia[99]

The **Chanter (or Choir) and People** sing the four Evening Psalms (140/141; 141/142; 129/130; 116/117) and the assigned hymns (*stichera troparia*) in the appointed tone(s).[100]

•⇒•

The Censing

Deacon

When the chanters start singing Psalm 140/141, the deacon is given the censer (also called thurible and *thymiaton*). He holds the censer in his right hand. The front end of the orarion is placed on his left forearm. Facing the priest, he raises the censer slightly and bids him to bless the offering of incense, "*Bless, Master, the incense* – Εὐλόγησον, δέσποτα, τὸ θυμίαμα.*" After the priest has blessed the offering of incense, the deacon stands in front of the Holy Table. As the chanters begin singing the second verse of Psalm 140, "*Let my prayer be set before you as* incense...," the deacon commences censing in the usual manner starting with the Holy Table. He exits the sanctuary through the

---

99 The first two verses of Psalm 140/141 read as follows: "Lord, I cry out to you; make haste to me. Give ear to my voice when I cry out to you. Let my prayer be set before you as incense, the lifting up of my hands as an evening sacrifice." These same two verses, however, are rendered differently in the service of Vespers: "Lord, I cry out to you; *hear me. Hear me, O Lord*. Lord, I cry out to you; *hear me*. Give ear to my voice when I cry out to you; *hear me, O Lord*. Let my prayer be set before you as incense, the lifting up of my hands as an evening sacrifice; *hear me, O Lord*." The words in *italics* are an interpolation, a remnant of cathedral office usage. These interpolations are, in fact, remnants the refrains which the people sang together with the chanters or choir, according to the cathedral office. Notice also that in the "liturgical" version, verse 1(a), "Lord, I cry out to you; *hear me. Hear me, O Lord*," is said twice. It was common for the precentor (*protopsaltis*) to sing the verse first, in order to identify the psalm, the tone, and melody of the refrain(s). The verse was repeated by the choir and the people.

100 Unfortunately, for the sake of brevity, many choose to omit the biblical verses in favor of the *troparia*. However, the time saved is negligible. For example, only the first two verses of Ps. 140/141 are sung melodically. The subsequent verses of the evening psalms are sung in quick rhythm. More time consuming are the stichera troparia, which, in some instances, are long and may, according to the typikon, amount to as many as ten in number in addition to the "Doxastikon" and the "Kai nyn." For the sake of brevity, the number of troparia in parish usage may be limited to six or four, depending on circumstances and need. It is far more important to create a prayerful setting, so that what is being read and sung conveys meaning and inspires the soul of the singer(s) and hearers. According to an ancient Greek maxim, "*The good is found not in quantity but in quality.*" The troparia are taken from the Octoechos or the Tridion or Pentecostarion and the relevant Menaion. The number of the troparia are determined by the typikon.

north door (closest to the Prothesis). When he has completed the censing, he re-enters the sanctuary by the south door.

> **NOTE 1:** *For the order of censing see the appropriate entry below.*
>
> **NOTE 2:** *In the absence of a deacon, the priest wears the phelonion, offers the prayer of incense, and performs the censing according to the set order.*

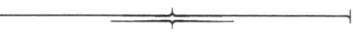

The Entrance Rites

When the Καὶ νῦν *troparion* is being chanted the priest and deacon prepare for the Entrance. The **priest** is vested with the *epitrachilion* and *phelonion*. He comes before the Holy Table and reads The Prayer of Entrance.[101] The **deacon** receives the priest's blessing and censes the Holy Table. The priest follows him around the Holy Table. The acolytes lead the procession through the north door. The procession comes directly to the middle of the solea. The **deacon** stands slightly to side and bids the priest to bless the Entrance. After the blessing, the deacon steps in front of the priest and draws closer to the iconostasis and censes the icons of the iconostasis. He then censes the priest and the people. When the chanters complete the hymn, the **deacon** raises the censer slightly and intones, *"Wisdom! Arise! (Σοφία! Ὀρθοί!).* He steps to the right of the priest as the *Evening Thanksgiving* – the ancient hymn, *"O Joyous Light... Φῶς Ἱλαρόν,"* is being sung.

The Evening Thanksgiving – "O Joyous Light...Φῶς Ἱλαρόν"

The **Priest and People** sing the Evening Thanksgiving. When the phrase, "ἐλθόντες ἐπὶ τὴν ἡλίου δύσιν... now that we are come to the setting of the sun...," is being sung, the deacon (or priest in the absence of a deacon) censes the icons of the Lord and the Theotokos and enters the sanctuary through the Holy Doors. He censes the Holy Table, steps to the left of the Table and censes the priest as he enters and then all other persons in the sanctuary.

---

101 Originally, the Prayer of Entrance was recited aloud by the priest standing in the midst of the congregation before he blessed the Entrance. This element in the prevailing practice also requires further study.

O Joyous Light: *St. Basil the Great in his treatise, On the Holy Spirit (29:73), makes reference to the hymn and describes it as ancient. As he notes, "Our fathers thought that they should welcome the gift of evening light with something better than silence, so they gave thanks as soon as it appeared. We cannot say who composed these words of thanksgiving at the lighting of the lamps, but the people use these ancient words... We praise Father, Son, and God's Holy Spirit...." It has been theorized that the hymn was originally sung antiphonally. Accordingly, the phrase, "ἐλθόντες ἐπὶ τὴν ἡλίου δύσιν... now that we are come to the setting of the sun and behold the evening light, we sing in praise to God the Father, Son, and Holy Spirit,"*[102] *was sung as a refrain – after the first and third verses of the hymn. In fact, the first and third verses use words of praise for the Lord Christ, whereas the second verse utters words of praise for the Holy Trinity. "O joyful light of the holy glory of the immortal Father, heavenly, holy, blessed Jesus Christ; now that we are come to the setting of the sun and behold the evening light, we sing in praise to God the Father, Son, and Holy Spirit. It is proper at all times to praise you in hymns with happy voice, O Son of God, who grants life: therefore, the world gives you glory."*

The Evening Prokeimenon

Deacon

When the hymn has concluded, the deacon faces the right choir and bids them to sing the Prokeimenon, saying: Ἑσπέρας Προκείμενον ... *The Evening Prokeimenon.*[103]

---

102 St. Basil the Great, On the Holy Spirit (Crestwood, NY 1980), 110.

103 The prokeimenon is a select verse from a particular psalm deemed appropriate to the occasion. It is sung three times, the third time after a specific verse from the same psalm. The prokeimenon of Saturday Vespers has two verses and in some traditions three. Some have speculated that in earlier times the prokeimenon may have been sung as a refrain after each verse or a group of verses from a psalm.

Chanters/Choir and People

Sing the Evening Prokeimenon. (Each day of the week has a prokeimenon. Some dominical feasts have their own special prokeimenon).[104]

If the Service Has Readings

[When a feast is assigned readings (αναγνωσματα), they are read immediately after the prokeimenon]

Reader

The lector announces the reading before each of the three assigned Old Testament pericopes. (For example, "*The reading is from [the Book of] Genesis*").[105]

Deacon

The deacon responds after each announcement with an exhortation, inviting the people to be attentive. He faces the people and says: "*Wisdom! Let us be attentive!* – Σοφία! Πρόσχωμεν!"

(If the reading is from the New Testament, a rare occurrence, the deacon says: "Πρόσχωμεν! Σοφία! Πρόσχωμεν!")

---

104 The seven prokeimena of the week are based on the weekly cycle of feasts and are meant to reflect the theme of the day. In addition to these daily prokeimena, feasts of the Lord have their own prokeimenon as do the Sundays of Great Lent. The Paschal Vigil Vespers with Liturgy (now celebrated on Holy Saturday morning) does not have a prokeimenon, nor do the Vespers of Christmas and Theophany. The regular Evening Prokeimena of the week are Saturday, Ps. 92/93:1; Sunday, Ps. 133/134:1; Monday, Ps. 4:4b (Septuagint) or 4:3b (Masoretic); Tuesday, Ps. 22/23:6; Wednesday, Ps. 53/54:1; Thursday, Ps. 120/121:2; and Friday, Ps. 58:10b-11b (Septuagint) or 59:9b-10 Masoretic). For the monastic practice on the prokeimena, see *The Great Horologion*, 13 and 189-90.

105 See Calivas, *Liturgy in Dialogue*, 227.

Part One: The Service of Vespers (ΕΣΠΕΡΙΝΟΣ)

The Fervent Litany or Entreaty[106]

Deacon

After the Entrance and the prokeimenon, the deacon exits the sanctuary in the usual manner and proceeds to the middle of the solea. Facing the sanctuary, he intones the petitions of the Fervent Litany ("Let us all say ... Εἴπωμεν πάντες...").

(If there is no deacon, the priest intones the petitions within the sanctuary, standing before the Holy Table).

Priest

The priest reads the Prayer of the Litany at the appropriate time in a low voice and intones the doxological ending (*"For you are a merciful and loving God... Ὅτι ἐλεήμων καὶ φιλάνθρωπος Θεὸς ὑπάρχεις...").*

---

[106] The title, *Fervent Litany*, derives from the Greek term, Ἐκτενὴς Δέησις, which means a fervent or earnest entreaty. The several petitions of the Litany bear witness to this. The first petition is addressed to the people and has two foci. First, it identifies the sources from which the prayer must emanate, namely, the worshippers' soul and mind: *"Let us all say from the depths of our soul and with all our mind"* (with all attentiveness). Say what? The petition gives the answer: "Let us say, Κύριε Ἐλέησον," which is the response to each of the subsequent petitions. The second and third petitions are directed not to the people but to God, the *Almighty Lord and God of our fathers*. This petition-plea for his love and mercy is intense: "*we pray you, hear us, and have mercy*." The next five petitions are addressed to the people to pray in all earnestness for the clergy; for the faithful and their needs; for the departed founders of God's holy churches and for all who have fallen asleep in the hope of resurrection; and for those who labor on behalf of the Gospel, those who look after God's holy churches, those who sing in them, and those who are present at the service awaiting God's plenteous mercies. The response to each petition is three Κύριε Ἐλέησον, sung earnestly. According to circumstance, additional petitions may be added to this litany for specific needs or special remembrances, as in the rites of baptism, marriage, and burial. In some instances, the second and third petitions are omitted, for example, when the Fervent Litany is intoned prior to the apolysis at daily Vespers. The Fervent Litany, as we shall see below, was used at stational Liturgies. From there it became part of the Divine Liturgy. Recently, the Holy Monastery of Vatopaidion on Mt. Athos published a small volume, Ἐκτενεῖς τῶν Ἑορτῶν (Karyes 2020), containing thirty-two fervent litanies based chiefly on a tenth-century Georgian manuscript. These litanies were once used in the environs of Jerusalem on major feast days at the Divine Liturgy. The form of these litanies is unique and unlike the fervent litany we know and pray. These litanies begin with a diaconal invitation, "Let us all say, Kyrie eleison," followed by a series of doctrinal declarations related to the given feast, each of which ends with the plea, "*We pray to you, Lord, hear us and have mercy*." These litanies are worthy of further study.

The Evening Prayer

Reader/People:

After the Fervent Litany and the *ekfonesis*, the reader and the people recite the Evening Prayer (*"Grant Lord ... Καταξίωσον, Κύριε..."*).[107]

The Dismissal (or Completion) Litany – Αἱ Δεήσεις or Αἰτήσεις[108]

Deacon

The deacon, still standing in the middle of the *solea* intones the petitions of the Dismissal or Completion Litany (*"Let us complete our evening prayer... Πληρώσωμεν τὴν ἑσπερινὴν δέησιν ἡμῶν..."*).

Priest

The priest intones the *ekfonesis* at the end of the litany.

The Peace, Bowing of Heads, and the Prayer of Inclination

Priest

Turns to the people and blesses them with his hand in the usual manner, saying, *"Peace be to all."*

> ***A Note on the Manner of Blessing:*** *When bestowing a priestly blessing, the priest configures the fingers of his right hand in a distinct manner and makes the sign of the cross with his raised right hand. When blessing the people, he faces them. He raises his right hand to eye level. Then lowers his hand to a point below his head, tracing the vertical line of the cross. He raises his hand again to chin level and moves it from his left to*

---

107 This same prayer forms the last portion of the Great Doxology found in the services of the Great and Small Apodeipnon and the Orthros. The prayer, as with the entire Great Doxology, is formed mainly by select verses from the Psalms.

108 The Ieratikon and other liturgical books refer to these petitions as δεήσεις (entreaties), αἰτήσεις (requests), or simply πληρωτικά (from the verb πληρώσωμεν, the first word in the first petition – *Let us complete...*). I refer to this series of petitions as the "Dismissal Litany" because it was once part of the dismissal rites of Vespers, Orthros, and other services as indicated by the first petition in the series, "Let us complete our evening (morning) prayer to the Lord."

his right, tracing the horizontal line of the cross. During these movements the fingers of his right hand are configured as follows: the index finger is held high and is joined with the middle finger, which is slightly bent to form the Greek initials IC (Ἰησοῦς – Jesus); the thumb is joined to the bent ring finger to form the Greek letter X; and the small (pinky) finger is bent to form the letter C. Together they form the initials XC (Χριστός – Christ).109 The movements of the hand should be conducted gracefully, without overstated motions.

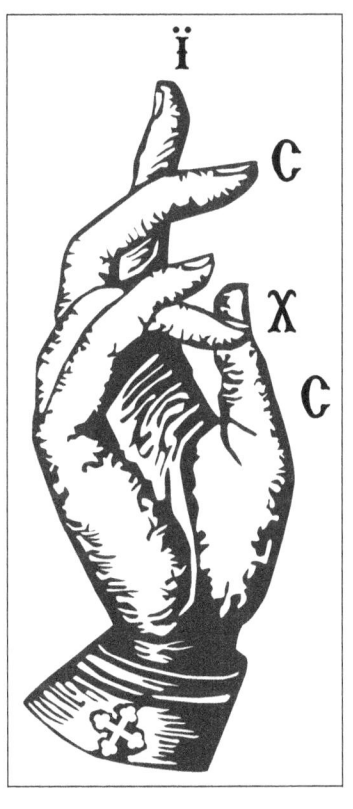

Deacon

The deacon, still facing the sanctuary, says: *"Let us bow our heads to the Lord"* and bows his head reverently. (*If there is no deacon* the priest, still facing the people, bids them to bow their heads.). When saying this bidding, **neither the priest nor the people directly face or bow low** before the icon of Christ on the iconostasis. They just bow their heads.

109This form of blessing (with minor variations) is depicted in many icons portraying the Lord and saints, particularly hierarchs and priests.

Priest

The priest turns and enters the sanctuary and, standing before the Holy Table, reads the Prayer of Inclination *("Lord our God, you bowed the heavens – Κύριε ὁ Θεὸς ἡμῶν, ὁ κλίνας τοὺς οὐρανούς...")* and intones its doxological ending, the *ekphonesis.*[110]

The Aposticha[111]

Chanter/Choir

Sing the designated aposticha troparia.

---

[110] Toward the end of every corporate service the celebrant pronounces a prayer of blessing, which is named the Prayer of Inclination (εὐχή τῆς κεφαλοκλισίας – prayer for the bending of the head). It is introduced by the priestly greeting, "Peace be to all" and the diaconal bidding, "Let us bow our heads to the Lord." The content of these prayers is dependent on the circumstances. At Vespers, the priest prays for the well-being of the faithful during the night: "Lord our God...look upon your servants...who have bowed their heads and inclined their necks...guard them at all times, both during this present evening and in the approaching night from every foe, from all adverse powers of the devil and from vain thoughts and evil imaginations. Blessed and glorified be the might of your kingdom..."

[111] In earlier times, Vespers concluded with the Prayer of Inclination followed by the Song of St. Symeon. The aposticha and apolytikia were added later. It became customary on major feasts and on Saturday evenings to hold a procession after the prayer of inclination (as for example, the procession with the *Epitaphios* (the image of Christ's burial shroud) on Holy Friday Vespers). During the procession a festal hymn was sung repeatedly as the clergy and the people departed from the church. This gradually led to the creation of the aposticha and the apolytikia which are now sung at the end of Vespers both on feast days and ordinary days, and on occasion at the end of an Orthros service. The aposticha are a set of troparia accompanied by verses taken from a select Psalm. The first of these hymns is never preceded by a psalm verse. The select Psalm for Saturday evenings is Ps. 92/93, verses 1a and 1b, and 5. See Ioannis Fountoulis, *Λογική Λατρεία* (Thessaloniki 1974/1984), 166-72. In monasteries an additional service was created and placed before the aposticha. This service is called the *Lite* (λιτή – prayer, entreaty, supplication). The Lite is celebrated on major feast days and always at vigils. The service commences immediately after the Prayer of Inclination with a procession of the clergy to the narthex as several festal hymns are chanted. At the narthex, a set of solemn intercessions and litanies are intoned by the clergy. The procession returns to the nave as the aposticha are chanted. The blessing of the bread follows. A shorter version of this monastic service gradually found its way into parish usage and is called *artoklasia*, about which we will speak below.

The Song or Prayer of St. Symeon – Trisagion Prayer – Apolytikion

Priest

When the aposticha have been concluded, the priest faces the people and intones the Song/Prayer of St. Symeon. (If a Hierarch is presiding, the prayer is intoned by him).[112]

Reader and People

Recite the Trisagion Prayers.[113]

Priest

"For yours is the kingdom ..."

Chanter/Choir and People

Sing the designated Apolytikion(a) and the Theotokion.[114]

---

[112] In current Greek practice, the Prayer or Song of Symeon (Luke 2:29-32) is intoned by the chief celebrant. In the Slavic tradition it is sung by the chanter/choir and the people. The latter reflects an earlier practice.

[113] The Trisagion Prayer(s) (Τρισάγιον) consist of the hymn, "*Holy God* - Ἅγιος ὁ Θεός;" the prayer, "*All-Holy Trinity* - Παναγία Τριάς;" and the Lord's Prayer. The Trisagion is also recited at the beginning or end of other services.

[114] Several theories have been put forth on the origins of the term, *apolytikion* - ἀπολυτίκιον - *dismissal hymn*. One suggestion is based on the position of these hymns in Vespers. They are sung at the very end, just prior to the apolysis or dismissal. A more probable reason, however, rests on the fact that in earlier centuries Vespers concluded with the Song of Symeon (Luke 2:29-32). The apolytikion was added to the service to serve as a recessional hymn – enhancing the formal exit of the worshippers from the church. The Song of Symeon contains the phrase, "Νῦν ἀπολύεις τὸν δοῦλον σου, Δέσποτα – Lord, now let your servant *depart* in peace." Accordingly, the term apolytikion is said to have derived from the verb ἀπολύω (to depart), which we find in the Song of St. Symeon. The apolytikion is considered by many as the principal hymn of a given feast or commemoration because it succinctly declares the nature, content, and meaning of the celebration. Every feast and every saint has an apolytikion. There are also sets of apolytikia for various categories of saints, which are sung when a particular saint does not have one. Apolytikia are sung at the end of Vespers, the beginning of the Orthros, the end of the Doxology, and before and after the Small Entrance at the Divine Liturgy. A theotokion is added to the apolytikia of saints and to the Resurrectional Apolytikia of Sundays at both Vespers and Orthros. On the feasts of the Lord and the Theotokos, however, the apolytikion of the respective feast is repeated three times without a *doxa* and *ke nyn* at both Vespers and Orthros. Also, they do not have a theotokion.

Apolysis

Deacon or Priest

Sophia!

Priest

"Ὁ ὢν εὐλογητός ... Blessed is He who is..."[115]

Deacon

Στερεῶσαι Κύριος ὁ Θεός ... Lord, God make firm the faith..."

Priest

"Glory to you, O God, glory to you."

"May Christ our true God (who),[116] as a good and loving God ..."

"Through the prayers ... Δι' εὐχῶν..."

B. DAILY VESPERS (WITHOUT AN ENTRANCE)

The service is celebrated in much the same way as Great Vespers.

The **priest** is vested with the rason and epitrachilion.

He starts the service in the same way. He reads the seven evening prayers while the Introductory psalm is being recited by the reader.

He intones the Great Synapte. After the ekphonesis, he offers the prayer for the offering of incense.

At the second verse of Psalm 140/141 he begins censing in the usual manner.

When the troparia are completed, the Evening Thanksgiving (*"O Joyful Light"*) is recited or intoned (not sung) by the priest or reader.

---

115 When the service of artoklasia is included in Vespers, we omit *"Blessed is He who is,"* and say instead, *"Let us pray to the Lord... May the blessing of the Lord and his mercy come upon you through his divine grace and love always, now and forever... Τοῦ Κυρίου δεηθῶμεν... Εὐλογία Κυρίου καὶ ἔλεος..."*

116 On Saturday evenings, Sunday mornings, the Feast of the Elevation of the Cross (September 14), and throughout the Paschal season, we insert the phrase, *"who rose from the dead."* All dominical feasts have a distinct phrase, which is inserted at this point. These phrases are listed in the Ἱερατικόν at the end of Vespers and are also found in the texts produced by the Narthex Press and GOA Digital Chant Stand.

The **deacon** introduces the Evening Prokeimenon and it is sung by the **chanters**, followed by the Evening Prayer, read by the **reader**.

The **priest** intones the Dismissal (Completion) Litany, gives the peace, and reads the Prayer of Inclination.

The aposticha are sung by the **chanter**, followed by the Song of St. Symeon and the Trisagion Prayers.

The **chanter/choir** sings the apolytikion(a) and the theotokion.

The priest intones the (short) Fervent Litany, starting with the petition, "Have mercy on us, O God."

After the ekphonesis of the litany, he performs the *apolysis*.

C. VESPERS ON THE SUNDAYS OF GREAT LENT

The service is celebrated on the evening of Cheesefare (Forgiveness) Sunday and on the five succeeding Sunday evenings of Great Lent.

The **priest** is vested with the exorasson and with an epitrachilion and phelonion of a dark "Lenten" color (dark purple).

The service begins in the usual manner and is conducted as above through the censing.

At the appropriate time, the **priest** performs the Entrance Rites as in the Great Vespers.

The Evening Thanksgiving (*"O joyful light..."*) is recited or intoned (not sung).

The **priest** introduces the Evening Prokeimenon.

The **chanter/choir** sings the Great Solemn Prokeimenon (*"Turn not away your face..."*).

The **priest** intones the Fervent Litany.

The **reader and the people** recite the Evening Prayer.

The **priest** intones the Dismissal or Completion Litany, gives the blessing of peace, and reads the Prayer of Inclination.

The **chanter/choir** sings the aposticha.

The **priest** recites the Song of St. Symeon.

The **reader** recites the Trisagion Prayers.

The **chanter/choir** sings the troparia: Hail, Theotokos Virgin…; O Baptist of Christ…; Pray for us, holy Apostles…; Beneath your tender mercy…" (prostrations are performed with each hymn, except the last).

The **reader/lector** says the Kyrie eleison forty times; "Glory to the Father… Now and…

Greater in honor than the cherubim… In the name of the Lord, father bless…"

Priest

Blessed is He who is, Christ our God…

Heavenly King, uphold our rulers…'Επουράνιε Βασιλεῦ…

The Prayer of St. Ephraim: "Lord and master of my life…" Each of the three verses of the prayer is accompanied by a deep prostration.

The apolysis…

D. DAILY VESPERS DURING LENT

The service commences in the usual manner.

The priest is vested with exorasson and epitrachilion (dark color).

After the Introductory Psalm and the Great Synapte, the **reader** (lector) recites the eighteenth kathisma of the Psalter.[117]

The **priest** says the Small Litany.

The **chanter/choir** sings the Evening Psalms with the prescribed troparia.

The **priest** censes at the appropriate time in the usual manner.

There is no entrance.

The **reader** recites the "*Fos ilaron.*"

The **priest** says, "*Esperas.*"

The **lector** reads the assigned prokeimena and the two Biblical lessons, one from the Book of Genesis and the other from the Book of Proverbs.

The **reader and the people** recite the Evening Prayer.

The **priest** intones the Dismissal Litany, offers the peace, and recites the prayer of inclination.

---

[117] For the sake of brevity, the Kathisma is often omitted in parish usage. However, it is said in its entirety when Vespers are celebrated with the Divine Liturgy of the Pre-Sanctified Gifts.

The **chanter/choir** sings the aposticha.

After the Prayer of St. Symeon and the Trisagion Prayers, the **chanter/choir** sings the four troparia, "*Hail, Theotokos Virgin...*" and the rest as above.

The service continues in the manner described above in **Section C** up to and including the Prayer of St. Ephraim.

The **lector** repeats the "Kyrie eleison" twelve times, recites the prayer, "*Παναγία Τριάς, τὸ ὁμοούσιον κράτος... Most Holy Trinity, consubstantial Power, undivided Kingship, the Cause of all good, be gracious even unto me, a sinner. Confirm and instruct my heart and take away from me every defilement. Enlighten my mind that I may ever glorify, praise, and worship you, saying: One is holy, one is Lord, Jesus Christ, to the glory of God the Father. Amen.*"[118]

The **reader** recites the hymn, "*Εἴη τὸ ὄνομα Κυρίου... Blessed is the name of the Lord, both now and to the ages,*" (thrice) and reads Psalm 33/34.

The **priest** conducts the apolysis.[119]

E. THE VESPERS OF
PASCHA SUNDAY AND RENEWAL (BRIGHT) WEEK

At the Vespers on Holy and Great Sunday of Pascha the **priest** is fully vested in brightly colored vestments. He holds the Paschal candle in his left hand and the censer in his right. He stands in front of the Holy Table and *censes* it three times. Then he intones the *opening doxology*, «Δόξα τῇ ἁγίᾳ καὶ ὁμοουσίῳ καὶ ζωοποιῷ καὶ ἀδιαιρέτῳ Τριάδι, πάντοτε ...»

"*Glory to the holy and consubstantial and life-creating and undivided Trinity, always, now and forever and to the ages of ages.*"

The **priest** sings the troparion, "Χριστὸς Ἀνέστη ... *Christ is risen...*" three times up to the words "*He has granted life,*" which are sung by the **chanter/choir**. The **priest** censes the front of the Holy Table as he sings the Χριστὸς Ἀνέστη.

The **priest** then intones the first of the four prescribed psalm verses and censes the front of the Holy Table. The **chanter/choir/people** sing the Χριστὸς Ἀνέστη. The **priest** repeats the procedure with the other verses standing before each side of the Holy Table. The **priest** then says, "Glory to the Father..." The **chanter/choir**, the Χριστὸς Ἀνέστη. The **priest**, "*ke nyn,*"

---

[118] This prayer is sometimes recited by the priest. If the text is available, it may be recited by all worshippers in unison.

[119] The text of the different Vespers services may be found on the internet in GOA Digital Chant Stand.

the **chanter/choir**, Χριστὸς Ἀνέστη. After the censing of the Holy Table, the **priest** censes the prothesis, the icons of the iconostasis, and the people from the Holy Doors. The Χριστὸς Ἀνέστη is sung again (tenth time) with greater fervor by all.

The **deacon (if one is present) or the priest** intones the Great Synapte and the ekphonesis.

The **chanter/choir** sings the Evening Psalms with the prescribed hymns.[120]

At the appropriate time the **priest** conducts the censing rites.

The **entrance rites** are performed as usual. However, instead of the censer, the deacon or priest carries the Evangelion.

After the *"Fos ilaron"* we sing the Great Prokeimenon, *"Τίς Θεὸς μέγας ... Who is so a great a god as our God..."* with the prescribed verses. The reading of the Gospel lesson follows.

The **Deacon (or priest)** intones, *"Καὶ ὑπὲρ τοῦ καταξιωθῆναι ἡμᾶς ... That we may be deemed worthy..."*

The **Chanter/Choir** sings *"Kyrie eleison"* (thrice)

The **Deacon (or priest)** intones, *"Σοφία! Ὀρθοί! Ἀκούσωμεν τοῦ ἁγίου Εὐαγγελίου ... Wisdom! Arise! Let us hear the holy Gospel."*

The **Priest** intones, *"Peace be to all...The Reading is from the Holy Gospel according to John ..."*[121]

When the Gospel lesson is completed, **the deacon or priest** intones the Fervent Litany.

The **reader** recites the Evening Prayer.

---

[120] If the Feast of St. George (April 23) falls before Pascha, the feast is transferred to Monday of Renewal or Bright Week. Hence, in addition to the resurrection troparia we also sing those of the feast of St. George, according to the prescribed order.

[121] According to custom, this pericope is read in several languages to emphasize the universality of the Gospel. The priest will arrange in advance and assign qualified persons for this purpose.

The **deacon (or priest)** intones the Dismissal Litany.

The **priest** gives the peace and recites the Prayer of Inclination with its ekfonesis.

The **chanter/choir** sings the Paschal aposticha and doxastikon.

The **priest** conducts the apolysis, at the end of which he exclaims, *"Christ is Risen!"* (3) and the **people** respond each time, *"Truly he is risen!"*

The **priest** says, *"Glory to his three-day resurrection!"*

The **people** respond, *"We venerate his three-day resurrection!"*

The **priest** says the *Christ is Risen* in its entirety.

The **people** respond, saying, *"Truly, the Lord has risen!"*[122]

F. ORDER OF VESPERS WHEN A HIERARCH PRESIDES

Receiving the Hierarch

The hierarch is received in the narthex by the clergy.[123] Previously, the priests and deacons are assembled in the sanctuary. They wear their rason and pectoral cross, if they have an office – offikion. When the hierarch arrives, the clergy process to the narthex, according to seniority and office – πρεσβεῖα καὶ ὀφφίκια. The deacon (or in the absence of a deacon, the youngest priest) holds the mandyas (μανδύας) and the senior priest the episcopal staff (ράβδος). The clergy stand on either side of the middle aisle in two lines, with the senior priests closest to the hierarch. The deacon assists the hierarch with the mandyas. (A deacon or an altar server holds the end of the mandyas when the hierarch processes). When the hierarch has put on the mandyas, the senior priest gives him the staff (ράβδος).

---

[122] The entire service is found in all the bilingual texts of *Holy Week and Pascha* currently in circulation published by Fathers George Papadeas, Spencer Kezios, N. Michael Vaporis, and online by Fr. Seraphim Dedes, GOA Digital Chant Stand.

[123] A hierarch is received in the same manner when presiding at an Orthros. It is wise for the priest to consult his hierarch on matters pertaining to the divine services in advance of his arrival to the parish. Most, if not all, the hierarchs have issued written instructions pertaining to these things. See, for example, the *Liturgical Guidelines for Hierarchical Services of the Metropolis of Boston*.

The Procession

After this, the clergy process down the middle aisle to the solea and stand on either side in two lines, with the senior clergy closest to the hierarch. The hierarch comes to the center of the solea and bows toward the sanctuary. As he blesses the people and the choirs, the chanters sing melodically, "Εἰς πολλὰ ἔτη, Δέσποτα."

The "Kairos" and the Beginning of the Service

When the hierarch has ascended the throne, the clergy proceed to receive his blessing. The senior priest with the deacon (if there is one), reverence and receive the blessing of the hierarch, kissing his hand. They enter the sanctuary through the Holy Doors and make a prostration before the Holy Table. The priest kisses the Evangelion and the Holy Table, the deacon only the Holy Table. The other clergy, two by two, follow the same procedure. When all the clergy have entered the sanctuary, the senior priest, wearing his epitrachilion, bows to the hierarch, turns and commences the service as outlined above. The other clergy, wearing the epitrachilion, stand on either side of the Holy Table according to seniority.

During the Service

The hierarch reads the Introductory Psalm and the three prescribed biblical readings, if the service has readings. (He may choose to assign the readings to others). At the appropriate times, he also recites the Evening Prayer, gives the Peace, and intones the Song of Symeon.

Before the Evening Psalms are sung, the kanonarchis (reader) stands in the middle of the solea, faces the hierarch and intones the words: "Κέλευσον, δέσποτα ἅγιε. Ἦχος..."

Censing

As the chanters begin singing the Evening Psalm (140/141), the deacon (or in the absence of a deacon the youngest priest) is given the censer. He bows reverently before the Holy Table and proceeds slowly – without censing – to exit the sanctuary from the north door. He comes before the hierarch, raises the censer slightly and says, "Master bless the incense – **Εὐλόγησον, δέσποτα, τὸ θυμίαμα**." When the hierarch has given the blessing, the deacon (or priest) censes him three times. Then he proceeds to the center of the solea and stands close to the Holy Doors. From there he censes the Holy Table three times[124] and then the icons in the prescribed manner. Then he turns and censes the hierarch nine times and then the choirs and the people in the usual manner.[125] When he has finished censing the people, he comes to the solea and again censes the hierarch nine times. He turns and censes the icons of the Lord and the Theotokos; he bows and enters the sanctuary via the south door. He censes the Holy Table, the prothesis, and all who are in the sanctuary.

The Entrance

At the entrance, the clergy proceed to the throne and stand on either side of the hierarch according to seniority. The deacon (or youngest priest) does the censing in the prescribed manner. The clergy continue standing at the throne through the first verse of the Evening Prokeimenon. They take their leave, according to seniority, by bowing to the hierarch. They enter the sanctuary through the Holy Doors and stand around the Holy Table as before.

If an Artoklasia is Celebrated

The service is conducted before the aposticha (see below). The sexton and his helper set an auxiliary table with the five (or more) loaves of bread in the middle of the solea together with a stand for the icon. The deacon (or priest) brings the epitrachilion and omophorion to the hierarch and assists in the vesting. The clergy prepare for the procession. They are given a lit candle to hold. One of the priests is assigned to hold the icon of the feast. The procession around the interior of the church (up and down the two side aisles) is led by the altar servers. The priest carrying the icon follows. The rest of the clergy, seniors first, follow him.

When the procession reaches the solea, the altar servers stand on either side of the auxiliary table. The priest brings the icon to the hierarch for veneration. Then he brings it to and places it on the stand. (In current practice the priest with the icon processes three times around the table before placing the icon on the stand). The clergy, as before, stand on either side of the throne according

---

[124] The older and more appropriate practice requires the deacon to re-enter the sanctuary and cense the Holy Table and the prothesis. Traditionally, all censing begins with the Holy Table. However, for reasons of practicality the older practice has been abandoned in parish usage.

[125] The censing of the hierarch nine times is a remnant of the Byzantine era and imitates the manner by which the emperor was honored.

to seniority. The deacon or the priests in rotation intone the petitions. Usually, the pastor of the church says the petition for the well-being of those who are offering the breads and reads the names of those for whom they are offered. (At an artoklasia we read the names only of the living). The hierarch reads the prayers and gives the peace. He also designates the priest who will chant the Θεοτόκε παρθένε... O Virgin Theotokos. When the hymn is completed, the senior priest or another brings one of the breads to the throne. The hierarch reads the prayer of blessing. By custom, each priest places his right hand on the shoulder of the priest closest to him as the hierarch recites the prayer. When the prayer is completed, we sing the troparion, Πλούσιοι ἐπτώχευσαν καὶ ἐπείνασαν... The wealthy have become poor... and the senior priest presents the blessed bread, according to custom, to each of the priests who kiss it. The clergy take leave of the hierarch in the usual manner, reverence the icon, and return to the sanctuary. The deacon (or youngest priest) helps the hierarch remove the omophorion and epitrachilion.

The Apolysis

1. After the Prayer of Symeon, the deacon (or youngest priest) brings the blessing cross to the hierarch and remains standing by the throne.

2. While the priest is saying the apolysis, the hierarch descends from the throne, reverences the festal icon, and enters the sanctuary. He says the Δι' εὐχῶν... and the priest ends with the Δι' εὐχῶν τοῦ ἁγίου Δεσπότου ἡμῶν...

3. **When an artoklasia is celebrated, we omit**, "Σοφία. Ὁ ὤν εὐλογητὸς."

Instead, the priest says: "Τοῦ Κυρίου δεηθῶμεν."

4. **The hierarch will give the blessing**: "Εὐλογία Κυρίου καὶ ἔλεος..."

5. **The priest will say the apolysis.**

G. THE SERVICE OF ARTOKLASIA

According to Parish Usage

At the Vespers of major feasts, it is customary to conduct the artoklasia (blessing of the loaves – litia) and to pray for the health of those celebrating the feast and are offering the gifts (five loaves, wheat, wine, and oil). The service originated in the monasteries as an integral part of a vigil. In monastic communities it is celebrated at the end of Great Vespers only when a vigil is scheduled. Its purpose is practical: to provide the worshippers with some blessed food and drink to help sustain them through the long hours of the vigil.

In an altered abbreviated form and for a different purpose, the service entered into parish worship. It is usually celebrated at Great Vespers of major feasts, accompanied by prayers for the well-being of the person(s) offering the gifts, although it is sometimes held at the end of the Orthros or the end of the Divine Liturgy. In parish usage the artoklasia is celebratory in nature, an act of thanksgiving for the rich and abundant blessings of God. It is offered on behalf of the living and especially for those who are celebrating a particular feast or are commemorating a special event; and do so in the company of their fellow parishioners. The blessed bread is broken and shared with all those present as a sign of brotherly affection. To make their joy complete, those who offer the artoklasia may also make additional gifts for the distribution of alms to the needy.

The rite commences immediately after the Prayer of Inclination and before the aposticha. The icon of the feast is carried in procession around the interior of the church and placed on the analogion (stand) in the middle of the solea. An auxiliary table is set before the analogion. On it are placed five loaves (ἄρτοι) which are offered by faithful who are celebrating the feast.[126] An artoklasia is always celebrated with five round loaves of (sweet) bread in imitation of the miracle of the feeding of the multitude (Mt. 14:14-21; Mk. 6:34-44; Lk. 9:10-17; Jn. 6:1-13). The consecratory prayer makes reference to the miracle. The blessed bread is cut (broken) and shared with all the congregants. The word artoklasia means "to break bread." It is broken so that it may be shared. Some say that the sharing of the gifts of the artoklasia is a remnant or reminder of the agape meals of the ancient church.

The consecratory prayer makes reference to additional offerings, namely, wheat (flour), wine, and oil. These offerings were usually distributed to the poor or were used for the needs of the church: the oil for the lamps; the wine for Holy Communion; and the flour for the preparation of prosphora. Keeping the tradition, in addition to the five loaves, some people bring one or more of these gifts to the church. If feasible, small containers with these gifts may be placed on the table.

[If a hierarch is presiding, the deacon or a priest will bring him his epitrachilion and small omophorion and assist him as he vests. This is done before the procession starts.

---

[126] More than the usual five loaves may be placed on the auxiliary table when more than one person, family, or group is offering an artoklasia at the same service.

The procession is led by the altar servers. The deacon (or in the absence of a deacon, the sexton or a senior altar server) holds the censer.

A priest carries the icon. If more than one priest is present, the pastor of the church asks one of the visiting clergy to carry the icon. The other priests are handed a lit candle and, according to seniority, follow behind.

The icon is brought to the center of the solea and is placed on the analogion. (In current practice the priest with the icon processes three times around the auxiliary table before placing the icon on the stand). During the procession, one of the priests or the chanter sings one of the troparia of the lite.

When the procession ends, the clergy, according to seniority, stand in front of the auxiliary table facing the sanctuary:

1. The deacon or the priests in rotation intone the fervent litany.

2. The parish priest usually says the petition commemorating those who are offering the gifts.

3. The senior priest says the prayer, *"Hear us, O God ... Ἐπάκουσον ἡμῶν ὁ Θεός..."* He also gives the peace.

4. The deacon (or junior priest) says, "Let us bow our heads to the Lord... Τὰς κεφαλὰς ἡμῶν τῷ Κυρίῳ κλίνωμεν..."

5. The senior priest (or another) says the prayer of inclination *"Most merciful Master... Δέσποτα πολυέλεε...."*

6. The priest, usually the one with the finest voice, chants the hymn, "Θεοτόκε Παρθένε ... *O Virgin Theotokos.*"[127] As he sings the hymn, he processes around the auxiliary table, censing the offerings from each side of the table. Then he censes the icons, the clergy, and the people in that order.

7. The senior priest reads the consecratory prayer, while one or two of the other priests lift up and hold one of the loaves. If there are more priests, each one stretches forth his right hand and places it on the right shoulder of the priest closest to him.

If the service is celebrated by only one priest, he intones the litanies, reads the prayers, sings the hymn, lifts up one of the loaves, and offers the consecratory prayer.

---

[127] If the service is celebrated during Renewal (Bright) Week or on the Apodosis of Pascha, we sing the hymn, *"Christ Is Risen..."*

If a hierarch is presiding, he will say the ekphonesis, give the peace, and say the prayer of supplication. He will select the priest who will chant the hymn. When the hymn is concluded, the senior priest will bring one of the loaves to the hierarch. The hierarch will read the consecratory prayer. Each priest, as above, places his right hand on the shoulder of closest priest.

If the service is celebrated within a Vespers Service, at the apolysis we omit, "Σοφία. Ὁ ὢν εὐλογητὸς..." and say instead, "Τοῦ Κυρίου δεηθῶμεν. Εὐλογία Κυρίου καὶ ἔλεος..."

If a hierarch is presiding, he will say, "Εὐλογία Κυρίου καὶ ἔλεος..." The priest will say the apolysis.

2. THE ORTHROS SERVICE (ΟΡΘΡΟΣ)

Introduction

The Orthros (Matins or Morning Service) is the longest service of the daily office, the most complicated, and the richest in biblical and festal material. In its received form it is a conflation of several distinct offices that trace their beginnings to the cathedral and monastic offices of past centuries.[128]

Fr. Robert Taft, the eminent liturgical scholar of the Byzantine Rite, makes the following observation: "Both traditions [cathedral and monastic] are inheritors of exactly the same ancient custom of beginning and ending the day with prayer. The monks rose earlier and prayed longer, so what was Matins and Vespers in cathedral usage was vigils and Vespers for the monks."[129] He goes on to say that eventually an original monastic office absorbed cathedral elements, including the Psalms of Praise (Lauds) 148-150. "Such a system," he notes, "starts with Nocturns as its pristine first service of the day and appends Lauds to it. Others seem to have started with cathedral Matins that included Psalms 148-150, and then added to the cursus a separate monastic night office. It is this pattern – two separate offices, one monastic (Nocturns), and one cathedral (Matins) – that is at the basis of all extant offices..."[130] Unlike today, in former times, as it happens in monasteries to this day, the Orthros began in the predawn hours.

128See Taft, *Liturgy of the Hours*, 273-91; and his *Beyond East and West*, 259-79.

129Taft, *Liturgy of the Hours*, 202.

130*Ibid.* 209. See also Fountoulis, Ἀκολουθία τοῦ Ὄρθρου, 18.

In the broadest of terms, the received Orthros service, essentially monastic in character, is made up of two distinct parts, one nocturnal the other a morning office. The first part, rooted in an ancient night office, is comprised of the Hexapsalmos, the *God is the Lord* (Θεὸς Κύριος), the kathismata, and the *Anavathmoi (Hymns of Ascent)*. The second part, anchored in an ancient morning service, consists of Psalm 50/51, the Biblical Odes and the Canon(s), the Psalms of Praise and the Doxology. Inserted between the two parts is the order of the morning Gospel which is introduced by two prokeimena, one variable and the other fixed. Starting with the *Typikon of Konstantinos Protopsaltis* (1838) the place of the Sunday morning Gospel changed, as we shall see below._

The received tradition has five different types of Orthros services, each with its own structure and many shared elements.[131] The five types are: the Sunday Orthros; the Daily Orthros (without Gospel); the Major Feast-day Orthros (with Gospel); the Lenten Daily Orthros; and the Orthros of Pascha and Renewal or Bright Week (Διακαινίσιμος Ἑβδομάς). The complete order or *taxis* ... τάξις for each of these types can be found in the more recent editions of the Ieratikon published by the *Apostolike Diakonia* of the Church of Greece.

In most instances, several liturgical books are needed to properly conduct the Orthros: the Ieratikon (containing the priestly prayers and petitions); the Horologion (containing the fixed elements); the Psalter; the Octoechos (and/or the Triodion and Pentecostarion in their proper season); the Menaion of each month; and the Evangelion. Happily, the texts published biannually by the Narthex Press and weekly by the online GOA Digital Chant Stand have greatly simplified the process for clergy, chanters, and readers by providing them with the order and text of the Sunday and feast-day Orthros services based on the received tradition and the prevailing practice of the Greek Orthodox Archdiocese of America.

A complete Sunday Orthros, sung and read according to the rubrics, could take upwards of three hours, something that is unsustainable in a parish. Because of its length, elements of the Orthros have been omitted, for example the canon, or are reduced, for example the number of troparia sung at the Praises (Αἶνοι; Lauds). The prevailing parish order of the service, when executed properly and rhythmically, can be accomplished in a little over an hour. Every effort should be made to preserve the dignity of the service.

---

131 See Fountoulis, Ἀκολουθία τοῦ Ὄρθρου, 14-18. For the basic structure and order of Vespers, Orthros, and the Hours see *The Festal Menaion* (68-97) and *The Lenten Triodion* (69-98).

A. THE SUNDAY ORTHROS

As Celebrated by One Priest with a Deacon.

(If there is no deacon, the priest, within the sanctuary, says the petitions assigned to the deacon).

The Priest begins the service wearing the exorasson and epitrachilion. (If he has already performed the "kairos," he may wear all his priestly vestments). The **Deacon** receives the priest's blessing and wears the three vestments of his office (sticharion, orarion, and the epimanika).

---

1. The Introductory Prayers

Priest

Stands before the Holy Table and reverences three times. He kisses the Evangelion and the Holy Table. He intones the opening doxology: "*Blessed is our God* – Εὐλογητὸς ὁ Θεὸς ἡμῶν…. and recites the prayer, "*Heavenly King …* Βασιλεῦ Οὐράνιε…[132]

Reader

The Trisagion Prayers

Every divine service and all personal devotions begin with an initial blessing praising God. In our received liturgical tradition we find three such initial blessings: (a) "Blessed is our God always, now and forever…." which is the most common with roots in the Palestinian monastic tradition; (b) "Blessed is the kingdom of the Father and of the Son, and of the Holy Spirit now and forever and unto the ages of ages…." now used mostly with sacramental rites, but was once the initial blessing for all services of the cathedral rite of Constantinople; and (c) "Glory to the holy and consubstantial and life-giving and undivided Trinity, always now and forever…" which originated in the monastic tradition. In private devotions, prayers are introduced with the blessing, "In the name of the Father, and of the Son, and of the Holy Spirit. Amen."

---

[132] The "Heavenly King" is omitted during the entire Paschal Season. It is replaced with the troparion *"Christ is Risen … Χριστὸς Ἀνέστη."* The "Heavenly King" is sung at Vespers and Orthros of the Feast of Pentecost. The priest begins the Orthros of Pentecost with the "Heavenly King" and thereafter every other Orthros service until the Sunday of Pascha the following year.

Strictly speaking, the prayer, "Heavenly King," belongs to the service of the Mesonyktikon which precedes the Orthros. However, since the Mesonyktikon is omitted in parish usage, it has become customary for the priest to begin the service with the prayer, "Heavenly King." The same prayer is used to introduce the Hours and the Apodeipnon and private devotions. The "introductory character" of the prayer, "Heavenly King," is based on Rom. 8:26: "Likewise the Spirit helps us in our weakness; for we do not know how to pray as we ought, but the Spirit himself intercedes for us with sighs too deep for words."

2. The Royal Office

Reader

Recites the three Royal hymns: "Lord, save your people … Σῶσον, Κύριε, τὸν λαόν σου…"

Priest

Intones the abbreviated Fervent Litany and the ekfonesis.

The Royal office originated in imperial monastic foundations (communities funded by imperial largesse). In gratitude, the community offered prayers for its benefactors. The result was the creation of an office comprised of two Royal Psalms (19/20 and 20/21), three royal hymns, and an abbreviated form of the fervent litany. With the collapse of the Byzantine Empire, the petition for the emperor and the royal family was replaced with a general petition on behalf of "all devout Orthodox Christians." The Royal Psalms have long since fallen into disuse in parish practice. However, they have been retained in the Orthros services of Holy and Great Week, when, according to ancient custom, they are intoned and not read. To quote Fr. Taft, "This is really a separate service, extraneous to the structure of matins. Because monks are fond of adding but only rarely subtract material from their offices, it has become permanently prefixed to Byzantine matins."[133]

---

[133] Taft, *Liturgy of the Hours*, 277.

3. The Enarxis (Beginning) of the Orthros

Reader

"In the name of the Lord, father, bless."

Priest

Intones the initial blessing, *"Glory to the holy... Δόξα τῇ ἁγίᾳ..."*

Reader

Recites the introductory verses and reads the Hexapsalmos (Ἑξάψαλμος).

Priest

According to the prevailing practice, the priest recites the twelve morning prayers during the reading of the Hexapsalmos. He stands in front of the Holy Table and reads them in a low voice.[134]

---

134 The rubrics in some *ieratika* instruct the priest to read the first three prayers in front of the Holy Table and the rest in front of the icon of Christ on the iconostasis. Others instruct him to read the first six in front of the Holy Table and the rest in front of the icon of Christ. No reason is given for this curious practice. Eleven of the prayers are directed to the Holy Trinity, as evidenced by the ekfonesis of each. The tenth prayer is directed to God the Father who is blessed together with the Son and the Holy Spirit. Why then are some of the prayers said outside the sanctuary in front of the icon of Christ, and is it necessary to do so? The prayers, as noted above, originated in the cathedral Orthros of Constantinople, the first part of which was conducted in the narthex with the clergy standing before the closed Royal Doors leading into the nave. After the initial blessing and the Great Synapte, the choir sang three antiphons and the people the refrains. On Sundays, when Psalm 118/119 was sung, at verse 170 of the Psalm, "Let my supplication come before you ...Εἰσέλθοι τὸ ἀξίωμά μου ἐνώπιόν σου, Κύριε," the royal doors were opened, and the people entered the nave, led by the clergy, one of whom held the processional cross with its three lit candles. The cross was brought to and placed on the *ambo* around which the service continued. The service around the ambo included the singing of the 8th Biblical Ode and the recitation of the synaxarion of the day, about which we will speak below. Then the choirs sang Psalm 50/51 with the troparion, "Having behold the resurrection of Christ." This was followed by the polyeleos (Psalm 134/135; 135/136), the *Ekloge* (a collection of psalmic verses appropriate to the feast), the Ninth Biblical Ode, the Psalms of Praise (148-150), and the Great Doxology. At this point the clergy entered the sanctuary. The Resurrectional Prokeimenon was sung and the morning (Eothinon) Gospel was read from the ambo. The service was concluded with diaconal petitions, the prayer of inclination, and the apolysis. Each of these several elements was accompanied by an appropriate priestly prayer. Hence as the service unfolded, some of the prayers were said in the narthex, some by the ambo, and others within the sanctuary. See Panayiotis Trembelas, Μικρὸν Εὐχολόγιον, volume 2 (Athens, 1955), 194-202; 208-47. It is possible for the priest to match the twelve prayers with the ekphoneses and recite them (or at least some of them) aloud in their appropriate place. If, however, this seems difficult, the priest should continue to read the twelve prayers in a low voice according to the prevailing practice in front of the Holy Table.

Priest

When the reader has finished reading the Hexapsalmos, the priest intones the Great *Synapte* or Great Litany and the ekfonesis.

Chanter/Choir

Sings, "*God is the Lord...Theos Kyrios*" (Θεὸς Κύριος), the Apolytikion (Ἀπολυτίκιον), and the Theotokion (Θεοτοκίον).[135]

The Hexapsalmos *(Six Psalms) is comprised of two staseis with three psalms each: 3, 37/38, and 62/63; and 87/88, 102/103, and 142/143. The history of the Hexapsalmos is complex. It is sufficient for our purposes to note that Psalm 62/63 is mentioned as the morning psalm in all the early sources and is found in the matins of all liturgical rites, East and West, except for the Chaldean. According to an earlier tradition, the Hexapsalmos was sung and not read as is the case today. The Six Psalms touch on various themes, including awakening from sleep; anticipating the new day with its burdens and trials but also its possibilities. Additional themes include expressions of thanksgiving, hope, and trust in God's faithfulness, in his plenteous mercy and compassion. According to tradition, everyone stands attentively in silence when the Hexapsalmos is read.*

The twelve prayers of the Orthros, *as with the seven prayers of Vespers, were adopted into the monastic office from the cathedral office of Constantinople as a result of the Studite synthesis. The prayers were read at different intervals of the service and not in sequence and inaudibly as they are today. A comparison of the ekfonesis of each prayer with those attached to the end of the several small litanies sheds light on the use of these prayers. For example, the first prayer was read after the Great Synapte; the second after the first kathisma of the Psalter; the eighth after the resurrectional Evlogetaria, the kathismata troparia of Psalm 118/119, which constitutes the Seventeenth Kathisma of the Psalter.*

The content or theme of each prayer also gives an indication of its place in the service. For example, the ninth prayer, with minor variations,

---

135 The *Theotokion* is a hymn in honor of the Theotokos and Ever-virgin Mary. The last in a series of hymns is usually dedicated to the Theotokos. On Wednesdays and Fridays, when the Church remembers the Passion of our Lord, the theotokion is replaced by a hymn that honors the Cross and the Theotokos; it is called *stavrotheotokion*. When we celebrate a feast of the Lord or the Theotokos, at the Theos Kyrios we sing only the apolytikion of the feast three times without a theotokion or a "δόξα" or a "καὶ νῦν." In parish usage, for the most part, the theotokion is selected from one of the eight "resurrectional" *theotokia* of the Octoechos, in accord with the tone of the apolytikion.

is similar to the prayer before the Gospel in the Divine Liturgy. Hence, it was (is) read before the Morning (Eothinon) Gospel of the Orthros. The tenth prayer is related to Psalm 50/51, the eleventh to the Psalms of Praise, and the twelfth to the Doxology or to the end of the service. In the manuscript tradition of the cathedral office these same prayers are identified as prayers of specific antiphons (first, second, third, etc.). Others have titles such as Prayer of the Gospel, Prayer of the 50th, Prayer of the Praises, Prayer of the Apolysis. The content of the prayers also sheds light on the time the service was celebrated and addresses some of its themes. The first three prayers and the eighth, for example, are nocturnal ("My soul yearns for you in the night…"). This is a clear indication that the first part of the Orthros was a nocturnal office. The next five prayers contain various themes such as: a renewed awareness upon awakening from sleep with prayers of thanksgiving for the night passed in safety and for the dawning of a new day; songs of praise for the true Light (Christ) that has dawned and grants salvation to the world; the joy that comes from corporate prayer; supplications for forgiveness and for grace to pray rightly. The ninth prayer, as already noted, asks for illumination to comprehend the message of the Gospel. The tenth is penitential. The eleventh echoes the Psalms of Praise, by which the entire created order offers praise to the Creator. The twelfth, asks God to keep the worshippers in a state of prayerful vigilance during the day.

Here, as in the case of the priestly prayers of Vespers, it would be more effective if the prayers were read aloud in their proper place. One of the purposes of the priestly prayers is to help inform and shape the conscience of the worshippers. Of course, if the prayers are not heard, their purpose is hindered.

The enarxis of the Orthros *reaches its pinnacle with the singing of the "Θεὸς Κύριος… God is the Lord…" and the apolytikia that follow. The Theos Kyrios is a short hymn of praise comprised of two verses, 27 and 26, of Ps. 117/118, which is a song of thanksgiving. Two other verses of the psalm, 22 and 24, have a prominent place in the liturgy of Holy Week and Pascha. In earlier times the entire psalm was sung and the God is the Lord was probably used as a refrain. In the prevailing order, the Theos Kyrios is sung initially without verse in the tone of the apolytikion. It is repeated three more times, preceded by three verses of Ps. 117/118:1, 10, and 23.*

In the Psalter According to the Seventy, translated by the Holy Transfiguration Monastery, verses 27 and 26 are rendered as follows: "God is the Lord and hath appeared unto us. Blessed is he that cometh in the name of the Lord." The Festal Menaion has a similar rendering, "The

Lord is God and hath appeared unto us: blessed is He that cometh in the name of the Lord." Versions of these two renderings are used in several translations of the Orthros. For example, GOA Digital Chant Stand has: "God is the Lord and He revealed Himself to us…" The Orthodox Study Bible, which uses the New King James Version, renders verse 27 differently: "God is the Lord, and he has given us light." The Revised Standard Version of the Bible has, "The Lord is God and he has given us light." In the first instance, the emphasis is on God, who appears or reveals himself to us. In the other, it is God who gives and sheds his light on us. In either case, the Church, gathered for morning prayer at daybreak, anticipates the coming of the light which overcomes the darkness and gives glory to God, who is the creator of the physical light, the sign of the True Light, Christ, "that enlightens every man coming into the world" (John 1:9).

The apolytikion or apolytikia that follow the Theos Kyrios introduce the festal element(s) of the day. In monasteries, the lamps are lit at this time, symbolizing the coming of the light, both the created and the uncreated light. In earlier times, the God is the Lord was sung only on Sundays and feast days. On all other days, and especially on fast days, the Alleluia was (is) sung with four verses (Isaiah 26:9a, 9b, 11b, 14b (or 15 in the Septuagint) from the Ode of the Prophet Isaiah (26:9-20), followed by the hymns to the Holy Trinity (Τριαδικά) in the tone of the week. Today, especially in parish usage, the Alleluia is sung only on certain days of the year and on the weekdays of Great Lent and Holy Week.

4. The Kathismata - Καθίσματα

Chanter/Choir

Sing the two sets of kathismata troparia or sessional hymns, followed by the resurrectional evlogetaria (Τὰ Ἀναστάσιμα Εὐλογητάρια).

Priest

Intones the Small Litany

The term καθίσματα *(plural of kathisma) comes from the verb καθίζω, which means to be seated. The plural is used to distinguish the hymns from the κάθισμα (singular) which refers to a section of the Psalter. The term sessional derives from the Latin verb sedere, which means to sit. The kathismata troparia or sessional hymns are sung after each reading of a* *kathisma of the Psalter. The Sunday Orthros has two kathismata of the Psalter, the Second (Psalms 9-16) and the Third (Psalms 17-23). In parish usage, however, the reading of these two sections of the Psalter has long since been abandoned. The assigned hymns, however, have been retained. The Sunday Orthros has two such sets of kathismata troparia in each of the eight tones for Sundays. The kathismata troparia in each of the tones have distinct melodies, many of which serve as model melodies (προσόμοια) for other festal kathismata troparia.*

The Evlogetaria: *except for rare occasions, the typikon assigns the Seventeenth Kathisma of the Psalter to the Sunday and Saturday Orthros (See Τυπικὸν τῆς τοῦ Χριστοῦ Μεγάλης Ἐκκλησίας, 19-20). It consists of Psalm 118/119, the longest of the psalms with 176 verses. It is structured on an alphabetical acrostic consisting of twenty-two sections, each containing eight poetic lines and each beginning with a successive letter of the Hebrew alphabet (22 x 8 = 176). Almost every line contains one of approximately eight terms for God's "Torah," (his law, testimonies, ways, precepts, statutes, commandments, ordinances, word). The psalm is divided into three staseis to form the Seventeenth Kathisma. Liturgically, Psalm 118/119 is also known as the Amomos (blameless) or Amomoi (from the first verse in the Septuagint Greek: "Μακάριοι οἱ ἄμωμοι ἐν ὁδῷ οἱ πορευόμενοι ἐν νόμῳ Κυρίου – Blessed are those whose way is blameless, who walk in the law of the Lord." As with every kathisma, the seventeenth also has kathismata troparia: the Evlogetaria – Εὐλογητάρια. The term or title comes from the twelfth verse of the psalm, which serves as the refrain – "Εὐλογητὸς εἶ, Κύριε, δίδαξόν με τὰ δικαιώματά σου – Blessed are you, O Lord; teach me your statutes"– sung before each hymn, except for the last two, which are introduced by Δόξα and Καὶ νῦν, respectively. There are two types of evlogetaria, the resurrectional and the funereal. The resurrectional honor the resurrection of Christ and are sung on Sundays; the funereal are sung on Saturdays, when the Church remembers the dead. The single exception to this rule is the Orthros of Great and Holy Saturday, when we sing the resurrectional evlogetaria.*[136]

---

[136] The funereal evlogetaria are sung at funerals (κηδεῖα) and memorials (μνημόσυνον). On feast days, the Seventeenth Kathisma is replaced with the polyeleos, which is comprised of two psalms, 134/135 and 135/136, and the ekloge, which is comprised of select verses from particular psalms that reflect the theme(s) of the feast. For reasons of practicality the polyeleos and the ekloge are often omitted in parish usage.

5. Hypakoe – Anavathmoi – Prokeimenon

Priest

Intones the Small Litany

Reader

Recites the Hypakoe (Ὑπακοή).

Chanter/Choir:

Sing the Anavathmoi (οἱ Ἀναβαθμοί).

Chanter/Choir

The festal Prokeimenon is sung immediately after the Anavathmoi.

The Hypakoe is a short hymn. Originally, it was sung by the precentor and then by the entire congregation under his direction. The name of the hymn, ὑπακοή, derives from the verb ὑπακούω, which means to listen attentively. The worshippers "listened attentively" to the precentor and then repeated the hymn under his direction, either fully or only its final phrase(s). The hypakoe is found only in the Orthros of Sundays and Great Feasts. (The same Orthros hymn is also found in the preceding Midnight Service). The Octoechos has eight such hymns, one for each of the eight tones. On Sundays, the hypakoe comes after the evlogetaria. On Great Feasts it is found after the third ode of the canon. Six of the eight hypakoe troparia of the Octoechos share a common theme, the Good News of Christ's resurrection delivered by the angel to the Myrrh-bearing Women, who in turn evangelized the Disciples. The other two troparia, those of the plagal 2nd and grave tones, address the cosmic significance of Christ's resurrection.

The Anavathmoi are a set of poetical compositions based on the Psalms of Ascents – Ἀναβαθμοί (also known as the Gradual Psalms or Songs of Degrees). Each of these fifteen psalms (119-133 Septuagint; 120-134 Masoretic) is prefaced by the term, "A Song of Ascents." They were probably a collection of pilgrimage hymns sung by pilgrims on their journey up to Jerusalem. These psalms also comprise the Eighteenth Kathisma of the Psalter, which, with some exceptions, is read at Vespers on all the weekdays of the year. In parish usage it is usually limited to *the weekdays of Lent. There are eight sets of Anavathmoi, one for each of the eight tones. Each set is divided into three antiphons, except for the pl. 4th which has four. Each antiphon in turn has three short troparia, which some attribute St. Theodore the Studite. The first two are poetical interpretations of one of the Psalms of Ascents. The Third hymn is a superb meditation on the Holy Trinity with an emphasis on the person, the divine attributes, and the economy of the Holy Spirit.* [137]

The Prokeimenon: *On Sundays and feast days the Morning Gospel is introduced by two prokeimena, the first of which is variable and the second fixed. The first prokeimenon is always festal in nature, a select verse from a particular psalm that reflects the theme of the feast. In earlier times the psalm from which the prokeimenon was drawn was sung in its entirety. In current practice the festal prokeimenon is sung three times. The third rendition is preceded by a select verse from the same psalm. The Sunday variable prokeimenon always has a resurrectional theme and is sung immediately after the Anavathmoi.*

The second, fixed prokeimenon, "Let everything that breathes, praise the Lord" (Psalm 150:6) is sung only on Sundays and feast days. Originally, the two Prokeimena, the variable and the fixed, were sung in succession, separated by a call to prayer and a prayer. The prayer has long since been omitted, except for its ekfonesis. This original order, however, has been altered in the Greek Church in accordance with the directives of the Typika of Konstantinos and Violakis. The Sunday Morning Gospel has been moved forward and is read after the 8th Ode of the Canon, about which we will speak below. The Slavic and other Orthodox churches have maintained the original order. On feast days the ancient order is maintained even by the Greek Church. [138]

---

[137] The hymns on the Psalms of Ascents are distributed as follows. The author meditates sequentially on three Psalms in each of the four primary tones, for a total of twelve Psalms (119-130/120-131). He repeats the same procedure in the four plagal tones, except that he adds a fourth antiphon in the plagal fourth tone, in which he meditates on the final three Psalms of Ascents (131-133/132-134).

[138] The festal prokeimenon is preceded by the first antiphon of the Anavathmoi of the Fourth tone, "*Since my youth...*'Ἐκ νεότητός μου..." which is based on Psalm 128/129. The second, fixed prokeimenon is sung immediately after the call to prayer, "Let us pray to the Lord," and the ekphonesis. The antiphon of the Fourth tone which is sung on feast days appears to have been selected randomly. Its place was solidified by its inclusion in the early printed liturgical books.

6. Kontakion and Synaxarion

Reader

Reads/intones the Kontakion and the Oikos.

Reader

Reads/intones the Synaxarion.

Kontakion and Oikos: *The Orthros service contains two hymns called the Kontakion and Oikos. The two hymns are found between the sixth and seventh Odes of the Canon in the Octoechos, Triodion, Pentecostarion, and Menaia. They are also found in the Menologion section of the Horologion. The word kontakion is derived from the Greek κοντός – a pole, rod, stick of wood – and identifies a genre of hymns that were written on parchment and rolled around a wooden stick. This form of poetry originated in the early sixth century and flourished until the eighth when a new form, the Canon, became more popular. Saint Romanos the Melodist is believed to be the originator of this early hymnographic form. Kontakia are considered homilies in verse, poetic sermons. A complete kontakion is comprised of several stanzas or strophes, from eighteen to thirty, each of which was called an oikos (from the Greek οἶκος – house). Every kontakion begins with a prelude or prologue (προοίμιον), called κουκούλιον (koukoulion), which summarizes the central theme of the poem. Eventually, as the kontakion was being displaced by the Canon, the term koukoulion was replaced with the word kontakion to identify the prelude. Every prelude (kontakion) and stanza (oikos) of a kontakion concludes with a refrain which is repeated by the people. Also, the first letter of every oikos of a complete kontakion formed an acrostic. Since the accession of the canon, only a remnant of the ancient hymnographic form remains in the Orthros: the prelude or kontakion, and the first stanza or oikos.*[139]

---

[139] A festal kontakion is also sung at every Divine Liturgy after the Small Entrance and at other services, including Holy Unction and the burial services. The best known complete kontakion is the *Akathist Hymn*, which many attribute to St. Romanos the Melodist. Its theme is the incarnation and is thought to be the kontakion of the Feast of the Annunciation. It is celebrated during the Lenten season and weekly in many monasteries. It consists of twenty-four *oikoi*, each of which begins with a successive letter of the Greek alphabet (twenty-four). The service of the Akathist is preceded by a complete Canon, attributed to St. Joseph the Hymnographer, and is set within the service of the Small Apodeipnon. The Horologion also contains the Kontakion of the Precious Cross, modeled on the Akathist hymn. Seminarians of Holy Cross of the eighties and nineties may recall that just before the Christmas break, the entire Kontakion of the Nativity of our Lord, authored by St. Romanos the Melodist, was celebrated in the school's chapel.

The Synaxarion: *(συναξάριον) provides the assembly with the names of the saints whose feast is being observed on a given day together with a brief account of their lives, or with a brief commentary on the event or mystery being celebrated. Each of the twelve Menaia contains a synaxarion for every day of the month. Synaxaria are also found in the Triodion and Pentecostarion, and in the Horologion. The Synaxarion is also known as the Menologion (from the Greek μήν – month). The Synaxarion is listed immediately after the kontakion and oikos. A complete listing of saints with an account of their lives together with the commentaries on the mysteries being celebrated is found in a multi-volume book with the same name, Synaxarion.*[140] *The Synaxarion is always evolving; it is open-ended. In it are inscribed the names and short biographies of every newly proclaimed saint of the Church.*

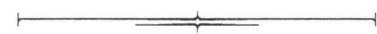

7. The Katavasiai – Αἱ Καταβασίαι – and the Canon

Chanter/Choir

Chants the assigned Katavasiai of the Odes (Ode 1, followed by Odes 3-8)

Katavasiai: *are part of the Canon, a form of hymnography, which came into prominence between the seventh and eighth centuries and, as already noted, gradually supplanted the kontakion. The Canon is closely related to the Biblical Odes (from the Greek, Ὠδή), also known as Songs or Canticles. The Biblical Odes formed a major portion of the Orthros in both the cathedral and monastic rites. The received monastic office has nine Biblical Odes, the latter of which consists of two odes. The nine odes in the received office are: (1) Ode of Moses (Exodus 15:1-19); (2) Song of Moses (Deut. 32:1-43); (3) A Prayer of Hannah/Anna (1 Kings 2:1-10–Septuagint or 1 Samuel 2:1-10–Masoretic); (4) A Prayer of Habakkuk/Abbacum (Habakkuk 3:2-19); (5) A Prayer of Isaiah (Isaiah 26:9-20); (6) A Prayer of Jonah (Jonah 2:2-9); (7) A Prayer of Azariah and the Holy Three*

---

140 Interestingly, among the liturgical reforms adopted by the monks of New Skete Monastery in Cambridge, New York, the synaxarion is also read at the beginning of every Vespers, so that worshippers are made aware of the commemoration(s) at the very beginning of the liturgical day. This, I believe, is an excellent concept and should be adopted officially by the Church.

Youths; and (8) The Song of the Holy Three Youths.[141] The Ninth Ode, is comprised of the Song of the Theotokos (Luke 1:46-55) and the Prayer of Zechariah, the father of St. John the Baptist (Luke 1:68-79).

Because of its penitential character, the Second Ode is sung only on Tuesdays of Great Lent. It recounts God's great benefits to Israel and Israel's faithlessness and rebellious forgetfulness of God, it's ingratitude and idolatrous behavior. On the other hand, the 9th Ode, the Song of the Theotokos is never omitted, except on Great Feasts when we sing the 9th ode of the canon. The full text of the Biblical Odes can be found in the Great Horologion in the Orthros service and in the Psalter after the twenty kathismata.

The katavasia is the concluding hymn in an ode of a canon. It may be the eirmos which is repeated as the katavasia or a special festal hymn which is added to the last troparion of the ode. On Sundays and feast days a katavasia is sung after each ode. It takes its name from the action of the choirs, which originally sang the katavasia in unison. They descended – came down – from their respective stasidia (stalls) to the center of the church to sing the katavasia in unison. The term is derived from the verb καταβαίνω – to step or go down.

The Biblical Odes and the Canon form the bulk of the Orthros service. However, as the Orthros service expanded it could not be sustained in its fullness in parish usage. Among the first deletions was the recitation or singing of the Biblical Odes, except for the ninth, the Song of Mary the Theotokos. Also suppressed were the canons, except in some local churches where the first and third odes are still sung. The katavasia alone is all that remains of the canon in most parishes today. The Typikon of Violakis has assigned several sets of festal katavasiai to different periods of the liturgical year.[142]

The Canon: *Before the appearance of the canon, it was customary to sing a short refrain between verses of the Biblical Odes. These refrains were*

---

141 The 7th Ode and the 8th Ode are inserted in the third chapter of the *Septuagint* Book of Daniel, between verses 3:23 and 3:24. In English and other translations of the Old Testament these passages are listed among the Apocryphal writings under the title, *The Prayer of Azariah and the Song of the Three Young Men*. In the *Septuagint* the 7th Ode accounts for verses 2-33 of the Book of Daniel; in the Apocrypha the 7th Ode constitutes verses 3-34. In the *Septuagint* the 8th Ode is based on verses 34-65 of the insert together with three additional verses created by a hymnographer. In the Apocrypha, the 8th Ode constitutes verses 35-65.

142 A collection of these sets is found in the *Reader's Manual* (Ἐγκόλπιον τοῦ Ἀναγνώστου) and the *Laypeople's Prayer Book* (Συνέκδημος). They are also available in the publications of Narthex Press and in GOA Digital Chant Stand. Of course, the sets are listed in one or more of the liturgical books: Octoechos, Triodion, Pentecostarion, or the Menaia.

eventually replaced by short hymns celebrating a particular theme of a feast(s). Thus was born the genre of hymns called the canon, the origins of which are attributed to St. Andrew of Crete (660-740). Every canon has a varying number of hymns in each ode and each canon is sung in one of the eight tones of Byzantine chant. The first hymn or troparion of each set is called the eirmos (εἰρμός – to be linked together in a series). In many printed editions the eirmos appears in quotation marks or in italics or both. The eirmos serves as the model hymn. It sets both the melody and the meter of each subsequent troparion in the set of hymns of each ode. Each of these hymns is introduced by a brief acclamation such as, "Lord, glory to your holy resurrection;" "Glory to you, O God, glory to you;" "Most holy Theotokos, save us;" "O Saint of God, pray for us." The penultimate hymn is introduced by "Glory to the Father..." while the last is introduced by, "Now and forever..." If two or more canons are to be sung, then the last two hymns of the last canon are considered as the penultimate and final hymns of the set. The eirmos usually reflects the theme of the corresponding Biblical Ode or of a particular festal theme.[143]

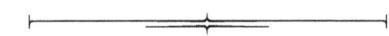

8. The Morning Gospel (Ἑωθινόν Εὐαγγέλιον)

The Orthros of every Sunday and major feast day includes a Gospel lesson – a significant feature. The Sunday morning cycle of readings is comprised of eleven lessons, each of which narrates an event related to the resurrection of Christ and his post-resurrection appearances and meals.[144] These pericopes are read in rotation in a recurring cycle of eleven weeks.[145] The cycle of readings commences annually on the Sunday of All Saints and ends on the Fifth Sunday of Lent the following year. The Orthros of the Feast of Pentecost (the eighth

---

[143] The Sunday Orthros in the Octoechos has three canons in each of the eight tones: the resurrectional or anastasimos, the stavroanastasimos, and the Canon of the Theotokos. To these a fourth is added, the canon of the saint or the feast of the day, which may come from the Menaion, Triodion or Pentecostarion. The Octoechos also contains two canons for each day of the week in the eight tones based chiefly on the weekly festal calendar. Additional canons may be added from the other books. On weekdays of Lent only two, three, or four odes are sung. In addition to the Orthros, we find canons in several other services, including the Mesonyktikon, Apodeipnon, the Supplications (Παρακλήσεις) to the Theotokos, Holy Unction, funerals, and other services.

[144] The order of the eleven Morning Gospels is as follows: the 1st: Matthew 28:16-20. The 2nd and 3rd: Mark 16:1-8 and 16:9-20 respectively. The 4th, 5th and 6th: Luke 24:1-12; 24:13-35 and 24:36-53 respectively. The 7th, 8th, 9th, 10th and the 11th: John 20:1-10; 20:11-18; 20:19-31; 21:1-14 and 21:14-25 in that order.

[145] For the history of the Eleven Morning (Ἑωθινά) Gospels see Panayiotis Skaltsis, Λειτουργικές Μελέτες, vol. 2 (Thessaloniki 2009), 275-93. The cycle of eleven lessons was solidified by the eighth century. The number of lessons (eleven) is based on the eleven post resurrection appearances of Christ to the eleven Apostles and the Myrrhbearers.

after Pascha) has its own festal pericope (John 20:9-23) as does the Orthros of Palm Sunday (Matthew 21:1-10, 15-17).¹⁴⁶ During the Paschal season, however, from the Sunday of Thomas to the Saturday before the Sunday of Pentecost, the eleven Sunday Orthros pericopes are read but not in their regular order. They are assigned to specific Sundays and feasts of the Paschal season.¹⁴⁷

A note on the contents of the Evangelion and the place of the Eothinon

The Evangelion contains two large collections of lessons totaling several hundred pericopes from the New Testament. The first, and by far the largest collection, is based on the movable cycle of feasts centered on Pascha. The pericopes or readings (ἀναγνώσματα) begin with the Gospel of John on the Sunday of Pascha.¹⁴⁸

The second collection is based on the fixed feasts, referred to as the Menologion, which starts on September 1, the beginning of the civil and ecclesiastical year in Byzantium. The Menologion contains pericopes for the Divine Liturgy of a given feast and another pericope for those feasts that also have a Gospel

---

146 The Orthros of the Sunday of Pascha does not have a Gospel lesson. Eventually, a lesson was added but not to the Paschal Orthros. It was included in the Intermediate Resurrection Service that precedes it. See Alkiviadis Calivas, *Great Week and Pascha in the Greek Orthodox Church* (Brookline, MA 1992), 110-1.

147 By tradition, the 2nd morning Gospel is read at the intermediate Resurrection Service before the Paschal Orthros (even though the typikon designates Matthew 28:1-20). On the Sunday of Thomas (second Sunday after Pascha) we read the 1ˢᵗ Morning Gospel at the Orthros and the 9ᵗʰ at the Divine Liturgy; on the Sunday of the Myrrhbearers (third Sunday), the 4ᵗʰ; on the fourth Sunday (the Paralytic) the 5ᵗʰ; on fifth Sunday (the Samaritan Woman) the 7ᵗʰ ; on the sixth Sunday (the Man Born Blind), the 8ᵗʰ; on the Feast of the Ascension, at the Orthros the 3ʳᵈ and at the Divine Liturgy the 6ᵗʰ; on the seventh Sunday (Holy Fathers) the 10ᵗʰ; and on the Saturday before Pentecost (Saturday of the souls) at the Divine Liturgy, the 11ᵗʰ. On the contents of the Evangelion, see Appendix A:2.

148 The Gospel lessons in the Evangelion are organized in four periods, starting with the Gospel of John on the Sunday of Pascha. It is read continuously, with few exceptions, every day up to and including the Sunday of Pentecost. Lessons from the Gospel of Matthew follow and cover a period of seventeen weeks (or less) depending on the early or late date of Pascha from one year to the next. The Matthean pericopes start on the day after Pentecost and end on the Friday after the Elevation of the Cross in mid-September. The pericopes from the Gospel of Luke begin on the Monday immediately following the Sunday after the Elevation of the Cross and end at the beginning of the Triodion. The Gospel of Mark is associated with Great Lent and is read on the Saturdays and Sundays of the Lenten period, except for the first Sunday. The Gospel of Mark (chapters 1-7) is also read on the weekdays from the 12ᵗʰ to the 16ᵗʰ week of Matthew and on the weekdays from 13ᵗʰ to the 17ᵗʰ week of Luke (chapters 8-14). As with the other Gospels, the "missing" passages in the continuous reading – *lectio continua* – of Mark are found in the services of Holy Week, Pascha, and the Menologion. For more on the Evangelion, including a short bibliography, see A. Calivas, "The Sunday Lucan Pericopes in the Byzantine Lectionary," in his *The Liturgy in Dialogue*. (Brookline, MA 2018), 225-42.

lesson assigned to the Orthros.

In addition to these two large collections, the Evangelion also contains two other smaller sets. The first is comprised of the eleven Morning (Ἑωθινά) Gospels assigned to the Sunday Orthros. The other consists of Gospel lessons assigned to sacramental rites and other services and a set of generic pericopes for various categories of saints. In the Evangelion the set of the eleven Morning Gospels is found at the end of the movable cycle, immediately after the pericopes of Holy Week. The Gospel lessons assigned to the sacramental rites and other services are found after the Menologion section.

The original position of the Morning Gospel in the received tradition is after the Anavathmoi and the two prokeimena, and before the canon. However, for pastoral reasons the *Typikon of Konstantinos Protopsaltis* (1838) relocated the Sunday Morning Gospel later in the service positioning it after the katavasia of the eighth ode of the canon. The change became fixed when the *Typikon of Violakis* (1888) adopted it. The change served a practical purpose. It made it possible for a greater number of worshippers to be present at the service to hear the Gospel. While the decision to transfer the reading to a later time had merit, the choice of place, however, was arbitrary and some would say odd, since it disrupts the orderly flow of the liturgical units that give shape to the Orthros.

If our Eparchial Synod were to consider some modifications to the structure of the Sunday Orthros to accommodate parish worship needs, the relocation of the Sunday Morning Gospel would be a good starting place. A sound and traditional choice would be to place the reading at the end of the service as it was in the ancient cathedral office of Constantinople. The Morning Gospel was read after the Great Doxology at the ambo,[149] followed by the fervent and dismissal litanies, the prayer of inclination, and the apolysis.[150] In fact, this order has been retained in the Orthros of Great and Holy Saturday, which in current practice is celebrated on the evening of Great Friday.[151]

By tradition, the Sunday Morning Gospel is always read by the senior priest,

---

[149] In his treatise on the Divine Liturgy, St. Germanos of Constantinople says that "the ambo manifests the shape of the stone at the holy Sepulcher [on which the angel sat after he rolled it away from the doors of the tomb], proclaiming the resurrection of the Lord to the myrrhbearing women." See Paul Meyendorff, *St. Germanus of Constantinople on the Divine Liturgy* (Crestwood, NY 1984), 63.

[150] See Panagiotis Trembelas, Μικρὸν Εὐχολόγιον, Β (Athens, 1955), 200-201 and Ioannis M. Fountoulis, Λογικὴ Λατρεία (Thessaloniki 1971), 322.

[151] See Ioannis M. Fountoulis, Ἀπαντήσεις εἰς Λειτουργικὰς Ἀπορίας, Ε (Thessaloniki 2004), 305-10.

if there is more than one serving. When reading the pericope, he stands at the right side of the Holy Table for symbolic reasons, the roots of which are in the Gospel narrative:[152] "And entering the tomb, they [the Myrrhbearers] saw a young man clothed in a long white robe *sitting on the right side*, and they were alarmed. But he said to them, 'Do not be alarmed. You seek Jesus of Nazareth, who was crucified. He is risen. He is not here. See the place where they laid him" (Mark 16:5-6).[153] In our liturgical tradition, both the ambo and the Holy Table are linked symbolically to the tomb of Christ from where the proclamation of the Good News began.

When a dominical feast (e.g., Christmas, Theophany), a feast of the Theotokos, or some other great feast falls on a Sunday, in place of the Eothinon, we read the Orthros Gospel of the feast standing at the Holy Doors facing the people. The one exception to this rule is the Sunday of Thomas also known as the Sunday of Antipascha. Although it is a dominical feast, it is clearly resurrectional in character. Therefore, the designated Orthros lesson, the First Eothinon, is read in the usual manner at the right side of the Holy Table.

If a deacon is present at the Orthros, he begins serving his role for the first time at this point of the service. Fully vested, he stands at his regular place, to the right and slightly behind the priest who stands in front of the Holy Table.

The Order of the Morning Gospel

(At the Conclusion of the Katavasia of the Eighth Ode)

Deacon (or Priest)

Let us pray to the Lord.

Chanter/Choir

Lord, have mercy.

Priest

For you are holy, our God...

Chanter/Choir

---

[152] According to St. Germanos, the Holy Table "corresponds to the spot in the tomb where Christ was placed...It is also the throne of God, on which, borne by the Cherubim, he rested in the body. At that table, at his mystical supper, Christ sat among his disciples and apostles... This table was prefigured by the table of the Old law upon which the manna, which was Christ, descended from heaven." Meyendorff, *St. Germanus*, 59.

[153] The priest should be fully vested when he conducts the office of the Proskomide and when he reads the Morning Gospel.

Says the Amen and sings the fixed prokeimenon, "Let everything that breathes praise the Lord." (3)

Deacon (or Priest)

"That we may be made worthy to hear the Holy Gospel, let us entreat the Lord our God." (When intoning this bidding, the deacon faces the people).

Chanter/Choir

Lord, have mercy (3).

Deacon (or Priest)

Facing the people says, "Wisdom! Arise! Let us hear the Holy Gospel."

Priest

Peace be to all.

Chanter/Choir

And to your spirit.

Priest

The Reading is from the Holy Gospel according to... (Matthew, Mark, Luke, or John).

Deacon (or Priest)

Let us be attentive!

Chanter/Choir

Glory to you, O Lord, glory to you.

Priest

Proceeds to the right side of the Holy Table from where he intones the assigned pericope. (If a deacon is present, he stands opposite the priest). When the priest has finished reading the assigned lesson, he comes before the Holy Doors, raises the Evangelion, and blesses the people. He returns to the Holy Table and places the book in its proper position on top of the folded antimension.[154]

Chanter/Choir

---

[154] The front and back covers of the Evangelion are usually adorned with two icons, the crucifixion and the resurrection of our Lord respectively. Starting with Saturday evening Vespers through Sunday and throughout the Paschal season up to the feast of the Apodosis of Pascha we display the icon of the resurrection. At all other times we display the icon of the crucifixion.

Glory to you, O Lord, glory to you.

The Resurrectional Troparion

Deacon

Recites or intones the troparion, "Having beheld the resurrection of Christ, let us worship the holy Lord Jesus, who alone is without sin..."[155]

Psalm 50/51 – The Troparia – Litany of Intercession

Chanter/Choir

Intones Psalm 50/51, *"Have mercy upon me, O God, according to your lovingkindness..."* (If there are two or more chanters, the verses of the psalm are sung antiphonally/responsively).[156] By tradition, verse 6 (or verse 8 in the Septuagint), *"Behold, you desire truth – Ἰδοὺ γὰρ ἀλήθειαν ἠγάπησας,"* is sung slower and with greater emphasis. At this point, the priest exits the sanctuary through the Holy Doors holding the Evangelion and comes to the center of the solea presenting it to the people for veneration.

Christ is the Word and Wisdom of God, the Revealer of truth and the hidden mysteries and purposes of God. Hence, the Evangelion, which narrates through its pericopes the entire Christ event, is the Church's par excellence icon of Christ. The presentation of the Evangelion for veneration at this point constitutes a symbolic gesture. It is an invitation to the people to draw near and worship the risen Christ—as the Apostles and the Myrrhbearers did (Matthew 28:17; Mark 16:9-14; Luke 24:52; John 20:17). Having just heard the good news of his resurrection, they are filled with gladness; they come forth, reverencing the Evangelion with joyous hearts to worship the Lord Jesus, risen from the dead. It is an act of faith, and expression of love, a renewal of hope.

Upon completion, the priest processes to the narthex and places the Evangelion on the proskynetarion (*προσκυνητάριον* – stand) so that it may be venerated by the faithful.[157] He then returns to the sanctuary through the Holy Doors. When the psalm is completed, the singers chant the three troparia.

Chanter/Choir

---

[155] In some churches the troparion is sung. It is also said on all other days of the Paschal season and on the Feast of the Exaltation of the Precious and Life-giving Cross (September 14)

[156] Psalm 50/51 is chanted only on Sundays. At other times it is recited by the Reader.

[157] Obviously, this is possible only if the Church has a second Evangelion. If there is only one, then it is brought directly back to the sanctuary after the people have venerated it.

Sings the three troparia of the psalm: *"Glory to the Father...At the prayers of the Apostles... Now and forever... At the prayers of the Theotokos... Have mercy upon me, O God...Jesus having risen from the tomb as he foretold..."*[158]

Deacon or Priest

Intones the **Intercessory Litany** (Σῶσον, ὁ Θεὸς τὸν λαόν σου...*O Lord, save your people and bless your inheritance...*). **If a deacon** is present, he exits the sanctuary via the north door and comes to the center of the solea. Facing the sanctuary, he raises his right arm slightly while holding the orarion and begins intoning the Litany of Intercession. When he has completed the commemorations, he bows reverently and enters the sanctuary via the south door.[159] **If there is no deacon, the priest intones** the litany from within the sanctuary, standing in front of the Holy Table.[160]

Chanter/Choir

---

158 On Great Feasts, the last troparion, *"Jesus having risen from the tomb,"* is replaced by a hymn of the feast. Some feasts also have special troparia for the first verse and sometimes for the second. Starting with the Sunday of the Publican and Pharisee (at the beginning of the period of the Triodion) and up to the Fifth Sunday of Great Lent, these hymns are replaced by three penitential troparia: *"Glory to the Father...Open unto me, O Giver of life, the gates of repentance...Now and forever...Guide me in the paths of salvation, O Theotokos...Have mercy upon me, O God... As I ponder in my wretchedness the many evil things that I have done, I tremble for the fearful day of judgment..."*

159 Despite the fact that the printed editions of the service have attempted to standardize the Litany of Intercession, it remains a "soft" element, open to expansion. Through the years, clergy have added the names of various local and other "favorite" saints to the earlier, shorter version of the litany. In the last several decades, the "official" list of saints has been expanded to include a long list of women saints, hitherto absent from the earlier versions. Significantly, the most recent (2004) Ἱερατικόν published by the *Apostolike Diakonia* of the Church of Greece contains the earlier, shorter and preferred version of the Litany of Intercession. A prolonged list of saints distracts the worshipper from the true intent of this Intercessory Prayer: a fervent entreaty to God the Father to save his people; bless his inheritance; look upon his world with mercy and compassion, exalt (raise) the *horn* (= strength, power, dignity) of Orthodox Christians; send down upon the congregants his rich mercy; and hear those who beseech him through the intercessions of the saints and by the mercy, compassion, and love of his only-begotten Son, the only merciful Lord. The deacon or priest must take care **not** to commemorate festal events at the end of the Litany, only the name(s) of the saint(s) of the day. Events related to the Theotokos or St. John the Forerunner are cited immediately after their commemoration in the Litany. For example: "Through the intercessions of our most pure Lady, the Theotokos and ever-Virgin Mary, *whose Nativity we celebrate (commemorate) this day...*"

160 Properly speaking, the Litany of Intercession is not truly a litany but a prayer, as evidenced by the ekfonesis that completes it. As such it should be intoned by the priest and not the deacon. However, in the course of time, having lost its identity as a prayer, it has been assigned to the deacon, if one is present, inasmuch as the deacon offers most, if not all, the litanies and petitions.

Sings the Κύριε ἐλέησον twelve (12) times.

Priest

Intones the ekfonesis of the litany.

The Ninth Biblical Ode and the Censing

Deacon or Priest

Following the ekfonesis, the deacon stands in the middle of the Holy Doors facing the people and intones the bidding: *"Let us honor in hymns and magnify the Theotokos and Mother of the Light – Τὴν Θεοτόκον καὶ μητέρα τοῦ Φωτός..."* If there is **no deacon**, the priest intones the bidding in the same manner. When intoning the bidding, the deacon or priest faces the people and **not** the icon of the Theotokos on the iconostasis. He is addressing the people, inviting them to sing praises to the Theotokos. Out of reverence, he may bow to the icon but only after the bidding.

Chanter/Choir

Sings the Ninth Biblical Ode, the Song of the Theotokos, with the usual *refrain-troparion* after each verse: *"My soul magnifies the Lord...More honorable than the Cherubim..."* At the conclusion of the Song of the Theotokos, the chanter/choir sings the appointed katavasia of the Ninth Ode. **On Great Feasts**, in the place of the Song of the Theotokos, we sing the eirmos and troparia of the Ninth Ode of the feast with its special megalynaria and katavasia.

Deacon or Priest:

As the chanter/choir begins singing the Song of the Theotokos, the deacon receives the **censer** and asks the priest to bless the offering of incense. Standing in front of the Holy Table he begins the censing of the Holy Table in the usual manner. Exiting the sanctuary from the north door, he comes to the center of the solea. He censes the icons on the iconostasis. Then he censes the chanters/choirs and proceeding down the middle aisle he censes the people, beginning with those on his left. He enters the narthex and censes the Evangelion (if one is there on a stand), the icons on the stands, and the people there. Returning to the nave through the middle aisle and moving forward to the solea, he censes the people, again on his left. Coming to the solea, he censes only the icons of the Lord and the Theotokos (Δεσποτικαὶ εἰκόνες). He returns to the sanctuary via the south door. He censes the Holy Table, the prothesis, the "diakonikon," the clergy, and all others in the sanctuary. *If there is no deacon*, the priest conducts the censing in the same manner.[161]

Regarding the Incensation at the Ninth Ode

The roots and purpose of the general incensation which takes place at this point in the Orthros are not clear. I suspect it is rooted in earlier preparatory rituals for the Divine Liturgy. Pseudo-Dionysios the Areopagite, for example, in his treatise, *The Ecclesiastical Hierarchy* (3:2), informs us that in his time (fifth-sixth century) the Divine Liturgy began with a general incensation of the church. "The hierarch, having said a sacred prayer at the divine altar, begins the censing there and then he makes the round of the entire sacred place. Returning to the divine altar, he begins the sacred singing of the psalms and the entire assembly joins him in this.... The chosen deacons, along with the priests, put on the divine altar the sacred bread and the cup of blessing...."[162]

The significance of the general incensation is two-fold. First, it is an honorific act, a way of showing respect for the sacred space in which the liturgy is celebrated, for the sacred icons that surround it, and for special furnishings (Holy Table, Prothesis) that are in it. It is also a sign of the presence of the Holy Spirit as suggested by the prayer of incense: "We offer you incense, O Christ our God, as an odor of spiritual fragrance. Receive it upon your heavenly altar, and send down upon us in return the grace of your all-holy Spirit."[163]

---

[161] Depending on the size of the church and other factors, it is possible to extend the censing in the following manner. After the censing of the icons, the deacon or priest proceeds down the middle aisle and before entering the narthex, he turns left and proceeds to the south aisle, all the while censing the people and the icons. He goes down the south (end) aisle toward the solea. Bowing before the Holy Doors, he proceeds to and goes down the north (end) aisle. He enters the narthex and censes as usual and returns to the nave via the middle aisle, censing the people on his left in the usual manner. On the meaning and purpose of the censing at the Ninth Ode see Appendix A:3.

[162] Pseudo-Dionysius: The Complete Works, The Classics of Western Spirituality (New York/Mahwah 1987), 210, 211.

[163] A similar concept appears in the Prayer of the Proskomide of the Divine Liturgy of St. Basil the Great: "Having received it [our reasonable sacrifice without the shedding of blood] upon your holy, heavenly, and ideal altar for an odor of spiritual fragrance, send upon us in return the grace of your Holy Spirit."

This practice, in different forms, continued through the centuries.[164] Eventually, it was attached to the end of the prothesis rite (proskomide), as indicated by a twelfth-thirteenth century diataxis.[165] By then the censing was conducted by the deacon or, in his absence, a priest.

The determinative *Diataxis of Philotheos Kokkinos* (14th century) contains the following rubric. After the apolysis of the prothesis rite, "the deacon receives the censer and proceeds to cense the Holy Table saying in a low voice the troparion, *"You were in the tomb bodily...;"* after which he recites Psalm 50/51 in its entirety while censing the entire sanctuary (ἱερατεῖον) and the temple (ναός). Returning to the Holy Bema (Sanctuary) he censes the Holy Table and the priest before returning the censer to its place."

The same rubric with some modifications accompanies the prothesis rite to this day. The deacon (or priest) is instructed to cense the Holy Table, the Sanctuary, the icons of the iconostasis, and the people from the Holy Doors, while reciting the three troparia attached to the end of the prothesis rite.[166] However, a brief and preferred version of this practice is to cense only to the Holy Table at the conclusion of the prothesis rite.[167] An extensive censing has already occurred at the Ninth Ode and will be enacted again at the Great Entrance of the Divine Liturgy.[168]

---

164 We learn, for example, the cathedral Orthros Service of Constantinople had an extensive incensation starting with the narthex, then the nave and the sanctuary. It was performed by a deacon or priest at the conclusion of the first part of the Orthros which was celebrated in the narthex. Following the incensation, the royal and other doors leading into the nave were opened and the clergy with the people entered the nave to continue the service. See Panayiotis Trembelas, Μικρὸν Εὐχολόγιον, vol. 2, 194-199. To this day, monastic communities conduct an extensive incensation of the temple prior to the commencement of Vespers and Orthros. This ancient practice is also evident during Holy Week, when the priest censes the entire temple while the Royal Psalms are intoned at the beginning of the Orthros.

165 See Trembelas, Μικρὸν Εὐχολόγιον, 5.

166 For the development and meaning of the prothesis rite see, Stelyios S. Muksuris, *Economia & Eschatology: Liturgical Mystagogy in the Byzantine Prothesis Rite* (Brookline 2013).

167 In monasteries where the Divine Liturgy is celebrated after the service of the Sixth Hour, the entire temple is censed during the course of the Sixth Hour. The same practice occurs at the Ninth Hour as the Beatitudes are sung when the Divine Liturgy of the Pre-Sanctified Gifts is celebrated after the Ninth Hour.

168 We do not cense during the Great Doxology.

What is the reason for censing at the Ninth Ode? It is conceivable that this incensation is related to the censing of the entire temple described by Pseudo-Dionysios, which was later attached to the end of the prothesis rite. If it is a remnant of the rite described by Dionysios, why was it attached to this particular unit of the Orthros? Perhaps, the answer lies in the second of the two canticles that comprise the Ninth Ode. In addition to the Song of the Theotokos, the Ninth Ode also contains the Prayer of the Righteous Zechariah (Luke 1:68-79), a prayer he uttered after the birth of his son, St. John the Baptist and Forerunner. This birth was foretold to Zechariah by an angel while he was performing his priestly duties, offering incense. "Now while he was serving as priest before God when his division was on duty, according to the custom of the priesthood, it fell to him by lot to enter the temple of the Lord and burn incense. And the whole multitude of the people were praying outside at the hour of incense. And there appeared to him an angel of the Lord standing on the right side of the altar of incense…" (Luke 1:8-11).

When the **chanter/choir** has concluded the katavasia of the Ninth Ode, we say the Small Synapte.

The Small Synapte:

Deacon or Priest

Intone the Small Synapte: "*Again and again, in peace let us pray to the Lord... Help us, save us... Remembering our most holy...*" (If a deacon is present, he exits the sanctuary via the north door to the solea, where he intones the petitions. In the absence of a deacon, the priest stands before the Holy Table and intones the petitions.

Priest

Intones the ekfonesis, "*For all the powers of heaven praise you...*" (Note that this is the concluding doxology – the ekfonesis – of the Eleventh Morning Prayer).169

169After the ekfonesis, the priest should remain at the Holy Table during the singing of "*Holy is the Lord...*" and "*Exalt the Lord...*" He bows reverently when he hears the words "*and worship at his footstool...*"

The Exaposteilaria (Ἐξαποστειλάρια)

Chanter/Choir

Amen, which is followed by:

"'Άγιος Κύριος ὁ Θεὸς ἡμῶν... Holy is the Lord our God." (twice)

"'Ὑψοῦτε Κύριον τὸν Θεὸν ἡμῶν καὶ προσκυνεῖτε τῷ ὑποδίῳ τῶν ποδῶν αὐτοῦ, ὅτι ἅγιος ἐστι...

Exalt the Lord our God, and worship at his footstool for he is holy."

Chanter/Choir

Sing the appointed Exaposteilarion and Theotokion.

A Note on the "Holy is the Lord our God" and the Exaposteilaria

According to Ioannis Fountoulis, "Holy is the Lord our God" was a type of prokeimenon before the Psalms of Praise. The verse, "Holy is the Lord our God," comes from Psalm 98/99, verse 9. Originally it was sung three times. In a later development it was sung twice together with an additional verse, "Exalt the Lord our God..." as it is today. The original form is maintained in the Orthros of Palm Sunday and Holy Saturday.

The verse, "Exalt the Lord our God, and worship at his footstool for he is holy," also comes from Psalm 98/99 (verse 5). Both verses, "Holy is the Lord" and "Exalt the Lord," are sung only on Sundays, never on weekdays. They are also omitted from the Orthros of the Sunday of Pascha.

Traditionally, the word "ὑποπόδιον–footstool" is understood to refer to the Cross. That this verse, "Exalt the Lord our God," is used as the entrance hymn (εἰσοδικόν) of the feast of the Exaltation of the Precious and Life-giving Cross attests to this interpretation.

As with other liturgical units of the Orthros, the "Holy is our God," was in time expanded to include additional hymns. There are two types of these hymns: the festal and the ordinary. The ordinary have a single theme: light –φῶς and as such are called photagogika. The photagogikon of the third tone, for example, says: "Send forth your light, O Christ my God, and illumine my heart..." The photagogika were once sung in ordinary, non-festal days, but have long since been limited to the Lenten season.

It is not difficult to know why the theme of light is connected to these hymns. The service is drawing to a close. In earlier days, especially in monastic communities, the Orthros ended at dawn with the appearance of the natural light, when the darkness of night is overcome.

The festal troparia by their very nature treat particular themes. The festal hymns acquired the name exaposteilaria. The exaposteilarion of the Feast of the Exaltation of the Life-giving Cross is a good example. "The Cross is the guardian of the whole earth; the Cross is the beauty of the Church; the Cross is the strength of kings; the Cross is the support of the faithful. The Cross is the glory of angels and the wounder of demons."

Some exaposteilaria creatively combine the theme of light with that of the feast. We see this, for example, in the penitential exaposteilarion of Holy Week: "I see your bridal chamber adorned, O my Savior, and I have no wedding garment that I may enter there. Make the robe of my soul to shine, O Giver of Light, and save me."

The Exaposteilaria of the Sunday Orthros: *Festal exaposteilaria are found in the Triodion, Pentecostarion, Menaia, and Horologion in their usual place, after the canon(s). The Octoechos, however, constitutes an exception. The exaposteilaria in the Octoechos are contained in an appendix and not in the main body of the text. The Octoechos has several types of exaposteilaria. The exaposteilaria of the Sunday Orthros are of special interest. There are eleven such hymns, all of which, together with their respective Theotokion, are sung in the second tone and are based on the meter and melody of the first hymn in the series, "Ταῖς μαθηταῖς συνέλθωμεν – Let us go up with the disciples." These hymns were composed by Emperor Constantine VII Porphyrogenitos (913-959). Each set is a brief poetic summary of the corresponding morning Gospel. They are sung in rotation in a successive cycle of eleven weeks, corresponding to the cycle of the eleven morning Gospels, so that, for example, the first of the eleven Sunday exaposteilaria always falls on the same Sunday as the first morning Gospel (Matt. 26:16-20).*

In addition to the eleven resurrectional exaposteilaria, the Octoechos also has a group of exaposteilaria together with their respective theotokion or stavrotheotokion for each day of the week in each of the eight tones based on the weekly festal calendar. Saturday has an additional exaposteilarion for the dead. The appendix also contains a series of eight photagogika, one for each of the eight tones for the ordinary days. The ending of each of these hymns changes according to the commemoration of the particular day in the festal calendar of the week.

The Triodion also has an appendix titled, "Hymns to the Trinity and Hymns of Light (φωταγωγικά) in the Eight Tones Sung during the Great Fast." These hymns are borrowed from the appendices of the Octoechos.

The word exaposteilarion is derived from the verb ἐξαποστέλλω – to send forth. The word photagogika is derived from the noun φῶς – light and the verb ἄγω – to lead. Both words are related to Christ, the True Light, who is implored to send forth or to lead us to his light. Some have suggested that the word exaposteilaria may also refer to the commissioning of the Holy Apostles whom Christ sent forth to proclaim the Gospel.

The Psalms of Praise or Lauds (148, 149, 150) – Οἱ Αἶνοι

Chanter/Choir

Sing the Psalms of Praise – Αἶνοι – in the appointed tone starting with the following "introductory verses."

"*Let everything that breathes praise the Lord.* Praise the Lord from the heavens; praise him in the heights. *To you, O God, is due praise.*"[170]

"Praise him, all his angels; praise him, all his host! *To you, O God is due praise.*"

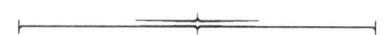

A Note on the Psalms of Praise (Οἱ Αἶνοι or τα Πασαπνοάρια)

The last three psalms of the Psalter, 148, 149, and 150, are called Psalms of Praise because of their content.[171] The word praise is used repeatedly. All created things together with all the peoples of the earth are called to give praise to the Author of life in joyful thanksgiving with song at all times and in every circumstance. According to the typikon, these communal hymns of praise are sung or intoned at every Orthros service. Regrettably, however, in parishes, for the sake of brevity, their use is limited to the two introductory verses and several additional verses, depending on the number of hymns attached to the Praises.

The two "introductory" verses, based on Psalm 148:1-2, are sung only on Sundays and feast days.[172] On ordinary days the Praises begin directly with the first verse of Psalm 148, "Praise the Lord! Praise the Lord from

---

[170] The text in italics is not found in the two verses of the biblical text but are refrains from the repertoire of the cathedral office.

[171] All classical liturgical rites of the East and West include the Psalms of Praise in the morning service. They were also part of temple worship in ancient Israel.

[172] On Sundays, after Psalm 150, we add two additional psalmic verses: "Arise, O Lord! O God, lift up your hand! Do not forget the humble to the end;" and "I will praise (confess) you, O Lord, with my whole heart; I will tell of all your marvelous works." These two verses are from Psalm 9:33 (in the Septuagint) or Psalm 10:12 and Psalm 9:1 respectively (in the Masoretic). When a feast of the Theotokos falls on a Sunday, these two verses are replaced by two others. When a feast of the Lord falls on a Sunday, they are omitted.

the heavens; praise him in the heights."

In current practice, these psalms are executed responsively, that is, their verses are sung one after the other, in accordance with the monastic tradition. Festal hymns are inserted between the last verses of Psalm 149 and 150.

In the cathedral office the Psalms of Praise were executed differently. Various refrains were sung by the people between verses of the psalms. Remnants of this practice have been retained in the two introductory verses. Notice the words in these two verses; they do not correspond fully with the biblical text of Psalm 148:1-2. The opening phrase "Let everything that breathes praise the Lord!" is not from Psalm 148, but is the last verse (6) of Psalm 150. Originally, it may have been sung by the precentor to signal the start of the Praises or to identify the refrain the people were to sing. The last phrase, "To you, O God, is due praise," is not found in any of the three psalms. It is, without doubt, one of the refrains in the repertoire of the cathedral office. The sources provide us with examples of other refrains, some of which have been retained in the received liturgical texts. The following are examples from the collection of refrains. "To him is due praise;" "Give glory to our God;" "Glory to you, O Holy Father;" "Son of God, have mercy on us;" "Spare us, O Lord;" and "Glory to you who has shown us the light."[173] The last refrain is now used to introduce the Great Doxology.

The Stichera Troparia (Hymns) of the Praises

Eventually, as hymnography developed and expanded, the refrains were replaced by an assortment of hymns, treating a variety of themes. The largest number of hymns were written by monastics.

On Sundays and feast days, sets of troparia are interpolated between the last several verses of the Praises. The interpolation of hymns begins with Psalm 149:9 or with verses from Psalm 150 depending on the number of troparia. The count always starts with the last verse and moves up to the fourth, sixth, eighth, or tenth preceding verse, according to the number of hymns assigned to the Orthros of the day.[174]

The Octoechos contains eight resurrectional praise hymns in each of the eight tones for the Sunday Orthros. Additional festal hymns are often

---

[173] See Trembelas, Μικρὸν Εὐχολόγιον, vol. II, 199.

[174] In parishes, depending on circumstances, the number of hymns is often limited to six or less.

added from the Triodion, Pentecostarion, or Menaia. When festal troparia are added to the repertoire, the resurrectional hymns (προηγοῦνται τὰ ἀναστάσιμα) always precede. If a feast of the Lord falls on a Sunday, the resurrectional hymns are omitted in favor of the festal hymns.[175]

The Doxastikon (Δοξαστικόν)

The Psalms of Praise conclude with two troparia. As usual, the Psalms of Praise, as with all sets of psalms, concludes with the verses, "Glory to the Father... Now and forever...." Gradually, hymns were written to accompany these verses, the so-called Δοξαστικόν-Doxastikon (troparion) followed by the καὶ νῦν (now and forever), which is usually a Theotokion.[176] *The doxastikon takes its name from the first word of the verse, δόξα, which means glory.*

The Octoechos contains eleven resurrectional idiomela doxastika written by Emperor Leo VI the Wise (886-912),[177] *the father of Constantine VII Porphyrogenitos. Each hymn is related to and paraphrases one of the eleven Sunday Morning Gospels. These hymns are found in the Appendix of the Octoechos and are listed after their corresponding resurrectional exaposteilarion under the title Eothinon A (1), Eothinon B (2), etc. Each hymn is sung in one of the eight tones of the Byzantine music in order starting with Eothinon A (1) in the first tone. The three additional doxastika (ninth, tenth, and eleventh) are sung in the pl. first, pl. second and pl. fourth tones respectively. These hymns are sung only on Sundays. They are omitted in favor of a festal doxastikon when a feast of the Lord, the Theotokos, or some other major feast (e.g. Sunday of the Holy Fathers) falls on a Sunday. They are also omitted on the Sundays of the Triodion and Pentecostarion. Most, if not all, feasts have their own doxastikon. The feasts of the Lord and the Theotokos usually have only one hymn (doxa/ke nyn).*

The "Now and forever..." (Καὶ νῦν)

In the course of time, as noted, a hymn was also added to the verse ke nyn. This hymn is usually a theotokion, a troparion dedicated to the Theotokos. It is usually sung in the tone of the preceding doxastikon, but

---

[175] The feasts of the Meeting of the Lord (February 2) and the Annunciation (March 25) are an exception because they are simultaneously Feasts of the Lord and the Theotokos.

[176] Normally, on feasts of the Lord or the Theotokos there is only one hymn. It is sung after the "Glory to the Father... Now and forever..."

[177] Leo VI the Wise is also known as the Philosopher because of his erudition and extensive writings. He was, however, a controversial figure. Upon his accession to the throne he banished Patriarch Photios to a monastery and later in the disputes that followed concerning the validity of his fourth marriage he deposed Patriarch Nicholas Mysticos who opposed it.

not always. It is usually sung in a quicker rhythm than the doxastikon.

On Sundays, except for rare occasions, we sing the familiar hymn, "'Ὑπερευλογημένη ὑπάρχεις, Θεοτόκε Παρθένε...You are Most-blessed, O Virgin Theotokos." During the Paschal season, to emphasize the joy of the Resurrection, it has become customary to replace this hymn with the resurrectional doxastikon, "Ἀναστάσεως Ἡμέρα... It is the day of the Resurrection…" When a feast of the Lord or the Theotokos falls on a Sunday, we sing the designated festal ke nyn. On weekdays we sing the appointed festal hymn.

The Great Doxology – Ἡ Μεγάλη Δοξολογία

The Orthros concludes with the singing of the Great Doxology, followed by a series of petitions, a blessing, the prayer of inclination, and the apolysis.

The Great Doxology is sung joyously every Sunday and on the feasts of the Lord, the Theotokos, and major saints.[178] By tradition, on Sundays the Great Doxology is sung in the tone of the week. On all other festal days in the tone of the doxastikon of the Praises. Traditionally, on the feasts of the Elevation and the Veneration of the Cross it is sung in the fourth tone.[179]

The Great Doxology is introduced by the refrain of the ancient cathedral office, "Δόξα σοι τῷ δείξαντι τὸ φῶς – Glory to you who has shown us the light." In earlier times, the doxology was timed to coincide with daybreak, with the appearance of the sun. This tradition holds true in monastic communities to this day. In parishes, however, the Orthros begins well after sunrise.

*On ordinary weekdays and during the first five days of Holy Week the doxology is not sung but read. It is preceded by the phrase, "Σοὶ δόξα πρέπει – To you is due glory…" The read doxology is referred to as the **Small Doxology**, the ending of which differs from that of the Great Doxology. Following the recitation of the Small Doxology the priest intones aloud the fervent and dismissal litanies, gives the peace, and recites the prayer of inclination, after which the chanter(s) sings the aposticha of the*

---

[178] The original Greek texts of the Great and Small Doxologies are found in the Horologion. Translations are available in the texts produced by the Narthex Press, GOA Digital Chant Stand, and the Divine Music Project.

[179] See Papayiannis, Σύστημα Τυπικοῦ, 76. In parishes of the Greek Archdiocese of America the doxology is rendered according to the musical abilities of the chanter or choir. Many choirs have been accustomed to sing the doxology only in the third tone. Perhaps, with the encouragement of the parish priest and the assistance of the music director chanters, choirs, and the people can learn to sing it in one or two other tones.

Praises. The priest then intones the blessing, "Ἀγαθὸν τὸ ἐξομολογεῖσθαι τῷ Κυρίῳ – It is good to give thanks to the Lord." The chanter recites the Trisagion Prayers, followed by the singing of the festal apolytikion, and the apolysis.

The Orthros of the Sunday of Pascha, the weekdays of Renewal Week, and the Apodosis of Pascha does not have a Doxology, Great or Small. Instead, we sing only the resurrectional doxastikon, "Ἀναστάσεως Ἡμέρα ... It is the day of the Resurrection…." followed by the hymn "Χριστὸς ἀνέστη ἐκ νεκρῶν ... Christ is risen from the dead….," which is sung three times.

The Great Doxology contains fifteen verses or stichoi, the majority of which are borrowed from the psalms or from other biblical sources. Some are ecclesial poetry inspired by Scripture. The verses are of unequal length and are divided into three sections. The first section has six verses as does the third; the second has three. The first section begins with the angelic hymn recorded in the Gospel of Luke (2:14), "Glory to God in the highest…" The verses that follow constitute a hymn of praise and thanksgiving to the Triune God with an emphasis on the economy of the Son, our Lord Jesus Christ, and a plea for mercy. In the second section the worshipper is conscious of God's gracious presence in the affairs of everyday life and offers praise to his Holy Name. The third section is comprised of verses that affirm God's mercy, compassion, and healing power and acknowledge him as the source of life, light, and forgiveness. The generations who take refuge in him recognize his loving care and exclaim, "Blessed are you, O Lord, teach me your statutes." This verse, the eleventh, is repeated three times. As mentioned initially, the Great Doxology is introduced by the ancient refrain, "Glory to you who has shown us the light." It concludes with the ancient hymn ""Ἅγιος ὁ Θεός ... Holy God, Holy Mighty, Holy Immortal, have mercy on us….," which is sung three times.

The Small Doxology differs from the Great Doxology in several ways. It has its own distinct introduction and order, it is comprised of sixteen verses, it does not include the hymn, "Holy God, Holy, Mighty, Holy, Immortal," and concludes with a doxological ekfonesis. The last seven verses, together with the ekfonesis, are identical to the Evening Prayer of Vespers, "Καταξίωσον, Κύριε ... Grant Lord, to keep us this evening (day or night) without sin…" The Small Doxology is also read at the services of the Great and Small Apodeipnon, but without the introductory phrase, "To you is due glory…"

The Concluding Hymn

On Sundays, the Great Doxology is followed by the familiar concluding hymn, "Σήμερον σωτηρία τῷ κόσμῳ γέγονεν – Today, salvation has come to the world…" According to the typikon, this hymn is sung on Sundays only when the tone of the week is one of the four authentic tones. When the tone of the week is one of the plagal tones, another hymn is assigned: "Ἀναστὰς ἐκ τοῦ μνήματος, καὶ τὰ δεσμὰ διαρρήξας τοῦ ἅδου, ἔλυσας τὸ κατάκριμα τοῦ θανάτου, Κύριε … Lord, having risen from the grave and having broken the bonds of Hades, you loosened the sentence of death…." Today, however, for reasons of practicality this rubric is rarely observed in parish usage. Over the decades, the people have become accustomed to and have, in many instances, memorized the familiar and now beloved troparion, "Today, salvation has come to the world…." On feast days we sing the apolytikion of the feast at the conclusion of the Great Doxology.

The Concluding Petitions and the Apolysis

In current Greek practice, the priest (or the priest with the deacon) recites the fervent and dismissal litanies inaudibly, standing before the Holy Table while the Great Doxology is being sung. The priest also gives the peace, reads the Prayer of Inclination, and recites the apolysis again in a low voice. It appears that this is done for the sake of brevity. However, the practice makes little sense and is indefensible.[180] Nonetheless, clergy are obliged to observe it until the Church decrees otherwise.

Biblical Readings

If the Divine Liturgy is not celebrated on a weekday, we read the Epistle and Gospel lessons assigned to the weekday system of readings at the end of the Orthros, and prior to aforementioned petitions. On the weekdays of Great Lent when the Divine Liturgy is not celebrated, we read a lesson from the Prophecy of Isaiah, listed in the Tridion at the end of the Orthros. This reading, together with its troparion and two prokeimena, was once part of the trithekte service of the cathedral office.[181]

---

[180] When the Orthros is conducted independently of the Divine Liturgy, it makes sense to intone and recite these things audibly because they are an integral element of the Orthros. However, if brevity is a concern, because the Divine Liturgy is to follow, with the local hierarch's permission, it is possible to eliminate the two litanies, both of which will be said at the Divine Liturgy that follows. In this way, the celebrants can also sing and pray the doxology. After the doxology and the concluding hymn, the priest gives the peace, recites the prayer of inclination, and conducts the apolysis aloud. This way there is a clear demarcation point between the Orthros and the Divine Liturgy.

[181] The rubrics concerning the daily readings at the Orthros are faithfully observed in the Chapel of the Holy Cross Greek Orthodox School of Theology.

A Note on Byzantine Music

The liturgical chant of the Orthodox Church is often referred to as Byzantine chant or Byzantine music.[182] It is characterized by a lofty and imposing dignity. It is one of the distinctive features of Orthodox worship. In its authentic forms it has the power to move souls, creating within the worshippers prayerful dispositions. Its melodic formulas and tonal characteristics have universal appeal and are capable of touching the emotions, inspiring the mind, gladdening the heart, and delighting the soul. Simultaneously, Byzantine music can generate tranquility and produce spiritual exhilaration. Above all, it enhances the beauty, symmetry, and eloquence of the ecclesial poetry it is intended to serve.

According to the specialists, Byzantine music is of composite origins, drawing especially from the musical traditions of ancient Greece. It is based on a system of eight standard tones or modes called ἦχοι. Of these, four are authentic or primary (κύριοι) tones and four are derivative or plagal (πλάγιοι). The four authentic tones have numerical names and are called sequentially, First tone (ἦχος Πρῶτος), Second (Δεύτερος), Third (Τρίτος), and Fourth (Τέταρτος). The plagal tones are preceded by the adjective plagal: plagal First (πλάγιος τοῦ Πρώτου), plagal Second (πλάγιος τοῦ Δευτέρου), plagal Third or more commonly Grave (Βαρύς), and plagal Fourth (πλάγιος τοῦ Τετάρτου). In some traditions the plagal tones are referred to in the ascending numerical order as: fifth, sixth, seventh, and eighth tone respectively. Each tone has a basic signature which corresponds to the first four Greek letter-numerals: α, β, γ, δ. The letters πλ. (for plagal) are assigned to the plagal tones, except for the pl. Third whose signature is βαρύς. Characteristically, every text which is intended to be sung always bears a tonal signature, even when in current usage some of these texts are recited and not sung.

Each tone has four basic elements: a scale (κλῖμαξ), an introductory motif called *apechema* (ἀπήχημα), dominant notes (δεσπόζοντες φθόγγοι), and cadences (καταλήξεις). The apechema identifies the tone and offers its basic tonal characteristic.

Authentic Byzantine music is executed vocally without instrumental accompaniment. The melody, sung by one or many voices is supported usually by the *ison* (holding note) which is also sung by one or several voices according

---

[182] The information in the note on Byzantine music has been gleaned from a variety of sources. On the state of Byzantine music after the fall of Constantinople see Romanos Karanos, "The Role of the Ecumenical Patriarchate in the Preservation and Development of Ecclesiastical Music after 1453," in *Evangelist, Shepherd, and Teacher: Studies in Honor of Archbishop Demetrios of America*, J. Skedros, M. Constas, and V. Limberis, editors (Brookline, MA 2020), 284-302.

to set rules. The ison serves to maintain the pitch and adds an element of rudimentary harmony. When executed properly, Byzantine chant is strikingly simple and beautiful.

The hymns in all the liturgical books fall into one of several categories and are chanted in one of three styles: the *heirmologikon* (ειρμολογικόν) in quick time with few florid passages; the *sticherarikon* (στιχηραρικόν), in moderate time with some florid passages; and the *papadikon* (παπαδικόν) in slow free-time with frequent florid passages. For example, the troparia of canons and stichera prosomoia (model hymn-melodies) are sung in the heirmologikon style. The stichera idiomela are chanted in the sticherarikon style. An example of a hymn sung in the papadikon style is the Cherubic Hymn.

The oldest manuscripts containing musical notations are dated no earlier than the middle of the tenth century. These mss fall under five basic types: *heirmologion, sticherarikon, asmatikon, psaltikon,* and *akolouthia.* The heirmologia mss, dating from the tenth to the fifteenth centuries, contain the heirmoi or eirmoi (model stanzas) for the odes of the canons in the various tones. The sticheraria contain the stichera troparia (*idiomela, prosomoia, and automela*) sung with psalms or psalm verses in Vespers, Orthros and other services. The asmatikon and psaltikon contained highly melismatic responsorial chants. The asmatikon was designed for choirs and chanters, while the psaltikon was intended for the precentor or protopsaltis (leader).

The *Akolouthia,* a new class of manuscripts, appeared in the fourteenth century. The anthology of chants in the Akolouthia was first compiled by Ioannis Koukouzelis, the great master of medieval Byzantine chant. It is the first liturgical book to collect in one volume the psalms and hymns of the daily Office and the three Divine Liturgies in musical notation. Koukouzelis and other composers of the Akolouthia introduced a new style of chant that included both simple and highly elaborate melodies. The new chant was intended primarily for monastic communities. This style, known as *kalophonic* or beautiful, lasted through the early part of the nineteenth century when it was supplanted by a new method using the original basic notation in a simplified form. It was developed chiefly by the Protopsaltis Gregorios Levites (+1822), the Chartophylax, Harmouzios (+1840), and Chrysanthos, the Metropolitan of Prousa (+1843) who published several studies explaining and interpreting the theory of Byzantine music.

The period immediately preceding the reforms of Chrysanthos was influenced greatly by Petros the Peloponnesian (+1777), the Lampadarios of the Great Church. A highly talented musician, he was himself an interpreter of the received tradition in neumatic (notation symbols) notation and melodic formulations. A chanter of considerable ability and a teacher at the Music School of the Ecumenical Patriarchate, he composed music for every conceivable liturgical use in each of the traditional styles. Especially important were his reconstructed and simplified melodic versions. Two of his chief works were his two *Anastasimataria*, one in slow time (ἀργόν) and the other in quick time (σύντομον).

The **Anastasimatarion** (Ἀναστασιματάριον), as the word indicates, is a musical book containing the neumanated text of the resurrectional troparia of the Octoechos. Other earlier composers of the Anastasimatarion were Ioannis Glykis (ca. 14th century), Manuel Chrysaphis (ca.1458), and Chrysaphis the Younger (ca.1655). Another significant figure in the developing story of Byzantine music is Ioannis Sakellaridis (1853-1938), a renowned protopsaltis and composer. He simplified the traditional melodies, liberating them from the melismatic over-extensions they had accumulated over the centuries. He also added harmony lines to many of his compositions – a clear innovation, frowned upon by the traditionalists.[183]

Scholars who have contributed to the promotion of Byzantine music studies include H.J.W Tillyard, Egon Wellesz, Carsten Hoeg, and Oliver Strunk. Dionysios Psarianos, the Metropolitan of Kozani, published numerous works pertaining to worship and sacred chant and in 1970 helped establish the Synodical Institute of Byzantine Musicology. Orthodox musicologists who have delved into the history and development of Byzantine music include Markos Dragoumis, Simon Karras, Gregorios Stathis, Dimitri Conomos, Milos Velimirovic, Spyros Peristeris, Ioannis Maragariotes, Michael Adamis, Diane Touliatos-Banker, and Alexander Lingas. Others, as Panagiotis Chrestou, a patristic scholar, and Constantine Trypanis and Kariofylis Mitsakis, both of whom are philologists, contributed greatly to the study of Byzantine hymnography. Finally, among the leading twentieth century interpreters of the Byzantine musical tradition whose works gained wide circulation in the Greek Church include the precentors of the Ecumenical Patriarchate: Konstantinos Pringos and Thrasyvoulos Stanitsas; and the Greek precentors Theodoros Vasilikos, Athanasios Karamanis, Harilaos Talliadoros, Emmanuel Hatzimarkos, Evangelos Georgiadis, Athanasios Pettas, and Lycourgos Angelopoulos.

The Byzantine musical idiom, with local variations and adaptations, is common to all the Orthodox Churches, with the exception of modern Russian church music. Although it maintains the technical terms of the standard system of eight tones, this music differs significantly from the traditional chant. Its basic elements and melodies, which feature harmonized singing, have been greatly influenced by western music.

---

[183] The Ὑμνωδία of Sakelarides was used by the students of Holy Cross for several decades in the classroom and in the chapel. In the early eighties it was replaced by the Anastasimatarion.

In North America, and other places where Orthodoxy was planted through immigration, the liturgical chant of the various Orthodox jurisdictions has been influenced by the received tradition of each. Among the pioneer composers and choir directors of the GOA were Nicholas Roubanis, George Anastasiou, and Christos Vrionides. Their compositions reflected the influence of Ioannis Sakellaridis.

In recent years, The National Forum of Greek Orthodox Musicians has worked diligently to promote creatively the traditional liturgical chant. Composers whose works are used today by many choirs include Frank Desby, Anna Gallos, Tikey Zes, Theodore Bogdanos, Demetrios Pappas, Dean Limberakis, George Athanasopoulos, George Demos, Kevin Lawrence, Nicholas Maragos, Steven Cardiasmenos, and Fr. Konstantinos Mendrinos. Happily, a new generation of church musicians is emerging to further the work of their predecessors. In its *Liturgical Guide Book*, which the Forum publishes annually, one will find an annotated bibliography of liturgical compositions in western notation.

We must not lose sight of the fact that all Orthodox Theological Schools and Seminaries have played an important role in fostering an appreciation for and promoting the knowledge and use of the traditional liturgical chant. With respect to Holy Cross, we are obliged to recognize with gratitude the efforts and contributions of the instructors who taught courses in and implanted a love for Byzantine music in the students from its inception in 1937 to the present day: Fr. Basil Efthimiou, Fr. George Tsoumas, Prof. Christos Vrionides, Prof. Panayiotis Nychis, Bishop Mark Lippa, Prof. Savas J. Savas, Fr. Nicholas Kastanas, Fr. Constantine Terss, Prof. Photios Ketsetzis, and Fr. Romanos Karanos.

To assure both continuity and creativity in the development of our church music in this land several key factors are essential. These include: a deep respect for our musical tradition; an in-depth knowledge of the tonal system, neumatic notations, and melodic formulas of Byzantine music; the production of excellent English translations of the hymnographic material; a deep appreciation for the ministry of song; and an acute awareness of the needs and temperament of present-day worshippers.

PART TWO
THE HOLY SACRAMENTS

The powers and mysteries of God's kingdom already experienced in the Church are manifested through the divine sacraments celebrated in faith. It is through these, as windows, that the risen and glorified Christ enters into the life of people to overcome sin and corruption and to bestow sanctification and immortal life.[1]

The sacraments – or the divine mysteries as the Orthodox prefer to call them – reveal and communicate the inexhaustible mystery of God's salvific activity. They are the singular manifestations of the one, unique mystery, who is Jesus Christ – the mystery hidden before all ages in God and already revealed in the Church (Ephes. 3:4-12). Hence, the sacraments constitute a single reality. They are not independent acts but distinct manifestation of the one Mystery, Christ.

Everything that Christ did once for all for the salvation of the world has now passed over into the sacraments of his Church. The sacraments manifest the radical renewal and transformation of human nature, human persons, and human life. Through the sacraments Christ becomes everyone's contemporary. Through them we encounter Christ – "the life of all" – in order to be made participants in and beneficiaries of the great mystery of salvation accomplished by him through his life, teachings, death, resurrection, and glorification.

---

[1] On the sacraments, see the excellent study of Dumitru Staniloae, *The Sanctifying Mysteries* (Brookline, MA 2012). On the connectedness of the sacraments to the Eucharist see Nenad Milosevic, *To Christ and the Church: the Divine Eucharist as the All-encompassing Mystery of the Church* (Los Angeles, 2012). See also Panagiotis Trembelas, Δογματική τῆς Ὀρθοδόξου Καθολικῆς Ἐκκλησίας, volume 3, 1-363 (Athens 1961).

The sacred and sanctifying sacraments confer their transformative power upon every believer through the operation of the Holy Spirit who makes Christ present to the Church. Christ celebrates the sacraments invisibly, performing them through visible organs and acts, that is, through hierarchs and priests, who are set apart by ordination to exercise his saving activity upon his people who are united to him and seek to grow and mature spiritually in him.[2] He also acts through material elements and through the prayers, gestures, and declarations that make up the sacred rites of the Church.

The holy sacraments are both inward and outward in character. They transmit redeeming and sanctifying grace by visible means. Material elements – water, oil, bread, and wine – are made into vehicles of the Spirit. Water, by way of example, is the dominant matter in baptism. Its natural properties as a source of cleanness, destruction, and life, bear the essential meanings of baptism: purification, death, and rebirth (Rom. 6:3-14; John 3:3-8).

Every sacrament embodies a particular gift and grants the recipient the possibility to realize the gift in its fullness. The sacraments, however, are neither magical nor mechanical operations. The grace given through the material elements is real, a divine gift by which each person is perfected in faith. But, the full effectiveness of the sacramental life is made manifest, to a greater or lesser degree, by the spiritual awareness, the depth of faith, and the genuine piety and commitment of each participant.[3] The realities which the holy sacraments confer remain active and are perfected only when they are interiorized and when the recipient becomes firmly set in what is good in the unity of the Church. Just as each sacrament has its outward signs, each Christian life has the capacity to become itself a sacrament, a revelation of divine love, truth, holiness, and beauty.

---

2   See Staniloae, *Sanctifying Mysteries*, 19.

3   On this point, St. Cyril of Jerusalem (*Procatechesis* 2) told the catechumens of his day, "Honesty of purpose makes you called: for though the body be here, yet if the mind be away, it avails nothing. Even Simon Magus once came to the laver of baptism. He was baptized, but not enlightened. His body he dipped in water, but admitted not the Spirit to illuminate his heart. His body went down and came up; but his soul was not buried together with Christ, nor with him raised. I mention such instances of falls, so that you may not fail."

The sacraments are founded on the words and actions of our Lord Jesus Christ and are, in a special way, a continuation and an extension of his saving ministry. The Orthodox Church recognizes seven sacraments or special acts that embody and communicate the new life in Christ to believers and are celebrated by the whole Church, clergy and laity together. These are: baptism, chrismation, the Eucharist, penance, ordination, marriage, and the anointing of the sick.[4] Of these seven sacraments, baptism, chrismation, and the Eucharist – the sacraments of initiation – hold a preeminent place.

In the mind of the Church the Eucharist was never counted simply as one sacrament among many, but as the very source and summit of the Church's life. All the sacraments were once inseparably bound to and determined by the Eucharist. This connectedness remains fully operative to this day in the instance of ordination. Hierarchs, priests, and deacons continue to be ordained during and within the Divine Liturgy. Traces of this connectedness can be found in the other sacraments as well. One result of this rupture, the separation of the Eucharist from the other sacraments, has been the blurring of the ecclesial and communal character of the sacraments.

Every sacrament is intensely personal, a unique and decisive event in the life of the one who receives it, but it is also intensely communal[5] The sacraments, by which the new life in Christ comes into existence and is sustained and advanced, belong to and are celebrated by the whole Church, by the clergy and people together. The power of the sacraments emanates from and within the community of faith, the Church. Salvation is not an individual affair but an ecclesial event. It comes through the Church, which is "the field of action of the Spirit of Christ."[6]

---

4   The numbering of the sacraments at seven appeared for the first time in the East at the dawn of the thirteenth century. The list became fixed and definite only in the seventeenth century. See Timothy Ware [Metropolitan Kallistos], *The Orthodox Church - New Edition* (London & New York 1997), 274-276. Also see Calivas, "The Lima Text as a Pointer to the Future: An Orthodox Perspective," in *Studia Liturgica*, Vol. 16, nos. 1-2 (1986), 80-91.

5   Many have come to equate personal with individual; and so sacramental celebrations and experiences have been individualized and privatized. However, every sacrament is an ecclesial event; it effects and concerns the entire ecclesial community, inasmuch as we are all members of the one Body, the Church (1 Cor. 12:20-27; cf. Ephes. 4:25).

6   The phrase is borrowed from the writings of Fr. Dumitru Staniloae.

1. The Sacrament of Holy Baptism

The Wondrous Gifts of Baptism

Baptism is the first and essential sacrament, the absolute decisive action for a Christian.[7] It is the frontier between two worlds, between two entirely different modes of being. It manifests the most radical change in the human condition and in human relationships. It accomplishes sacramentally both a death and a new birth. Hence, the baptismal font is both a tomb and a womb, in which the "old man" is buried and the "new man" is born. In the words of St. Paul, "We [are] buried with him through baptism into death, that just as Christ was raised from the dead by the glory of the Father, even so we also should walk in the newness of life (Rom. 6:4).

In baptism we partake in the death, burial, and resurrection of Christ and are incorporated into him, to share in his deified humanity, to come under his rule, and to be like him.[8] The clearer the image of Christ is in us, the more perfect we become, because perfection is nothing more than the realization of the purpose for which we have been made. And we have been made to be in Christ and to become like him by grace. Baptism, in the words of Fr. Dumitru Staniloae, puts the one who is baptized into an intimate relationship not with Christ alone, but with the Father and the Holy Spirit, the entire Holy Trinity.[9]

Through baptism we become a new creation (2 Cor. 5:17). We experience in faith a new birth from above brought about by water and the Holy Spirit: "Unless one is born of water and the Spirit, he cannot enter into the kingdom of God. That which is born of the flesh is flesh, and that which is born of the Spirit is spirit" (John 3:3-6). The eternal God takes us unto himself as a father

---

7 On the rites and the theology of baptism see Alexander Schmemann, *Of Water and the Spirit* (Yonkers, NY, 1974) and (Metropolitan) Maximos Aghiorgoussis, "Some Preliminary Notations of Baptismal Ecclesiology: Baptism and Eucharist, Constitutive of the Church as Communion," in his *The Image of God* (Brookline, MA 1999), 75-111. See also E. J. Yarnold, *The Awe-Inspiring Rites of Initiation: Baptismal Homilies of the Fourth Century* (Collegeville, MN 1772 and 1994); Robin Jensen, *Baptismal Imagery in Early Christianity: Ritual, Visual, and Theological Dimensions* (Grand Rapids. MI 2012); and the respective entries by K. W. Noakes, E. J. Yarnold, and W. J. Grisbrooke in *The Study of Liturgy* (London/New York 1992), Chapter II – Initiation, 112-144 and 152-154. See also the collection of articles in Σειρά Λογική Λατρεία (Volume 13): Τό Ἅγιο Βάπτισμα - Ἡ ἔνταξή μας στήν Ἐκκλησία τοῦ Χριστοῦ (Athens 2002); and Σειρά Ποιμαντική Βιβλιοθήκη (Volume 6): Τὸ Ἅγιον Βάπτισμα (Athens 2003).

8 In his *Baptismal Instructions* (2:11), St. John Chrysostom says, "Baptism is a burial and a resurrection. For the old man is buried with his sin and the new man is resurrected, being renewed according to the image of his Creator. We put off the old garment, which has been made filthy with the abundance of our sins; we put on the new one, which is free from every stain. What am I saying? We put on Christ himself."

9 Staniloae, *Sanctifying Mysteries*, 50.

his children and admits us into an area of non-death. The Triune God draws us into his beauty, glory, and unending life to free us from the old manner of life corrupted by evil and deception, to give us his kingdom which is to come and to render us unshakable in our fidelity to the commandments and to the values of the Gospel.

Saint Peter describes the passage from what is old to what is new which baptism accomplishes with these moving words: "You are a chosen race, a royal priesthood, a holy nation, God's own people, that you may declare the wonderful deeds of him who called you out of darkness into his marvelous light. Once you were not a people but now you are God's people; once you had not received mercy but now you have received mercy" (1 Peter 2:9-10).

Baptism incorporates us into Christ, but also into his mystical Body, the Church, where the powers of the age to come are at work. The Church is the environment in which we apprehend salvation and share in the saving acts of Christ that we may persevere in the exercise of righteous actions: thinking and doing all those things that are pleasing to God. The Church provides us with all things necessary to strengthen our will for holiness as God's people.

In his address to the newly-baptized – the neophytes – St. John Chrysostom reminds them of God's benevolence and of the many graces of baptism. He said, "Blessed be God, who alone does wonderful things [Ps. 71/72:18], who does all things and transforms them. Before yesterday you were captives, but now you are free and citizens of the Church; lately you lived in the shame of yours sins, but now you live in freedom and justice. You are not only free, but also holy; not only holy, but also just; not only just, but also sons; not only sons, but also heirs; not only heirs, but also brothers of Christ; not only brothers of Christ, but also joint heirs; not only joint heirs, but also members; not only members, but also the temple; not only the temple, but also instruments of the Spirit...You have seen how numerous are the gifts of baptism. Although many men think that the only gift it confers is the remission of sins, we have counted its honors to the number of ten."[10]

---

10 St. John Chrysostom, *Baptismal Instructions*, 3:5, in the series, *Ancient Christian Writers*, Vol. 31 (New York/Ramsey, NJ, 1963), 57. P.W. Harkins, the translator of the text, makes the following observation. "Chrysostom never swerves from the New Testament, and all the fruits he enumerates except the last are mentioned either in the Gospels or the Pauline Epistles.... Only the term "instruments of the Spirit" is not found as such in the Scriptures, but it flows directly from the notion of temple, since it is the grace of the Spirit which makes us temples of Christ." p. 232, note 9. In another passage, Chrysostom notes that the "mystic cleansing...does not have one name but is spoken of in many and varied ways. It is called a bath of regeneration (Titus 3:5), an enlightenment (Heb. 6:4-6; 10:32), a baptism (Gal. 3:27), a burial (Rom. 6:4), a circumcision (Col. 2:11), a cross (Rom 6:6)." *Baptismal Instruction* 9:12. We can add the name resurrection to the list (Col. 2:12).

2. Children and the Church: The Pre-baptismal Rites for Infants

The First-, Eighth-, and Fortieth-day Rites

The Church has a special love for infants and children, because the Lord said of them: "Let the little children come to me, and do not forbid them; for such is the kingdom of heaven" (Matt. 19:14). In fact, the Orthodox Church has three special services for infants that are closely linked to baptism.[11] The Church offers prayers for newborn infants on the *first, eighth, and fortieth day after birth.*

On the *first day*, the Church gives thanks to God for the safe delivery of the mother and celebrates joyously the birth of a new human being. Praying for the well-being of the mother and the newborn infant, the Church also lays claim to the child in the name of Christ. Children born to Christian parents are considered *catechumens* or peripheral members of the Church until they are fully incorporated into her life through baptism.

On the *eighth day* the Church emphasizes the worth of the human being by confirming on the newborn infant a personal identity through the bestowal of a name chosen by the parents; the name with which the child will be known and baptized and with which he or she will receive the sacraments and all other

---

11 For an analysis of the pre-baptismal rites for infants see Schmemann, *Of Water and the Spirit*, 131-47 and Calivas, *Aspects of Orthodox Worship*, 138-55. See also Peter A. Chamberas, *Baptism and Chrismation: Beginning our Christian Life in the Orthodox Church* (Manchester, NH 1993). Although the three rites for infants have significant spiritual and pastoral value, they are seldom used today, except for the *rite of the fortieth day*, which still has currency among a large segment of the faithful. For a variety of reasons, the first-day and eighth-day rites have fallen into disuse in most places. However, nothing prevents parish clergy from reviving them through sound instruction and by making them available to those who ask for them. In fact, for practical reasons, the two services (first day and eighth day) may be combined into one and performed by the priest in the home at the invitation of the parents on the eighth day after birth. There, in the presence of the parents and other family members he reads the prayers of the two rites, appropriately adapted. However, it is important to note that more is required of the Church than simply promoting the use of these services. To be fully responsive to today's needs, the Church must also take a good look at the content of these rites and reformulate the prayers in order to erase misconceptions regarding human sexuality and the natural functions of the human body and other ambiguities, including strange sounding and accusatory language. Take, for example, the words in the last prayer of the first day rite. "Lord our God, you graciously consented to descend from heaven and to be born of the Holy Theotokos and Ever-Virgin Mary for the salvation of us sinners. *Knowing the frailty of human nature, according to the multitude of your mercies forgive your servant (N) who today has given birth.... Look down from heaven and have regard for our weakness, as we are under judgment, and forgive your servant (N) and the entire household in which the child was born...*" The language of the prayer is perplexing, to say the least, and joyless. One could see the influence of Levitical laws on cleanness and uncleanness (Lev. 12 and 15) in play here, even as Christ has freed us from the ceremonial law and its material observance.

blessings of the Church at every stage and circumstance of life. By tradition, the child is given a saint's (Christian) name as a sign of his/her identity with the faith community.[12]

Through the rite of naming the Church acknowledges, emphasizes, and affirms the uniqueness of the newborn infant. The infant is not just the bearer of human nature but is a person who is unique, unrepeatable, and beloved by God whose image the child bears. For this reason, parents should give careful thought when selecting the name.

The prayer for the conferral of the name also reveals another truth. The infant will also be sealed with the name of Christ so that he or she may be identified with him and become both in name and in essence a Christian, a faithful disciple of Christ. "Lord our God, we pray and entreat you let the light of your countenance shine upon this your servant (N), and let the Cross of your Only-begotten Son be sealed in his (her) heart and thoughts…. And grant, Lord, that your holy Name will remain indelible in him (her) so that in due time may be joined to your holy Church and be perfected through the awesome mysteries of your Christ…." (Prayer of the Eighth-Day Rite). In other words, together with a personal name, the infant is sealed with, bears, and is called by the grandest of all names, Christian.[13]

The rite for the naming a child on the eighth day is based in part on Mosaic Law (Lev. 12:1-5) and in particular on the accounts in the Gospel of Luke concerning the infant John who would later become the Forerunner and Baptist (Luke 1:59) and the infant Jesus (Luke 2:21). Significantly, however, the Levitical requirement of circumcision, central to the Mosaic Law, is omitted from the rite. From the time of the Apostles (Acts 15) the Church abrogated the requirement of circumcision as a mark of identity and inclusion. Baptism replaced circumcision. Baptism confers upon us a new identity and introduces us into a new community. Every baptized person is clothed with Christ (Gal. 3:27) and is incorporated into his mystical body, the Church.

---

12 Christian discipleship is more than a name. For this and other pastoral and theological issues related to baptism, see Calivas, "The Lima Statement on Baptism," in *St. Vladimir's Theological Quarterly*, 27:4 (1983), 257- 63.

13 The name Christian was first given to the disciples of Christ in Antioch: "And in Antioch the disciples were for the first time called Christians" (Acts 11:26). Saint John Chrysostom, speaking to the catechumens preparing for baptism, tells them they are about to acquire a great dignity, "Henceforth, through the kindness of God, you will be called a Christian and one of the faithful…. Soon you will put on Christ. You must act and deliberate in all things with the knowledge that he is everywhere with you." (*Baptismal Instructions* 1:44).

Rite of the Fortieth Day After Birth

The service of the fortieth day after birth is an important communal event. The mother and the child are welcomed into the faith community after the period of the mother's confinement.[14] The Church rejoices with the parents and offers prayers of thanksgiving for the creation of a new life.

The earliest extant *Euchologion* of the Byzantine rite, the eighth-century *Barberini Codex*, has only two pre-baptismal prayers for newborn infants. The first is a prayer for the naming of a child on the eighth day and the second is entitled, "A Prayer at the Time When a Child Enters the Church on the Fortieth Day of its Birth." This latter prayer likens the churching of the infant to the presentation of Christ to the Temple on the fortieth day after his birth by Mary, his holy Mother, in fulfillment of the Mosaic Law (Luke 2:22-38; cf. Lev. 12:6-8); and supplicates God for the child's safe-keeping until the day of his/her baptism. Clearly, the service of the fortieth day was established in imitation of the New Testament event described in the Gospel of Luke.

The *Barberini Codex* presents us with two important facts. The first is that in the eighth century the Church had not yet established a first-day rite or a rite for the purification of the mother. These prayers were introduced centuries later when severe ascetical attitudes were in vogue and the Levitical regulations were revived.[15] The prayers for the purification of the mother were added to the fortieth-day rite in the eleventh-twelfth centuries. Over time, the title of the fortieth-day rite was changed from the churching of a child to Prayers

---

14   In the Old Testament (Lev. 12) a woman at child birth was considered unclean because of her bodily discharge and was confined for forty days, the period of her purification. Through the years various cultural taboos have been connected to the period of confinement, many of which have little to do with the Orthodox faith. The period of confinement should focus on the safe delivery of the mother and the joy of childbirth, and not be burdened with archaic concepts of physical impurity. "If anyone is in Christ, he is a new creation; old things have passed away; behold, all things have become new." (2 Cor. 5:17). The time of confinement should move beyond the limiting social attitudes of the past which focused on exclusion from domestic duties and social activities. It should be seen as a period of family bonding, a time to experience anew the joys of marriage and childbearing, a time to reflect on the gift of parenthood. It should also be a time for the mother to rest and recuperate from the stresses of pregnancy and the pains and anxieties of labor; and for the husband to assume the responsibilities and learn the joys of fatherhood. More importantly, the time of confinement, if in fact it is observed fully in our time due to the hectic pace of modern life, should not be construed as a kind of excommunication – an exclusion of the mother from the church and Holy Communion – even if temporarily. For these reasons, I believe, the prayers of the pre-baptismal rites should be reviewed so that their language may reflect more accurately modern sensibilities about bodily functions and express better the Orthodox understanding of human sexuality, conception, birth, and the blessings of family.

15   According to the manuscript evidence, the Rite of the First Day was introduced only in the fourteenth century.

for a Woman in Child-bed after Forty Days (Εὐχαὶ εἰς γυναῖκα λεχὼ μετὰ τεσσαράκοντα ἡμέρας). Informally, Greek people refer to the fortieth day service as "σαραντισμός," derived from the Greek word "σαράντα" which means forty. The term is also used to indicate the time when the woman's menstrual flow and confinement are completed and her "churching" is at hand.

The original form of the eighth-day and fortieth-day rites was very simple, consisting of a single prayer. The eighth-day rite retained its original simplicity. The first and fortieth-day rites, however, were gradually transformed into services through the addition of hymns, ceremonial actions, and additional prayers, most of which reflect the purity codes of the Old Testament. As a result, the joyous character of both rites was eclipsed by the themes of physical impurity and forgiveness.

The received rite of the fortieth day was built around the third prayer in the present rite, which is a variation of the prayer for the "churching of an infant" found in the *Barberini Codex*. The second prayer was added in the twelfth century and shortly thereafter the first prayer of the present rite was introduced into the service. Both the first part of the first prayer and the second prayer ask for the purification of the mother from physical and spiritual impurities. The second part of the first prayer asks for blessings upon the newborn infant. Finally, a fourth prayer was added, which is a prayer of blessing and thanksgiving. The service opens with the Trisagion Prayers, the apolytikion of the day and a hymn to the Theotokos. After the aforementioned prayers, the priest receives the infant in his arms and enters the nave to present the child to the Lord, reciting the Prayer of St. Symeon (Luke 2:29-32), followed by the apolysis.

Significantly, through the pre-baptismal rites the child is considered a catechumen, a candidate for baptism, as we read in one of the prayers: "Do you, O Lord, who preserve children, bless this infant together with his/her parents and sponsor and grant that, in due season, he (she) may be united, through water and the Spirit of the new birth, unto the holy flock...which is called by the name of your Christ."

3. Celebrating the Service of the Fortieth Day

For a number of reasons, it is often difficult in our day for parents to bring their newborn infant to the church for the service on exactly the fortieth day after birth. The priest should be sensitive and accommodating. The service can be performed on any day and time of the week – on the fortieth day after birth or the closest to it. In smaller parishes, the service is often conducted on Sundays or feast days after the Divine Liturgy with the entire congregation in attendance. This is particularly difficult – not to say impractical – in larger parishes because of time constraints. When the family calls the priest to make arrangements for the service, he should suggest, if possible, that all members of the family be present (husband, siblings, godparents, etc.).

The priest meets the parents in the narthex of the church, where the service will take place. The priest wears his exorasson and epitrachilion.[16] He stands before the open royal doors leading into the nave and faces "west" (toward the entrance of the church). He calls the mother to come forward holding the child in her arms. The husband stands by her side and any other family members, if present, on either side.

The priest welcomes the family and invites all who are present to join him in prayer. He asks for the name of the mother and the child. Then, facing the sanctuary he says:

Priest

Blessed is our God – Εὐλογητὸς ὁ Θεὸς....

Recites the Trisagion Prayers together with those present

[Recites or sings the apolytikion of the day and of the Theotokos]

Priest

Turning to and facing the mother, he asks her to bow her head and says, "Let us pray to the Lord." Placing his hand gently upon the mother's head, he reads the first prayer of the service. The first prayer has two parts.[17] The first part is a prayer for the mother, and the second for the infant. When he comes to the words, "*And bless the child born of her...*" he turns his attention to the infant. As he says these words, he blesses the infant with his hand in the usual manner making the sign of the cross over the child.

---

16 If the service is being conducted immediately after the Divine Liturgy, the priest retains all his vestments.

17 There are two important concerns regarding this prayer. First, it presupposes that the mother is an Orthodox Christian. If she is not, the prayer cannot be read, at least not in its original form because it makes reference to the partaking of the Holy Mysteries, referring essentially to the reception of Holy Communion. Yet, for pastoral reasons, we cannot and should not ignore the mother who in faith has brought her child to receive the blessings of the Church. The prayer could be adjusted easily for such occasions by omitting the reference to the Holy Mysteries and by changing the phrase, "cleanse your servant (N) from every sin," to "...bless your servant (N) whom by your will have preserved..." Second, if the newborn child has died before the fortieth day, only the first part of the prayer is read and concludes with the assigned *ekfonesis*.

Priest

Gives the blessing of peace and calls for the bowing of the head. He reads the second prayer.[18] Then he proceeds to the other prayers.

Priest

Reads the third and fourth prayer with the appropriate introductions as noted in the text of the service.

Priest

Conducts the rite of entrance.[19] After the fourth prayer, the priest takes the infant from the mother with great care and holds him/her in his arms. He faces the sanctuary and at the entrance to the nave he raises the child to some extent gently, making the sign of the cross with him/her, saying, *"Ἐκκλησιάζεται ὁ δοῦλος (ἡ δούλη) τοῦ Θεοῦ ... The servant of God (N) is churched in the Name of the Father and of the Son an ..."* Then proceeding into the nave, he says, *"Εἰσελεύσομαι εἰς τὸν οἶκόν σου ... I shall enter into your house, I shall worship toward your temple."* And he adds, *"The servant of God (N) is churched...."*

Priest

Having reached the middle of the nave, he pauses and says: *"Ἐν μέσῳ Ἐκκλησίας ὑμνήσω σε ... In the midst of the congregation I will praise you."* And he adds, *"The servant of God (N) is churched ..."*

Priest

He proceeds forward and reciting the Prayer of St. Symeon, *"Νῦν ἀπολύεις τὸν δοῦλόν σου, Δέσποτα ... Lord, now let your servant depart in peace..."* he enters the sanctuary through the south door and processes behind the Holy Table and exiting the sanctuary from the north door, he stands by the Holy Doors and says the apolysis.

---

18 The subject of the second prayer is the mother. If, however, the mother is not an Orthodox Christian, the second prayer is omitted because its contents do not fit the circumstance. In addition, if the infant has died, or for some reason has already been baptized, the priest concludes the service after the second prayer.

19 Before starting the entrance, the priest instructs the parents to follow him into the church, to reverence the icon of Christ on the iconostasis, and to wait in front of the Holy Doors to receive the child.

Priest

After the *apolysis*, he presents the child to the mother and offers her and the father his blessings and good wishes.[20]

Admittance to the Sanctuary

According to current liturgical practice, male infants only are brought into the sanctuary while female infants are brought before the Holy Doors. This practice is, in fact, a late development, which is recorded in the more recent codices and printed Euchologia.[21] Saint Symeon of Thessaloniki (+1429), for example, tells us that in his time, due to the dangers of infant mortality, most children were baptized by the fortieth day after birth. Hence, at the time of churching all baptized infants were admitted to the sanctuary, regardless of gender. Only the unbaptized were brought before the Holy Doors. Thus, baptism, not gender, determined entrance into the sanctuary. Today, infants are baptized well after the fortieth day. The current practice which distinguishes between male and female children and excludes female babies from the sanctuary is untenable and untraditional, as earlier codices did not make such a distinction. As St. Paul says, there is neither male nor female, for all are one in Christ (Gal. 3:28). Hence, gender should not be an obstacle because men and women are recipients of the same grace. Therefore, all infants, regardless of gender, should be admitted to the sanctuary. St. Symeon of Thessaloniki makes note of the fact that the fortieth day churching of infants constitutes an offering; and he adds, what better space could be more appropriate for the dedication of the infant to God than the sanctuary?[22]

Dealing with Stillbirth, Death, and Miscarriage

In the event the child does not survive birth or dies before the fortieth day, the Fortieth-day Rite, as noted above, is read in part for the mother. In such

---

20   According to the rubrics in the *Great Euchologion*, after the *apolysis* the priest lays the infant before the Holy Doors or before the icon of Christ. The mother (or the godparent) reverences thrice and takes up the child. This practice has long since been abandoned. Instead, the priest simply hands the child to the mother wishing her, the father. and their child every blessing that comes from above.

21   See Trempelas, Μικρὸν Εὐχολόγιον, 270-3.

22   Some codices include elaborate rubrics which instruct the priest with the infant in hand to enter the sanctuary via the south door. Circling the Holy Table, he bows, inclining the infant on each of the four sides of the Table as a sign of veneration. See Trempelas, *ibid*. The Slavonic *Great Book of Needs – The Holy Sacraments* also mentions this practice in a note, attributing the gesture to St. Symeon of Thessaloniki.

cases, it is incumbent upon the priest to show great sensitivity. He consoles and comforts the mother (and father) appropriately, allowing the mother to express her grief and sorrow over the loss of her baby.

The received prayer for miscarriage is deficient and vexing.[23] A miscarriage, like stillbirth, produces physical pain, emotional stress, mental anguish, and spiritual suffering. The current prayer for miscarriage needs revision. A prayer for stillbirth does not exist. We also have no prayer for infertility, a sensitive prayer that would give hope and solace to a woman or a married couple who desire parenthood. The Eparchial Synod may wish to commission a small group of qualified persons to formulate such prayers.

In the case of a willful abortion or of a self-induced miscarriage, the priest should introduce the parents to the Sacrament of Penance. After proper spiritual guidance and an act of contrition, the priest reads the Prayer of Absolution, or uses the Prayer after an Abortion found in the Euchologion at the end of the fortieth day service, which also needs to be revisited.

4. Infants and Baptism

No one is born a Christian. Christians are made through a series of acts that culminate in the rites of initiation: baptism, chrismation, and the Eucharist. The Church baptizes infants and children, not because they are born sinful or bear guilt, but that they may share with us the joys and gifts of the new life in Christ. St. John Chrysostom says it best: "We baptize even infants, although they are sinless, that they may be given the further gifts of sanctification, righteousness, filial adoption, and inheritance; that they may be brothers and members of Christ and become dwelling places of the Holy Spirit."[24]

Baptism is always preceded by a period of instruction that focuses on gaining an understanding of the Church's dogmas, ethics, liturgy, and discipline. However, in the case of infants, the period of instruction comes after baptism, carried out both in the home and in the church. Christian parents are responsible to "bring up [their children] in the training and the admonition of the Lord" (Ephes. 6:4); and the parish is obliged to provide not only competent instructors for the young, but also a nurturing environment where the truths of the faith are lived and acted upon in concrete ways so that the young may learn that "faith apart from works is barren" (James 2:20).

---

23 See Calivas, *Aspects of Orthodox Worship*, 152-4.

24 St. John Chrysostom, *Baptismal Instructions*, 3:6.

The baptism of infants is performed on the explicit profession of faith by the parents, the sponsor (godparent), and the faith community itself, all of who must be fully devoted to the Church's faith and committed to providing an environment of continued Christian witness for the child, both in the home and in the local parish.

These several points are summed up nicely in the writings attached to the name of Dionysios the Areopagite, which appeared in the fifth or sixth century. Concerning infant baptism and its rituals, he says the following.

> Despite their inability to understand the divine things, infants are nevertheless admitted to that sacrament of sacred divine-birth and to the sacred symbols of the divine communion. In effect, the hierarch may be seen to teach divine things to those not yet capable of understanding them, to pass on the sacred tradition to those unable to grasp it…. [Yet] our knowledge is far from being commensurate with the divine mysteries, many of which remain beyond our grasp and with a meaning outside our power to understand…. Many elude even the highest beings…. But let me set down what our blessed teachers have passed down to us…. Children raised up in accordance with holy precepts will acquire the habits of holiness. They will avoid all the errors and all the temptations of an unholy life. Understanding the truth of this, our divine leaders decided it was a good thing to admit children, though on the condition that the parents of the child would entrust him to some good teacher who is himself initiated in the divine things and would provide religious teaching as the child's spiritual father and as the sponsor of salvation. *Anyone thus committed to raise the child up along the way of a holy life is asked to agree to the ritual renunciations and to speak the words of promise…. In effect what is said is this: I promise that when the child can understand sacred truth, I shall educate him and shall raise him up by my teaching in such a way that he will renounce all the temptations of the devil, that he will bind himself to the sacred promises and will bring them to fruit….* When the hierarch admits the child to a share in the sacred symbols it is so that he may derive nourishment from this, so that he…may acquire a holy an enduring life.[25]

---

25 Pseudo-Dionysios, *Ecclesiastical Hierarchy*, Chapter Seven: III, 11. The italics have been added for emphasis.

5. The Rite or Service of Holy Baptism

An Introduction

The Baptismal Rite of the Orthodox Church, in its essential form, has been in continuous use for the greater part of two millennia.[26] It contains the fundamental liturgical elements employed by the early Church for the making of a Christian, a process which began with the candidate's enrollment in the catechumenate.[27]

The essential purpose of the ancient catechumenate was to reform and re-socialize the candidates for baptism through instruction and rites of exorcism. The enrollment included an inquiry into the candidate's personal life, status, and occupation, as well as the seriousness of their intentions. A candidate was always accompanied by a sponsor, a respected member of the community, who testified on the candidate's behalf.[28] The instruction included regular lessons based on the Scriptures, the Creed, and ethical living. Normally, the sessions ended with a prayer of exorcism,[29] the aim of which was to help free the

---

26 On the historical development of the rite of baptism and its rubrical elements see Ioannis Fountoulis, "Τὸ Ἅγιον Βάπτισμα - Ἱστορικό-Τελετουργικὴ Θεώρηση," in his Τελετουργικὰ Θέματα, Vol. 1 (Athens 2002), 177-208.

27 See M. Dujarier, *A History of the Catechumenate: the First Six Centuries* (New York, 1979).

28 In infant baptism the sponsor's role as witness no longer applies, but the role as guarantor remains. Hence, in Greek the sponsor is called ἀνάδοχος, that is, a person who undertakes a specific role. In this case the sponsor assumes the role of guarantor and spiritual guide. Concerning the awesome responsibility of sponsors, St. John Chrysostom made the following observation: "If, then, those who go surety for others in the matter of money make themselves liable for the whole sum, those who go surety for others in matters of the spirit and on an account, which involves virtue should be much more alert. They ought to show their paternal love by encouraging, counseling, and correcting those for whom they go surety." *Baptismal Instructions*, 2:15.

29 The exorcisms were usually conducted by persons assigned the task, the exorcists, who comprised one of the minor orders. See canon 24 of the local Synod of Laodicea (ca 343). By the *Penthekte* Synod (692), this order and that of doorkeeper had already fallen into disuse.

candidates from the physical, psychological, and spiritual forces that stood as obstacles to their full conversion, especially the habits and addictions of the pagan culture that held sway over them (Cf. Ephes. 6:10-17).[30]

The prayers, hymns, readings, and symbols of the received rite retain elements of these features and express the theology of baptism contained in the New Testament and the writings of the Church Fathers. The rite consists of three major parts, each with its own distinctive features and characteristics. The present single rite is, in fact, a combination of several separate, but interdependent rites that were conducted over a period of several days, weeks, and months.[31]

Part 1: The first part of the received rite is preparatory in nature. It is usually referred to as the *catechesis* - *κατήχησις*. In Christian antiquity the rites that comprise this part of the service were celebrated during the period of instruction which was called *catechesis* (meaning oral instruction). The first part of the service contains the following six elements: a prayer for the making of a catechumen (one receiving instruction); a set of exorcism prayers offered in the name of Christ against the pernicious assaults and the divisive powers of the devil, who deceives and lures the unwary into a graceless life; renunciations of the devil and his works; expressions of allegiance to Christ as King and God; a profession of faith through the recitation of the Nicene-Constantinopolitan Creed; and a prayer or call to baptism.

The parents, with the sponsor(s), play a key role in the performance of these rites, inasmuch as both assume the responsibility before God and the ecclesial community to help bring and guide the incipient faith of the child to maturity.

---

30 The practice of expelling evil spirits through prayer was common among Jews and pagans. It was adopted also by Christians based chiefly on the example of Christ, the pre-eminent Exorcist, ("And he healed many who were sick with various diseases, and he cast out many demons..." (Mark 1:34); and on Christ's instructions to his disciples: "And he called to him his twelve disciples and gave them authority over unclean spirits, to cast them out, and to heal every disease and infirmity" (Matt. 10:1). In addition to the exorcisms in the baptismal liturgy, the Euchologion also contains many additional prayers for the expulsion of evil powers from the possessed and from those under the curse of an evil-eye (βασκανία) – for those under the influence of malevolent and evil individuals with obsessive jealousy and psychotic feelings of envy. Exorcisms, however, should be used sparingly and cautiously for persons with mental health issues so as not to contribute to their neurosis. While we do not doubt the efficacy and value of these prayers, we should focus less on the demonic and more on Christ's boundless love and healing power, which engender hope. For more on the subject see *Exorcism through the Ages*, St. Elmo Nauman, editor (New York, 1974). The volume contains an informative essay by Fr. George Papademetriou, "Exorcism and the Greek Orthodox Church," 43-72.

31 On the meanings of the sacred actions, elements, and symbols of the baptismal rites see the catechetical or baptismal instructions of St. Cyril of Jerusalem, *Lectures on the Christian Sacraments*; St. John Chrysostom, *Baptismal Instructions*; and St. Nicholas Cabasilas, *The Life in Christ*.

Hence, it is important to have the parents accompany the sponsor(s) and be present with him/her when these rites are being performed.

Part 2: The second part is the Service of Baptism proper. It is focused almost entirely on the baptismal font. It includes a series of petitions; a prayer of invocation for the consecration of the baptismal waters, that they may be given the power of spiritual fertility; the blessing of the "Oil of Gladness" and the anointing with it of both the water and the child. This first anointing of the child (or the adult catechumen) is a sign of the restoration of the fallen, corrupt nature which we all bear at birth. It is also symbolic of becoming an athlete for Christ.[32] The anointing of the font/water is a sign of the presence of the Holy Spirit over the face of the baptismal waters (cf. Gen. 1:2).

When these rites have been accomplished, the candidate is baptized with three immersions and emersions using the liturgical formula: "*The servant of God (N) is baptized in the name of the Father. Amen. And of the Son. Amen. And of the Holy Spirit. Amen.*" This formula is based on the Lord's commandment recorded in the Gospel of Matthew (28:19). The threefold immersion and emersion is the adequate symbol of participation in Christ's three-day burial and resurrection.

The newly illumined Christian is then robed in a white garment, the symbol of innocence, regeneration or rebirth, of newness, kingship, and future immortality. White is the color of royalty, hence St. John Chrysostom calls it a royal robe and likens it also to a marriage robe: "I am continually exhorting you to keep the marriage robe in its integrity, that with it you may enter forever into this spiritual marriage. And what takes place here is a spiritual marriage.... For in this way you will draw the Bridegroom to a fuller love and you yourselves will shine forth with increasing radiance and luster as time goes on, because grace increases more and more with the good deeds we do."[33] The white baptismal garment is a symbol of the many gifts that baptism bestows upon persons of faith. It is intended to remind all Christians of their responsibility to remain whole and blameless, and faithful to their baptismal pledge.

At this point in the service, the second sacrament, Chrismation, is administered by the priest, who anoints the neophyte with the Holy Chrism or *Myron* – the consecrated oils. The priest uses the liturgical formula, "*The seal of the gift of*

---

32 In ancient times athletes, especially wrestlers, rubbed their bodies with oil to strengthen them and to make them slick so that they could not be easily grasped by their opponent. Likewise, every athlete for Christ sees to it that he or she does not become an easy prey of demonic powers. In other words, the anointing of the whole body is seen as a preparation for the life-long struggle against the temptations of the demonic forces that attempt to ensnare and destroy. Today, in the case of adult baptism, for reasons of modesty, the anointing with the Oil of Gladness should be limited to the actions performed by the priest when he applies the blessed oil in the prescribed order.

33 Chrysostom, *Baptismal Instructions*, 4:3 and 6:23-25. Cf. Rev. 3:4-5, 18.

the Holy Spirit. Amen." The chrism is the very emblem of the real presence of the Holy Spirit. When anointing, the priest applies the chrism to the senses and to other parts of the body signifying the indwelling presence of the Holy Spirit by whose grace the new Christian grows continuously into the image and likeness of God. The Holy Spirit is the fount of all wisdom, of every good gift, and of untold divine riches. Baptism and chrismation cause a mysterious new and hidden life to flow in us. The more we become aware of the Spirit's presence in us, the more we shine with godliness; the more we become Christ-like.

In the ancient Church, baptism was immediately followed by the celebration of the Divine Liturgy, the sacred rite by which the Orthodox Church celebrates *the sacrament of the Eucharist*, the central mystery of the Church, the source and summit of her life. The newly illumined Christians, holding lighted candles,[34] process from the baptistery to the nave to join the community already gathered for the Eucharist. Vestiges of these ancient practices form the next sequence of actions in the baptismal rite. The neophyte is given *a cross* to wear, in order to remind him/her to also hold its saving mystery in the heart. A procession around the font follows as all sing the ancient baptismal hymn: "*As many as have been baptized into Christ, have put on Christ. Alleluia*" (Gal. 3:27). This is followed by two *readings*, one from the Epistle of St. Paul to the Romans (6:3-11) and the other from the Gospel of St. Matthew (28:16-11). The former explains the meaning of baptism, while the latter recalls the Lord's command to the Church to go into the world to make disciples of all nations, baptizing them, and teaching them the commandments of God. After this, the neophyte receives *Holy Communion*, the Body and Blood of our Savior, "the medicine of immortality and the antidote against death, enabling us to live forever in Jesus Christ."[35] Jesus Christ gives us His life – His flesh and blood (John 6:31-58) – as food so that "we may be partakers of the divine nature" (2 Peter 1:4).

Part 3: When a set of petitions has been intoned, the neophyte participates in *three additional rites* that in antiquity were conducted eight days after baptism. First, *the neophyte is washed* symbolically on the forehead to indicate that the visible signs of the mysteries (oils, etc.) have become inner realities, which is to say the very essence of one's life. Second, to emphasize this, the *priest lays his hand upon the neophyte's head and prays* that the person be strengthened by the Holy Spirit to live a graceful life. Finally, *the neophyte is tonsured*. The tonsure is both an offering and a sign. It is an offering of one's self that does not require the mutilation or humiliation of the human body. It is also a sign

---

34   Light is the sign of warmth, knowledge, and life.

35   St. Ignatius of Antioch, *Letter to the Ephesians*, 20.

of servitude and obedience. Through the tonsure the new Christian proclaims his/her willingness and readiness to serve God with faithful devotion by continually renouncing the false values of the fallen world.[36]

6. Celebrating the Received Service of Baptism

The received Service of Baptism, as already mentioned, is comprised of several interrelated parts and rites which have their beginnings in Christian antiquity. These rites were initially celebrated at different intervals and stages during the process by which converts were received, prepared, catechized, and baptized. The process usually lasted several months and, in some places, up to three years. From the eighth century on, the several constituent parts of the rite were coalesced into a single service at a time when infant baptism had already become the norm. The Church uses this same service for both adults and children.

The following rubrics have in mind the baptism of infants and children as celebrated by one priest. Where necessary, a note is added for adult baptisms.

Well before the day of the service, the priest should meet with the parents and sponsors to discuss the meaning of the sacrament, parental expectations and responsibilities, and details pertaining to the service. Additionally, the priest should explain the role of the sponsor(s) and emphasize the need that this person must be an Orthodox Christian in good standing with the Church and parish. The priest should also make certain that the church office has the correct scheduled date and time of the service and the necessary documents and information to complete the baptismal certificate, which will be signed and given to the parents on the day of the service.

---

36 It is customary for the family to mark the baptism of a beloved member with a modest celebratory meal. Following the service, family and friends gather to honor the neophyte with a meal, which is itself a symbol of sharing and fellowship. Recall, for example, the events described in the Book of Acts at Philippi. Paul and Silas were jailed and were saved through divine intervention. Paul baptized the jailer and his family. "Then he [the jailer] brought them [Paul and Silas] up into his house and set food before them; and he rejoiced with all his household that he had believed in God" (Acts 16:34).

Preparations

To perform the service in an orderly and meaningful fashion the priest will require the assistance of an experienced sexton (*neokoros*) and chanter.[37]

Most churches have a movable baptismal font. For reasons of practicality, the font may be placed on one side of the nave or in the middle of the solea. Some churches have a small baptistery or a font which is fixed off to the side of the nave. A few churches have a baptistery for adult baptisms, some of which can also be used for infants. If it is practical and convenient, a small *proskynetarion* or stand may be placed directly in back of the portable font, upon which the Evangelion is placed. Some fonts also have a holder for three candles.

In addition to the font, an auxiliary table is needed. It is positioned in an inconspicuous place close to the font. The sexton places several items on the table, including the vessel containing the Holy Chrism and the cross of the *Agiasmos* (the blessing of water). He also places on it the items brought by the sponsor (or parents): a small container of olive oil, a bar of soap, a hand towel, baptismal candles, a new inner garment of the child, and the child's baptismal cross.[38] For purposes of convenience, the censer hanging from a stand is also placed next to auxiliary table.

The church must also have a space which is adequately equipped for the undressing and dressing of the child at the appropriate times. This place should not be in direct proximity to the font so as to avoid confusion and distractions.

Before the service begins, the sexton should see to it that all the items are in place for an orderly celebration of the sacrament. Besides the items mentioned above, the sexton should make certain that the font is filled with enough water; additional pitchers of hot and cold water should also be available to add to the font as needed and for the washing of hands after the baptism by the priest and sponsor; a hand towel is hung on the rings of the font; and the censer is lit and available.

---

37 The priest must see to it that the sexton and chanter are familiar with the service and are properly trained to fulfill their respective roles so that the service may be conducted in an orderly and dignified fashion.

38 The cross is placed on the auxiliary table only if the priest intends to place the cross on the child after being fully dressed with the new baptismal garments. Otherwise, the cross is left with the new baptismal garments and placed on the child by those appointed to dress the child.

The priest also needs to make certain that the vessels for the preparation and distribution of Holy Communion are in order.

When the service is completed, the sexton makes certain that the baptismal water is appropriately disposed of in the χωνευτήριον – *honefterion* (dry well), the font is properly cleaned, and, where applicable, returned to its place.

The priest also prepares the certificate of baptism in advance of the service.[39] When the service is completed, he and the sponsor sign the certificate. The original is placed in a marked envelope and given to the parents (or the sponsor), reminding them that it is an official document. Copies of the certificate are handled in accordance with the instructions of the metropolis. The priest makes certain that the relevant information is recorded in the parish registry book of baptisms.

7. The Order of the Service of Baptism

Preparatory Notes

The priest stands before the Holy Table wearing his exorasson and a white or bright colored epitrachelion.[40] If he is serving alone, without a deacon, he reads in a low voice the deprecatory prayer, the text of which is located in the service of baptism after the Great Litany: "'Ο εὔσπλαγχνος καὶ ἐλεήμων Θεός.... *O God, compassionate and merciful, who tests the hearts and reins, and alone knows the secrets of men....*"[41]

After the prayer and before starting the service, the priest welcomes the people and asks them to join him in prayer as they all prepare to participate

---

39   The information required for the certificate should be obtained from the parents well in advance of the service together with a copy of the child's birth certificate. The information on the certificate should be typed or written in good penmanship.

40   In earlier times the priest wore all his priestly vestments. In current practice only the epitrachelion and phelonion are required. It would be good, if it is feasible, for the priest to make a set of these two articles from washable material to be used only for baptisms.

41   Such prayers are found in only two sacraments, baptism and the Eucharist. A similar prayer is also found in the Service of the Great Agiasmos (The Great Blessing of the Water on the eve and Feast of Theophany). Through these prayers the celebrant recognizes his unworthiness and implores God to empower him to celebrate the holy mysteries by granting him humility and the forgiveness of sins. In the Euchologion this prayer is found after the Great Litany with a rubric instructing the priest to read it in a low voice while the deacon intones the litany. However, when there is no deacon or another priest present, the lone celebrant, for reasons of practicality, reads the prayer before the start of the service, as initially noted.

in the making of a new Christian. He also says a few words about the meaning and the gifts of holy baptism, reminding the people to take the opportunity to reflect upon and renew their own baptismal pledge as they listen carefully to the prayers and hymns of the service.

The first part of the service, generally referred to as the "*Catechesis,*" is normally conducted in the narthex.[42] The priest invites the parents, one of whom holds the child, and the sponsor(s) to join him in the narthex for the start of the service.[43] They proceed to the narthex and stand by the royal doors facing the sanctuary. There, the priest briefly addresses the parents and the sponsor(s) regarding the significance of the rites that are about to take place, and that they, on behalf of child, will affirm the Church's faith through the *apotaxis, syntaxis,* and the recitation of the Creed. To assist the sponsor in this task, the priest should have in hand a laminated card or small pamphlet with the questions and responses of the apotaxis and the syntaxis and the text of the Creed. Before starting the service, the priest asks the parents and the sponsor for the name of the child.

The Catechesis

The Enarxis (The Entrance)

Priest

Blows on the face of the child and seals him/her, making the sign of the cross with his hand in the usual manner over the child's head saying each time, "Εἰς τὸ ὄνομα τοῦ Πατρός... *In the Name of the Father...*" These actions are repeated three times.[44]

---

42 The use of two different spaces is based on ancient practice. The baptistery had two large chambers: one contained the baptismal font and the other a space where the catechumens gathered for instruction and for the performance of the Catechesis. Following baptism, the neophytes were led into a third space, the nave of the church for the celebration of the Eucharist.

43 Experience has taught me that a child feels more comfortable and less stressed when held by one of the parents during the Catechesis. The sponsor may hold the child after the recitation of the Creed, as long as the child remains calm.

44 Saint Nicholas Cabasilas explains this initial breathing as a sign of life. "So far is the catechumen from life and from being a son and an heir, that he is still enslaved to the tyrant.... Therefore, the celebrant breathes into his face, for the inbreathing from above is a symbol of life," *The Life in Christ* (Book Two: 3: b). The idea of breathing as a sign of life is based on the Genesis narrative, "Then the Lord God formed man of dust from the ground and breathed into his nostrils the breath of life; and man became a living being" (Gen. 2:7).

Priest

Faces the sanctuary and says aloud the opening doxology, "*Blessed is our God –* Εὐλογητὸς ὁ Θεός...."[45]

The Prayer of Inscription

Priest

Turns toward the child, places his hand on the child's head, and begins to read the "Prayer for the making of a Catechumen," also called the "Prayer of Inscription."), "'Ἐπὶ τῷ ὀνόματί σου.... *In your name, O Lord, God of truth...*"[46]

---

[45] I have omitted the rubrics regarding certain gestures, clothing, and footwear which one finds at the start of the Catechesis in the Euchologia. These rubrics are appropriate for adult catechumens and not for infants; they also mention garments that belong to another era. The rubrics are not appropriate for infant baptism or for our times. However, the symbolism of the rubrics should not be lost. In earlier days, the catechumens were stripped of their outer garments to symbolize the collapse of the façade of their alleged independence and self-sufficiency. With hands at their side and wearing a single garment, without a belt, with heads uncovered and feet unshod, the catechumen's true status is revealed—a subordinate of the ruler of this world, whom they were about to renounce, in order to gain true freedom and the status of sonship. Then, with hands raised, the catechumens surrender themselves to Christ to come under his rule.

[46] Originally, the Prayer for the Making of a Catechumen was read over the candidate on the very day he or she was officially accepted into the ranks of the catechumenate and, as the prayer indicates, had their name recorded in the registry book of the church: "*Inscribe him (her) in your Book of Life and unite him (her) to the flock of your inheritance.*" The same prayer is found in the earliest extant Euchologion, the eighth-century *Barberini Codex*. It is titled, "Εὐχὴ εἰς τὸ ποιῆσαι κατηχούμενον – *A Prayer for the making of a catechumen.*" In his *Procatechesis: 1*, St. Cyril of Jerusalem writes, "Already is there upon you the savor of blessedness...already you are gathering spiritual flowers...already are you at the entrance-hall of the King's house.... Thus far, your names have been given in, and the roll-call made for service."

The Exorcisms[47]

Immediately after the Prayer of Inscription, we find three exorcisms, the first two of which are directed to the devil. As such, they are not prayers in the strict sense but a sharp rebuke of the devil and his minions.[48] The third prayer is addressed to God, who is entreated to search out and expel the unclean spirits and giving victory to the catechumen over them. In earlier times, adult

---

[47] The three exorcism prayers are part of a larger collection. These three have survived due to their inclusion in the printed Euchologia. The same three exorcisms, bearing the titles "ἀπορκισμός α, β, γ," are included in the *Barberini Codex*. Other manuscripts and printed editions use the terms ἀφορκισμός *and* ἐξορκισμός. An exorcism prayer was said over the catechumens after each session of instruction. A careful reading of the three exorcisms gives the impression that they were read at different intervals. For example, the first exorcism contains the words, "Be gone and depart from the sealed, *newly-elect* soldier of Christ our God...." This indicates that the prayer was used in the initial stages of the catechumenate. The second exorcism could be interpreted to reflect a mid-point in the preparation process, "Depart hence from him (her) that has been newly-sealed in the name of our Lord...Be gone and depart from him (her) that is being prepared for holy illumination..." The third exorcism, which is also softer in language, appears to reflect nearness to the time of baptism. "That, having obtained mercy from you, he (she) may be counted worthy of your immortal and heavenly Mysteries." The subject matter of the three exorcisms is essentially the same: the rebuke and abjuration of the devil and his works. As with most prayers, they contain an anamnestic formula which, in this case, acknowledges the power of God to cast out demons (Mark 1:32-34; cf. Matt. 8:16-17) and a petitionary formula which asks God to bless the catechumen with strength and power to overcome the influences of demonic forces.

[48] A new service for infants? Exorcisms are an essential part of the baptismal liturgy. However, the exorcisms in the received rite were written for adult converts coming mostly from pagan backgrounds and are hardly fit for infants and young children. Yet, until such time as they are studied and adjusted to reflect the realities of infant baptism, we are obliged to use them. There is evidence that an attempt was made in the sixteenth and seventeenth centuries to adapt them for infants. The efforts, however, did not bear fruit. The time has come to revisit the issue. In recent years, the Roman Catholic Church, after Vatican II, created two different rites of Christian initiation, one for adult converts and another for children. I believe it is necessary and proper for the Orthodox Church to do the same, that is, to undertake the creation of a new service of baptism for infants and children based on the received tradition, relevant scholarly research, and sound theological reflection using concepts, language, and imagery that are suitable to the rite, but also comprehensible to modern worshippers, whose conception of the material world and the shape of reality is far more different than those of previous generations. See, for example, Fr. Philip Zymaris, "Theological Bubble Language: A Literalist View of the Fall and Its Connection to the Denigration of the Human Condition," in the Acts of the December 7, 2018 Annual Conference of the Institute for Studies of Eastern Christianity: *Fully Human - Theological Anthropology and Human Flourishing in the 21st Century* (presently under publication).

catechumens were exorcized frequently as they prepared for baptism.⁴⁹ The exorcisms in the received rite were not read sequentially, one after the other, as we do today but at different stages of the catechumenate.

In his address to the catechumens, St. John Chrysostom explained the purpose of the exorcisms: "For this rite does not take place without aim or purpose; you are going to receive the King of heaven to dwell within you. This is why, after we have admonished you, those appointed to this task take you and, as if they were preparing a house for a royal visit, they cleanse your minds by those awesome words, putting to flight every device of the wicked one and making your hearts worthy of the royal presence...."⁵⁰

The Reality of Evil

The exorcisms bring us before the stark, pervasive reality of evil,⁵¹ not only as the absence of the good but as a personal presence – a real, dark, irrational, sinister, and seductive personal presence,⁵² which the Scriptures call: "the god of this world" (2 Cor. 4:4); "the Devil and Satan;" the deceiver of the whole world (Rev. 12:7-9), "who disguises himself as an angel of light" (2 Cor.11:14), in order to blind the mind of unbelievers (2 Cor. 4:4). The prophet Isaiah calls this irrational personal force Lucifer (Day Star – Ἑωσφορός). Isaiah further states that Lucifer is a fallen angel who sought to usurp the throne of God, in order to make himself like the Most High (Is. 14:12-14).⁵³ Jesus speaks of the devil as a murderer, the one who "brought death to man from the beginning – ἀνθρωποκτόνος ἦν ἀπό ἀρχῆς" and as the father of lies. The devil, Jesus also said, is the one

---

49 Egeria, for example, in her *Diary of a Pilgrimage* (46), notes the following. "It is the custom here [Jerusalem], throughout the forty days on which there is fasting, for those who are preparing for baptism to be exorcised by the clergy early in the morning, as soon as the dismissal from the morning service has been given at the Anastasis."

50 John Chrysostom, *Baptismal Instructions* 2:12.

51 See John S. Romanides, *The Ancestral Sin*, George S. Gabriel, trans. (Ridgewood, NJ 2002), 69-101.

52 Schmemann, *Water and the Spirit*, 20-7.

53 Concerning the devil, St. John Climacus says, "The fallen Lucifer is the prince of demons," i.e., the cohort of fallen angels, the demonic powers who are at war with God. In *The Ladder of Divine Ascent*, Step 14, On Gluttony.

who "has nothing to do with the truth, because there is no truth in him. When he lies, he speaks according to his own nature, for he is a liar and the father of lies (John 8:44).[54]

The devil is the worker of evil in will and energy. He is the first and ultimate sinner, who introduced the germ of anti-life into God's good creation. He tempted, deluded, and corrupted the progenitors of our race, Adam and Eve, offering the appearances of life and the promise of eternity (Gen.3:1-7). Instead of life, however, the progenitors encountered death (Gen. 3:19). Breaking their communion with God, the sole fountain and giver of life, our ancestors became aware of their mortality. Led astray by the devil, they rebelled, and like him they betrayed their Creator: "And so death spread to all men; and because of death, all men have sinned" (Rom. 5:12; cf. 1 Cor. 15:21-22; Heb. 2:14-15).

This decisive passage (Rom 5:12), according to the Greek Fathers, tells us that the progenitors of the race have bequeathed us a fallen, weakened, and diseased nature which makes the occurrence of sin predictable because of our fear of death. The progenitors bequeathed us mortality – with all its implied limitations – and not their guilt. We are not their co-transgressors or sharers in their guilt.[55]

Saint Cyril of Alexandria explains the original or ancestral sin in this way. "How did many become sinners because of Adam? What are his missteps to us? How could we, who were not yet born, all be condemned with him? … We became sinners through Adam's disobedience in such a manner as this. He was created for incorruption and life, and the manner of his existence he had in the garden of delight was proper to holiness. His whole mind (nous) was continuously beholding God; his body was tranquil and calm with all base pleasures being still. For there was no tumult of alien disturbances in it. But because he fell under sin and slipped into corruptibility, pleasures and filthiness assaulted the nature of the flesh, and in our members was unveiled a savage law. Our nature, then, became diseased by sin through the disobedience of one, that is, of Adam. Thus, all were made sinners, not by being co-transgressors with Adam, something which they never were, but by being of his nature and falling under the

---

[54] For a concise explanation of the nature and the wicked works of the devil and his minions see St. John of Damascus, *Exposition of the Orthodox Faith*, Book II: IV, in the *Nicene and Post-Nicene Fathers*, Vol. ix.

[55] See Romanides, *Ancestral Sin*, 159-69. Meyendorff, *Byzantine Theology*, 143-6. T. Ware, *The Orthodox Church*, 218-25.

law of sin... Human nature fell ill in Adam and subject to corruptibility through disobedience, and therefore, the passions entered in."[56]

Theodoret of Cyrus explains this same truth in a more simple and direct way. "Having become mortal [Adam and Eve] conceived mortal children, and mortal beings are necessarily subject to passions and fears, to pleasures and sorrows, to anger and hatred."[57]

Our mortality makes us vulnerable and susceptible to the wiles of the devil (Ps. 128/129:1-2), as the Epistle to the Hebrews affirms (Heb. 2:14-15). The devil holds the power of death by which he subjects people to lifelong bondage through the fear of death. Fear of death leads to compensatory acts of self-assertion and pride. The devil exploits peoples' fears and passions, leading them to ruinous deeds and evil acts, both personal and collective.[58]

However, our fallen nature is not beyond redemption, as the very words of the Lord affirm: "For God has so loved the world that he gave his only begotten Son, that whoever believes in him should not perish but have everlasting life. For God did not send his Son into the world to condemn the world, but that the world through him might be saved" (John 3:16-17). As we pray at the Divine Liturgy, "God does not overlook the sinner but has set repentance as the way of salvation" (Prayer of the Trisagion Hymn; cf. Heb. 9:26-28). Through the proper exercise of the will, everyone is open to the operations of divine grace from which salvation and eternal life flow.

Indeed, as Fr. Dumitru Staniloae affirms, our Orthodox faith offers people a sure remedy for the desperate dread of death which makes us prey to the evil one. He notes, "Death in Christ is a means for our elevation from this incomplete and fleeting life – into which we have descended – to the life without death, to the plenitude of life through the encounter with Christ beyond death, after we have lived in part with him here. And we have the certainty of our encounter with him, of surpassing our death, in his victory over death through the resurrection."[59]

---

56 Cyril of Alexandria, *Commentary on Romans*, P.G. 74, 788-9, cited in Romanides, *Ancestral Sin*, 167-8.

57 Cited by Meyendorff, *Byzantine Theology*, 145.

58 For an engaging discussion on evil see the short essays of eight contemporary Christian thinkers in Sin, Death, and the Devil, Carl E. Braaten and Robert W. Jenson, editors, (Grand Rapids Michigan, 2000).

59 Staniloae, *The Experience of God: The Fulfillment of Creation*, vol 6 (Brookline, MA 2013), 7-8. In this volume Fr. Staniloae offers the reader valuable insights on the Orthodox understanding of death, the immortality of the soul, judgment, hell, the resurrection of the body, prayers for the dead, the relics of saints, the second coming of Christ.

Indeed, moral failures and all manner of human weaknesses do not have the last word because sin and death have been overcome in Christ: "For as in Adam all die, so also in Christ shall all be made alive" (1 Cor. 15:22). The last enemy, death, has already been defeated through the death and resurrection of Christ. Life has been liberated! Death has become the gateway to another mode of existence for those who hear, believe in, and do the will of God: "Just as we have borne the image of the man of dust, we shall also bear the image of the man of heaven" (1 Cor. 15:49).

Evil is Not Proper to Human Nature

Another biblical passage, also key to our understanding of the human condition, is found in the story of Cain and Abel. Sibling rivalry, jealousy and resentment tormented the soul of Cain. God, in his inscrutable wisdom and boundless love, speaks to Cain and through him to all people: "Why are you angry, and why has your countenance fallen? If you act rightly, will you not be accepted? And if you do not act rightly, sin is couching at the door; its desire is for you, but you must master it" (Gen. 4:7; cf. 1 John 3:11). This passage clearly indicates that evil is not intrinsic, nor proper to human nature. As St. John Climacus puts it: "Evil or passion is not something naturally implanted in things. God is not the creator of passions."[60] True! But nature, as it has been said, "can be habituated through the passions to act in evil ways." Nor is death an instrument of divine wrath. God is not vengeful and vindictive or the source of corruptibility and death. The devil is. God brought nothing evil into existence.

Yet death exists. The universe and all that is in it are finite. God alone is immortal and the source of all life. The story of Adam and Eve, the progenitors of the race, as told in the book of Genesis, describes the creation, nature, and destiny of the human race (Gen. 1, 2, 3). Succumbing to the temptation of the devil and the allure of his false promise, "You will not die…. You will be like God," the progenitors disobeyed God's command and breaking their communion with him, they confronted their mortality. By eating the "forbidden fruit" they surrendered and forfeited the gift of eternal life which God had bestowed upon them, "For in the day that you eat of [the tree of knowledge of good and evil] you shall die" (Gen. 2:15-17; 3:1-24).

---

60 John Climacus, *Ladder*, Step 26, On Discernment.

However, hidden behind the divine admonition lies a compassionate purpose, which is expressed succinctly in a funeral prayer.[61] The prayer states that God, because of his great love and compassion, allows death "so that evil should not become immortal – ἵνα μὴ τό κακόν ἀθάνατον γένηται."[62]

God's compassionate purposes are fulfilled in the death and resurrection of Christ, through whom light shown in the darkness and hope sprang forth from Hades. "Christ also died…that he might bring us to God (1 Peter 3:18). We die in the promise of resurrection. At the consummation of the age, the dead will be made whole again. The unity of body and soul, broken and dissolved by death, will be healed and restored. "Death is swallowed up in victory" and the perishable will put on the imperishable and the mortal will put on the immortal (1 Cor. 15:52-53).

Satan and his legions have power over us to the degree we allow them. We read in the Book of Baruch (2:8): "Each of us, from the thoughts of his wicked heart" turns away from God and becomes disobedient and sinful (cf. 1 John 3:4-10). Through the misuse of free will each of us becomes an imitator of Adam and Eve.

In other words, sin is the product of a misguided, free, personal mind and will. Sin is always a personal act and never an act of nature.[63] It is also more than the misuse of freedom. As St. Maximos the Confessor avers, sin is a diversion: "Evil is the diverting of the activities of the powers implanted in nature from their purpose and nothing else."[64] Sin is a distraction. It

---

61 This prayer is found in the common burial service and in the service when the soul desires release from the body (Εὐχή εἰς Ψυχορραγόντα). The prayer reads in part: "Lord our God, in your inexpressible wisdom you created man out of the earth, and gave him a comely form and a fair appearance as a precious and heavenly being, befitting your glory and sovereignty, since you made him in your image and likeness. But he transgressed against your command and having received the image, violated it. *So that evil should not become immortal,* in your love, as God of our Fathers, you ordained that this compounding and mingling, this unbreakable bond, should by your divine will be severed and dissolved: that the soul should make its way to where it had its origin to await the common resurrection, while the body returns to the elements out of which it was composed…"

62 Many years ago, at one of the named annual lectures at Holy Cross, the lecturer, a scientist, compared the insidious power of evil to cancer. Cancer, he said, is caused by mutation of the genetic material of normal cells, which results in uncontrolled cell division. These cells develop in ways that "defy" death; they keep growing without limit, even if slowly. Listening to the speaker, it struck me that evil is, indeed, like cancer. Left to its own devices, evil attacks and destroys human beings so that it may become immortal. Hence God, in his compassionate purposes, allows death *so that evil should not become immortal.*

63 Meyendorff, *Byzantine Theology,* 143.

64 Cited in Dumitru Staniloae, *The World: Creation and Deification* (Brookline 2000), 151.

hinders us from fulfilling our God-given personal purpose and ultimate destiny, which is to become by grace what Christ is by nature. We call this gift theosis or participation in the divine life (2 Peter 1:4).[65]

The words of God to Cain also confirm that the devil is a predator, a crouching beast hungering to devour the unwary (1 Peter 5:8). The struggle against the ruler of this world is relentless. It defines the nature of the spiritual warfare in which we are all embroiled. As the Psalmist asserts, we have been brought forth in iniquity, into a fallen world (Ps. 50/51:7). And so, the first and last line of defense against the ferocious predator – the devil – is to be united in faith with Christ and to do good. In other words, we must act rightly, which is to say we must obey the commandments; keep the righteous judgements of God; and dwell on his precepts, which are a lamp to our feet and a light to our path (Ps. 118/119:105-106).

If we are of God and abide in him, we will hear his voice and keep his commandments and discern the spirit of truth from the spirit of error (1 John 4:1-6). The lines of defense, however, begin to blur when a person sets themselves up haughtily as the sole arbiter of good and evil (Gen. 2:1-7). As strong as the temptations that enter one's mind may be, the power of sin is not invincible. It can and must be mastered. However, the power to check evil, repent of it, and be healed cannot be achieved through one's efforts alone, but with the help of divine grace through a deep personal relationship with Christ (Ephes. 6:10-19).[66] *This grace-filled relationship enables persons to overcome their sinful impulses and desires, and their repressed fears and anxieties which are the stuff of which their sinful thoughts and deeds are made.*

It is for these reasons that the baptismal rites of the Church begin with exorcisms. They remind us that the ability to overcome the wiles of the Devil must begin with the acknowledgement that evil exists not simply as the absence of the good, but, as Fr. Alexander Schmemann taught, "as the presence: the presence of something dark, irrational and very real, although the origin of that presence may not be clear and immediately understandable." And he continues, "Behind the dark and irrational presence of evil there must be a person or persons. There must exist a personal world of those who have chosen to hate God, to hate the light, to be against. Who are these persons? To these questions the Church gives no precise answers...The answer is veiled in symbols and images which tell of initial rebellion against God...The origin of evil is viewed here not

---

65 On the subject of theosis see Norman Russell, *Fellow Workers with God: Orthodox Thinking on Theosis* (Crestwood, NY 2009).

66 Staniloae, *Creation and Deification* 147-62.

as ignorance and imperfection but, on the contrary, as knowledge and a degree of perfection which makes the temptation of pride possible. Whoever he is, the Devil is among the very first and the best creatures of God. He is so to speak, perfect enough, wise enough, powerful enough to know God and not to surrender to him—to know him and yet to opt against him, to desire freedom from him...But since this freedom is impossible in the love and light which always lead to God and to a free surrender to him, it must of necessity be fulfilled in negation, hatred and rebellion."[67]

Parental Responsibility – Guarding the Heart

St. John Climacus states clearly that "among children no evil is found, nothing deceitful, no insatiable greed or gluttony, no flaming lust."[68] *Hence, in the case of infant baptism the exorcisms and the renunciations in the received rite should be understood and interpreted accordingly.*

---

67 Alexander Schmemann. *Of Water and the Spirit* (New York 1974), 22, 23. Regarding the human condition the following passage from the *Apologia pro vita sua* (first edition, p. 242-243) of John Henry Newman, the 19th century cleric, theologian and philosopher is also of interest. The passage was given to me by Metropolitan Savas of Pittsburgh, to whom I offer my thanks. Although the passage is long, it is worth repeating for its fascinating prose. The italics have been added for emphasis. "To consider the world in its length and breadth, its various history, the many races of man, their starts, their fortunes, their mutual alienation, their conflicts; and then their ways, habits, governments, forms of worship; their enterprises, their aimless courses, their random achievements and acquirements, the impotent conclusion of long-standing facts, the tokens so faint and broken of a superintending design, the blind evolution of what turn out to be great powers or truths, the progress of things, as if from unreasoning elements, not towards final causes, *the greatness or littleness of man, his far-reaching aims, his short duration, the curtain hung over his futurity, the disappointments of life, the defeat of good, the success of evil, physical pain, mental anguish, the prevalence and intensity of sin, the pervading idolatries, the corruptions, the dreary hopeless irreligion, that condition of the whole race, so fearfully yet exactly described in the Apostle's words, "Having no hope and without God in the world,"—all this is a vision to dizzy and appal; and inflicts upon the mind the sense of profound mystery, which is absolutely beyond human solution.* What shall be said to the heart-piercing, reason-bewildering fact? I can only answer, that either there is no Creator, or this living society of men is in a true sense discarded from his presence. Did I see a boy of good make and mind, with the tokens on him of refined nature, cast upon the world without provision, unable to say whence he came, his birthplace or his family connections, I should conclude that there was some mystery connected with his history, and that he was one, of whom, from one cause or other, his parents were ashamed. *Thus only should I be able to account for the contrast between the promise and the condition of his being. And so I argue about the world; if there be a God, since there is a God, the human race is implicated in some terrible aboriginal calamity. It is out of joint with the purpose of its Creator. This is a fact, a fact as true as the fact of its existence; and thus the doctrine of what is theologically called original sin becomes to me almost as certain as that the world exists, and as the existence of God."*

68   Climacus, *Ladder of Divine Ascent*, Step 1, Renunciation of life.

The exorcisms, first and foremost, should remind parents, sponsors, and the entire faith community of the pervasive presence of evil in the world. The family, together with the church community, constitute the frontline of defense in the unseen warfare. They are tasked with the responsibility to protect every child in their care from the debasing, deadly effects of sin by developing in them the facility for virtue[69] and creating for them a loving environment in which they may develop into mature and wholesome human beings and faithful disciples of Christ (Ephes. 6:4). Parents, sponsors, and the faith community as a whole, are obliged to teach every child, by word and deed, how best to practice their special gifts as followers of Christ. In this they will have life, and have it more abundantly (John 10:10).

Alexander Solzhenitsyn, the Russian novelist and thinker, inspired by the

---

69 In addition to the commandments and the virtues voiced by the Lord in the Beatitudes and the Sermon on the Mount (Matt. 5:1-7:29), lists of virtues are contained in the apostolic *Letters* and in the writings of the Fathers. Saint Paul, for example, speaks of the virtues as the "fruits of the Spirit" (Gal. 5:22) and lists several of them (Gal. 5:22-23; cf. 1 Cor. 6:9-10): joy, peace, patience, kindness, goodness, faithfulness, gentleness, self-control (temperance), humility, faith, hope, and "above all these things, love, which binds everything together in perfect harmony" (Col. 3:14; cf. 1 Cor. 13:1-13).

To this list we can add other virtues found in the writings of the desert fathers and other ancient Christian writers: prudence, detachment (the readiness to turn away from worldly concerns and an excessive attachment to material things), discernment (the ability to distinguish between the thoughts inspired by God and the suggestions of the evil one), obedience, compunction (to be conscious of one's sinfulness and God's abundant mercy), godly sorrow (which nourishes the soul with hope through repentance), simplicity, stillness (inner peace, mental quietude – listening to the word of God), prayer, and dispassion (to uproot sinful passions, or, to re-educate them so that they may be exercised in accordance with their original beauty).

The brief comment of St. Mark the Ascetic on the difference between the commandments and the virtues is worth noting. He writes, "The Lord is hidden in his own commandments, and he is to be found there in the measure he is sought. Do not say, 'I have fulfilled the commandments, but have not found the Lord'.... Fulfilling a commandment is one thing, and virtue is another, although each promotes the other. Fulfilling a commandment means doing what you are enjoined to do; but virtue is to do it in a manner that conforms to the truth.... Always do as much good as you can, and at a time of greater good do not turn to a lesser. For it is said that no man who turns back is fit for the kingdom of heaven." *The Philokalia*, Vol. 1, 123, 124.

Liturgical texts also contain references to virtues and vices. The brief, well-known Prayer of St. Ephraim, for example, lists five vices to flee from and five virtues to seek after. "Lord and Master of my life, give me not a spirit of sloth, vain curiosity, lust for power, and idle talk. But give to me, your servant, a spirit of prudence, humility, patience, and love. Lord and King, grant me to see my own faults and not to condemn my brother: for you are blessed to the ages of ages."

teachings of the Lord[70] *and based on his own painful experiences in the forced labor camps of the Soviet Union, made the following insightful observation in his masterpiece,* The Gulag Archipelago: *"The line separating good and evil passes not through states, nor between classes, nor between political parties either – but right through every heart – and through all human hearts."*

Indeed, according to our biblical and patristic tradition, the heart is not simply the physical organ which sustains our biological life. It is also perceived as the spiritual center of one's being, of one's deepest and true self, made in the image of God. At the innermost part of the heart is the nous (νους) or the intellect, which is the highest faculty of the human person. Distinguished from reason, the nous is the organ of contemplation and communion with the life-giving presence of God, which is to say his divine energies. The nous is the eye of the heart, which is enabled by grace to see and contemplate the unsearchable riches of Christ (Ephes. 3:7-21). The heart is the inner temple, the dwelling place of God in the Spirit (Ephes. 2:21-22), in which the communion of the divine and the human is being accomplished (John 14:20-21, 23-24).[71] *Indeed, according to the Lord's promise, the pure in heart will see God (Matt. 5:8; Heb. 12:14; Ps. 23/24:3-6).*

The misuse and abuse of one's free will, however, can cause the heart to turn into a dark place of betrayal, disobedience, unfaithfulness, and defilement; a den of iniquity and the lair of vices (Mark 7:21-23; 1 Cor. 6:9-10; Gal. 5:19-21).[72] *Hence, guarding the heart from immorality, from evil thoughts, desires, and actions is critical, if one is to grow "to the measure of the stature of the fullness of Christ" (Ephes. 4:13).*

---

70 "And [Jesus] called the people to him again and said to them…. Do you not see that whatever goes into a man from outside cannot defile him, since it enters not his heart…. For from within, out of the heart of man, comes evil thoughts…" (Mark 7:14-23; cf. Matt. 15:10-20).

71 These definitions (heart and nous) are drawn from *The Philokalia*, Vol. 1 (London and Boston 1979), 361.

72 We find lists of vices in the Scriptures and in the writings of Christian writers. Christ said that vices flow out of the heart and defile the human person (Mark 7:20-21). Saint Paul denounces immoral behavior or vices as unbecoming and warns that those who practice them will not inherit the kingdom of heaven (1 Cor. 6:9; Gal 5:21; cf. Matt. 7:21-23). He calls the vices, "works of the flesh" (Gal. 5:19), which is to say, works of an imprudent mind, perverted will, and insensible heart. The vices are sometimes listed in two categories: non-physical and physical. In the first category we find: evil thoughts, wickedness, hate, strife, dissension, deceit, coveting, envy, slander, anger, malice, blasphemy, foolishness, despondency, sloth, idle talk, falsehood, conceit, lust for power, and pride which is the source of all evil. In the second category are: gluttony, avarice, greed, lust, licentiousness, fornication, adultery, perversions, murder, theft, sorcery, idolatry, drunkenness and the like.

A guarded and vigilant heart produces the desire for God which in turn gives rise to the practice of virtues, the chief of which is love – ἀγάπη (1 John 4:7-21; 1 Cor. 13:1-13).[73] *And so we pray at the Divine Liturgy, "Instill in us also reverence for your blessed commandments, so that having conquered all sinful desires, we may pursue a spiritual life, thinking and doing all those things that are pleasing to you" (Prayer before the Gospel).*

Parental responsibility can be summarized by the concise definition of the essence of the spiritual life given by St. John Climacus. He highlights the need for a deep personal relationship with Christ and faithful adherence to the Orthodox faith in the pursuit of a virtuous life. He writes, "A Christian is an imitator of Christ in thought, word, and deed, as far as is humanly possible, and believes rightly and blamelessly in the Holy Trinity.[74] *A friend of God is the one who lives in communion with all that is natural and free from sin and who does not neglect to do what good he can. The self-controlled man strives with all his might amidst the trials, the snares, and the noise of the world, to be like someone who rises above them."*[75]

Bishop Gerasimos of Abydos, the reposed "elder of America," says it more plainly and directly: "The earliest faith begins with our mothers. It is our mothers who plant the seeds that become the first roots of faith in the innocent, open hearts of childhood. After that comes the life of faith that develops in the Church, nourished by sacred Tradition, sacred Scripture, and liturgical experience. Sacred Tradition broadens, deepens, illumines and strengthens our first child-like faith. Each life of faith has its own history. The history of faith is the history of mankind. With faith we can withstand the spirit of the world which attempts, at each historical stage, to uproot our faith in God – the living God who is active in the life of the world – without giving us anything positive for the meaning of our life. In the faith that comes from our mothers and from sacred Tradition, we learn many things about the person of Christ, about God and man, and about the relationship of man with God – truths which many prophets

---

73 On guarding the heart see the homilies of St. Isaiah the Solitary, "On Guarding the Heart" and St. Hesychios the Priest (Sinai), "On Watchfulness and Holiness." Both texts are in *The Philokalia*, Vol. 1, 21-8 and 161-98, respectively.

74 "*As far as is humanly possible.*" Each person is unique and unrepeatable, different in character, talents, abilities, and potentialities. In the pursuit of holiness, however, everyone is called to excel in earnestness, each according to their God-given powers and capacities. What matters most is the earnest and genuine effort, even when the result may differ. See, for example, the parable of the seeds recorded in the Gospel of Mark: "And other seeds fell into good soil and brought forth grain, growing up and increasing and yielding thirtyfold and sixtyfold and a hundredfold" (Mark 4:8; cf. Matt. 13:23).

75 Climacus, *Ladder*, Step 1.

and saints of the Church and even angels sought to learn (Ephes. 3:10-12, 14-21; 1 Peter 1:10-12)."[76]

The Fourth Prayer and the Apotropaic Act of Breathing

The title and content of this prayer are of special interest. In some printed Euchologia it has no title, while in others it is identified simply as "a fourth prayer." In the *Barberini Codex*, however, it bears the title, "*Prayer after the making of a catechumen for him who is about to be baptized – Εὐχὴ μετὰ τὸ ποιῆσαι κατηχούμενον πρὸς τὸν πρὸς ὥραν βαπτιζόμενον.*" The prayer has two parts, the first of which is clearly an exorcism which includes the apotropaic act of *breathing*.[77] The second part, unlike the preceding three prayers of exorcism, contains a direct plea to God to introduce the candidate into the *"holy flock of Christ,"* by making him (her) an honorable member of the Church. This second section is also replete with baptismal imagery: "make him (her) a sanctified *vessel;* a *son (daughter) of light;* and an *heir* of the kingdom; that he (she) may keep the *seal* unbroken and preserve the *garment* undefiled." Immediately after this prayer the priest conducts the *apotaxis* and the *syntaxis*, the renunciation of the devil and the attachment or adherence to Christ.

The title of the prayer and its place in the service raise a question about its nature and purpose. The content of the prayer suggests it is a summary of all the prebaptismal prayers. Was it used in emergency situations as Fountoulis suggests, or was it used when the adult catechumenate had all but disappeared

---

76 Gerasimos Papadopoulos Bishop of Abydos, "The Hierarchical Prayer of Jesus Christ" in *Bishop Gerasimos of Abydos the Spiritual Elder of America*, Peter A. Chamberas, ed. (Brookline, MA 1977), 41-2.

77 Apotropaic (= to ward off evil). The apotropaic act of breathing (or blowing) in this instance has a double meaning: to put the devil to flight and to cleanse the soul. The priest performs this act by breathing crosswise on the face of the candidate after which he says the words, "Drive out from him (her)...." The ritual is repeated three times. The prayer further identifies the unclean spirits that are being rebuked: "the spirit of error, of evil, of idolatry, of covetousness, of lying, and of all uncleanness that operates according to the coaxing of the devil." As mentioned earlier, in other instances, the act of breathing is a sign of life (Gen. 2:7) and of divine presence (John 20:22).

and the practice of daily or frequent exorcisms over the candidates was no longer in force?⁷⁸ Could it be that it was read immediately after the Prayer for the Making of a Catechumen in the case of infants and children?⁷⁹

Priest:

Reads the *fourth prayer*. About half way through, when he comes to the phrase, *"Ἐξέλασον ἀπ' αὐτοῦ.... Drive out from him (her) every evil and unclean spirit hiding and nesting in his (her) heart,"* the prayer is interrupted. The priest performs an apotropaic gesture: *breathing* crosswise on the child's face or head. The phrase is intoned three times, preceded each time by the breathing.⁸⁰

On sin, apotropaic rituals, and little children

Originally, the formula *"Drive out from him/her every evil and unclean spirit"* was meant and used for adult catechumens, not infants and children. Nonetheless, as already noted, we are obliged to perform the rite as we have received it until such time as the Church decrees otherwise. The formula rests in the belief that evil spirits hide and nest in the bodies of those preparing for baptism.

The concept behind this formula is difficult to explain when applied to infants and little children. It implies that every infant and child, who bears the image of God (Gen. 1:27) and the light of Christ (John 1:9), also houses within their heart evil and unclean powers waiting to strike and lead them astray. This concept is inconsistent with what the Church says about infants. The prayer of the rite of eighth day after birth, for example, says: "Let the light of your countenance shine within your servant and let the Cross of your only begotten Son be sealed in his (her) heart and in his/her thoughts...and grant, O Lord, that your holy name shall remain indelible upon him (her)...."

---

78 Ioannis M. Fountoulis, Τελετουργικὰ Θέματα (Athens 2002), 302.

79 The title of the prayer suggests that it was used after the making of a catechumen at a time close to baptism. According to ancient ritual practices in Constantinople (ca. fifth century) and elsewhere, the catechumens who were approved for baptism, called φωτιζόμενοι – *the illumined* – made their baptismal renunciations and pledges and professed the Faith (Creed) on Great Friday before the patriarch, bishop, or priest. They were baptized on Great Saturday night at the Paschal Vigil. The special intensified process of training for the φωτιζόμενοι began on the fourth week of Lent (the day after the Sunday of the Veneration of the Cross), at which time special petitions were added for them at divine services. The rites on Great Friday were attended by adult candidates and older children capable of participating in the proceedings.

80 On apotropaic rituals see Appendix B:2.

It is true that in his First Epistle, St. Peter the Apostle tells us that the devil, our adversary, prowls about like a lion seeking to tempt, ensnare, and kill (1 Peter 5:8). But he is addressing adults – not infants and little children – admonishing them to resist the devil and his machinations through vigilance by placing themselves under the mighty hand, the rule, of God (1 Peter 5:6, 9).

We are earth and dust, created by God out of matter which he brought into being out of nothing. Hence, being mortal we are perishable by nature and are exposed to change and corruption and the wiles of the devil. We live under the tyranny of sin. Christ alone, who was incarnate by the Holy Spirit and the Virgin Mary, was born outside the tyranny of sin.

As pervasive as evil is, it does not belong to the essential nature of the created order. It is a parasitic force. Everything that God made is good; not perfect but very good (Gen. 1:4-31). In his great goodness, God has called all people to become perfect (Matt. 5:48), to transcend by grace the boundaries of their creaturely existence through their union with him (Rom. 8:11-17). Indeed, "creation itself will be set free from its bondage to decay and obtain the glorious liberty of the children of God" (Rom. 8:18-22).

Evil entered the world through the deliberate misuse of free will, the wondrous gift which God bestowed upon angels and human beings. Satan, a fallen angel, the god and ruler of this age (2 Cor. 4:4; John 12:31), is the worker of evil. He is the primary cause of corruption and sin through his will and energy. According to the biblical story (Gen. 3:1-24), Satan tempted the progenitors of our race. In their willful disobedience of the commandments, our progenitors defiled the world and caused the state of existence we call the Fall, which may be defined as estrangement and separation from God—a condition in which death has dominion over all (Rom. 5:12-21; Heb. 2:14-18).

Our inner world is beset by a profound sense of alienation, failure, and lack of fulfillment. We are in a state of continuous unrest, deeply wounded by the hereditary cosmic corruption. We are driven by an arrogant demanding subjectivity – by unbridled pride – and the controlling preservation instinct. Our God-given vocation to become gods by grace, as St. Athanasios affirms, is continually thwarted by the devil and his legions. Through their evil devices, we succumb to our passions – the distorted faculties of the soul – and commit sin. Mortal sins (1 John 5:16) hinder our progressive growth "to the measure of the stature of the fullness of Christ" (Ephes. 4:13).

Sin is born of desire; it is made manifest in willful acts. Rational, conscious, self-determining persons commit sins, not infants and little children. Sin is born of temptations that come from within, prompted by our desires, as St. James tells us: "Let no one say when he is tempted, 'I am tempted by God;' for God cannot be tempted with evil and he himself tempts no one; but each person is tempted when he is lured and enticed by his own desire. Then desire when it is conceived gives birth to sin; and sin when it is full-grown brings forth death" (James 1:13-15).

Hence, infants, as St. John Chrysostom argues, are sinless because they are free from personal sins, even as they bear the wounds of the Fall, the broken and distorted image of God in us. Their hearts, to be sure, are not the nesting place of evil spirits but of God's transforming grace. To assert that evil and impure spirits are hidden and nesting in a child's heart is to compromise the Church's teaching that evil is extrinsic to human nature.

On another note, it is significant that no mention is made of original sin or of inherited guilt in the baptismal service. In fact, the latter concept is alien to our Orthodox theological tradition. The phrase "forgiveness of sins" (note the plural), is mentioned only three times in the entire service. In each instance, the reference is to willful transgressions committed knowingly by rational persons and not by infants or little children.

The Apotaxis and Syntaxis

At this point, attention is focused on the candidate for baptism – the catechumen. Through a series of answers to questions posed by the priest, the catechumen chooses of his own free will to renounce the devil and all his works *(apotaxis)*; to accept Christ as Lord, God and Savior *(syntaxis)*; and to profess the Orthodox faith by reciting the Creed. Through these actions the catechumen both seals and gives voice to his (her) personal conversion and regeneration. The apotaxis and syntaxis summarize the catechumen's experiences of deliverance from darkness and the renewal of life through the knowledge of the truth and union with Christ.

Of course, in the case of infant baptism, the awesome responsibility of the apotaxis and syntaxis falls on the sponsor, but also on the parents under whose care the child will grow to maturity. The sponsor becomes the child's spiritual father/mother. Together with the parents, the sponsor assumes the role of a reliable guide in the faith. Parents and godparents together become the guarantors of the child entrusted to their care. By example and counsel, they are called to lead the child into the paths of righteousness, into a life lived in continuous newness as he or she mirrors more and more the image of Christ.[81]

The apotaxis is crucial even in the case of infant baptism. Through the apotaxis the parents and sponsor acknowledge the pernicious presence of the devil

---

81 See Staniloae, *Sanctifying Mysteries*, 44-5.

in the world, who preys on the innocent and the credulous, but also on the prideful and self-absorbed, deceiving and corrupting his victims. Through the renunciations parents and sponsor affirm their readiness to protect the child, by God's grace, from the wiles of the devil as the child grows to maturity. This is an awesome responsibility and a most arduous task, since from our youth many passions war against us.[82] No one is immune to sin, to the temptations of the devil.

The apotaxis and syntaxis consist of two sets of questions and answers. The first set is in the present tense while the second in the aorist past tense.[83] The second set is followed by a third question to which the sponsor gives an affirmative answer. The sponsor confesses his/her belief in Christ as King and God followed by the recitation of the Creed.

The apotaxis begins with the instruction of the priest to the sponsor. He is asked to face toward the "west," that is, to look away from the sanctuary, which by tradition, at least in theory if not always in practice, faces the east. The west is where the sun sets and is therefore perceived as the place of darkness. The devil dwells in darkness and is himself darkness.

1. The Apotaxis—Renunciations

Priest

Turns to the sponsor and provides him/her with a copy of the text of the renunciations, the pledges, and the Creed. He begins the questioning.

Priest

"*Do you renounce Satan and all his works ... Ἀποτάσσῃ τῷ Σατανᾷ καὶ πᾶσι τοῖς ἔργιοις αὐτοῦ....*"[84]

Sponsor

Responds, "*I renounce him. – Ἀποτάσσομαι.*"

This form of questioning is repeated twice more for a total of three.

---

82 See Psalm 128/129:1-2 and the first antiphon of the fourth tone of the Sunday Orthros.

83 In current circumstances the second set of questions (past tense) may be superfluous. Should the Church decide, the second set could be omitted since the several rites of catechism are no longer conducted at different intervals but simultaneously.

84 The word ἀποτάσσω means to take leave of or to part from someone or something. In this instance it means to renounce, refuse, repudiate, or abjure the evil one.

Then the priest begins another series of questions which is also repeated three times [85]

Priest

"*Have you renounced Satan? - Ἀπετάξω τῷ Σατανᾷ;*"

Sponsor

"*I have renounced him. - Ἀπεταξάμην.*"

The priest then tells the sponsor to perform the apotropaic act of breathing and spitting

Priest

"*Then breathe and spit upon him. - Καὶ ἐμφύσησον καὶ ἔμπτυσον αὐτῷ.*"

Sponsor

Facing west, he or she blows (and spits) in the air three times as a sign of disdain, contempt, and utter repudiation.

•——•

2. The Syntaxis – Adherence or Allegiance

The sponsor and parents turn toward the "east" and face the sanctuary.[86] **The priest begins a new set of questions – a new threefold interrogation.**

Priest

Do you join yourself to Christ? - Συντάσσῃ τῷ Χριστῷ;"[87]

Sponsor

"*I do join myself to Christ. - Συντάσσομαι.*"

This dialogue and the one that follows are repeated three times.

---

85 In times past, saying or repeating something three times was a way of confirming and sealing one's word. It signified finality and permanence.

86 The sun rises from the east. Hence the east is the place of light. It serves as a symbol of light and life. God is light—uncreated light. He dwells in unapproachable light. Jesus is the True Light, the Light of the world, who dispels the darkness.

87 The word συντάσσω has several meanings: to put in order, to bring into line, to associate with or to pledge allegiance to someone. As a military term it meant to put (troops) in array or in order for battle. It also means to be under the command of a superior. Hence the question may be translated and stated in several ways, as for example: "Do you join Christ?" … "Do you unite yourself to Christ?" … "Do you pledge allegiance to Christ?"

Priest

"Have you joined yourself to Christ? – Συνετάξω τῷ Χριστῷ;"

Sponsor

"I have joined. – Συνεταξάμην."

Looking directly at the sponsor, the priest again asks in all earnestness

Priest

And do you believe in Him? – Καὶ πιστεύεις αὐτῷ;"

Sponsor

"I believe in Him as King and God. – Πιστεύω αὐτῷ ὡς Βασιλεῖ καὶ Θεῷ."

3. The Creed

Immediately after the syntaxis the sponsor is invited to recite the Creed.[88]

The Creed of the Orthodox Church — Τὸ Σύμβολον τῆς Πίστεως ("Τὸ Πιστεύω") – *was promulgated by the First and Second Ecumenical Synods, which were convened in Nicaea (325) and Constantinople (381) respectively. It is a concise formulation of the Church's faith.*[89]

---

88 Orthodox parents may join the sponsor in the recitation of the Nicene-Constantinopolitan Creed.

89 Originally, creeds were recited at baptisms. However, in the struggles against heresies the Creed was eventually introduced into the Divine Liturgy to be recited by all the people in unison as an expression of their fidelity to the true faith. It is said that Patriarch Peter the Fuller (+488), the Monophysite Patriarch of Antioch, was the first to start the practice. The introduction of the Creed into the Eucharistic rites of Constantinople began with Patriarch Timothy (511-517). It was inserted into the Divine Liturgy after the Great Entrance and the kiss of peace and before the anaphora. In the Eucharistic setting the Creed was usually said in the plural form (*We believe*) but in time the text reverted back to the original singular form used in the baptismal rite (*I believe*). See Hugh Wybrew, *The Orthodox Liturgy* (Crestwood, NY 1990), 84-6.

4. The Final Interrogation

Priest:

Turns to the sponsor and asks again, "Have you joined yourself to Christ? – Συνετάξω τῷ Χριστῷ;"

Sponsor

"I have joined. – Συνεταξάμην."

Priest

"Then bow down before him and worship him. – Καὶ προσκύνησον αὐτῷ."

Sponsor

"I bow down before the Father and the Son and the Holy Spirit, the Trinity, one in essence and undivided. – Προσκυνῶ Πατέρα, Υἱόν, καὶ Ἅγιον Πνεῦμα, Τριάδα ὁμοούσιον καὶ ἀχώριστον."

5. The Call to Baptism and the Apolysis

At this point the sponsor may take the child, as long as the child remains calm.

Priest

Exclaims aloud the ekfonesis: "Blessed is God who wills that all should be..." – "Εὐλογητὸς ὁ Θεός, ὁ πάντας ἀνθρώπους...."

Chanter

Amen.

Priest

Let us pray to the Lord.

Recites the prayer – the call to Baptism, "Sovereign Master, Lord our God, call your servant (N) to your holy Illumination..." "Δέσποτα, Κύριε, ὁ Θεὸς ἡμῶν, προσκάλεσαι τὸν δοῦλόν σου τρὸς τὸ ἅγιόν σου φώτισμα...."

Then he recites the small apolysis of the Catechesis.

An Important Rubric

Priest

When the *apolysis* is completed, the priest instructs the parents and the sponsor to follow him into the nave and to come to and stand at the right side of the baptismal font. The priest then proceeds into the sanctuary and puts on his *phelonion*. He exits the sanctuary and comes to the baptismal font. He receives the censer from the sexton and censes the font, the iconostasis, and the people.

Chanter

After the apolysis of the Catechesis, as the priest, sponsor and parents enter the nave, the chanter sings the apolytikion of the feast of Theophany. During the Paschal season, he sings the Kontakion of Pascha.[90]

The Service of Baptism – Proper

1. The Enarxis

Priest

Raises the Evangelion over the baptismal font (Κολυμβήθρα) and blesses it crosswise in the usual manner as he intones the opening doxological formula: *"Blessed is the kingdom ... Εὐλογημένη ἡ βασιλεία....* [91]

Then, he presents the Evangelion to the sponsor and parents for reverencing. After this, he instructs them to be seated with the child until he calls them up again.

Priest

Intones the Great Synapte or Great Litany with the added petitions for the water and the candidate.[92]

---

90 The Euchologion does not contain such a rubric. The practice developed over time to bridge the silence between the end of the Catechesis and the beginning of the service of baptism.

91 As usual, during the Paschal season we sing the Paschal troparion after the opening doxology.

92 As already noted, if a deacon is present, the Great Synapte is said by him. As the deacon intones the Litany the priest recites in a low voice the prayer of deprecation, *"Loving and merciful God..."*

2. The Blessing of the Baptismal Font with the Associated Words and Actions

A Note on the Consecratory Prayer

The prayer for the blessing of the font is addressed to Christ and constitutes a solemn act of praise, thanksgiving, and adoration of him, whose goodness is infinite. It begins with words of praise and thanksgiving for the Son of God through whom all things were made, the wonders of which are beyond telling. The prayer also gives thanks for the wonders of divine providence, which include the loving care of creation and most especially the divine plan of salvation, climaxing in the incarnation of the Son of God, who dwelt among us and sanctified the waters of the Jordan River thereby crushing the power of the devil.

Following the remembrance of all that has come to pass for our sake, the prayer invokes (*epiclesis*) the Lord's blessing upon the baptismal water through the descent of the Holy Spirit so that it may be given the grace of redemption and the blessing of the Jordan, making it a fountain of immortality filled with angelic might and inaccessible to hostile powers; a gift of sanctification and adoption, a bath of regeneration and a garment of incorruption.

The prayer then invokes the Lord's blessing upon the candidate, that through baptism, being buried in the likeness of Christ's death, the candidate may become a partaker of his resurrection – renewed according to the image of him who created him/her. The prayer ends with a plea that the candidate, having guarded the gift of the Holy Spirit, may increase the measure of grace entrusted to him/her.[93]

Water is the primordial element of creation (Gen. 1:1) and the primary symbol of baptism because it signifies naturally all that baptism is. Water cleanses, water destroys (death), and water is life-giving. The baptismal waters are the source of purification; and the baptismal font is the place in which the mystery of death and rebirth are accomplished (John 3:3, 5). Through the baptismal waters we become participants in the death and resurrection of Christ (Rom. 6:3-14). We put off the old man in order to put on the new man (Col. 3:9-10). We become a new creation (2 Cor. 5:17).

Salvation is not to be saved from the material world but from evil (John 17:15). God created only one world, this vast cosmos of which we are a part. He created it out of nothing, the result of his uncreated will and energy; a

---

[93] The cosmology set forth in this admittedly beautiful doxological prayer is based on an antiquated world view of a three-tiered universe, heaven above the earth and hades below it. It also contains some archaic imagery which may be incomprehensible to many. See Calivas, *Aspects of Orthodox Worship*, 155-6.

world which in the beginning was very good, a gift of life for communion with God. The present evil in the world is parasitic and not part of the nature of the created order. It is the work of Satan and his cohorts, all fallen angels. As Fr. Romanides puts it, "Satan is the cause of the post-creation imperfections of the world."[94] Therefore, when we invoke the grace of the Holy Spirit upon the baptismal water, we do so not to replace it because the material world is profane, impure and defiled, but, as Fr. Schmemann tells it, "To restore it and to fulfill it as a means of communion with God. The water is consecrated to show and to be all that which matter is meant to be: a means to an end... the gift of the world as communion with God, as life, salvation, and deification."[95]

Priest

Raises his hand(s) and intones the opening phrase of the prayer for the blessing of the baptismal waters, "*You are great, O Lord and marvelous are your works ... Μέγας εἶ Κύριε, καὶ θαυμαστὰ τὰ ἔργα σου....*" This is said three times.

Chanter

At the end of each declaration, he sings "*Glory to you, O Lord, glory to you ... Δόξα σοι, Κύριε, δόξα σοι.*"

Priest

Continues the recitation of the prayer. When he reaches the phrase, "*Do you, therefore, O loving King ... Αὐτὸς οὖν, φιλάνθρωπε Βασιλεῦ....*" the priest intones the words as he dips his fingers in the water blessing it crosswise in the usual manner. The words and the action are repeated three times. At the end of each, the **chanter** sings, Amen.

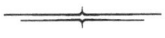

> ***A practical note:*** *While dipping his hand in the water, the priest is also able to judge its temperature. Accordingly, he will tell the sexton to add hot or cold water to the font, in order to bring the temperature to a tolerable degree of warmth for the comfort of the child (or adult catechumen).*

---

94 Romanides, *Ancestral Sin*, 60.

95 Schmemann, *Of Water and the Spirit*, 49-51. The priest prays that all hostile powers flee from the baptismal water ("Let not a demon of darkness conceal itself in this water..."), so that through the presence of the Holy Spirit it will be set apart and restored to its original purpose: "show this water to be a water of redemption, a water of sanctification... a bath of regeneration... a fountain of life."

Priest

Again, takes up the recitation of the prayer. When he comes to the phrase "*Let all adverse powers be crushed ... Συντριβήτωσαν ὑπὸ τὴν σημείωσιν...*" he intones the words as he blesses the water by dipping the *Cross of the Agiasmos* into the water crosswise. Immediately after each recitation, he also breaths upon the water crosswise.[96] The ritual is performed three times. At the end of each action, the **chanter** sings, *Amen*.

Priest

Concludes the prayer of blessing of the font.

3. Preparing the Child for Baptism

Priest

At this point, the priest asks the sponsor to come forward and to stand to his right at the right side of baptismal font.[97] He also asks the designated person(s) to take the child, disrobe it, and bring it to him naked, wrapped in the large sheet and towel usually provided by the sponsor.

Sexton

Assists the priest to pin his vestments in a way that will facilitate his movements for the ritual actions that follow. The priest also rolls up his sleeves.

Sexton

Brings the small bottle, vessel, or container of *olive oil*, which the sponsor has provided, and gives it to the priest.

Priest

Receives the vessel and breathes upon it three times and gives it to the sponsor to hold. The sponsor stands to the right of the priest.

---

96 The use of the cross used for the Agiasmos is suggested by the text: "Let all adverse powers be crushed beneath the sign of *the image* of your precious Cross." However, in many places the use of the Cross has been dispensed with. The priest blesses only with his hand.

97 At this point, if the sponsor is a male, he should take off his jacket and roll up his sleeves, so that his clothing may not be soiled.

4. The Anointing of the Font and the Child with the Oil of Gladness[98]

Priest

Reads the prayer for the oil, "*Master, Lord God ... Δέσποτα, Κύριε, ὁ Θεός....*" He blesses the oil with his hand making the sign of the cross over it as he says the words, "*Do you yourself bless also this oil by the might ... Αὐτὸς εὐλόγησον καὶ τοῦτο τὸ ἔλαιον...*"

Priest

When he finishes the prayer, he takes the vessel from the sponsor. Holding it in his right hand he *pours some oil into the font crosswise*, as he intones the words: "*Let us be attentive... Πρόσχωμεν!*" The words and action are repeated three times.

Chanter

Responds by singing, "*Alleluia... Ἀλληλούϊα*" (three times after each pronouncement).

Priest

Intones the doxological formula, "*Blessed is God, who enlightens and sanctifies... Εὐλογητὸς ὁ Θεός, ὁ φωτίζων καὶ ἁγιάζων...*"

Priest

Instructs the sponsor to cup his/her hands, right over left, holding them over the font. He pours some oil into the cupped hands of the sponsor and instructs him/her how to anoint the child with the oil at the appropriate time.

---

98   The term, "*Oil of Gladness,*" is derived from the verse the priest uses to commence the first anointing of the catechumen, "The servant of God (N) is anointed with the Oil of Gladness, in the name of the Father..." The Church uses olive oil for a variety of purposes for its symbolic value. In antiquity olive oil was used widely for medicinal purposes. Hence, it became the essential element of the sacrament of Holy Unction. Oil was also used in lamps to provide light. Therefore, it came to symbolize light and by extension knowledge, illumination, truth, and joy. In ancient times athletes rubbed oil on their bodies to strengthen them and to make them slippery (a form of armor), so that it would be difficult for their adversaries to grasp and hold them. In the Old Testament persons and objects were consecrated through the pouring of anointing oil (Ex. 29:7; 30:25-31). The pouring of oil on the baptismal water signifies the consecrating presence of the Holy Spirit who gifts the water with spiritual power and life – reminiscent of the creation narrative, "In the beginning God created the heavens and the earth...and the Spirit of God was moving over the face of the waters" (Gen. 1:1, 2). The oil is also a sign of reconciliation and salvation, as noted in the prayer, "Master, Lord God of our fathers to those who were in the ark of Noah you sent a dove, bearing in its beak an olive twig, a token of reconciliation and of salvation from the flood." For more on the use of oil see *The Oil of Gladness: Anointing in the Christian Tradition*, Martin Dudley and Geoffrey Rowell, eds. (Collegeville, MN 1993).

The designated person(s) bring the child to the priest. He unfolds the sheet and towel in which the child is wrapped and commences *the anointing of the child with the Oil of Gladness* on various parts of the body.[99]

Holding the three fingers of his right hand in the manner by which he crosses himself, the priest dips them into the oil held by the sponsor in his/her cupped hands. He anoints the child crosswise with the blessed oil on the parts of the body specified in the text. Each anointing is accompanied by an appropriate verse.[100]

The anointing begins with the forehead with the liturgical formula *"The servant of God (N) is anointed with the Oil of Gladness in the Name of the Father... Χρίεται ὁ δοῦλος (ἡ δούλη) τοῦ Θεοῦ...."*

Priest

When he completes the anointing, he wipes his hands on the sheet covering the child. He picks up the child gently holding him/her under the armpits. The child should be facing forward with its back to the priest. He holds the child over the font and invites the sponsor to commence the anointing as previously instructed by the priest.

Sponsor

Quickly begins anointing the body of the child with the oil as previously instructed by the priest. When the anointing is finished, the sponsor steps back.

Sexton

Immediately drapes the baptismal sheet/towel over the outstretched hands of the sponsor, who will receive the child from the priest after it has been baptized.

---

99 Inasmuch as each human being is a unique embodied personal existence – soul and body – the anointing of specific parts of the body signifies the healing of the impaired faculties of the soul and the bodily senses. This is emphasized by the biblical verses which accompany each anointing, as for example, the breast: *"For the healing of body and soul;"* the ears, *"For the hearing of faith;"* the hands, *"Your hands have made me and fashioned me;"* the feet, *"That he (she) may walk in the ways of your commandments."*

100 The parts of the body which the priest anoints are not the same in all the texts. The longest list I have encountered includes: the forehead, breast, ears, nose, lips, hands, feet, soles, and the back between the shoulders.

5. The Baptism – The Triple Immersion and Emersion

"The source of every evil stream was once cured by Elisha, the very wise prophet. He treated the waters; their taste had the plague of bareness (2 Kings 2:19-22). But even though the waters were cured and changed, they did not know how to purify sins and renew the spirit. However, baptismal waters learned this: they both purified all men and they were for all who were born a bath of rebirth."[101]

The baptismal font is both a tomb and a womb. It is the place in which the "old man" is buried and the "new man" is born. In baptism we partake of the death, burial and, resurrection of Christ and are incorporated into him to share in his deified humanity, to come under his rule, and day by day grow to become like him, as we read in the prayer for the blessing of the baptismal waters. *"You have granted us rebirth from on high by water and the Spirit (cf. John 3:3-6). Manifest yourself in this water, Lord, and grant that he (she) who is baptized in it may be transformed, casting off the former creature... to be clothed in the new which is renewed in the image of his/her Creator (cf. 2 Cor. 5:17; Ephes. 4:22-24). Thus, being buried in the likeness of your death through baptism, he (she) may likewise became a partaker of your resurrection (cf. Rom. 6:3-11), and having guarded the gift of the Holy Spirit, and increased the measure of grace entrusted to him/her may receive the prize..."* (cf. Ephes. 4:7, 13).

Baptism also incorporates us into the Church, the mystical body of Christ (cf. Acts 2:41), which is itself a sacrament, the very sign of Christ's presence in the world. In baptism we are united not only with Christ but also with his people. We are baptized into a faith community to share its life, doctrines, values, vision, and mission. We enter into and are received by the Church, not just by accepting some theoretical principles, but through a bodily act – baptism – by which we are graced with the newness of life, vivified and sanctified by the Holy Spirit, so that we ourselves may become a sacrament, a sign of the resurrectional life. *"I have been crucified with Christ. It is no longer I who live, but Christ lives in me; and the life which I now live in the flesh I live by faith in the Son of God, who loved me and gave himself for me"* (Gal. 2:20).

---

101 St. Romanos the Melodist, *Kontakion on Baptism*, strophe 8.

The rite of baptism is centered on the example of Christ (Matt. 3:13-17; 28:19-20) and especially on the words of Christ (John 3:5 and Matt. 8:19). Thus, the triple immersion in water and the Trinitarian formula became the constituent elements of the sacrament from the earliest days.[102]

The Greek word βαπτίζω means to dip, immerse, or plunge into water (or some other liquid). It does not necessarily mean to submerge. In the case of adult converts when it is feasible the whole body is immersed. In the case of infants, it is sufficient to immerse the body in the water up the shoulders and to pour water with the hand over the head of the infant.[103]

The Trinitarian formula which has come down to us, based on the command of Christ (Matt. 28:19), is the following:

Βαπτίζεται ὁ δοῦλος (ἡ δούλη) τοῦ Θεοῦ (δεῖνα) εἰς τὸ ὄνομα τοῦ Πατρός. Ἀμήν. Καὶ τοῦ Υἱοῦ. Ἀμήν. Καὶ τοῦ Ἁγίου Πνεύματος. Ἀμήν.

The servant of God (N) is baptized in the name of the Father. Amen. And of the Son. Amen. And of the Holy Spirit. Amen.

---

102 By way of example see *The Didache*, chapter 7: "Regarding baptism, baptize thus. After giving the foregoing instructions, baptize in the name of the Father and of the Son and of the Holy Spirit in running water. But, if you have no running water, baptize in any other; and, if you cannot in cold water, then in warm. But, if the one is lacking, pour the other three times on the head in the name of the Father and Son and Holy Spirit. But before the baptism, let the one who baptizes and the one to be baptized fast, and any others who are able to do so. And you shall require the person being baptized to fast for one or two days." Admittedly, the complete immersion of an adult is preferable but as the author of the *Didache* points out it is not always feasible or practical. The symbolism of a complete immersion is obvious, as we read in the writings of Pseudo-Dionysios: "[I]t is quite appropriate to hide the initiate completely in the water as an image of death...By his triple immersion and emersion he imitates, as far as the imitation of God is possible to men, the divine death of one who was three days and nights in the tomb, the life-giving Jesus..." *Ecclesiastical Hierarchy*, Chapter One: *iii*, 5. As archeological and iconographical evidence suggests, fonts often were (and are) too shallow to permit total immersion. See, *Study of Liturgy*, 137; J. G. Davies, *The Architectural Setting of Baptism* (London 1962); R. Krautheimer, *Early Christian and Byzantine Architecture* (Baltimore, MD 1965).

103 When baptizing an older child who cannot be picked up or is unable to fit into the regular baptismal font, or when baptizing an adult and the church does not have a large enough font, it is best to do something like the following. Bless the water in the regular baptismal font. Place an auxiliary large plastic or metal container which is fairly wide and a foot, or so, deep next to the font. This container should be stored and used only for this purpose. After the first anointing with the Oil of Gladness have the child or the adult step into the container. Then, with a large pitcher draw water from the consecrated font and pour it over the head of the candidate three times using the Trinitarian formula.

Priest

When the anointing of the body has been completed, he holds the child upright and facing forward ("east"), he begins the triple immersion. ***He immerses the child after each invocation and raises him/her again.*** (After each immersion or after the third he pours water over the head of the child).

Priest

When he has completed the baptism, he places the child in the outstretched arms of the sponsor on which the baptismal sheet or towel is spread out. He gently dries the face of the child and covers him/her with the sheet. The priest dries his hands on the corner of the sheet. The sexton gives him his service book.

Chanter

Immediately after the triple immersion and emersion, he sings the verses of Psalm 31/32. In current practice, it is customary to sing only the first verse three times: "Μακάριοι ὧν ἀφέθησαν αἱ ἀνομίαι, καὶ ὧν ἐπεκαλύφθησαν αἱ ἁμαρτίαι ... Blessed are they whose transgressions are forgiven, and whose sins are covered."[104]

The Office of Chrismation

As I have noted elsewhere, chrismation is the second of the three sacraments of initiation, in which the entire mystery of the new life in Christ is made manifest and accessible.[105] It is conferred on the newly baptized (adult or infant) immediately after baptism to impart the gift of the Holy Spirit and signify the Spirit's indwelling presence. The *chrism* – a mixture of olive oil, wine, and a large number of prescribed aromatic substances symbolizing the diverse gifts of the Holy Spirit – is prepared and consecrated in a special service periodically on Holy Thursday by the Ecumenical Patriarchate and distributed to parishes by the local hierarch. Chrism is also used to consecrate churches and to receive baptized converts from certain other churches.

---

104 Psalm 31/32 is counted among the penitential psalms. Its emphasis on the confession of sin and on God's readiness to forgive and heal the repentant sinner may be appropriate for adult baptisms but not for infants, in view of what was said above about infants and sin. Perhaps, the Church may wish to consider replacing this verse with another from the same psalm for infant baptisms: "I will instruct you and teach you the way you should go; I will counsel you with my eye upon you" (verse 8); or (verse 11), "Be glad in the Lord, and rejoice, O righteous, and shout for joy, all you upright in heart."

105 See the entry, "Chrismation" in *The Cambridge Dictionary of Christianity*, Daniel Patte, ed. (Cambridge University Press, 2010), 210.

The oils of chrism are consecrated only by a hierarch. The priest administers the sacrament by anointing the neophyte with the pre-sanctified *Holy Myron* (Μύρον, *aromatic oil*), another name for the chrism. Through the ritual anointing, which signifies the coming of the Holy Spirit, the events of the Jordan (Mark 1:9-11) and of Pentecost (Acts 2:1-4) become a personal experience for every neophyte.[106] The anointing is also an act of ordination. The neophyte enters into the order of the laity, which is one of the constitutive orders of the Church together with those of the episcopate, presbyterate, and diaconate.[107]

Chrismation is also called the *Seal* or *Sphragis* (Σφραγίς). Through the ritual anointing the neophyte is sealed or branded, marked forever as the servant and friend of Christ, as one who belongs to his flock (cf. 2 Cor. 1:22; 1 John 2:20, 26-27.). Hence, Chrismation is sometimes called the perfecting anointing because it confers the visitation of the divine Spirit, who acts to make us Christ-bearers and transparencies of God.[108]

The gift being bestowed at Chrismation is one, the Holy Spirit: "Beware of supposing this to be plain ointment. For as the Bread of the Eucharist, after the invocation of the Holy Spirit, is mere bread no longer, but the Body of Christ, so also this holy chrism is no more simple ointment, nor common, after the invocation, but the gift of Christ; and by the presence of his Godhead, it causes in us the Holy Spirit…. And while the body is anointed with visible chrism, your soul is sanctified by the holy and life-giving Spirit."[109]

---

106 See St. Cyril of Jerusalem, *Lectures on the Christian Sacraments*, Mystagogical Catechesis III:1-2: "Having been baptized into Christ and put on Christ, you have been made conformable (σύμμορφοι) to the Son of God…. Being therefore made partakers of Christ, you are properly called *christs* (χριστοί), and of you God said, 'Touch not my christs', or anointed. Now you were made *christs* by receiving the emblem (ἀντίτυπον - *antitype*); and all things were in a figure wrought in you because you are images (εἰκόνες) of Christ. He also bathed himself in the river Jordan…. He came up from them and the Holy Spirit in substance lighted upon him, like resting upon like (τῷ ὁμοίῳ ἐπαναπαυομένου τοῦ ὁμοίου). In the same manner to you also, after you had come up from the pool of sacred streams, was given the chrism (χρίσμα), the antitype (emblem) of that wherewith Christ was anointed; and this is the Holy Spirit."

107 See Calivas, *Church, Clergy, Laity, and the Spiritual Life*, 18-21.

108 See, for example, Pseudo-Dionysios, "The Ecclesiastical Hierarchy," 4:484A – 485A in *Pseudo-Dionysios: The Complete Works* (The Classics of Western Spirituality – New York and Mahwah, NJ, 1987), 231-2.

109 Cyril, *Mystagogical Catechesis* III, 3.

The Prayer and the Anointing

Priest

Having completed the triple immersion and emersion, he reads the prayer of the Holy Myron over the newly baptized infant which is still in the arms of the sponsor: "Εὐλογητὸς εἶ, Κύριε, ὁ Θεὸς ὁ Παντοκράτωρ, ἡ πηγὴ τῶν ἀγαθῶν… *Blessed are you, Lord God Almighty, source of all good things…*" (The same procedure applies to adults).[110]

Sexton

Brings and holds the vessel with the Holy Myron.

Priest

Removes the applicator from the vessel and begins anointing the body of the newly baptized starting with the forehead. He marks it with the sign of the cross as he intones the liturgical formula: "Σφραγὶς δωρεᾶς Πνεύματος Ἁγίου. Ἀμήν. …*The seal of the gift of the Holy Spirit. Amen.*" After the forehead, the priest also anoints the breast, ears, and nostrils, repeating each time the same exact formula, "Σφραγὶς δωρεᾶς… *The seal of the gift…*"[111]

The Robing[112]

Sexton

Gives the priest the baptismal garment or more usually another new article of clothing (an undershirt) provided by the sponsor (or parents).

Priest

Takes the garment and places it on the newly baptized saying, "Ἐνδύεται ὁ δοῦλος (ἡ δούλη) τοῦ Θεοῦ (Ὄνομα)… *The servant of God (Name) is clothed…*"

---

110 For practical reasons, the true order of the service at this point has been truncated. Immediately after the baptism, the neophyte is anointed with the Holy Myron, tonsured, and robed. The priest reads the associated prayers sequentially in a low voice while the child is being dressed. In spite of the prevailing "short cut" practice, the maintenance of the proper liturgical order should always be preferred and followed.

111 Some also anoint the lips, hands, feet, and back. However, the more limited anointing is in keeping with the ancient practice recorded in the *Mystagogical Catecheses* (III, 3-4) of St. Cyril of Jerusalem: "You were first anointed on your forehead…then on your ears…then on your nostrils…then on your breast…"

112 In ancient times at adult baptisms the robbing preceded the anointing for reasons of modesty. This order is still found in many Euchologia. The robbing after baptism and before chrismation is symbolic of the new and restored nature that is now ready and capable of receiving the Holy Spirit.

Chanter

Sings the troparion of the robbing three times, "Χιτῶνά μοι παράσχου φωτεινόν... *Give unto me a shining robe...*"

Priest

As the hymn is sung, he directs the assigned attendant(s) to take the child and dress him/her in the baptismal garments.[113]

Chanter

According to custom, after the hymn of robbing, he sings the *katavasiai* of the Feast of the Exaltation of the Cross and during the Paschal season, the katavasiai of Pascha.

Priest and Sponsor

Wash their hands over the font with the assistance of the sexton. The sponsor then returns to the pew and sits with the parents, awaiting further instructions from the priest. The priest enters the sanctuary and prepares the vessels for the distribution of Holy Communion from the reserved Sacrament. He returns to the font and recites in a low voice the prayers of ablution.[114] Then he invites the sponsor to come forward and asks him/her to stand on the other side of baptismal font facing him. He gives the sponsor a candle to hold. He recites the prayer of the tonsure, which also contains words of blessing for the sponsor. The priest also invites the parents or two other persons to come forward to hold candles and participate in the procession around the font.

---

[113] Traditionally, baptismal garments are white (Ecclesiastes 9:8). See St. Cyril, *Mystagogical Catechesis* IV: 8: "Before you came to baptism, your works were vanity of vanities. But now, having put off the old garments, and put on those which are spiritually white, you must be continually robed in white; we mean not this, that you must always wear white raiment; but with truly white and glistening and spiritual attire, you must be clothed withal, that you may say with the blessed Isaiah [61:10], 'My soul shall exult in my God; for he has clothed me with the garments of salvation, he has covered me with the robe of righteousness'". Also, by tradition, the sticharion of a hierarch and priest is usually white or another bright color since symbolically it is considered an extension of the baptismal garment. Significantly, the words of the prophet Isaiah cited above are said when a hierarch or priest wears the sticharion.

[114] These prayers and the prayer for the tonsure belong to the rites of the eighth day after baptism. They have now been incorporated into the baptismal rite for the sake of brevity. In many places their related rituals are performed out of sequence.

NOTE: *From this point on to the end of the service, there are many variations both in the printed texts and in the practices of local churches. What follows is based, to the degree possible, on the original structure of the baptismal rite. The subsequent elements are related to the Eucharist and to the rites of the eighth day after baptism, which were once integral to the baptismal rite. Hopefully, at some point in the future, our Eparchial Synod will establish a proper common practice.*

The Procession

When the child has been dressed in the baptismal garments, he or she is brought to the priest by the attendant(s). The priest places the baptismal cross around the neck of the child. For reasons of practicality, the priest may choose to have the attendant(s) put the cross on the child. The child is then given to the sponsor to hold, if practicable.[115] The participants gather around the baptismal font, holding candles. The sponsor stands opposite the priest. The other two stand to the right and left of the font facing each other. At the signal of the priest, they process slowly around the font three times singing the baptismal troparion, "Ὅσοι εἰς Χριστόν.... *As many as have been baptized into Christ have put on Christ. Alleluia*" (Gal. 3:27). The troparion is sung three times. Then we say "Glory to the Father.... Now and forever.... have put on Christ. Alleluia. Δύναμις!" Then we sing the entire troparion again. During the circular procession around the font, the priest censes. After the third round he censes the icons on the iconostasis and the people. Then, depending on the position of the font in the church, he leads the sponsor and the parents to the steps in front of the Holy Doors. The sponsor stands in the middle holding the child with the parents on either side. All face the sanctuary. The priest enters the sanctuary. Of course, if the church has a baptistery or a permanent font within a chapel or a chapel-like setting, these movements are applied accordingly. In other words, the movements should be suited to the setting.

Remnants of the Eucharistic

The baptismal troparion, "Ὅσοι εἰς Χριστόν," the two biblical readings, and the fervent litany that follow are all remnants of the Eucharistic celebration, which until late antiquity completed the rites of initiation. Following baptism and chrismation, the neophytes were led from the baptistery into the church with

---

[115] If the child is uneasy and crying, it is best for the mother or father to hold the child while standing next to the sponsor. Common sense should prevail.

song to join the faithful at the Eucharistic celebration where they would hear the Word of God, participate in the service, and receive Holy Communion. The procession that is conducted around the font is a remnant of the procession that took place from the baptistery into the nave.

Scripture Readings

The first biblical lesson is from the Epistle of Paul to the Romans (6:3-11). It is introduced by a *prokeimenon*, verses from Psalm 26/27:1. The second lesson is from the Gospel of Matthew (28:16-20). Both pericopes are replete with baptismal motifs. The two pericopes are also read at the Divine Liturgy of the Pascal Vigil,[116] which in antiquity was considered the foremost time for the celebration of the baptismal rites. The chanter or reader, as usual, reads the Epistle, receives the peace, and sings the prokeimenon of the Gospel, i.e., the alleluia with the appropriate verses. The priest gives the blessing of peace and reads the Gospel lesson in the usual manner.

The Fervent Litany

Immediately after the Gospel lesson, the priest stands in front of the Holy Table and intones the assigned petitions of the fervent litany.

Holy Communion

Following the fervent litany, the chanter sings the communion hymn, "*Taste and see that the Lord is good. Alleluia.*"[117] The priest comes forward and administers Holy Communion to the neophyte.[118]

The Eighth-Day Rites

The rites that follow were once performed on the eighth day after baptism but are now part of the same baptismal service and are conducted immediately after the administration of Holy Communion. In earlier times, during the entire week after baptism the neophytes were taught the meaning of the three

---

116 To be precise, at the Divine Liturgy of the Paschal Vigil, Chapter 28 of the Gospel of Matthew is read in its entirety and not just verses 16-20.

117 This communion hymn is mentioned in the *Mystagogical Catechesis* of Cyril of Jerusalem, V: 20.

118 To administer communion, the priest places a tiny amount of the eucharistic elements from the Reserved Sacrament on the communion spoon by mingling a bit of wine with a tiny morsel of the Pre-sanctified Gifts. If, however, the baptism is held immediately after the Divine Liturgy, he administers Holy Communion directly from the chalice in the usual manner.

holy sacraments in which they had just participated. They were also exhorted to strive in life for spiritual excellence through the practice of virtuous actions commensurate to the grace they have received.[119] During the week they also refrained from bathing. The purpose of this was to allow the baptismal oils and the chrism with which their bodies were anointed to be absorbed internally, so that the mysteries they signified would become inner realities. The rites of the eighth day are three: the ablution (washing), the laying on of hands, and the tonsure, all of which are accompanied by prayer.

The Ablution

After Holy Communion has been administered, the sexton gives the priest a clean cloth (a towel) the end of which has been dipped in clean water. The priest proceeds to "wash," wipe gently the face of the child, saying the following words: *"Ἐβαπτίσθης, ἐφωτίσθης, ἐμυρώθης, ἡγιάσθης, ἀπελούσθης.... You have been baptized; you have been illuminated; you have been anointed with chrism; you have been sanctified and washed, in the name of the Father and of the Son and of the Holy Spirit. Amen."* The priest returns the cloth to the sexton.[120]

The Laying on of Hands

After this, the priest gives the blessing of peace and bids the people to bow their heads. Then he says, "Let us pray to the Lord," and proceeds to read the prayer, *"Κύριε ὁ Θεός, ὁ ἐκ τοῦ πληρώματος τῆς κολυμβήθρας... Lord our God, who through the fullness of the baptismal font..."* As he begins reading the prayer, the priest places his right hand on the head of the neophyte. "... and as you blessed David the king through the prophet Samuel, so bless the head of your servant (N) by the hand of me the sinner..." The prayer is a prayer of blessing ("...and let your blessing rest upon his/her head..."); and an invocation (epiclesis) of the Holy Spirit ("...visiting him/her with your Holy Spirit, that he (she) may increase unto maturity...").

---

119 See for example, Cyril, *Mystagogical Catechesis* III:7: "Having been anointed, therefore, with this holy myrrh (μύρον), keep it unspotted and unblemished in you, pressing forward by good works, and becoming well-pleasing to the leader of your salvation, Christ Jesus, to whom be glory forever and ever. Amen."

120 The prayers for the ablution were read earlier in anticipation, while the child was being dressed with the baptismal garments.

The Tonsure

The last act is the tonsure. The priest snips a bit of the neophyte's hair crosswise with a small scissor, the edges of which should be blunted for reasons of safety. He gives the snips of hair to the sexton who disposes them in the font. When performing the tonsure the priest uses the formula, *"Κείρεται ὁ δοῦλος (ἡ δούλη) τοῦ Θεοῦ (Ο)... The servant of God (N) is shorn in the name of the Father..."* As noted initially, the tonsure is a sign of servitude. It also constitutes an offering which does not require the mutilation of the human body. For reasons of brevity, some clergy read the prayer for the tonsure in anticipation while the child is being dressed.[121]

The Apolysis

After this the priest conducts the apolysis in the usual manner.

He offers the parents and the sponsor his blessings and best wishes and bids the parents to receive their child, now newly baptized and illumined, from the sponsor. By custom the parents kiss the hand of the sponsor as a sign of respect and gratitude.

The priest may also wish to give the parents a small icon – a gift from the parish to the neophyte. The child's birthday and date of baptism may be inscribed on the back of the icon.

The Baptismal Certificate

The priest makes certain the sponsor signs the *Baptismal Certificate*. He gives the original signed certificate to the sponsor(s) in a marked envelope so that they may give it to the parents for safe-keeping. It is an official document. Copies of the certificate are deposited in the church office and the proper entry is made in the Baptismal Registry Book of the parish. A copy of the certificate is forwarded to the local metropolis.

---

121 As previously noted, many priests today perform the tonsure immediately after they have anointed the child with the holy chrism and not at the end of the service, thus fusing the "eighth-day rites" to the rite of baptism.

The Service for an Adult Baptism

The received rites of baptism are meant for the unbaptized children of Orthodox parents and for non-Christians, for converts from other religions (Judaism, Islam, Hinduism, Buddhism, etc.), for pagans, for sectarians, and for heretics in the strict sense.[122] A sufficient period of instruction in the dogmas, morals, discipline, and liturgy of the Church should precede the baptism of adult converts. The candidate should have a sponsor, preferably of the same sex, who attests to the candidate's good character and affirms the earnest desire of the candidate to receive holy baptism and to be counted a member of the Orthodox Church. The sponsor also pledges to help the candidate grow in the life of Christ within the Church. At the service the sponsor will assist with the anointing of the candidate. According to ancient custom, an adult candidate should fast for several days before the baptism.

The candidate should be instructed to bring suitable garments, including a modest bathing suit or gown and an appropriate baptismal suit or dress to be worn after baptism.

For adult baptisms, the priest makes the same preparations for the service as he does for infants. The catechesis is conducted in the usual place and manner, except that the renunciations and the adherences are performed by the candidate, who also recites the Creed.

---

[122] See Alkiviadis Calivas, "Receiving Converts into the Orthodox Church: Lessons from the Canonical and Liturgical Tradition," in his, *Liturgy in Dialogue*, 141-201. Given the opportunity to receive an adult convert from another religion through baptism, the received baptismal rites, *with the local hierarch's permission*, could be celebrated as they were intended, at different stages in the initiation process. What follows is a broad outline only for *the reception and baptism of a convert from another religion or no religion*: The Prayer of Inscription is read over the candidate at the beginning of the period of instruction. The three exorcisms are read at different intervals during the instruction period. On the day before or on the day of baptism, the priest reads the fourth prayer (the exorcism) and conducts the rites of renunciation and adherence, the candidate recites the Creed, followed by the call to baptism. At the appropriate time, the candidate changes into the garment agreed upon in preparation for the baptism. The priest conducts the rites of the font, the anointing with the Oil of Gladness, the baptism, the robing, and the chrismation. After the baptism, the neophyte changes into his/her baptismal garments and returns to the nave with the sponsor to participate in the Divine Liturgy and receive Holy Communion. Meanwhile, the priest begins the Divine Liturgy with the Prayer of the Trisagion after which the choir or chanter sings the baptismal hymn, "*As many as have been baptized into Christ...*" At the conclusion of the Divine Liturgy, before the apolysis, the priest calls the candidate forward and conducts the rites of the eighth day. After the apolysis the priest says words of welcome and blessings to the neophyte and invites the congregation to welcome the newly-baptized Christian into the community. If it is doable, the eighth-day rites may be conducted on the eighth day after baptism; if not they could be conducted at the end of the Divine Liturgy on the same day of the baptism.

As indicated above, in the absence of a baptismal font fit for an adult, the church should have a special movable wide and fairly deep container into which the candidate can step in easily. The container should be placed next to the baptismal font. The water is sanctified in the baptismal font according to the prescribed rituals. At the appointed time the candidate is anointed with the Oil of Gladness and steps into the container and faces the sanctuary. The priest draws water from the font with a pitcher three times. Using the baptismal formula, "*The servant of God (N) is baptized in the name of the Father. Amen. And of the Son. Amen. And of the Holy Spirit. Amen.*" He pours water over the head of the candidate three times, as he invokes each of the three divine Names. A sufficient amount of water should be used to simulate, to the degree possible, an immersion.

Immediately after the baptism, the neophyte is robed. The priest reads the Prayer of the Holy Chrism/Myron and anoints the neophyte with the holy chrism in the manner noted above. Similarly, the remainder of the service is conducted as previously noted.

Clinical Baptism

In an emergency, when the life of an unbaptized infant, child, or adult is in danger of imminent death, the priest uses a modified version of the baptismal rite. If the clinical baptism is to take place in a hospital, the priest must take care to follow the instructions of the staff.

The priest wears his exorasson or anteri and an epitrachelion. If it is necessary to wear a hospital gown and mask, the priest may wear only the epitrachilion. In some cases he may be required to also use disposable gloves. He discards the gloves, mask, and gown after the baptism according to hospital procedures.

In some instances the infant in danger may be in an incubator. In other instances the person to be baptized may be under the constant supervision of nurses and physicians. In such instances, the priest must use good judgment and common sense.

To perform the service, the priest takes with him a small bottle with olive oil and another filled with Holy Water (from the *Great Agiasmos*).[123] If water from the Great Agiasmos is not available, the priest blesses and uses ordinary clean water.

The service for a clinical baptism may vary from the simplest form to a longer form, depending on the circumstance.[124]

---

123 From year to year, parish clergy usually reserve one or more bottles of the *Great Agiasmos*, which is consecrated annually on January 6, the feast of Theophany or Epiphany.

124 See Ioannis Fountoulis, Τελετουργικὰ Θέματα, Vol. 1 (Athens, 2002), 313-7.

The short form when time is of the essence

Priest

"Εὐλογημένη ἡ Βασιλεία.... Blessed is the kingdom...."

Priest

Breathes three times on the person, saying, "'Εξέλασον ἀπ' αὐτοῦ (αὐτῆς).... Expel from him (her) every evil and impure spirit...."

Priest

"Sovereign Master, Lord our God, call your servant (N) to your holy illumination and count him/her worthy of the great grace of Holy Baptism. Fill him with the power of your Holy Spirit for union with your Christ, that he (she) may no longer be a child of the body, but a child of your kingdom, through the goodness and grace of your only-begotten Son with whom you are blessed together with your all-holy, good, and life-creating Spirit, now and forever and unto the ages of ages. Amen."[125]

Priest

Takes the bottle with the water from the Great Agiasmos (holy water from the Service of the Greater Blessing of the Waters) and pours or sprinkles drops of water on the head of the person as he invokes each divine Name when he intones the baptismal formula, "Βαπτίζεται ὁ δοῦλος (ἡ δούλη.... The servant of God (N) is baptized in the name of the Father. Amen. And of the Son. Amen. And of the Holy Spirit. Amen."

Priest

*Sings in a low voice, "Ὅσοι εἰς Χριστόν.... As many as have been baptized **into** Christ have put on Christ. Alleluia."*

Priest

Have mercy on us, O God, according to your steadfast love, we pray you, hear us and have mercy.

Again we pray for mercy, life, peace, health, and salvation of your newly-illumined servant (N), for his/her sponsor, parents, and all who have gathered here for this holy sacrament.

---

125 This is the last prayer of the catechesis, the call to baptism.

For you are a merciful and loving God and to you we give glory, to the Father, and the Son, and the Holy Spirit. Amen.

Priest

Turns to the newly baptized and making the sign of the cross over him/her says: "*The grace of our Lord Jesus Christ and the love of God and Father and the communion of the Holy Spirit be with you (N).*

Priest

Performs the apolysis.

The longer form when circumstances permit

Priest

"Εὐλογημένη ἡ Βασιλεία…. Blessed is the kingdom…."

Reads the Prayer of Exorcism, "'Ο ὤν Δέσποτα, Κύριε, ὁ ποιήσας τὸν ἄνθρωπον…. *Sovereign Master and Lord, you created man in your own image….*"[126]

After this, if time and circumstances permit, the priest performs the renunciations, the adherence and the Creed. If the candidate can answer for themselves let them do so, if not let the sponsor or the parents or another Orthodox Christian do it. If time does not permit, recite only the Creed.

Priest

Reads the prayer, "Sovereign Master, Lord our God, call your servant (N) to your holy illumination and count him/her worthy of the great grace of holy baptism. Fill him with the power of your Holy Spirit for union with your Christ, that he (she) may no longer be a child of the body, but a child of your kingdom, through the goodness and grace of your only-begotten Son with whom you are blessed together with your all-holy, good, and life-creating Spirit, now and forever and unto the ages of ages. Amen."

Priest

If time permits, he recites the *Prayer for the Oil of Gladness* and *anoints* the person with the oil on the forehead using the liturgical formula. If time is of the essence, he omits the prayer but anoints the child/adult with the oil.

---

126 This is the fourth prayer – the exorcism in the received rite of baptism.

Priest

Takes the bottle with water from the Great Agiasmos and pours or sprinkles drops of water on the head of the person as he invokes each divine Name when intoning the baptismal formula, "Βαπτίζεται ὁ δοῦλος (ἡ δούλη)... *The servant of God (N) is baptized in the name of the Father. Amen. And of the Son. Amen. And of the Holy Spirit. Amen.*"

Priest

Sings in a low voice, "Ὅσοι εἰς Χριστόν.... *As many as have been baptized into Christ have put on Christ. Alleluia.*"

Priest

Have mercy on us, O God, according to your steadfast love, we pray you, hear us and have mercy.

Again we pray for mercy, life, peace, health, and salvation of your newly-illumined servant (N), for his/her sponsor, parents, and for all who have come together for this holy sacrament.

For you are a merciful and loving God and to you we give glory, to the Father, and the Son, and the Holy Spirit. Amen.

Priest

Turns to the newly baptized and making the sign of the cross over him/her says: "*The grace of our Lord Jesus Christ and the love of God and Father and the communion of the Holy Spirit be with you (N).*"

Priest

Conducts the apolysis.

Important Notes:

The priest takes time to talk with the neophyte depending on his/her age and the parents or other relatives of the neophyte. He comforts and counsels them accordingly.

The priest also discreetly takes the essential information to complete a baptismal certificate when he returns to his office. He records the baptism in the Parish Registry of Baptisms with an appropriate note. He retains the original certificate and gives it to the parents or the next of kin, when he deems it appropriate. He reports the baptism to the local metropolis as he is obliged to do with all baptisms he performs.

Should the person survive, the priest completes the service as indicated below at which time he gives the parents or the next of kin the certificate of baptism.

*If the person who has undergone a clinical baptism survives, he or she is brought to the church to be anointed with holy chrism and to complete the other rituals of the service. In such instances, **no** immersion takes place! The service begins with the Prayer for Chrismation followed by the anointing of the body with the holy chrism. If the surviving person is an infant or child, he or she is undressed from the waist up and is wrapped in a sheet or blanket. After the anointing the child is dressed in the baptismal garments and the service continues to the end as described above. If the surviving person is an adult male, he wears a shirt sufficiently open at the collar; if an adult female, she wears a blouse or dress sufficiently open at the collar, so that it is easy for the priest to anoint the upper chest of the neophyte with the chrism.*

The So-Called Aero-Baptism Performed by a Lay Person

In an extreme emergency when no priest is available and a child or an adult is in danger of imminent death, it may happen that a lay person baptizes the person in the name of the Holy Trinity. In the case of infants this is usually done by lifting the child in the air three times, hence the term aero-baptism. The priest is obliged to examine the circumstances of such a baptism carefully. In any case, should the child or adult survive, the entire service of baptism is performed by the priest in the church.

The Reception of Converts by Chrismation

The Greek Orthodox Archdiocese of America has a rite of conversion by which non-Orthodox Christians with valid baptism (by economy or otherwise) are united to the Orthodox Church. The service of reception is included in *The Priest's Handbook*.[127] Other jurisdictions have similar rites. Forms of the service are also found in liturgical texts published by individuals.

For more on the canonical and liturgical tradition regarding the reception of converts see my article, "Receiving Converts into the Orthodox Church: Lessons from the Canonical and Liturgical Tradition," in my study, *Liturgy*

---

[127] *The Priest's Handbook* (New York, 1987) was issued by Archbishop Iakovos as a guide for priests.

in Dialogue.[128] The article concludes with a proposed service of reception by chrismation for non-Orthodox Christians whose churches and confessions affirm the doctrine of the Holy Trinity and the divinity of Christ and baptize by water in the name of the Father and of the Son and of the Holy Spirit.[129]

The proposed service has been submitted respectfully to the Holy Eparchial Synod of the Greek Orthodox Archdiocese of America for study and approval.[130] The proposed service is an expanded version of the one found in *The Priest's Handbook*. Its structure is based on the rite promulgated by the Synod of 1484 and the rite in the *Barberini Codex*.

Regarding the reception of Oriental Orthodox Christians, the historical and canonical record is clear, however ambiguous the relations between the churches may be in any given time. The standard or normative practice for reception of these Christians was established by the Penthekte Ecumenical Synod and confirmed by the liturgical practice of the Church.[131] In accordance, therefore, with the decision of the Penthekte Synod, Nestorian and Monophysite Christians should be received by a confession of faith and a *libellus* only, having first been properly catechized.[132]

---

128 The volume, *The Liturgy in Dialogue*, was published by Holy Cross Orthodox Press in 2018. In it the reader will find references to the works of several other authors who have also written on the subject. The article discusses the prevailing approaches to reception, analyzes the historical record, explores the principle of ecclesial economy, examines the question of heresy, and analyzes the several services of reception now in use among the Orthodox jurisdictions in America, and, as noted, offers for review a new Service for the Reception of Converts into the Orthodox Church.

129 A comprehensive list of these churches and confessions, as determined by the Holy Eparchial Synod, hopefully would be appended to this or any other service approved by the synod. Such a comprehensive list already exists and is appended to the service adopted by the Antiochian Archdiocese of America. The list includes the Roman Catholic Church and more than fifty Protestant denominations.

130 See Calivas, *The Liturgy in Dialogue*, 197-201.

131 Full communion with the Oriental Orthodox remains an unfinished task, even though the Churches in recent times have affirmed their fundamental agreement in the understanding of the apostolic faith and tradition. See Thomas FitzGerald and Emmanuel Gratsias, eds., *Restoring the Unity of Faith: the Orthodox-Oriental Theological Dialogue* (Brookline, MA 2007).

132 A *libellus* is a brief written and signed document in which the convert recants heretical beliefs and professes the Orthodox faith.

PART THREE
THE DIVINE LITURGY

1. A Brief Introduction

The Divine Liturgy is the sacred rite (service) by which the Orthodox Church celebrates the sacrament of the Holy Eucharist, which was instituted by our Lord and Savior Jesus Christ at the Last (or Mystical) Supper to perpetuate the remembrance of his redemptive work and to establish continuous intimate communion between himself and his faithful people.[1]

Through the Divine Liturgy we remember and celebrate with joy and thanksgiving the whole mystery of the divine economy – God's household plan for the salvation of the world – from creation to the incarnation, and especially the passion, resurrection, glorification, and second coming (Parousia) of the Son and Word of God.[2]

---

[1] The earliest account of the Last Supper is in 1 Cor. 11:23-26 (and 10:16-21), followed by the accounts in the Synoptic Gospels, Matthew 26:26-29; Mark 14:22-25; and Luke 22:17-20. The Gospel of John does not mention the Eucharist in the account of the Last Supper but contains a significant brief discourse in eucharistic terms on the bread of life that Jesus gives (John 6:51-58); and the bread he gives is his own consecrated body (John 6:51, 17:19; Heb. 10:10).

[2] For more on the Divine Liturgy see Alkiviadis Calivas, *Aspects of Orthodox Worship* (Brookline, MA, 2003), 162-226 and *The Liturgy in Dialogue* (Brookline, MA, 2018), 19-103. See also Alexander Schmemann, *The Eucharist* (Crestwood, NY, 2003). Τὸ Μυστήριον τῆς Θείας Εὐχαριστίας, Σειρὰ Ποιμαντικὴ Βιβλιοθηκὴ 8 (Athens 2004). Hugh Wybrew, *The Orthodox Liturgy* (Crestwood, NY 1990).

At every Divine Liturgy we are embraced by the boundless love of the Triune God; and we engage the mystery of the Cross – the sacrifice of the incarnate Word and Son of God, "for whom and by whom all things exist" (Heb. 2:10)[3] – and the Empty Tomb. Christ tasted death for everyone (Heb. 2:9), in order to "deliver all those who through the fear of death were subject to lifelong bondage" (Heb. 2:15) through his resurrection.

At every Divine Liturgy we also meet the crucified and risen Christ and are united with him. He is made present to us through "the writings of the prophets and the memoirs of the apostles,"[4] and the sacramental sign of bread and wine, of which we partake for the forgiveness of sins and life eternal. Immersed in the mystery of our salvation, we joyfully "speak to one another in psalms and hymns and spiritual songs, singing and making melody in [our] heart to the Lord, giving thanks always for all things to God the Father in the name of our Lord Jesus Christ, submitting to one another in the fear of God" (Eph. 5:19-21).[5]

The Eucharist is the "sacrament of sacraments,"[6] the great and final mystery (sacrament), since it is not possible to go beyond it or add anything to it. "*After the Eucharist,*" said St. Nicholas Cabasilas, "*there is nowhere further to go.... For in it we obtain God Himself, and God is united with us in the most perfect way.*"[7] Thus in former days, as we learn from Dionysios the Areopagite, every sacrament was completed by the Eucharist. "For scarcely any of the hierarchic sacraments can be performed without the divine Eucharist as the high point of each rite, divinely bringing about a spiritual gathering to the One for him who receives the sacrament, granting him as a gift from God its mysterious perfecting capacities, perfecting in fact his communion with God."[8]

The Eucharist is the central act of the Church. In and through it the Church actualizes herself as the Body of Christ. Thus, the whole life of the local community or parish is centered essentially on the weekly celebration of the

---

3 We will say more below on the Eucharist as sacrifice.

4 St. Justin the Martyr, *1 Apology*, 67.

5 Among the many hymns and songs that speak of the mystery of the incarnation, cross, and resurrection, by way of example, is the resurrectional *apolytikion* of the plagal First tone: "Let us the faithful, praise and worship the Word, coeternal with the Father and the Spirit, born for our salvation from the Virgin; for he willed to be lifted upon the Cross in the flesh, to endure death, and to raise the dead by his glorious resurrection."

6 Pseudo-Dionysios, *The Ecclesiastical Hierarchy*, 3:1.

7 Nicholas Cabasilas, *The Life in Christ* (Yonkers, NY 1974), 114, 116 (Fourth Book: 1, 3).

8 Dionysios, *Ecclesiastical Hierarchy*, 3:1. See also, Cabasilas, *Life in Christ*, 116: "Wherefore the Eucharist, alone of the sacred rites, supplies perfection to the other Mysteries." For more on the relationship of the sacraments to the Eucharist see Nenad Milosevic, *To Christ and the Church: The Divine Eucharist as the All-Encompassing Mystery of the Church* (Los Angeles, 2012).

Eucharist on the Lord's Day – Sunday. At the Divine Liturgy we gather together as God's People to confess our common faith; express our indissoluble unity in love; learn and live another new, true way of life; receive the seeds of sanctity to bear fruit commensurate to the gift; and experience in faith the transformation of our being by communing the Lord Christ sacramentally as members of his body, the Church. Thus, through the Eucharist we continually advance and perfect the new life which was bestowed upon us at baptism. The effect of the Eucharist is to make of each one a dwelling of the Holy Spirit.

Attendance at and participation in the Divine Liturgy is an essential requirement of the Christian life, not in fulfillment of a vague religious obligation, but for the inestimable privilege of glorifying God as partakers of divine grace. As St. Maximos the Confessor says, we come to the Eucharist that we may partake "of the grace of the Holy Spirit which is present there…. This grace transforms and changes each person who is found there and in fact remolds him in proportion to what is more divine in him…even if he does not himself feel this because he is still among those who are 'children' in Christ, unable to see either the depths of the realities or the grace operating in it."[9]

Put another way, as an ancient text of the Church affirms, "Let no one fail to attend … Let no one deprive the Church of one of her members!… You must not scatter yourselves outside the Church by failing to assemble there…. Do not deprive the Savior of his members, do not rend, do not scatter his Body."[10] According to this account, absence from the Divine Liturgy is seen as a dismemberment of the Body of Christ.

The Divine Liturgy is accomplished through the shared action of all the people of God; the clergy and the people together celebrate the Divine Liturgy through their different roles, functions, duties, and distinct responsibilities. Everyone is vital and everyone has a role in the celebration of the liturgy. No one is a mere spectator; everyone exercises a liturgical ministry, however small.

In the Eucharist we become concelebrants with Christ, who is invisibly present among his people in fulfillment of his promise (Matt. 18:20). He is the One who offers and is offered, the One who receives and is distributed (Prayer of the Cherubic Hymn). Christ celebrates the Divine Liturgy invisibly, performing it, as he does all the sacraments, through visible organs and acts; that is, through sacred rituals and through hierarchs and priests who are set apart by ordination to exercise Christ's saving activity on his people who are united to him in faith and seek to grow in him.

---

9 St. Maximos the Confessor, *Mystagogy* 24, in *Maximos Confessor: Selected Writings*, trans. George C. Berthold, Classics of Western Spirituality (New York, 1985), 206-7.

10 *The Didascalia of the Twelve Apostles*, 13. See Lucien Deis, *Springtime of the Liturgy*, trans. Matthew J. O'Connell (Collegeville, MN 1979), 176-7.

The honor and the responsibility placed upon hierarchs and priests in the exercise of their liturgical functions are truly humbling, for "to serve [God] is great and awesome even for the heavenly powers." The clergy, after all, are frail and imperfect human beings, perishable earthen vessels. Yet, Christ "has entrusted to [them] the celebration of the liturgical sacrifice without the shedding of blood" – the Eucharist. It is he who "enables [them] by the power of the Holy Spirit so that, vested with the grace of priesthood, [they] may stand before his Holy Table to celebrate the mystery of his holy and pure Body and his precious Blood"[11]

A priest may not celebrate the Divine Liturgy alone – by himself and for himself – because no ordained person realizes his priesthood in himself, but in the community.[12] The presence of another person representing the people, the community, is required because it is in their name that he offers the Eucharist. Indeed, hierarchs and priests pray for, and on behalf of the people but also with the people. They do this in the Name of Christ and not as the people's delegates. It is Christ who empowers them with priestly grace to enact the sacred rituals.

The Divine Liturgy is, first and foremost, an act of the Triune God, who takes his people unto Himself, as a father his children. In and through the Divine Liturgy the participants experience the real presence of Christ and meet and are embraced by the self-giving of the Triune God – Father, Son, and Holy Spirit. At the liturgy God admits us to an area of non-death that we may share in his life and joy. Hence, our action at the liturgy can be understood only as an *offering-in-return* (ἀντιπροσφορά, *antiprosfora*), as the response of a humble heart to the unfathomable mystery of God's irresistible beauty, goodness, and love with which he has embraced us through the incarnation of his Son, our Lord and Savior Jesus Christ.

At its deepest levels our *offering-in-return* is an act of *kenosis*, an act of self-emptying. It is the laying aside of our egotistical, rebellious, prideful, and self-centered spirit with all its negative impulses and irrational attitudes that consume us. At the Divine Liturgy we enact our own personal *kenosis*, our willingness to lose our life in order to gain it (Mark 8:35). Through the bread and wine, the appropriate symbols of human life, we offer our life to God in exchange for his. In receiving the Body and Blood of Christ, we receive eternity for temporality. Through the Eucharist we become partakers "of the divine nature" (2 Peter 1:4).

---

11 The several quotations are taken from the Prayer of the Cherubic Hymn.

12 For the priest as celebrant of the Eucharist see Dumitru Staniloae, *The Sanctifying Mysteries* (Brookline, MA 2012), 105-11.

The Divine Liturgy is a complex act of rhythmic sound and movement, characterized by a sense of harmony, beauty, and mystery. The liturgy is structured around five solemn processions, which today are abbreviated forms of earlier more elaborate ceremonies.[13] The principle behind the development of the liturgy's ceremonial splendor rests on the notion that our earthly worship reflects the joy and majesty of the heavenly worship.[14] Hence, every component and element of the liturgy should be enacted and celebrated in a manner befitting the wondrous mystery that we experience in faith: "*God in men and God among gods (Θεὸς ἐν ἀνθρώποις καὶ ἐν μέσῳ θεῶν), who have received deification from him.*"[15]

The Eucharist is a banquet, a feast of thanksgiving and joy. Celebrating the Eucharist, we touch eternity. When we partake of Holy Communion we are in Christ and Christ is in us, according to his promise: "He who eats my flesh and drinks my blood abides in me and I in him" (John 6:56). Eternity penetrates our finitude – our creaturehood with all its limitations and frailties – to heal the harmful evil impulses and delusions of the mind, the passions of the heart, and the wounds of the soul. In our communion with Christ, the agape, goodness, and holiness of the Triune God illumine and overcome the darkness in us, so that, degree by degree, we may become sons and daughters of the Light (Ephes. 5:8-9; 1 Thess. 5:5; 1 John 1:5-7) and inheritors of his promises (Ephes. 1:10-14; Col. 1:11-14).

Through the Eucharist, the messianic kingdom becomes real to the people of God assembled in faith. At the Divine Liturgy the divine Bridegroom of the Church calls his people – however imperfect they may be personally and collectively – to sit with him in the heavenly places (Ephes. 2:6; Col. 3:1). We are raised to where Christ is so that he – in whose image we have been made and who strive earnestly in faith to attain his likeness – may set his seal upon our souls and bodies so that we may receive inwardly by grace what is his by nature: incorruptibility and immortality; gifts that will be made manifest in

---

13   The five processions are the two solemn entrances, the so-called Small Entrance and the Great Entrance; the two "lesser" entrances, the procession of the Evangelion to the ambo and the procession of the Holy Chalice to the nave for the distribution of Communion to the people; and finally, the formal procession-departure of the clergy and the people from the church at the conclusion of the service. Today, for example, the Evangelion is processed to the ambo only when a deacon is present and the formal departure from the church has all but disappeared.

14   For example, in the Prayer of Entrance we read these words: "Master and Lord our God, you have established in heaven the orders and hosts of angels and archangels to minister to your glory. Grant that the holy angels may enter with us that together we may serve and glorify your goodness."

15   St. Symeon of Thessaloniki, *Dialogos*, 94, in *Patrologia Graeca (PG)* 155, 285.

the end times when the kingdom of God appears in glory (Rom. 8:11, 14-17; 1 Cor. 15:50-58; 1 Peter 1:3-5). Then the degree of our personal holiness or lack thereof, now veiled, will be disclosed outwardly (Matt. 25:31-46).

The image of God in us may be broken, disfigured, distorted, and wounded by our sins and imperfections, but it can never be lost. Consequently, in the inner chambers of our souls resides a deep longing for love, freedom, and life – for whatever is lovely, true, and pure. That is why our conscience cries foul when we assault the authenticity and dignity of our humanity through sinful acts and moves us to seek forgiveness, mercy, and compassion. Unlike the image, the likeness of God in us may be lost and destroyed through ignorance, apathy, neglect, recklessness, contempt, and all manner of evil.

The likeness of God is attained through a conscious personal struggle to acquire, by grace, a virtuous and righteous life – to become godlike, each according to his/her capacity. In other words, to be fully and authentically human we must labor through faith to grow the image; to mature into the likeness of God; to attain union with God (theosis).[16] This life-long effort for the attainment of holiness has been implanted in our nature by our Creator. It is strengthened in many ways, and especially through prayer, ascesis, works of love, and regular active participation in the Divine Liturgy. At the Eucharist we are immersed into and participate in the mystery of our salvation and share in the awesome, precious, and life-giving mysteries of Christ, his Body and Blood, unto the forgiveness of sins and life eternal.

Interpreting the Divine Liturgy

Before all else, it is important that both the clergy and the people have a clear understanding of what the Church is saying and doing at the Divine Liturgy.[17] In the absence of good instruction, people are apt to invent their own meanings through private reflection or by borrowing the thoughts of others. However, not all private meanings, whether personal or borrowed, are sound, valid, or edifying, especially when they are based on erroneous assumptions, false ideas, and irrational superstition.

The Church has always explained and interpreted her liturgical rites either in the form of catechetical homilies or in the form of liturgical commentaries. In fact, the Byzantine liturgical tradition boasts a durable liturgical genre,

---

16 Recall the pithy dictum of St. Athanasios on the meaning of theosis, "God became a human being that we might be made gods," (*On the Incarnation*, 54.) As Metropolitan Kallistos (Timothy) Ware points out, to understand the doctrine of theosis or deification, we must first know of the distinction between God's divine essence and his divine energies. Our union with God is possible only with his divine energies and not with his divine essence. See Ware, *Orthodox Church*, 218-25, 231-38.

17 See Calivas, *Liturgy in Dialogue*, 87-91.

the mystagogical commentaries of the Divine Liturgy.[18] These works seek to give a theological explanation not only of the sacraments but of the ritual actions that make up the liturgical celebration. These mystagogical works are integral to the Byzantine liturgical tradition and remain popular among a large segment of the population to this day.

Clergy and catechists, however, must be judicious in their use of symbolic interpretations and avoid the use of excessive representational symbolisms – especially when they are extravagant, exaggerated and baseless – in explaining the sacred rite of the Divine Liturgy, and for that matter, any sacred rite of the Church.

Unfortunately, most congregants today, largely due to what they have heard and read, understand the Divine Liturgy more in terms of a drama, as a ritual reenactment of the life of Christ through gestures and actions, than as an unfolding vision of God's reign and the fulfillment of the Church as the mystical Body of Christ. The Eucharist is more than theater, more than a performance. It is the remembrance of God's redemptive activity and the Church's appropriation of its benefits through prayers of thanksgiving and with hymns of praise for what the Triune God has done and continues to do for the life and salvation of the world.

Symbolization should not be the sole exegetical and hermeneutical method of understanding and explaining the Divine Liturgy. We must also teach the history, development, and structure of the liturgy and explain the meaning of its prayers, petitions, and hymns, as well as its ritual actions and even its rubrics. In other words, we must study the text, understand it, and explain exactly what we are saying and doing at the liturgy, engaging the worshippers in the mystery of salvation.

More will be said on the theology of the Eucharist when we analyze and discuss the development of the several components and ritual actions that comprise

---

18 The terms mystagogy and mystagogical are derived from the Greek verb μυω, which means to initiate into the mysteries. The Greek Fathers used the terms to refer to the holy sacraments, especially baptism, chrismation, and the Eucharist, and other sacred rites. The terms were used in two ways: to refer to the performance of the ritual action or to explain the mystery hidden and celebrated in the sacred rites. One could say that mystagogy is a way of doing theology – liturgical theology. Included among the several mystagogical commentaries are the catechetical homilies of Theodore of Mopsuestia, Cyril of Jerusalem, and John Chrysostom; the commentaries of Ambrose of Milan, Pseudo-Dionysios, Maximos the Confessor, Germanos of Constantinople, Nicholas Cabasilas, and Symeon of Thessaloniki. See Enrico Mazza, *Mystagogy: A Theology of Liturgy in the Patristic Age* (New York, 1989). For a summary of the Byzantine mystagogical works and their value see John Klentos, "Mystagogy for a New Generation: Interpreting Liturgy for the Twenty-first Century," in *Evangelist, Shepherd, and Teacher*, 303-21. Also, on symbol and reality in the Divine Liturgy, see Pavlos Koumarianos, "Σύμβολο καὶ πραγματικότητα στή Θεία Λειτουργία" in *Σύναξη* 71 (1999), 22-37.

the liturgy. What follows is a broad outline of the structure and elements of the sacred service.

Structure, Components, and Ritual Actions of the Divine Liturgy

The celebration of the Divine Liturgy involves the whole person, body and soul. It engages not only the soul, but also the mind, emotions, imagination, and all the senses: hearing, seeing, smelling, tasting, and feeling or touch. The verbal and non-verbal elements of the divine service fit together harmoniously, weaving a pattern of prayer that embraces the whole person. On the verbal side we hear Scripture lessons and are called to ponder their message as we listen to a homily that explains their meanings and the teachings of the faith. We hear eloquent prayers of praise, thanksgiving, intercession, and confession. We invoke the Father to send the Holy Spirit upon the worshippers and the Gifts being offered so that the congregants may be Spirit-bearers and the eucharistic elements become the Body and Blood of Christ. We listen and respond appropriately to litanies, petitions, acclamations, greetings, and invitations. We hear and sing various hymns, songs, and psalms. We are made aware of creedal statements and recite with attentiveness the Creed and the Lord's Prayer.

On the non-verbal side, we exchange the kiss of peace, we are caught up in processions, and we engage in various ritual actions and gestures. An assortment of symbols – incense, light, icons, making the sign of the cross, bowing, etc. – heighten our awareness and perception of spiritual realities.

The Divine Liturgy is enacted within a sacred space, the temple (the ναός or church building), which itself is a sign and mirror of the kingdom, of the age to come when creation itself will be delivered from the bondage of corruption (Rom. 8:18-25). In its setting, content, and ritual actions, the liturgy becomes the gateway to heaven, a place of mystery flooded by the presence of God. The earth encounters heaven, as the emissaries of Prince Vladimir of Kiev said of their experience of the Divine Liturgy in Constantinople (ca. 987): "And the Greeks led us to the edifice where they worship their God, and we knew not whether we were in heaven or on earth. For on earth there is no such splendor or such beauty, and we are at a loss how to describe it. We only know that God dwells there among men, and their service is fairer than the ceremonies of other nations, for we cannot forget that beauty."

Whether we find ourselves in a great cathedral or in a tiny chapel, it is incumbent upon the clergy as leaders of the worshipping community to make every effort to create an environment in which the beauty and holiness of God shine forth so that the souls of the faithful may be set aflame.

The Divine Liturgy is comprised of two distinct but inseparable parts. The first is centered on the so-called Small Entrance and the *ambo* (ἄμβων–pulpit) with the public reading of the Holy Scriptures and the homily. Since the eighth century, the Small Entrance is preceded by the *enarxis* and the antiphons or the Typika. The reading and explication of the scriptures are followed by a series of petitions and prayers. The first part of the Divine Liturgy is a Christianized version of synagogue worship. It is called the Liturgy of the Word or the *proanaphora*, or the Liturgy of the Catechumens, a term that should be avoided.

The second part of the Divine Liturgy, the Eucharist proper, is centered on the Holy Table and is derived from the seven actions of the Lord at the Last Supper,[19] which have been translated into the four actions of the Eucharist proper: (a) the offering *(proskomide)* and the transfer of the Gifts (Great Entrance); (b) the *Anaphora*, the great Eucharistic Prayer which includes the offering of the eucharistic elements, the sacrifice of praise, the consecration of the Holy Gifts, and the intercessions; (c) the elevation and fraction of the Lamb; (d) and the distribution of Holy Communion.

The two parts are linked together by the two Prayers of the Faithful. The true link, however, between the two parts of the Divine Liturgy which makes them inseparable is found in the words of the Lord in the Gospel of John (15:3), *"You are already made clean by the word which I have spoken to you. Abide in me, and I in you."* The proanaphora or the Liturgy of the Word is thus more than instructional. Above all, it is a call to repentance, an act of purification, and an opening and a conversion of the heart. Likewise, the kiss of peace, which precedes the Creed and the *anaphora*, is also a preparation for the Eucharist. It is a preliminary condition for the offering of the great Eucharistic Prayer; it is an act of reconciliation based on the words of the Lord in the Gospel of Matthew (5:23-24): *"...first be reconciled to your brother, and then come and offer your gift."*

The Byzantine Rite, which constitutes the final unification of liturgical practice in the Orthodox Church, has three Divine Liturgies: The Divine Liturgy of St. John Chrysostom (CHR), The Divine Liturgy of St. Basil the Great (BAS), and

---

19 "Now as they were eating, Jesus took the bread, and blessed, and broke it, and gave it to the disciples and said, 'Take eat; this is my body." And he took a cup, and when he had given thanks, he gave it to them, saying, 'Drink of it, all of you; for this is my blood of the covenant..." (Matthew 26:26-28). The seven actions are: he took bread, blessed, broke it, and gave it; and he took a cup, gave thanks, and gave it to them. On the covenantal nature of the Eucharist and the words of institution in each of the four narratives on the Last Supper see Calivas, *Liturgy in Dialogue*, 38-40.

the Divine Liturgy of the Pre-Sanctified Gifts (PRES).[20] In current practice, the Divine Liturgy of St. Basil is celebrated ten times annually.[21] The Pre-Sanctified is celebrated on Wednesdays and Fridays of Great Lent and on the first three days of Holy Week.[22] The Divine Liturgy of St. John Chrysostom is celebrated every Sunday and Feast Day, except when the typikon orders the celebration of the Divine Liturgies of St. Basil the Great or of the Pre-Sanctified Gifts.[23]

2. The Structure of the Divine Liturgies of Saints Basil and John Chrysostom

Both BAS and CHR constitute a complex act of movement, sound, and sight and are characterized by a sense of harmony, beauty, dignity, and mystery. They are outwardly identical in form and are structured around several solemn entrances, which today are abbreviated forms of earlier, more elaborate ceremonies. Their structural components include: the reading and exposition of Holy Scripture; petitions for and the dismissal of the catechumens; the

---

20   The Divine Liturgy of St. James the Brother of the Lord (Ἰακώβου τοῦ Ἀδελφοθέου) was the principal liturgy of both Antioch and Jerusalem before the liturgies of Constantinople (BAS and CHR) became universal in the Orthodox Church. It is now celebrated once or twice a year on the feast of St. James which is celebrated on October 23 and on the Sunday after Christmas. See John D. Witvliet, "The Anaphora of St. James," in Paul F. Bradshaw, editor, *Essays on Early Eastern Eucharistic Prayers* (Collegeville, MN), 153-72).

21   The ten times are: the five Sundays of Great Lent, the Vigils of Pascha, Christmas, and Theophany, Holy Thursday, and on January 1, the feast of St. Basil. When the feast of Christmas or Theophany falls on a Sunday or Monday, the feast has only one Divine Liturgy. There is no vesperal Divine Liturgy, only a morning Divine Liturgy. In this instance the Divine Liturgy of St. Basil is celebrated in the morning.

22   In former times PRES was also celebrated on Holy Friday and on Wednesdays and Fridays of the year. It was also celebrated on other occasions in the context of other services such as weddings and coronations. For more on PRES see the excellent comprehensive study of Stefanos Alexopoulos, *The Presanctified Liturgy in the Byzantine Rite: A Comparative Analysis of its Origins, Evolution, and Structural Components* (Leuven-Paris-Walpole, MA, 2009).

23   The Divine Liturgy of St. John Chrysostom can be celebrated on any day of the year, except for certain days: Wednesday and Friday of Cheesefare Week, unless the Feast of the Presentation of the Lord or of a major saint happens to fall on either of these days; the five week-days (Monday-Friday) in each of the six weeks of Great Lent, unless the feasts of the Presentation and the Annunciation happen to fall on a weekday; on Holy and Great Monday, Tuesday, Wednesday, and Friday, unless the Feast of the Annunciation happens to fall on any of these days; and when the service of the Great Hours of Christmas or Theophany happens to fall on a Friday.

kiss of peace. and the recitation of the Nicene-Constantinopolitan Creed; the Great Eucharistic Prayer, called the *Anaphora*; and the preparation for and distribution of Holy Communion. Elaborate opening rites (the *enarxis*) and a series of dismissal rites (the *apolysis*) embrace the whole action.[24]

To the casual observer there is little, if any, difference between BAS and CHR, especially since the prayers of the priest in current practice are said in a low voice or inaudibly.[25] The more observant participant, however, will notice that while the two liturgies "sound" almost the same and share an identical structure or framework, BAS is lengthier than CHR. Even the casual observer cannot help but notice that it takes the priest longer to read some of the prayers and that the choir tends to prolong some of the hymns. However, to fully appreciate the differences between the two liturgies one must do more than watch the clock. One must learn to be an attentive listener and a careful reader of the texts of the two services. Then the similarities and the distinctive characteristics and features of each will become apparent.

The received texts of both BAS and CHR contain twenty priestly prayers of varying length whose doxological endings (ἐκφωνήσεις) are the same.[26] The received texts also contain the same prescribed ritual actions and gestures, the same diaconal litanies, responses and hymns of the people, and the same

---

24 The dismissal rites originally included a recessional. The clergy and the people entered the church together in solemn procession with song to begin the Divine Liturgy. So also, at the conclusion of the divine service, the clergy and the people exited the church together with song.

25 The recitation of prayers in a low voice or inaudibly has a long and complex history. It originated in East Syria and prevailed throughout the Eastern Church by the end of the eighth century, in spite of imperial legislation to the contrary. Today, with varying degrees of success, many local Churches are encouraging the clergy to recite all or some of the prayers aloud and most especially the Anaphora. For a comprehensive treatment of the subject, see Georgios N. Filias, Ὁ Τρόπος Ἀναγνώσεως τῶν Εὐχῶν στὴ Λατρεία τῆς Ὀρθοδόξου Ἐκκλησίας (Athens 1997). For a brief account, see Calivas, *Aspects of Orthodox Worship*, 214-17.

26 See, for example, the text of the two Divine Liturgies in parallel columns together with a brief but informative introduction in Ioannis Fountoulis, Βυζαντιναὶ Θ. Λειτουργίαι Βασιλείου τοῦ Μεγάλου καὶ Ἰωάννου τοῦ Χρυσοστόμου (Thessaloniki 1978). To the twenty prayers of the Divine Liturgy, we should add another, the Prayer of the Prothesis. While this prayer is now said at the conclusion of the Service of Proskomide, which is performed before the Divine Liturgy at the Prothesis or Preparation Table, the Prayer of the Prothesis is prefixed to the text of BAS in the manuscripts. Also, the dismissal blessings have not been counted among the twenty prayers, since they were originally part of the rituals at the *skeuophylakion,* where the leftover consecrated Gifts were returned and consumed by the appointed persons.

rubrical information. Of the twenty priestly prayers, eleven are common to both liturgies, while nine are different.[27]

The nine different prayers in the received texts include the Prayer for the Dismissal of the Catechumens and the two Prayers for the Faithful. These two prayers bridge the two parts of the Divine Liturgy, the Liturgy of the Word and the Eucharist proper.[28] The focal point of the first part, the proanaphora, is the reading and the explication of the Word of God. The focal point of the second part, the Eucharist proper, is the transfer of the eucharistic elements to the Holy Table, their consecration, and their reception in Holy Communion.

The other six different prayers in BAS and CHR include the Prayer of the Proskomide, the holy Anaphora, the Pre-Communion Prayer (before the Lord's Prayer), the Prayer of Inclination, the Prayer of Thanksgiving after Communion, and the Prayer of the Skeuophylakion (today at the Prothesis). While all these prayers are related to the Anaphora, three in particular are especially important: the Prayer of the Proskomide, which anticipates the Epiclesis; the Pre-Communion Prayer which reiterates the effects or fruits of Communion presented in the Anaphora; and the Thanksgiving Prayer after Communion, which expands on the benefits of Holy Communion.[29]

From this list of prayers, the chief difference between BAS and CHR rests chiefly in the second part of the Divine Liturgy, the Eucharist proper. These differences are both external and internal. The prayers differ not only in length, but also in content, and this is especially true of the holy Anaphora.

---

27   Of the eleven common prayers, one, the Prayer before the Gospel, is not found in the *Barberini Euchologion*. It was added around the tenth century to both formularies. The other ten have been supplied by BAS. These are the prayers of the three antiphons, the Prayer of Entrance, and the Prayers of the Trisagion Hymn, the Incensing, the Fervent Litany, the Cherubic Hymn, Before the Elevation of the Lamb (the consecrated Bread), and Behind the Ambo. In the early manuscript tradition CHR did not have prayers for the three Antiphons, the Cherubic Hymn, or the *Skeuophylakion*. They were supplied by BAS. In the *Barberini Euchologion* CHR has its own original prayers for the Entrance, the Trisagion, the Cathedra, and Behind the Ambo. In later manuscripts these were supplanted by the prayers in BAS. Also, in the *Barberini Euchologion* BAS and CHR each has a Prayer for the Cathedra (or *synthronon*). However, these prayers were omitted in the printed Euchologia, since the ascent to the synthronon was eventually abandoned in most Greek Churches and the synthronon itself gradually disappeared from the apse of the sanctuary in most churches. BAS and CHR have similar dismissal rites which are not found in the early manuscripts. These rites end with the Prayer of the Skeuophylakion. In the received text of CHR, the Prayer of the Skeuophylakion is an original creation. It was added to CHR after the ninth century.

28   In many catechetical manuals the two parts of the Divine Liturgy are referred to as the Liturgy of the Catechumens and the Liturgy of the Faithful. The former designation is unfortunate and should be avoided.

29   On the effects, fruits, and benefits of Holy Communion see Calivas, *The Liturgy in Dialogue*, 50-64.

As Andre Jacob has shown in his comprehensive but as yet unpublished doctoral dissertation on the Divine Liturgy of St. John Chrysostom, CHR is incomplete in the earliest extant *Euchologion* of the Byzantine rite, *Barberini Codex – 336*, and in other early mss.[30] According to Robert Taft, the celebrant was obliged to refer to the complete formulary of BAS for the prayers common to both Divine Liturgies.[31] By the eleventh century, however, CHR appears in a complete form in the euchologia, its missing prayers supplied by BAS. And equally important, CHR is now listed first, having supplanted BAS as the chief liturgy of the Byzantine Rite.[32]

3. Diataxeis or Manuals of Rubrics

In times past, as I have noted initially, the order and the directives for the performance of the ceremonials and rituals of the divine services were passed down orally, except for some general written rules.[33] Even now, when the rubrics of a given service are spelled out, an oral tradition is presupposed because no rubric is complete or capable of transmitting all the nuances of a particular liturgical act, ceremony, gesture, or movement. The liturgical rules, called rubrics in English, from the Latin *rubrica*, meaning red, were written in red ink to distinguish them from the priestly prayers, diaconal litanies, and hymns in the various texts.

The collections of liturgical directives – manuals of rubrics – are called *Diataxeis* (Διατάξεις). They began to appear after the tenth century. The directives initially were placed at the beginning of the service books and later, as they appear today, were interpolated at the appropriate places within the text. Of the many diataxeis that appeared between the twelfth and fourteenth centuries, none proved to be more influential and lasting than the two composed by Philotheos Kokkinos, twice Patriarch of Constantinople (1353-1355 and 1364-1376). He wrote these two documents while he was the abbot (*hegoumenos*) of the Great Lavra on Mt. Athos. They reflect, in part, monastic practices.

The two *Diataxeis* of Philotheos, the *Diataxis of the Diaconate* and the *Diataxis of the Divine Liturgy* gained universal recognition as part of the liturgical reforms that took place in the wake of the Hesychastic Controversy. The two *Diataxeis* of Philotheos were gradually incorporated into the text of the divine services

---

30 Andre Jacob, *Histoire du formulaire grec de la liturgie de Saint Jean Chrysostome* (unpublished doctoral dissertation, University of Louvain 1968). Parenti and Velokovska, *L'Eucologio Barberini*, 24-41.

31 Taft, *Great Entrance*, xxxi-xxxii.

32 On the ascendancy of CHR see Calivas, *Liturgy in Dialogue*, 19-64.

33 On the *Diataxeis* see Robert F. Taft, *The Great Entrance* (Rome 1978), xxxv-xxxviii. Calivas, *Aspects of Orthodox Worship*, 98-100.

of the daily office and the Divine Liturgy of the Greek Church, starting with the first printed edition of the three Divine Liturgies by Demetrios Doukas in 1526.[34] To this day these rubrics retain their vitality even though changes have occurred through the centuries.

4. The Preparatory Rites for the Divine Liturgy

> *When the priest is to celebrate the Divine Liturgy, he must be at peace with all, have a pure heart, fast from the preceding evening, and remain in a spirit of vigilance and joyful expectation until the service.*[35]

In preparation for the celebration of the Divine Liturgy a hierarch, priest, and deacon perform three rites before the start of the service: (a) the *"kairos,"* (b) the vesting, and (c) the washing of the hands.

A. The "Kairos" or the Preparatory Prayers

The *"kairos – καιρός"* is a brief service by which the clergy prepare themselves for the celebration of the Divine Liturgy through a series of prayers and actions which, at their core, constitute an act of contrition. The title of the service, kairos, is probably derived from the brief dialogue exchanged by the deacon and priest just prior to the start of the Divine Liturgy, when the deacon utters the words of the psalmist to the priest, *"It is time for the Lord to act – Καιρὸς τοῦ ποιῆσαι τῷ Κυρίῳ"* (Psalm 118/119:126).[36]

Originally, the kairos was a simple act that included three prostrations before the Holy Doors and a solemn entrance into the sanctuary.[37] Prostrations signify

---

34 Demetrios Doukas, editio princeps, Αἱ Θεῖαι Λειτουργίαι τοῦ Ἰωάννου Χρυσοστόμου, τοῦ Βασιλείου Μεγάλου, καὶ τῶν Προηγιασμένων. Γερμανοῦ Ἀρχιεπισκόπου Κωνσταντινουπόλεως, Ἱστορία ἐκκλησιαστικὴ καὶ μυστικὴ θεωρία (Rome 1526).

35 See the introductory comment of Philotheos Kokkinos in his "Διάταξις τῆς Θείας Λειτουργίας," in Trembelas, Αἱ Τρεῖς Λειτουργίαι Athens 1935), 1. For more on the kairos see Ioannis Fountoulis, Ἀπαντήσεις εἰς Λειτουργικὰς Ἀπορίας, vol. 2 (Thessaloniki, 1975), 123-26. Also see Casimir Kucharek, *The Byzantine-Slav Liturgy of St. John Chrysostom* (Allendale, NJ 1971), 218-33.

36 *The Liturgy of the Orthodox Church*, translated by Archbishop Athenagoras (Kokkinakis) and published by the Archdiocese of Thyatira and Great Britain (London, 1979) renders the same passage differently, "It is time *to serve* the Lord..." *The Divine Liturgy according to St. John Chrysostom*, published by the Russian Orthodox Greek Catholic Church of America (now the Orthodox Church in America – New York, 1967) renders the passage, "It is time *to begin the service* to the Lord..." A Uniate text has, "It is time *to sacrifice unto the Lord...*" in Kucharek, *The Byzantine-Slav Liturgy*, 334.

37 We find a trace of this simple act in a hierarchical celebration of the Divine Liturgy. The concelebrating priests, having received the blessing of the hierarch, proceed directly to the Holy Gate, bow deeply, enter the sanctuary, bow, and reverence the Evangelion and the Holy Table.

penitence but also deep reverence and awe. In Greek a prostration is called a μετάνοια (*metanoia*), which means repentance.[38]

At some point, the Trisagion Prayers and a series of penitential troparia were added. By the twelfth century, a new ritual was introduced: the reverencing of the holy icons on the iconostasis by the celebrant(s), starting, of course, with the icon of Christ.[39] Gradually, this ritual act was accompanied with an appropriate hymn for each of the icons, which the celebrant(s) recites before reverencing the icon. In a further development, as evidenced by the fourteenth-century *Diataxis of Philotheos Kokkinos,* a prayer of access was also added to the service. The penitential troparia and the prayer of access, which are part of the received rite, express the essential character of the service: an acknowledgment by the celebrant of his failures and inadequacies and a plea for God's grace so that he may be made worthy to offer the Holy Eucharist:

> *Lord, stretch forth your hand from the height of your holy dwelling and strengthen me to conduct your service so that, standing uncondemned within your fearful sanctuary (τῷ φοβερῷ σου βήματι), I may offer the sacrifice without the shedding of blood; for yours is the power...*[40]

Following the prayer, the priest conducts the *apolysis*. Then he turns and bows to the people asking humbly for their forgiveness. He proceeds to the north door of the iconostasis and enters the sanctuary, saying the words of the psalmist, "*I will enter into your house, I will worship toward your holy temple in the fear of you...*" (Psalm 5:7). He comes to the Holy Table, where he makes three prostrations and reverences the Evangelion and the Holy Table.

The service of kairos provides us with an example of the gradual development of a simple act into a rite, into a complex service of words and ritual actions

---

38   There are two forms of prostrations, the small and the great. The small is done with a bending of the knees and a bowing of the head and body. The second is done by bending down on the knees with the hands supporting the body as the forehead touches the ground. The latter form is used mostly during penitential periods. Prostrations are normally accompanied by words of contrition. The most frequently used phrase is: "*God, be merciful to me a sinner*" (Luke 18:13).

39   In early documents there is no mention of icons. The veneration and censing of icons appear in later diataxeis and printed editions. It has been suggested that through the veneration of the holy icons, the celebrant is seeking the support, prayers, and blessings of the saints as he prepares for the Eucharistic service.

40   Typically, in Greek, the sanctuary is called ἱερὸν βῆμα (sacred *bema*). The word *bema* designates a dais or a raised place, and in particular a raised apse, a feature of the basilica-type building – a longitudinal roofed hall, with or without aisles, and terminated and dominated by a raised apse or platform, the *bema*. With the peace of Constantine, local church communities adopted the basilica as the basic architectural style for their worship space. Often, the sanctuary is identified simply as the ἱερόν (the sacred space), the word bema is omitted but implied. The raised platform in Jewish synagogues is also called a bema.

whose structure possesses a life of its own.⁴¹ The transformation of a simple act into a service, as a rule, is meant to expand on and explain further the elemental meanings of a particular act. In the case of the kairos, the purpose of the expansion was to accentuate two contrasting themes: the unworthiness of the celebrant and the plenteous mercy of God.

While one could say that the kairos is a private office, a priest's personal prayer of preparation, it is nonetheless always conducted publicly, which is to say openly in the presence of the congregation. This is especially significant because a priest or hierarch may not celebrate the Divine Liturgy alone, whether in a private space or in a church. There must always be another person present to represent the people. The Divine Liturgy is an act of the whole Church and not of an individual cleric.

The Service of Kairos

When the time for the celebration of the Divine Liturgy approaches, the priest enters the Church wearing the exorason. He proceeds into the nave and stands before the Holy Doors facing the sanctuary and begins the service of kairos.⁴²

The Enarxis:

Priest

"*Blessed is our God ... Εὐλογητὸς ὁ Θεὸς ἡμῶν...*"

"*Heavenly King ... Βασιλεῦ Οὐράνιε...*" It is followed by the Trisagion Prayers.⁴³

---

41   See, for example, the two essays of Robert Taft, "The Structural Analysis of Liturgical Units" and "How Liturgies Grow: The Evolution of the Byzantine Divine Liturgy," in his *Beyond East and West: Problems in Liturgical Understanding* (Second revised and enlarged edition – Rome 2001), 187-232.

42   The *kairos* is not associated with the Orthros or any other service of the daily office. The rite is related directly to the Divine Liturgy, even though in current Greek practice it is often conducted during the first part of the Orthros at the kathismata or during the singing of the canon. However, in most churches in America the chanters do not sing the canon. When a hierarch is the celebrant, the kairos is conducted before the troparia of the praises (the Αἶνοι) of Orthros, at which point the Orthros is suspended while he performs the kairos. The Orthros is resumed once the hierarch enters the sanctuary. Today, some hierarchs have simplified the ritual. Originally, between the end of the Orthros or the end of the Hours and the start of the Divine Liturgy there was a break in the proceedings. It was during this interval that the clergy conducted the kairos. For practical reasons, many clergy today conduct the kairos before the Orthros begins, a practice that is especially helpful and recommended for the newly ordained.

43   The prayer, "*Heavenly King*" is omitted during the Paschal season and is replaced by the *troparion*, "*Christ is risen from the dead...*" "*Heavenly King*" and the Trisagion Prayers, which are comprised of the "*Holy God...*" "*All-holy Trinity...*" and the "*Lord's Prayer,*" are used as introductory prayers in a number of services, including the Hours of the daily office. If a deacon is present, the Trisagion Prayers are recited by him.

The Three Penitential Troparia[44]

Priest

"Have mercy upon us... Ἐλέησον ἡμᾶς..."

"Glory to the Father... Lord have mercy on us... Δόξα... Κύριε ἐλέησον..."

"Now and... Open the gate... Καὶ νῦν... Τῆς εὐσπλαγχνίας..."[45]

The penitential *troparia* are meant to remind the clergy that they conduct the divine services not because of any personal merit or gift, but by the grace and love of God: *"You did not choose me, but I chose you and appointed you that you should go and bear fruit"* (John 15:16). Hence, every clergyman must approach his liturgical ministry with fear and trepidation but also with faith and hope in the tender mercies and steadfast love of God.

The Veneration of the Icons and the Troparia

Having recited the three troparia, the priest (and deacon, if one is present) comes before each of the four icons of the iconostasis in turn, prostrates before each, and kisses each as he recites the appointed troparia.[46] This ritual extends and accentuates the priest's sense of contrition and dependence on God's boundless love. He is mindful that no one has holiness in himself; it comes from Christ, the only holy One, who pours himself upon us:

---

44 If a deacon is present, the penitential troparia are said in turn by the priest and deacon. The same holds true when a hierarch is the celebrant. The three penitential troparia of the office are borrowed from the Octoechos: the first two are kathismata troparia of the Monday Orthros in the period of the *plagal* second tone; the third is a kathisma troparion of the Thursday Orthros in the same period.

45 At this point, the Holy Doors are opened as a sign of God's favor. If a deacon is present, he proceeds to the doors and opens them. If a priest serves alone, he opens the doors or a person within the sanctuary opens them. (Regarding the doors of the *iconostasis* take note of the following tradition: during all of Renewal or Bright Week the Holy Doors and the two side doors of the *iconostasis* remain open. From the Sunday of Thomas to the feast of the Apodosis of Pascha, only the Holy Door (central doors) remains open. The open doors are meant to emphasize symbolically the power and joy of Christ's resurrection by which the gates of Hades were torn asunder and humanity was delivered from the bonds of death. "It is the day of the Resurrection, let us be radiant...for Christ God has brought us from death unto life, and from earth unto heaven as we sing the triumphal hymn..." (Paschal Canon, Ode One).

46 When venerating the icons, we recite the *apolytikion* of the saint or of the event depicted. For the icon of Christ, we recite the hymn, "We venerate your most pure image..." This hymn is the apolytikion of the Feast of Orthodoxy celebrated on the First Sunday of Lent, when we commemorate the restoration of the holy icons following the final victory of the Orthodox over the iconoclasts in 843. For the icon of the Theotokos we say the hymn, "Being the fountain of tenderness...." which is borrowed from the Octoechos, a kathisma troparion of the Monday Orthros in the period of the second tone.

"We venerate your most pure image, O Good One, and ask forgiveness for our transgressions, O Christ our God. Of your good will you were pleased to ascend the cross in the flesh and to deliver your creatures from bondage to the enemy. Therefore, with thanksgiving we cry aloud to you: You have filled all things with joy, O our Savior, for you did come to save the world."

We also venerate the icons of the Theotokos, St. John the Baptist, and the patron saint of the church.[47] We do so to manifest our love for them and for all the saints, as we seek to emulate their heroic devotion to God and their unwavering desire to acquire the mind of Christ, which is the vocation of every Christian. In addition, we call upon the saints to come to our aid as benevolent intercessors, so that we also may grow in the image and likeness of Christ our God.[48] Furthermore, the veneration of the icons emphasizes the truth that the saints, together with all the living faithful, are part of the one mystical Body of Christ, the Church. At every Divine Liturgy we ascend to the heavenly Jerusalem to concelebrate the mystery of our salvation together with the angels and the saints in the presence of "Jesus, the mediator of a new covenant" (Heb. 12:22-24; cf. Rev. 4:1-11).

Priest at The Icon of Christ

"We venerate your holy Icon… Τὴν ἄχραντον εἰκόνα σου…"

Priest at The Icon of the Theotokos

"Being the fountain of tenderness… Εὐσπλαγχνίας ὑπάρχουσα πηγή…"

---

47 The hymn of St. John the Baptist is the apolytikion of his feast day, January 7. The hymn of the saint in whose memory the church is dedicated is the apolytikion of the saint's feast.

48 In his challenging reflection on sainthood, "Men, Monks, and Making Saints," which appeared on the website *Public Orthodoxy* (December 2019), which is the online publication of the Orthodox Christian Studies Center of Fordham University, Fr. John Chryssavgis writes, "Saints are completely and consistently human – neither superhuman nor semi-divine." When synods act to recognize holiness, they do so on what the clergy and the people, as the conscience of the Church, refer to them. On the process by which saints are recognized in the Orthodox Church see Peter Chamberas and John Chryssavgis, *The Recognition of Saints in the Orthodox Church: Past and Present* (Newfound Publishing: Hebron, NH, 2021); K. Papadopoulos, "Γιὰ τὴν διακήρυξη τῶν Ἁγίων" in Σύναξη, vol. 102 (2007); George Tsetsis, "'Η διαδικασία ἐντάξεως Ἁγίων στὸ ἑορτολόγιο κατὰ τὴν πρᾶξη τοῦ Οἰκουμενικοῦ Πατριαρχείου," in Ὀρθοδοξία (2001); Stylianos Papadopoulos, Διαπίστωση καὶ Διακήρυξη τῆς Ἁγιότητας τῶν Ἁγίων (Katerini 1990); P. Papageorgiou, "Ἀνακήρυξις Ἁγίων ἐν τῇ Ὀρθοδόξῳ Ἐκκλησίᾳ" in Γρηγόριος Παλαμᾶς, vol. 43 (1960); Amilka Alivizatos, "Ἡ Ἀναγνώρισις τῶν Ἁγίων ἐν τῇ Ὀρθοδόξῳ Ἐκκλησίᾳ," in Θεολογία, vol. 19 (1941-1948), 18-52; Also see the brief but informative article, "The Saints of the Orthodox Church," on the website of the Greek Orthodox Archdiocese of America.

Priest at The Icon of the Baptist

"The memory of the just... Μνήμη δικαίου..."

Priest at The Icon of the Patron Saint of the Church

(The *apolytikion* of the saint) or of the event which the local church honors (*apolytikion* of the feast, e.g., of the Transfiguration, the Dormition of the Theotokos, et.al.).[49]

The Prayer

Having venerated the icons, the priest stands before the Holy Doors and faces the sanctuary. He bows reverently and raising his hands slightly he recites the devotional prayer with a contrite heart. As already noted, through the prayer he confesses his weakness and unworthiness to celebrate the august sacrament of the Eucharist and asks God for the strength that comes from above that he may worthily accomplish his priestly office: "to offer unto [God] gifts and spiritual sacrifices for [his] sins and for the errors of the people."[50]

Priest

"Let us pray to the Lord. Τοῦ Κυρίου δεηθῶμεν."

"Lord, stretch forth your hand... Κύριε, ἐξαπόστειλόν μοι..."

The Apolysis

The priest conducts the apolysis, at the end of which he commemorates the saint whose Divine Liturgy is about to be celebrated (St. John Chrysostom or St. Basil the Great) and remembers also the saint(s) of the day.

The Forgiveness

When the apolysis is concluded, the priest turns and bows to the people asking for their forgiveness. This act is repeated twice more during the Divine Liturgy, at the Great Entrance before the procession of the Gifts and before the priest receives Holy Communion. The bowing before the people and before one's concelebrants, if any are present, asking for forgiveness and pardon is an essential element of the preparatory rite and is based on the dominical command: "So if you are offering your gift at the altar, and there remember

---

49 The term "*patron - προστάτης*" is used to identify the saint chosen by the founders of the community as their special advocate in whose honor the church edifice is dedicated. The custom probably originated from the ancient practice of celebrating the Eucharist over the tomb of martyrs on the anniversary of their martyrdom. This practice also gave rise to the custom of placing relics of a saint(s) in the Holy Table when the church is consecrated by the hierarch.

50 From the Prayer of the Proskomide in CHR.

that your brother has something against you, leave your gift there before the altar and go; first be reconciled to your brother, and then come offer your gift" (Matthew 5:23-24). The principle of mutual love and reconciliation is also at the heart of the exchange of the kiss of peace at the Divine Liturgy.

Entrance into the Sanctuary

After this, the priest enters the sanctuary through the south gate (the side door on the right) and comes before the Holy Table, as he repeats the words of the psalmist, "*I will enter your house... Εἰσελεύσομαι εἰς τὸν οἶκον...*" (Psalm 5:7). In earlier times, the priest recited the remaining verses of Psalm 5:7-12. In current Greek practice, however, we say only the seventh verse.

In some printed editions of the Greek ieratika, verse seven is augmented with a doctrinal phrase which reads: "I will enter your house, I will worship toward your holy temple in the fear of you, *one God in three Persons, the Father, the Son, and the Holy Spirit, now and forever. Amen.*"[51] In the most recent edition of the ieratikon of the Church of Greece, this phrase is omitted.

Standing before the Holy Table, the priest makes three prostrations and says each time these words: "*God, be merciful to me a sinner... Ὁ Θεὸς ἱλάσθητί μοι τῷ ἁμαρτωλῷ...*" (Luke 18:13). These words were spoken first by the Publican in the Lord's Parable, The Publican and Pharisee, recorded in the Gospel of Luke (18:9-14). The clergy repeat these words many times and on different occasions in the performance of their liturgical duties. Following the prostrations, the priest kisses the Evangelion and the Holy Table and proceeds to vest.

Entrance into and conduct within the sanctuary should never be casual or indifferent but always worshipful and reverential. When entering, moving about, or standing in the sanctuary, clerics should bear in mind the Lord's words to Moses at the Burning Bush on Mount Horeb (Exodus 3:1-6). It was there that God revealed himself to Moses and called him to his service and told him the place on which he was standing was *holy ground* (Exodus 3:5). And so, he told him, "Put off your sandals from your feet" (Exodus 3:5). In other words, stand here humbly in a manner befitting the place that marks the appearance of your God. And so, it is with us who serve in the sanctuary; it is a sacred space and holy ground *(γῆ ἁγία)*. Entering and serving in it, we are called to set aside every pretense, pettiness, and idle talk.[52]

---

51 Most priests of my generation use this formula.

52 By tradition, whenever a priest enters an Orthodox church, he goes into the sanctuary. There, he bows and venerates the Holy Table, kissing it and the Evangelion which rests upon it.

B. The Service of Vesting

As I have noted elsewhere, according to tradition, the essential garments or vestments of the priestly office are conferred at the time of ordination.[53] Since ordinations are accomplished in a hierarchical order successively from one order to the next, a candidate for ordination appears before the ordaining hierarch wearing the liturgical vestments of his order. When the ordination to the higher office is completed, the vestments of the new order are added to those of the previous order, with one exception, the appointment of a subdeacon.

In the case of a subdeacon (ὑποδιάκονος), the candidate or ordinand appears before the hierarch with a cloak or *himation* (a *rason* or robe), which is the liturgical garment of the reader and chanter, the first of the minor orders. When the initial requirements of the rite have been fulfilled, the cloak is removed and the new subdeacon is clothed with a *sticharion* (στιχάριον), the liturgical garment of the subdeacon, which is also the basic vestment of all three major orders of the priesthood.

When a deacon is ordained, in addition to the *sticharion*, he is given the *orarion* (ὀράριον), the characteristic vestment of the diaconate and, in more recent times, he also receives the *epimanika* or cuffs (ἐπιμάνικα).[54]

In the same way, in addition to the sticharion and epimanika, a priest is also vested with the *epitrachilion* (ἐπιτραχήλιον),[55] the *zone* (ζώνη – belt), and the *phelonion* (φελώνιον). The epitrachilion is the distinctive vestment of the priest and hierarch and is worn at every divine service.

---

53 Calivas, *Church, Clergy, Laity and the Spiritual Life*, 99-102. See also the collection of articles on sacred vestments and the external attire of clergy in Τὰ ἱερὰ Ἄμφια καὶ ἡ ἐξωτερικὴ περιβολὴ τοῦ Ὀρθοδόξου Κλήρου in Σειρά Ποιμαντική Βιβλιοθήκη, volume 5 (Athens 2002).

54 The *epimanika*, now worn by deacons, priests, and hierarchs, were originally worn only by hierarchs.

55 The *epitrachilion* is a long liturgical scarf, i.e., a broad cloth worn around the neck that falls to the feet. The two sides are held together usually by decorative buttons. Some believe the epitrachilion is derived from the orarion, which a deacon wears on his left shoulder and hangs to the feet on either side. According to this theory, at the ordination of a priest, the orarion was turned and placed around the neck of the priest to become the epitrachilion. Hence its name: ἐπι-upon + τράχηλος-neck).

Similarly, in addition to the vestments conferred upon the priest, a hierarch also receives the *sakkos* (σάκκος) in place of the *phelonion*,[56] the *epigonation* (ἐπιγονάτιον),[57] and the *omophorion* (ὠμοφόριον)*,* the latter being the distinctive vestment of the episcopate, worn at every divine service together with the epitrachilion. The hierarch also receives the pastoral staff (ῥάβδος) and the mitre (μίτρα).[58]

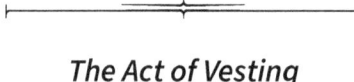

The Act of Vesting

The vesting "prayers" or, more correctly, the biblical verses used for each article reflect the symbolic meaning of each priestly vestment; meanings that are beneficial and uplifting for both the clergy and the people.

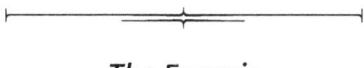

The Enarxis

"Blessed is our God... Εὐλογητὸς ὁ Θεὸς ἡμῶν..."

---

56 Originally, the *sakkos* was an imperial ceremonial garment. The first evidence of the sakkos as a eucharistic vestment is recorded in the twelfth century by the renowned canonist Theodore Balsamon. Initially, it was worn only by the Ecumenical Patriarch, a privilege bestowed by the emperor. It was worn only three times annually, at Pascha, Pentecost, and Christmas. The privilege was later extended to the other patriarchs and to certain metropolitans and archbishops. By the sixteenth century the sakkos, together with the mitre, was worn by all hierarchs. Patriarchs and hierarchs wore the phelonion through the eleventh century, at which time the hierarch's phelonion acquired a distinct feature. It was decorated with a pattern of crosses and was called *polystaurion* (πολυσταύριον = many crosses). Today, many-crossed phelonia are often worn by priests, a practice that would not have been allowed centuries ago.

57 The *epigonation* may be conferred on a presbyter as a sign of honor, when, for example, he receives the office (ὀφφίκιον) of oikonomos and/or protopresbyter.

58 Like the *sakkos*, the imperial *mitre* or crown also became a liturgical article, the normal liturgical head covering of hierarchs.

The Vesting

Taking each article in turn, the priest blesses and kisses it as an act of reverence.

The Sticharion

"Ἀγαλλιάσεται ἡ ψυχή μου ἐπὶ τῷ Κυρίῳ.... My soul shall rejoice in the Lord, for he has clothed me with the garment of salvation; he has covered me with the robe of gladness, as a bridegroom he has set a crown on me; and as a bride adorns herself with jewels, he has adorned me...." (Isaiah 61:10).[59]

---

*The **sticharion** symbolizes the baptismal garment which is given to all neophytes as a sign that they have been clothed with Christ (Gal. 3:27), "the author and perfecter of our faith" (Heb. 12:2). We draw our identity from Christ and strive "to grow up in every way into him" (Ephes. 4:15). The baptismal garment is the outward sign, the emblem of the new life; the garment of salvation and the robe of gladness of all who "were buried with Christ by baptism into death, so that as Christ was raised from the dead by the glory of the Father [they] too might walk in the newness of life" (Rom. 6:4).*

As the antitype of the baptismal garment the sticharion is meant to remind clergy and laypeople alike that by virtue of their baptism they are a new people who, by God's grace, are able "to see the deformity of evil and virtue's shining beauty as they truly are."[60] Because of its relation to the baptismal garment and in keeping with ancient tradition, the sticharion should be white (or some other bright color).[61]

The verse which accompanies the wearing of the sticharion, Isaiah 61:10, was deemed appropriate to convey the relationship of the sticharion to the baptismal garment. In the preceding verses Isaiah refers to the emergence of Zion from the ashes of destruction and speaks of the appearance of a new priestly people. Christians also have emerged from darkness into the light through baptism. "Once we were no people, but now we are God's people, a chosen race, a royal priesthood, a holy nation" (1 Peter 2:9-10). We rejoice heartily in the Lord, who has clothed us with

---

59 Some older printed editions of the ieratikon often preface each biblical verse with a call to prayer, "Let us pray to the Lord." The phrase, however, is unsuitable because what follows is not a prayer but an avowal, an affirmation.

60 St. John Chrysostom, *Baptismal Instructions*, 4:14.

61 Immediately after baptism, the neophyte is traditionally clothed with a white or bright garment, a fact which the accompanying hymn underscores: "Grant me a shining bright robe, you who clothe yourself with light as with a garment, O most merciful Christ our God." On the symbolic value of color in clerical vestments see Appendix C:2.

the garment of salvation and covered us with a robe of righteousness and joy. The marital imagery (groom – bride) in verse ten also speaks metaphorically of our intimate union with Christ, which baptism confers and which we must constantly nurture through ascesis by engaging the struggle "against the rulers of the darkness of this age" (Ephes. 6:12).

The Epitrachilion:

"Εὐλογητὸς ὁ Θεός, ὁ ἐκχέων... Blessed is God who pours forth his grace upon his priests, as myrrh upon the head, that runs down the beard, the beard of Aaron, that runs down the border of his robe" (Psalm 132/133:2).

*The **epitrachilion**, as initially noted, is the distinctive vestment of priests and hierarchs. It signifies the grace of priesthood. It is worn around the neck and falls down to the feet. This particular psalm verse (132/133:2) makes reference to the anointing oil which Moses poured on the head of Aaron, his brother to consecrate and ordain him a priest of the Most High (Exodus 29:7). The grace of priesthood is like the anointing oil, rich and plentiful; it is poured out and covers the ordained completely. The shape of the epitrachilion and the manner by which it is worn reflect the words of the psalmist.[62] It is also said that the tassels that adorn the bottom borders of the epitrachilion symbolize the souls of the faithful the Lord has placed in the care of his priests and hierarchs.*

The Zone (ζώνη – belt or girdle)

"Εὐλογητὸς ὁ Θεός, ὁ περιζωννύων με δύναμιν... Blessed is God who girds me with strength and makes my way blameless" (Psalm 17/18:32).[63]

The belt – a wide cloth band that ties in the back – serves both a utilitarian and a symbolic function.[64] On the one hand, it keeps the sticharion and

---

62 Saint Germanos of Constantinople in his treatise of the Divine Liturgy, *Ecclesiastical History and Mystical Contemplation* (18), gives a very different interpretation: "The epitrachilion is the cloth which was put on Christ at the hands of the high priest, and which was on his neck as he was bound and dragged to his passion."

63 Some sources add verse 33: "He made my feet like hind's feet and set me secure on the heights."

64 On rare occasions, one may come upon a cloth belt that fastens in front with an ornate buckle.

epitrachilion in place and on the other, it reminds the priest, and for that matter every faithful Christian, that the Lord God is the source of all virtue, godliness, and strength. He is the one who equips his servants – the one who girds them – with strength to withstand the assaults of the wicked. He is the one who guides and makes straight our way so that we are able to pursue the path to life, the blameless way of living which leads to the kingdom.

Whatever good we are able to accomplish, we do because the Lord enlightens and strengthens us, as St. Paul confessed: "For I am the least of the apostles, unfit to be called an apostle because I persecuted the church of God. But by the grace of God I am what I am, and his grace toward me was not in vain. On the contrary I worked harder than any of them, though it was not I, but the grace of God which is in me" (1 Cor. 15:9-10; cf. Phil. 4:12-13).

In earlier times the belt was also a piece of military equipment on which the sword has fastened. Hence it came to be associated with vigilance and action. To "gird one's self" or to "gird one's loins" came to mean attentiveness and preparedness for action in the struggle "against principalities, against powers, against the rulers of the darkness of this age" (Ephes. 6:12; cf. 1 Peter 1:13-16).

The Epimanika

For the right cuff: "'Η δεξιά σου, Κύριε, δεδόξασται ἐν ἰσχύι ... Your right hand, O Lord, glorious in power, your right hand, O Lord, shatters the enemy. In the greatness of your majesty, you overthrow your adversaries" (Exodus 15:6-7).[65]

For the left cuff: "Αἱ χεῖρές σου ἐποίησάν με καὶ ἔπλασάν με ... Your hands have made and fashioned me; give me understanding that I may learn your commandments" (Psalm 118/119:73).

*Originally, the **epimanika** were worn only by hierarchs. Gradually, they also came to be worn by priests and deacons. In the case of hierarchs and priests the epimanika are worn over the sticharion, while deacons wear them under the sticharion.*

As the two respective verses indicate, the epimanika are meant to remind the clergy and the people that we are created beings. The Triune God has made and fashioned us and the cosmos we inhabit. He made us in

---

[65] These verses are from the Song of Moses (Exodus 15:1-19), which comprises the First of the Nine Biblical Odes.

his own image and likeness and has adorned us with every gift. He alone gives wisdom and understanding to those who seek to walk by his law and keep his testimonies. Moreover, the verses remind us that in every circumstance of life and in all our doings we are never alone. By our side we have the mighty warrior, the holy one, and the worker of wonders, the Triune God whose judgments are just.

The Epigonation

"Περίζωσαι τὴν ρομφαίαν σου ἐπὶ τὸν μηρόν σου, δυνατέ... Gird your sword upon your thigh, O Mighty One, with your glory and your majesty. And in your majesty ride prosperously because of truth, humility, and righteousness" (Psalm 44/45:3-4).

*The **epigonation** is worn on the right by hierarchs and by priests who have an office (ὀφφίκιον). In the case of hierarchs this diamond-shaped vestment is put on last, attached to the sakkos; in the case of priests it hangs from the neck or the belt by a cord and is put on before the phelonion (or the epitrachelion).*[66] *In both instances, it rests on the right knee as the name of the article indicates (επι = upon + γόνατον = knee).*

The verses for the epigonation are drawn from Psalm 44 (45), which is characterized as a royal wedding song. Liturgically, this psalm is used extensively at feasts and divine services dedicated to the Theotokos. The two verses speak to and extol the king's military prowess and his ability to govern wisely. The same verses supply the symbolism behind the epigonation. They speak of the need for vigilance ("gird your sword"), in other words, be ready for battle, be prepared to engage in spiritual warfare. Our weapon, however, is not a military sword that aims to kill and maim. It is rather "the sword of the Spirit, which is the word of God" (Ephes. 6:17); and "the word of God is living and powerful, and sharper than any two-edged sword, piercing even to the division of soul and spirit, and of joints and marrow, and is a discerner of the thoughts and intents of the heart" (Heb. 4:12). The word of God judges, forgives, heals, and saves.

The epigonation should remind hierarchs and priests that preaching the word of God at every Divine Liturgy and sacred service with fervor and joy is of paramount importance. No opportunity should be lost to

---

66 It is more practical for a priest to put on the epigonation after he has worn the sticharion followed by the epitrachelion. Then, when he puts on the belt, he can maneuver the cord of the epigonation in a way that it stays fixed. Some priests choose to hang the epigonation from the belt. This however is less effective.

tell the story of God's goodness, even briefly, and to recount his manifold blessings and his providential love for the world.

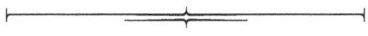

The Phelonion

"Οἱ ἱερεῖς σου, Κύριε, ἐνδύσονται δικαιοσύνη καὶ οἱ ὅσιοί σου ἀγαλλιάσονται ... Your priests, O Lord, will be clothed with righteousness and your saints will rejoice" (Psalm 131/132:9).

*The **phelonion** is the second of the two distinctive vestments worn by priests, the other being the epitrachilion. On occasion, the phelonion is also worn by hierarchs in place of the sakkos together with the small omophorion.*[67] *The phelonion resembles a cloak that is gathered up in the front. In earlier versions, the front opening of the phelonion was lower. For reasons of practicality the higher front opening prevailed.*

The verse selected to accompany the wearing of the phelonion is from a royal and messianic psalm which commemorates the election of Zion as God's dwelling place and the desire (unfulfilled) of David to build there a temple for the God of Israel. The psalmist envisions those who will serve and worship in the temple: priests, first, who will be clothed with righteousness and, second, the devout faithful who will be filled with joy. True worship and authentic service are marked by righteousness and joy. Gathered around the Risen and Reigning Lord, our hearts are filled with joy and gladness as we celebrate the mystery of our salvation.

What is the righteousness with which priests are clothed? For that matter, what is "the righteousness of God" that we must all become (2 Cor. 5:21)? As I have noted elsewhere, the righteousness of which the scriptures and the liturgy speak is God's just action, his saving deeds – his redemptive, restorative, and transformative works.[68] *The righteousness with which the celebrants are clothed and which we must all become is the holiness, mercy, loving-kindness, and goodness of God revealed in Jesus Christ – realities which we must pursue, perfect, and practice by grace, because apart from the Lord we can do nothing (John 15:5).*

---

67 As already noted, hierarchs wore the phelonion through the twelfth century, when the sakkos was bestowed honorifically on leading prelates, starting with the patriarch of Constantinople. When vesting with the omophorion the hierarch says: "*Upon your shoulders, O Christ, you brought our fallen nature to the Father*" (Cf. Hebrews 2:10-15 and 10:11-25).

68 Calivas, *Church, Clergy, Laity*, 1-18.

The Sacred Vestments of the Orthodox Clergy

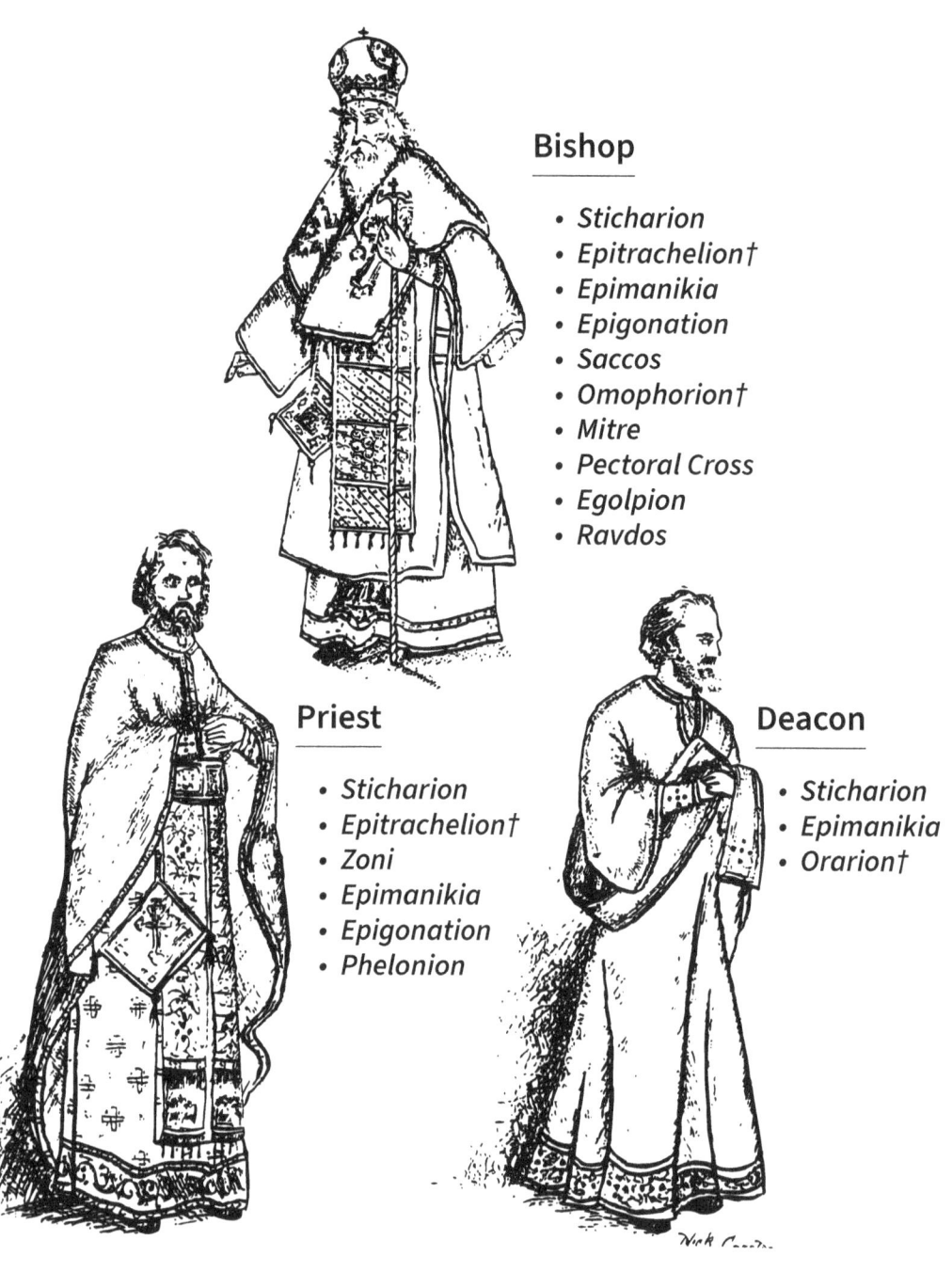

Bishop

- *Sticharion*
- *Epitrachelion†*
- *Epimanikia*
- *Epigonation*
- *Saccos*
- *Omophorion†*
- *Mitre*
- *Pectoral Cross*
- *Egolpion*
- *Ravdos*

Priest

- *Sticharion*
- *Epitrachelion†*
- *Zoni*
- *Epimanikia*
- *Epigonation*
- *Phelonion*

Deacon

- *Sticharion*
- *Epimanikia*
- *Orarion†*

The Pectoral Cross

"Ὅστις θέλει ὀπίσω μου ἐλθεῖν ... If any man would come after me, let him deny himself and take up his cross and follow me" (Mark 8:34; Matt. 16:24; Luke 9:23).

---

*The **pectoral cross** is worn only by hierarchs and by priests who have an office and are authorized.[69] The pectoral cross is not a decorative item but a sign of true discipleship: self-denial and obedience to Christ, the Suffering Servant and the Man of Sorrows who was wounded for our transgressions, and bruised for our iniquities; who bore our griefs and carried our sorrows (Isaiah 53:4-5).*

A Note for the Deacon: If a deacon is present, he presents himself to the priest with his vestments in hand saying: "Bless Master, the sticharion and the orarion." Having received the blessing of the priest, he proceeds to vest using the same biblical verses noted above for the sticharion and epimanika. For the orarion, he says the following verse: *"Ὁ θέλων γενέσθαι μέγας ἐν ὑμῖν, ἔσται ὑμῶν διάκονος... Whoever would be great among you, must be your servant"* (Matthew 20:26).[70]

---

[69] In addition to the pectoral cross a hierarch wears the *encolpion* (ἐγκόλπιον), an oval medallion suspended from the neck with a chain and bearing an enameled icon of Christ or the *Theotokos*. It is also known as the *Panagia*. The encolpion is also worn in public, outside the liturgy as an emblem of the episcopal office. On rare occasions a relic may be placed within the encolpion. When putting on the encolpion the hierarch says: *"Create in me a clean heart, O God, and put a new and right spirit within me"* (Psalm 50/51:10). When the encolpion is worn with a pectoral cross, it rests on the left side over the heart. By the fifteenth/sixteenth century all hierarchs began to wear a *mitre* (μίτρα), which is in the form of an imperial crown decorated with medallions and topped with a cross. When placing the mitre, the hierarch says, *"You have placed on his head a crown of precious stones"* (Psalm 20/21:3). When the hierarch is given and takes his *pastoral staff* (ῥάβδος), also called *pateritsa* (πατερίτσα), he says, *"The Lord sends forth from Zion your mighty scepter. Rule in the midst of your foes"* (Psalm 109/110:2).

[70] Vesting "prayers" for the deacon are found in only some editions of the *Euchologion* and only for the sticharion and epimanika but not for the orarion. The present verse for the orarion is found in a sixteenth-century manuscript and has been included in the more recent edition of the ieratikon of the Church of Greece. See the note in *Ieratikon* (Athens 2004), 340. The ieratikon of 1995 used a different phrase: *"Holy, holy, holy, Lord Sabaoth, heaven and earth are filled with your glory"* (Isaiah 6:3).

C. The Washing of the Hands (ἡ Νίψις τῶν χειρῶν – the Lavabo)

When the priest is fully vested, he washes (rinses) his hands[71] as he recites the words of the psalmist: *"Νίψομαι ἐν ἀθῴοις τὰς χεῖράς μου ... I will wash my hands in innocence; I will go about your altar, O Lord, that I may proclaim with the voice of thanksgiving, and tell of all your wondrous works. Lord I have loved the habitation of your house and the place where your glory dwells..."* (Psalm 25/26:6-12).[72]

The washing or rinsing of the hands by the celebrant(s) is strictly symbolic in nature and has no practical value.[73] It is reminiscent of the requirements of the Old Testament priesthood, "When they go into the tent of meeting, or when they come near the altar to minister...they shall wash with water..." (Exodus 30:17-21). It is also an outward manifestation of the requirements of the new life in Christ: "put away all malice and all guile and insincerity and envy and all slander" (1 Peter 2:1). Or, as St. Cyril of Jerusalem (+386) – the first witness to this practice – tells it succinctly, "[It is] not at all because of bodily defilement; for we did not set out for the Church with defiled bodies. This washing of hands is a symbol that you ought to be pure from all sinful and unlawful deeds.... Washing them we represent the purity and blamelessness of our conduct."[74]

---

71 Many churches have an anteroom with a sink, the pipes of which usually allow the water to go directly into the ground. If a sink is not available, the celebrant follows the ancient order. A subdeacon (if there is one), or the sexton or another altar server pours water over the hands of the celebrant into a bowl.

72 The rubrics call for the celebrant to recite verses 6-12 of the psalm. Often, however, only verses 6-8 are said.

73 For more on the lavabo see P. Trembelas, *Τρεῖς Λειτουργίαι*, 77, and especially R. Taft, *The Great Entrance*, 162-77.

74 Cyril of Jerusalem, *Mystagogical Catechesis* 5:2. The full text reads as follows. "You saw the deacon give the priest water to wash, and the presbyters who stood round God's altar. He gave it, not at all because of bodily defilement; no; for we did not set out for the Church with defiled bodies. But this washing of hands is a symbol that you ought to be pure from all sinful and unlawful deeds; for since the hands are a symbol of action, by washing them we represent purity and blamelessness of our conduct. Have you not heard the blessed David opening this mystery and saying, *I will wash my hands in innocence; so I will go about your altar, O Lord?* The washing therefore of hands is a symbol of immunity from sin." The psalm verse in Cyril's description is the same as the one in the received rite of washing. The symbolic character of the act is also highlighted in the *Apostolic Constitutions* (Book 8:11), a fourth-century church order: "But let one of the subdeacons bring water to wash the hands of the priests, which is a symbol of the purity of those souls that are devoted to God." The same is true of the fifth- to sixth-century corpus, Pseudo-Dionysios, *The Ecclesiastical Hierarchy*, 3:3,10: "With his extremities thus purified he preserves the utter purity of his conformity to God.... Those who approach this most holy sacred act are obliged to be purified even from whatever last fantasies there are in their souls."

Ceremonial ablutions are a common religious occurrence. Such washings were practiced by the temple priests, as already noted, and by pious Jews before meals and prayers, and as Robert Taft notes, "especially before the thanksgiving at the end of meals which so obviously parallels our Eucharist."[75] The washing of hands before the celebration of the Divine Liturgy as practiced by the clergy may well have its roots in these Judaic ritual practices.

The lavabo by priests as conducted presently, after vesting and before the prothesis rites, appears for the first time in the *editio princeps* of Demetrios Doukas (1526). Prior to that, at least through the twelfth century, the washing was performed both at episcopal and presbyterial liturgies after the transfer of the Holy Gifts, as demonstrated by the rubrics in the earliest sources (Cyril of Jerusalem, Apostolic Constitutions, and Pseudo-Dionysios) and in the euchologia of the tenth to the twelfth centuries.[76] Initially, the lavabo was part of the proanaphoral rites.[77]

In post-twelfth century sources the rite begins to appear before the Great Entrance during the singing of the Cherubic Hymn. By the end of the fourteenth century the lavabo at episcopal liturgies was conducted, as it is today, before the Entrance.

Strangely, the *Diataxis of Philotheos Kokkinos* and most euchologia before the *editio princeps* of Doucas do not mention the lavabo in presbyteral liturgies, despite the evidence of its existence after the entrance in the earlier sources. During the thirteenth to fourteenth centuries, the rite for priests was transferred to its present place, before the prothesis rite. This change may be related to and coincide with the transfer of the prothesis rite to before the Divine Liturgy.

---

75   Taft, *Great Entrance*, 164. See, for example, the act of Christ at the Last Supper (John 13:4-12).

76   For example, St. Cyril places the washing just before the kiss of peace. while the Apostolic Constitutions have it immediately after, as does Pseudo-Dionysios (*Eccl. Hierarchy*. 3:10).

77   To this day, when a subdeacon is present at a Divine Liturgy, he joins the procession at the Great Entrance in the very last position so that after the Gifts have been deposited on the Holy Table, the celebrant may turn to him to execute the lavabo. This is especially evident at a diaconal ordination.

The preponderance of the evidence from the sources indicates that every celebrating hierarch and priest participated in the lavabo. It is also evident from the sources that the subdeacon was and continues to be the main minister of the rite, a fact borne out by the rite of appointment *(χειροθεσια)* of a subdeacon.[78] We read, for example, in the *Apostolic Constitutions*, "Let one of the subdeacons bring water to wash the hands of the priests" (Book 8:11).

The biblical verses (Psalm 25/26:6-12) attached to the lavabo are found in almost all the sources beginning with the first witness to the rite, the *Mystagogical Catechesis* of St. Cyril of Jerusalem.[79] The verses constitute a confession of faith by which the priest recognizes his many weaknesses but also the tender mercies of God: "Sweep me not away with sinners... but redeem me and be gracious to me." The washing gives expression to the celebrant's desire to retain his integrity, to stand on level ground and not to stumble. Moreover, the priest expresses wonder and gratitude for the gift of priesthood that has been bestowed upon him; the gift that allows him to go about the altar of the Lord and to tell the people the wondrous deeds of God. While washing his hands, the priest confesses that his heart is aflame with the love of God's habitation, his holy house where his glory dwells. There, more than at any other place, the celebrant senses his nearness to the Triune God, who is his hope, refuge, and protection.[80]

---

78 The rite of appointment (χειροθεσία) of the subdeacon requires the candidate to come before the ordaining hierarch carrying a small pitcher of water, a small bowl, and a napkin or small towel draped on his shoulder. At a prescribed point during the rite, the subdeacon pours water as the hierarch washes his hands over the bowl and dries them with the napkin (towel). The napkin or towel is then placed on the shoulder of the subdeacon and not over his head as has become the practice.

79 See Taft, *Great Entrance*, 172-5.

80 This phrase is based on the final brief prayer of the *Apodeipnon*-Compline: "The Father is my hope; the Son is my refuge; the Holy Spirit is my protection; O, Holy Trinity, glory to you."

5. The Office of the Proskomide at the Prothesis

In the divine figure and action of the holy proskomide we see Jesus himself and we contemplate the one Church. Through him, who is the true light, she (the Church) acquires eternal life, and is illumined and constituted. On the one hand, he is in the center through the Bread; on the other hand, his mother is at his right through the particle, while the saints and the angels are at the left. And, below him is the entire devout assemblage (ἄθροισμα) of those who have believed in him. There is a great mystery here: God in men and God among gods (Θεὸς ἐν ἀνθρώποις καὶ ἐν μέσῳ θεῶν), who have received deification from him, who is true God by nature, and who was made flesh for their sake. The future kingdom is here too, and the revelation of eternal life: God with us, both seen and partaken (Θεὸς μεθ᾿ ἡμῶν ὁρώμενός τε καὶ μεταλαμβανόμενος)

– St. Symeon of Thessaloniki (+1429).[81]

The *Proskomide (Προσκομιδή)* is the sacred service through which the eucharistic elements – the bread and the wine – are prepared for the Eucharist by the priest who is fully vested. The service is conducted at the *prothesis (Πρόθεσις = προθέτω, to place or set before)* before the start of the Divine Liturgy, usually during the Orthros. The prothesis is the table where the sacramental elements are set forth. Today, the prothesis is located within the sanctuary on the "northeast" side, to the left of the Holy Table. In rare instances it is located in a small chamber apart from the sanctuary to the left of the Holy Table.

A. The Prothesis

The earliest sources tell us that the Eucharistic elements, the bread and the wine, were presented and set upon the Holy Table but with no further details about where, when, and by whom they were prepared and brought to the Table. Saint Justin the Martyr, for example, in his description of the liturgy on the Lord's Day, written around 150 A.D., notes the following: "When the lector has finished, the president addresses us and exhorts us to imitate the splendid things we have heard. Then we stand and pray.... When we have finished praying, bread, wine, and water are brought up. The president then prays and gives thanks, according to his ability, and the people give their assent with an Amen" (*1 Apologia*, 67).

---

81   Symeon of Thessaloniki, *Dialogos,* 94, in *Patrologia Graeca (PG) 155, 285.*

Almost three centuries later, Theodore of Mopsuestia (+428) in his *Mystagogical Catechesis*, a series of homilies most likely delivered in Antioch, gives us additional information: "It is the deacons who bring out this oblation [on patens and in chalices]...which they arrange and place on the awe-inspiring altar...[having previously] spread linens on the altar...[And afterwards] they stand on both sides and fan the air above the Holy Body so that nothing will fall on it."[82]

The Dionysian writings (fifth-sixth century) provide similar evidence: "The chosen deacons, along with the priests, put on the divine altar the sacred bread and the cup of blessing.... The *covered* divine bread is brought forward together with the cup of blessing. The divine kiss of peace is exchanged."[83] We learn from this account that the gifts are brought and set on the Holy Table by deacons and priests, that the bread is covered for protection, and that the gifts are transferred before the exchange of the kiss of peace.[84]

Saint Germanos of Constantinople (+733), in his treatise on the Divine Liturgy, gives us more details.[85] From him we learn that the preparation of the gifts took place "on the altar located in the skeuophylakion, which signifies the place of Calvary (Golgotha), where Jesus was crucified."[86] The skeuophylakion of Hagia Sophia – the Great Church – was a circular building located to the northeast of the church. According to St. Germanos, the skeuophylakion came to symbolize Golgotha[87] and was thus identified with the Passion of our Lord, an association that is highlighted by the use of sacrificial language in the

---

82 Theodore of Mopsuestia, *Mystagogical Catechesis*, Homily 15, cited in Taft, *Great Entrance*, 35-36 and in Wybrew, *Orthodox Liturgy*, 53. For a series of patristic and liturgical texts outlining the development of the prothesis rite see F. E. Brightman, *Eastern Liturgies* (Gorgias Press - Piscataway, NJ, 2004), 539-51.

83 Pseudo-Dionysius, *Ecclesiastical Hierarchy*, Chapter 3, II and 3, III: 8. The italics were added for emphasis. Brightman who was able to reconstruct a sketch of the Syrian Liturgy from the fifth to eighth centuries also indicates that the gifts were brought to the Holy Table by deacons. See his *Eastern Liturgies*, 482.

84 Saint Maximos the Confessor, who also wrote a commentary on the Divine Liturgy, makes no mention of a prothesis rite or prayer. The prothesis prayer was added sometime between Maximos (+662) and the *Barberini Codex* (late eighth century). The *Codex* contains two prothesis prayers, one for BAS and another for CHR. The CHR prayer fell into disuse as the actions at the prothesis gradually evolved into a separate rite or service.

85 Germanos, *Ecclesiastical History and Mystical Contemplation*, chapters 20-22 and 36. The original Greek text together with an English translation, introduction and commentary was published by Paul Meyendorff, *St. Germanus of Constantinople on the Divine Liturgy* (Crestwood, NY, 1984), 71 and 85.

86 *Ibid*. 36.

87 Golgotha (a Hebrew name which means the place of a skull) is the place where Jesus was crucified (Matt. 27:33, Mark 15:22, Luke 23:33, and John 19:17).

preparation of the Eucharistic elements.[88] Eventually, this led to the placement of the icon "Extreme Humility" at the prothesis.

Three centuries later, Nicholas of Andida in his commentary on the Divine Liturgy, the *Protheoria* (Προθεωρία – ca. 1055-1063), would associate the prothesis with the incarnation of Christ, an idea which led to the placement of the icon of the Nativity of Christ at the Prothesis.[89] Saint Symeon of Thessaloniki (+1429) also associated the skeuophylakion with the Nativity of Christ saying that it "represents Bethlehem and the cave."[90]

The skeuophylakion (σκευοφυλάκιον: σκεῦος = *vessel*, φυλάκιον = *treasury*), as indicated by the name, was the storehouse or treasury where the sacred vessels and the vestments of the clergy were kept. It was also the place where the faithful deposited their gifts of bread and wine before they entered the church.[91]

According to the descriptions in Germanos' treatise, the eucharistic elements were prepared in the skeuophylakion after the clergy had vested and before the start of the Divine Liturgy. This is a significant new development. Previously, the gifts were prepared immediately before their transfer in what later would be called the Great Entrance. During Germanos' time the gifts were transferred to the sanctuary by deacons (Chapter 37)[92]. After the distribution of Communion, what remained of the consecrated Holy Gifts was returned to the skeuophylakion, where the leftovers were consumed by the clergy.[93]

From a ninth-century interpolation in the text of St. Germanos (chapter 22),[94] we learn that the gifts were prepared by a priest with the assistance of deacons or subdeacons in what by then had become an elaborate ceremony known as the proskomide. We will say more about this below.

---

88 Germanos, *Ecclesiastical History*, 21: "The piece which is cut out with the lance signifies that "Like a sheep he is led to the slaughter…." (Isaiah 54:7); 22: "The wine and the water are the blood and the water which came from his side…"

89 See Wybrew, *Orthodox Liturgy*, 140.

90 See Trembelas, *Τρεῖς Λειτουργίαι*, 156, note 45.

91 For more on the offering of the gifts see Taft, *Great Entrance*, 16-34.

92 Meyendorff, *St. Germanus*, 87.

93 In late antiquity, if the portions of the leftover Holy Gifts were large, sober and mature children were called to assist. Today, only the clergy consume the leftover Holy Gifts at the prothesis. If a deacon(s) is present, the task usually falls on him.

94 See Meyendorff, *St. Germanus*, 12, 73.

From architectural studies of the early churches of Constantinople we learn that the skeuophylakion was a separate building adjacent to the church.[95] By Taft's description, the skeuophylakion was the building where the liturgy began and ended.[96] Byzantine sources, according to Taft, almost never use the terms prothesis and diakonikon, especially with reference to St. Sophia. Often in euchologia (prayerbooks) the three terms were used interchangeably. In fact, Constantinopolitan churches had no auxiliary chambers called pastophoria (παστοφόρια – παστός=*chamber*) anywhere in the church before the early tenth century.[97] Thereafter, the prothesis and the diakonikon, where feasible, gradually became pastophoria or side chambers of the sanctuary, the prothesis on the left side and the diakonikon which served as a sacristy on the right.

In due course, the skeuophylakion began to disappear. Finally, for various practical considerations the prothesis was relocated and placed in the sanctuary[98] to the left of the Holy Table, the "northeast" side of the church, where we see it today in the form of a free-standing adorned credence (table) or as a decorated shelf within a niche. The prothesis is used exclusively for the preparation of the gifts. Even though the skeuophylakion has long since disappeared, the term is still found in some liturgical texts. For example, the prayer in both BAS and CHR immediately after the Prayer behind the Ambo (Ὀπισθάμβωνος Εὐχή) in some editions bears the title, "Εὐχὴ λεγομένη ἐν τῷ σκευοφυλακίῳ – Prayer said in the skeuophylakion."[99]

---

[95] For more on the skeuophylakion see Taft, *Great Entrance*, 185-91. See also Thomas F. Mathews, *The Early Churches of Constantinople: Architecture and Liturgy* (Pennsylvania State University, 1977), 158-9. Rowland J. Mainstone, *Hagia Sophia: Architecture, Structure and Liturgy of Justinian's Great Church* (New York, 1988), 137. The stored vessels included patents or discs (δίσκοι), cups or chalices (ποτήρια), lances (λόγχαι), veils (καλύμματα), scripture texts, processional crosses (σταυροί), liturgical fans (ριπίδια), baskets (κανίσκια, κάνιστρα) to collect the gifts of the people, and other paraphernalia. The skeuophylakion of Hagia Sophia also had an oven, which according to evidence was used to prepare the Holy Chrism and to consume by fire the Eucharistic Gifts that had spoiled. It was not used to bake the prosphora. See Taft, *Great Entrance*, 191, note 49.

[96] Taft, *Great Entrance*, 189.

[97] The liturgical disposition of the churches of Greece and Syria was different. For example, the prothesis chambers were common as pastaphoria adjacent to the sanctuary or as chambers by the narthex.

[98] Such practical considerations include smaller church buildings and Eucharistic celebrations by a single priest.

[99] See Trembelas, *Τρεῖς Λειτουργίαι*, 156 and 194. Other later editions have the title, "Εὐχὴ εἰς τὸ Συστεῖλαι τὰ Ἅγια – Prayer at the Consummation of the Gifts."

In our liturgical tradition the term *prothesis* designates the place in the church where the eucharistic gifts are prepared. In times past it also designated the ritual preparation of the gifts. However, commencing with the twelfth century the term *proskomide* was used to specify the ritual preparation of the gifts.[100]

B. The Proskomide

The proskomide is the service by which the sacred gifts, the bread and wine, are prepared for the Eucharist. The earliest sources say little about the preparation of the gifts or about how they were set forth on the Holy Table. We do know that the faithful, clergy and laity alike, brought their offerings – a small loaf of bread, or a flask of wine, or some other gift – and deposited them in the skeuophylakion or some other place.[101] The offered breads were probably placed in baskets. The deacons were charged with the reception and preparation of the gifts. The preparation, in fact, consisted of two actions: the selection of a loaf of bread and setting it on a patent *(discos)*, and filling the cup(s) with wine and water.

In time, these simple, functional acts were embellished and ritualized with ceremonials, biblical verses, hymns, and prayers. The authors of the Byzantine liturgical commentaries[102] – the *mystagogical catecheses* – explained the various rites of the Divine Liturgy according to their own distinct theological insights and symbolic interpretations, often with an allegorical, anagogical, or representational view of the liturgy.[103]

Saint Germanos, for example, explained the Holy Liturgy using a multilayered symbolic system held together in a dynamic synthesis. He saw the bread of

---

100 For a comprehensive study on the prothesis rites see Stelyios S. Muksuris, *Economia and Eschatology: Liturgical Mystagogy in the Byzantine Prothesis Rite* (Brookline, MA 2013) and Thomas Pott, *Byzantine Liturgical Reform: A Study of Liturgical Change in the Byzantine Tradition* (Crestwood, NY 2010), 197-228. Also see Schmemann, *Eucharist*, 107-12.

101 On the offering of gifts by the faithful see Taft, *Great Entrance*, 16-43. The offerings were made without fanfare much as it is done in contemporary practice. Other gifts may have included oil for the lamps, candles, incense, food and coins and other non-liturgical gifts for the charitable activities of the community.

102 The genre includes the treatises of Cyril of Jerusalem, John Chrysostom, Theodore of Mopsuestia, Pseudo-Dionysios, Maximos the Confessor, Germanos of Constantinople, Nicholas and Theodore of Andida, Nicholas Cabasilas, and Symeon of Thessaloniki.

103 See Meyendorff, *St. Germanus,* 23-52. Hans-Joachim Schulz, *The Byzantine Liturgy: Symbolic Structure and Faith Expression* (New York, 1986); Enrico Mazza, *Mystagogy: A Theology of Liturgy in the Patristic Age* (New York, 1989); and Rene Bornert, *Les Commentaires Byzantins de la Divine Liturgie du VII - au XV siècle* (Paris 1966). As I have noted elsewhere, symbolic interpretations of the Divine Liturgy have a long and complex history. However, they are not entirely trouble-free, especially when they are excessively realistic or exaggerated. (Calivas, *Liturgy in Dialogue*, 87-91).

the many contained in a basket. The priest then takes the lance and with it proceeds to incise the loaf crosswise (σταυροειδῶς χαράξας) saying the words, "As a sheep led to the slaughter..." (Isaiah 53:7).[108] The priest then places the oblation on the discos and pointing over it, he says, "He does not open his mouth..." (Isaiah 53:7-8). The priest then takes the cup and the deacon pours wine and water into it saying, "Blood and water poured from his side... (John 19:34-35).[109] After this the priest places the cup on the table "and pointing at the bread, the sacrificed Lamb, and the wine, the blood poured out, he says: 'There are three who bear witness, the Spirit, the water and the blood, and the three are one (1 John 5:8) now and ever and to the ages.'"[110] Following this, the priest takes the censer, adds incense, and says the Prayer of the Prothesis.

From this description we learn several things. By the ninth century a priest presided at and conducted, in part, the rite of the proskomide. He traced/cut the sign of the cross over the prosphoron and placed it on the discos as he recited the words of Isaiah. A deacon or subdeacon was also present and played an active role. The deacon selected the bread of offering (προσφορά) and gave it to the priest. The deacon also poured the wine and water into the cup while reciting the appropriate words. The actions performed by the deacon are certainly a vestige of the earlier practice when deacons were charged with the preparation of the gifts.

By the ninth century the words from the prophecy of Isaiah (53:7-8) were firmly associated with the preparation of the offering bread and the words from the Gospel of John (19:34-35) were associated with the preparation of the cup. There is no mention in Germanos of any other commemorations or the placement of additional bread particles on the discos. There is, however, a reference to an offering of incense and to a prayer.

---

108 In the earlier chapter (21) Germanos clearly states that the offering is a piece of bread extracted from a whole loaf. The interpolated text, however, is not as clear. In any case, the priest, much as he does today, extracted the Amnos from a whole loaf.

109 By citing this event and the flow of blood and water from the side of the crucified Lord the Evangelist sought to emphasize the reality of Jesus' death.

110 Meyendorff, *St. Germanos*, 73. This may be a symbolic reference to baptism and the Eucharist.

In the *Barberini Codex* the text of the Divine Liturgy of St. Basil begins and ends with prayers recited at the skeuophylakion. The first of these prayers bears the title, "Prayer which the priest says in the skeuophylakion when placing the breads on the discos." This prayer is, in fact, the same Prayer of the Prothesis mentioned in the text of Germanos: "*O God, our God, who did send the Heavenly Bread, the food of the whole world, our Lord Jesus Christ...*" This prayer, which dates to the seventh century, concludes the rite of the prothesis to this very day.[111]

The interpolated text in Germanos' treatise provides another important detail. The offering bread or prosphora which is placed on the discos is referred to as "*the slaughtered (sacrificed) lamb.*" The term or name, *Lamb*, no doubt, derives from the prophecy of Isaiah. But the name or title, *Lamb*, is also mentioned in the Gospel of John. It is applied by St. John the Baptist to Jesus Christ when he saw him coming to him, "*Behold, the Lamb of God, who takes away the sin of the world*" (John 1:29). The title "Lamb of God" for Jesus identifies him with the Suffering Servant of Isaiah who "is led to slaughter as a lamb and bears our sins." It also connects Jesus' own passion and death with that of the Passover lamb: "For Christ, our paschal lamb, has been sacrificed" (1 Cor. 5:7). In the euchologia and ieratika the piece of bread extracted from the prosphoron and placed on the discos to be offered and consecrated is referred to as the *Amnos* (Ἀμνός = Lamb).

Thus, as Thomas Pott observes, the amnos becomes "the antitype of the immolated Son of God."[112] The amnos, however, signifies more. The sacrificed Son of God, as the seal imprinted upon the offering bread indicates, is also the conqueror, the victor over sin, corruption, and death. The crucified Christ is also the risen Christ, who "led captivity captive" (Psalm 67/68:18). Thus, the amnos at the prothesis anticipates the anaphora and the consecration of the gifts. It confirms the truths proclaimed in the anaphora: "Descending through the cross into Hades – that he might fill all things with himself – he loosed the pangs of death. He arose on the third day, having made for all flesh a path to the resurrection from the dead, since it was not possible for the Author of Life to be a victim of corruption" (*Anaphora* of BAS).[113]

---

111 See Pott, *Byzantine Liturgical Reform*, 200-3. Muksuris, *Economia and Eschatology*, 38-40.

112 Pott, *Byzantine Liturgical Reform*, 203.

113 Compare the words of the hymn which the priest recites at the conclusion of the prothesis rites: "In the tomb with the body; in Hades with the soul, as God; in Paradise with the thief; and on the throne with the Father and the Holy Spirit were you, O Christ, filling all things, yourself uncircumscribed."

The Prothesis Rite – the preparation of the bread and the cup(s), the offering of incense, and the Prayer of the Prothesis – remained relatively unchanged until the twelfth century when a series of new elements were introduced into the rite. These included a more elaborate preparation of the bread and cup,[114] the use of multiple loafs, the placement of additional particles of bread on the discos commemorating the saints and the living and the dead, the appearance of the asterisk (ἀστερίσκος-*small star*), the ritualized covering of the discos and the chalice with veils, the larger of which is called the *aer* (ἀήρ), and the prayer for the blessing of the incense. The new components were eventually formalized by the *Diataxis of Philotheos Kokkinos* in the fourteenth century and stabilized by the invention of the printing press and the publication of liturgical texts, which led to the standardization of the Orthodox liturgy, save for minor local variations.[115]

The Service of the Proskomide at the Prothesis

Prior to the service, the priest or deacon uncovers and arranges the sacred vessels (ἱερὰ σκεύη) and the other essential articles positioned on the prothesis table. These include the discos or paten (δῖσκος, δισκάριον), the chalice (cup - ποτήριον), the lance (λόχγη),[116] the asterisk, the veils (καλύμματα), the communion cloth or napkin (μάκτρον),[117] and the communion spoon (λαβίς). In addition, he makes certain the two cruets (bottles) are filled, one with fresh water and the other with sweet red wine. When the vessels have been properly arranged, the priest, deacon, or sexton places a tray with the prosphoron (prosphora) on the table in front of the discos and chalice.

The prosphora or prosphoron is a round loaf of leavened bread made only of wheat flour, yeast, salt, and water.[118] It is imprinted with a special seal or

---

[114] By the end of the twelfth century the preparation of the Lamb and the Cup approximated the form we know today. Pott, *Byzantine Liturgical Reform*, 207-10.

[115] *Ibid.* 226-33.

[116] The sacred vessels, including the asterisk, lance, and communion spoons, should be washed from time to time with soap and water and when necessary re-plated professionally.

[117] The priest must see to it that the church has a sufficient number of communion cloths. They should be washed and ironed frequently. The wash-water should be deposited in a dry well or directly into the earth by a tree or plant.

[118] The shape and size of the bread has varied through the centuries according to local customs.

offering as a sign of the incarnation but also of the passion of the Lord and as a true memorial of the Mystical (Last) Supper.[104] The Son of God, he says, in his goodness took on flesh (matter) and gave himself as an offering, a ransom and atonement for the life and salvation of the world. Citing the Gospel of John, Germanos notes that he who assumed the entirety of our human nature, except for sin, is the Bread which came down from heaven; and when eaten gives eternal life (John 6:51). Germanos also identifies the bread of offering with the Suffering Servant of Isaiah 53:7 and with the Cross, citing Jeremiah 11:19 (Septuagint version: "Δεῦτε καὶ ἐμβάλωμεν ξύλον εἰς τὸν ἄρτον αὐτοῦ – Come, let us place a stake in his bread").[105]

The reference to the Suffering Servant is of special interest because the words of Isaiah became decisive in the preparation of the bread. Here is what Germanos says: "The piece which is cut (ἀποκείρεσθαι) with the lance signifies the Crucified Lord who "like a sheep [was] led to the slaughter, and like a lamb that before its shearers is dumb" (Isaiah 53:7). From this we learn that, at the time of Germanos, the bread offered was no longer a whole loaf, but a piece extracted from a loaf. We also learn that a small lance-type implement was used to extract the piece and that the implement was identified with the lance used to pierce the side of the Lord at the crucifixion.[106] Additionally, when removing the piece, the words of Isaiah were pronounced.

Germanos also provides information about the cup. He likened the wine and water that are poured into the cup to the blood and water which came from the side of the crucified Lord. Finally, the bread and the cup correspond to the Mystical Supper at which the Lord spoke the words, "Take, eat... Drink of it..." He further declares that through these gifts Christ makes us communicants of his death, resurrection, and glory.

In the ninth century an additional text was interpolated into Germanos' original treatise (Chapter 22).[107] This added text is an even richer source of information on the development of the rite of the proskomide. According to this text, the priest is handed a loaf of bread by a deacon or subdeacon from

---

104 Meyendorff, *St. Germanus*, (chapters 20-22), 71-73.

105 *Ibid*, (chapters 20 and 21) 71.

106 On the introduction and use of the lance see Taft, *Pre-communion Rites*, 348-50; Pott, *Byzantine Liturgical Reform*, 202-6; and Muksuris, *Economia and Eschatology*, 40-1. The introduction of the lance into the rite of the Proskomide is connected to the feast commemorating the transfer of the relic of the lance (spear) used at the Crucifixion. The transfer of the relic from Jerusalem to Constantinople took place in the year 614. The relic was revered by the populace as having touched the very Body of the crucified Christ. Annually, on Great Friday, it was displayed in Hagia Sophia where it was reverenced by the faithful. See Juan Mateos, *Le Typikon de la Grande Eglise*, vol. II (Rome, 1963), 78.

107 Meyendorff, *St. Germanos*, 71-72.

THE PROSKOMIDE

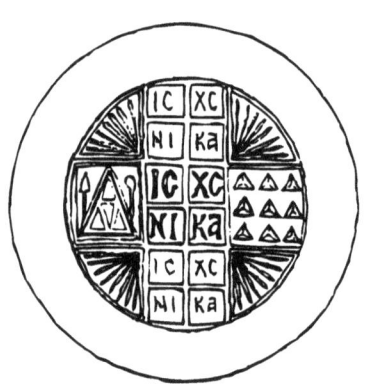

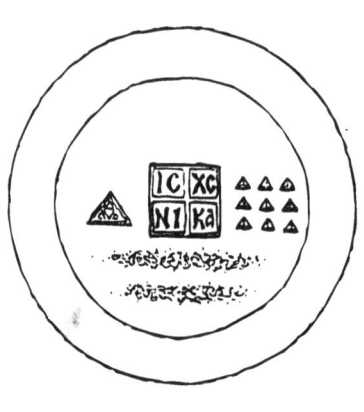

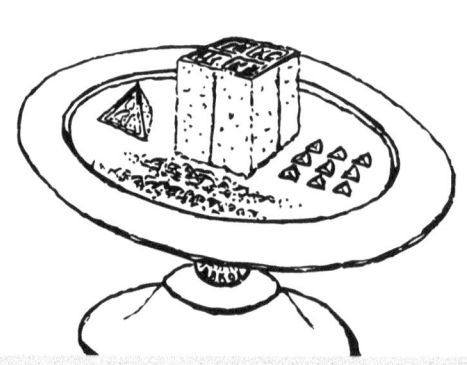

stamp, which bears, among other things, an imprint of the cross within a square and the Greek letters and the word: IC XC NIKA (IC = *Jesus*, XC = *Christ*, NIKA = *Conquers*) above and below the horizontal line separated by the vertical line of the cross (see the drawing).[119]

The sacred vessels are placed in the middle of the prothesis table, with the discos on the right (left hand of the priest) and the chalice on the left (right hand of priest).[120] The folded veils are usually placed to the right of the vessels. The folded asterisk is placed upon them while the lance rests on them or next to them. The cruets are usually to the left of the vessels (priest's right hand).

The Enarxis

The **priest** approaches the prothesis fully vested having first performed the lavabo. He makes three small prostrations saying, "*May God be merciful to me a sinner... Ὁ Θεὸς ἱλάσθητί μοι τῷ ἁμαρτωλῷ...*"

Priest

"*Εὐλογητὸς ὁ Θεὸς... Blessed is our God...*"

Then he takes the prosphoron with both hands while holding the lance in his right hand, lifts it to eye level and recites the hymn, "*Ἐξηγόρασας ἡμᾶς ἐκ τῆς κατάρας τοῦ νόμου ... You have redeemed us from the curse of the law by your precious blood...*"[121]

---

119 For more on the prosphoron and seal see the George Galavaris, *Bread and the Liturgy: the symbolism of the early Christian and Byzantine bread stamps* (University of Wisconsin Press, 1970).

120 To avoid cluttering the table with tiny crumbs falling from the prosphora during the preparation of the Amnos and the commemorations, the priest should place a communion cloth under the discos and chalice. When the commemorations have been completed, he lifts the cloth carefully and gives it to the sexton to properly dispose of the scraps. Instead of the cloth, the priest may use a tray to accomplish the same goal. It is important that the prothesis table be kept clean and free of bread crumbs.

121 This hymn is not mentioned in the diataxeis before the thirteenth century but is recorded in the fourteenth-century *Diataxis of Philotheos Kokkinos*. In the earlier versions of the service this troparion was recited before the opening doxology. However, since it is not an extraneous element of the service it should be said after the opening doxology. The hymn is borrowed from the Orthros of Great Friday (kathisma of the fifteenth antiphon). Some earlier versions of the service also contain the hymn "*Bethlehem be prepared ... Ἑτοιμάζου Βηθλεέμ*," as an introductory hymn to the service. This hymn is from the Forefeast (*παραμονή*) of Christmas and is a later addition to the service. Its inclusion was prompted by the idea that the prothesis represents Bethlehem, the place of Christ's birth. This imagery also drew the icon of the Nativity to the prothesis. However, as initially noted, the prothesis rite is clearly related to the passion of the Lord and the icon proper to the prothesis is the "Extreme Humility."

The Remembrance and the Sealing of the Prosphoron

The **priest** places the prosphoron on the tray. Holding the lance in his right hand he makes the sign of the cross over the prosphoron with the lance three times. Each time he repeats the words, *"Εἰς ἀνάμνησιν τοῦ Κυρίου ... In remembrance of our Lord and God and Savior Jesus Christ...."*[122]

Up to this point, as St. Nicholas Cabasilas observes, the bread of the prothesis, though separated from other loaves, remains only bread. Once it is sealed with the sign of the cross and the words *"In remembrance of our Lord..."* are spoken over it by the priest, the bread acquires a new characteristic; it is dedicated to God. It is an offering, a προσφορά.[123] While it is still only bread at this point, it is nonetheless special; it has a new identity, it is the bread of offering. Furthermore, the words, *"In remembrance..."* apply not only to the bread but also to the entire Divine Liturgy in which we remember the Lord Christ and all his saving deeds, especially his passion, resurrection, and glorification, the very cause of our salvation.[124]

Preparation of the Amnos and the Cup

The lamb is excised from the central part of the seal, the square piece, which bears the imprint containing a cross and the words IC XC NIKA. It is excised with five incisions, the latter of which is used to lift the lamb from the *prosphoron*. Each incision is accompanied by a phrase from the Messianic verses contained in the Prophecy of Isaiah 53:7-8, which are also recorded in the Book of Acts 8:32-33. In fact, the words used are taken from the passage in Acts which corresponds to the Septuagint text of Isaiah.

After the lamb is excised, the celebrant inverts it and cuts it crosswise, parting it just below the crust. These incisions are made to facilitate the breaking of

---

[122] These words became a fixed element of the rite by the twelfth century, if not earlier. They echo the command of the Lord at the Mystical Supper, "Do this in remembrance of me," which is recorded by St. Paul (1 Cor. 11:24) and St. Luke (22:19) in their respective descriptions of the Last Supper. Christ instituted the Eucharist at the Supper to perpetuate the remembrance of his redemptive work and to establish a continuous intimate communion between himself and those who believe in him. The Eucharist is Christ himself. Sacramentally, we receive the sacrificed, risen, and glorified body of the Lord, which he gives to his people for the forgiveness of sins and life eternal.

[123] Cabasilas, *Commentary on the Divine Liturgy*, 1:6, 11. In the rare instance when, for some reason, the extracted piece cannot be used, it is set aside to be eaten by the priest (or deacon) when the leftover consecrated elements are consumed at the end of the Divine Liturgy. In such rare instances, the priest is obliged to extract a new lamb and repeat the ritual actions. The presence of three lambs on the prosphoron seal serves a practical purpose, to meet problems such as the one just mentioned. This is especially helpful when an additional prosphoron is not available.

[124] *Ibid.* 1:7.

the Holy Bread before Communion. As with other utilitarian acts, it also was ritualized. It is accompanied by sacrificial language based, in part, on the testimony of St. John the Baptist recounted in the Gospel of John: "*Sacrificed is the Lamb of God, who takes away the sin of the world, for the life of the world and its salvation.*"[125] In later times a second phrase was added to accompany the second incision: "*By your Crucifixion, O Christ, the power of the enemy was crushed; neither angel nor man has saved us, but the Lord himself...*"[126]

Cutting and Excising the Lamb – Amnos

The **priest** inserts the lance (or a sharp knife) into the prosphoron at the right (priest's left) of the seal IC XC NIKA. Cutting deep along the right border (IC/NI) of the square, he says, "*As a sheep led to the slaughter ... Ὡς πρόβατον ἐπὶ σφαγὴν ἤχθη.*" Cutting along the border of the left side (XC/KA) of the square he says, "*And as a blameless lamb before its shearers is dumb, so he opens not his mouth ... Καὶ ὡς ἀμνὸς ἄμωμος...*" Cutting along the upper side, he says, "*In his humiliation his judgment was taken away ... Ἐν τῇ ταπεινώσει...*" Cutting along the lower side, he says, "*Who shall declare his generation ... Τὴν δὲ γενεὰν...*"

After this the priest extracts the piece of bread in front of the amnos. Then he inserts the lance at the bottom of the amnos and lifts it up saying, "*For his life was taken away from the earth .... Ὅτι αἴρεται ἀπὸ τῆς γῆς ἡ ζωὴ αὐτοῦ...*"[127]

Inverting the amnos (crust down), he lays it on the discos and cuts it crosswise, taking care not to break the crust. He says, "*Sacrificed is the Lamb of God, who takes away the sin of the world, for the life and salvation of the world ... Θύεται ὁ Ἀμνὸς τοῦ Θεοῦ.*" According to current practice, while making the second of the crosswise incisions, he adds the words, "*By Your crucifixion, O Christ ... Σταυρωθέντός σου Χριστέ...*"

When these actions have been completed, the priest inverts the amnos again (imprint or crust up) and places it in the middle of the discos (see the drawing).

Piercing the right side of the *amnos* with the lance under the letters *IC*, he

---

125 John 1:29. The naming of Jesus as the lamb of God brings to mind Isaiah's Man of Sorrows, the Suffering Servant (Isaiah 53:1-12).

126 The adoption of this second phrase is relatively new. It is not found in the early Greek or Slavic euchologia nor is it included in the recent *Ieratikon of the Church of Greece* or in the Ieratikon published by the Monastery of Simonopetra of Mt. Athos. Nonetheless, there is no reason to omit it. It affirms our belief that salvation comes from God alone and not from men or angels. Here we have an example of liturgical "expansion."

127 Theodore of Mopsuestia interpreted the transfer of the gifts of bread and wine to the Holy Table symbolically. He identified the procession of the gifts with the funeral cortege of the crucified and dead Christ. This symbolic interpretation may have led to the association of the gifts with the Passion – with the immolated Christ, who was once dead and now lives and is glorified.

says, "*One of the soldiers pierced his side with a spear and at once there came out blood and water. He who saw it has borne witness and his witness is true ... Εἷς τῶν στρατιωτῶν λόγχῃ τὴν πλευρὰν αὐτοῦ ἔνυξε, καὶ εὐθέως ἐξῆλθεν αἷμα καὶ ὕδωρ...*" (John 19:34-35).

The Cup or Chalice

As the **priest** says the words, "*and at once there came out blood and water,*" he takes the cruets with the wine and water and pours a sufficient amount of wine and some water into the cup.¹²⁸ After this, the priest blesses the cup saying, "*Blessed is the union of your holy things ... Εὐλογημένη ἡ ἕνωσις τῶν ἁγίων σου...*" (To protect the cup from contamination while he completes the proskomide, he places a temporary cover on it).

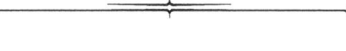

AN IMPORTANT NOTE

If a deacon is present, he assists the priest during the performance of the proskomide by saying the prescribed biddings in the Ieratikon. More importantly, according to tradition, as noted in the Euchologion, the deacon pours the wine and water into the cup. Accordingly, the deacon takes up the cruets and says to the priest, "Bless, Master, the holy union." The priest responds, "Blessed is the union of the holy things..." after which, the deacon pours the wine and water into the cup.

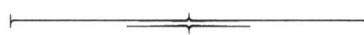

The Commemoration of the Saints and the Living and the Dead

The earliest witness to the multiplication of particles of bread on the discos commemorating the Theotokos and the saints and the living and the dead is an eleventh-century manuscript. The multiplication of particles constitutes the most significant development in the prothesis rite after the ninth century.¹²⁹

The impetus for the multiplication of particles probably came from the Prayer of the Prothesis, which reads in part: "Bless this offering, and accept it upon your heavenly altar. *Remember those who offered it and those for whom it was offered.*" Since all the offering breads could not be placed on the discos, save

---

128 Some scholars have argued that ordinary water was poured into the chalice only when the prothesis rite was transferred to the beginning of the Divine Liturgy. Earlier, when the rite was conducted at the Great Entrance, they say, warm water was poured into the chalice. Warm water was added again to the chalice after the consecration and before the reception of Holy Communion. More will be said about this below in reference to the *zeon* (hot water).

129 On the multiplication of particle see Muksuris, *Economy and* Eschatology, 136-63. Pott, *Byzantine Liturgical Reform*, 210-16.

one or a portion of one, the church prayed that God would bestow his rich mercies upon all those who brought a gift and upon those for whom the gift(s) was offered.

This general petition led to a ritual action: the placement of tiny particles on the discos from the offerings. Two general petitions, one for the living and the other for the dead, accompanied the placement of the particles. In a final development the general petitions were augmented with the commemoration of particular names: for the well-being of the living and for the repose of the dead.[130] All this was accomplished by invoking the prayers and supplications of the Theotokos and the saints, "*Through their prayers, O Lord, accept this sacrifice upon your heavenly altar.*"[131] The particles for the living and the dead were and continue to be placed in front of the amnos – representing God's people who stand humbly before him supplicating his rich and abundant mercies.

The multiplication of particles was finalized when additional particles were added to the discos commemorating the saints who intercede on behalf of the people. However, the saints are more than intercessors; they are also the beloved, revered, and honored members of the Church community. Thus, it came about that small triangular pieces of bread were placed on either side of the amnos in honor and in memory of the saints, starting with the Theotokos. In fact, the Theotokos and the saint(s) of the day were the first of the saints to gain a fixed place in the prothesis rite.[132]

The Theotokos holds the place of honor because of her distinct role in sacred history – her unique relationship to the Lord as both mother and servant. The triangular particle in her honor and memory is positioned on the discos to

---

130 Pott (*Ibid.* 213) suggests that the commemoration of names at the prothesis probably began in monasteries where the benefactors of the community, both living and dead, were remembered in prayer. In time, the commemorations also included the names of the hegoumenos and the living and deceased members of the community.

131 This phrase has now been attached to the commemoration of the Theotokos. Pott (215-6) argues that by omitting the phrase, "*Through their prayers,*" the "saints no longer [have] the function of interceding for the forgiveness of the faithful who [are] being commemorated, but rather [are] themselves commemorated in their own honor and memory." However, in the anaphora of both liturgies, BAS and CHR, the commemoration of the saints ends with the phrase, "*at whose supplications visit us, O God,*" thus emphasizing the intercessory role of the saints. For more on the commemoration of the saints see Muksuris, *Economia and Eschatology*, 136-40. For the commemoration of the saints in Vespers, Orthros, prothesis, and Divine Liturgy see James C. Skedros, "Having Remembered all the Saints: Liturgical Commemoration of the Saints in Middle and Late Byzantium," in *Evangelist, Shepherd, and Teacher: Studies in Honor of Archbishop Demetrios of America*, J. Skedros, M. Constas, and V. Limberis, editors (Brookline, MA 2000), 341-52.

132 Pott, *Byzantine Liturgical Reform*, 214.

the right of the amnos, since the right side is regarded as the place of honor.[133] Certainly, this notion gave rise to the use of the psalm verse, *"The Queen stands on your right side…"* when the particle in her honor is placed on the discos.

Extracting the Particles in Honor of the Theotokos, the Angels, and the Saints

The seal of the prosphoron contains the figure of the cross within a large circle. The vertical bar of the cross as already mentioned, contains three squares, each with the same distinct inscription, IC XC NIKA. The horizontal bar on either side of the middle square contains two square imprints, one with a small triangular piece on the right side and another with nine smaller triangular pieces on the left (see figure). The triangular imprint on the right will be cut and placed on the discos in honor and in memory of the Theotokos. The nine smaller triangles on the left will also be cut and placed on the discos in hierarchical order in honor and in memory of the angels and the saints.[134]

The Theotokos

The **priest** cuts the larger triangle on the right side of the seal with the lance. He thrusts the lance into the two sides and into the bottom of the triangle along its borders. When cutting the piece, he says, *"Εἰς τιμὴν καὶ μνήμην τῆς ὑπερευλογημένης … In honor and memory of our most blessed Lady, the Theotokos and ever-Virgin Mary. Through her prayers, O Lord, accept this sacrifice upon your heavenly altar."*

Then lifting up the particle with the lance, he places it on the right side of the lamb. When he places it on the discos, he says: *"Παρέστη ἡ βασίλισσα ἐκ δεξιῶν σου… The Queen stands on your right side, arrayed in garments of gold and of diverse colors"* (Psalm 44/45:10; Septuagint text).[135]

---

133 In scripture and tradition sitting or standing at one's right is a sign of special honor. See, for example, Psalm 110:1, Mark 16:19, Rom. 8:34, Ephes. 1:20, 1 Peter 3:22, and Matt. 25:32-34.

134 In times past, as it is done today in Slavic and other churches, four small prosphora were placed on the prothesis: the first is in honor of Christ, the second in honor of the Theotokos, the third in honor of the saints, and the fourth is for the living and the dead. In Russia, prior to the reforms of Patriarch Nikon, five or even seven small loaves were used. In contemporary Greek practice all the particles are usually extracted from one prosphoron. However, the priest may choose to use more than one prosphoron. It is well-known that the prosphoron from which the particles are extracted is cut into small pieces together with a sufficient number of additional prosphora for the antidoron, the blessed bread which is distributed to the congregation at the end of the Divine Liturgy. When a Pre-Sanctified Divine Liturgy is to be celebrated, the Greek priest is obliged to use two prosphora. He extracts the Amnos for the Liturgy which is about to be celebrated from one prosphoron and from another the Amnos for the Pre-Sanctified Liturgy.

135 The triangular piece in honor of the Theotokos should be of a moderate or proportionate size. The amnos is always the prominent piece on the patent.

The Saints

The **priest** cuts the nine smaller triangular particles in honor of the saints and places them on the discos on the left of the amnos. The saints are divided into several categories and are commemorated in hierarchical order. The particles are placed in three descending columns or lines, with the first three closest to the amnos.[136] The fourth, fifth, and sixth particles make up the middle column, while the seventh, eighth, and ninth particles comprise the outer column.

The **priest** removes the first small triangular particle and places it on the left side of the amnos,[137] saying: *"In honor and memory of the Archangels Michael and Gabriel and of all the heavenly host."*[138] *Removing the second small triangle, he places it below the first, saying: "Of the honorable and glorious Prophet, Forerunner, and Baptist John, of the glorious prophets..."*[139]

The succeeding particles are dedicated in honor of the following several categories of saints: the holy Apostles (3); the holy fathers and ecumenical teachers (4); the First-Martyr Stephen and all the glorious martyrs (5); the venerable and righteous ascetics (6); the wonder-workers and healers (7); the righteous ancestors Joachim and Anna...and the saint(s) of the day (8); and the holy father whose liturgy is being celebrate (9).[140]

Regarding the practice of commemorating the saints and the living and the dead, St. Symeon of Thessaloniki says the following: "A discussion has come down to us from the fathers that the particles provide great advantage: for they are there in place of the persons for whom they are offered, and the offering is made on their behalf to God, just as the priest says in offering them, 'Receive,

---

136 As Pott notes (218-9), moved by pietistic impulses, the list of saints grew longer and longer. The tendency toward excess was finally corrected by Philotheos Kokkinos through his Diataxis. The prothesis rite became more or less fixed. Local churches have introduced some minor variations. Most versions of the rite, however, have remained faithful to the spirit of Philotheos Kokkinos.

137 Sometimes, it is difficult to extract each particle individually from the seal. In such instances, the priest may cut out the portion containing the nine small triangles and place it on the discos. He may also score the crust of the portion with the lance by making two vertical and two horizontal lines between the triangles thus giving the appearance of distinction or separateness.

138 Some euchologia omit the commemoration of the angelic host. The first particle is dedicated to St. John the Baptist and the second to the prophets of the Old Testament.

139 The phrase *"in honor and memory"* is not repeated for each of the succeeding particles but is understood, as indicated by the syntax in the original Greek in each commemoration.

140 In some instances, local churches differ in the sequence of the categories of saints and in the number of names in each category. Often some commemorations reflect local usages and traditions. The longer the list of saints becomes the more recent is its origin.

Lord, this offering.' The offerings for the saints, then, are for their glory and honor. The particles for the faithful departed are for the forgiveness of sins, and the union of divine grace, while those for the living, provided they lead lives of repentance, are for the deliverance from errors, for the forgiveness of sins, and for the hope of eternal life."[141]

The Commemoration of the Diptychs (the Living and the Dead)

For the Living: The priest retains the portion of the prosphoron he extracted to gain access to the amnos. He uses it to commemorate the names of the living and the dead by taking tiny particles from it and placing them in front of the lamb in two groups side by side with a space between them. The particles for the living are placed on the right side of the lamb (left of the priest) and the particles for the dead on the left (right of the priest).[142]

First, the priest commemorates the living, saying: "*Remember, Loving Master all Episcopates of the Orthodox, our Archbishop (Name)... Μνήσθητι, Δέσποτα φιλάνθωπε, πάσης Ἐπισκοπῆς Ὀρθοδόξων, τοῦ Ἀρχιεπισκόπου ἡμῶν (δεῖνος)...*" As he remembers the hierarch, the presbyterate and the diaconate, and every order of the clergy, he extracts a particle and places it on the right side of the discos (his left). He continues to extract additional pieces as he finishes the general commemorations of the living.

When he has finished the general commemoration, he continues to pray for the living whom he wishes to remember and for those for whom he has been asked to pray by reciting their baptismal name.[143]

For the Dead: The general commemoration of those who have fallen asleep follows: "*In blessed memory and for the forgiveness of sins of... Ὑπέρ μνήμης καὶ ἀφέσεως...*" Again, he extracts particles for the dead and places them on the left side of the discos (his right).

When he has finished this general petition, he prays for those whom he wishes to remember and for other departed Orthodox Christians for whom he has been asked to pray by reciting their baptismal name.

The priest also remembers in prayer the hierarch(s) who ordained him.

---

141 Symeon of Thessaloniki, *Explanation of the Divine Temple,* cited in Taft, *The Communion, Thanksgiving, and Concluding Rites* (Rome 2008), 715. Also see S. Hawkes-Teeples, *The Praise of God in the Twilight of the Empire: The Divine Liturgy in the Commentaries of Symeon of Thessaloniki (+1429),* (Rome 1997) unpublished doctoral dissertation.

142 In some depictions of the discos, the particles of the living and the dead are placed in two rows. The upper row closest to the lamb is for the living and the second row for the dead.

143 When praying for the living and the dead we use baptismal names. Nicknames should be avoided.

The priest concludes the commemorations of the living and the dead by imploring God not to forsake him: "*Remember, Lord, my unworthiness also, (N) the presbyter... Μνήθητι, Κύριε, καὶ τῆς ἐμῆς ἀναξιότητος ...*"

Important Note

If a hierarch is presiding at the Eucharist, the priest prepares the eucharistic gifts up to and including the commemoration of the saints. He also excises a small particle and places it in front of the amnos as he prays for the well-being of the hierarch, "Remember, loving Master all Episcopates of the Orthodox, our Archbishop (Name)..." At the appropriate time, the hierarch will complete the remembrances of the living and the dead and cover the gifts. When the hierarch is at the prothesis commemorating the diptychs, the priest stands to his right. By tradition, when the hierarch remembers the priest by saying his name, the priest kisses the hierarch's shoulder as a sign of respect and gratitude for the hierarch's prayer on his behalf.

The Offering of Incense:

When the preparation of the gifts has been completed, the deacon or in the absence of one the sexton or altar server brings the censer to the priest, who blesses the offering of the incense and recites the prayer: "*We offer incense to you, Christ our God... Θυμίαμά σοι προσφέρομεν, Χριστὲ ὁ Θεὸς ἡμῶν...*"[144]

Covering the Gifts

After he has blessed the incense, the priest proceeds to cover the gifts. First, he takes the star, opens it, and holds it over the censer as the deacon or sexton censes it.[145] Then he places it on the discos. After this he takes each of the three veils in turn and follows the same procedure. He places the first veil over the

---

144 Censing at the prothesis was introduced around the ninth century to accompany the prothesis prayer. By the twelfth century it was moved forward and associated with the covering of the gifts. A blessing prayer for the offering of incense was also added. The incense prayer dates to at least the tenth century. Today, the same prayer is said twice, once at the prothesis and a second time at the Divine Liturgy when the Evangelion is about to be censed as the "Alleluia" is sung. For practical reasons the second recitation is often omitted.

145 This passage, which is found in most *ieratika*, is in conflict with the earlier image of the prothesis as Golgotha. It reflects a later development when the prothesis was seen in terms of the manger or the cave of Bethlehem, the birthplace of Christ. As a result, the icon of the Nativity of Christ began to displace the icon of the Extreme Humility, which depicts the Passion of Christ.

discos and the second over the chalice.[146] He covers both vessels with the third large veil called the *aer*. For each of the aforementioned articles, the priest says the following biblical verse as he places them on the discos and the cup:

The Asterisk[147]

"And the star came to rest over the place where the child was… Καὶ ἐλθὼν ὁ ἀστὴρ…" (Matt. 2:9).

Or we say:

"By the word of the Lord the heavens were made, and all their host by the breath of his mouth – Τῷ λόγῳ Κυρίου οἱ οὐρανοὶ ἐστερεώθησαν καὶ τῷ πνεύματι τοῦ στόματος αὐτοῦ πᾶσα ἡ δύναμις αὐτῶν" (Psalm 32/33:6), which is more appropriate.[148]

The veil for the discos

"The Lord reigns… Ὁ Κύριος ἐβασίλευσεν…" (Psalm 92/93:1).

The veil for the chalice

"Your virtue, Christ… Ἐκάλυψεν οὐρανούς…" (Based on Habakkuk 3:3).

The large veil, the aer (ἀήρ)

"Cover us with the shelter of your wings… Σκέπασον ἡμᾶς…" (It is based on Psalm 16/17:8).[149]

---

146 Sometimes, the discos and chalice are supplied with decorative metal covers which take the place of the two veils.

147 The asterisk is first mentioned in late eleventh-century sources. However, it appears in liturgical books only in the fourteenth century. The asterisk serves a practical purpose. It consists of two bent metal pieces which are joined at the center. When it is opened and placed on the discos it forms a firm structure over the bread particles, a base upon which the veil rests safely. It was introduced precisely for this reason, to prevent the particles from being disturbed and scattered by the veil. In time, it was given the name "asterisk" and identified symbolically with the star of Bethlehem (Matt. 2:19).

148 Cabasilas mentions both verses. The new *Ieratikon of the Church of Greece* has replaced the Matthean verse with the psalmic verse, which is also found in the *Ieratikon of the Monastery of Simonopetra*. The psalmic verse is found in several manuscripts and is compatible with the diaconal bidding which precedes it, "*Master, make firm – Στερέωσον, δέσποτα.*" This psalmic verse is more appropriate rather than the Matthean verse. This change in the ieratika of the Church of Greece and Simonopetra provides us with an example of liturgical restoration.

149 The same phrases appear at the end of some prayers of supplication. See, for example, the Supplicatory Prayer of the Orthros which is also found in the service of the *Lite* and the *Artoklasia*, "*O God, save your people – Σῶσον ὁ Θεὸς τὸν λαόν σου…*"

Censing of the Gifts

When the vessels have been covered, the **priest** takes the censer and censes the gifts saying: *"Blessed is our God, who is thus pleased. Glory to you! – Εὐλογητὸς ὁ Θεὸς ἡμῶν, ὁ οὕτως εὐδοκήσας, δόξα σοι..."* (He says this three times. If a deacon is present, the deacon adds the phrase, "Now and forever and unto the ages of ages. Amen"). After this the priest recites the Prayer of the Prothesis.

The Prayer of the Prothesis

"O God, our God ... Ὁ Θεός, ὁ Θεὸς ἡμῶν..."

As already mentioned, the initial preparation of the eucharistic elements was purely functional. The act was embellished and ritualized in the seventh century with the addition of the prothesis prayer. According to the sources, the prayer was recited by a priest in the skeuophylakion after the deacon(s) had placed the offering bread on the discos and had filled the cup(s) with wine and water.[150] Significantly, the focus of the prayer is on the offering bread; the cup is not mentioned.[151] This focus remained constant through the ages, even as the ritual actions of the Prothesis Rite developed.

The brief preface of the prayer is based on the Gospel of John in which Jesus identifies himself with the Bread of Life sent from heaven by the Father for the life of the world (6:25-59). The prayer reads in part, *"O God, our God, who did send the heavenly Bread, the food of the whole world, our Lord and God Jesus Christ..."* The prayer also declares that Jesus, the Bread of Life, is the Savior, Redeemer, and Benefactor, the one who blesses and sanctifies all those who believe in him. He is the food of the world, the unique nourishment of the entire cosmos and especially of every human being who comes into the world. The short preface is followed by an epiclesis. God is asked to bless the offering of the Church (*"εὐλόγησον τὴν Πρόθεσιν ταύτην..."*) that it may be received upon the heavenly altar. The intercessory part of the prayer contains two petitions. God is asked to shed his goodness and mercies upon those who have offered the gifts and upon those for whom they were offered. The priest, praying for all, also beseeches God to preserve the clergy and the people blameless as they celebrate the Divine Eucharist. The prayer's concluding doxology is addressed to the Persons of the Holy Trinity, the majestic name of whom is sanctified and glorified by the worshipping community.

---

[150] The addition of a prayer is a further indication of the gradual ritualization of the rite, which was originally performed only by deacons.

[151] The omission of the cup in the prayer may be due, as Pott and others have suggested, to the fact that the cup was still being prepared at the Great Entrance, as originally practiced.

The Apolysis

Immediately after the prayer, the **priest** recites the standard small *apolysis* (dismissal prayer) as prescribed in the Ieratikon. Following the apolysis, the priest kisses the covered gifts, first the discos (bread), then the chalice, and then the cross at the center of the aer.[152] If a deacon is present, he kisses the end of the aer.

Censing the Holy Table

Immediately after, the **deacon** or in the absence of a deacon, the **priest** censes the Holy Table. This is considered an honorific act in preparation for the Divine Liturgy.[153] While censing, the priest (or deacon) recites the three prescribed hymns, which are a later addition to the rite.[154]

C. THE PRELIMINARIES

1. As the time for the celebration of the Divine Liturgy approaches

The **priest** and **deacon**, if one is present, stand before the Holy Table in their usual place.[155] The priest, lifting his hands slightly recites the prayer, "*Heavenly King, the Comforter, the Spirit of truth…*"[156]

Then, the priest and deacon alternately recite the following two biblical verses. If there is no deacon, the priest says everything. First, the angelic hymn is recited three times: "*Glory to God in the highest, and on earth peace, among men with whom he is pleased.*" (Luke: 2:14). At each recitation, the priest and deacon bow, making a small prostration.[157]

---

152 The amnos always takes precedence over the chalice. Hence, the discos is always reverenced first.

153 The rubrics in many euchologia and ieratika extend the censing to include the icons of the iconostasis and the people. This extended form of censing, however, was already performed during the Orthros at the Ninth Ode. Another similar censing seems redundant. Also, we do not cense at the Great Doxology of Orthros. At the conclusion of the prothesis rite, we cense only the Holy Table and the sanctuary

154 Some editions of the prothesis rite contain only one hymn, the first: "*In the tomb with the body; in Hades with the soul, as God….*" Other editions omit them entirely. Some euchologia and ieratika contain a rubric that requires the deacon or priest to recite Psalm 50/51 during the censing at the conclusion of the prothesis rite.

155 Most often, this occurs when the choir or chanter starts singing the Great Doxology.

156 The prayer is omitted during the entire Paschal season and is reintroduced on the eve of the Sunday of Pentecost.

157 In some ieratika the rubrics have the concelebrating clergy perform the three small prostrations after the biblical verses have been recited. In this instance, the clergy repeat the words of the repentant Publican, "*God, be merciful to me a sinner - Ὁ Θεὸς ἱλάσθητί μοι τῷ ἁμαρτωλῷ*" (Luke 18:13) at each prostration.

Second, the psalm verse is said twice: "*O Lord, open my lips and my mouth shall show forth your praise*" (Ps. 50/51:15).

After this, the priest kisses the Evangelion and the Holy Table. The deacon kisses the Holy Table.

The priest prayerfully concentrates on the mystery that he is about to celebrate. At this point, some *Ieratika* contain the following rubric: "The priest raises his hands slightly and says humbly, "*Lord, Lord open to me the door of your lovingkindness.*"

2. If a deacon is present

The deacon bows his head to the priest and says, "*It is time for the Lord to act; bless, Master.*" The priest lays his right hand on his head and blesses him saying, "*Blessed is our God…*"

The deacon again says, "*Pray for me, Master.*" The priest responds saying, "*May the Lord direct your steps unto every good work.*" The deacon again says, "*Remember me, holy Master.*" The priest responds saying, "*May the Lord God remember you in his kingdom…*" The dialogue ends here. The deacon takes leave of the priest and exits the sanctuary via the north door. He proceeds to the solea and stands before the Holy Doors. At the appropriate time, he intones the bidding for the start of the Divine Liturgy, "*Master, bless.*"

A NOTE

In some euchologia and ieratika the order of the preliminaries is reversed. The blessing of the deacon precedes the prayers and prostrations. Either order is acceptable. Of course, in the absence of a deacon the dialogue between the priest and deacon is omitted.

If two or more priests are concelebrating, they gather before the Holy Table according to seniority and recite the aforementioned prayer and biblical verses in rotation and make the three small prostrations in unison. Then the senior priest bows to the others. The senior priest stands in front of the Holy Table. The second in rank stands to his right on the side of the Holy Table and the third to his left, and so forth.

6. CELEBRATING THE DIVINE LITURGY

In the following paragraphs we will focus on the units that comprise the Divine Liturgy by tracing their development through the centuries and mining their meanings.[158] The aim of this exercise is to provide the celebrant with a better understanding of what he is doing and why he is doing it. The Divine Liturgy, however, is more than ceremonials; it is a prayer. Above all, it is an event, an encounter with the living God. As such, it is a transformative experience for all those who celebrate it in faith.

The Divine Liturgy is celebrated by all the people of God, clergy and laity together. The people are not dispensable spectators but essential concelebrants. At the liturgical assembly every faithful person stands before God as a liturgical minister, each with their respective role.

Most, if not all, official texts of the Divine Liturgy presuppose the celebration is being performed by a single priest with a deacon. These texts also assign various responses and hymns to the people (λαός), led by a chanter or choir.[159] Because very few parishes are graced with the presence of a deacon, I will concentrate on the actions of the priest and offer remarks for the deacon when necessary.

---

158 Renewal and reforms that are sound and meaningful can come about only through a real, objective knowledge of the historical development of liturgical rites. This knowledge constitutes the most effective methodological tool for meaningful discussions on liturgical renewal and reform. Professor Nicholas Denysenko, the distinguished liturgist and Orthodox theologian, drawing from certain principles of liturgical history, has recently provided us with a new order of the Divine Liturgy, which he carefully developed, reflecting his academic competences and pastoral sensitivities. His commendable effort affords us the basis for a meaningful dialogue regarding the process and implications of liturgical renewal and the revisions and modifications it may suggest and require. See Nicholas Denysenko, "The Divine Liturgy – A New Order," in *Worship*, vol. 95 (January 2021), 12-33.

159 We are obliged to respect, honor, and support the important ministry offered by choirs, chanters, and readers who enrich our liturgical experiences through the exercise of their God-given talents. Emulating their devotion, every worshipper should aspire to participate in the actions of the liturgy by fulfilling his/her ministry of prayer and song, however limited the role. On this point, choirs and chanters at the suggestion of the priest can be very helpful. They can encourage the people's participation in worship by helping them learn how to follow their lead in singing in a low voice the simple, well-known responses, refrains, and hymns of the liturgy. Congregational singing, when done well, is not a distraction. On the role of the laity in the Church, see Nicholas Afanasiev, *The Church of the Holy Spirit* (Notre Dame, IN 2007), 33-79. See also Ioannis Karmiris, *The Status and Ministry of the Laity in the Orthodox Church* (Brookline, MA, 1994); Emmanuel Clapsis "The Laity in the Orthodox Church," in his *Orthodoxy in Conversation: Orthodox Ecumenical Engagements* (Geneva and Brookline, MA 2000); Calivas, *Church, Clergy, Laity, and the Spiritual Life*, 6-21).

A. THE ENARXIS

From the extant sources we learn that the Divine Liturgy, in its earliest form, began with the Readings, which were preceded by a gathering of the clergy and the people. In due course, the gathering itself was formalized and ritualized into what we now call the Small Entrance, which for several centuries marked the beginning of the service, called the *Enarxis*.[160]

At some point between 630 and 730 A.D., probably at the beginning of the eighth century, a new element or unit was attached to the enarxis, the office of the three antiphons.[161] This unit has its roots in the daily cycle of worship of the cathedral office of Constantinople.[162] Within a couple of centuries, two additional elements were also introduced to the enarxis: the initial blessing

---

[160] See Brightman, *Eastern Liturgies*, for an outline and text of the Byzantine Liturgy before the seventh century (527-34); ninth century text of CHR, BAS and PRES (309-352); and the received text of CHR and BAS (prayers), 353-411. Each of the sections is prefaced by a brief note providing the sources from which the texts are drawn.

[161] The antiphons are not cited by St. Maximos the Confessor (+662) in his description of the Divine Liturgy but are mentioned in the commentary of St. Germanos of Constantinople (+733). The antiphons were originally associated with the stational liturgies of Constantinople. The *Typikon of the Great Church* lists sixty-eight such liturgies, which featured a grand procession through the streets of the city. In time, the number of these liturgies was reduced. They were used to celebrate certain feasts and events from as early as the fifth century. The service began with the Orthros in one church. From there the clergy and the people processed to the designated church for the Divine Liturgy using antiphonal psalmody and stopping at three or more places (stations) to invoke God with litanies and prayers. On a limited number of occasions, the office of the three antiphons was sung at the halfway point of the procession. Sometime between the seventh and eighth centuries this office was attached to the enarxis of the Divine Liturgy. See John F. Baldovin, *The Urban Character of Christian Worship: The Origins, Development, and Meaning of Stational Liturgy* (Rome 1987), 205-26. For a brief account see Calivas, *Aspects of Orthodox Worship*, 69-77.

[162] In the beginning, the office of the antiphons was conducted by a priest(s). The hierarch arrived and waited in the narthex until the antiphons were concluded. Then, accompanied by clerics and people, he performed the entrance rite. To this day, a hierarch remains on the episcopal throne, outside the sanctuary, until the antiphons have been completed. Then, he moves to the center of the *solea*, performs the rites of the entrance, and enters the sanctuary.

or doxology,[163] and the *Great Synapte* or Great Litany.[164] These elements – the opening doxology, the litany, and the antiphons – have for centuries constituted the enarxis or the introductory part of the Divine Liturgy.[165]

In his *Commentary* on the Divine Liturgy (II, 12), St. Nicholas Cabasilas reminds us that when we come before God, we must first recognize the inaccessibility and grandeur of his glory and be filled with wonder and awe. He writes, "Thus, doxology has first place in any intercourse with God, and it is for this reason that the priest glorifies God before any prayer or sacred homily. But why does he glorify the three-fold nature of God and not his unity? For he does not say 'Blessed be God' or 'Blessed be the kingdom,' but distinguishes between the Persons. 'Blessed be the kingdom of the Father and the Son and the Holy Spirit.' It is because it was through the Incarnation of the Lord that humankind first learned that God was three Persons, and the mystery which is being performed is centered on the incarnation of the Lord, so that from the very beginning the Trinity must shine forth and be proclaimed."

---

163 The initial blessing or doxology, "*Blessed is the kingdom...*" began to appear in manuscripts of the Divine Liturgy in the tenth century. However, it appears to have been in existence at least a century earlier. It is mentioned by St. Theodore the Studite (+826). In fact, this particular initial blessing is identified with the Studite typikon. Every divine service begins with a brief doxological formula.

164 The Great Synapte was placed at the beginning of the service after the eleventh century. Previously, it was said before the transfer of the Gifts, associated with the prayers of the faithful before the Great Entrance. The synapte has left traces of its earlier position in the Dismissal or Completion Litany which is now intoned immediately after the Great Entrance. In any case, the present position of the Great Litany seems out of place. The Divine Liturgy begins not with songs of praise and thanksgiving but with a series of requests. Saint John Climacus teaches us that "prayer is by nature a dialogue and a union of man with God.... Heartfelt thanksgiving should have first place in our book of prayer. Next should be confession and genuine contrition of soul. After that should come our request to the universal King. This method of prayer is best" (*The Ladder*, step 28 – On Prayer). When the Church embarks on a serious program of liturgical renewal and reform, the present position of the Great Synapte should be evaluated. Indeed, the entire enarxis should be carefully studied, restoring to it its initial dynamic character. In the spirit of the words of St. John Climacus, after the opening blessing, the Church may wish to consider inserting select verses from Psalm 144/145 to be sung by the people. This psalm extols God as King whose greatness, majesty, love, and mercy are unsearchable. His kingdom is everlasting, enduring throughout all generations. Righteous in all his ways, he is near to all who call upon him in truth. He hears their cry and fulfills the requests of those who fear him.

165 In the case of vesperal liturgies, as, for example, at the vigils of Pascha, Christmas, and Theophany, the antiphons are omitted. Instead, the Divine Liturgy begins with the first part of the vesper service up to and including the entrance and the assigned Old Testament readings (if there are any). The liturgy proper begins immediately after with a call to prayer, the Trisagion Prayer, and the thrice-holy hymn, "Holy God, Holy Mighty, Holy Immortal..." or the baptismal hymn, "As many as have been baptized into Christ..."

For more on the Kingdom of God, For more on the Kingdom of God see Appendix C:3.

(a) Initial blessing

When the preliminaries have been completed, the **priest** stands reverently in front of the Holy Table and collects himself, physically, mentally, emotionally, and spiritually. He concentrates on the mystery which is about to unfold over which he is called to preside by virtue of his ordination. Having kissed the Holy Table and the Evangelion at the conclusion of the preliminary rites, he lifts the Evangelion holding it upright in both hands; and with it he blesses the Holy Table crosswise over the folded *antimension*[166] as he intones the initial blessing or doxology, "*Blessed is the kingdom... Εὐλογημένη ἡ Βασιλεία...*"[167] After this, he places the Evangelion vertically on top of the folded antimension which is permanently found on the Holy Table.[168]

On the Sunday of Pascha and all of Renewal Week we sing the Paschal Hymn with the assigned verses immediately after the initial blessing. The priest also censes. From the Sunday of Thomas to the Apodosis of Pascha, the Paschal hymn is sung three times after the initial blessing.

---

166 The two actions are not mentioned in the *Diataxis of Philotheos Kokkinos* or in the early manuscripts and printed editions. At some point, they entered into printed ieratika and euchologia. Of the two gestures, the making of the sign of the cross over the folded antimension with the Evangelion appears to be an old tradition. The rubric regarding the lifting of the Evangelion with both hands is strictly functional. The act has no hidden meaning, symbolic or otherwise. The rubric is meant to inform the priest how to raise the Evangelion from its vertical, flat position to an upright, vertical position so that the blessing of the Holy Table may be accomplished with ease. Eventually the rubric, "ὑψῶν τὸ ἱερὸν Εὐαγγέλιον," was interpreted to mean lift up the Evangelion, hold it high. This, however, invites the question, "how high" and has led some clerics to employ exaggerated gestures. In keeping with tradition, the Evangelion should be lifted slightly above the Holy Table, without overstated actions. See Fountoulis, *Ἀπαντήσεις εἰς Λειτουργικὰς Ἀπορίας*, vol. 3 (Athens 1976), 181-2.

167 In some manuscripts and printed editions, we find rubrics which instruct the celebrant to intone the initial blessing with reverence, fervor, and joy and with a raised loud voice, as for example the rubric, "'Ο ἱερεὺς ἐκφωνεῖ λαμπρὰ τῇ φωνῇ μετὰ φόβου, ὑψοῖ τὴν φωνήν, λαμπρῶς καὶ μεγαλοφώνως." See Trembelas, *Τρεῖς Λειτουργίαι*, 22. In this particular rubric the verb lift or raise (ὑψοῖ) refers to the raising of the voice and not to the Evangelion.

168 In earlier times, the Evangelion was brought into the church from the skeuophylakion at the Small Entrance. Eventually, however, it was permanently placed on the Holy Table, lying vertically flat on the folded antimension. As noted earlier, each outer cover of the Evangelion is engraved with an icon: one with the Resurrection and the other with the Crucifixion. On Sundays and during the entire Paschal season, the Evangelion is turned so that the icon of the Resurrection is displayed. At all other times, the icon of the Crucifixion is face up.

People (λαός)

Amen.

Important Note

In the texts of the Divine Liturgy the parts assigned to the people are so marked, even when they are executed by chanters and/or choirs. In line with this venerable tradition, the responses assigned to the people will be marked accordingly.

(b) Great Synapte[169]

Immediately after the initial blessing, the **priest** intones the Great Synapte, starting with the petition, "*In peace let us pray to the Lord.*"[170]

People (Choir or Chanter)

Respond to each petition, "*Lord, have mercy… Κύριε, ἐλέησον.*"

To the bidding, "*let us commit ourselves and one another,*" the response is "*To you, O Lord … Σοί, Κύριε.*"

---

[169] The Great Synapte or Great Litany, as has been already noted, consists of a series of eleven petitions in three categories (general petitions; petitions for ecclesial and civil persons, and communities; and petitions for specific needs). The word *synapte* comes from the verb συνάπτω, which means to tie or join together. In this instance, it refers to the series of petitions that are joined together. The Great Synapte is also called τὰ Εἰρηνικὰ or the *Peace Petitions*, from the fact that the first three petitions contain the word peace. The synapte is addressed to the people, inviting them to think about, meditate on, and pray for specific things. In some texts we find the petition, "*For all pious and Orthodox Christians, let us pray to the Lord*" inserted before the petition for the local hierarch. This petition began to appear in Greek liturgical texts after the fall of Constantinople in 1453 as a substitute for the petition for the imperial family – τῶν εὐσεβεστάτων βασιλέων. In later times, a new general petition for civic leaders was formulated and added to the Great Synapte in keeping with the apostolic exhortation to pray "for all who are in authority that we may lead a quiet and peaceable life in all godliness and reverence" (1 Tim.2:2). The petition, "For all pious and Orthodox Christians," is unnecessary. It is out of place and superfluous. The people are prayed for in two of the fixed petitions of the Great Synapte: "For our Archbishop (N), the honorable presbyters… *and for all the clergy and the people*, let us pray to the Lord;" and "For this city…and every city and land (χώρα), *and for the faithful who live in them.*" Besides, liturgical protocol excludes the remembrance of the people before the ecclesial authorities. See Fountoulis, Ἀπαντήσεις, vol. 3, 128-31.

[170] Litanies are usually said by a deacon. However, in the absence of a deacon, the priest intones them from within the sanctuary while standing in front of the Holy Table.

(c) Office of the Antiphons and the Office of the Typika

As I have noted earlier, the psalms are used extensively in all the services of the Church, often in combination with ecclesiastical compositions. Psalmody for the Divine Liturgy is found in three key parts of the service: at the beginning (antiphons or *typika*), in connection with the readings (*prokeimena* and alleluia), and at Communion (*koinonikon*).

The office of the antiphons has its roots in the cathedral typikon. It consists of three psalms, which are sung antiphonally, that is with a brief refrain after each verse. These responses were for the most part ecclesiastical compositions rather than biblical verses. Each psalm ended with the small doxology, a repetition of the refrain and an abbreviated form of the refrain. The psalm verses are intoned by the singer(s), while the people sing the appointed refrain, with or without the lead of the choir or chanter. In the beginning, each psalm was sung in its entirety. In time, however, for the sake of brevity, the psalms were limited to four verses for the first two antiphons and three for the third, ending with the small doxology, "Glory to the Father and the Son and the Holy Spirit, now and forever…"

The psalm of each antiphon is preceded by the so-called Small Litany, which consists of the following elements: an invitation to prayer, "*Again and again in peace let us pray to the Lord;*" a plea for God's help and mercy; a commemoration of the Theotokos and the saints; a call for a personal and communal commitment to Christ; and a prayer recited by the priest.[171] These same elements have been appended to the Great Synapte. When the Great Synapte was transferred to the beginning of the Divine Liturgy, it replaced the Small Litany of the first antiphon. The Small Litany precedes the second and third antiphons.

---

171 The content in each of the three prayers suggests that they are not original to the antiphons. The first prayer, for example, is similar in content to the two Prayers of the Faithful in CHR. The second prayer is identical with the first part of the prayer behind the *Ambo*, which is a prayer of blessing. The third prayer reflects the promise of the Lord to grant the requests of those who are gathered in his Name, an indication of its connection to a series of petitions. At some point, the entire inaugural part of the Divine Liturgy will require careful study and reform.

The cathedral office assigned Psalms 91/92, 92/93, and 94/95 respectively to the three antiphons for Sundays.[172] The refrain for the first antiphon (91/92) is "Ταῖς πεσβείαις τῆς Θεοτόκου... *By the intercessions of the Theotokos...*" The same refrain is sung after the small doxology. The refrain of the second antiphon (92/93) is, "Σῶσον ἡμᾶς, Υἱὲ Θεοῦ...*Save us, o Son of God...*" The refrain for the small doxology is the troparion, "Ὁ μονογενὴς Υἱὸς καὶ Λόγος τοῦ Θεοῦ... *Only begotten Son and Word of God...*"[173] The refrain of the third antiphon (94/95) is always the apolytikion of the day.[174] In times past, the small doxology (Glory to the Father and to the Son and to the Holy Spirit, now and forever...) of the third antiphon was said after the small entrance using the apolytikion and the kontakion of the day as the refrains. Today, the small doxology is omitted after the third antiphon. We sing the apolytikion (or apolytikia) of the day and the kontakion after the entrance but without the small doxology. The common entrance hymn, "*Come, let us worship and bow before Christ*," comes from the sixth verse of Psalm 94/95, which is the psalm of the third antiphon.

With the ascendance of the monastic typikon and the gradual disappearance of the cathedral typikon, the office of the antiphons was gradually replaced with the Office of Typika from the monastic office. The use of antiphons was limited to dominical, Marian, and other important feast days, each of which has its own set of antiphons.[175] These festal sets of antiphons are found in the respective liturgical books in which the service of the feast is contained (Menaion, Triodion, or Pentecostarion).[176]

---

172 In current practice these three psalms are used for weekday Liturgies: First antiphon, Ps. 91/92: 1, 2, 4, 15; second antiphon, Ps. 92/93: 1a, 1b, 4, 5; and third antiphon, Ps. 94/95:1, 2, 3-4.

173 This is a lovely Christological hymn which encapsulates in poetic form articles of the Creed related to the Son of God: Christ, the only begotten Son and Word of God, who is one of the Holy Trinity, humbled himself and became incarnate from the holy Theotokos and ever Virgin Mary, without undergoing change. He was crucified and by his death he vanquished death. Glorified with the Father and the Holy Spirit, he is the Savior of the world. The hymn was composed at the time of Emperor Justinian and introduced into the liturgy by him before 540.

174 For the sake of brevity, at the entrance we sing the apolytikion only once, preceded by one or all three of the verses of the third antiphon. The apolytikion is repeated again after the entrance. In bilingual parishes the apolytikion could/should be sung first in Greek and after the entrance in English or vice-versa.

175 For example, on the feast of the Nativity of Christ the three antiphons are: Ps. 110/111:1, 2, 3, 9; Ps. 111/112:1, 2, 3, 4; Ps. 109/110:1, 2, 3a. The Entrance hymn is from Ps. 109/110: 3b-4. The Communion Hymn is from Ps. 110/111:9a.

176 One can also find the festal antiphons in the *Almanac of the Ecumenical Patriarchate* which is published annually. Another source is the bulletin of directives published annually by the National Forum of Greek Orthodox Musicians. See also the relevant entries in Konstantinos Papagiannis, *Σύστημα Τυπικοῦ* (Athens 2006).

The prevailing Greek practice, however, has restored the antiphons for parish usage on Sundays and weekdays.[177] Sadly though, in many parishes the verses of the psalms are omitted. The chanter or choir sing only the traditional refrains. (In these two instances we have an example of liturgical restoration on the one hand, and of liturgical reductionism on the other). The designated verses of the psalms should always be intoned and not omitted. It is incumbent upon the priest to correct the error and supply the singer(s) with the appointed psalm verses.

Monastic communities, the Slavic Church, and other Orthodox Churches use the antiphons only on major feast days, following the rule of the monastic *Typikon of St. Savas.* On Sundays and weekdays, they sing the typika. This order is reflected in the Octoechos, Triodion, and Pentecostarion. The Octoechos, for example, after each Orthros service has a section with the title, "Ἐν τῇ Λειτουργίᾳ – *In the liturgy*" with the rubric, "Τὰ Τυπικά, καὶ οἱ Μακαρισμοί – *The Typika and the Beatitudes.*" This section contains a set of eight hymns (for Sundays) and six hymns (for weekdays). These hymns are interpolated between the verses of the Beatitudes in the tone of the week. On a given feast, the hymns are taken from the odes of the canon.[178]

The Typikon contains two psalms: 102/103 and 145/146 and the Beatitudes.[179] The verses of the psalms are sung alternately by the singers in their entirety without a refrain between the verses. Psalm 102/103 is sung in the plagal fourth tone as the first antiphon; Psalm 145/146 is sung in the second tone in place

---

177 According to current practice, for Sundays (in an attempt to bring together the two traditions, the cathedral and monastic), the first and second antiphons are comprised of verses from Psalms 102/103 and 145/146 from the office of the typika (monastic) with the refrains of the cathedral office, "By the intercessions…" The third antiphon is Psalm 117/118. The selected verses for each antiphon are: Ps. 102/103:1, 2, 19, 22; Ps. 145/146:1-2, 5, 6, 10; Ps. 117/118:1, 4, 24. I see no reason why the chanter could not alternate between these three psalms and those in note 191 above, which were once the Sunday antiphons of the cathedral office.

178 The Triodion and Pentecostarion often direct the singers to use the hymns in the Octoechos in the tone of the week or to use the hymns in the third and sixth odes of the canon of a given feast from the Menaion.

179 These three elements constitute the first part of the Office or Service of the Typika. The full service contains additional hymns, prayers, psalms, and the Creed. The complete office is found in the *Horologion* after the service of the mid-Sixth Hour. On fast days, the office is said after the Ninth Hour. The entire office is rarely used in parishes. In monastic communities it is celebrated on days when there is no liturgy. Hence it is found in the *Horologion* after the Sixth Hour because, according to the monastic Typikon of St. Savas, the Divine Liturgy is celebrated after the Sixth Hour (See Calivas, *Aspects of Orthodox Worship*, 92-94). The typika always precede the Liturgy of the Pre-Sanctified Gifts and are inserted into the service of the Ninth Hour. For an English translation of the office with rubrics see *The Great Horologion* (Holy Transfiguration Monastery, Boston 1997), 140-8 and 174-80.

of the second antiphon. The Beatitudes are taken from the Gospel of Matthew (5:3-12a) and are sung in the tone of the week in place of the third antiphon.[180] On Sundays the first six verses of the Beatitudes are sung sequentially; between the remaining verses and the small doxology, we insert the designated hymns. On weekdays, the hymns are inserted after the eighth verse. The priest makes the small entrance at the beginning of the small doxology.

Although the antiphons have become the standard practice in the Greek Church, there is nothing that prohibits the use of the typika service. In fact, it would be a refreshing and pleasing change for the worshippers to hear them from time to time. To help the congregation pray the typika, copies of the psalm verses and the Beatitudes should be available in the pews. It goes without saying that the singers should be prepared to perform them well.[181]

The Beatitudes are of special importance. Hearing and absorbing their meaning, the people are given succor and comfort on their pilgrimage toward the blessed way of life. As a statement of faith in God's graciousness toward those who strive to live under his rule, the Beatitudes describe the resplendent gifts and the invincible joy of the new life received at baptism; the life which all faithful people are called to nurture and advance to maturity day by day (Ephes. 4:13). The Beatitudes assure us that the joy Christ gives is a present unassailable possession of all those who seek in earnest the kingdom of God through their union with him and one another (John 15:9-12; 17:13).

---

[180] For an inspired concise reflection on the Beatitudes see Nicholas Cabasilas, *The Life in Christ* (Crestwood, NY, 1974), 176-89. See also Kyriaki K. FitzGerald, *Happy in the Lord – the Beatitudes for Everyday: Perspectives from Orthodox Spirituality* (Brookline, MA 2000).

[181] Because Psalm 102/103 is long, one could make an allowance and limit the number of verses for the sake of brevity. Also, because many chanters or choirs are unfamiliar with or unable to sing properly the hymn-refrains attached to the Beatitudes, the hymns may be intoned or omitted, if necessary.

B. THE SMALL ENTRANCE[182]

Actions and Prayer[183]

Priest

As the chanter or choir sings the third antiphon with the designated apolytikion (or the Beatitudes of the typika), the priest bows before the Holy Table, reverences, and picks up the Evangelion with both hands. He holds it up at eye-level and processes around the Holy Table.[184] The altar servers holding candles lead the procession. The priest follows and exits through the north

---

[182] The term, S*mall Entrance*, began to appear in liturgical texts after the thirteenth century. The term became fixed with its inclusion in the *Diataxis* of Philotheos Kokkinos. Previously, it was called First Entrance, a term used initially by St. Maximos the Confessor (*Mystagogy*, chapters 8 and 9). It was also called: Entrance with the Evangelion or simply Entrance (Εἴσοδος). In some texts we find the terms Entrance of the Patriarch or Entrance of the Hierarch. The two latter terms, in fact, are descriptive of the liturgical action at a hierarchical liturgy. Hierarchs made their entrance into the nave (now into the sanctuary) after the third antiphon, preserving the ancient custom.

[183] As already noted, the present actions are a remnant of the more striking ancient entrance rite. In earlier times, the clergy and the people gathered in the courtyard and narthex and entered the church together to begin the Divine Liturgy. The entrance was preceded by a prayer recited aloud by the chief celebrant (hierarch or priest). The entrance into the church was accompanied with a hymn called the Εἰσοδικόν or *Entrance Hymn*, usually an appropriate psalm verse. At Hagia Sophia, the many doors leading into the church were opened and the people entered from all sides of the building. The emperor and his entourage and the patriarch with the clergy entered via the Royal or Beautiful Gate, the central doors of the narthex. During the procession the Evangelion, which is the icon par excellence of the Christ, is carried high, in the manner by which the Scripture scrolls are carried in the liturgy of the synagogue. Holding the Evangelion aloft serves a twofold purpose: it is a way of showing honor and respect for God's word and a sign of Christ's presence among his people.

[184] If a deacon is present, the priest gives the Evangelion to the deacon, who receives it from the priest as he kisses his hand. The deacon processes in front of the priest. He holds the Evangelion at eye level. When he comes to the solea, he stands in front and to the right of the priest. When the priest has finished the Prayer of Entrance, he stands in front of him and offers him the Evangelion to reverence. Then, standing to his side, he says, "Bless, Master, the holy Entrance." The priest, as with all blessings, raises his hand and makes the sign of the cross in the usual manner. After the priest has offered the blessing, the deacon stands in front of him facing the holy doors. He raises the Evangelion and intones the bidding, "*Wisdom! Let us be attentive! ... Σοφία! Ὀρθοί!*" As the chanter or choir sings the entrance hymn, the deacon enters the sanctuary through the Holy Doors and enthrones the Evangelion on the Holy Table. He then stands at his usual place within the sanctuary.

door of the sanctuary and comes to the solea.¹⁸⁵ There, he faces the sanctuary and recites the Prayer of Entrance, "Δέσποτα Κύριε, ὁ Θεὸς ἡμῶν... *Master and Lord our God, you have established in heaven the orders and hosts of angels...*" (For what and where heaven is see Appendix C:4).

The Prayer of Entrance is common to both BAS and CHR. In the *Barberini Codex*, however, CHR has its own distinct prayer which reads as follows: "Maker and Benefactor of all creation receive the Church as she draws near to accomplish that which is good and beneficial for each person. Lead us all to perfection and make us worthy of your kingdom. By the grace, mercy, and love for us of your only begotten Son, with whom you are blessed, together with your all holy, good, and lifegiving Spirit, now and forever and to the ages of ages." After the tenth century for unknown reasons the original prayer of CHR was set aside in favor of the entrance prayer of BAS. This prayer entreats God, the Creator of the heavenly bodiless powers, to send forth his holy angels so that they may join the worshippers as concelebrants, that together – people and angels – may serve and glorify the goodness of God. The worship of the church is thus associated with the heavenly liturgy. The rite of entrance, as Fr. Alexander Schmemann taught, signifies an ascent, the drawing near of the Church to the place where Christ is, the heavenly sanctuary.¹⁸⁶ At the Divine

---

185 In current liturgical language the term solea (σολέας) refers to the large space in front of the sanctuary, which may or may not be a raised platform. On the right side of the solea is the episcopal throne and on the left the ambo or pulpit. In the Byzantine arrangement of the church, the episcopal throne was in the sanctuary, located in the center of the apse behind the Holy Table. It was moved out to the solea after the fall of Constantinople at the place where the emperor's throne was once situated. On either side of the solea, in traditional churches, are the two chant stands. Laypeople come forward and receive Holy Communion on the solea. The rite of matrimony, funerals and other services are also conducted on the solea. In former times, the term designated the protected passageway between the ambo which stood in the middle of the church and the central or holy doors of the sanctuary.

186 The Prayer of Entrance is common to both BAS and CHR. In the *Barberini Codex*, however, CHR has its own distinct prayer which reads as follows: "Maker and Benefactor of all creation receive the Church as she draws near to accomplish that which is good and beneficial for each person. Lead us all to perfection and make us worthy of your kingdom. By the grace, mercy, and love for us of your only begotten Son, with whom you are blessed, together with your all holy, good, and lifegiving Spirit, now and forever and to the ages of ages." After the tenth century for unknown reasons the original prayer of CHR was set aside in favor of the entrance prayer of BAS. This prayer entreats God, the Creator of the heavenly bodiless powers, to send forth his holy angels so that they may join the worshippers as concelebrants, that together – people and angels – may serve and glorify the goodness of God. The worship of the church is thus associated with the heavenly liturgy. The rite of entrance, as Fr. Alexander Schmemann taught, signifies an ascent, the drawing near of the Church to the place where Christ is, the heavenly sanctuary. At the Divine Liturgy we come to experience the power and glory of the risen and reigning Christ who sanctifies the worshippers through his presence. Schmemann, *The Eucharist*, 49-63.

Liturgy we come to experience the power and glory of the risen and reigning Christ who sanctifies the worshippers through his presence.

Priest

When he completes the prayer, he holds the Evangelion in his left hand and proceeds to bless with his right hand facing the sanctuary as he says, *"Εὐλογημένη ἡ εἴσοδος τῶν ἁγίων σου ... Blessed is the entrance of your sanctuary (or Blessed is the entrance of your saints)."*[187]

Entrance hymn (Εἰσοδικόν) and refrain (ἐφύμνιον)

Priest

Having offered the blessing, he raises the Evangelion and intones the bidding, *"Wisdom! Let us be attentive! ... Σοφία! Ὀρθοί!"* Then he invites the people to join him in singing the entrance hymn with its refrain together with the chanter and choir: *"Δεῦτε προσκυνήσωμεν... Come, let us worship..."* followed by the refrain *"Σῶσον ἡμᾶς... Save us, O Son of God..."*[188]

---

[187] This blessing was introduced into the text at the end of the twelfth century. Its meaning – especially the phrase, *"τῶν ἁγίων σου"* – is open to interpretation. The key word ἁγίων, in the second person plural, is the possessive case of both the masculine and neuter nouns: οἱ ἅγιοι (holy ones, saints) and τὰ ἅγια (holy things, holy place, sanctuary) respectively. The question is, what entrance (εἴσοδος) is the priest blessing? Is it the entrance of God's holy people (saints) or is it the entrance into the holy place, the temple, the sanctuary? If τῶν ἁγίων σου is neuter, the blessing concerns the sanctuary. If, on the other hand, τῶν ἁγίων σου refers to the holy ones, the blessing is related to the people and their entrance into God's presence. Most English translations have adopted this latter view. In the Epistle to the Hebrews (10:19), however, we meet the same phrase, εἴσοδος τῶν ἁγίων. "'Ἔχοντες οὖν, ἀδελφοί, παρρησίαν εἰς τὴν εἴσοδον τῶν ἁγίων ἐν τῷ αἵματι τοῦ Ἰησοῦ ... Therefore, brethren, since we have confidence *to enter the sanctuary* by the blood of Jesus..." In this and in other similar texts of the Old Testament the word τῶν ἁγίων is construed as the possessive case of τὰ ἅγια. Hence it is understood to mean a sanctuary, a holy place, as in the "Holy of Holies – τὰ Ἅγια τῶν Ἁγίων." (Cf. Psalm 59/60:6 and Ps. 62/63:2). In an ekphonesis of Orthros and in the Prayer of the Trisagion Hymn of the Liturgy we meet a similar phrase: *"Ὁ Θεὸς ὁ ἅγιος, ὁ ἐν ἁγίοις ἀναπαυόμενος ... Holy God, who is resting among the holy ones (among the saints) or who is resting in your holy dwelling place."* Now, the holy place may be heaven or the temple; it may also be God's holy people, his devout adherents. God rests or dwells in heaven and his glory in the temple (Ps. 11:4; 1 Chron.7:1; Is. 66:1-2; Matt.6:9); he also rests in his holy ones, his saints (John 14:23; 1 Cor. 3:16; Ephes. 2:19-22; 3:16-19). Because our liturgical texts are replete with biblical words and phrases, we should follow the Septuagint and New Testament context of biblical Greek to help interpret and translate challenging texts. See Taft, "Translating Liturgically," in *LOGOS*, vol. 39:2-4 (1998), 173; and Fountoulis, Ἀπαντήσεις, volume 5, 375-9.

[188] According to a strict interpretation of the rubrics, priests sing the entrance hymn and its refrain only when there is a concelebration. Otherwise, the hymns are sung by the chanters or the choir. However, since most worshippers know the common entrance hymn by heart, it makes sense for the priest to invite the people to join him and the singers in chanting the refrain together ("ὅλοι μαζύ - all together").

Procession into sanctuary

Priest

As he sings the hymn, he bows reverently. Then, as he sings the refrain, "*Save us, O Son of God...*" he processes into the sanctuary through the Holy Doors and enthrones the Evangelion on the Holy Table, resting it on the folded antimension.

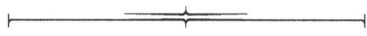

Important Note: *At no time does a priest cense after his entrance into the sanctuary. Only a hierarch does, inasmuch as this is, at least theoretically, his first entrance into the sanctuary. Through this censing the hierarch pays homage to and honors the sanctuary and the temple, and all that is in them.*

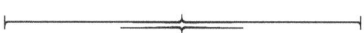

Hymns after the Entrance: Once the priest has entered the sanctuary, we sing the designated festal apolytikion (or apolytikia) of the day, the hymn of the church, and the kontakion of the feast or of the period. These hymns are usually sung by the chanter or choir. However, at a concelebration the festal apolytikion is sung by the clergy as is the kontakion. In any case, should the priest wish to lead the congregation in singing some of these hymns, he should consult first with the chanter or choir. On all dominical feasts we do not sing the apolytikion of the church. Also, if a memorial service (Μνημόσυνον) is scheduled, the priest sings the kontakion of the dead (Μετὰ τῶν ἁγίων ἀνάπαυσον... *With the saints give rest...*) before the designated kontakion.

C. THE PRAYER OF THE TRISAGION HYMN

Priest

Immediately after the kontakion, the priest calls the people to prayer intoning the customary exhortation, "*Let us pray to the Lord.*" If a deacon is present, the call to prayer is said by him while facing the people. After the response, "*Lord have mercy*,"[189] the priest recites the Trisagion Prayer aloud in a prayerful voice

---

189 Regarding this response, Cabasilas (*Commentary*, II:13) says the following: "Whereas the priest askσ them to pray for so many different things, the faithful, in fact, ask for one thing only – mercy. Why? ... It is because this prayer implies both gratitude and confession. Secondly, to beg God's mercy is to ask for his kingdom, that kingdom which Christ promised to give to those who seek for it, assuring them that all things else of which they have need will be added to them..." (Cf. Matt. 6:33).

and intones the ekphonesis at the end of the prayer.[190] Then the chanters or choir together with the people sing the Trisagion Hymn. This is the proper liturgical order.

Today however, for the sake of brevity, the call to prayer is often followed immediately by the ekphonesis of the prayer. The prayer is recited by the priest in a low voice while the choir sings the Trisagion Hymn. In this instance, when the priest completes the prayer, he recites the Trisagion in a low voice three times, bowing each time before the Holy Table. In fact, he is duplicating what the chanter or choir is doing.[191]

It seems inappropriate and makes no sense to call the people to prayer when no prayer is offered, at least in their hearing. For the reasons that follow, this prayer, as with most other prayers of the Divine Liturgy, should be read aloud by the priest in a prayerful voice. We must not forget that liturgical prayers bear and transmit the Church's faith. As such, they have the power to inform, influence, and gradually transform the attentive worshipper, including the priest.

The Trisagion Prayer is the same in both BAS and CHR. The earliest version of CHR, however, has a different prayer, original to CHR.[192] Eventually, the Trisagion of BAS supplanted the prayer of CHR. This probably occurred between the tenth and eleventh centuries when CHR was in the process of replacing BAS as the chief eucharistic liturgy of Constantinople.[193] In fact, the prayer of BAS is richer and more comprehensive in scope than the original prayer in CHR.[194]

---

190 If a deacon is present, he says the last phrase of the ekphonesis, "And unto the ages of ages," while facing the people. This is the only instance when a deacon completes the ekphonesis of a prayer. It is a remnant from an earlier time. It was used to give a signal to the chanters/choir to start the Trisagion Hymn. For more on the development of this peculiar practice see, Trembelas, Τρεῖς Λειτουργίαι, 41-5 (note 9).

191 Here, as in other instances, the priest repeats what the people are singing. This duplication began to appear when the practice of reciting the prayers inaudibly and usually out of sequence began to take root. As a result, the clergy no longer joined the people in chanting the appointed hymns. Instead, at the conclusion of the prayer the clergy simply recite and replicate inaudibly what the people are singing aloud.

192 For the text of this prayer see Parenti and Velkovska, *Eucologio Barberini*, 26 and Trembelas, Τρεῖς Λειτουργίαι, 45.

193 In the eleventh century *Euchologion* of Constantinople – *Hagiasmatarion* and *Archieratikon* – CHR begins with the prayers for the catechumens. All previous prayers are borrowed from BAS. See Miguel Arranz, *L'Euchologio Constantinopolitano Agli Inizi del Secolo XI* (Rome, 1996), 499.

194 The Prayer of CHR is centered mostly on the orders of the angelic host, each of which offer hymns of praise to the only Holy One who exists in insuperable glory.

The prayer begins with two pronouncements, the first of which (Ὁ Θεὸς ὁ ἅγιος, ὁ ἐν ἁγίοις ἀναπαυόμενος) may be interpreted in two ways. The prayer declares that God dwells in a holy place, in a place of unapproachable light, the nature of which transcends human understanding (1 Tim. 6:16). The same declaration may be interpreted to mean that God rests among the saints, which is to say among those who seek his face (Ps.27:8) that they may partake of his holiness (Heb. 12:10). The prayer also states that the angelic host glorify him perpetually with the thrice-holy hymn for the majesty of his being and for his mighty deeds. Accordingly, the holy angels supply us with an image of true worship, which is essentially an act of praise and thanksgiving. It is an encounter with the holy and an experience of the eternal. It results in the establishment of a personal relationship with the Creator, which is of benefit both to the worshipper and to all creation (Rom. 8:18-23).

The prayer also contains two doctrinal affirmations which are closely related. The prayer affirms the Church's belief that God freely created all things, both visible and invisible, out of nothing (*ex nihilo* - ἐκ τοῦ μὴ ὄντος), out of his limitless love and wisdom; a theme which will be repeated in the anaphora.[195] This means that creation is a gift ordered by a benevolent and loving God. And the gift he brought forth is very good (Gen. 1:31), not perfect. It also means that the cosmos has an absolute beginning and is therefore subject to dissolution, to death. According to St. Maximos the Confessor, "Every creature is a composite of substance and accident and in constant need of divine Providence since it is not free from mutability."[196] God alone is perfect and deathless since he alone has life in himself (John 5:26).

As Metropolitan John of Pergamon (Zizioulas) avers in one of his essays, "there is no eternal and immortal element in the nature of creation, all of them – including souls, species, and matter – having had a beginning can be extinguished, for they have no natural capacity for survival. Creation taken in itself constitutes an entity surrounded and conditioned by nothing. Time and space came into being together with creation. The space-time structure of the universe is experienced by everything and everyone in the world as the means by which entities acquire their being and at the same time their non-being. There is no natural affinity between creation and God. He is the only eternal

---

195 The theme of *ex nihilo* creation is also stated explicitly in the Anaphora of CHR and implied in the Prayer of the Proskomide and the Anaphora of BAS.

196 See his, *Chapters on Love* 4:6, in George Berthold, *Maximus Confessor: Selected Writings* (New York 1985), 76.

and immortal being."[197] Or as Fr. Georges Florovsky taught, the very existence of the world is a mystery and a miracle of divine freedom. God alone is mighty and eternal. All created things were brought into existence and are sustained in existence solely by the grace and pleasure of God, by his sovereign will.[198]

The link between God and creation that secures the communication of life between them is, according to Metropolitan John, the human being (ὁ ἄνθρωπος – man and woman). As the Prayer of the Trisagion affirms, human beings have been created by God in his image and likeness and are adorned by him with all the gifts of his grace (i.e. with divine qualities). These gifts are not enumerated in the prayer. Saint Maximos the Confessor, however, reflecting on the creation of the human being names four of these gifts. "In bringing into existence a rational and intelligent nature, God in his supreme goodness has communicated to it four of the divine attributes by which he maintains, guards, and preserves creatures: being, eternal being, goodness, and wisdom. The first two of these he grants to the essence, the second two to its faculty of will; that is, to the essence he gives being and eternal being, and to the faculty of volition he gives goodness and wisdom in order that what he [God] is by essence the creature might become by participation.... But creatures, because they all have existence...do have contrary qualities. To existence is opposed nonexistence, to aptitude for goodness and wisdom is opposed vice and ignorance. For them to exist forever or not to exist is in the power of their maker. To share in [God's] goodness and wisdom or not to share depends on the will of the rational being."[199]

This means that human beings are endowed with another divine gift, freedom. The elemental exercise of freedom lies in one's conscious decision and desire to fulfill his/her vocation. The vocation of every human being is to transcend the limitations of creaturehood and to share in the plenitude of divine life.

---

197 Select phrases from John D. Zizioulas, "Preserving God's Creation: Three Lectures on Theology and Ecology," in *King's College Theological Review*, volumes 12 (1989) and 13 (1990). For a Greek translation of the lectures see Ἰωάννου Ζηζιούλα, Ἡ Κτίση ὡς Εὐχαριστία - Θεολογικὴ προσέγγιση στὸ πρόβλημα τῆς οἰκολογίας (Athens 1992). See also George Papademetriou, *The Nature of Man According to the Holy Fathers* (Synaxis Press – B.C. Canada 2004), 51-60, and John Meyendorff, *Byzantine Theology*, 129-137.

198 Georges Florovsky, "St. Athanasius' Concept of Creation," in *Studia Patristica*, vol. 6 (1962), 36-57, which is also found in volume four of his collected works, *Aspects of Church History* (Belmont, MA 1975), 39-62. See also volume three of his works, *Creation and Redemption*.

199 *Chapters on Love* (3:25, 27), 64, 65.

However, human beings are also free to neglect and even reject their high calling. They exist within two contrasting realities, the way of death and the way of life (Deut. 30:15-19). As I have noted elsewhere, one way leads to death and perdition, and the other to life and holiness.[200] Tragically, the progenitors of the race chose the way of death, subjecting humanity to the tyrannizing power of corruption and death which hold sway over us. The horror and fear of death overwhelm our natural emotions and are the root cause of our disobedience (Heb. 2:14-15; Rom 5:12).

Yet, that which humanity failed to do, God accomplished through the incarnation of his only-begotten Son and Word, our Lord and Savior Jesus Christ, the God-Man (Θεάνθρωπος).[201] Or as the anaphora of CHR states succinctly, "You brought us into being out of nothing, and when we fell, you raised us up again. You did not cease doing everything until you led us to heaven and granted us your kingdom to come." Christ, the God-Man, bore all our infirmities and endured all things, even death on the Cross, for the life of the world. Raised from the dead, he cracked the fortress of death and took "captivity captive" (Ps. 67/68:18). In Christ, the risen and reigning Lord, all human nature has been fully and completely cured from a lack of wholeness and mortality (1 Cor. 15:21-22; Rom. 8:18-23).

As awesome and true as this mystery is, no one can be compelled to believe in God or to obey his commandments. Salvation comes through a living and dynamic personal relationship with Christ through the Church. Through her teachings the Church is constantly reminding people of their true vocation and ultimate destiny. Through the sacraments her faithful members experience from now the blessings of the kingdom which is to come in glory.

The remaining parts of the Trisagion Prayer offer the worshipper additional statements regarding God's divine economy. The Triune God who is holy and most holy and beyond comprehension is also benevolent and compassionate beyond measure.[202] His love for the world and humankind is boundless. He does not condemn, nor does he overlook sinners. Rather, he offers salvation to all who heed the call to repentance (Mark 1:15) – who recognize, acknowledge, and reveal the true state of their soul to him who is the source of forgiveness and healing. In the words of St. Maximos, the Confessor, "God who yearns for the salvation of all and hungers after their deification, withers their self-conceit.... He does this so that they may prefer to be righteous in reality rather than appearance... genuinely pursuing a virtuous life in the way that the

---

200 Calivas, *Church, Clergy, Laity and the Spiritual Life*, 119-20.

201 See Calivas, *Aspects of Orthodox Worship*, 14-6, 23-9.

202 1 John 4:16-19.

divine Logos wishes them."[203]

The prayer also contains a series of petitions that offer the worshipper an opening to the loving-kindness of the Triune God. The initial petition is simultaneously a declaration, "You give wisdom and understanding to the supplicant." Both wisdom and understanding are gifts that come from above, from the Father of Lights. Through them we come to know and practice what is pleasing to God. Thus, true wisdom should always be sought out and cherished because "the wisdom from above is first pure, then peaceable, gentle, open to reason, full of mercy and good fruits, without uncertainty or insincerity" (James 3:17).

The additional petitions in the prayer include a plea for forgiveness of the voluntary and involuntary transgressions of the worshippers, for the sanctification of their whole being, body and soul, and for grace to worship and serve God in holiness all the days of their lives.

Of special note is the fact that of the several initial prayers of the Divine Liturgy, the Prayer of the Trisagion Hymn is the first to speak of the origins of the world and of humankind and the first to call the worshippers to repentance and to ask for the forgiveness of their sins and transgressions. As Christ began his public ministry with a call to repentance (Matt. 4:17), so does the Divine Liturgy. It calls upon the worshippers to be heedful and contrite. Contriteness and repentance, however, are more than a change in attitude. They are the fruit of a conscious choice to live under the rule of God. And this is not a once-for-all static decision. It requires continuous vigilance and unwavering fidelity to Christ.

Repentance involves a radical change in the way one exists, thinks, and acts. And this is beyond one's own capacity to accomplish. It is a gift bestowed by Christ, who takes the penitent to himself to give him/her a new and clean heart. A virtuous life, however, is more than the occasional display of conventional morality. It is anchored in the constant struggle for truth and in the deliberate choice to be a humble imitator of Christ, in spite of the temptations that surround us and the failures that afflict us. *"From my youth many passions have warred against me, but my Savior, help me and save me"* (Antiphon of the fourth tone).

---

[203] *Philokalia*, vol. 2, 181.

D. THE THRICE-HOLY HYMN – Ὁ ΤΡΙΣΆΓΙΟΣ ὝΜΝΟΣ

The Thrice-Holy Hymn, or *Trisagion*, is an ecclesiastical composition based on the angelic hymn in Isaiah's vision of the heavenly liturgy (Is. 6:3). It is often called the liturgical Trisagion to differentiate it from the biblical Trisagion, which is the angelic hymn recorded in the Prophecy of Isaiah: "Holy, holy, holy is the Lord of hosts [Sabaoth]; the whole earth is full of his glory" (Is. 6:3). The biblical Trisagion, as we shall see, is a fixed element of the anaphora in both BAS and CHR.

The origins of the Thrice-holy Hymn are connected to a devastating earthquake that struck Constantinople in the mid-fifth century (ca. 450). Tradition has it that during this disastrous earthquake people gathered round imploring God for mercy (Κύριε, ἐλέησον ἡμᾶς). Suddenly, a young boy was swept up into heaven where he heard the song of the angels. Upon his return, he told the people the words of the song he heard: "*Holy God, Holy Mighty, Holy Immortal.*" The people, filled with astonishment and wonder, began to sing this simple powerful hymn, adding their words of supplication "*have mercy on us* – ἐλέησον ἡμᾶς."

Thereafter, the Trisagion was chanted at stational liturgies and penitential processions, usually as a refrain to select psalm verses.[204] The hymn began to appear in the Divine Liturgy in the fifth century, well before the addition of the antiphons. By the sixth century it was permanently incorporated into the divine service, initially as the usual entrance hymn (εἰσοδικόν).[205] When the antiphons were added to the Divine Liturgy, the Trisagion retained its original position, sung always before the Epistle and Gospel.[206] No longer an entrance

---

204 At stational liturgies the Trisagion was sung by the people as a refrain after each verse or group of verses of a psalm, which as a rule was Psalm 79/80, a prayer for deliverance. At each of the three stations the presiding hierarch invoked God's mercies and compassion upon the people – God's vineyard which he himself planted by his power – with the words of verses 14 and 15 of Psalm 79/80, "*Lord, Lord look down from heaven...*" To this day, at every hierarchical liturgy, the hierarch blesses the congregation with the same words between repetitions of the Trisagion Hymn. The Trisagion is also sung during various liturgical processions, retaining its original function.

205 The Trisagion Hymn has retained its introductory character at the vigil Divine Liturgies of Pascha, Christmas, Theophany, and Holy Thursday. Immediately after the Old Testament readings of the vesper service, the priest intones the call to prayer followed by the prayer and the Trisagion Hymn, which in the vigils of Pascha, Christmas and Theophany is replaced by the baptismal hymn, "*As many as have been baptized into Christ have put on Christ. Alleluia.*"

206 In earlier times, the Eucharistic liturgies of Constantinople also contained an Old Testament lesson. Once the Trisagion Hymn became a fixed element of the liturgy, the Old Testament reading was read before the trisagion as it is today in the vigil Divine Liturgies of Holy Thursday, Pascha, Christmas, and Theophany.

hymn but a fixed element of the liturgy,[207] it was introduced, as in current practice, by a call to prayer and a prayer – the Prayer of the Trisagion – in which God is implored to accept the thrice-holy hymn from the lips of sinful people who beseech his tender mercy and goodness, confident that God hears the prayer of humble penitents.[208]

The Trisagion is a hymn of exaltation in praise of the one true God who is holy, mighty, and immortal. Of these three, holiness is the principal attribute of God, as emphasized in the anaphora of BAS.[209] Holiness refers to God's transcendence and otherness as well as to his moral perfection, boundless love, and righteousness. The Trisagion is also a penitential hymn recited and sung by a people who recognize their imperfections, limitations, and mortality as well as their ultimate dependence on a gracious and loving God. Mindful of God's perfections and cognizant of their own failings, the people humbly petition the only Holy One, "*Have mercy on us.*" Reciting or singing the hymn is not only an act of faith in the power and majesty of God but also an act of contrition.

Initially, the Trisagion was understood to refer to God the Father, who is the cause (αἰτία) and the principle (ἀρχή) of the divine nature, which is in the Son and in the Holy Spirit. However, because of the foundational belief of Christians that God is Trinity; that God is one in essence (οὐσία) in three hypostases (ὑποστάσεις),[210] it did not take long to also interpret the hymn in a Trinitarian manner ascribing the words Holy God to the Father, Holy Mighty to the Son, and Holy Immortal to the Holy Spirit.[211]

---

207 On the feasts of Pascha, Christmas, Theophany, and Pentecost the "Holy God" is replaced by the baptismal hymn, "As many as have been baptized into Christ..." which was also used as a processional hymn. It was sung when the newly baptized were led from the baptistery into the nave of the church to join the gathered assembly for the Eucharist. On the feasts of the Elevation of the Life-giving Cross (September 14) and the Sunday of the Veneration of the Cross (Third Sunday of Lent) in place of "Holy God" we sing, "*We venerate your Cross, Master...*"

208 On the development of the order (τάξις) of the Trisagion, see Trembelas, Τρεῖς Λειτουργίαι, 40-5, and Fountoulis, Ἀπαντήσεις, vol. 3, 136-9 and vol. 5, 22-5.

209 "With these blessed powers, Master who love humankind, we sinners also cry aloud and say: You are holy and all-holy and there are no bounds to the majesty of your holiness. You are holy (ὅσιος) in all your works for you have disposed all things for us in righteousness and true judgment..."

210 See John Meyendorff, *Byzantine Theology* (New York 1979), 180-90.

211 For example, see the doxastikon of the aposticha of the Kneeling Service of Pentecost. "Come, O you people, let us worship the Godhead...Holy God, who created all things through the Son, with the cooperation of the Holy Spirit. Holy Mighty, through whom we have known the Father, and through whom the Holy Spirit came into the world. Holy Immortal, the Comforting Spirit, who proceeds from the Father and rests in the Son. O Holy Trinity, glory be to you."

A Note on the Trisagion Hymn and the Acclamations at a Hierarchical Liturgy

When a hierarch presides at the Divine Liturgy, the Trisagion Hymn is sung five times in the following order. The chanter/choir sings it twice. The third time it is sung by the clergy within the sanctuary. It is sung again (fourth) by the chanter/choir. The clergy sing it for a fifth time. The chanter/choir sings the Δόξα and καὶ νῦν... Ἅγιος Ἀθάνατος ἐλέησον ἡμᾶς. Then the clergy (or another appointed person) sing the hymn in florid style from within the sanctuary in four "parts:" Holy God... Holy Mighty... Holy Immortal... Have mercy on us." After each of the first three parts, the presiding hierarch blesses the people with the dykerotrika repeating the words of the psalmist, "Lord, Lord, look down from heaven..." (Psalm 79/80:14-15). When the fourth part is completed, the deacon or priest says, Δύναμις, and the chanter/choir sings the trisagion again. After this the deacon or priest faces the congregation standing at the Holy Doors and says, "Lord, save the devout – Κύριε, σῶσον τοὺς εὐσεβεῖς." The hierarch with clergy sings it once. The deacon repeats the ekphonesis twice more; each time the chanter/choir sings it. Then the deacon says: "And hear us," which is sung melodically by the hierarch. Immediately after, the deacon or priest proclaims the acclamation(s), the φήμη (pheme) for the hierarch, according to the order set by the Charter of the Archdiocese. The pheme or acclamation was originally sung before the Trisagion at the beginning of the liturgy, announcing the entrance of and praying for the long life of the emperor and the patriarch. Hence, in earlier texts we find the initial proclamation, "Lord, save the emperors – Κύριε, σῶσον τοὺς βασιλεῖς," referring to the imperial family.

E. PRAYER OF THE CATHEDRA – ΕΥΧΗ ΤΗΣ ΚΑΘΕΔΡΑΣ

A version of the dialogue we now find in the *Ieratikon* following the Trisagion Hymn was introduced into the Divine Liturgy as early as the late fourth century when the entrance of the clergy into the sanctuary and their ascension to the synthronon was ritualized. In current practice the dialogue between the deacon and priest is recited in a low voice while the Trisagion Hymn is being sung. If a deacon is not present, the priest says only the verses assigned to him as he proceeds to the synthronon, which is also referred to as the *high place* or *bema*. The rubrics and the dialogue in the received rite read as follows:

The celebrants bow three times before the Holy Table. Then the deacon says:

Deacon

Command, Master.

As the celebrants go to the synthronon, the priest says:

Priest

Blessed is he that comes in the name of the Lord.

Deacon

Master, bless the *cathedra* (throne) on high.

Priest

Blessed are you on the throne of glory of your kingdom, who are seated upon the Cherubim, always, now and forever, and to the ages of ages. Amen.

The priest then stands on the right side of the high place, the center being reserved for the hierarch.

The brief ceremony of access to the cathedra can be understood and appreciated only when its origins are known.

In the original entrance rite of the Divine Liturgy, after the Prayer of Entrance was recited by the chief celebrant, the people poured into the nave as the clergy processed to the sanctuary and took their place on the synthronon which was reserved for the hierarch(s) and priests.[212] By conciliar decision, deacons and lower clergy do not sit on the synthronon.[213]

The entrance ritual came to an end when the hierarch ascended to the throne, *the cathedra* – καθέδρα, and the concelebrating clergy stood or sat on either side of him according to rank. If a hierarch was not present, the cathedra

---

212 On every level of ecclesial life, the Church functions both hierarchically and synodically and the synthronon gives expression to this. The hierarch is the head of the local church. He is the source of its orderly life. However, he does not possess an autonomous power but presides over the local church in concert with his principle co-workers and associates, the priests, and the synthronon signifies this reality. The Church requires the ministry of the πρῶτος (the first), but also of the many. The two ministries are essential and coincide. One does not exist without the other (Canon 34 of the Holy Apostles). The word *synthronon* means to sit with, hence, to administer jointly.

213 Canons 18 of Nicaea, 7 of the Penthekte Council, and 20 of Laodicea.

remained vacant. The celebrating priests sat in their places according to rank and seniority, with the first in order to the right of the throne. When all were settled, the chief celebrant (hierarch or priest) gave the peace. Immediately after, the designated scripture lessons were announced and read.

The earliest extant Prayer of the Cathedra in both BAS and CHR is found in the *Barberini Codex*. It is a prayer of blessing and reflects the original order of the rite: "Lord and Master, God of the powers, save your people and grant them peace (εἰρήνευσον) by the power of your Holy Spirit, through the sign (τύπου) of the precious cross of your only-begotten Son with him you are blessed to the ages of ages. Amen."[214]

In his treatise on the Divine Liturgy, St. Germanos (+733) gives a different emphasis to the rite of the cathedra. There is no mention of a blessing. Rather, the emphasis is placed on the symbolic presence of the glorified Christ among his people. This same theme is emphasized in the received text. Germanos notes, "The *bema* (τὸ βῆμα)[215] is a concave place, a throne on which Christ, the King of all, presides with his apostles, as he says to them: You shall sit on thrones judging the twelve tribes of Israel.[216] The cathedra points to the second coming, when Christ will come sitting on the throne of glory to judge the world, as the prophet says: Thrones were set for judgment over the house of David."[217] In other words, the synthronon, occupied by the hierarch and priests serves as a tangible image of the transforming presence of Christ among his people. Christ is the exalted Lord who will come again in glory to judge the living and the dead.

According to the Constantinopolitan liturgical plan the synthronon occupied the apse of the sanctuary.[218] In cathedrals, such as Hagia Sophia, and in other large churches the synthronon consisted of an impressive semicircular tier of benches or steps with a cathedra at the center.[219] The cathedra or throne

---

214 Parenti and Velkovska, *L'Eucologio Barberini*, 5 (BAS) and 27 (CHR).

215 The word *bema* means a raised step or platform. It is also known as the high place. The bema describes the elevated area which contained the synthronon.

216 Matt. 19:28.

217 Ps. 121/122:5

218 In the Syrian liturgical plan, the synthronon and ambo are located in the center of the nave. See Peter Cobb, "The Architectural Setting of the Liturgy," in *The Study of Liturgy*, Jones, Wainwright, Yarnold, and Bradshaw eds. (New York and London 1992), 528-42. Louis Bouyer, *Liturgy and Architecture* (Notre Dame 1967).

219 See Thomas F. Mathews, *The Early Churches of Constantinople: Architecture and Liturgy* (Pennsylvania State University Press 1977); Rowland, J. Mainstone, *Hagia Sophia: Architecture, Structure and Liturgy of the Justinian's Great Church* (New York 1988); and Richard Krautheimer, *Early Christian and Byzantine Architecture* (Baltimore 1965).

was reserved for the hierarch. In later times the synthronon was reduced to a throne with simple benches on either side for the priests. Today, few Greek parish churches have a synthronon and where it exists it is rarely used.[220]

Because the synthronon is rarely found in parish churches today, some editions of the *Ieratikon* re-focused the rite on the prothesis directing the priest to say the words, "Blessed is he that comes in the name of the Lord," while facing the prothesis in anticipation of the Great Entrance.[221] The same texts direct the priest to say the other phrase, "Blessed are you on the throne of glory of your kingdom..." in front of the Holy Table.

Happily, newer editions and translations of the *Ieratikon* have retained the original order.[222] In any case, the rite of access to the cathedra has lost its original dynamic character and meaning. Rituals that have been disrupted by change should be carefully studied and prudently modified to fulfill a real purpose, otherwise they can easily fall prey to the harmful effects of ritual formalism, which give rise to subjective ill-considered interpretations.

F. SCRIPTURE READINGS (ΑΝΑΓΝΩΣΜΑΤΑ)

When the Trisagion Hymn has been completed, the deacon stands by the Holy Doors, faces the people, and exhorts them to be attentive. If there is no deacon, the priest pronounces the exhortation from the synthronon or from the Holy Doors. The admonition to pay close attention (πρόσχωμεν)[223] is pronounced before the readings in order to alert the people and to emphasize

---

220 Through the course of time the reason for and the meaning of the synthronon has become blurred. As a result, many priests rarely use it, if ever. In churches where a synthronon exists, it is often occupied by altar servers, which of course distorts its purpose and meaning and cannot be called a synthronon.

221 See, for example, the 1977 edition of the *Ieratikon of the Church of Greece.* Unfortunately, this same directive is found in the Holy Cross translation of CHR (1985). However, the new bilingual edition of CHR published by the Greek Orthodox Archdiocese of America (2015) has the correct order.

222 A synthronon is not an absolute requirement. Church edifices have existed without one for centuries for the lack of adequate space or for some other reason. For the synthronon to serve a real purpose, it must be used properly. Otherwise, why have one?

223 In other instances, the word ὀρθοί - *stand aright (stand well)* is used in place of πρόσχωμεν. These exhortations at different intervals of the service are meant to bring the worshippers, clerics and people alike, to attention, to be as servants whose eyes look to the hand of their masters to do them service (cf. Psalm 122/123:2).

the manner by which they are called to hear and receive the message of the Holy Scriptures, which contain the wisdom of God. For this reason, the word Σοφία – Wisdom is also added to the exhortation for attentiveness.[224]

As noted earlier, before the eighth century the Divine Liturgies of Constantinople had three readings, one from the Old Testament and two from the New Testament. By the eighth century the Old Testament reading had already disappeared from the Eucharistic liturgies. The readings were now limited to two, one from the Apostolos and the other from the Evangelion.[225]

The Apostolos

The reading from the Apostolos is preceded by the prokeimenon, which is introduced by an appeal for attention. The prokeimenon (*προκείμενον*)[226] is comprised of verses from a particular psalm, the content of which bears some relevance to the reading or the feast of the day and as such can be a source of inspiration for the preacher.[227] Eventually, the prokeimenon was limited to two verses of a psalm, the first of which was probably sung as a refrain. According to tradition, the reader intones the prokeimenon and the appointed pericope from the solea.[228] Strict conformity to the canons requires the Apostolos (Epistle) be read by a duly appointed reader.

---

[224] "What is this wisdom," Cabasilas asks? And he responds: "It is the sum of those thoughts which are in accord with the service, which should occupy those full of faith when they behold the ceremonies and listen to the prayers, so that they are concerned with no purely human sentiment…But this is far from easy to achieve. That is why we should keep constant watch on ourselves, and behave with circumspection" (*Commentary* II, 21).

[225] See above Part One – The Liturgical Books. See also Calivas, *Liturgy in Dialogue*, 225-42.

[226] The word is derived from the verb πρόκειμαι which means to lie before, to set before or in front of. Some have interpreted the word to mean before (*προ*) the text (*κείμενον*).

[227] For example, the *prokeimenon* and the accompanying verse for the Nineteenth Sunday are taken from Psalm 117/118:14 and 18 respectively: "The Lord is my strength and my song … The Lord has chastened me sorely." The Epistle Lesson is from 2 Corinthians 11:31-33; 12:1-9, in which St. Paul recounts his hardships, sufferings, and humiliations but also his extraordinary spiritual experiences and unique visions and revelations. Yet he boasts of nothing, except his weaknesses. "If I must boast," he writes, "I will boast of the things that show my weakness," that the power (grace) of Christ may rest upon me. Indeed, Christ alone is the apostle's strength and his song. Verses of Psalm 117/118 are also found in texts of several other services.

[228] From the inscriptions in the Apostolos, we learn that every prokeimenon was chanted according to an assigned tone (ἦχος). This tradition has been retained in some instances. For example, the prokeimenon of the Apostolos in the funeral service, "Μακαρία ἡ ὁδός… *Blessed be the way…*" is always chanted. From the text of the Pre-Sanctified Divine Liturgy we learn, in addition to the tone of the prokeimenon, the number of the psalm was also inscribed and perhaps even announced as it happens in the present practice.

Deacon or Priest

Let us be attentive – Πρόσχωμεν.

Priest

Peace be to all – Εἰρήνη πᾶσι.[229]

Reader

And to your spirit.

Intones the verses of the Prokeimenon.

Deacon or Priest

Wisdom – Σοφία.

Reader

Intones the title of the Epistle (The reading is from the *Acts of the Apostles*... is from the *Epistle of Paul to the*...).[230]

Deacon or Priest

Let us be attentive – Πρόσχωμεν.

Reader

Intones or reads the appointed pericope from the Apostolos. Today, the more common practice is to read the pericope.

When the reading is completed, the lector turns toward the priest to receive his blessing.

Priest

Peace be to you.[231]

Reader

And to your spirit.[232]

---

[229] In the prevailing Greek practice this blessing is omitted. Hence it is placed in brackets. The peace is now offered before the reading of the Gospel. The peace before the Apostolos is a remnant of the ancient entrance rite.

[230] The Apostolos is read from the solea facing the people or, if need be, from the chanter's stand. In the cathedral church of Hagia Sophia biblical lessons were read from the ambon which was situated in the center of the nave.

[231] The form, "Peace be to you, the reader," is found only in some recent editions.

[232] This response is wrongly omitted. Every priestly blessing is followed by a response from the recipient(s). Liturgical etiquette requires it.

The Evangelion

Of all the liturgical books of the Orthodox Church the Evangelion is the object of special honor. It is venerated as the icon of Christ par excellence. It is kissed, carried in procession, enthroned on the Holy Table, and reverenced with other honorific acts. Its covers are overlaid with a thin metal sheet (gold or silver plated) or bound in special leather or fabric with metal fittings and adorned with graphic material and stones. It is censed and escorted with lit candles. The readings are preceded by song, prayer, blessings, and acclamations. And while the lections of the Apostolos and Prophetologion are read by lectors and chanters, the Gospel is proclaimed only by deacons, priests, or hierarchs.

The Alleluia – Ἀλληλούϊα

The Alleluia should never be sung hurriedly. It acts as a prelude to the Gospel. It sets the tone, the manner by which the Word of God should be heard and received – with joy and thanksgiving. As such, the Alleluia should be sung gloriously and not as an afterthought.[233]

Alleluia is the Greek form of the Hebrew word Hallelujah, which means "Praise the Lord." As with the Hebrew words *Amen*, *Sabaoth*, and *Hosanna*, it has not been translated but retains its original form. The word is found in many psalms, the Book of Tobit (13:18), and the Book of Revelation (19:1-6). The latter verses from Revelation describe the heavenly liturgy. "And from the throne came a voice crying, 'Praise our God, all you his servants, you who fear him, small and great.' Then I heard what seemed to be the voice of a great multitude, like the sound of many waters and like the sound of mighty thunderpeals, crying, '*Alleluia!*' For the Lord our God the Almighty (ὁ παντοκράτωρ) reigns" (Rev. 19:5-6).

The *Alleluia* is a song of praise, thanksgiving, and joy. It was adopted by the Church at an early date and incorporated into all of its services, including the daily office, the holy sacraments, and other occasional services. It is found in the burial rites and abounds in the services of Lent and Holy Week.[234]

According to the rubrics, the Alleluia before the Gospel is meant to be sung nine times, in three sets of three. The second and third sets are preceded by a psalm verse. On Sundays and feast days, the psalm verses for the Alleluia

---

[233] All Gospel lessons in every service are preceded by the *Alleluia*, with one exception. At the vesperal Divine Liturgy of BAS at the Paschal Vigil (now celebrated on Holy Saturday morning) in place of the *Alleluia* we sing verses from Psalm 81/82 with verse 8 as the refrain, "*Arise O God, judge the earth ... Ἀνάστα ὁ Θεὸς κρῖνον τὴν γῆν...*" During the singing of Psalm 81/82, the priest spreads laurel leaves throughout the church. See Calivas, *Great Week and Pascha in the Greek Orthodox Church* (Brookline, MA 1992), 113-4.

[234] In Roman usage, the Alleluia is said at Mass and the daily office throughout the year except in Lent and has been omitted from the burial rites.

are listed in the Apostolos immediately after the appointed pericope. For weekdays, the verses are listed in the introductory section of the Apostolos under the heading, "Prokeimena of the Apostolos and the Alleluiaria of the Evangelion."[235] This list also contains the communion hymn for each weekday.

The Censing

The Evangelion, as already noted, constitutes the icon of Christ *par excellence*. For this reason, it is censed reverently before it is read. The purpose of the censing is to honor Christ, whose words we are about to hear. He is the word and wisdom of God; and to all who receive him and believe in his Name, he will give them power to become children of God (John 1:12).

In the absence of a deacon, the censing is conducted by the priest.[236] The correct order is to perform the censing while the Alleluia is being sung. At no time should the censing occur while the Apostolos is being read. Everyone, clergy and laity alike, should listen attentively to the Epistle lesson. No one should be distracted. To do otherwise would be disrespectful. The rubrics in most texts call for the deacon (or priest) to cense the Holy Table, the sanctuary and those in it. It is sufficient, I believe, and more appropriate to cense only the Evangelion in keeping with the original purpose of the act.

Blessing of the Deacon

If a deacon is present, he is charged with reading the designated Gospel pericope. He comes before the Holy Table and kneels on one knee at the right of the priest asking for his blessing so that he may be enabled to proclaim the Gospel with power. The priest places his right hand on the head of the deacon and recites the appropriate blessing. The deacon rises and the priest hands him the Evangelion. The deacon reverences the hand of the priest and in response to the blessing he has received, he says, "Amen. Amen. Amen. Be it unto me according to your word."[237] When the chanter or choir sings the Alleluia, the deacon proceeds to the ambo (pulpit) exiting the sanctuary via the north door preceded by altar servers holding lit candles. The dialogue between the priest and deacon is found in all the Ieratika and in the new bilingual edition of CHR of the Greek Orthodox Archdiocese of America (GOA).

---

235 For more on the prokeimena and alleluiaria see Evangelos Antoniadis, Περὶ τῶν ἐν ταῖς ἱεραῖς ἡμῶν ἀκολουθίαις Προκειμένων καὶ Ἀλληλουϊαρίων (Athens 1934).

236 Germanos of Constantinople in his treatise on the Divine Liturgy (Chapter 30) describes the thurible (censer) in symbolical terms. He writes, "The censer demonstrates the humanity of Christ, and the fire, his divinity. The sweet-smelling smoke reveals the fragrance of the Holy Spirit which precedes. For the censer denotes sweet joy..."

237 Luke 1:38.

When the deacon has completed the reading, he processes to the Holy Doors preceded by the altar servers. There, he hands the Evangelion to the priest and both enter the sanctuary.

Prayer of the Gospel (Εὐχὴ τοῦ Εὐαγγελίου)

The Prayer of the Gospel was added to both BAS and CHR around the twelfth century. Most likely, it was borrowed from the Divine Liturgy of St. Iakovos (James-JAS), the Brother of the Lord.[238] The same prayer, with minor differences, is also found in the Orthros service, the ninth in the series of the twelve prayers of Orthros. According to proper order, it should be read before the morning (Ἑωθινόν) Gospel on Sundays and feast days when the Orthros has a Gospel reading (ἀνάγνωσμα).

The significant difference, however, in this prayer, which is a shared prayer with JAS, the Orthros, BAS, and CHR, is found in the ekphonesis. The ekphonesis in JAS is addressed to the Father; in the Orthros it is addressed to the Trinity; and in BAS and CHR to the Son, our Lord Jesus Christ.[239] In BAS and CHR there are only four prayers addressed to the Son: the Prayer of the Gospel; the Prayer of the Cherubic Hymn; the Prayer of the Fraction, "Lord Jesus Christ, our God, hear us from your holy dwelling place;" and the prayer at the prothesis before the apolysis, "Christ our God, you are the fulfillment…" (CHR); "The mystery of your dispensation, O Christ our God…" (BAS).[240]

The Prayer of the Gospel has a special message for the clergy. It underscores the significance of the preaching ministry and indicates that the sermon or homily is an integral part of the Divine Liturgy. We read the words: "Shine in our hearts, loving Master, the pure light of your divine knowledge and open the eyes of our mind that we may comprehend the message of your Gospel." Effective preaching helps the people delve into the mysteries of the faith contained in the Scriptures and Tradition (cf. Luke 24:13-35).

---

238 On the Antiochian-Jerusalem Liturgy of St. James see John D. Witvliet, "The Anaphora of St. James," in Paul F. Bradshaw, ed., *Essays on Early Eastern Eucharistic Prayers* (Collegeville, MN 1997), 153-72.

239 In the ekphonesis of JAS we read: "For you, O God, and your only-begotten Son and your all-holy Spirit, are the herald of good tidings (ὁ εὐαγγελισμός) and the illumination, savior, and guardian of our souls and bodies, now and forever and to the ages of ages." The ekphonesis of the prayer in Orthros reads: "For you are our sanctification and to you we offer glory, to the Father and the Son, and the Holy Spirit, now and forever…" In BAS and CHR the ekphonesis reads: "For you, Christ our God, are the illumination of our souls and bodies, and to you we offer glory, together with your Father who is without beginning, and your all-holy, good, and life-creating Spirit, now and forever…."

240 The title of the prayer, "Εὐχὴ εἰς τὸ συστεῖλλαι τὰ Ἅγια," suggests that it was prayed when the remaining Holy Gifts were consumed.

The prayer also contains words which highlight the essence of the spiritual life: "Instill in us also reverence for your blessed commandments, so that having conquered all sinful desires, we may pursue a spiritual life, thinking and doing all those things that are pleasing to you." The spiritual life is not about abstract feelings and obscure notions. It is centered on a Person, our Lord and Savior Jesus Christ, the God-Man (Θεάνθρωπος), who illumines all. The activities that fuel and energize the spiritual life begin with a deep reverence for the commandments which are summarized and set forth in the Decalogue (Ex. 20:1-20; Deut. 5:6-21), the Sermon on the Mount (Matt. 5-7), and the Last Supper discourses (John 13:1- 17:26). By following the commandments, the Spirit of God empowers us to overcome our sinful desires (Rom. 8:1-9).

Simply put, the spiritual life is nothing more than the pursuit of virtue and goodness, i.e. thinking and doing all those things that are pleasing to God. Or, as St. Maximos the Confessor taught: "Our mind is in the middle of two things, each one active at its own work, the one at virtue, the other at vice, in other words between angel and devil. The mind has the power and strength to follow or oppose the one it chooses.... The perfect soul is the one whose affective drive is wholly directed to God."[241] At its core, the spiritual life is a kenotic act, the readiness to surrender one's self freely to the Author of life, to be sustained by his transforming grace and unconditional love. As we move, even falteringly, from death to life and from glory to glory, we become little by little a source of joy and love.

Unfortunately, for reasons of brevity this lovely prayer is seldom read aloud. It is said by the priest in a low voice during the singing of the Trisagion. Should the Church decide to renew and reform aspects of the sacred service, I would support a change in the rubrics and have the entire congregation recite the prayer together with the priest, who at the end would intone the ekfonesis, as we do with the Lord's Prayer.

The simplicity and directness of the prayer touch the heart and penetrate the soul. Reading it altogether aloud would make the worshippers more alert and receptive, more aware of the transforming power of God's word. As a result, the worshippers would be reminded again to resist and abhor the wickedness of the fallen world and embrace with growing fervor the righteousness of God, so that day by day they may become doers of God's word and not just listeners of it.

---

241 Maximos the Confessor, *The Four Hundred Chapters on Love*, The third Century, 92, 98.

Proclaiming the Gospel

In earlier times, the Gospel was proclaimed from the *ambo* (pulpit). Today, this custom is observed only when a deacon is present. In current practice when serving alone, the priest reads the Gospel from the Holy Doors facing the people, usually from a moveable lectern placed there by the sexton or another altar server.[242]

For its symbolic value, if feasible, the priest may process to the ambo with the Evangelion to proclaim the Gospel pericope from there. However, to avoid misunderstandings the priest should first consult with his hierarch on this matter. The procession to the ambo suggests movement, the coming of the Lord to his people. Saint Germanos, in his treatise on the liturgy (Chap. 31), says, "The Gospel (τὸ εὐαγγέλιον) is [a sign] of the coming of God, when he was seen by us…no longer speaking to us through a cloud and indistinctly, as he did to Moses…nor appearing through dreams as to the prophets, but he appeared visibly as a true man. He was seen by us as a gentle and peaceful king who descended quietly…and we have beheld his glory, glory as of the only-begotten Son, full of grace and truth…."

Priest

When the Alleluia has been sung, the priest stands at the Holy Doors facing the people and says:

Wisdom! Arise! Let us hear the holy Gospel.[243]

And blessing the people with his right hand in the usual manner, he says:

Peace be with all.

People

And with your spirit.

Priest or Deacon

The reading is from the Holy Gospel according to (Matthew, Mark, Luke, or John).[244]

---

242 In most monasteries and many Slavic churches the lectern is placed in the middle of the solea.

243 When reciting the bidding in Greek, it is important for the priest to pause after the word Σοφία! The bidding has two distinct commands: Σοφία! and Ὀρθοί! Of course, the same is true in English.

244 Note, in the original text of the four Gospels and in our liturgical texts the name of each Evangelist is not preceded by the title "Saint."

Priest

Let us be attentive.[245]

People

Glory to you, O Lord, glory to you.

*And the **priest** (or **deacon**)[246] reads (or intones) the prescribed pericope. Upon its completion, the priest kisses the Evangelion, blesses the people with it, and returns it to the Holy Table, as the people sing:*

People

Glory to you, O Lord, glory to you.[247]

G. THE HOMILY OR SERMON

To proclaim the Gospel with power and conviction is one of the fundamental and indispensable activities or ministries of the Church, the responsibility for which rests chiefly on the clergy and more specifically on hierarchs and priests.[248]

While the message of the Gospel may be understood directly or immediately – inasmuch as the word of God speaks by and for itself – its deeper meanings are drawn from the explanations provided by the preacher, who is charged to open the scriptures in order to stir the souls of the faithful and contribute to their edification in the faith. The priest-preacher is authorized to "bear witness to the light," to preach and to teach not his own ideas, opinions, and thoughts but the "words of eternal life" (John 6:68). Or as the psalmist puts

---

245 In the Slavic tradition, the bidding, "Let us be attentive," is said after the "Glory to you, O Lord…"

246 If a deacon reads the pericope, the priest blesses him after its completion, saying: "Peace be to you." After the reading the deacon processes to the Holy Doors and hands the Evangelion to the priest.

247 This acclamation is a brief song of praise and should be sung joyously. The acclamation is sung after every reading of the Gospel with one exception. At the Orthros of Holy Friday, now sung on Holy Thursday night (Service of the Twelve Gospels) after each Gospel reading, we sing, "Δόξα τῇ μακροθυμίᾳ σου, Κύριε, δόξα σοι – *Glory to your long-suffering, O Lord, glory to you.*" Here, the focus of our praise is the forbearance of God, the inscrutable condescension of our Lord and Savior.

248 See Calivas, "The Presbyter and the Essential Activities of the Church," in *Church, Clergy, Laity, and the Spiritual Life*, 65-87.

it, the priest-homilist is obliged to *"Proclaim the good news of God's salvation from day to day. Declare his glory among the nations, his wonders among all peoples"* (Psalm 95/96:2-3).[249]

The sermon is an integral part of the Divine Liturgy – and for that matter of every liturgical service.[250] Hence sermonizing should never be neglected or depreciated. On the importance of the liturgical homily and its relation to the Divine Liturgy see Appendix C:5.

H. FERVENT LITANY, CATECHUMENS, PRAYERS OF THE FAITHFUL, AND ANTIMENSION

In the received text of the Divine Liturgy three different sets of litanies and prayers follow the Biblical readings and the homily, namely, the Fervent Litany, the Litany and Prayer for the Catechumens, and the two prayers for the faithful.

The **deacon** intones the Fervent Litany.

The **priest** recites the Prayer of the Litany.

The **deacon** intones the Litany of the Catechumens.

The **priest** recites the Prayer of the Litany.

The **deacon** calls the faithful to prayer

The **priest** recites the First Prayer of the Faithful.

The **deacon** again, calls the faithful to prayer.

The **priest** recites the Second Prayer of the Faithful.]

---

249 The second verse of Psalm 95/96, *"Proclaim the good news of his salvation from day to day,"* is used as the *eisodikon* on the Feast of the Annunciation. The troparia of the ninth ode in the Orthros of the same feast are introduced by a *megalynarion* with a similar theme: "O earth, announce good tidings of great joy; O heavens, praise the glory of God." Both texts capture succinctly the essence of the liturgical homily.

250 This truth is affirmed by the Scriptures (Acts 2:42; 6:2-4; cf. Luke 24:25-32) and the writings of the Fathers. See, for example, the testimony of St. Justin the Martyr (Apology 1:67): "On the day named after the sun, all who live in city or countryside assemble. The memoirs of the apostles or the writings of the prophets are read for as long as time allows. *When the lector has finished, the president addresses us and exhorts us to imitate the splendid things we have heard.* Then we all stand and pray...." (The italic is for emphasis).

The Fervent Litany (ἐκτενὴς δέησις = earnest prayer)²⁵¹ and its prayer of supplication is found in many services, including Orthros and Vespers, and in a modified form in baptismal, wedding, and funeral rites.²⁵² The litany is an insistent, earnest entreaty, an urgent plea for God's measureless love and abundant mercy on behalf of God's people who find themselves in various circumstances. It includes petitions for the clergy, for the living and deceased, and for those who do good works and serve the Church and its mission to the world.

The litany's fervent, earnest character is illustrated in two ways. First, by the three passionate pleas which are addressed to God: "we pray you, hear us, and have mercy." Second, by the triple Κύριε ἐλέησον sung by the people after each petition. In former times, the singing of the Κύριε ἐλέησον was sung with raised hands and open palms to accentuate further the earnestness of the supplication. The Fervent Litany has both a hopeful and penitential tone, echoing Psalm 50/51, the foremost penitential psalm.

The structure of the Fervent Litany and the style of the petitions suggest that it has two distinct parts. The petitions in the first part are addressed to God and in the second part to the people.²⁵³ In the mss, the number

---

251 An act of earnest prayer is mentioned in Acts 12:5 on behalf of the Apostle Peter who was in prison: "προσευχὴ δὲ ἦν ἐκτενῶς γινομένη ὑπὸ τῆς ἐκκλησίας πρὸς τὸν Θεὸν περὶ αὐτοῦ... but *earnest* prayer for him was made to God by the church."

252 See the note on this litany in the vesper service, Ierotelestikon, Part One.

253 There are two petitions addressed to God, the first of which addresses God as the "*God of our fathers* - Ὁ Θεὸς τῶν πατέρων ἡμῶν." This phrase is used throughout the Old Testament and refers to the forebears in the faith. The same petition refers to God as the Almighty (παντοκράτωρ). It is a divine name or title and is used to describe the absolute, all-powerful ruler of all. The title is found in the Old Testament and mentioned in the Book of Revelation (1:8, 4:8, 16:7, and 19:5). It also appears in the first article of the Symbol of Faith (Creed) where it is ascribed to God the Father, "the Almighty, Creator of heaven and earth and all things visible and invisible." The title is also applied to Christ and specifically to the icon that adorns the main dome of a traditional Orthodox temple. There, Christ is presented as *Pantokrator* because, he is the One "through whom all things were made." In addition to *Pantokrator*, Christ is *Savior*: "For us and our salvation, he came down from heaven." He is also the impartial *Judge*: "He will come again to judge the living and the dead..."

On another note, compare the petition for the clergy in the Fervent Litany with that in the Great Litany. The petition in the Fervent Litany appears to have monastic roots. We pray for the hierarch and the priests but also for priest-monks (ἱερομονάχων), deacon-monks (ἱεροδιακόνων), and monastics (μοναχῶν), and for all the brotherhood in Christ (καὶ πάσης τῆς ἐν Χριστῷ ἡμῶν ἀδελφότητος), a reference, no doubt, to the particular monastic community. A monastic community is referred to as a brotherhood (or sisterhood) - **ἀδελφότης**.

of petitions in the second part vary, which suggests that the received form of the litany is a shortened version of an earlier, extended form of supplication.[254]

The Fervent Litany is not original to the Divine Liturgy. It was an integral part of processions and stational liturgies, from which it was introduced into the Divine Liturgy. This occurred before the eighth century, inasmuch as the Prayer of the Fervent Litany was already included in BAS and CHR in the Barberini Codex, gr. 336. Today, for reasons of brevity, it is usually recited by the priest inaudibly.[255] The Fervent Litany provides the priest the opportunity to pray for specific needs of the community and its members. In such circumstance, were the litany to be said aloud, it could help sensitize the worshippers to the special needs of others.[256]

The Litany and Prayer for the Catechumens: Praying for and invoking blessings over the catechumens is an old tradition. The essential elements of this unit of the Divine Liturgy were set down by the fourth century, if not earlier. The Constitutions of the Holy Apostles (Ἀποστολικαὶ Διαταγαί) or simply the Apostolic Constitutions, a fourth-century church order, for example, contains the following instructions after the readings at the Divine Liturgy. "Catechumens pray, and let all the faithful pray for them saying, 'Lord have mercy upon them.' And let the deacon bid prayers for them…. 'Rise up, ye catechumens…and bow down your heads.' And let the bishop bless them with this blessing…. And after this, let the deacon say, 'All catechumens depart in peace.'"[257]

The same order appears in our received text. The priest (or deacon) exhorts the catechumens to pray silently ("Catechumens, pray to the Lord").[258] As the priest offers petitions on their behalf, the faithful

---

254 See Kucharek, *Byzantine-Slav Liturgy*, 446-57.

255 Sadly, because the Fervent Litany is usually said inaudibly, it has been omitted from many bilingual editions. The same is true of the Litany of the Catechumens and the first or both Prayers of the Faithful. The more appropriate thing to do – until the time liturgical reforms are properly introduced – is to include the entire official text of the Church in every edition and place the parts which have been relegated to inaudible recitation in a smaller font.

256 For example, petitions can be offered for a variety of reasons and occasions, both happy and sad, such as: the health and wellbeing of graduating seniors, or members of the community who are seriously ill, or victims of a recent tragedy or calamity. In the spring of 2020, for example, during the terrible Covid-19 (Coronavirus) pandemic, the Church created two special petitions for God's blessings upon the doctors, nurses, hospital staff, first-responders, researchers, volunteers, and essential workers who were risking their lives in the service of the general public.

257 *Constitutions of the Holy Apostles*, Book 8 (VI).

258 In former times, the catechumens knelt as the community prayed for them.

intercede for the catechumens by responding Κύριε ἐλέησον. In addition to being supplicatory, the petitions are also didactic. They remind the catechumens as well as the people who are praying for them of the fundamental purpose of the catechumenate: "Let us, the faithful, pray for the catechumens; that the Lord will have mercy upon them; that he will teach them the word of truth; that he will reveal to them the gospel of righteousness; that he will unite them to his holy, catholic, and apostolic church...." When the petitions are finished, the catechumens are called to bow their heads to receive the priest's blessing in the form of a prayer. If a hierarch is present, the prayer is read by him. Immediately after this, the priest or deacon bids the catechumens to depart ("Those who are catechumens depart.... Let none of the catechumens remain").

In more ancient times similar dismissals were also made for three other categories of persons who were not allowed to remain for the Eucharist, the energumens (ἐνεργούμενοι), the penitents (μετανοοῦντες), and the competentes (φωτιζόμενοι).²⁵⁹ Petitions and prayers for the energumens and penitents disappeared from the Divine Liturgy centuries ago. The catechumens and competentes, however, continue to be prayed for. Prayers for the competentes have been preserved in all three Liturgies, CHR, BAS, and PRES. The petitions for the competentes are added to those of the catechumens after the Third Sunday of Great Lent, which marks the mid-point of the Lenten season.²⁶⁰

Unfortunately, in current practice the petitions and prayer for the catechumens are read inaudibly at best or simply eliminated as anachronistic. However, an argument can be made for the retention of these petitions and requires serious attention. See Appendix C:6

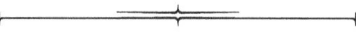

---

259 *Constitutions*, Book 8 (VI, VII, VIII, and IX). The term *energumen* was used of demoniacs and others possessed with abnormal mental and physical states. The community treated them with care, imitating of the example of Christ (Matt. 4:24; 8:16-17, 28; 9:32; 12:22; 15:22-28; Mark 5:2-19; Luke 8:26-39). *Penitents* were those who had committed grave sin and were separated from the worshipping community by location, posture, dress and appearance until they were readmitted to Holy Communion. The *competentes* were catechumens who qualified for, and were admitted to, the final stage of preparation for baptism. Prayers for the energumens and penitents were removed from the text of Divine Liturgy as early as the eighth century. Regarding those who were excluded from the Eucharist proper and Communion, see Pseudo-Dionysios, *Ecclesiastical Hierarchy*, chapter three, III: 5-7.

260 In the early Church, Pascha was considered the most appropriate time for conferring the sacrament of Holy Baptism. The catechumens who qualified for baptism at the Paschal feast, the *competentes*, underwent an intense period of preparation during Great Lent and were prayed for separately especially during the latter part of the Lenten season and all of Holy Week.

The Two Prayers of the Faithful

All three Divine Liturgies of the Byzantine rite (BAS, CHR, and PRE) contain two prayers for the faithful. The prayers were once preceded by the Great Litany, which is now found at the beginning of the Divine Liturgy. This litany is the common prayer of the community of the faithful, namely the Church, which prays for the common and universal needs of the Church and the world.

The first of the prayers was offered inaudibly by the celebrant as the deacon said the petitions. The subject matter of the first prayer concerns the clergy who are presiding at the service. In CHR the celebrant prays for himself and for all who stand at the Holy Altar with him, asking for the forgiveness "of our sins and for the errors of the people."[261] Acknowledging that he is appointed to this ministry by God, the celebrant asks that he be enabled by the power of the Holy Spirit to call upon the Triune God "at all times and in all places" to offer supplications on behalf of the people and that together with them and for them offer the sacrifice without the shedding of blood, and to do this with a clear conscience.

The second prayer was and should continue to be said aloud.[262] The second prayer focuses chiefly on the people, who like the clergy, must be counted worthy to stand before God. The celebrant first prays that God may cleanse him (and all who stand at the Holy Table with him) from every defilement of flesh and spirit (2 Cor. 7:1) so that he (they) may draw near to the Holy Table without condemnation. Then he prays for all the people asking God to "grant [them] progress in life, faith, and spiritual discernment." He also beseeches God to bestow upon them three special blessings: to "always worship [God] with reverence and love; partake of the Holy Mysteries without blame or condemnation; and become worthy of God's heavenly kingdom.[263]

---

261 Liturgical etiquette requires of the celebrant to speak kindly of the people (errors) and sternly of himself (sins).

262 The opening phrase of the prayer, "Again and oftentimes we fall down before you..." is of interest. It indicates that the people knelt during the prayer and the litany that preceded it. However, kneeling was (is) prohibited on Sundays. Was this prayer used on Sundays? The answer is yes. Originally CHR was the weekday Liturgy of Constantinople. When CHR supplanted BAS and became the regular Sunday Liturgy, the priestly prayers were no longer being read aloud.

263 As I have noted elsewhere (*Liturgy in Dialogue*, 92-3), the two prayers in BAS are not prayers of the faithful but clerical prayers of access. Robert Taft has argued that the two prayers in BAS are not primitive elements of BAS, at least in their present position. The two originally formed a single prayer, the original access prayer of BAS which was replaced by the so-called Prayer of the Cherubic Hymn ("*No one is worthy ... Οὐδεὶς ἄξιος...*"). Juan Mateos maintains that the three prayers of the antiphons in both BAS and CHR are, in fact, the original prayers of the faithful in BAS, in the order, 3, 1, and 2, the last being a prayer of benediction.

The two Prayers of the Faithful are the links that hold the two parts of the Divine Liturgy together.

A Special Note – The Priest as Spokesperson: These two prayers and others that follow, such as the Prayer of the Proskomide, underscore the representative role of the celebrant priest or hierarch at the Divine Liturgy. These prayers, written in the first-person plural, are said by the celebrant as the spokesman of the people and of his fellow clergy: "Again, we bow before you and pray to you…hear our supplication…and grant that we may stand before your Holy Altar without blame or condemnation. Grant also, O God, progress in life, faith, and spiritual discernment to the faithful who pray with us, so that they may worship you with reverence and love…"

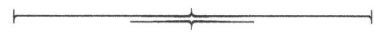

Unfolding the Eiliton or Antimension

The ritual act which brings us to the very threshold of the second part of the Divine Liturgy, the Eucharist proper, entails the unfolding of the *eiliton* or *antimension (εἰλητόν - ἀντιμήνσιον)*.

Following the Fervent Litany, according to the rubrics in most texts of the Divine Liturgy, the priest is instructed to lift the Evangelion, make the sign of the cross over the folded antimension, and place it on the upper part of the Holy Table in front of the *artophorion*.[264] Obviously, if the Fervent Litany and the Litany of the Catechumens are omitted, the antimension is unfolded immediately after the reading of the Gospel.

Space permitting, the Evangelion should be positioned in a flat vertical position.[265] If it can be helped, the Evangelion should not be positioned horizontally on the Holy Table. The horizontal position is used only on Holy and Great Friday to symbolize the death of Christ.[266] At all other times, the

---

264 Spreading the *eiliton* or *antimension* well before the Great Entrance is probably based on an early tradition which required the deacons to perform the task before they departed for the skeuophylakion to fetch the Gifts.

265 Following an old tradition, some clergy choose to place the Evangelion in a standing position in front of the artophorion. This, however, requires great care. The Evangelion must be made very secure so that it will not fall forward on the Gifts or backwards on the artophorion.

266 Long before the epitaphios was introduced into the rituals of Holy Friday, the Evangelion was used to depict the burial of Christ. It was carried on the shoulder of the priest in a horizontal position with a cloth wrapped around it.

Evangelion is enthroned on the Holy Table flat, in an upright/vertical position. When the Evangelion has been properly positioned, the priest carefully unfolds the antimension and spreads it on the Holy Table. See Appendix C:7.

I. THE GREAT ENTRANCE

Deacon or Priest

Let us, the faithful, again and again in peace pray to the Lord. Help us, save us, have mercy on us, and protect us, O God by your grace.

(The chanters or choir respond accordingly)

The **priest**, in an audible voice, reads the Second Prayer of the Faithful and intones its doxological ending: *"That, ever-guarded by your might ... Ὅπως ὑπὸ τοῦ κράτους σου πάντοτε φυλαττόμενοι..."*

People - Choir or Chanter:

Amen.

Sing the Cherubic Hymn: *"Οἱ τὰ Χερουβὶμ μυστικῶς εἰκονίζοντες ... We who mystically represent the Cherubim..."*

Priest

As the Cherubic Hymn is being sung, the priest stands before the Holy Table and in a low voice recites with great care the prayer, "Οὐδεὶς ἄξιος ... No one bound by sinful desires..."

When he completes the prayer, the priest, with raised hands, recites the Cherubic Hymn in a low voice.[267] *On Sundays and during the entire Paschal season he also recites the Paschal troparion, "Ἀνάστασιν Χριστοῦ θεασάμενοι ... Having beheld the resurrection of Christ...."*

Then he takes the censer and censes the Holy Table and the sanctuary. Coming out a little from the Holy Doors, he censes the icons on the iconostasis and the people in the usual manner.[268] *As he censes he recites Psalm 50/51. If it is a weekday when the*

---

267 According to the current practice, the rubrics have the priest recite the hymn three times through a mistaken reading of earlier directives. The early manuscripts and *diataxeis* order the celebrant to recite the hymn only once upon completion of the Prayer of the Cherubikon. The act itself is redundant since it duplicates what is being said by the people/singers. The *Diataxis* of Philotheos Kokkinos makes the following note. "And when [the prayer] has been completed, they stand together [deacon and priest] and pray the Cherubikon, saying it quietly to themselves. And while they are saying it, they make three reverences; then they proceed to the prothesis." At some point in time, the directive for three reverences was misunderstood and thought to apply to the hymn as well, and so a new practice was begun.

268 In keeping with ancient tradition, the Slavic practice assigns the censing to the deacon, if one is present. For more on this practice see below, the Rite of Censing.

Paschal Hymn is not chanted, Psalm 50//51 is preceded by the recitation of the bidding, "Come let us worship... Δεῦτε προσκυνήσωμεν...."

When the censing is complete, the priest stands before the Holy Table and makes three small prostrations, saying each time, "'Ο Θεός, ἱλάσθητί μοι τῷ ἁμαρτωλῷ... God, be merciful to me a sinner."[269] *Then he kisses the antimension and the Holy Table and makes another prostration. Turning toward the people, he bows and asks them for forgiveness, saying,* Ἀδελφοί, συγχωρήσατέ μοι [τῷ ἁμαρτωλῷ] ... "My brothers and sisters, forgive me [a sinner]" *or some similar words.*

After this, the priest proceeds to the prothesis. He censes the covered gifts, bows, and kisses them. Then, lifting the aer he places it on his shoulders, saying, "Ἄρατε τὰς χεῖρας ὑμῶν εἰς τὰ ἅγια καὶ εὐλογεῖτε τὸν Κύριον ... Lift up your hands to the holy place and bless the Lord. Ps. 133/134: 2)."[270] *To secure the aer, the priest ties a slip knot in front of him with the ribbons hanging from the two corners of the aer. Then he lifts the covered discos and chalice head-high holding each securely with his left and right hand respectively.*[271]

When the chanter/choir sings "'Ως τὸν Βασιλέα τῶν ὅλων ὑποδεξόμενοι ... So that we may receive the King of all...." *the priest makes the Great Entrance. Preceded by altar servers carrying the processional cross, candles, ripidia, and censer, the priest*

---

269 According to current Greek practice, if a deacon is present, he stands opposite the priest during the censing. Together they bow before the Holy Table. The deacon kisses only the Holy Table. He then turns to the priest, bows and says, "May the Lord God remember your priesthood." He also turns to the people and asks for their forgiveness.

270 This psalm verse (Ps. 133/134:2) was added because the word ἅγια was associated with the Holy Gifts (τὰ ἅγια δῶρα). In the original sense of the psalm, however, the word ἅγια refers to the holy place, the sanctuary. If a deacon is present, the priest places the aer on the shoulders of the deacon and gives him the covered paten (discos), saying *"Lift up your hands to the holy place and bless the Lord."* The priest takes the covered chalice. As the deacon and priest process they proclaim, one after the other the exclamation, *"May the Lord God..."* When the procession reaches the solea, the deacon enters the sanctuary through the Holy Gate. He stands to the right in front of the Holy Table and says to the priest as he enters, *"May the Lord God remember your priesthood..."* And the priest says to the deacon, *"May the Lord God remember your diaconate..."* The priest places the chalice on the Holy Table, takes the discos from the deacon and places it next to the chalice and removes the covers. Then he takes the aer from the shoulders of the deacon and covers the gifts with it. A dialogue between the deacon and priest follows. When it is concluded, the deacon receives the priest's blessing and exits the sanctuary to intone the litany. The dialogue is found in all texts of the Divine Liturgy at the conclusion of the Great Entrance rites and before the Litany of Completion – the so-called Πληρωτικά or Αἰτήσεις.

271 In the most recent edition of the Ieratikon of the Church of Greece, the editor has inserted two additional psalm verses. When lifting the discos: *"Ἀνέβη ὁ Θεὸς ἐν ἀλαλαγμῷ, Κύριος ἐν φωνῇ σάλπιγγος...God has gone up with a shout, the Lord with the sound of a trumpet"* (Ps. 46/47:5). When lifting the chalice: *"I will take up the cup of salvation and call upon the name of the Lord... Ποτήριον σωτηρίου λήψομαι καὶ τὸ ὄνομα Κυρίου ἐπικαλέσομαι"* (Ps. 115:3/116:13).

exits the sanctuary via the north door.[272] The procession passes through the north aisle and the middle aisle of the nave. When the servers arrive at the center of the solea, they split into two lines facing each other, allowing room for the priest to proceed into the sanctuary through the Holy Doors. When the priest enters the sanctuary, the servers bow before the sanctuary and enter it via the north and south doors respectively. The server with the censer enters first and stands to the side of the Holy Table, ready to give the censer to the priest.

Once the procession starts, the chanter/choir remains silent. As the priest processes through the church, he proclaims aloud, "Πάντων ὑμῶν μνησθείη Κύριος ὁ Θεὸς ἐν τῇ βασιλείᾳ αὐτοῦ πάντοτε, νῦν καὶ ἀεὶ καὶ εἰς τοὺς αἰῶνας τῶν αἰώνων ... May the Lord God remember all of you in his kingdom always, now and forever and to the ages of ages."[273] When he reaches the solea, the priest turns to the people as he finishes the exclamation and bows his head toward them. Through this gesture the priest acknowledges the people on behalf of whom he has just entreated God, "May the Lord God remember all of you...." The gesture, however, does not include a blessing of the people with the Gifts. In fact, at no time are the Gifts used for blessing. Having acknowledged the people, the priest turns and enters the sanctuary through the Holy Door.

When the priest enters the sanctuary, he deposits the Gifts on the open antimension. He places the discos on the right (his left) and the chalice on the left (his right). When placing the Gifts on the Holy Table, he recites the apolytikion of Holy Friday, "'O

---

272 In a concelebration, when a hierarch and several priests and deacons are present, the senior deacon carries the discos and the senior priest the chalice. If a second deacon is present, he carries the censer. The remaining priests also process according to seniority, usually carrying additional chalices or some other implement or vessel. In keeping with the ancient tradition, the hierarch does not process but stands at the Holy Doors to receive the Holy Gifts. Originally, the deacons alone carried the gifts and the other liturgical paraphernalia in the procession. Today, the processional cross, candles, ripidia, and censer are carried by altar servers. Earlier, the deacons carried the veils, the covers for the discos and chalice and the aer–epitaphios. A subdeacon carried the χερνιβόξεστον (the vessel for water to wash the hands within a hand basin or bowl). Today, this practice occurs only when a subdeacon is to be ordained to the diaconate. The candidate-subdeacon holds the χερνιβόξεστον and joins the procession last, after all the other clergy.

273 Is it, "Remember us all" or "Remember all of you?" In the manuscripts, the Diataxeis, and the early printed editions of the Divine Liturgy we find the plural pronoun of the second person "ὑμῶν – you." "Remember all of you" is the preferred form, not because it is older but because it corresponds more faithfully to the role of the clergy, who pray for the people. In fact, commemorations at the Great Entrance are a result of popular piety. The first mention of commemorations pronounced aloud appears in a 12th-13th century Diataxis. They are said aloud by the priest to assure the people of his prayers. At concelebrations priests greet one another with a similar greeting, "May the Lord God remember *your* priesthood in his kingdom." See Calivas, *Aspects of Orthodox Worship*, 193-9.

εὐσχήμων Ἰωσήφ ... The noble Joseph..."[274] *The priest removes the veils from the paten and chalice, folds them, and lays them to one side of the Holy Table. He removes the aer from his shoulders, holds it over the censer, and then drapes it over the Gifts. Then, he takes the censer and censes the Gifts three times, saying,* "Ἀγάθυνον, Κύριε ... Do good to Zion, Lord..." *(Ps. 50/51:18-19).*

People

As the priest passes through the nave, the people bow their heads, cross themselves, and say in a whisper, *"Remember us, Lord, in your kingdom...Μνήσθητι ἡμῶν, Κύριε, ἐν τῇ βασιλείᾳ σου."*

People (Chanter or Choir)

When the priest finishes the exclamation, "May the Lord God remember all of you..." the chanter or choir resumes and completes the Cherubic Hymn, *"Ταῖς ἀγγελικαῖς ἀοράτως δορυφορούμενον τάξεσιν. Ἀλληλούϊα, Ἀλληλούϊα, Ἀλληλούϊα ... Invisibly escorted by the angelic hosts. Alleluia. Alleluia. Alleluia."*

A Brief Explanation of the Elements that Comprise the Great Entrance

The Great Entrance *marks the beginning of the second part of the Divine Liturgy, the Eucharist proper. It is comprised of several elements which were combined over the course of time into a single liturgical unit. The original simple functional act – the transfer of the unconsecrated Gifts from the skeuophylakion to the sanctuary – grew gradually into the grand ritual of the Great Entrance, perhaps the most impressive sensory experience of the entire service.[275] The growing splendor of the ritual had an effect on the piety of the clergy and the people, even in the smallest of churches.*

Gradually, the simple transfer of the Gifts was embellished with various symbolic or allegorical interpretations, the earliest of which is that of Theodore of Mopsuestia who saw in the procession of the Gifts an image of Christ being led to his passion and burial.[276] The linen cloth which was

---

274 The recent bilingual edition of the Divine Liturgy by the GOA omits this hymn.

275 For more on the development of the Great Entrance rites see the classic work of Robert Taft, *The Great Entrance* Rome 1978). See also A. Schmemann, *The Eucharist* (Crestwood, NY 1988), 112-31. H. Wybrew, *The Orthodox Liturgy* (Crestwood, NY 1990). A. Calivas, *Aspects of Orthodox Worship*, 193-204.

276 Saint Maximos the Confessor interpreted the Great Entrance as a figure of the incarnation of Christ, while St. Nicholas Cabasilas saw it as Christ's triumphal entry into Jerusalem. Nicholas of Andida, Pseudo-Sophronios, and St. Symeon of Thessaloniki followed the line of Theodore of Mopsuestia, as did St. Germanos of Constantinople who added a second image, Christ's descent into Hades.

carried and placed on the Holy Table was equated with the burial cloth of Christ. Eventually, it became the epitaphios, a large, embroidered cloth depicting the burial of Christ.[277] It was carried by deacons in the solemn procession of the Gifts. In small parish churches, the epitaphios was small in size and carried by the deacon or priest by draping it over the head or tied around the shoulders. In time, the use of the epitaphios was limited to Holy Week and the Paschal period. The aer, also a large veil, took its place. The aer is used to cover the Gifts and is carried in procession draped around the shoulders or the arm of the deacon or the priest. It serves a purely functional purpose – a protective cover for the Gifts.

As in other similar instances, the aer has attracted various symbolic interpretations, the chief being that it represents the stone that covered the tomb of Christ. While such representational interpretations of utilitarian acts and articles may stir the imagination, they are typically disconnected from the text, from what is actually being said and done. From time to time such interpretations have led to ritual actions that are difficult to explain or justify.

The Cherubic Hymn. Our earliest sources indicate that the transfer of the Gifts was conducted with little or no fanfare, without song or commemorations. In its primitive form the Great Entrance was performed in silence, as we do at the Divine Liturgy of the Pre-Sanctified Gifts. Gradually, a chant sung by the singers and the people was added to accompany the procession. Initially, the chant was a psalm, most probably Psalm 23 (24),[278] with the alleluia as a refrain. Soon the psalm was sung antiphonally, that is, with a troparion which was added to the original refrain, alleluia.

Sometime between the eighth and tenth century the psalm was abandoned in favor of the troparion, the earliest of which is the celebrated Cherubic Hymn which was introduced into the Divine Liturgy by a decree of Emperor Justinian in the year 573-574. Since then, it continues to be sung at every Divine Liturgy, except for those of Holy Thursday and the Paschal Vigil.[279] Originally, the hymn was sung three or more times without interruption as the prayers and rituals of the Great Entrance

---

277 The funeral cortege symbolism also led to the use of Holy Friday hymns as the Gifts are deposited on the Holy Table.

278 "The earth is the Lord's and all its fullness.... And the King of glory shall come in.... Who is the King of glory? The Lord of hosts, He is the King of glory." Psalm 50/51 and Psalm 117/118 were also used as Entrance chants.

279 On Holy Thursday we sing the Communion Hymn, "Receive me today, Son of God, as a partaker of your mystical Supper...." At the Paschal Vigil we sing the hymn, "Let all mortal flesh keep silence...."

were being accomplished. Eventually, the hymn began to be chanted only once in the florid style to which we have become accustomed.

Although it is a single grammatical unit, the hymn is nonetheless split into two parts. The practice of interrupting the hymn began sometime between the thirteenth and fourteenth century when a new element, the commemorations, was introduced into the Great Entrance rite. The contemporary Greek practice interrupts the hymn after the phrase, "that we may receive the King of all."

The Cherubic Hymn serves a two-fold purpose. It calls upon the worshippers to be watchful and attentive as imitators of the angelic host who offer the heavenly worship. The hymn also instructs the people to "lay aside all the cares of life" and adapt a proper state of mind as befits those who will offer the Anaphora and will receive in Holy Communion the Lamb of God, the Lord of lords, and the King of kings (Rev. 17:14).[280]

The Prayer of the Cherubikon *(Οὐδεὶς ἄξιος – No one is worthy).[281] The origins of the prayer are uncertain. It is not original to the Constantinopolitan liturgical tradition and appears to have been borrowed from the Alexandrine Divine Liturgy of St. Gregory the Theologian (GREG) in which the prayers, including the anaphora, are addressed to Christ and not to the Father. The prayer is found in the eighth-century Barberini Codex BAS under the title, "Prayer which the priest recites for himself while the Cherubika are being said."[282] The prayer, however, is missing from two tenth-century manuscripts.[283] At some point the prayer was also introduced into CHR, probably when it became the chief liturgy of Constantinople. The prayer is addressed to the Son of God which, as already noted, is the distinctive characteristic of GREG.*

The prayer is written in the first person singular and not in the usual first-person plural, a clear sign of its strictly personal devotional character. For this reason, it should always be read in its original form by the celebrant, even if other priests are concelebrating.[284] In such instances the concelebrants follow the recitation quietly or recite it themselves in

---

280 For a brief description of the Cherubic Hymn – the text and its interpretation, see Calivas, Aspects, 199-202.

281 For more on the prayer see Taft, *Great Entrance*, 119-48. Trembelas, Τρεῖς Λειτουργίαι, 71-76. The title of the prayer is derived from its use. It is recited during the chanting of the Cherubic Hymn. Some manuscripts have a slightly modified title.

282 Note the use of the plural, Cherubika – Χερουβικά.

283 In an eleventh-twelfth century codex the prayer is found only in CHR.

284 The use of the plural form distorts the character of the prayer. Here, the celebrant prays for himself and not as the spokesman of his fellow clergy.

a very soft voice. The prayer was probably used initially by the clergy for personal devotional purposes. In time, it passed into the Euchologia and settled into its present position in both BAS and CHR.[285]

Through this powerful, moving prayer the celebrant is placed before the inscrutable, awesome mystery of Christ, the Son and Word of God, who for our sake freely became a human being without alteration or change. His power is limitless, love immeasurable, holiness ineffable, and goodness infinite. Before the greatness of Christ's majesty, the celebrant remains awe-struck. He is humbled and moved to acknowledge his complete unworthiness: "No one bound to sinful desires and pleasures is worthy to approach, draw near, or minister to you, the King of glory. To serve you is great and awesome even for the heavenly powers." The celebrant bows before Christ and entreats him fervently: "Do not turn your face away from me or reject me from among your children but make me, your sinful and unworthy servant, worthy to offer you these gifts."

The celebrant recognizes fully that the priesthood with which he is clothed belongs to Christ; he does not hold it on his own merit or account. Christ is the only High Priest and Lord of all. The priesthood is Christ's precious gift to the Church, which in turn confers it upon frail persons, hierarchs and priests, so that the "mystery of [Christ's] holy and pure Body and precious Blood," the Eucharist, may be rightly performed for the salvation of the world and the sanctification of God's people. The Eucharist is accomplished by the power of the Holy Spirit. Hence, the celebrant invokes the Spirit – a personal epiclesis – to enable him to stand blamelessly before the Holy Table to enact the liturgical sacrifice without the shedding of blood (ἀναίμακτος θυσία) together with and for the people.

The ending of the prayer contains four participles which point to an important teaching on the Eucharist: "For you are the One who both offers (ὁ προσφέρων) and is offered (προσφερόμενος), the One who accepts (προσδεχόμενος) and is distributed (διαδιδόμενος), Christ our God..."[286] As Fr. Alexander Schmemann observes, "As we offer again and again our life and our world to God, we discover each time there is nothing else to

---

285 According to Taft, the prayer is probably of monastic origin. He notes, "From the length and tenor of the prayer we would suspect it to be a devotional addition of monastic origin that eventually was accepted in the Great Church." See his *Great Entrance*, 134.

286 The last two participles in the *Barberini Codex* BAS are different: ὁ ἁγιάζων καὶ ἁγιαζόμενος – the One who hallows (consecrates) and is hallowed (consecrated). In his treatise on the Divine Liturgy, St. Germanos of Constantinople mentions only the first two participles. In fact, the four participles in the received text were lifted from a fifth-century (ca. 400) Holy Thursday homily of Theophilos of Alexandria. In the mid-twelfth century this passage occasioned a theological controversy, about which see Taft, *Great Entrance*, 135-40.

be offered but Christ himself – the Life of the world, the fullness of all that exists. It is his Eucharist, and He is the Eucharist…. We are included in the Eucharist of Christ and Christ is our Eucharist."[287]

The Prayer should be recited in a prayerful low voice with the head bowed, since it constitutes a personal devotional act. As a rule, priestly prayers are recited with bowed head.

The Rite of Censing[288] Who is responsible for censing at the Great Entrance, the presiding hierarch, priest, or the deacon? Of course, the question is moot when a priest serves alone without a deacon. The contemporary Greek practice is ambivalent. In some texts the rubrics assign the task to the deacon while, in others, to the presiding priest or hierarch.

In the early sources, however, there is no ambiguity. The task is assigned to the deacon, who conducts the censing while the priest recites the Prayer of the Cherubikon. When applicable, this older practice should be restored. Among other things, it permits the deacon to exercise a basic function of his office and allows the celebrant to concentrate on the prayer. And, from a practical perspective, it saves a little time so that other parts of the rite may be performed more calmly, without haste.

The current order of censing – Holy Table, sanctuary, iconostasis, people – began to take root in the fourteenth century when the prothesis in most, if not all, churches was located in the sanctuary or in a side room next to the sanctuary. It appears that the original object of the incensation was the Holy Gifts. The Gifts were prepared and censed in the skeuophylakion. During their transfer to the sanctuary at the Great Entrance, a deacon held the censer. After the Gifts were placed on the Holy Table they were censed again in preparation for the anaphora.

According to tradition, every incensation begins with the Holy Table. Thus, when the prothesis was relocated and incorporated into the sanctuary, the incensation of the Gifts was preceded by the censing of the Holy Table. Eventually this led to the grand incensation we have become accustomed to at the Great Entrance: Holy Table, prothesis, sanctuary, iconostasis, and people.

The purpose of the incensation is essentially honorific, an act of reverence. Everyone and everything is being made ready to welcome the precious Gifts (τίμια Δῶρα) that will be offered, consecrated, distributed, and communed. In fact, the current practice requires three incensations which have come out of the original simple incensation. They are: the

---

287 Alexander Schmemann, *For the Life of the World* (Crestwood, NY 1973), 35-6.

288 See Taft, *Great Entrance*, 149-62.

great incensation, the censing of the Gifts at the Prothesis, and the censing of the Gifts after they have been deposited on the Holy Table.

During the great incensation the priest recites Psalm 50/51 in a low voice. To emphasize and extend the penitential themes in the preceding prayers of the faithful and of the Cherubic Hymn, clergy began to recite various penitential hymns as a form of spiritual exercise.[289] In late medieval times Psalm 50/51, the Church's preeminent penitential prayer supplanted such hymns and became a fixed element of the rite of incensation at the Great Entrance.

The Lavabo or washing of hands, as noted above, was once part of the Great Entrance rites, or, as others believe, part of the proanaphoral rites, especially when it was performed after the Great Entrance. In current practice it is conducted before the service of the proskomide. Some hierarchs, however, continue to perform the lavabo at the Great Entrance after the censing and before the entrance or after the Gifts have been placed on the Holy Table. In the latter instance, the lavabo is counted as part of the proanaphoral rites.

The Commemorations at the Great Entrance came about as a result of popular piety. Nicholas Cabasilas' description of the procession indicates as much. "The priest goes on, surrounded by candles and incense, until he comes to the altar. This is done, no doubt for practical reasons; it was necessary to bring the offerings which are to be sacrificed to the altar… During this ceremony we must prostate ourselves before the priest and entreat him to remember us in the prayers, which he is about to say. For there is no other means of supplication so powerful, so certain of acceptance, as that which takes place through this most holy sacrifice, which has freely cleansed us from our sins and iniquities."[290]

To assure the people of their prayers, the clergy began to say in a low voice the common general commemoration, "May the Lord God remember all of you in his kingdom," while the Cherubic Hymn was being sung. Gradually, the common commemoration began to be made aloud. The first mention of commemorations pronounced aloud appears in a Diataxis of the twelfth-thirteenth century. The practice, however, became

---

[289] In former years, it was common among older priests to add one or more penitential troparia after the recitation of Psalm 50/51. In keeping with the theme of the Great Entrance as a portrayal of the burial of Christ, some priests, for example, recited the long but moving *doxastikon* of the aposticha for the Vespers of Great and Holy Friday. Such well-meaning additions may please the priest but do not add to the solemnity of the Great Entrance rite. What the Church has ordered is sufficient.

[290] Cabasilas, *Commentary on the Divine Liturgy* (24). St. Nicholas Cabasilas was born in Thessaloniki in 1322 or 1323.

routine only after the fifteenth century with the spread of the printed editions of the Divine Liturgy.

In a later stage of development, but not before the end of the eighteenth century, the simple commemoration was amplified to include ecclesial and civil authorities and other classes of the faithful, first at episcopal and much later at presbyteral liturgies.[291] The expanded commemorations are, in fact, out of place at the Great Entrance. They have long-since been omitted at presbyteral liturgies in the Greek Orthodox Archdiocese and in other churches.

The pronouncement of the commemoration aloud also led to the interruption of the Cherubic Hymn. To avoid discordant sounds, the hymn was stopped at some point so that the simple commemoration could be spoken aloud before the procession was concluded. The pause in the hymn served another practical purpose. By interrupting the hymn so that a portion of it would be said after the commemorations, the priest has time to complete the final rites of the Great Entrance unhurriedly.

One final point on the commemorations. In some recent editions of the service, the commemoration reads, "May the Lord God remember all of us (πάντων ἡμῶν) in his kingdom." In the manuscripts, Diataxeis, and early printed editions of the Divine Liturgy, however, the commemoration employs the plural pronoun of the second person – ὑμῶν, you. "May the Lord God remember all of you (πάντων ὑμῶν) in his kingdom." This form should be preferred over the other, not because it is older or found in most liturgical documents, but because it corresponds to the role of the clergy who are tasked to pray for the people, entreating the Triune God on their behalf.[292]

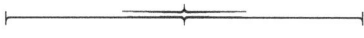

---

291 See Trempelas, Τρεῖς Λειτουργίαι, 82.

292 See Calivas, *Aspects of Orthodox Worship*, 193-4.

J. THE PROANAPHORAL RITES

The dialogue of the priest and deacon after the Great Entrance

(The dialogue pertains only if a deacon is present, otherwise it is omitted).

After the Gifts have been placed on the Holy Table and censed, the priest, in the received text, turns to the deacon, and says:

Priest

Remember me, brother and concelebrant.

Deacon

May the Lord God remember your priesthood in his kingdom, now and forever and to the ages of ages. Amen.

Pray for me, holy Master.

Priest

The Holy Spirit will come upon you, and the power of the Most High will overshadow you.

Deacon

May the selfsame Spirit minister together with us all the days of our life.

Remember me, holy Master

Priest

May the Lord God remember your diaconate in his kingdom always, now and forever...

This dialogue is found in all the official texts of the Divine Liturgy.[293] It is original to the Byzantine Eucharistic rite and is found in other traditions as well in a similar form.[294] It has been in use as early as the tenth century but in a form different from the one in the received text. The manuscripts do not contain the first part of the dialogue, which is probably a remnant or a variation of the greeting which the priest and deacon now exchange after their entry into the sanctuary with the Gifts. The original dialogue began with the second part, "*Pray for me....*" However, it was not the deacon but the

---

293 For more on the dialogue see Taft, *Great Entrance*, 285-310.

294 The Divine Liturgy of St. James (Iakovos - JAS), for example, contains the following dialogue: The main celebrant turns to his concelebrants and says: "Magnify the Lord with me and let us exalt his Name together." And they answer, "The Holy Spirit shall come upon you and the power of the Most High shall overshadow you."

principal celebrant (hierarch or priest) who initiated the dialogue. Turning to his concelebrants he said, "*My brothers and concelebrants, pray for me.*" And they responded in the words of the Angel Gabriel to the Virgin Mary, "*The Holy Spirit will come upon you....*" (Luke 1:35). In a later development, the principal celebrant again addressed his concelebrants saying, "*May the selfsame Spirit minister together with us...*" This order is found in the *Diataxis* of Philotheos with the priest initiating the dialogue and the deacon responding.

Saint Symeon of Thessaloniki (+1429) explains the purpose of the dialogue with these words. "The bishop, with head bowed, asks the prayers of all because he knows himself, and trembles and is seized with fear before the task before him [the anaphora], and because he is fulfilling the precept of the apostle, who says: "Confess your sins to one another," and "Pray for one another." For he does not put his trust in himself, since he too is a man."[295]

For some unknown reason, the original form of the dialogue was altered in the sixteenth century. The roles of priest and deacon were reversed. The words of the chief celebrant were placed on the lips of the deacon and the deacon's words (or those of the concelebrants) on the lips of the celebrant. The altered order began to appear in manuscripts of the period and, more importantly, it was incorporated into Doucas' *editio princeps* (1526). Eventually, it passed into all Greek texts.

The original order has been retained by the Slavic, Antiochian, and other Churches.[296] Hopefully, the original form of the dialogue will soon be restored to the Greek texts as well. It is more fitting and proper to pray the words of the angel for the principal celebrant (ὁ προεστώς) who will pray the Anaphora and recite the words of consecration rather than for the deacon who is not empowered to do so.

One further point: The dialogue underscores the crucial role of the Holy Spirit in worship. It is through the power and inspiration of the Holy Spirit that the priest is able to perform and fulfill his priestly ministry and his functions as presider at the Divine Liturgy and every other sacred service.

---

295 Cited by Taft, *Great Entrance*, 282-3.

296 See, for example, *The Divine Liturgy of St. John Chrysostom* (OCA) and *The Liturgikon – the Book of Divine Services for the Priest and Deacon* (Antiochian Archdiocese).

The Completion or Dismissal Litany – Αἱ Αἰτήσεις – Supplications[297]

When the Cherubic Hymn is completed, the priest standing in front of the Holy Table begins the Litany of Completion or Dismissal. (If a deacon is present, he takes leave of the priest, goes out the north door, stands in his usual place, and intones the litany).[298]

Priest (or Deacon):

Let us complete our prayer to the Lord – Πληρώσωμεν τὴν δέησιν ἡμῶν τῷ Κυρίῳ.[299]

People

Lord, have mercy...

Priest

For a perfect, holy, peaceful, and sinless day, let us ask the Lord.

People

Grant this, O Lord.

> ***The Litany of Completion*** *receives its name from the petition that introduces it, "Let us complete our prayer."*[300] *In the Divine Liturgy this Dismissal Litany is comprised of a call to prayer ("Let us complete our prayer…"), a petition related to the Holy Gifts ("For the precious Gifts here presented…"),*[301] *and two additional petitions borrowed from the Great Synapte ("For this holy house… For our deliverance…"). It also includes the plea which in former times included the command to rise ("Help us,*

---

297 For more on the Litany of Completion see Taft, *Great Entrance*, 311-49.

298 According to the early sources, the deacon mounted the ambo which was in the center of the nave to intone the litanies. He faced the sanctuary. When the ambo fell into disuse or was moved to the side of the nave, the deacon continued to intone the litanies from the solea, near the center of the nave.

299 The Αἰτήσεις are also found in the services of Vespers and Orthros and are introduced by the same bidding, "Let us complete (conclude) our *evening (morning)* prayer to the Lord." In the Vespers and Orthros, the two adjectives define the time or the hour of prayer, evening and morning respectively.

300 In some Greek texts the litany is referred to as the Πληρωτικά, derived from the first word of the initial bidding, "Πληρώσωμεν (let us complete) τὴν δέησιν ἡμῶν τῷ Κυρίῳ." It is also called the Dismissal Litany because the Αἰτήσεις were originally used as a series of concluding requests preceding the final blessing and dismissal (apolysis – ἀπόλυσις). The Αἰτήσεις are meant to prepare, arm, and predispose the worshippers for their reentry into the affairs of everyday life with all its burdens but also its promises.

301 This is probably a primitive introduction to the Prayer of the Proskomide.

*save us, have mercy on us...").*³⁰² *At the core of the litany are the six Αἰτήσεις or Supplications that follow, beginning with the entreaty, "For a perfect, holy, peaceful, and sinless day, let us ask the Lord...."*³⁰³ *The litany ends with the familiar exhortation, "Commemorating our most holy, pure... Lady, the Theotokos...with all the saints, let us commend ourselves and one another and our whole life to Christ our God." The ekfonesis that follows is the concluding doxology of the Prayer of the Proskomide.*

In all the official texts of BAS and CHR, the six Αἰτήσεις are repeated a second time within the litany that precedes the Lord's Prayer. We will say more about this later.

*Except for the last Αἴτησις, each supplication/petition ends with the plea unique to the Αἰτήσεις: "let us ask the Lord – παρὰ τοῦ Κυρίου αἰτησώμεθα."*³⁰⁴ *The last of the supplications ends simply with the verb αἰτησώμεθα, "let us ask." The six supplications receive their name from the noun αἴτησις – αἰτήσεις (plural), which comes from the verb αἰτησώμεθα (αἰτέω), which means to ask, beg, request.*

The six supplications (Αἰτήσεις), which comprise the heart of the Dismissal Litany (the Litany of Completion), address the spiritual welfare and needs of the faithful. They recommend broadly the manner by which the struggles and trials of everyday life should be met and surmounted. The supplications remind us that life is very precious, a lovely but fragile gift. It should not be wasted in frivolities, discordant tensions, debilitating anxieties, crippling fears, paralyzing resentments, or selfish inclinations. Rather, each life should be enriched and perfected through introspection, a contrite and forgiving heart, and a peaceful and joyful disposition filled with hope and an openness to others. Because life is unpredictable, we ask God to grant us a peaceful life, without shame or suffering, and a

---

302 In former times the people knelt during the litanies. The command to rise from prayer was inserted in this petition: "Help us, save us, have mercy on us, *raise us up*, and protect us, O God, by your grace." When the practice of kneeling during the petitions fell into disuse, the command to rise was omitted. We find it, however, in the Vespers or Kneeling-Service of Pentecost.

303 In the Divine Liturgy the Αἰτήσεις are always part of a larger litany.

304 When translating the supplications into English, we must take care not to use two prepositions in the same Αἴτησις, for and of. We must choose one or the other. For example: "An angel of peace...let us ask *of* the Lord." Or, "*For* an angel of peace, a faithful guide, a guardian of our souls and bodies, let us ask the Lord." Care also must be taken when we recite the last supplication. The Greek original is very clear. The petition is simple and ends with the verb "αἰτησώμεθα – let us ask." Hence, we must not use the ending of the previous petitions, "let us ask the Lord."

Christian end. As we work day by day to organize our lives according to the high calling to which we have been summoned, we ask for the guidance and protection of our guardian angel, so that our actions and decisions may be sound so that we may have "a good defense before the awesome judgment seat of Christ." We are moved to act in this manner because we are certain that "through our Lord Jesus Christ we have obtained access to [God's] grace in which we stand, and we rejoice in our hope of sharing the glory of God. More than that, we rejoice in our sufferings, knowing that suffering produces endurance, and endurance produces character, and character produces hope, and hope does not disappoint us because God's love has been poured into our hearts through the Holy Spirit which has been given to us" (Rom. 5:1-5).[305]

From where and when was the Litany of Completion introduced into CHR and BAS? The evidence is not immediately clear. However, on the basis of comparative liturgics, Taft has concluded that "the litany first entered CHR and BAS via PRES before the Our Father…. Later, the litany came to be said after the Great Entrance in CHR and BAS. If we have to hazard a guess as to when this might have occurred, it was probably after 615."[306] *Fountoulis notes that the litany was initially intoned after the Gospel and before the dismissal of the catechumens, as is in the case of JAMES. The litany was transferred later to its present position when the catechumenate slowly waned and finally disappeared. The repetition of the Αἰτήσεις before the Lord's Prayer came about under the influence of PRES.*[307]

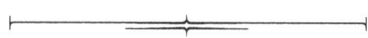

---

305 For a brief but excellent edifying article on the mystery of suffering see Emmanuel Clapsis, "Suffering in God's Beloved Creation" in *Evangelist, Shepherd, and Teacher*, 376-92.

306 Taft, *Great Entrance*, 335.

307 Ioannis Fountoulis, Ἀπαντήσεις εἰς Λειτουργικὰς Ἀπορίας, Γ (Thessaloniki 1976), 173-8. Parts of the litany can be traced to earlier documents as, for example, the fourth-century *Apostolic Constitutions*.

The Prayer of the Proskomide

Following the Litany of Completion, the priest offers the Prayer of the Proskomide (Εὐχὴ τῆς Προσκομιδῆς)[308]

CHR and BAS each has its own distinct prayer. Besides being longer, the prayer in BAS is replete with biblical formulas and images, a sign of its late reworking. While distinct in content, both prayers share a common purpose: the preparation the celebrant(s) for the offering of the anaphora.[309] The prayer in both liturgies contains a fervent plea for access to the Holy Table (the altar) so that the celebrant(s) may properly perform his sacred duties. "Enable us to offer you gifts and spiritual sacrifices for our own sins and the failings of your people. Deem us worthy to find grace in your sight so that our sacrifice may be pleasing to you, and that the good Spirit of your grace may rest upon us and upon the gifts presented and upon all your people."[310] In fact, as the last phrase of the prayer indicates, the prayer and all that will come after it – the kiss of peace and the Creed – are meant to prepare the clergy and the people for the anaphora. As St. Nicholas Cabasilas explains it:

> The priest places the offerings upon the altar. Then, finding himself on the threshold of the consecration, and about to begin the august sacrifice, he now thoroughly prepares himself, purifying himself by prayer and getting ready for the sacrifice; not only does he do this, but he also prepares all those present, and puts them in a disposition of grace by prayer, mutual charity, and a profession of faith. For in these is contained the whole of the preparation ordained by our Lord, when

---

308 For more on the Prayer of the Proskomide see Taft, *Great Entrance*, 350-373; and Pavlos Koumarianos, "Πρόθεση, Προσκομιδή, Προσφορά" in Θεολογία, vol. 70, Β-Γ (1999). In many editions of the Divine Liturgy, the Prayer of the Proskomide is placed between the petitions and the Αἰτήσεις, to be read by the celebrant while the deacon intones the Αἰτήσεις.

309 The parallel prayer in BAS has two parts. The first, as in CHR, accentuates the plea for access; the second is centered on the offering of the Gifts. "Look down upon us, O God, and behold this our service. Receive it as you received the gifts (τὰ δῶρα) of Abel (Gen. 4:4), the sacrifices (τὰς θυσίας) of Noah (Gen. 8:20-21), the burnt offerings (τὰς ὁλοκαρπώσεις) of Abraham (Gen. 22:13), the priestly offerings (τὰς ἱερωσύνας) of Moses and Aaron (Exod. 9:31-37), and the peace offerings (τὰς εἰρηνικάς) of Samuel (1 Sam. 11:14-15 – Α΄ Βασιλειῶν 11:14-15). Even as you received from your Holy Apostles this true worship (λατρείαν), so now, in your goodness, accept these gifts from the hands of us sinners, O Lord…" (cf. Heb. 11:1-40, 12:1-2). The Old Testament offerings foreshadow the sacrifice of the Cross and the true worship, the Eucharist, through which we continuously encounter Christ – crucified, raised from the dead, and glorified – in his personal immortal presence, who lives to make intercession for us (Heb. 7:24).

310 The prayer in BAS has a similar plea. "Through the greatness of your mercy accept us as we draw near to your holy altar, so that we may be worthy to offer to you this reasonable sacrifice without the shedding of blood for our sins and for the errors of your people."

he said: Be ready [Matt. 24:44]. Here are both faith and works; the one is seen in the profession of faith which we make [the Creed], the other in that charity which is the end of every good work and the peak of all virtue [the kiss of peace].[311]

The prayer is not an offertory prayer. This being the case, what are we to make of prayer's title, Prayer of the Proskomide? The word proskomide is often used as a synonym for the anaphora, the great Eucharistic Prayer. Hence, as Juan Mateos, the eminent liturgist, explains it, "The whole prayer is in intimate relation with the offering (anaphora) to come, but is not in itself an offering. That is, we do not offer now, but pray that the offering we are about to make in the anaphora will not be vitiated by our unworthiness to approach the altar. The direct object of the petition is worthiness to offer; the acceptance of the coming offering is a consequence of this."[312]

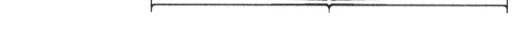

The Peace and the Kiss of Peace (Love) – Ὁ Ἀσπασμός

The kiss of peace was an essential element of Christian worship from the beginning and is mentioned in all the ancient liturgical sources. It was exchanged by all the worshippers according to a prescribed order, as it happens in a number of parishes today. We know from the sources that the "memoirs of the apostles and the writings of the prophets" were read at the gatherings of the early Christian communities and that the exchange of the "holy kiss" had become an integral part of their assemblies based on the urgings of St. Paul, "Greet one another with a holy kiss" (Rom. 16:16; cf. 1 Cor. 16:20; 2 Cor. 13:12; 1 Thess. 5:26).[313]

Where the kiss is no longer practiced – because of centuries of neglect – an effort should be made to restore it in a manner that is both fitting and dignified.[314] *Even a simple gesture of bowing to one another would suffice.*

---

311 Cabasilas, *On the Divine Liturgy*, III, 25.

312 Cited by Taft, *Great Entrance*, 357.

313 See also 1 Peter 5:14: "Greet one another with the kiss of love." The kiss is also mentioned by St. Justin the Martyr in his description of the Eucharist, "When we finish praying, we greet one another with a kiss. Then bread and a cup of wine mixed with water are brought to him who presides over the brethren" (1 Apology, 1:65).

314 I am not suggesting that we adopt the ancient and medieval practice (kissing on the mouth) mentioned by St. John Chrysostom which was customary among relatives and close friends in antiquity. As customs changed, the kiss was gradually abandoned. Where the kiss has been reintroduced successfully, people use a simple handshake or some other acceptable expression of communality and friendship. The important thing is for the congregants to experience through the ritual the truth that they are all members of the one Body of Christ, sons and daughters of the same household of God, and inheritors of the same promises.

The congregants should be taught to greet one another with the words: "Christ is in our midst," and the response, "He is and always shall be."

The exhortation, "Let us love one another," without some kind of ritual expression carries little weight and is less effectual as a sign of mutual forgiveness and fraternal love – the very purpose for which the kiss was incorporated into the Eucharist in the first place.[315] Of course, I am not suggesting that the exchange is a panacea for the hurts that afflict us; it is not a magical potion. However, the very gesture of reaching out to someone in the name of Jesus has the power to soften the heart and contribute to the building of community. With proper instruction and encouragement, the priest with the people can restore the ancient practice in a fashion that is appropriate to their parish for the benefit of all. To prevent the exchange from deteriorating into an empty gesture, the priest should remind the people, now and then, of its meaning and significance.

As an expression of mutual love, the kiss becomes an act of abjuration, a form of renunciation of the devil who is the father of lies and the source of enmity, deceptiveness, and divisiveness. Thus, the kiss, as an expression of fraternal affection and concern, constitutes the continual renewal of our baptismal pledge: the renunciation of Satan, the tempter and separator.

In preparation for the anaphora and the reception of Holy Communion, everyone, clergy and laity alike, should open their hearts humbly to receive and share the transforming power of Christ's love. The kiss of peace is a sign of reconciliation and agape,[316] the latter being the essential characteristic of the Christian, "By this all men will know that you are my disciples, if you have love (ἀγάπη) for one another" (John 13:35). According to St. Maximos the Confessor, the kiss also mirrors the future age, "The spiritual kiss which is extended to all prefigures and portrays the concord, unanimity, and identity of views which we shall all

---

315 When a priest serves alone, having no other priest with whom to exchange the peace, the rubrics instruct him to kiss the covered gifts. The practice probably came about to compensate for the decline and disappearance of the ritual kiss. Some Ieratika even have the deacon kiss the end of his orarion.

316 St. Cyril of Jerusalem (*Mystagogical Catecheses*, V, 3) underscores the meaning of the kiss as a symbol of reconciliation. "The deacon cries aloud, 'Receive one another; and let us kiss one another.' Think not that this kiss ranks with those given in public by common friends. It is not such. This kiss blends souls one with another, and solicits for them entire forgiveness. Therefore, this kiss is the sign that our souls are mingled together, and have banished all remembrances of wrongs.... The kiss therefore is reconciliation...." The same point was made three centuries earlier in the *Didache* (14:2): "Come together on the Lord's day.... Anyone who has a quarrel with his fellow should not gather with you until he has been reconciled, lest your sacrifice be profaned."

*have among ourselves in faith and love at the time of the revelation of the ineffable blessings to come."*³¹⁷

Through the kiss we enact ritually the Lord's exhortation: "So if you are offering your gift at the altar, and there remember that your brother has something against you, leave your gift there before the altar and go; first be reconciled to your brother, and then come and offer your gift" (Matt. 5:23, 24). The position of the kiss before the creed and the anaphora, according to the Orthodox liturgical tradition, is based on this exhortation of the Lord.

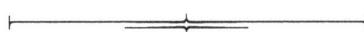

The priest turns toward the congregation and standing just beyond the Holy Doors, he blesses the people in the usual manner with his right hand.

Priest

Peace be to all (with all) – Εἰρήνη πᾶσι.

People

And to (with) your spirit.

Still facing the people, the priest invites, exhorts them, to express their love for one another. He raises his hands slightly with open palms in a gesture of welcome, openness, and readiness to embrace. He says the following. (If, however, a deacon is present, the deacon speaks the words, as the priest lifts his hands).

Priest (or Deacon)

Let us love one another, that with one mind we may confess.³¹⁸

People

Father, Son, and Holy Spirit: Trinity, one in essence and undivided.³¹⁹

---

317 Maximos the Confessor, *Mystagogy*, 17. The ritual kiss is also mentioned by Pseudo-Dionysios, *Ecclesiastical Hierarchy*, Chapter Three, 2.

318 The latter phrase, "that with one mind we may confess," appears to be a later addition to the proclamation, perhaps as late as the twelfth century.

319 The hymn is a doctrinal formula, a Trinitarian confession. It fulfills the exhortation to confess in unison the basic dogma of the faith. The hymn is first mentioned in mss of the twelfth century. Initially, it was sung by the clergy and later adopted by the people. In recent times, chanters often replace the hymn with the psalm verses at a concelebration, in order to cover the extra time it takes to complete the kiss. As well-intentioned as this may be, I believe it is ill advised. It is an unbefitting response to the exhortation, "that with one mind we may confess."

The priest returns to the Holy Table and bows before the covered Gifts. Then he kisses the Gifts: first the discos, then the chalice, and last the Holy Table in that order.

Priest

As he kisses the gifts, he says in low voice,

I will love you, O Lord, my strength; the Lord is my foundation, my refuge, and my deliverer (Ps. 17/18:1-2a).[320]

•—⁓—•

In the Orthodox tradition the kiss of peace is exchanged within and among the different orders of the Church: laypeople with laypeople,[321] deacons with deacons, priests with priests and hierarch(s), and hierarchs with hierarch and priests.[322]

•—⁓—•

If two or more priests are concelebrating with a hierarch or with another senior priest they proceed around the Holy Table and await the return of the hierarch or the senior priest who reverences the Gifts and moves to the right of the Holy Table. The priests proceed according to descending seniority. First, they kiss the covered Gifts and then they exchange the kiss with the hierarch or the senior priest. Each priest stands to the right of his senior and awaits to embrace the priest(s) who come after him. When the kiss has been exchanged by all, the concelebrants return to their places around the Holy Table.

If more than one deacon is serving, the deacon(s) within the sanctuary goes to the deacon who is in the nave to exchange the kiss.

•—⁓—•

---

320 The practice of kissing the covered Gifts according to the prescribed manner together with the recitation of the two psalm verses appears first in the *Diataxis* of Philotheos Kokkinos (See Trembelas, Τρεῖς Λειτουργίαι, 10-1; and Taft, *Great Entrance*, 386-8.

321 In the ancient church men and women sat or stood separately in the assemblies. Hence the kiss was exchanged between men and men and women with women. In the Roman Catholic tradition, the kiss is given before Communion in a descending or hierarchical manner. The kiss originates in the sanctuary and is passed by the celebrant to other ministers who pass it to the laity, and they to one another.

322 As I have noted elsewhere, the collegiality of the hierarch and his priests is emphasized at the Divine Liturgy in two ways: by the synthronon and the kiss of peace. The concelebrating priest alone exchange the kiss with the hierarch and with one another. This is especially significant because the kiss in the tradition of the Orthodox Church is exchanged only among those of the same order. See Calivas, *Church, Clergy, Laity, and the Spiritual Life*, 28

The Symbol of Faith or the Creed – Τὸ Σύμβολον τῆς Πίστεως

Priest or Deacon:

The doors! The doors! In wisdom, let us be attentive – Τὰς θύρας! Τὰς θύρας! Ἐν σοφίᾳ πρόσχωμεν.

The **people** recite the Creed.

The **priest** recites the Creed with the people. During the recitation he lifts the veil (aer) over the Gifts.

It is claimed that the Creed was introduced into the Divine Liturgy first in Antioch by the Monophysite Patriarch Peter the Fuller (ca. 489). However, the earliest authentic reference indicates that the Creed was introduced into the liturgy by Patriarch Timothy of Constantinople (ca. 511) and placed in the position it now holds, after the kiss and before the anaphora.[323]

Previously, the Creed was recited only at baptismal rites by catechumens who were deemed ready and worthy of Holy Baptism as a sign of their acceptance of the Church's faith and their devotion to it.[324] Hence, the recitation of the Creed at every Divine Liturgy, in some sense, constitutes a renewed affirmation of our baptismal pledge centered on the conscious personal confession of the fundamental truths of the Orthodox faith. Thus, as it has been suggested, the Creed is no longer only a test of belief for those entering the Church but also a test for those already within the Church, a solemn confirmation of their continued commitment to what the Church has always believed, taught, and proclaimed.[325]

---

323 See Taft, *Great Entrance*, 396-407. Trembelas, *Τρεῖς Λειτουργίαι*, 92. Wybrew, *Orthodox Liturgy*, 84-6.

324 In addition to the Divine Liturgy and the baptismal rite, the Creed is also recited daily at the Apodeipnon (Compline) and the Midnight office.

325 Dom Gregory Dix, *The Shape of the Liturgy* (London 1949), 485-6. In the words of St. Maximos the Confessor, "The profession by all of the divine symbol of faith signifies the mystical thanksgiving to perdure [to last] through all eternity for the marvelous principles and modes by which we are saved by God's all-wise Providence on our behalf. Through it those who are worthy are confirmed as grateful for the divine favors, for otherwise they would have no other way of returning anything at all for the numberless divine blessings toward them." (*Mystagogy*, 18). Saint Maximos understands the Christian life as an eternal liturgy of thanksgiving in God's presence. For a discussion on the Orthodox faith proclaimed in the Creed, see Thomas Hopko, *The Orthodox Faith: Doctrine*, vol. 1 (Crestwood, NY 1970), expanded and republished in *Doctrine and Scripture* in the series, *The Orthodox Faith,* vol. 1 (Crestwood NY 2016).

The Creed of the Orthodox Church was promulgated by the First (325) and Second (381) Ecumenical Synods.[326] It was accepted by the whole Christian world and considered immutable.[327] This Creed has come to be known as the Nicene-Constantinopolitan Creed, after the two cities (Nicea and Constantinople) in which the first two Ecumenical Synods were held.

Although the fundamental truths of the faith are recounted in the prayers of the Divine Liturgy and especially in the anaphora of both liturgies and in particular in BAS, the recitation of the Creed by each worshipper (note the singular form, "I believe") allows each person to publicly affirm and proclaim their belief in and devotion to the essential elements of the Orthodox faith.

The Creed is meant to be said by all the worshippers in unison and not be a sole reader. In fact, according to some sources the Creed was sung or intoned by all. We find, for example, in some sources the diaconal command: "Τὰς θύρας, τὰς θύρας, πρόσχωμεν καὶ τὸ σύμβολον ψάλλωμεν – The doors, the doors. Let us be attentive and let us sing the Creed."

The Command, "The Doors!" *To what doors does the command make reference? As evidenced by the remarks of St. Maximos the Confessor, the command, "The doors," originally referred to the church doors. "The closing of the doors which takes place after the sacred reading of the Holy Gospel and the dismissal of the catechumens signifies the passing from material things which will come about after that terrible separation and even more terrible judgment and the entrance of those who are worthy into the spiritual world, that is, into the nuptial chambers of Christ, as well as the complete extinction of our senses of deceptive activity."[328] Saint Maximos used the opportunity to lift the thoughts of the worshippers by attaching a symbolic meaning to the purely utilitarian act of closing the church doors.*

It was common practice in antiquity to close the doors of the church after the dismissal of the catechumens. We read, for example, the following

---

326 Creedal statements (the rule of faith) were and continue to be essential to ecclesial life. As Jaroslav Pelikan notes, "Like the development of the canon of the New Testament, the evolution of Christian creeds is an essential and unavoidable part of the history of early Christian doctrine.... Creedal statements of faith were an integral element in the determination of apostolic continuity.... The standard of faith needed to be condensed into a rule that could be learned and confessed." In *The Christian Tradition: A History of the Development of Doctrine: 1 the Emergence of the Catholic Tradition (100-600)* (University of Chicago Press 1971), 158-159.

327 See Archbishop Peter L'Huiller, *The Church of the Ancient Councils: The Disciplinary Work of the First Four Ecumenical Councils* (Crestwood, NY 1996), 105-6.

328 Maximos, *Mystagogy*, 15.

rubric in the Apostolic Constitutions (ca. 375-380): "and let the deacons stand at the doors of the men, and the sub-deacons at those of the women, that no one go out, nor a door be opened, although it be for one of the faithful, at the time of the oblation."[329] Saint John Chrysostom explains the reason for the exclusion: "We celebrate the mysteries with closed doors and keep out the uninitiated, not that we have convicted our rites of any weakness, but that many are still imperfectly prepared for them."[330]

The initial purpose of the exclamation, "The doors! The doors!" was to alert the doorkeepers (πυλωροί – gatekeepers) and subdeacons to make certain that all the catechumens and other unauthorized persons had departed and the doors of the church were shut so that no one could enter or leave. With the gradual disappearance of the catechumenate, the ritual shutting of the church doors fell into disuse as did the minor order of doorkeeper.

"In Wisdom, Let Us be Attentive…"

The diaconal command, "The doors," is followed immediately by another, "In wisdom, let us be attentive." The two Greek words, σοφία (wisdom) and πρόσχωμεν (be attentive), are used interchangeably in the liturgy and serve the same purpose. They are invitations and warnings to pay attention.[331]

In this instance, the word wisdom appears in a new form, "ἐν σοφίᾳ – *in wisdom.*" Taft claims "the effect of this new formula was to change the warning into an introduction to the creed."[332] The faithful are invited to recite the Creed in wisdom, which is to say, in all earnestness, being attentive to all they know and have been taught about the holy mysteries of the faith. As St. Paul tells it, "Your faith should not be in the wisdom of men but in the power of God.... We speak the wisdom of God in a mystery, the hidden wisdom which God ordained before the ages for our glory" (1 Cor. 2:5, 7).

In light of this, why not change the diaconal command, "The doors.... In wisdom...." to say something like this: "Let us be attentive! That we may reaffirm our faith in all earnestness, with confidence and certainty."

---

329 *Apostolic Constitutions*, Book 8:11.

330 Chrysostom, *On Matthew* 23:3.

331 See Taft, *Great Entrance*, 405.

332 Ibid. 407.

Waving the Aer During the Creed

The current practice of lifting and waving the aer over the Gifts during the Creed is relatively new. It is not found in any manuscripts or editions of the Divine Liturgy before the sixteenth century.[333] In any case, the lifting of the aer served a practical purpose. The Gifts had to be uncovered in preparation for their consecration and communion.

The lifting of the aer may have its beginnings in Syria (ca. sixth century), where the cloth covering the Gifts was lifted and lowered over them frequently during the anaphora, unquestionably for practical reasons.[334] Before long, the act attracted a symbolic meaning. The cloth was equated with the veil in St. Peter's vision (Acts 10).[335]

Here, we have another example of connecting events of salvation history symbolically to parts or acts of the Divine Liturgy. A vivid imagination is capable of inventing all sorts of symbolic and allegorical associations, correlations, and connections to basic utilitarian rituals and actions. Instead of limiting these tendencies we seem to encourage them, adding layer upon layer of arbitrary and ambiguous symbolisms. I was told once by an astute student, "I enjoy the symbolisms. They speak to another part of me, my imagination." I find no fault with this statement. The whole person participates in the act of worship, including one's imagination. However, exaggerated symbolisms that emanate from an unbridled imagination are not helpful. Once, another intelligent student told me that he was taught to see in the waving action, the banner of Orthodoxy waving proudly and majestically in the wind as the

---

333 See, for example, the elaborate rubric in the GOA 2015 bilingual edition of the Divine Liturgy (p. 47), which in addition to the "shaking" of the aer "above" the gifts, instructs the celebrant to "make the sign of the Cross over the Holy Gifts with the aer when the words, 'He was crucified for us,' are heard." This rubric is borrowed from the latest edition of the *Ieratikon* published by the Apostolike Diakonia of the Church of Greece. Other rubrics instruct the priest to withdraw the aer at the words: "He rose on the third day;" still others at the words: "He ascended into heaven;" and others at the Creed's conclusion. These rubrics serve no real purpose and are hard to explain and justify.

334 Taft, *Great Entrance*, 418-9.

335 The veil began to acquire various other symbolic names. It was called aer (ἀήρ = *air*) because it was a substitute for the ripidia which protected the gifts by causing the air to move. It was also called νεφέλη, for the bright cloud (νεφέλη) that overshadowed the participants at the event of the Transfiguration (Matt. 17:5; Luke 9:34). It also received the name ἀναφορά because it was used to cover the holy offering (Gifts) and ἀνώτατον πέπλον or supreme veil, for its considerable size. Around the fourteenth century, the aer began to be embroidered with the image of the dead Christ and acquired the name ἐπιτάφιος. In time, however, the epitaphios and the aer became two different cloths. The epitaphios was used and displayed on Holy Friday and Holy Saturday and placed on the Holy Table throughout the Paschal season until the Apodosis of Pascha. The aer retained its original purpose. See Trembelas, Τρεῖς Λειτουργίαι, 95.

Creed is proclaimed! (Are there no bounds to the use of imagination?) The Creed speaks for itself and has no need of symbolic gestures to highlight its significance and truths.

As in many other instances, liturgical actions and allegorizing explanations may obscure rather than clarify meanings. Not every new ritual action or symbolic interpretation is a positive contribution. At some point in the near future when discussions on liturgical renewal and reform take place, the waving ritual should be thoroughly studied and evaluated. In many respects the waving ritual has become a withered form. We give greater emphasis to the waving ritual than we do to restoring the kiss of peace among the people as an act of mutual love and respect. From the beginning the exchange of the kiss was an important element of the eucharistic celebration, the waving was not.[336]

We learn from the *Apostolic Constitutions* (late fourth century) that the Gifts on the Holy Table were carefully attended lest they be defiled by insects. "Let the deacons bring the gifts to the hierarch at the altar; and let the priests stand on his right hand and on his left.... But let two of the deacons, on each side of the altar, hold a fan, made up of thin membranes, or of the feathers of the peacock, or of fine cloth, and let them silently drive away the small animals

---

336 Strangely, the symbolic interpretations attached to the waving ritual are related mainly to the resurrection of Christ. However, the waving ritual takes place before the anaphora, in which the actions and words of the Lord at the Mystical (Last) Supper are remembered as are his crucifixion, burial, resurrection, and exaltation. The prevailing explanation of lifting of the aer as a symbol of the resurrection upends the historical sequence of events.

that fly about, that they may not come near the cups."³³⁷ The liturgical fans, called *ριπίδια* (*ripidia*), gradually evolved into today's *exapteryga*. They are often placed behind the Holy Table, a tangible reminder of their former function.

The first witness to the lifting of the aer in Byzantine sources is a tenth-century codex, according to which the aer is lifted after the Creed: "*Μετὰ τὸ σύμβολον, αἴρεται τρίτον, καὶ τρίτον ἀφαίρεται ἐκ τῶν ἁγίων δώρων τὸ κάλυμμα* - After the Creed, the veil is lifted from the Gifts three times and removed."³³⁸ From additional sources, we learn that the aer was lifted and lowered horizontally over the Gifts three times when the deacon intoned, the triple command, "Let us stand well! Let us stand in awe! Let us be attentive!" In other words, the triple lifting of the aer coincided with the triple command in preparation for the anaphora, "that we may present the holy offering in peace."

The fourteenth-century *Diataxis* of Philotheos Kokkinos clearly states that the aer is lifted when the deacon intones the triple formulation and adds a further detail: the priest recites the Trisagion hymn as he lifts the aer. "*Ὁ διάκονος, Στῶμεν καλῶς. Τοῦ δὲ παρὰ τοῦ διακόνου λεγομένου, ὁ ἱερεὺς αἴρει τὸν ἀέρα ἀπὸ τῶν ἁγίων κατὰ μικρὸν ὑψῶν αὐτὸν καὶ λέγων, Ἅγιος ὁ Θεός, ἅγιος ἰσχυρός, ἅγιος ἀθάνατος. Καὶ τοῦτον ἀσπαζόμενος μετατίθησιν* - Deacon, Let us stand well. As the deacon says this, the priest lifts the aer a little over the gifts saying Holy God,

---

337 *Apostolic Constitutions*, Book 8:12. At some point, the portrait of deacons holding and waving the fans was perceived as an image of the heavenly liturgy, of the Cherubim and Seraphim who stand round the heavenly throne glorifying God. For additional sources describing the practice of waving see Trembelas, Τρεῖς Λειτουργίαι, 93-6 and Taft, *Great Entrance*, 420-2. Trembelas believes the covering of the Gifts and the lifting of the aer are rooted in and serve the same purpose as the waving of the ripidia. After a while, these utilitarian acts were clothed in symbolisms. Prof. Ioannis Mesoloras, for example, writing more than a century ago, refers to three such symbolic interpretations, which he calls "highly forced and totally allegorical." He writes, "The waving of the aer, as some say, denotes the earthquake that took place during the resurrection of the Lord. Consequently, at this point they also interpret the opening of the Holy Doors or the drawing of the veil as denoting iconically the rolling away of the stone from the door of the tomb. And the other interpretation, that the waving of the aer over the gifts denotes the descent of the grace of the Holy Spirit is also highly allegorical. The invocation of divine grace for the transubstantiation [μετουσία - a term rarely used by the Orthodox] will occur later at the proper time." See his, Ἐγχειρίδιον Λειτουργικῆς τῆς Ὀρθοδόξου Ἀνατολικῆς Ἐκκλησίας (Athens, 1895), 151, note. These interpretations have been handed down through the generations in one form or another. Often, more attention is paid to these explanations than to what is actually being said and done at the divine service. Fortunately, no one has attempted to connect the waving of the aer to the wave offering in the Old Testament (Exodus 29:24-26; Lev. 7:30). The description in the *Apostolic Constitutions*, as mentioned above, informs us that the ripidia were made of various materials (thin membranes, feathers of the peacock, or fine cloth). Today, having lost their original purpose, most, if not all, ripidia (exapteryga) are made of metal and in some cases of wood, too heavy to hold aloft and wave with any efficiency as in times past.

338 Taft, *Great Entrance*, 420.

Holy Mighty, Holy Immortal. And kissing it he sets it aside." Although it is not said explicitly, the priest probably held the aer in a horizontal position and not vertically. Philotheos' rubrics seem to imply that the priest lifted the aer up and down three times, saying Holy God at the first movement, Holy Mighty at the second, and Holy Immortal at the third.

The first reference connecting the aer to the Creed is found in a treatise of St. Symeon of Thessaloniki (+1429). He writes, "They hold the sacred veil on the gifts (κρατοῦσι δὲ τὸ ἱερὸν κάλυμμα ἐπὶ τῶν δώρων ἕως ἂν τὸ ἱερὸν ἐκπληρωθῇ Σύμβολον...) until the Creed is completed since it is necessary that everything concerning Jesus be clearly confessed, and in this way to see him uncovered."[339] Symeon's description, however, is not clear and is open to interpretation. Taft believes Symeon is implying that the raised aer was held over the gifts during the Creed.[340] The text, however, could also mean that the veil was kept on the gifts until the Creed was completed. If the latter reading is correct, in Symeon's time the aer was raised and removed after the Creed.

The first direct witness to the prevailing practice is found in a fifteenth-century codex.[341] By the end of the sixteenth century the waving of the aer during the Creed had become a common practice.[342]

Note: *When the priest completes the waving, he withdraws the aer, folds it and sets it aside with the other veils. He does* **not** *wave the folded aer over the gifts when he says, "Let us stand well…"* **nor** *does he bless the people with it when he exclaims, "The grace of our Lord…"*

Note: *In some places, seasonal or sanitary conditions necessitate the covering of the cup after the aer has been removed. In recent times, special small round decorated covers are available for purchase for such a purpose. The priest would do well to purchase several of these small covers. They can be used appropriately at the prothesis as well as at the Holy Table to protect the cup. A folded communion cloth can serve the same purpose.*

---

339 Symeon of Thessaloniki, "Περί τε τοῦ Θείου Ναοῦ," (85), in *PG* 155, 732.

340 Taft, *Great Entrance*, 421.

341 Ibid. 423.

342 For example, in the *Εὐχολόγιον τὸ Μέγα* (second edition, Venice 1862), 61, edited by Spyridon Zervos, an Archimandrite of the Ecumenical Patriarchate, the rubric pertaining to the aer is simple and direct: "The priest lifts the aer open over the Gifts and moves it; [after the Creed] the priest withdraws the aer from the Gifts and puts it aside in a near place."

The Aer at a Hierarchical Divine Liturgy

The practice of waving the aer over the head of the hierarch at a hierarchical liturgy is not mentioned in any *archieratika* (service book of hierarchs) before the seventeenth century.[343] Taft suggests the original size of the aer may have resulted in the practice. "The aer was so large that, as many sources indicate, several ministers had to assist in removing it from the Gifts. Then they undoubtedly had to lift it over the head of the main celebrant and fold it behind him. This at least is prescribed in the rubrics of the Russian liturgical reform of 1666-1667, which state that the aer is removed over the head of the hierarch and folded behind him."[344] To facilitate this movement, the hierarch probably had to lower or bow his head. Eventually, this led to the hierarch placing his head under the aer when it was being lowered or waved over the Gifts, as in the current practice.[345] To this day, regardless of the size of the aer, it is always removed over the head of the hierarch. Eventually, the act attracted a symbolic meaning. It is looked upon as an example of the hierarch's submission to the Orthodox faith. However, the true manifestation of one's commitment and faithfulness to the Orthodox faith is in one's free and open recitation of the Creed.

---

343 Trembelas, Τρεῖς Λειτουργίαι, 93.

344 Taft, *Great Entrance*, 423.

345 Significantly, the *Archieratikon* (Thessaloniki, 2004), 35, edited and published by the late eminent professor of canon law and liturgy, Metropolitan Panteleimon Rodopoulos, makes no reference to the aer ritual, even though it provides detailed directions regarding the kiss of peace among the clergy.

K. THE ANAPHORA

The Divine Liturgy celebrates and communicates the mystery of salvation. The anaphora or Great Eucharistic Prayer reveals both the purpose for which the Church celebrates the Divine Liturgy and the gifts the people hope to receive from it. The anaphora is the very heart and center of the Divine Liturgy. It is its most essential element.

Introductory Dialogue to the Anaphora

Priest

Let us stand well! Let us stand in awe! Let us be attentive! That we may present the holy offering in peace. (*This is said by the deacon, if one is present and serving*).[346]

People

Mercy, peace, a sacrifice of praise.[347]

---

346 The anaphora is introduced by an exhortation, an appeal to the people to stand aright, that is, in a good and proper manner with reverence and the fear of God, with seriousness of purpose, and a humble heart. The admonition appears in fourth-century documents and in the *Barberini Codex*. Cabasilas (fourteenth century) connects the bidding to the Creed and the anaphora. "Let us stand firm on this profession [the Creed], he [the priest] seems to say, lest we should be thrown off our balance by the persuasive arguments of heretics. 'Let us stand in fear' [awe]; for the danger to those who allow in their minds any doubt or hesitation, concerning matters of faith, is very great. And he goes on to say: Thus, standing firm in faith let our offerings to God proceed as is proper. What does 'as is proper' mean? It means in peace." (*Commentary*, 26).

347 In the received text the response of the people reads, "A mercy of peace, a sacrifice of praise." The form, "a mercy of peace," is obscure, if not unintelligible, and was probably created to provide rhetorical and stylistic balance with the phrase, "a sacrifice of praise." The *Barberini Codex* has a simple form, "mercy, peace – ἔλεος, εἰρήνη." The phrase, "a sacrifice of praise" (Heb. 13:15), was added later. The more primitive form of the response, "mercy, peace, a sacrifice of praise," should be preferred (in Greek, "ἔλεον, εἰρήνην, θυσίαν αἰνέσεως" – accusative form). The accusative form in Greek makes clear that the response constitutes the direct object of the admonition. (Trembelas, Τρεῖς Λειτουργίαι, 95-6). All expressions of mercy, love, and kindness flow out of a soul that is filled with inner peace. Only such a soul is capable of offering a sacrifice of praise. A soul at peace is itself an offering pleasing to God. Hence one could make the case that a linkage exists between the response and the kiss of peace. See Cabasilas (*Commentary*, 26). For more on the response see Calivas, *Aspects of Orthodox Worship*, 204-7.

Priest

The grace of our Lord Jesus Christ, and the love of God and Father, and the communion of the Holy Spirit, be with all of you (2 Cor. 13:14).[348] (*As he says this, the priest turns, faces the people, and blesses them with his hand in the usual manner*).[349]

People

And with your spirit.

Priest

Let us lift our hearts.[350] (*As he says this, the priest looks slightly up and raises his hands with open palms, as a sign of focusing the heart, which is to say concentrating one's whole being on God. The gesture has its origins in St. Paul's admonition in 1 Timothy 2:8: "I desire that in every place the men should pray, lifting holy hands…"*).

People

We lift them up to the Lord.

Priest

Let us give thanks to the Lord. (*As he completes the bidding, the priest turns and faces the Holy Table and crossing his hands he bows his head toward the Holy Table. He does **not** bow to the icon of Christ.*)

---

348 The apostolic blessing is not a primitive element of the Divine Liturgy. It is not mentioned by St. Cyril of Jerusalem but appears in other documents of the late fourth century (see Trembelas, Τρεῖς Λειτουργίαι, 96-7). The liturgical form of the blessing is slightly different from the original biblical text, which reads as follows: "'Ἡ χάρις τοῦ Κυρίου Ἰησου Χριστοῦ καὶ ἡ ἀγάπη τοῦ Θεοῦ καὶ ἡ κοινωνία τοῦ Ἁγίου Πνεύματος μετά πάντων ἡμῶν … The grace of the Lord Jesus Christ and the love of God and the communion of the Holy Spirit be with you all" (2 Cor. 13:14). Cabasilas (*Commentary*, 26) explains the blessing as follows. "This prayer is taken from the Epistles of St. Paul. It procures for us the benefits of the Holy Trinity – every perfect gift. And it asks from each of the Divine Persons his special gift: from the Son grace, from the Father love, from the Holy Spirit communion…. We pray thus in order that we may not lose that which we have received but may keep it forever."

349 The priest performs this blessing in the usual way with his right hand and never with the blessing cross, or the folded aer, or any other object.

350 The bidding and its response are primitive elements of the liturgy. They are found in all ancient rites in a variety of forms, such as: "Lift up the mind (νοῦς, νοῦν);" "Lift up your mind;" "Lift up your hearts;" "Let us lift up our minds and hearts." The bidding echoes the Old Testament exhortation "Let us lift up our hearts and hands to God in heaven" (Lamentations 3:41; cf. Ps. 62/63:4). *At this point, the people should be encouraged to lift up their hands and eyes to indicate that their thoughts and heart are centered on the Lord from where our help comes.* The Triune God is our hope and keeper (Ps. 120/121:1-2, 5).

People

It is proper and right.[351]

The introductory dialogue between the priest and the people which introduces the anaphora serves to remind us that all our prayers and offerings must be characterized by sincere interior dispositions, such as mercy, peace, thanksgiving, and praise. Otherwise, our offerings become empty, formalistic acts and our prayers hollow words. The response – mercy and peace – mean that we are able and willing to share in God's infinite forgiving, healing, compassionate, and steadfast love, which alone breaks through all our human failings and limitations. This peace and mercy are a gift that comes from our Lord Jesus Christ and results in our communion with God. However broken we may feel or be, we must never despair because God sees and loves everyone as sons and daughters having adopted us through the incarnation of his Son. Sharing in God's peace and mercy, we share in his joy (John 17:13). In this way we become a eucharistic people, filled with unfeigned love and boundless gratitude for God's gift of communion and life. Thus, we are made capable of offering him our sacrifice of praise: "Lord God Almighty, you alone are holy. You accept a sacrifice of praise from those who call upon you with their whole heart..." (Prayer of the Proskomide CHR).

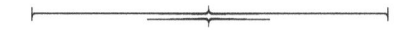

The Anaphora or Eucharistic Prayer

Priest

bowing his head, he begins to read the anaphora aloud, "*It is proper and right to hymn you, to bless you, to praise you, to give thanks to you, and to worship you...*

---

[351] In some editions, a Trinitarian formula was added to the original simple response. The addition reads, "It is proper and right to worship the Father, and the Son, and the Holy Spirit: the Trinity, one in essence and undivided." The addition was probably created to cover the priest's inaudible recitation of the initial part of the anaphora. It should not be used. It is better the people hear the words of the prayer. (At this point, the deacon returns to the sanctuary).

The principal difference between BAS and CHR rests chiefly in the second part of the Divine Liturgy. The differences are both external and internal. The prayers differ not only in length but also in content, and this is especially true of the holy anaphora.³⁵²

The anaphora of BAS is powerful in its unity of thought, theological depth, and rich biblical imagery. It is decidedly creedal in nature. It contains a grand litany of titles and attributes of the three Persons of the Holy Trinity and their particular role and mode of being. It provides a stirring account of the divine economy and the blessings that are derived from it; and it has one of the most beautiful, harmonious, and comprehensive formulas of intercession.

The anaphora of CHR by contrast is shorter and less rhetorical. It is characterized by its simplicity, directness, and clarity. It is also marked by the absence of literal biblical passages, which is typical of the more primitive forms of liturgical prayer.³⁵³

The anaphora in both CHR and BAS is addressed to God the Father.³⁵⁴ While it is said by the presiding hierarch or priest by virtue of his ordination, it is not his prayer but the prayer of the whole Church. He offers it on behalf of, for and with the people. For this precise reason the Ecumenical Patriarchate long ago ordered that it be said aloud at every eucharistic celebration so that the people may hear and participate, that they may be inspired guided by it.³⁵⁵

The anaphora is a single prayer and not a series of prayers and hymns. This unity or singleness is key to understanding and appreciating its purpose, essence, and power to inform and transform God's faithful people. Not one of its several components is dispensable or superfluous. Each element of the anaphora is essential because they are interdependent; together they form the whole.

The anaphora is introduced by a simple but powerful command: "Εὐχαριστήσωμεν τῷ Κυρίῳ...Let us give thanks to the Lord." To which the people respond, "It is proper and right."

The anaphora begins with two pronouncements or affirmations. First, the worshipping community declares that nothing is more essential, more fitting and right in life than to bless, praise, and give thanks to God

---

352 See Calivas, *The Liturgy in Dialogue*, 24-9.

353 Ibid., 38-64.

354 The exception to this rule is the anaphora of the Divine Liturgy attributed to St. Gregory the Theologian, which is addressed to the Son rather than the Father.

355 See Calivas, *Aspects of Orthodox Worship*, 214-7.

for his ineffable goodness and glory, which are expressed in his creative, providential, and redemptive activity: "It is proper and right to hymn you, bless you, praise you, thank you, and worship you, in every place of your dominion…" (CHR). Second, the worshipping community blesses[356] God by acknowledging the divine attributes and perfections of the Godhead, the One God existing in three hypostases: "For you, O God, are ineffable, inconceivable, invisible, incomprehensible, existing forever, and always the same, you and your only begotten Son, and your Holy Spirit" (CHR).

Thanksgiving *So significant is the act of thanksgiving that the entire sacrament is called Eucharist – Εὐχαριστία – Thanksgiving. Giving thanks constitutes the first action of the worshipping community in imitation of Christ's action at the Last Supper: "The Lord Jesus on the night when he was betrayed took bread, and when he had given thanks, he broke it and said…." (1 Cor. 11:23-24).*[357]

After recalling and recounting the creative and redemptive activity of the Triune God,[358] we offer him thanks (εὐχαριστοῦμεν σοι) for all things both known and unknown and for blessings seen and unseen that have been bestowed upon us. Knowledge always precedes thanksgiving. We give thanks for things we know and intuit; and that which we know by faith is that everything in life is from God and the manifestation of his ineffable power and boundless love.

Fr. Alexander Schmemann captures the meaning of thanksgiving superbly with these words: "In thanksgiving we recognize and confess above all the divine source and the divine calling of our life. The prayer of thanksgiving affirms that God brought us from nonexistence into being, which means that he created us as partakers of Being, i.e., not just something that comes from him, but something permeated by his presence, light, wisdom, love – by what Orthodox theology, following St. Gregory Palamas calls divine energies and which makes the world called to and capable of transfiguration into a new heaven and a new earth, and the ruler of creation, man, called to and capable of theosis, partaking of the divine nature…. Thanksgiving is the sign, or better still, the presence, joy, fulness, of knowledge of God, i.e., knowledge as meeting, knowledge

---

356 To bless (εὐλογέω) God means to praise, honor, exalt, and worship him (cf. Ps. 102/103; 103/104).

357 Cf. Matthew 26:27; Mark 14:23; Luke 22:19).

358 In recounting the divine economy BAS includes Old Testament references. In BAS the Christ event is described principally in terms of St. Paul's theology in Philippians (2:5-11); Galatians (4:4-7); and Romans (5:12-21).

as communion, knowledge as unity."[359]

If, indeed, everything that exists is from God, what are we to make of evil? Fr. Schmemann provides one answer through the following perceptive words. "Sin and evil are essentially and above all a mystery, because evil does not and cannot have its own existence (for everything that exists is from God, and hence is very good).... Evil according to one of the Church Fathers, is unsown grass. But while it is not sown, not created by God, it is: it possesses a terrible destructive power, so that it can be said about the world itself that it "lies in evil" (1 John 5:19). There is no explanation of this mystery in the Christian faith.... And the Church, while not explaining it, convicts sin, in the original, seminal meaning of the word, to convict: the Church and only the Church exposes sin as sin, evil as evil.... The Church convicts sin through her thanksgiving. Through it she recognizes the vital essence of evil, the source of sin is un-thankfulness.... Not giving thanks is the root and the driving force of that pride...the sin that tore man away from God.... And thus, only thanksgiving convicts, i.e., exposes sin as the falling away of love from thanksgiving."[360]

The Triumphal Hymn (ἐπινίκιος ὕμνος) and the Proclamation of the Holiness of God

The second action unfolds into a proclamation of the holiness of God. The people join the angelic hosts to proclaim with joy and thanksgiving the holiness and majesty of the Triune God. "...even though thousands of archangels and tens of thousands of angels stand around you, the Cherubim and Seraphim, six-winged, many-eyed, soaring aloft upon their wings" (CHR).

Priest

Singing the triumphal hymn, exclaiming, proclaiming, and saying.[361] (*As he says this, the priest takes the asterisk from the discos. Making the sign of the cross over the discos with it, he cleans the ends of the asterisk with the mousa (sponge), folds it, kisses it, and places it on the folded veils. If a deacon is serving, he removes the asterisk*).[362]

---

359 Schmemann, *Eucharist*, 185, 176.

360 Ibid, 186-9.

361 The four verbal expressions which describe the manner by which the angelic host proclaim the triumphal hymn (ἄδοντα-singing, βοῶντα-exclaiming, κεκραγότα-crying out, and λέγοντα-saying), bring to mind the four living creatures ("like a lion, like an ox, the third with the face of a man, and the fourth like a flying eagle") in the vision of the heavenly worship recounted by St. John in the Book of Revelation (4:6-11).

362 Tracing the sign of the cross over the discos with the asterisk is not mentioned in the *Diataxis of Philotheos Kokkinos.* However, kissing the asterisk is part of the rubric.

People

Holy, holy, holy, Lord Sabaoth, heaven and earth are filled with your glory. Hosanna in the highest. Blessed is he who comes in the name of the Lord. Hosanna in the highest. (*The hymn is (should be) sung by the clergy and people together in unison signifying their participation in the heavenly liturgy*).[363]

Priest

after the hymn is sung, he continues reciting the anaphora, "Together with these blessed powers, Master, who love humankind, we also exclaim and say, Holy are you…"

---

[363] *The angelic hymn, also called the Biblical Trisagion* (thrice-holy hymn), is found in the prophecy of Isaiah (6:1-3; cf. 1 Kings 22:19; Ezek. 1:4-21; Rev. 4:6-8). It is an ancient element of the Divine Liturgy. (See Cyril of Jerusalem, *Mystagogical Catechesis* V, 6). In our liturgical language the hymn is often referred to as the "*triumphal hymn – ἐπινίκιος ὕμνος.*" As it happens in other instances, the triumphal hymn of the liturgy differs from the biblical text in several ways. The hymn was changed to include the words '*heaven and*' to the original phrase "the whole earth is full of his glory." In the same phrase, the pronoun *his* was changed to the second person, *your* glory. The Greek text has retained the Hebrew words *Sabaoth* (hosts) and *Hosanna* (a fervent cry which means, "we pray, save now" – as in Psalm 117/118:25). The acclamation, "Blessed is he who comes in the name of the Lord. Hosanna in the highest," is a later addition to the original angelic hymn recorded in Isaiah. The acclamation is from Psalm 117/118:26. According to the Gospel of Matthew (21:9), these words were exclaimed by the crowd as Jesus entered Jerusalem before the Passion (Cf. Mark 11:1-10; Luke 19:28-38; and John 12:12-18). In fact, the acclamation is borrowed verbatim from Matthew 21:9 with one exception. The opening phrase in Matthew, "Hosanna to the Son of David" has been changed to read "Hosanna in the highest." In both the Matthean account and the liturgical hymn the acclamation Hosanna is a greeting of welcome; but not a trite, casual, or empty greeting. Rather, it is filled with hope and expectation. It is a cry of adoration with a fervent plea – "Save us!" In the vision of Isaiah, the thrice-holy hymn is sung by two six-winged Seraphim. BAS is in accord with Isaiah but adds that the Seraphim are joined by angels, archangels, thrones, dominions, principalities, authorities, powers, and the many-eyed Cherubim, and every creature of reason and understanding. In CHR, the hymn is sung by thousands of archangels, and tens of thousands of angels, the Cherubim and Seraphim. For more on the orders and names of the heavenly host see Col. 1:16; Ephes. 1:21; and Pseudo-Dionysios, *Celestial Hierarchy*, chapters 6–13).

The Anamnesis

From the proclamation of God's holiness, the anaphora proceeds to the *anamnesis (ἀνάμνησις)*,[364] which in CHR consists of the following remembrances: (a) God's providential saving activity (*You so loved your world that you gave your only begotten Son so that everyone who believes in him should not perish, but have eternal life*); (b) the actions of the Lord at the Last Supper (*When he had come and fulfilled for our sake the entire plan of salvation, on the night in which he was delivered up, or rather when he delivered himself up* for *the life of the world, he took bread...*); (c) the saving command ("Do this...") by which the Eucharist was established (*Remembering, therefore, this saving command*).[365] The *anamnesis* also includes (d) the Words of Institution, the words spoken by the Lord over the bread and the cup at the Last Supper: "*He took bread in his holy, pure, and blameless hands, and giving thanks...he gave it to his holy disciples and apostles saying...*"[366]

---

364 The *anamnesis* or remembrance of the Church is not merely a psychological calling to mind of past events but an actual participation in the paschal presence of Christ, who said, "Lo, I am with you always, even to the end of the age" (Matt. 28:20). We affirm that his promise is fulfilled in the liturgy: "Where two or three are gathered together in [his] name, [he] is there in the midst of them" (Matt. 18:20). See Calivas, *Aspects of Orthodox Worship*, 177-80.

365 CHR does not quote the command of the Lord directly but after the words of institution uses the phrase, "Remembering therefore, this saving command." BAS, on the other hand, citing Luke 22:19 and I Cor. 11:24, includes the command: "*Do this in remembrance of me.*" BAS also paraphrases 1 Cor. 11:26: "For as often as you eat this Bread and drink this Cup, you proclaim my death, you confess my resurrection." The command, "Do this" is not mentioned by either Matthew or Mark.

366 BAS introduces the words of institution with the phrase, "He gave it to his holy disciples and apostles saying." The phrase is repeated before the Bread and the Cup.

The Words of Institution

Priest

Take, eat, this my Body...[367]

People

Amen.

Priest

Likewise, after partaking of the supper, he took the cup...[368]

---

[367] From a nineteenth-century Euchologion we learn that it was customary among the clergy to point to the discos and chalice respectively with the right hand, palm open, when the words of institution were being pronounced. The gesture, however, was frowned upon by others as being superfluous and antithetical to the Orthodox ethos probably because it seemed to suggest the Roman Catholic belief that the words of institution have a consecratory character. In fact, the demonstrative pronouns, "this is my Body...this is my Blood," do not refer to the eucharistic gifts on the Holy Table but are part of the anamnesis. (See Εὐχολόγιον τὸ Μέγα, S. Zervos, ed. (Venice 1862), 63, note. (A facsimile of this Euchologion has been produced by the publishing house, Astir, Al & E. Papadimitriou, Athens 1992). Eventually, the objection led to the omission of the gesture because it is not mentioned in most Greek Ieratika and their English equivalents. The gesture, however, is mentioned in a twelfth-century diataxis and recorded in the fourteenth-century *Diataxis of Philotheos Kokkinos*: "Ὅταν δὲ ἐκφωνήσῃ ὁ ἱερεύς, Λάβετε, φάγετε, ἁπτόμενος ὁ διάκονος τοῦ ἰδίου ὀραρίου δείκνυσι σὺν τῷ ἱερεῖ καὶ αὐτὸς τὸν ἅγιον δίσκον. Ὡσαύτως καὶ ὅταν τὸ ἅγιον ποτήριον δείκνυσιν ὁ ἱερεὺς λέγων, Πίετε ἐξ αὐτοῦ πάντες, δείκνυσι καὶ ὁ διάκονος σὺν αὐτῷ...*Further, when the priest proclaims, Take, eat, the deacon, with his orarion in hand, also points toward the holy discos together with the priest. Likewise, as the priest points to the holy chalice when he says, Drink of this all of you, the deacon also points to the holy chalice with him.*" (See Trembelas, Τρεῖς Λειτουργίαι, 11 and 108). The ancient Greek Liturgy of St. Mark (Egyptian rite) contains the diaconal biddings, Ἐκτείνατε (*stretch out your hands*) and Ἔτι Ἐκτείνατε (*Again. Stretch out your hands*), which are said at the Words of Institution. The bidding was directed to the priests and, as some argue also to the people. See Τρεῖς Λειτουργίαι, 108. Fountoulis, Θεία Λειτουργία τοῦ Ἀποστόλου Μάρκου (Thessaloniki, 1977), 18, 52. F. E. Brightman, *Eastern Liturgies* (Oxford, 1896/ facsimile Gorgias Press 2004), 132.

[368] This sequence ("after supper") follows the Pauline (I Cor. 11:25) and Lucan (Lk. 22:20) accounts of the Last Supper. In Matthew and Mark, the blessing of the Bread and Cup follow one another: "And as they were eating, he took bread... and he took a cup..." (Mark 14: 22-23; Matt. 26:26). BAS does not contain the words "after supper." Also, the introduction to the Cup in BAS is different from CHR and from the biblical accounts of the Last Supper: "Likewise he took the cup of the fruit of the vine, and having mingled it and given thanks, blessed and hallowed it, he gave it..."

Priest

Drink of this, all of you; this is my Blood...[369]

People

Amen.

Priest

The *anamnesis concludes* with a remembrance of all that was accomplished for our sake through *the cross, the tomb, the resurrection, the ascension, the enthronement, and the second and glorious coming of Christ.* "Remembering, therefore, this saving command and all that has been done for our sake...."

The Offering and the Sacrifice of Praise

Priest

Offering to you these gifts from your own gifts, at all times and in all places... (*In the prevailing practice, as the priest says these words, he crosses his right hand over his left, and holding the discos in his right hand and the cup in his left, he lifts them a little over the Holy Table*. If a deacon is serving, he usually lifts the Gifts as the priest intones the words of offering).[370]

People

We praise you, we bless you, we give thanks to you, and we pray to you, Lord our God. (*The hymn should be sung by all the worshippers, clergy and people alike, in unison*).

Offer or Offering: As I have noted elsewhere, in a small number of late manuscripts and in all printed editions of BAS and CHR the original adverbial participle προσφέροντες (offering) was changed to a verb προσφέρομεν (we offer).[371] *The reasons for the change are not known, nor do we know who authorized it. In recent years, attempts have been made to restore the participle with little success.*

The entire anamnesis in the manuscript tradition of BAS and CHR comprised one complete sentence with only one set of active verbs, those that constitute the sacrifice of praise. The original sequence in outline

---

369 The Words of Institution in both BAS and CHR are the same. Significantly however, they differ slightly from the versions recorded in the four biblical accounts of the Last Supper (Matthew 26:26-29; Mark 14:22-25; Luke 22:19-21; 1 Cor. 10:16-17, 11:23-26). In other words, they are not drawn verbatim from any of the four biblical versions of the words of institution.

370 For more on the key phrase "κατὰ πάντα καὶ διαπάντα ..." see Appendix C:9

371 Calivas, *Aspects of Orthodox Worship*, 209-212; and *Liturgy in Dialogue*, 94-96.

form was: Remembering [and] offering ... we praise you, we bless you, we give thanks to you and we pray to you, Lord our God. According to the original text, the object of the remembrance and the offering is the sacrifice of praise, "we praise you, we bless you, we give thanks to you..." The modification in language may appear unimportant, but it is not. Changing the original participle, offering, to a verb, we offer, dramatically altered the object of the people's action. The oblation or offering is now identified not with the sacrifice of praise – the initial intent – but with the Holy Gifts which are raised by the priest for dramatic emphasis.[372] This latter ritual act came about gradually as a result of the change in language, "We offer to you these gifts..." The new wording prompted and gave rise to the new ritual to accentuate the idea of offering. What we now offer is not the sacrifice of praise but the eucharistic elements.

The shift in language has diminished the significance of the sacrifice of praise. It has become just another hymn. But it is not just another ordinary hymn. It is the summit and climax of the Church's prayer. It is the Church's unique offering, the only possible response to the Father for the Paschal mystery that he renders present in and through the sacramental Gifts.

St. Nicholas Cabasilas says it best: "The Church says, 'We make this oblation mindful of your benefits.' Surely this is thanksgiving, to honor with our holy offerings the Benefactor for the good things he has given us. Thus, expressing her thanksgiving even more clearly, she adds 'In offering this oblation we praise you, we bless you...' This then is the purpose of the offering of the holy gifts – to praise, to give thanks, and to supplicate, as we have said at the beginning; so that the sacrifice we offer is at once eucharistic and supplicatory."[373] Indeed, as we read in the Epistle to the Hebrews, on our part sacrifice is essentially an act of self-giving, the climax of which is continual praise: "Through him then let us continually offer up a sacrifice of praise (θυσίαν αἰνέσεως) to God, that is, the fruit of lips that acknowledge his name" (Heb. 13:15; cf. Ps. 49/50:14, 23).[374]

---

[372] The current practice is relatively new. It is not mentioned in any of the early manuscripts. In fact, the *Diataxis of Philotheos Kokkinos* requires the priest and deacon only to point to the Gifts. See Trembelas, *Τρεῖς Λειτουργίαι*, 11 and 110. The elevation is first mentioned in two manuscripts of the seventeenth century. It is not noted in the 1862 Εὐχολόγιον τὸ Μέγα or in the more recent Ἀρχιερατικόν of Metropolitan Panteleimon Rodopoulos.

[373] The italics were added for emphasis. Cabasilas, *Commentary*, 49. See also P. Trembelas, Ἀπὸ τὴν Ὀρθόδοξον Λατρείαν μας (Athens, 1970), 288-9.

[374] For more on the Eucharist as sacrifice see Staniloae, *Sanctifying Mysteries*, 94-105. See also Schmemann, *Eucharist*, 204-211; Calivas, *Aspects of Orthodox Worship*, 184-188 and 210-213; and Appendix C:9.

The Epiclesis (Invocation or Earnest Request)

The sacrifice of praise concludes with a petition: *"and we pray to you, Lord our God."* This petition introduces the *epiclesis*, i.e., the fervent plea to God the Father to send down his Holy Spirit upon the gathered people and upon the Gifts they have set forth on the Holy Table. (*After the sacrifice or hymn of praise has been completed, the priest says:*).[375]

Priest

Once again we offer to you this spiritual worship without the shedding of blood, and we beseech and pray and entreat you: Send down your Holy Spirit upon us and upon the Gifts here presented.[376]

Priest

And make this Bread the precious Body of your Christ. (*As he says these words, the priest makes the sign of the cross over the Amnos in the usual way*).[377]

People

Amen.[378]

Priest

And that which is in this Cup, the precious Blood of your Christ. (*As he says these words, the priest makes the sign of the cross over the chalice*).

People

Amen.

---

375 At this point, Churches in the Slavic tradition interrupt the natural flow of the *epiclesis* with the insertion of hymns and prayers from the service of the Third Hour, the central theme of which is the Descent of the Holy Spirit (Pentecost). The addition of these elements is an unnecessary distraction.

376 If a deacon is serving, he will gesture toward the discos with his right hand holding the orarion and say, "Bless, Master, the Holy Bread," followed by the other biddings recorded in the *Ieratikon*.

377 In place of the verb *make* (ποίησον), BAS has the verb ἀναδεῖξαι (*show forth* or *declare*): "We pray and call upon you, O Holy of Holies, that by the favor of your goodness your Holy Spirit may come down upon us and upon the gifts now offered, to bless, hallow, and *show/declare* (ἀναδεῖξαι) this Bread to be the precious Body of our Lord and God and Savior Jesus Christ.... And this cup to be the precious Blood of our Lord...." Interestingly, BAS places the verb, "to show," on the lips of Jesus in the account of the Last Supper: "In the night in which he gave himself up for the life of the world, he [Jesus] took bread into his holy and pure hands; and having *shown* (ἀναδείξας) it to you, God and Father...." In BAS, we ask the Father to send down the Holy Spirit upon us and upon the Gifts that he may bless them, sanctify them, and show (declare) them to be what they really are, the Body and Blood of Christ.

378 If a deacon is serving, he leads the people in pronouncing the Amen.

Priest

Changing them by your Holy Spirit (*As he says these words, the priest makes the sign of the cross over the discos and the chalice*).[379]

People

Amen. Amen. Amen.

The Whole Action of the Divine Liturgy Depends on the Holy Spirit.

As the incarnation of the eternal Logos was accomplished by the Holy Spirit, so also is the change of the eucharistic gifts realized.[380] *The Holy Spirit makes the crucified, risen, and glorified Christ really present to us in the eucharistic elements. Through his transforming and sanctifying power, the eucharistic elements become, in a real but mysterious way, the Body and Blood of Christ – which is to say, the living and glorified Christ in all his fullness – through which our entire being is nourished and transfigured.*[381] *In other words, in Holy Communion we share in the deified humanity of the incarnate Word and Son of God.*

The change of the eucharistic elements, however, is not physical but mystical and sacramental. The bread and wine preserve their natural properties and qualities. Yet, when we partake of them, we commune the true Body and Blood of Christ, according to his own words, "This is my body…." (note the realism of his words – Matt. 26: 26, 28; Mark 14:22-24; Luke 22:19-20; 1 Cor. 11:24-25; John 6:51-56). To the eye and taste they remain bread and wine, but "let your faith be your stay," says St. Cyril of Jerusalem. And he continues, "Instead of judging the matter by taste, let faith give you unwavering confidence that you have been privileged

---

379 Notably, this formula is not found in BAS. Instead, we find the words, "Shed for the life and salvation of the world." Starting with some manuscripts of the fifteenth century and in some later printed editions of the *Ieratikon*, editors have added the formula of CHR at this point. This formula in CHR, however, is incompatible with the text of BAS and has no place in it. See Trembelas, Τρεῖς Λειτουργίαι, 183.

380 Saint John of Damascus underscores this point. "For just as God made all that he made by the energy of the Holy Spirit, so also now the energy of the Spirit performs those things that are supernatural and which is not possible to comprehend unless by faith alone. 'How shall this be,' said the holy Virgin, 'seeing as I know not a man?' And the Archangel Gabriel answered her: 'The Holy Spirit shall come upon you and the power of the Highest shall overshadow you.' And now you ask, how the bread became Christ's body and the wine and water Christ's blood. And I say to you, the Holy Spirit is present and does those things which surpass reason and thought." *An Exact Exposition of the Orthodox Faith*, Book 4:13.

381 See Calivas, *Aspects of Orthodox Worship*, 180-4.

to receive the Body and Blood of Christ."³⁸² *The epiclesis is not a magical formula or act. The bread and wine do not change their empirical existence. The change is seen by the eyes of faith. This experience, however, is not subjective fancy but the fruit of a living and dynamic faith (Heb. 11:1-3).*

As Fr. Staniloae tells it, "The Savior himself has assured us that he is really present in the Eucharist together with his body and blood; he has also assured us of the various meanings of this presence and explained how it is possible…. If, in the other mysteries, Christ is present invisibly through his activity, in the Eucharist he is present through his very body and blood in the forms of bread and wine. Through this sacrament he gives himself completely to the members of the Church, that is, to the Church herself, because inasmuch as Christ fulfills his intention of abiding within those who believe, he constitutes and upholds the Church completely as the extension of his body."³⁸³

Every Divine Liturgy is a renewal and confirmation of the constant coming of the Holy Spirit. He is ever present in the Church, animating and vivifying it; transforming it into the Body of Christ and liberating and perfecting its members. At the Divine Liturgy we experience the continuation of the mystery of Pentecost, "send down your Holy Spirit upon us…." In the Eucharist we acknowledge again and again that we bear the seal of the Holy Spirit; we are Spirit-bearers. Put another way, the new life received at baptism through water and the Spirit is continuously advanced and perfected at every Eucharist celebrated in faith through the continuous coming of the Holy Spirit.

In the changed elements of the bread and wine, creation itself is freed from its transitory, finite, and mortal character; it becomes Spirit-bearing. Material things come to bear divine perfections, as revealed in the incarnation of the Logos and in the change of the eucharistic elements.³⁸⁴ We are not saved from the material world but with it (Rom.

---

382 Cyril of Jerusalem, *Mystagogical Catechesis*, IV: 5 and 6.

383 Staniloae, *Sanctifying Mysteries*, 84, 83. Recall the words of institution in the Synoptic Gospels and 1 Cor. 11:21-23; and the words of the Lord on the Bread of Life in John 6:51-57.

384 Regarding sacramental matter, St. John of Damascus says, "[B]read and wine are employed for God knows man's infirmity. For in general man turns away discontentedly from what is not well-worn by custom. And so, with his usual indulgence he performs his supernatural works through familiar objects. And just as, in the case of baptism, since it is man's custom to wash himself with water and anoint himself with oil, he connected the grace of the Spirit with the oil and the water and made it the water of regeneration. In like manner since it is man's custom to eat and to drink water and wine, he connected his divinity with these and made them his body and blood in order that we may rise to what is supernatural through what is familiar and natural." *Exposition of the Orthodox Faith* Book IV: 13.

8:18-23). *While the age to come will reveal the comprehensive renovation, transfiguration, and glorification of humankind and the cosmos, the radical freedom from the bondage of corruption with all its limitations is made known to us through Christ's resurrection and the perfecting grace of the Holy Spirit, both of which are present to us in the sacraments, and particularly in the Eucharist.*

The Gifts, Fruits, Benefits or Effects of Holy Communion

Priest

(*continues praying the anaphora*) So that they may be to those who partake of them for vigilance of soul, forgiveness of sins, communion of your Holy Spirit, fulfillment of the kingdom of heaven, boldness before you, not for judgment or condemnation (CHR).

As I have noted elsewhere, the tradition of enumerating the gifts, effects, fruits or benefits of Holy Communion in the anaphora – a trait common to all ancient liturgies – is based on the New Testament references to the Eucharist.[385] *The Matthean account of the Last Supper, for example, names one such benefit or fruit of Communion: the forgiveness of sins (Matt. 26:28). The synoptic Gospels stress the covenantal and messianic nature of the Eucharist.*[386] *In the discourse on the Bread of Life, the Gospel of John (6:22-59) maintains that the Eucharist is true food and that Communion results in an intimate union with Christ and grants eternal life.*

St. Paul, whose "First Letter to the Corinthians" provides the earliest account of the Lord's Supper, emphasizes the real presence of Christ in the elements. Additionally, he stresses the eschatological character of the Eucharist, which is also the source of ecclesial unity. Furthermore, St. Paul encourages the faithful to exercise discernment, fraternal love, and

---

385 See Calivas, *Liturgy in Dialogue*, 19-64.

386 "This is the blood of the covenant, which is poured out for many" (Mark 14:24; cf. Matt. 26:28). The Lucan account (22:20) declares the covenant new (ἡ καινὴ διαθήκη ἐν τῷ αἵματί μου): "This cup which is poured out for you is the new covenant in my blood" (cf. 1 Cor. 11:25). Through his life and sacrificial death – his self-giving – Christ sealed and established a new bond between God and humanity; he inaugurated a new covenant community, the Church (cf. Exodus 24:3-8; Is. 53:12; Jer. 31:31-34, 32:38-41). At every eucharistic celebration the people renew their identity as the "chosen race, a royal priesthood, a holy nation, God's own people" (1 Peter 2:9). By consuming the Divine Gifts in faith Christ assimilates us to himself and gives us his divine and eternal life. We touch eternity and experience in faith the eschatological union of Christ and the Church. The future becomes a present reality.

vigilance, and warns them against partaking of Communion unworthily.

In keeping with tradition, the anaphora in both BAS and CHR also specifies the gifts and benefits of Holy Communion. Even a cursory reading of the two texts reveals that the effects and benefits in each are different. The anaphora of BAS emphasizes the ecclesial dimensions of Communion, while the anaphora of CHR gives greater prominence to personal benefits.

It is also clear that in both BAS and CHR, "communion of the Holy Spirit" is the fundamental gift and key to understanding the effects of Holy Communion because God's saving activities are accomplished and perfected by the Holy Spirit. As St. Irenaeus taught, "Through the Spirit [we] ascend to the Son, and through the Son to the Father."[387]

According to the anaphora of BAS,[388] those who partake of the one Bread and Cup receive essentially two gifts: the communion of the one Holy Spirit, by which the unity of God's people is continually accomplished, and the realization of the eschatological hope to find mercy and grace together with all the saints with whom we constitute the Church: "May we find mercy and grace with all the saints who through the ages have been well-pleasing to you...." By sharing in the consecrated elements, we are made to realize sacramentally the eschatological mystery of unity in diversity: "And unite all of us to one another who become partakers of the one Bread and Cup in the communion of the Holy Spirit." Nourished, empowered, and perfected by our participation in the one Bread and Cup we are called to become an epiphany of divine love and the image of the new community gathered and living under the rule of the risen Lord. In addition to the gift of unity, BAS specifies other effects of receiving Communion. These are recounted in three prayers: pre-Communion and post-Communion prayers, and the prayer at the skeuophylakion.[389]

In CHR the gifts of Holy Communion are related to the expectation of the kingdom and are meant to contribute to the continuous spiritual regeneration of the believers, sustaining them in a state of watchfulness and expectation, and at the same time giving them a foretaste of the

---

387 St. Irenaeus, *Against Heresies*, V. 36.2.

388 The effects or benefits of Holy Communion in BAS are stated thusly: "And unite all of us to one another who become partakers of the one Bread and Cup in the communion of the Holy Spirit. Grant that none of us partake of the holy Body and Blood of your Christ for judgment or condemnation. Instead, may we find mercy and grace with all the saints who through the ages have been well-pleasing to you..."

389 On the fruits of Communion in BAS see Calivas, *Liturgy in Dialogue*, 46-50.

blessedness that is to come.[390]

The anaphora of CHR lists seven effects of Communion: vigilance of soul, forgiveness of sins, communion of (in) the Holy Spirit, fulfillment of the kingdom of heaven, filial boldness and confidence, defense against unworthiness, which brings judgment and condemnation, and rejoicing in the saints.[391] *Of the seven fruits, as noted earlier, communion of the Holy Spirit is primary. The Holy Spirit unites those who partake of the Eucharist to Christ and keeps them vigilant, alert, and sober in expectation of the kingdom which is yet to come in fullness.*[392] *The Holy Spirit is also the source of forgiveness, purification, and sanctification. He is the pledge and guarantee of the future life, the "fulfillment of the kingdom of heaven" (Rom. 8:10-17; 2 Cor. 1:21-22, 5:1-5; Ephes. 1:13-14; cf. 1 Thess. 2:12:28; 2 Peter 1:11). Moreover, those who partake of Holy Communion are given the courage to come before God with boldness and confidence, free to speak before him as sons and daughters (Rom. 8:16-17).*

A note on the forgiveness of sins in both BAS and CHR

The theme of forgiveness is found in many prayers of the Divine Liturgy. It is, in fact, a fruit of Communion, but not for everyone.[393] Sin as such does not render a person unworthy of the Eucharist – for there is no one who lives and does not sin – but the willful, habitual attachment to sin, especially to grave or mortal sin, does. "All wrongdoing is sin, but there is sin which is not mortal" (1 John 5:17). Whether Communion brings forgiveness and sanctification or judgment and condemnation depends on the interior state and disposition of the recipient. Those burdened with heinous sins and addictions ought not to approach (1 Cor. 11:27-29). Grievous sins cut persons off from the Church and are subject to the discipline of penance, which is meant to heal and restore not to punish or humiliate.

Both BAS and CHR include warnings against the unworthy reception of Communion not only as a result of individual guilt that comes from secret sins but also of negligence and the absence of both personal and communal

---

390 On the fruits of Communion in CHR, Ibid. 50-3.

391 See Taft, *Precommunion Rites*, 114-28.

392 For more on the meaning and purpose of vigilance see Calivas, *Liturgy in Dialogue*, 60-3.

393 *Ibid.* 52-3.

works of righteousness (Matt. 25:31-46). From the beginning, the invitation to Communion was accompanied by warnings against improper inner dispositions and behaviors, such as impiety, immorality, irreverence, fractiousness, spiritual laziness, lack of charity, avarice, and habitual attachments. The warnings are meant to chasten and correct those who would commune in an unworthy and undiscerning manner, profaning the mysteries and bringing judgment to themselves (1 Cor. 11:27-29).[394]

The Commemorations of the Anaphora
Holy Communion and the Saints

Priest

(*Continues praying the anaphora*) "Again, we offer to you this spiritual worship for those who have reposed in the faith: forefathers, fathers, patriarchs, prophets, apostles, preachers, evangelists, martyrs, confessors, ascetics, and every righteous spirit made perfect in faith, especially for our most holy, pure, blessed, and glorious Lady, the Theotokos and ever-virgin Mary...for St. John the prophet...for the most praiseworthy Apostles...(*here the priest adds the name(s) of the saint(s) of the day*), and for all your saints, *through whose supplications visit us, O God.*"

Both BAS and CHR mention the saints in relation to the effects of Communion. The relationship, however, is understood and expressed differently in the two liturgies.[395] In BAS Holy Communion brings the earthly worshippers into fellowship with the saints – the first fruits of Christ's redemption – to share with them God's mercy and grace, both now and in the age to come. As St. Nicholas Cabasilas observes, "It is as if one said: Give us the grace which you have already given to the saints; sanctify us as you have already sanctified so many of our race."[396]

In CHR, on the other hand, the Holy Gifts are offered in honor of the saints, in whom the Church delights and at whose supplications the assembly awaits God's blessings and protection. The offering of the Holy Gifts on behalf of the saints is understood as an act of love for the saints and as a thanksgiving for the sanctification that God has bestowed upon them. The saints' passion for God,

---

394 *Ibid.* 53-4.

395 On the commemoration and the categories of saints in the anaphora, *Ibid.* 56-60.

396 Cabasilas, *Commentary on the Liturgy*, 4:33.

their fortitude and devotion, their simplicity and meekness serve as powerful examples of Christian living. They fill us with hope. Hence the offering of the Holy Gifts in their honor is also an act of intercession. We call upon the saints to intercede on our behalf. "In the saints," Cabasilas says, "the Church finds that which she seeks and obtains that for which she has prayed: the kingdom of heaven."[397]

When the **priest** has completed the general commemoration of the several categories of saints, he continues praying the anaphora, commemorating by name the Theotokos, St. John the Forerunner, the Holy Apostles,[398] and the saint(s) of the day. First, he intones aloud the name of the Theotokos:

Priest

"Especially for our most holy, pure, blessed and glorious Lady, the Theotokos and Ever-virgin Mary."[399]

In response, the people sing a hymn honoring her person, her unique role in the divine economy, and her special, unique relationship to Christ as servant and mother.

---

397 *Ibid.*

Concerning the honor due to the saints and their relics, St. John of Damascus says: "To the saints honor must be paid as friends of Christ, as sons and heirs of God. In the words of John, the theologian and Evangelist, 'As many as received him, to them he gave power to become sons of God'…and the Lord in the Holy Gospels says to his apostles, 'You are my friends. Henceforth I call you not servants, for the servant knows not what his lord does'…. Surely also the saints are gods and lords and kings…. Now I mean gods and lords and kings not by nature, but as rulers and master of their passions, and as preserving a truthful likeness to the divine image according to which they were made, and as being united to God of their own free will and receiving him as an indweller and becoming by grace through participation with him what he is himself by nature…. Christ the Lord made the remains [relics] of the saints to be fountains of salvation to us, pouring forth manifold blessings and abounding in oil of sweet fragrance…. Let us raise monuments to them and visible images, and let us ourselves become, through imitation of their virtues, living monuments and images of them…. Let us give honor to the Mother of God…the prophet and forerunner John…the apostles as the Lord's brothers… the martyrs…the holy fathers, the ascetics…. Also let us honor those who were prophets before grace, the patriarchs and just men who foretold the Lord's coming…. Let us carefully review their life and let us emulate their faith and love and zeal and way of life, and endurance of sufferings and patience even to blood, in order that we may be sharers with them in their crowns of glory." *Exposition of the Orthodox Faith* Book IV: 15.

398 These three names – the Theotokos, St. John the Baptist, and the Holy Apostles – are always mentioned in every apolysis and in every other supplicatory prayer in which the saints are invoked.

399 The ekphonesis of the Theotokos was introduced in the fifth century to uphold the doctrine of the Third and Fourth Ecumenical Synods.

People

Sing the appointed *megalynarion* in honor of the Theotokos, usually the well-known hymn, *"It is truly right to bless you..."* On feasts of the Lord and the Theotokos, we sing the *eirmos/katavasia* of the ninth ode of the festal Orthros. When we celebrate BAS, we sing the hymn, *"All of creation rejoices in you..."*[400]

The Censing

Priest

At this point, the priest is given the censer. He censes three times before the Holy Table.[401] He holds the censer in his hand *as he continues praying the anaphora.* When he completes the commemorations of the dead ("Grant them rest, O our God, where the light of your countenance keeps watch"), he gives the censer back to the altar server. However, if a deacon is present, the priest gives him the censer when he completes the initial censing. The deacon then proceeds to and stands behind the Holy Table and censes quietly until the priest has completed the commemoration of the dead. While censing, the deacon also remembers in a low voice those whom he wishes of the dead and of the living.[402] (In earlier times the names of the living were commemorated after the commemoration of the local hierarch).[403]

The Antidoron

As the priest completes the commemorations of the dead and the living, the altar server brings him the antidoron while the chanter/choir is singing the megalynarion. The priest takes the tray(s) and raises it over the Holy Gifts saying, "Great is the name of the Holy Trinity, now and forever and to the ages

---

400 This hymn is from the Sunday Orthros: the period of the pl. fourth tone, the theotokion of the second kathisma.

401 What is the purpose of the censing at this point? Many assume it to be in honor of the consecrated Holy Gifts. But it is not. If it were, it would have occurred earlier, immediately after the consecration. The censing at this point is connected with the commemoration of the saints, who offer prayers on our behalf. The practice is based on the Book of Revelation: "And another angel came and stood at the altar with a golden censer; and he was given much incense to mingle with the prayers of all the saints upon the golden altar before the throne; and the smoke of the incense rose with the prayers of the saints from the hand of the angel before God" (Rev. 8:3-4; cf. 5:8). The censing is also offered in prayer for the deceased who rest among the just. For this same reason we offer incense at funerals and memorial services when we commemorate the names of the deceased. In current practice, the priest instinctively censes the gifts first before he begins the commemoration of the saints and the deceased as he holds the censer in his hand.

402 This is a remnant of an earlier practice, long since abandoned, when the deacon proclaimed aloud the diptychs of the dead.

403 See Trembelas, Τρεῖς Λειτουργίαι, 123.

of ages. Amen." He does not bless the antidoron with his hand nor does he touch the tray to the chalice. Technically, the antidoron is usually comprised of the remnants of the blessed bread(s) used at the Prothesis Rite.[404]

The Intercessions and Diptychs of the Anaphora

In the Byzantine tradition, the commemorations and intercessions in the anaphora begin with the dead – the saints and the deceased members of the community – who are prayed for appropriately. Immediately after the dead have been prayed for, the intercessions move to the living, praying for various categories of people, the needs of the world, and the many concerns and needs of the Church and her people.

The intercessions which conclude the anaphora have the same basic structure in CHR and BAS. The intercessions in CHR, however, are succinct while those in BAS are more comprehensive and inclusive. In fact, BAS presents us with one of the most beautiful and harmonious formulas of intercession. Unfortunately, the intercessions in both liturgies are rarely heard by the congregation because, according to current practice, they are usually said in a low voice while the megalynarion is being sung. All of this is done for the sake of brevity. This practice, however, diminishes the intercessory role of the Church and the people. According to the biblical admonition, we are expected to pray for one another and for the needs of the world (James 5:16; cf. 1 Thess. 5:25; Heb. 13:18; Luke 6:28).

Nothing and no one should escape the concern of the Church, because she is God's eternal witness, the sign of his Kingdom in the midst of the contradictions and anomalies of the fallen world.[405] The Church welcomes all and prays for all as intercessor in the image of the Lord Christ, the unique Mediator. The Church intercedes for all in order to heal the brokenness of the world and bring about everyone's return from the estrangement of their own authenticity. The image of the Church as intercessor is especially evident in the intercessions of the anaphora, and notably in the comprehensive intercessions of BAS. One could say that the intercessions in BAS constitute a roadmap or guide for robust pastoral activity. The intercessions also sensitize the hearts of the worshippers to the needs and hopes of people. The intercessions have the ability to break down barriers and inspire each congregant and the community as a whole to want to accomplish godly works (Matt. 5:16; cf. Ephes. 2:10; 1 Peter 2:12; 1 Tim. 6:17-19). For these reasons the intercessory part of the

---

[404] See Fountoulis, Ἀπαντήσεις εἰς Λειτουργικὰς Ἀπορίας, vol. 2, 19-23.

[405] See Calivas, *Aspects of Orthodox Worship*, 122-4.

anaphora should also be said aloud.

In the prevailing practice only two intercessions are said aloud, one for the hierarch and the other for the those whom each worshipper has in mind.

Priest

Among the first remember, Lord, our Archbishop (Name) – (Metropolitan or Bishop); grant him to your holy churches in peace...

This commemoration/intercession serves a twofold purpose. It is the sign by which the priest and the people acknowledge the authority of the hierarch as the chief shepherd of the local church and demonstrates their communion with him.[406]

If more than one priest is serving, the commemoration is intoned by all the priests in unison. If a hierarch is presiding, he will commemorate his immediate superior first. Then the priest(s) will commemorate the hierarch presiding at the liturgy.

Priest (or Deacon)

And remember those whom each one of us has in mind, and all the people.

People

And all the people (for each and all) – Καὶ πάντων καὶ πασῶν. (After this, the priest should pause briefly to allow the people time to remember in prayer those whom each has in mind).

A note on the Diptychs

Diptychs is the name of the two-leaved (=*diptychs*) folded tablet containing two lists of names, one of the living and the other of dead for whom prayers were said at the liturgy. The last ekphonesis, "And remember those whom each one of us has in mind," concludes not only the anaphoral intercessions but also the diptychs of the living, which were read aloud by the deacon, a practice which lasted through the eleventh century. Today, for the most part, the diptychs are recited aloud only at liturgies at which patriarchs and primates of churches preside and on other solemn occasions. In fact, the inclusion or exclusion of the name of the head of an autocephalous church from the diptychs of a local church is a sign of communion between the churches or the lack of. Each autocephalous church has its own official diptychs containing the proper

---

406 See Calivas, *Church, Clergy, Laity, and the Spiritual Life*, 22-9.

names of the dead and the living, including members of other local churches.[407]

A note on the Second Megalynarion.

The fairly recent practice by some chanters to sing a second megalynarion in honor of a particular feast at this point is totally unfounded and is of little value. It has no place in the service and should not be practiced.

Priest

continues praying the anaphoral intercessions in a low voice: Remember, Lord, this city in which we live...."

Priest

And grant that with one voice and one heart..." (The *ekphonesis* concludes the anaphora. It is the same in both CHR and BAS. At this point, if a deacon is present, he bows to the priest, exits the sanctuary from the north door and goes to the center of the solea to intone the pre-Communion petitions).

People

Amen.

Priest

And the mercies of our great God and Savior, Jesus Christ, be with all of you" (Titus 2:13; 2 John 3; 2 Peter 1:1), *while exclaiming this blessing, the priest moves just beyond the Holy Doors, faces the people and blesses them with his right hand in the usual manner.*

As the anaphora was introduced by an "apostolic blessing" so it ends with another. The blessing also acts as an introduction to the pre-Communion unit of the liturgy.

---

407 For the nature, origins, history, and liturgical use of the diptychs see the exhaustive study of Robert F. Taft, *A History of the Liturgy of St. John Chrysostom: The Diptychs*, Vol. IV (Rome 1991).

L. THE PRE-COMMUNION RITES

The pre-Communion rites contain several elements: a litany, a pre-communion prayer, the Lord's Prayer, the peace, and a prayer of inclination.

The Litany

Priest (or Deacon)

Having commemorated all the saints, again and again, in peace let us pray to the Lord.

People

Lord, have mercy.

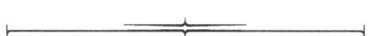

The pre-Communion litany in its present form contains twelve petitions, four of which constitute its primitive nucleus. The additional eight petitions, the Αἰτήσεις, are borrowed from the dismissal or completion litany and appear between the third and fourth petitions of the original nucleus. The Αἰτήσεις were interpolated into the original text perhaps as early as the fifth century and certainly by the eighth century because they are mentioned in the Barberini Codex. It has been argued by some that the introduction of the Αἰτήσεις into this litany was influenced by PRES, where they appear immediately after the Great Entrance and before Holy Communion. This theory, however, has been disputed by others. It has also been suggested that the petitions found their way into the pre-Communion rites as a result of infrequent Communion. It seems that many non-communicants would leave the service before Communion.[408] And the Αἰτήσεις served the role of transitioning them from the assembly into the world to attend to the affairs of daily life.

Even a cursory reading of the petitions indicates that the four original petitions are related to Holy Communion while the Αἰτήσεις are not. It is also uncharacteristic of the Byzantine liturgical tradition to use the exact same prayer or litany twice in the same service.[409] Besides, the practice of infrequent Communion has been overcome in recent years in most of our parishes and few people depart from the service before the apolysis.

---

408 See Robert F. Taft, *A History of the Liturgy of St. John Chrysostom: The Precommunion Rites* (Rome, 2000) 99-103. For more on the litany in PRES see Stefanos Alexopoulos, *The Presanctified Liturgy in the Byzantine Rite*, 236-46.

409 One may cite the Small Litany which is repeated several times in the liturgy and in other services. However, the core of each litany is not the call to prayer but the prayer itself and it is always different in each litany.

For these reasons, the Αἰτήσεις could (should) be omitted from the pre-Communion litany. In fact, the new bilingual edition of the Divine Liturgy approved by the GOA, though it contains the complete received version of the litany, the Αἰτήσεις are italicized and printed in a smaller font. They are also accompanied with a footnote that states, "These petitions were not originally included.... That is why they are rightly omitted today."[410]

The first petition is a call to prayer. It connects the present action with that which preceded it, namely, the remembrance or commemoration of the saints. The petition also acts as bridge. Having recalled the saints, their fervor and saintliness, the congregants are invited to focus their attention and prayer on the end purpose of the anaphora: the reception of the consecrated Holy Gifts. This end purpose is addressed in the second and third petitions, which in reality are not two but one, separated into two for emphasis. The priest bids the people to pray for the consecrated Holy Gifts, but for what purpose? The answer is in the third petition: "That our loving God, having accepted them at his holy and heavenly altar, may in return send down upon us the divine grace and the gift of the Holy Spirit." The last of the four original petitions hearkens back to the anaphora, reminding the people of what was asked for: "the unity of the faith and the communion of the Holy Spirit." It concludes with an invitation to all the people to commit or entrust their whole life to Christ, both as persons and as community. This ending is the same as the one in the Small Litany.

The Pre-Communion Prayer

In the extant manuscripts and most printed editions the pre-communion prayer is inserted between the Αἰτήσεις; it is introduced with the following rubric, "the priest bows and prays." The prayer was read in a low voice while the deacon intoned the petitions. The more recent editions of the Ieratikon, however, locate the prayer in its proper place, after the litany and before the Lord's Prayer. The same holds true for the pre-communion prayer in BAS and PRES. The purpose of these prayers is the same: the preparation of the clergy and the people for the reception of Holy Communion. The prayers, however, differ in content. The prayers in BAS and PRES are longer and more detailed.[411] The prayers in CHR and BAS share a common feature: they incorporate into the prayer elements from

---

410 *The Divine Liturgy of Saint John Chrysostom* (Brookline, MA 2015), 61. The Holy Cross faculty translation (1985) had already omitted them.

411 For the Pre-Communion Prayer in PRES see Alexopoulos, *Presanctified Liturgy*, 243-6. Alexopoulos argues convincingly that the prayer in PRES is based on the Prayer of the Proskomide and Pre-Communion Prayer of BAS.

their respective anaphora by reiterating the effects and benefits of Holy Communion.

The Pre-Communion prayer of CHR begins with an affirmation, "We entrust to you, loving Master, our whole life and hope," and a plea, "and we beseech, pray and entreat you: Grant us to partake of your heavenly and awesome Mysteries…with a clear conscience." The first three verbs in the plea are taken directly from the epiclesis, "παρακαλοῦμεν σε, δεόμεθα, καὶ ἱκετεύομεν." The awesome Mysteries are clearly identified as the consecrated Holy Gifts resting "at (on) this sacred and spiritual Table." The prayer further states the purpose for which one receives Communion and the effects of it: "for the remission of sins, forgiveness of transgressions, communion of the Holy Spirit, inheritance of the kingdom of heaven, boldness before you, and not unto judgment or condemnation." This is a reiteration of the effects of Holy Communion as stated in the anaphora. Missing from the list of gifts is "vigilance of soul," which has been replaced by the phrase, "a clear conscience." The list also contains a gift not recorded in the anaphora, "forgiveness of transgressions."[412]

The pre-Communion prayer in BAS is broader and more passionate. It starts with an acknowledgment that we do not know how to thank God appropriately. Thus, we ask him to "teach us to thank [him] properly for the benefits which [he] has performed and still performs for us." The prayer continues with a plea to God, who graciously accepted our offerings, to "purify us from every defilement of flesh and spirit, and to teach us how to perfect our sanctification in [his] fear."[413] The purpose of this is to be found worthy at every Eucharist to receive a portion of the Holy Gifts

---

412 Here, as in many other liturgical texts, we come upon various words or terms that describe the evil inclinations of the heart (Gen.6:5; cf. Jer. 16:12, 17:9-10, 18:12) and the wrongful deeds (sins) we commit willfully or in ignorance which defile us and separate us from the holiness and goodness of God. Sin is born of temptations that come from within or are prompted by another person(s) or by some circumstance. The decision to act wrongfully is fed by self-deceit and the rationalizations we devise to support our rebellious spirit. The words that describe these inclinations include the general term, sin – **ἁμαρτία** (which means to miss the mark, to go astray, to fail) and several other terms such as: transgressions (to break or defy the law = πλημμελήματα, παραπτώματα, παραβάσεις); trespasses (παραβάσεις); debts (ὀφειλήματα); offences (πλημμελήματα); iniquities (ἀνομίαι, ἀδικίαι); errors, failings, mistakes (ἀγνοήματα, παραπτώματα); disobedience (παρακοή); infidelity (ἀπιστία); guilt (ἐνοχή).

413 The introductory words of the prayer proclaim rightly that our salvation depends on God. Yet, salvation cannot be forced on us. It is accomplished only through the exercise of two essential but unequal wills, the divine and the human. We are not passive or powerless spectators in the unfolding mystery of the divine economy but active participants – we are God's fellow-workers. Every person is a work in progress. Hence, we pray daily: "Lord, give us grace and power to perfect our salvation in fear and trembling through the help of your Christ" (Sixth Prayer of the Orthros).

with a pure conscience,[414] *so that we may be united with the Holy Body and Blood of the Father's Only-begotten Son, our Lord Jesus Christ, thus sharing in his life. The reception of the Holy Gifts bestows on us two gifts: Christ comes to dwell in our hearts so that our bodies may become the temple of the Holy Spirit. The prayer then sets forth the Pauline warnings. It turns us inwardly to see and address our many weaknesses and errors so that we may humbly turn to God to ask him "to let none of us be guilty of these... nor be infirm in soul and body by partaking of the [Mysteries] unworthily. "Enable us," we continue, even to our last breath, to receive the Holy Gifts worthily, "as a support on the road to eternal life and an acceptable defense at the dread judgment seat of your Christ." Here, we are brought before the end times to contemplate the final judgment. Reiterating partially themes of the anaphora, we pray: "that we also, together with all the saints...may become partakers of eternal good things, which [God] has prepared for those who love [him]."*

The pre-communion prayer in both CHR, BAS, and PRES does not end in the usual manner, with a doxological ekfonesis. Instead, the prayer ends with another petition – a fervent plea that we may be made worthy to dare call the God of heaven, Father, and to say the Lord's Prayer.[415] *Thus the Lord's Prayer is incorporated into and completes the pre-Communion prayer.*

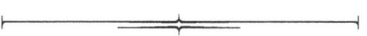

---

414 Corruptive behavior is a betrayal of both the faith and the ethical teachings of the Church and jeopardizes one's standing with the Church. As someone once said, "It is not sin that renders the Eucharist inadmissible but the attachment to sin and the refusal of the medicine of immortality." Saint Basil was asked once, "Which is the greatest sin?" And he replied, "The one that enslaves you." Before approaching Communion, we must examine and listen to our conscience. It is our guardian. It knows all our secrets and shows us the things we must uproot. When we heed our conscience, we fulfill Christ's commandments. See St. Isaiah the Solitary (+491) "On Guarding the Intellect: Twenty-Seven Texts;" and St. Mark the Ascetic (early fifth century), "On those who think that they are made righteous by works: two hundred and twenty–six texts," in *The Philokalia*, Vol. I (London and Boston 1979), 21-8 and 125-46 respectively.

415 Interestingly, the plea repeats two themes which are mentioned in the pre-communion prayers and are also listed among the fruits or gifts of Communion: filial confidence or boldness (παρρησία), and freedom from judgment (ἀκατακρίτως).

Priest

And make us worthy, Master, with confidence (παρρησία) and without fear of condemnation (ἀκατακρίτως), to dare call you, the heavenly God, as Father, and to say... [the Lord's Prayer].

People

Recite the Lord's Prayer.

The Lord's Prayer

The earliest witness to the use of the Lord's Prayer in worship, apart from the New Testament, is found in The Didache of the Twelve Apostles.[416] In addition to the text of the prayer in its Matthean redaction, the Didache also includes a rubric instructing the people to recite the prayer thrice daily. "And do not pray as the hypocrites, but as the Lord directed in his Gospel, 'thus shall you pray: Our Father...for thine is the power and the glory forever.' Three times in the day pray thus."[417]

There is no direct evidence for when exactly the Lord's Prayer was incorporated into the Divine Liturgy as part of the pre-communion rites. Saint Justin the Martyr (ca. 150) makes no mention of the prayer in his description of the Eucharist in his First Apology (ch. 65, 66 and 67). The first to mention the use of the Lord's Prayer in the pre-communion rites is St. Cyril of Jerusalem (+386). He writes, "Then, after these things [the anaphora], we say that prayer which the Savior delivered to his own disciples, with a pure conscience styling God our Father.... After this the priest says, Τὰ ἅγια τοῖς ἁγίοις."[418] By the end of the fourth century the Lord's Prayer is found in the pre-communion rites of all the ancient liturgies of the East.[419]

---

416 The version of the Lord's Prayer with which we are familiar is recorded in the Gospel of Matthew (6:9-13). A slightly different and shorter version is found in the Gospel of Luke (11:1-4). In both versions the familiar concluding doxology is missing, as it is in the *Mystagogical Catechesis* of St. Cyril of Jerusalem. However, a form of the doxology is found in a few ancient mss of Matthew and in the *Didache*.

417 *Didache*, 8:2.

418 *Mystagogical Catechesis*, V: 11-8. St. Cyril also provides us with a brief explanation of the introduction and the seven requests of the prayer.

419 On the use of the Lord's Prayer in the Eucharist see Taft, *Precommunion Rites*, 129-54. On its meaning see, among others, Alexander Schmemann, *Our Father* (Crestwood, NY 2002) and Joachim Jeremias, *The Lord's Prayer* (Philadelphia 1964).

Several theories have been proposed to explain the appearance and place of the Lord's Prayer in the Divine Liturgy. One theory is related to the baptismal rites. According to the Apostolic Constitutions (Book 7:45), the newly-baptized recited the Lord's Prayer immediately after their baptism and the anointing with Holy Chrism and just before their participation in the Eucharist. Having attained the gift of adoption and sonship through baptism and chrismation and instilled with filial courage and boldness, the neophytes were now able to address the God of heaven as Father. Gradually, the Lord's Prayer passed into the Divine Liturgy and was integrated into the pre-communion rites so that it may be recited by all the congregants in preparation for the reception of Holy Communion. This was considered especially appropriate since the Lord's Prayer was understood as a summary of the entire Gospel and a source for the continual upbuilding of Christian faith and morals.[420]

Others have suggested that several requests in the prayer commended its assignment to the pre-communion rites. St. Cyril of Jerusalem, for example, connects the request for our "daily bread" to the Bread of the Eucharist. "This common bread is not super-substantial bread, but this Holy Bread is super-substantial, that is, appointed for the substance of the soul. For this Bread does not go into the belly to be cast out into the draught, but is diffused through all of you, for the benefit of body and soul…."[421]

The Lord's Prayer is also a reminder of the dominical admonition. Jesus said, "Man shall not live by bread alone, but by every word that proceeds from the mouth of God" (Matt. 4:4). The bread we eat daily is essential for our biological existence but is unable to satisfy our deepest longings and hunger. Only the Living Bread can do that (John 6:48-58).

Forgiving and receiving forgiveness are essential prerequisites for the worthy reception of Holy Communion as is the desire to live a godly life in all earnestness. These requirements are addressed in the Lord's Prayer. We pray that the God of heaven will forgive us our sins as we commit to open our hearts to forgive those who sin against us. We also pray to be delivered from the machinations of the evil one – from the temptations that weaken our will and lead us astray. Hence, we can say that the Lord's Prayer "seems to have entered the pre-communion rite as a prayer for forgiveness and reconciliation in preparation for Communion."[422]

---

420 See Taft, *Precommunion Rites* 141-5.

421 Cyril of Jerusalem, *Mystagogical Catechesis*, V:15.

422 Taft, *Precommunion Rites*, 195.

That the Lord's Prayer is found in the account of the Eucharist preserved by St. Cyril of Jerusalem, it is safe to assume that it was already part of the liturgy well before the latter part of the fourth century.

The Doxology of the Lord's Prayer

As noted earlier, the Matthean and Lucan versions of the Lord's Prayer do not contain a doxological ending. In fact, the doxology in some mss of Matthew is, as some have noted, of liturgical origin and an interpolation into the text.[423] The editors of the Orthodox Study Bible have inserted the better-known version of the doxology into the text of Matthew: ""Ὅτι σοῦ ἐστὶν ἡ βασιλεία καὶ ἡ δύναμις καὶ ἡ δόξα εἰς τοὺς αἰῶνας. Ἀμήν.... For yours is the kingdom and the power and the glory forever. Amen."

By the eighth century, if not much earlier, the doxology was further amplified with the addition of the names of the Holy Trinity.[424] This new formula with its trinitarian character has come down to us and continues to be recited or intoned as the ekfonesis of the Lord's Prayer: ""Ὅτι σοῦ ἐστὶν ἡ βασιλεία καὶ ἡ δύναμις καὶ ἡ δόξα, τοῦ Πατρὸς καὶ τοῦ Υἱοῦ καὶ τοῦ Ἁγίου Πνεύματος, νῦν καὶ ἀεὶ καὶ εἰς τοὺς αἰῶνας τῶν αἰώνων. Ἀμήν... For yours is the kingdom and the power and the glory, of the Father and the Son and the Holy Spirit, now and forever and to the ages of ages. Amen.

---

423 *Ibid.* 151.

424 See the text of BAS in the *Barberini Codex* in Parenti and Velkovska, *L'Eucologio Barberini gr. 336*, 20.

The Peace and the Prayer of Inclination

The greeting, bidding, and prayer that follow are consistent with the Byzantine liturgical tradition which calls for a blessing at the end of a service or a unit of a service. The pre-communion unit ends with this three-fold action. There is evidence that the celebrant raised and extended his hand over the people as he read the prayer of blessing at the conclusion of a service. As Taft tells it, CHR and BAS had three such blessings: the first concluded the Liturgy of the Word, which disappeared from the service long ago.[425] The third, and final blessing, exists in a different form, that which we know as the Prayer Behind the Ambo (Ὀπισθάμβωνος εὐχή). The second prayer is found at the conclusion of the pre-communion rite. Its place in all three liturgies has been preserved but not without a problem in CHR.

Priest

Peace be to all.

People

And to your spirit.

Priest (or Deacon)

Let us bow our heads to the Lord.

People

To you, O Lord.

Priest

Recites the Pre-Communion Prayer:

"We give thanks to you, invisible King…" **(CHR)**

or

"Master, Lord, Father of compassions and God of every consolation…" **(BAS)**

Priest

The ekphonesis, "Through the grace, compassion, and love for humankind…"

---

425 Taft, *Precommunion Rites*, 157

By comparing the text of the Prayer of Inclination in CHR with that of BAS, PRES, and JAMES it can be shown that it is not in harmony with the occasion – preparation for Holy Communion.[426]

As I have noted elsewhere, to understand the problem with the prayer in CHR we have to clarify the meaning of two key words in the original Greek: the noun προκείμενα and the verb ἐξομάλισον (ἐξομαλίζω).[427] *The noun προκείμενα (plural) has several meanings. In this prayer it could refer to the circumstances of life that lie before (ahead) or it could refer to that which has been set before us. Some have understood the word to mean the latter, and therefore believe that it refers to the Gifts that are set before us on the Holy Table.*

However, this interpretation fails to take into account two things. First, in our liturgical texts the word προκείμενα never appears alone when it used to refer to the Holy Gifts. It is accompanied by one or more words, such as τὰ προκείμενα δῶρα. Second, the word ἐξομάλισον, which means to make smooth, precludes us from interpreting προκείμενα to mean the Holy Gifts. To do so would necessitate a change in the meaning of the verb, as some translators have done, in order to justify the prayers position in the pre-communion rites.

Correctly understood and translated, the prayer reads as follows: "Therefore, Master, make smooth and beneficial for us all, whatever lies ahead, according to the need of each: sail with those who sail…."

With all of the above in mind, we may conclude that the prayer in CHR is unrelated to the reception of Holy Communion; it makes no reference to the Eucharist or to Communion. The question, however, remains. Why was it placed at this point? It has been suggested that the word προκείμενα was, at some point in time, misapplied to the eucharistic elements and resulted in its placement in the pre-communion rites. Taft on the other hand proposes a different, more persuasive explanation. The prayer was intended to meet a new need: the withdrawal of non-communicants from the liturgy before the distribution of Communion.

The gradual decline in the reception of Holy Communion in Late Antiquity eventually introduced a hitherto unfamiliar distinction in the eucharistic assembly: communicants and non-communicants, which is to say, people who attend the Divine Liturgy but do not receive the Holy Mysteries and those who do. Because the distribution of Communion took a fair amount of time, many non-communicants apparently were leaving the church before the final dismissal. Liturgical decorum, however, demands

---

426 For more on the prayer see *Ibid.* 155-97.

427 See Calivas, *Aspects of Orthodox Worship*, 222-5.

that no one leave the assembly without being properly dismissed. The Inclination Prayer in CHR appears to be a prayer of blessing for the non-communicants, thereby putting order into their casual departure from the assembly.

Whatever the reason for the existence of this prayer in the pre-communion rites, one thing is clear: it is unsuitable for the purpose for which it is placed in this position. Also, few people today leave before the conclusion of the service. It is, therefore, appropriate to suggest that at some point in the liturgical renewal process attention be given to this prayer. To meet its purpose the prayer could be modified appropriately, or a new prayer could be composed, or it could be replaced with the pre-communion prayer of BAS. Already, as we have seen, several prayers of CHR have been borrowed from BAS. However, until such time, we are obliged to continue praying the prayer in the received text.

The received prayer, however, should not be completely discarded; its contents are meaningful. In fact, the intercessory part of the prayer with which it concludes could be amplified to include additional petitions for the needs of the people. It could be reformulated so that it may be included in the repertoire of Prayers Behind the Ambo, the collection of which exists in mss and in some printed editions of the liturgy. But more will be said about these prayers below.

M. THE COMMUNION RITES

This unit of the Divine Liturgy contains several elements, starting with a Communion prayer, which is addressed to Christ. The same prayer is found in all three Divine Liturgies of the Constantinopolitan or Byzantine Rite.[428]

Priest

Recites the Communion prayer: Lord Jesus Christ, our God, hear us from your holy dwelling place and from the glorious throne of your kingdom. You are enthroned on high with the Father and are also invisibly present among us. Come and sanctify us, and let your pure Body and precious Blood be given to us by your mighty hand and through us to all your people.

Priest (or Deacon)

Let us be attentive.

---

[428] For a full discussion on the Communion rites see Taft, *Precommunion Rites*, 199-526 and his *The Communion, Thanksgiving and Concluding Rites*, vol. VI (Rome, 2008).

Priest

Bows reverently and with deep awe holds the Lamb with the thumb, index and middle fingers of both hands and elevates it saying, "The Holy Gifts for the holy people of God – Τὰ Ἅγια τοῖς ἁγίοις."

People

Sing the hymn, "One is Holy, one is Lord, Jesus Christ, to the glory of God the Father. Amen."

People

Sing the assigned Communion (Κοινωνικόν) hymn.

As the people sing the Communion Hymn the priest prepares the Holy Gifts for distribution through a series of manual acts. The clergy partake of the Holy Gifts first within the sanctuary. But first, a few comments on the elements that comprise the Communion rites.

The Communion Prayer

In his description of the Divine Liturgy, St. Cyril of Jerusalem makes no mention of a Communion prayer at this point in the service. After the Lord's Prayer, he tells us that the priest immediately exclaimed, "Τὰ Ἅγια τοῖς ἁγίοις." However, by the mid-eighth century, as evidenced by the *Barberini Codex*, this particular prayer was already part of the Communion rites in all three liturgies: BAS, CHR, and PRES. It has been suggested that the prayer was interpolated first into BAS as early as the seventh century and from BAS it passed into CHR and PRES. In fact, in the *Barberini Codex*, the prayer in BAS bears the title, "Prayer of the Elevation of the Bread," even though there is no mention of the elevation in the text. The title probably came about when the prayer was inserted into the liturgy just before the elevation and because in some mss the priest is instructed to read the prayer while holding the Amnos aloft at the elevation.[429] Essentially, the prayer is a communion prayer and contains several powerful images.

The prayer is addressed to our Lord Jesus Christ, exalted and enthroned on high with the Father. He is implored to come down from his holy dwelling place and throne of glory so that he may sanctify his people. Though enthroned on high, he is nonetheless simultaneously present invisibly among his gathered people as he promised, "Lo, I am with you always" (Matt. 28:20; cf. Matt. 18:20). Given that he is the one who is offered and at the same time the one who offers, he is beseeched, as the true celebrant of the mysteries, to grant communion of his

---

429 See Trembelas, *Τρεῖς Λειτουργίαι*, 131.

most pure Body and Blood by his mighty hand to the celebrants and through them to all the people.[430] The last image accentuates the fact that Communion is a gift offered by Christ himself. Hence Communion is not "taken" but "received."

The Elevation – ἡ "Ὕψωσις – and its Significance

The elevation is preceded by an admonition, "Πρόσχωμεν – *Let us be attentive*," which is pronounced by the deacon or, in the absence of one, by the priest.[431] Everyone is called to attention, to be still. Everyone is called to set their minds on the great mystery because the moment for Communion is at hand.

The rubrics for the ritual act are simple. First, the priest is told to bow three times as he repeats the words of the Publican, "*Ὁ Θεὸς ἱλάσθητί μοι τῷ ἁμαρτωλῷ – God, be merciful to me a sinner.*" After this, the priest is told to hold the Lamb with both hands and to raise or hold it aloft. Some mss and printed editions of the Ieratikon include more precise details: "The priest takes up the Holy Bread (the Lamb) in both hands," or "The priest lifts the Lamb holding it with the three fingers of both hands [thumb and two fingers]."[432] The priest is also told to perform the act with deep reverence. The elevation of the Lamb had become a fixed ritual of the liturgy by the end of the fourth century, if not earlier.

The rubrics do not regulate how high the Holy Gifts are raised. They simply state, "The priest lifts/raises (ὑψοῖ) the Lamb." We learn from the sources that the ritual served a specific purpose. Together with the accompanying exclamation, "Τὰ Ἅγια τοῖς ἁγίοις – *The Holy Gifts for the Holy People of God,*" the elevation of the Amnos constituted the original invitation or call to Communion.

---

430 The event of the feeding of the multitude, which has eucharistic connotations, provides us with similar imagery: "and taking the five loaves and the two fish he looked up to heaven and blessed, and broke and gave the loaves to the disciples and the disciples gave them to the crowds" (Matt. 14:19; cf. Mark 6:41, Luke 9:16).

431 In the early mss, prior to the elevation, the deacon is instructed to place his orarion crosswise around himself, front and back. The *Diataxeis of Philotheos Kokkinos* on the other hand places the act just prior to Communion. Modern *Ieratika* give the rubric well before the elevation, at the Lord's Prayer. This is the least suitable place because it becomes a distraction to the congregation. It is best for the deacon to perform this act immediately after he has reentered the sanctuary. The act is clearly utilitarian in nature; it gives the deacon greater freedom to perform the manual acts of the Communion rites. As it usually happens, attempts have been made to interpret the act symbolically.

432 In some later rubrics the priest is instructed to lift the Lamb and make the sign of the cross with it over the discos. Such an act, however, has no meaning or purpose.

In order to emphasize the invitation, the Amnos was lifted and shown to the people.[433] The act of "showing the Amnos" lasted, at least, through the fourteenth century. Cabasilas mentions it in his *Commentary* (4: 36), "He [the priest] takes the Bread of Life, *and showing it to the people*, summons those who are worthy to receive it fittingly."[434] However, as the frequency of Communion diminished the reason for showing the Lamb was gradually forgotten.[435] In current practice, the elevation is barely visible to the people, if at all; its purpose and meaning have been lost on both the clergy and the people. It would be beneficial for the people to be reminded of the meaning of the elevation and the words that attend it.

Personal preparedness

The decline in frequent Communion came about gradually. Following the peace of Constantine, the awesome sacredness of Communion was increasingly emphasized over and against the personal worthiness of the communicant, a concept that found its way into liturgical texts: "It [Communion]is a burning coal that sears the unworthy." In addition to one's inner preparation and the observance of the Eucharistic fast (to eat nothing from the last meal of the day to the time of Communion), additional external ascetical expressions of piety were also promoted as essential for participation in the sacrament. These included strict fast rules, abstinence from sexual intercourse, compulsory confession, and other devotional acts. Some have suggested that the strong emphasis on personal worthiness deterred many, fearful of condemnation, from receiving frequently. The strict fast rules led many to connect Communion with the great fast periods of the year (Great Lent/Holy Week, the fast of the Apostles, the Dormition fast, and the fast of Christmas which slowly expanded to forty days). Thus was born the idea that Communion should be received four times or less a year.

Happily, in our days, thanks to the reemergence of devotional piety centered on the Eucharist, many families have espoused the practice of frequent Communion.

Of course, the challenge before every communicant is to maintain a deep reverence for and have a clear understanding of what Holy Communion is and means. The reception of Communion should not be reduced to an empty habit, a hollow custom. Adults and even children – in language and imagery proper to their age – should be taught to value Communion as an extraordinary event, an act of faith, and a wondrous gift that is given freely by God and

---

433 See Trembelas, Τρεῖς Λειτουργίαι, 131.

434 It is not clear from the sources how the Amnos was shown to the people. Most probably, the celebrant held it aloft in a way that avoided spillage.

435 See Calivas, *Church, Clergy, Laity, and the Spiritual Life*, 115-8; and 124-8.

not something one earns. The basic preparation for Communion is the daily struggle to bring one's will freely into conformity with the divine will and to love in a way that enables us to identify with Christ and with the sufferings of the least among us.

Not for adoration but for consumption

The elevation of the Amnos should not be interpreted as a form of eucharistic adoration. The Orthodox Church does not practice eucharistic adoration, at least not as it is understood and practiced in the Roman Church – as an extra-liturgical devotional practice.[436] The consecrated Holy Gifts are presented and offered not for adoration but for consumption: "Take eat...Drink of this...." Nevertheless, Orthodox Christians know intuitively the awesome, sacred character of the Holy Gifts. In their presence they bow and cross themselves reverently fully aware of their sacred identity – the Body and Blood of Christ.

Not a blessing object

On another note, as already mentioned, the Holy Gifts should never be thought of or used as a blessing "object." The clergy should avoid making the sign of the cross with the Gifts over the people at the Great Entrance or when exhibiting the chalice before and after Communion.

Τὰ Ἅγια τοῖς ἁγίοις

The manual act of elevating the Lamb is accompanied by the words, "*Τὰ Ἅγια τοῖς ἁγίοις – The Holy Gifts for the Holy People of God.*" The exclamation, spoken reverently by the priest as he lifts the Lamb, is both an invitation and a warning.

The exclamation summons the faithful to Communion, to partake of the "*holy things – τὰ ἅγια.*" The "holy things" are none other than the Holy Gifts: the gifts of bread and wine prepared and offered to God by the people in praise of and in thanksgiving for his mighty acts. They are the gifts which God receives and consecrates and are offered back to us for the forgiveness of sins and life eternal.

We offer up human food – the emblems of our humanity – in order to receive the Food of Life, the Body and Blood of the incarnate Son of God (John 6:55-59). In exchange for our fleeting mortal life we receive and partake of the divine life (2 Peter 1:4); we are given the gifts of incorruptibility and immortality. "Then Jesus said to them, Truly, truly, I say to you, unless you eat the flesh of the Son of Man and drink his blood, you have no life in you; he who eats my

---

[436] Eucharistic adoration is practiced by Roman Catholics, at least since the sixteenth century, in the belief that the consecrated reserved host encased in a monstrance is truly the Body of Christ and therefore of his real presence. Eucharistic adoration is an extra-liturgical devotional practice.

flesh and drinks my blood has eternal life, and I will raise him up at the last day" (John 6:53-54).

The invitation to Communion is simultaneously a warning. The "holy things" are for the "*holy ones - τοῖς ἁγίοις.*" The unworthy are advised to stay away. "Let not everyone come to receive," writes Cabasilas in his *Commentary* (4: 36), "but only those who are worthy, for holy things are for the holy only." Or as the plea in one of the private devotional pre-communion prayers says, "let not these Holy Gifts be to my judgment because I am unworthy...."

This cautionary approach to Communion was known and practiced from the start. St. Paul, for example, makes reference to it when he wrote these words to the Corinthians: "Whoever eats the bread and drinks the cup of the Lord in an unworthy manner will be guilty of profaning the body and blood of the Lord.... For anyone who eats and drinks without discerning the body eats and drinks judgment upon himself" (1 Cor. 11:27, 29). And he continued, "Let a man examine himself, and so eat of the bread and drink of the cup" (1 Cor. 11:28). A similar warning is embedded in the anaphora. We read in CHR, "So that [these Holy Gifts] may be for those who partake of them for vigilance of soul...[and] not for judgment or condemnation." Or as it is said in BAS, "Grant that none of us may partake of the holy Body and Blood of your Christ for judgment or condemnation."

But Who are the Holy Ones, the ἅγιοι, to whom Communion is Given?[437]

From the earliest days the term *saints - ἅγιοι,* as we know from the Epistles of St. Paul and others, was applied to the faithful, to those set apart by baptism who conscientiously strive to live their lives in accordance with the will of God. Here is how Cabasilas explains it. "Those whom the priest calls holy are not only those who have attained perfection, but those also who are striving for it without having yet obtained it.... The faithful are called saints because of the holy thing of which they partake, because of him whose Body and Blood they receive.... As long as we remain united to him and preserve our connection with him, we live by holiness, drawing to ourselves, through the Holy Mysteries the sanctity which comes from that Head and that Heart. But if we should cut ourselves off, if we should separate ourselves from the unity of this most holy Body, we partake of the Holy Mysteries in vain, for life cannot flow into dead and amputated limbs."[438]

---

437 See Taft, *Precommunion Rites*, 234-40.

438 Cabasilas, *Commentary*, 4:36.

Who Then Can Receive Holy Communion?

Saint Justin the Martyr (ca. 150) gives the following concise response: "This food we call eucharist, and no one may share it unless he believes that our teaching is true, and has been cleansed in the bath of forgiveness for sin and of rebirth, and lives as Christ taught."[439] According to this ancient maxim, to partake of the Holy Mysteries one must be baptized, espouse the faith of the Church, and walk in the newness of life (Rom 6:4). Or, as Cabasilas, puts it: "Christians, if they have not committed [mortal] sins as would cut them off from Christ and bring death, are in no way prevented, when partaking of the Holy Mysteries, from receiving sanctification, not in name alone, but in fact, since they continue to be living members united to the Head."[440]

Cabasilas' words, in part, are based on 1 John 5:16-17. The Apostle, Evangelist and Theologian John distinguishes between two kinds of sin, those which do not lead to death and those which do (mortal sins). The former, even when repugnant, are forgiven. The deadly mortal sins, however, are beyond forgiveness, not because God is incapable of forgiving them, but because the transgressors are in a continual and willful state of denial and disobedience; they deliberately reject the truth, love, and grace of God; they blaspheme against the Holy Spirit (Matt. 12:31-33).

One is Holy, one is Lord, Jesus Christ...

The invitation to Communion requires a proper response. Byzantine and ecclesial etiquette demands it. In light of our human weaknesses, frailties, and failings there could be only one, simple, direct, and appropriate response: "One alone is holy." Indeed, as Cabasilas tells it, "No one has holiness of himself. It is not the consequence of human virtue but comes to all from [God] and through him."[441] The response includes a Christological formula which affirms the divinity of Christ: "One is Holy, one is Lord, Jesus Christ, to the glory of God the Father. Amen."[442]

We believe and confess in the Creed that the Church is holy, even though she is not yet perfect. The holiness of the Church, however, is not derived from, nor is it dependent upon, the moral and pious life of its members, but from it being the mystical Body of Christ. The Church is holy because its Lord is holy. The Church is holy because it is the event of truth and the fact of the incarnation of

---

[439] Justin, *Apologia* 1:65-6. Note Justin's use of the word eucharist. It identifies both the sacred service and the sacramental elements – "this food we call eucharist."

[440] Cabasilas, *Commentary*, 4:36.

[441] Ibid.

[442] A similar Christological formula is found in the Great Doxology, "For you alone are holy, you alone are Lord, Jesus Christ, to the glory of God the Father. Amen."

the Son of God. Through the Church God calls all human beings to repentance and bestows upon them the gift of sanctification. Until the Final Judgment, the righteous as well as the sinful are included in the Church. Every member of the Church is a work in progress. Everyone, as Metropolitan John Zizioulas tells it, "is a potential saint, even if he appears to have been or continues to be a sinner."[443] Every believing member of the Church, however deficient or feeble their faith and inner life may be, still bears a trace of holiness, however faint. Everyone has the capacity to grow. It is incumbent upon us to reach out in order to help them grow their faith and strengthen their conscience. (Cf. Matt. 13:23; Mark 4:8; John 14:22).

The response, "One is Holy," was added to the pre-communion rites in the fourth century, if not earlier. The Christological formula is based on Phil 2:11, "Jesus Christ is Lord, to the glory of God the Father." The response includes a concluding "Amen" and an opening affirmation, "One is holy" the exact origins of which are unclear, although we meet the title "Holy One of Israel," in the Old Testament.[444]

The Communion Hymn – Τὸ Κοινωνικόν – Koinonikon

Immediately after the call to Communion, the people sing the Koinonikon during which the priest performs several manual acts.

In current practice the Communion hymn is comprised of one or two biblical verses, most often from a psalm, ending with a triple Alleluia.[445] Basically, the *Koinonikon* covers the manual actions and communion of the clergy and, after the call to communion is announced, the communion of the people. While it serves a utilitarian function in the first instance, the essential purpose of the koinonikon is to prepare the minds and hearts of the faithful for the reception of the Holy Mysteries. In time, a new type of koinonikon was also introduced. It was and is sung on major feast days, the aim of which is to connect and associate the reception of Communion to a given feast. This connection, however, is not always evident.

---

443 Metropolitan John Zizioulas, "Communion and Otherness," in *SVTQ*, 38, 4 (1994), 354. Elsewhere, he makes the same point. "The Church *depicts* the end time in history.... The Church in history is clearly not identical with the kingdom of God. The trauma of history means that along with the rest of the world, Christians struggle with evil, and the way of the cross is this struggle. The Church is not the society of those who have overcome evil but of those who are struggling against evil. The holy Church is full of sinners, being made holy. Therefore, we must say that the kingdom of God is *depicted* in the Church. This iconological ontology is key." In *John D. Zizioulas: Lectures in Christian Dogmatics*, Douglas H. Knight, ed. (London 2008), 136.

444 See Taft, *Precommunion Rites*, 246-48. The title "Holy One of Israel," is found in: 2 Kings 19:22; Isaiah 1:4, 10:22, 12:6, and 41:14; Jeramiah 50:29; Psalm 71:22; and Psalm 89:18.

445 On the joyful, celebratory, and doxological nature of the Alleluia see Fountoulis, Ἀπαντήσεις εἰς Λειτουργικὰς Ἀπορίας, vol. 5 (Athens 2003), 32-42.

In ages past, the principal koinonikon of the Jerusalem Church was Psalm 33/34 with verse 8 serving as the response, "Taste and see that the Lord is good."[446] As for Constantinople, Psalm 148:1 served as the original fixed koinonikon with "Alleluia" as the response.[447] In fact, to this day Psalm 148, because of its doxological character, is the common Sunday koinonikon. Gradually, Constantinople added three other psalms to form a broader basic repertory: Psalm 33/34:8 for PRES; Psalm 115/116:13 for Marian feasts; and Psalm 32/33:1 for the feasts of saints.[448] By the tenth century the repertory was expanded to include twenty-two koinonika for Sundays and feast days.[449] Of the several Communion hymns only two are non-biblical: the koinonika of Holy Thursday and Holy Pascha. These are ecclesial compositions.[450]

Originally, the koinonikon was a full psalm, the verses of which were sung by the chanter and the assigned refrain or response by the people. The response sung by the people came to be identified as the koinonikon.[451] By the twelfth century the koinonikon was no longer a full psalm but the single verse of the psalm, which initially was the response sung by the people.

---

446 For example, St. Cyril of Jerusalem notes the following in his *Mystagogical Catechesis* (V, 20): "After this you hear the chanter with a sacred melody inviting you to the communion of the Holy Mysteries, and saying, *O taste and see that the Lord is good.*" This is also the *Koinonikon* in PRES.

447 See Taft, *Precommunion Rites*, 305.

448 *Ibid.*

449 For a list of the psalms in the repertory see Taft, *Precommunion Rites*, 302-307. See also pages 264-267 for the list of the common koinonika and the koinonika of the fixed and movable cycle of feasts in the received tradition which is based on the original repertory of twenty-two koinonika. One can also find a list of the common koinonika based on the weekly calendar of feasts in the introductory part of the Apostolos. The Apostolos also contains the koinonikon of a particular feast at the end of the assigned pericope of the feast. The koinonikon for a given feast is also found in the *Typikon*, the digests of the *Typikon*, and in the liturgical books in which the service of the feast is contained. See Fountoulis, Ἀπαντήσεις, vol. 4, 90-7, in which he provides a list of the twenty principal koinonika and their use in the liturgy. Also, Trembelas, Τρεῖς Λειτουργίαι, 147-8.

450 The Holy Thursday koinonikon, "*Receive me today as a partaker of your Mystical Supper ... Τοῦ Δείπνου σου τοῦ Μυστικοῦ...*" is also used as a private pre-communion prayer. It should be noted that some Greek versions have interpolated the words, ὅταν ἔλθῃς – *when you come*, into the last phrase of the hymn. This addition is not supported by the sources and first appeared in a manuscript of the sixteenth century. The last phrase should read: "remember me, Lord, in your kingdom." The Paschal koinonikon is, "*Receive the Body of Christ, taste of the immortal source (fount, spring), alleluia – Σῶμα Χριστοῦ μεταλάβετε, πηγῆς ἀθανάτου γεύσασθε. Ἀλληλούϊα.*"

451 On the history of the koinonikon see Taft, *Precommunion Rites*, 262-318.

Today, the koinonikon is sung by the chanter or choir several times, usually in a slow melodic form. When there are many lay communicants, it has become customary in the Greek practice during the Communion of the people to sing the troparion/koinonikon of Holy Thursday, *"Τοῦ Δείπνου σου τοῦ Μυστικοῦ,"* in place of the regular koinonikon. This practice is a late development and requires further review.

Looking forward to the time when liturgical reforms are seriously contemplated, a comment of Fr. Taft bears repeating. He wrote, "In modern times, pastoral efforts have led to an increase in the frequency of communion. But only in a few places has it dawned on anyone to restore the original popular communion psalmody. Instead, various less than satisfactory stratagems are employed to "cover" the distribution of communion with less suitable chants."[452] The late eminent liturgist, Professor Ioannis Fountoulis, expressed similar sentiments, with which I also agree.[453]

---

452 Taft, *Precommunion Rites*, 318.

453 Fountoulis, Ἀπαντήσεις, vol. 4, 94-6. Tradition provides us with ample examples of additional suitable koinonika, which may be used alternately during the Communion of the people; verses that can be easily learned by chanters, choirs, and the people. The process should begin with the restoration of a full psalm, the verses of which would be sung by the precentor. The "main" verse, the koinonikon, would be sung by the choir and the people antiphonally, after each verse or group of verses. Fountoulis suggests the following psalms: Psalm 22/23:5 ("You prepare a table before me…"); Psalm 33/34:8 ("Taste and see…."); Psalm 33/34:5 ("They looked to him and were radiant…"); Psalm 144/145:15 ("the eyes of all look expectantly to you, and you give them their food…").

The Manual Acts Performed by the Priest

Immediately after the elevation and before Communion, the priest kisses the Amnos[454] and enacts four manual acts: the fraction, the commingling or union, the zeon, and the comminution.

The Fraction – ἡ κλᾶσις – ὁ μελισμός[455]

All three Liturgies, BAS, CHR, and PRES, and for that matter all classical eucharistic rites, include a fraction or the breaking of the consecrated Bread.[456] The fraction of the Amnos, according to tradition, is based on the actions of the Lord at the Last Supper: "*Now as they were eating, Jesus took bread, and blessed it, and broke it (ἔκλασεν), and gave to the disciples…*" (Matt. 26:26; cf. Mark 14:22; Luke 22:19; and 1 Cor. 11:24).[457]

The initial fraction (*κλᾶσις or μελισμός*) is followed by another, the comminution (*ὁ διαμερισμός*). The purpose of both is purely functional. To be distributed so that all may share it, the Amnos has to be broken and apportioned. But as it often happens, functional acts are often clothed with iconic and symbolic meanings. Accordingly, some see the fraction in iconic terms, as an imitation of the Lord's action at the Last Supper. Others see it in symbolic terms: either as a sign of the Lord's passion[458] or as a sign of the unity of all believers in the one Body of Christ.[459]

---

454 This devotional custom is mentioned in the sources as early as the fourth century. However, it is not universally practiced.

455 For the history and meaning of the fraction see Taft, *Precommunion Rites*, 319-79.

456 In the early church the term "*breaking of bread – ἡ κλᾶσις τοῦ ἄρτου*" was synonymous with the Eucharist (Luke 24:35; Acts 2:42, 46).

457 The same four actions – taking bread, blessing, breaking, and partaking – are mentioned in two other New Testament accounts: the supper at Emmaus at which the risen Christ revealed himself to the two disciples (Luke 24:30), and the multiplication of the loaves, an event with Eucharistic connotations (Matt. 14:16, 15:36; cf. Mark 6:41, 8:6; Luke 9:16; and John 6:11). Also see John 21:13. In his classic study, *The Shape of the Liturgy* (Glasgow 1949), 48-102, Dom Gregory Dix advances the theory that the seven actions of Jesus at the Last Supper as they relate to the bread and cup were reproduced in the *four-action shape* of all the ancient eucharistic rites: the preparation and transfer of the Holy Gifts to the Holy Table; the anaphora; the fraction; and Communion.

458 See Taft, *Precommunion Rites*, 371-73. Trembelas, *Τρεῖς Λειτουργίαι*, 132-3.

459 1 Cor. 10:16-17: "The bread which we break, is it not a participation in the body of Christ? Because there is one bread, we who are many are one body, for we all partake of the one bread." We find a similar image in the *Didache*: "As this broken bread was once scattered upon the mountain tops and after being harvested was made one, so let your Church be gathered together from the ends of the earth into your kingdom (chapter 9:4)

The fraction or breaking of the Amnos is performed with a liturgical formula, which expresses the functional character of the melismos: "Μελίζεται καὶ διαμερίζεται ὁ Ἀμνὸς τοῦ Θεοῦ ... The Lamb of God is broken and distributed; broken but not divided; forever eaten, yet never consumed; but sanctifying those who partake."[460] The formula contains the two technical terms which describe the double fraction or breaking which the Amnos will undergo, first the μελισμος (broken) and after the διαμερισμος (apportioned).

The *Barberini Codex* contains no such formula. It appears, however, in later manuscripts and with unfailing frequency from the twelfth century on. The formula underscores the purpose of the fraction. The Amnos is broken so that it may be distributed and eaten. The melismos formula also highlights a significant theological truth. The Bread which is broken is not divided; it is not dismembered but remains whole. Everyone partakes of the one and same bread, even though it is apportioned; they partake of the one and same Body of Christ (1 Cor. 10:17).

The idea of unity and oneness was emphasized from the earliest days as St. Ignatius of Antioch indicates: "Come together in common, one and all without exception in charity, in one faith and in one Jesus Christ, who is of the race of David according to the flesh, the son of man and Son of God, so that with undivided mind you may obey the hierarch and the priests, and break one Bread which is the medicine of immortality and the antidote against death, enabling us to live forever in Jesus Christ."[461] Also, though eaten repeatedly, the Bread is never consumed, never spent or exhausted. Rather, it is the source of sanctification for those who partake of it worthily.

The minister of the fraction is always the presiding celebrant, hierarch or priest. He lifts the Amnos, says the melismos formula, and performs the fraction by breaking the bread over the discos into four pieces. He also arranges the four pieces on the discos in the form of a cross.

ΙΣ

ΝΙ ΚΑ

ΧΣ

---

460 As mentioned earlier, in some manuscripts the priest is directed to say the melismos formula aloud after the "Εἰς Ἅγιος" as he performs the fraction, serving as a further invitation to Communion. On the development and forms of the melismos formulas see Taft, *Precommunion Rites*, 350-71. Trembelas, Τρεῖς Λειτουργίαι, 133-4.

461 St. Ignatius, *Epistle to the Ephesians*, 22.

The priest (or hierarch) holds the Amnos aloft with his two hands and breaks it along the incisions under the crust. First, he breaks the Amnos in two down the middle. Then turning the Amnos carefully he breaks again down the middle. The four pieces are placed on the discos (paten) crosswise. The four-piece fraction became a common practice from the twelfth/thirteenth century on.

According to the rubrics in the received tradition, the portion stamped ΙΣ or IC is placed in the Chalice for the commingling-union. The portion marked ΧΣ is for the Communion of the higher clergy (hierarchs, priests, deacons). The other portions NI KA are for the Communion of the minor orders and the people, all of whom commune outside the sanctuary.[462]

The Commingling or Union – ἡ ἀνάμιξις – ἡ ἕνωσις

(If a deacon is present, he says to the celebrant, "Master, fill (complete) the Holy Cup (Chalice).")

*Immediately after the fraction or melismos, the priest takes the topmost portion stamped with the letters ΙΣ **or IC** with his right hand and making the sign of the cross over the Chalice with it, he drops it into the Chalice, saying:*[463]

Priest

Πλήρωμα Πνεύματος Ἁγίου. Ἀμήν ... The fullness of the Holy Spirit. Amen.

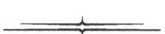

This simple formula is the earliest recorded in the sources. It is found in the *Barberini Codex* (CHR) but with the introductory preposition Εἰς which was eventually dropped in later mss. The standard formula (without the preposition) appears in mss from the eleventh century on, if not earlier, and in the *Diataxis* of Philotheos Kokkinos.

A new version of the formula began to appear in some mss of the fourteenth century. More importantly the new formula was adopted by Doukas in his *editio princeps* of the three Divine Liturgies which he published in 1526. The new formula found its way into the received Greek text and in many of its English translations: "Πλήρωμα πίστεως Πνεύματος Ἁγίου. Ἀμήν ... The fullness of

---

462 As it often happens, local traditions and needs determine the strict application of rubrics such as these. For example, the portion stamped **XC** is meant for the clergy. However, when a priest is the sole celebrant, does he consume the entire portion or only a part of it? This and other questions will be addressed below.

463 The rubric to place the uppermost portion (IC/ΙΣ) in the Cup begins to appear in the sixteenth century and became the standard practice by the eighteenth. Previously, the rubrics did not designate a particular portion, only that a portion of the Amnos, the Bread, be placed into the Cup. See Trembelas, Τρεῖς Λειτουργίαι, 136. Taft, *Precommunion Rites*, 382-4.

faith of the Holy Spirit. Amen." Taft suspects "that the πίστεως gloss came to be interpolated as a result of an assimilation to the *zeon* formula."[464] Minor variants of the standard and later formulas are recorded in some mss throughout the centuries.[465]

The most recent *Ieratikon* of the Church of Greece has the ancient, standard version as does the recent bilingual edition of the Divine Liturgy of the GOA (Πληρωμα Πνευματος Αγιου. Αμην. – *The fulness of the Holy Spirit. Amen,*). The same text is also found in Slavic and other texts.

What purpose does the union or commingling of the Cup serve? Theodore of Mopsuestia provides us with a succinct answer. The union he says, is "to show that the Body and Blood are inseparable, that they are one in virtue, and give the same grace to those who receive them." The union is meant to emphasize that in Communion we receive the glorified and deified Body and Blood of the Risen Lord.[466] Hence, the union or commingling symbolizes the resurrection of the Lord.

In addition, as the pleroma formula indicates, the union is completed by the Holy Spirit, by whom the resurrection of Christ was realized and the eucharistic elements are changed into his Body and Blood. By partaking of Christ's deified Body and Blood we are graced with the communion of the Holy Spirit, "which is the guarantee of our inheritance until we acquire possession of it (Ephes. 1:13).[467]

The origins of the commingling are uncertain. Some have proposed that it is based on the ancient custom of *"eulogies – ευλογίαι,"* i.e. sending a piece of the consecrated Bread to neighboring local churches as a sign of unity.[468] Others have suggested that the act was derived from the ritual action of the Presanctified Liturgy, when prior to Communion the consecrated Bread is added to the unconsecrated chalice.[469]

Today, in many large parishes Communion is often distributed by two or more priests (or deacon). Obviously, this necessitates the use of two or more

---

464 *Ibid.*, 390.

465 For a full discussion on the formula see Taft, *Precommunion Rites*, 384-98.

466 Cited by Taft, *Ibid.* 428.

467 *Ibid.* 431-2.

468 *Ibid.* 398. Closely related to the *eulogies* is the *fermentum*, defined by Taft as "the Late-Antique Roman usage in which a piece of the previously consecrated Eucharistic Bread (the fermentum) from the pope's mass was sent on Sundays as communion to the priests of the Roman *tituli*... and put in the consecrated chalice as a symbol of ecclesial communion and of the oneness of the eucharistic banquet." *Ibid.*

469 Trembelas, Τρεῖς Λειτουργίαι, 135.

chalices. In such instances, what does the celebrant do with the unconsecrated chalices? The answer is given in a fourteenth century *Archieratikon* (ca. 1380): "The patriarch, having cut the Holy Bread, takes the upper particle and divides it proportionately to the number of chalices and drops a piece into each of the chalices, making the sign of the cross with it over the chalice and saying, "The fullness of the Holy Spirit." And the deacon says, amen."[470] In other words, the celebrant performs the union or commingling with each chalice. He takes the upper portion (IC) and apportions it according to the number of chalices. He makes the sign of the cross over each chalice as he drops a piece into it, repeating each time the *pleroma* formula. This practice, however, has long since been abandoned. Instead, in such instances the clergy usually follow the practice of intinction (dipping), about which we will speak below.

The Zeon – τὸ ζέον

The word *zeon* is derived from the verb ζέω which means to boil, to bubble up, to be hot, warm, or fervent. The name is applied both to the hot water and to the manual act by which the hot water is poured into the consecrated chalice(s).[471] In some sources the hot water is also called θερμόν – *thermon* (hot water).

The act of pouring hot water into the consecrated chalice is common to all three liturgies of the Byzantine rite – BAS, CHR, and PRES. In the Byzantine tradition, water is added to the chalice twice, first at the Prothesis Rite during the preparation of the Holy Gifts, and second after the commingling and before Communion. This second pouring is not found in any other tradition. It is unique to the Byzantine rite.

As St. Justin the Martyr bears witness, the Church consecrated a mixed chalice from the start.[472] It was customary in antiquity to partake of wine diluted with water, either regular or hot water. The institution narrative in the anaphora of BAS attests to the practice. At the Last Supper Jesus is said to have hallowed a mingled cup: "Likewise, he took the cup of the fruit of the vine, and having mingled it (κεράσας),[473] offering thanks, blessing and sanctifying it, he gave it to his holy disciples and apostles saying..."

---

470 Cited by Taft, *Precommunion Rites*, 383-4.

471 Taft deals at length with the *zeon* rite. *Ibid.* 441-502.

472 Justin, *First Apology*, 65: "Then bread and a cup of wine mixed with water are brought to him who presides over the brethren." So deep-rooted is the tradition that Canon 32 of the Penthekte Synod attributes the practice to the Apostles and condemns those who fail to uphold it. The canon concludes with these words. "If, therefore, any bishop or presbyter fail to follow the procedure taught by the Apostles, to mix water with wine, and thus to offer the pure sacrifice, let him be deposed..."

473 In modern Greek, wine is called κρασί from κρᾶσις, which is derived from the verb κεράννυμι – κεράσω (future), which means to mix, mingle, often of diluting wine.

It is not clear if the chalice was mixed with cold or hot water at the prothesis. However, from the ninth century, if not earlier, the chalice is mixed with hot or boiling water before communion. The second mixing was eventually ritualized with blessing formulas in the eleventh century.[474]

What purpose does the infusion of hot water serve? It is purely a symbolic act which gives expression to and upholds a theological truth, namely, that in Communion we partake of the risen, living, and glorified Body of Christ, the one which was once dead but now lives. The *Protheoria*, a liturgical commentary authored by Nicholas and Theodore of Andida (1085-1095), describes the zeon rite in these words: "At this point a small vessel of hot water is brought, and some of it is mixed in the cups or chalices on the holy altar…. The warm water, poured in at communion time, thus makes the image complete, so that when the communicants touch the rim of the cup, they touch as it were the divine side."[475] In other words, the zeon becomes the sign of the indwelling presence of the Holy Spirit who imparts life-giving warmth to the consecrated eucharistic elements. Interestingly, according to this text, the faithful were still communing directly from the chalice, "…when the communicants touch the rim of the cup."

If a deacon is serving, he takes the zeon and addresses the celebrant saying, *Bless, Master, the zeon*. If there is no deacon, an altar server brings the zeon to the priest (or hierarch).

Priest

Blessing the zeon says:

Blessed is the warmth of your Holy Gifts (τῶν ἁγίων σου) always, now and forever and unto the ages of ages. Amen…. Εὐλογημένη ἡ ζέσις τῶν ἁγίων σου πάντοτε, νῦν καὶ ἀεὶ καὶ εἰς τοὺς αἰῶνας τῶν αἰώνων. Ἀμήν.

Or:

Blessed is the fervor of your saints…. Εὐλογημένη ἡ ζέσις τῶν ἁγίων σου…

---

474 *Ibid.* 501-502. Trembelas, *Τρεῖς Λειτουργίαι*, 137. By the ninth century the preparation of the eucharistic elements was transferred from the Great Entrance to before the start of the Divine Liturgy. Could it be that the second infusion of hot water into the cup came about as a result of this transfer? The cup had to be warmed or rewarmed before Communion.

475 Nicholas and Theodore of Andida, *Protheoria*, PG 140, ch. 36 (464B), cited in Hans-Joachim Schulz, *The Byzantine Liturgy* (New York, 1986), 97 and in Taft, *Precommunion Rites*, 453.

Once again, we are faced with a dilemma. How are we to understand and translate the phrase τῶν ἁγίων σου in this instance? Is it the second person plural in the possessive case of the masculine noun ἅγιοι (holy ones/saints) or of the neuter noun ἅγια (holy things)? If it is the former (masculine noun) then the second translation above, "Blessed is the fervor of your saints," is appropriate. If, however, it is the neuter noun then the translation, "Blessed is the warmth of your holy things (Gifts), is appropriate.

Unfortunately, there is no unanimity among the various English translations. Some favor the first, while others the second. I believe that context is key. The entire rite of the zeon, including its symbolic meaning and purpose, is centered on the consecrated eucharistic elements. What we are blessing and acknowledging is the warm, living, and deified Body and Blood of Christ resting in the chalice. Hence, "Blessed is the warmth of your Holy Gifts (things)," is the preferred translation. I substituted the word Gifts for the word "things" to be consistent with the accepted translation of the early call to Communion, "Τὰ ἅγια τοῖς ἁγίοις – The Holy Gifts for the holy people."

The priest pours the needed amount of the zeon into the chalice or chalices on the Holy Table, saying,

Priest

Ζέσις Πνεύματος Ἁγίου. Ἀμήν…. The warmth of the Holy Spirit. Amen.[476]

If a deacon is serving, he pours the zeon into the chalice(s).

The zeon rite concludes at this point. The Communion of the clergy and the people follows. However, before Communion is distributed a second breaking of the Bread takes place, the comminution or διαμερισμός.

The Comminution – ὁ διαμερισμός

The last of the manual acts which the priest performs before receiving Holy Communion is the comminution, which is performed in two stages. First in relation to the communion of the clergy, and second in relation to the communion of the people.[477]

---

476 This is the older and more correct version, which appears in the more recent editions of the Divine Liturgy. It has replaced the text found in the earlier printed editions: "Ζέσις πίστεως πλήρης Πνεύματος Ἁγίου, Ἀμήν…. Fervor of faith, fullness of the Holy Spirit. Amen." See Trembelas, Τρεῖς Λειτουργίαι, 136-7. The phrase is meant to emphasize the sanctifying presence of the Holy Spirit.

477 For a rich and comprehensive treatment of the communion rites see Robert F. Taft, *History of the Liturgy of St. John Chrysostom*, vol. VI, *The Communion, Thanksgiving, and Concluding Rites* (Rome 2008).

According to the rubrics, the priest breaks the portion of the Amnos marked ΧΡ (or **ΧΣ**, ΧC) into two pieces. He will commune the one piece and give the other to the deacon. Of course, this presupposes that a deacon is present and serving. In all instances, the Bread and Cup are always administered to the deacon(s) by the priest.

However, in most Greek Orthodox parishes in America there is just one priest who serves alone. According to the usual practice, the priest cuts a small piece from the portion ΧΡ and places it in the palm of his right hand. This procedure will be discussed in greater detail below.

When a hierarch is the chief celebrant, the clergy receive the Holy Bread and the Cup from him in the traditional manner and order.[478]

At a presbyteral concelebration (συλλείτουργον) Communion is received in one of two ways. According to one practice, the chief celebrant (ὁ πρῶτος τῇ τάξει) breaks the portion of the Amnos marked ΧΡ (or ΧΣ) into several pieces corresponding to the number of clergy who are to partake of the Holy Mysteries. He cuts the pieces with his fingers or with the liturgical lance (λόγχη), and places them on the front outer rim of the discos. Each priest approaches according to seniority to partake of the Bread and the Cup by himself.

According to the second practice, prevalent in the GOA, each priest approaches the Holy Table according to seniority and himself cuts a piece from the portion ΧΡ (ΧΣ) and places it in his right palm. Then, having partaken of the Holy Bread, the priest immediately approaches the Cup.

In some traditions, the celebrating priests receive the Holy Bread in turn but do not commune until all have received their portion of the Amnos. To make room for the others, the clergy circle the Holy Table. After this, each priest approaches the Cup.

Priests who are present in the sanctuary without participating in the liturgy, but still wish to partake of Holy Communion may do so after those who took part in the service. They wear an epitrachilion over their rason.

---

478 When a hierarch presides, the clergy move forward according to seniority to receive Communion from the hand of the hierarch. They circle around the Holy Table coming to the hierarch from his left. Each priest approaches and stands to the right of the hierarch with hands extended and with the right palm open and resting on the left palm. As the hierarch places a portion of the Amnos in his open hand, the priest kisses the hierarch's hand and carefully circles the Holy Table. Coming to the rear of the Table with head bowed, he consumes the portion of the Holy Bread. After this, he comes to the front of the Table and cleans his palm with the *mousa* (sponge) over the antimension. He stands to the hierarch's left and places the communion cloth under his chin as the hierarch offers him the Cup, from which he takes one sip. Then he moves to the side until all the clergy have received Communion.

When the priest(s) has communed, he prepares the consecrated Holy Gifts for distribution to the people. Basically, this involves the comminution of the remaining portions of the Amnos, about which we will speak below under the subtitle, *Distributing Communion to the People*.

The Order for Receiving Communion

By tradition, hierarchs, priests, and deacons receive Communion first at the Holy Table. Sub-deacons, readers, and chanters together with the people receive communion after the clergy in the nave. The higher clergy partake of the Holy Gifts separately, the Bread first and then the Cup, in the manner described in the Last Supper narratives. Today, the lower clergy and the people receive the sacred Gifts with a spoon.

The manner by which the clergy receive Communion today was, in fact, the general custom, practiced by all, clergy and laypeople alike, at least through the middle of the twelfth century, when communion under both species with a spoon became the general practice for the people.[479]

Saint Cyril of Jerusalem, for example, provides us with a vivid description of the ancient practice of Communion by the people. "Approaching, therefore, come not with your wrists extended, or the fingers open; but make your left hand as if a throne for your right…And having hollowed your palm, receive the Body of Christ, saying after it, Amen. Then after you have with carefulness hallowed your eyes by the touch of the Holy Body, partake thereof; giving heed lest you lose any of it.… Then after having partaken of the Body of Christ, approach also the Cup of his Blood; not stretching forth your hands, but bending and saying in the way of worship and reverence, Amen, be hallowed by partaking also of the Blood of Christ. And while the moisture is still upon your lips, touching it with your hands, hallow both eyes and brow and the senses. Then wait for the prayer and give thanks unto God, who has accounted you worthy of so great mysteries."[480]

The precedence given the clergy to receive first should not be construed as a form of clericalism. Rather, it accords with long established societal norms which the Church and the people continue to honor. Whether one receives first or last, everyone receives the very same Holy Mysteries, a truth which St. John Chrysostom is quick to point out: "All things are equal between us and you, even the very chief of blessings. For I do not partake of the Holy Table with greater abundance and you with less, but each partakes of the same equally.… For I do not partake of one Lamb and you of another, but all partake

---

479 See, for example, Panagiotis Skaltsis, "Ο τρόπος Κοινωνίας δια της λαβίδος" in www.Orthodoxia.Info June 14, 2020.

480 St. Cyril of Jerusalem, *Mystagogical Catechesis*, V: 21-22.

of the same one."[481]

The Forgotten Practice

To emphasize the fact that Holy Communion is a gift which is received and not taken, everyone, including patriarchs and hierarchs, received the Holy Gifts from the hand of another. The oldest extant *Diataxis* (eleventh century) of a patriarchal liturgy, for example, describes the order of Communion as follows. "And after having divided enough (of the consecrated bread) and wiped and shaken his hands lest perchance a pearl (=μαργαρίτης)[482] be left on them, he (the patriarch) descends from the platform (βῆμα) and bows three times to the east...with him bows the priest (ἱερεύς – which in this instance could mean hierarch) who is supposed to give him Communion, and both mount the platform and kiss the Holy Altar. And first the hierarch, having stretched forth his hands, receives.... Then...he takes the other particle and gives it to the one that gave Communion to him.... And the archdeacon gives the chalice to the priest and the hierarch, after turning to him and bowing, communicates... and [then] the hierarch communicates him.... And thus, the hierarch goes and gives Communion to those in the sanctuary. And after...he goes off (to give Communion to the people).[483]

Similar rubrics are found in mss of presbyteral liturgies. A twelfth-century *Euchologion*, for example, contains the following directive. "Then he [the presiding priest] pours the hot water into the chalice, as much as is needed. Next, if he is alone, he receives the Lord's Body. But if when there are several priests, the first among them, having received communion, gives it to the others, who kiss his hand and cheek. And he likewise receives the Eucharist from one of the others. And in like manner they give the chalice

---

481 St. John Chrysostom, *Homily 4:4 on 2 Thess.*, PG 62: 492. The *Apostolic Constitutions* (Book 8: xiii), a late fourth-century document, gives a brief description on the order of Communion. "And after that, let the hierarch partake, then the presbyters, and deacons, and subdeacons, and the readers, and the singers, and the ascetics; and then the women, the deaconesses, and the virgins, and the widows; then the children and then all the people in order with reverence and godly fear, without tumult." The order described here has the higher clergy receive first and then the members of the lower clergy. The children first and the adult members of the assembly follow. The *Apostolic Constitutions* is of Syrian origin and contains valuable information, including a brief outline of the Divine Liturgy as celebrated in the fourth century (Book 2: 57) and the full text with rubrics (Book 8: 5-15)). Prof. Ioannis Fountoulis prepared and published a text of the Divine Liturgy described in Book 8 suitable for liturgical use. This text is in the series, Κείμενα Λειτουργικῆς (13), Θεία Λειτουργία τῶν «Ἀποστολικῶν Διαταγῶν» (Thessaloniki 1978).

482 To this day, a small particle of the consecrated Bread is often called a pearl (μαργαρίτης), something precious and of untold value (Matt. 13:46).

483 Cited in Taft, *Communion*, 99.

to one another.... And when the priests, as we have said, have finished, the archdeacon says, 'Deacons, let us approach.'"[484]

That Communion is given and not taken is emphasized by the Communion prayer: "Lord Jesus Christ, our God, hear us from your holy dwelling place.... Come and sanctify us and let your pure Body and precious Blood be given to us by your mighty hand and through us to all your people." The image is clear. Christ is the one who offers and distributes. The image portrayed in this prayer is powerful. Christ is the one who offers Communion first to the clergy "by his mighty hand" and then to the people by the hand of the clergy.

This ancient practice fell into disuse by the fifteenth century, except for hierarchical liturgies when the hierarch self-communicates but imparts communion to the concelebrating priests and deacons. The practice of self-communication has unintentionally weakened the understanding of Communion as a gift offered and received. Some would argue that the practice has also weakened the synodal character of ecclesial life, giving greater emphasis to the hierarchical.

Thankfully, most, if not all, priests (and hierarchs) have retained the traditional manner by which the Holy Bread is received, even when self-communicating. To indicate that Communion is a gift, the priest breaks off a portion of the Amnos and places it in the open palm of his right hand, which he then rests on his left. After reciting the established formula, he consumes the Body of the Lord. It is as if the Lord himself placed a piece of the Amnos in his hand, giving him the Gift of life.

---

[484] *Ibid.* 105.

The Communion of the Clergy

When the chalice(s) has been mingled with the zeon, the priest prepares to receive the Holy Mysteries. By custom, the priest first recites the extra-liturgical devotional prayers. Then he seeks forgiveness from the people and from those in the sanctuary. After which, he approaches the Holy Table, bows three times, and proceeds to receive the Body of the Lord followed by the Cup.

The Devotional Communion Prayers

As I have noted elsewhere, the Pauline admonition gave rise to the creation of many Communion prayers in addition to those original to the Divine Liturgy.[485] Beginning with the tenth century and more especially with the emergence of rubrical manuals (diataxeis) in the twelfth and thirteenth centuries, one or more of these extra-liturgical devotional prayers gradually found their way into the communion ritual of the liturgy.[486] The Barberini Codex does not include any extra devotional pre- or post-Communion prayers. It contains only those that are integral to the rite.

The devotional prayers have been codified in two collections, the first of which is the set of prayers that has been interpolated into the text of the three liturgies: CHR, BAS, and PRES. The second collection is the anthology of private prayers that comprise the Office of Holy Communion

---

485 Calivas, *Liturgy in Dialogue*, 37-8; 55-6.

486 Interestingly, the new bilingual edition of the Divine Liturgy of the GOA inserts the following note, "These prayers and hymns are not part of the Divine Liturgy but are said out of piety," p. 69.

(Ἀκολουθία τῆς Θείας Μεταλήψεως) which represents the Athonite tradition of the fourteenth century.[487]

The number of prayers and hymns that comprise the first collection – the devotional pre-communion prayers – varies in both the manuscripts and the printed editions of the Divine Liturgy.[488] The basic structure in the official Greek text was established in the fourteenth century by Philotheos Kokkinos in his Διάταξις τῆς Θείας Λειτουργίας. The set contains two prayers, two didactic (admonitory) verses, and three hymns.[489]

The most famous of the prayers is the first, "I believe and confess, Lord…" This prayer was originally two separate confessional prayers, one concerning the divinity of Christ ("I believe and confess, Lord, that you are truly the Christ, the Son of the living God, who came into the world to save sinners, of whom I am the first"); and the other concerning the Real Presence ("I also believe that this is truly your pure Body and that this is truly your precious Blood"). The two prayers were eventually joined to form a single devotional prayer, which includes three additional elements: the recognition of one's unworthiness, a plea for mercy and forgiveness, and a supplication to be found worthy to partake of the Holy Mysteries.

In some parishes, it is customary for the congregation to recite this prayer together. In one sense, it is good for the people to recite the prayer in unison for its confessional and devotional value. In another sense, the shared recitation amounts to ritual formalism when people who are not receiving Communion join in the reading. Nevertheless, the common recitation of the prayer has a salutary effect on all, both communicants

---

[487] The *Office of Holy Communion* is found in most *Ieratika*, the Great *Euchologion*, and the *Horologion*. For a brief description of the service see Calivas, *Liturgy in Dialogue*, 37-8.

[488] Robert Taft traces the origins and use of these prayers in his *Communion*, 148-88.

[489] In addition to the first well-known prayer, "I believe and confess Lord…" which tradition attributes to St. John Chrysostom, the set includes a shorter second prayer, "Loving Master, Lord Jesus Christ, my God, let not these gifts be to my condemnation…but for the cleansing and sanctification of soul and body…" This prayer echoes the Pauline admonition in 1 Cor. 11:26-29. The two didactic verses, "Behold, I draw near to divine Communion…." and "Tremble, O man, as you behold…" are attributed to St. Symeon Metaphrastes (+c.984). Of the three hymns in the set, the most famous is the Holy Thursday troparion, "Receive me today, Son of God, as a partaker of your mystical Supper/…" The other two hymns are borrowed: one, "You have smitten me with yearning…" is from the ninth ode of the second canon of the Feast of the Transfiguration; the other, "How shall I, who am unworthy enter the splendor of your saints…" is from the ninth ode of the Canon of Holy Tuesday. In some mss, including the *Diataxis of Philotheos Kokkinos*, the priest and deacon recite these prayers while holding the Holy Body in their hands, the priest standing before the Holy Table and the deacon facing him from the back of the Table. Upon completing the prayers, they consume the Holy Bread.

and non-communicants, because it sensitizes the heart and mind of the worshipper to the wonders and benefits of Holy Communion.

Strikingly, greater emphasis has been placed on the personal devotional prayers than on the communal pre-communion and post-communion prayers which are integral to the rite. These prayers are usually recited inaudibly by the priest, thwarting the very purpose for which they exist: to remind people that Communion is not a matter of personal piety but a communal act and event. Communion is a gift given to and received in common by all of God's people for the realization of the Church as the Body of Christ of which we are all members.

The interpolated devotional prayers are strictly personal in nature. They originated in monastic circles in the late Middle Ages and share a common theme or characteristic. They are, for the most part, penitential and describe Communion in terms of individual piety – an ascetical act for the increase of one's spiritual consciousness and sensibilities.[490]

For sure, every sacrament is intensely personal, a unique event in the life of the one who receives it. But every sacrament is also intensely communal because every sacrament belongs to and is celebrated by the whole Church. The power of each sacrament emanates from within the Church. The Eucharist, for example, is a communal event. Holy Communion is the moment in and through which the participants are united not only to Christ but also to one another who share in Christ's risen and glorified Body. To paraphrase Metropolitan John Zizioulas, through the Eucharist Christ brings the many into himself, giving his own body for their sustenance and unites them in his eschatological assembly.[491]

---

490 The tendency toward atomization that began in the post-iconoclastic period affected liturgical piety. As Fr. Alexander Schmemann notes: "Without being noticed, the receiving of Communion was subordinated to individual piety, so that piety was no longer determined by the Eucharist as in the early Church. Instead, the Eucharist became an instrument of piety, an element of asceticism, an aid against demons. The change here was not a reduction of the place and significance of Communion, but a change in the way it was experienced and understood. It was included within the general scheme of monasticism as an ascetical act and a form of self-edification. In this sense the view of the Eucharist as the actualization of the Church as the people of God and as the eschatological feast of the kingdom was not denied or disputed. The emphasis simply shifted to the view of Communion as a beneficial ascetical act. The Eucharistic service was now seen as an opportunity to receive spiritual succor. This was in fact a change in liturgical piety." In his *Introduction to Liturgical Theology*, 141-2. Metropolitan John Zizioulas argues that the tendency toward individual piety appeared as early as the third century in Alexandria. See *John D. Zizioulas, Lectures in Christian Dogmatics*, Douglas H. Knight, ed. (London, 2008), 126-32.

491 Zizioulas, *Lectures in Christian Dogmatics*, 128.

The ecclesial dimensions of Communion are especially emphasized in the anaphora of BAS: "And unite us all to one another who become partakers of the one Bread and the Cup in the communion of the one Holy Spirit... that we may find mercy and grace with all the saints who through the ages have pleased you." The anaphora of CHR gives greater prominence to personal benefits.[492]

Great care must be given not to construe Holy Communion as a meritorious act, as something one earns through austere ascetical practices. Holy Communion is a gift, given freely by God to those who thirst for him and his righteousness. Asceticism properly understood is an essential component of the Christian life. However, it should not be associated with deprivation and miserly attitudes toward life but used as an antidote to egocentric individuality through the practice of discernment, prayer, fasting, hospitality, charity, and faithful adherence to the teachings of the Church.[493] The ascetic struggle is never strictly personal, inasmuch as a Christian never struggles or prays as an individual but as a member of the Body of Christ. Equally, no one receives Holy Communion as an individual but as a member of the Church, the household of God.

Asking Forgiveness

From the people: Before approaching the Holy Table to receive Communion, the priest turns to the people and then to those in the sanctuary and asks for their forgiveness. When performing these actions, the priest by custom opens his hands and bows to the people saying, "My brothers and sisters forgive me a sinner." When bowing to a fellow priest or deacon, the priest says, "My brother and concelebrant, forgive me a sinner." The forgiveness act and gestures are a sign of reconciliation based on the Lord's saying recorded in the Gospel of Matthew 5:23-24.

From God: Then the priest approaches the Holy Table and asks forgiveness from God. He bows or makes three small prostrations, repeating each time the plea of the Publican, "*God, be merciful to me a sinner – Ὁ Θεός, ἱλάσθητί μοι τῷ ἁμαρτωλῷ.*"[494]

---

492 See Calivas, *Liturgy in Dialogue*, 42-53.

493 See The Monks of New Skete, *In the Spirit of Happiness: Spiritual Wisdom for the Living* (Boston 2001), 72-93.

494 The order of reception by the clergy in Slavic usages is slightly different from the Greek. It appears to follow a practice which developed during the 16-17th centuries.

Reception of Communion by the Priest

Priest

Approaching the Holy Table and after bowing three times, the priest says:

Behold, I approach Christ, our immortal King and God ... Ἰδοὺ προσέρχομαι Χριστῷ τῷ ἀθανάτῳ Βασιλεῖ καὶ Θεῷ ἡμῶν.

Then the priest breaks off a piece from the portion ΧΣ (or ΧC) and places it in his right palm. Then placing the left hand under his right, he bows his head and says:

The precious and most holy Body of our Lord, God, and Savior, Jesus Christ, is imparted to me (N) the unworthy presbyter (or priest) for the forgiveness of my sins and for life eternal. ...Μεταδίδοταί μοι τῷ ἀναξίῳ πρεσβυτέρῳ (or ἱερεῖ) τὸ τίμιον καὶ πανάγιον Σῶμα τοῦ Κυρίου καὶ Θεοῦ καὶ Σωτῆρος ἡμῶν, Ἰησοῦ Χριστοῦ, εἰς ἄφεσίν μου ἁμαρτιῶν καὶ εἰς ζωὴν αἰώνιον.[495]

*The **priest** consumes the Holy Bread with fear and care. He wipes his right palm with the mousa over the discos and proceeds to partake of the Cup. If a deacon is present, he will administer Communion to him according to the order outlined in the Ieratikon.*

*With the communion cloth (μάκτρον) in his hands, the **priest** takes the Holy Chalice in his hands and raises it to his lips, saying:*

Again, the precious, most holy, and life-giving Blood of our Lord and God and Savior, Jesus Christ is imparted to me, (N), the unworthy presbyter (or priest) for the forgiveness of my sins and life eternal. – Ἔτι μεταδίδοταί μοι (δεῖνι) τῷ ἀναξίῳ πρεσβυτέρῳ (or ἱερεῖ) τὸ τίμιον καὶ πανάγιον καὶ ζωηρὸν Αἷμα τοῦ Κυρίου καὶ Θεοῦ καὶ Σωτῆρος ἡμῶν Ἰησοῦ Χριστοῦ εἰς ἄφεσίν μου ἁμαρτιῶν καὶ εἰς ζωὴν αἰώνιον.[496]

---

495 Take note of the prescribed formula and gesture. Both are meant to emphasize that Communion is a gift to be received and not taken. The formula is clear: "The precious and most Holy Body of our Lord...is imparted to me...." The gesture as well as the formula are consistent with and give expression to the words in the prayer of the Elevation: "Lord Jesus Christ, our God.... Come and sanctify us, and let your pure Body and precious Blood be given to us *by your mighty hand*...."

496 In G.W.H Lampe, *Patristic Greek Lexicon,* the adjective ζωηρόν is translated both as living and as life-giving.

*The **priest** communes once from the Chalice in silence. Then with the communion cloth he wipes the rim of the Holy Chalice from where he drank. After which he kisses the chalice, saying:*

This has touched my lips; it will take away my iniquities and cleanse my sins ... Τοῦτο ἥψατο τῶν χειλέων μου καὶ ἀφελεῖ τὰς ἀνομίας μου καὶ τὰς ἁμαρτίας μου περικαθαριεῖ.[497]

***An important note:** The recent editions of the Greek Ieratikon and the new bilingual edition of the Divine Liturgy published by the GOA have removed the formula, "in the name of the Father and the Son, and Holy Spirit," which was said by the clergy when partaking of the Cup. The pertinent rubric in the new translation of the GOA makes this clear: "He [the priest] communes once from the Chalice in silence." The phrase "in silence" is deliberate; it is intended to eliminate the use of the trinitarian formula. The rubric also instructs the clergy to "commune once" from the Cup, thus doing away with the previous practice.[498]*

Originally, the clergy and the people partook of the Chalice only once, accompanied with a simple formula, such as "the Blood of Christ, the Cup of life," as described in the Apostolic Constitutions (Book 8:13): "Let the bishop partake, then the presbyters and deacons…and then all the people in order.… And let the bishop give the oblation, saying, 'The Body of Christ'; and let him that receives say, 'Amen'. And let the deacon take the Cup; and when he gives it, say, 'The Blood of Christ, the Cup of life'; and let him that drinks say, 'Amen.' And let the thirty-third [thirty-fourth] psalm be said, while the rest are partaking; and when all, both men and women, have partaken, let the deacons carry the remains into the vestry [εἰς τὰ παστοφόρια]."[499]

The trinitarian formula began to appear in mss of the thirteenth and fourteenth centuries. We learn from at least one of these sources that the formula was said twice, once after partaking of the Bread and again after partaking of the Cup. More and more, however, the formula was

---

[497] This declaration is an adaptation of Isaiah 6:7. It appeared first in mss of the fifteenth century. The imagery in Isaiah 6:6-7 was used earlier in relation to the communion spoon: "Then flew one of the Seraphim to me, having in his hand a burning coal which he had taken with *tongs* (λαβίδι) from the altar. And he touched my mouth and said…" The word tongs – λαβίς was deemed appropriate for the communion spoon because it is the implement which holds the "burning coal," Holy Communion.

[498] I believe that communing once from the Chalice is the practice of the Ecumenical Patriarchate.

[499] See Fountoulis, Ἀπαντήσεις εἰς Λειτουργικὰς Ἀπορίας, vol 2, 15-8.

confined to the Cup. Eventually, the formula led to the introduction of the "triple" partaking of the Cup, as each sip was associated successively with one of the Persons of the Trinity: "In the name of the Father, and of the Son, and of the Holy Spirit. Amen." The practice of the triple sip with the formula was firmly established when Philotheos Kokkinos included it his Diataxis. Even so, it was not universally practiced. By removing the trinitarian formula and the triple sipping, the new bilingual edition of the Divine Liturgy has, in effect, restored the more primitive practice.

The Communion to the People

Immediately after the priest has communed, he prepares the chalice(s) for the distribution of Communion to the people. If a deacon is present, he assumes the role, unless directed differently.

The διαμερισμός.

According to the prevailing Greek practice, the priest places into the chalice the two remaining pieces of the Amnos, those marked NI and KA, and whatever remains from the portion XP from which the clergy communed. Then with the communion spoon, he performs the second comminution (the διαμερισμός), by breaking the portions of the Amnos into many smaller pieces for the communion of the people.[500]

When more than one chalice is needed. If more than one chalice is used to distribute Communion to the people,[501] the priest prepares the unconsecrated chalice(s) by what is called "consecration by contact."[502] One way to accomplish this, perhaps the oldest, is to pour a small amount of the precious Blood from the consecrated chalice directly into each unconsecrated chalice, to which the priest adds one or more of the remaining portion(s) of the Amnos. In this instance, the communion cloth should be available to wipe the lip of each chalice to avoid dripping or spillage.

---

500 In some traditions the second comminution is performed differently. The priest cuts the remaining portions of the Amnos into small pieces with the lance on a wooden or other type of tray or discos. The pieces are then transferred into the chalice(s). In some traditions, the priest breaks the Amnos into small pieces with his fingers over the chalice, dropping them into the chalice.

501 While several chalices may be placed on the Holy Table for communing the people, only one is consecrated according to ancient custom. Saint Ignatius of Antioch, for example, writes in his letter to the Philadelphians: "Be zealous, then, in the observance of one Eucharist. For there is one flesh of our Lord, Jesus Christ, and one chalice that brings union in his blood. There is one altar, as there is one hierarch with priests and deacons…" (*Philadelphians* 4).

502 On the matter of consecration by contact see Stefanos Alexopoulos, *Presanctified Liturgy*, 257-63; and Taft, *Precommunion Rites*, 435-39.

There are also two other ways the priest can consecrate by contact. He can place all the portions of the Amnos directly into the consecrated chalice and then transfer portions of the Amnos into the unconsecrated chalice(s) with the communion spoon. Or, he can partially immerse or dip (intinction) each of the remaining portions of the Amnos separately into the consecrated chalice and place each into one of the unconsecrated chalices.[503]

When the transfer has been completed, each cleric offering Communion breaks the portion of the Amnos in his respective chalice into small pieces with the spoon. On the history and use of the communion spoon see Appendix C:11.

An important note: Of the many particles on the discos we believe and affirm that only the Amnos is consecrated and offered for Holy Communion.[504] Today, the number of communicants in many parishes is fairly large. Hence, to avoid giving people particles of unconsecrated bread, only the Amnos should be placed into the chalice(s).[505] Saint Symeon of Thessaloniki explains the reason. "It should be known that in the communion of the most awesome mysteries the priest must offer and receive not from the particles, but from the Lord's Body [the Amnos], and must likewise give communion from it to those coming forward.... But since every one of the faithful should receive communion in both the

---

503 A similar practice is used for the preparation of the Amnos for PRES and for the reserved sacrament. The consecrated Amnos is dipped a little in the consecrated chalice and is set on a discos or some other appropriate vessel crust down and properly covered until its use. Or, the consecrated Amnos is held crust down and is signed by tracing the incisions with the precious Blood using the Communion spoon.

504 See Fountoulis, Ἀπαντήσεις, vol. 2, 176-81.

505 This matter is addressed by St. Nikodemos in the *Pedalion/Rudder* (note on canon 28 of the *Penthekte* Synod). He cites the comments of St. Symeon of Thessaloniki (+1429), the last of the great Byzantine liturgical commentators: "That is why Symeon of Thessaloniki says that priests must be very careful not to administer Communion to Christians by giving them these fragments but must be sure to give them pieces of the very body of the Lord itself. If those who are about to commune are numerous, let them not place the fragments [particles] in the Holy Chalice, in order to avoid making a mistake and administering the communion to anyone by giving them the fragments; instead, let them leave them on the holy disc, and after administering the communion to the Christians, then let them put them forth... For notwithstanding that the fragments were united with the Blood and the Body of the Lord, they did not actually become a part of the Lord's body."

Body and the Blood, taking the Lord's Body with the Blood in the spoon, let the priest give communion in this way to the one coming forward."[506]

If, however, only a few people are expected to receive, the priest may place the Amnos into the chalice together with all the particles. In such instances the priest leaves the portions of the Amnos whole so that he may easily distinguish the Amnos from the particles. He performs the comminution as each person approaches, by cutting a piece from the Amnos with the spoon and together with the precious Blood offers it the communicant.

When communing infants and little children, the priest should give them the tiniest possible particle of the Holy Bread, so that they may swallow it with ease.

The Call to Communion

When the chalice(s) has been properly prepared, the priest covers it with the communion cloth. He may leave the communion spoon in the chalice or place it on top of it.[507] *If a deacon is serving, the priest gives him the chalice to proclaim the invitation to commune.*

In former times when Communion was distributed separately to the people, the priest (or hierarch) administered the Holy Bread and the deacon offered the Holy Chalice. Presenting the chalice to the deacon at this point is a vestige of that ancient practice. If the deacon is not giving Communion, he returns the chalice to the priest. Unless the priest and the deacon both give Communion, I think it makes sense to dispense with the exchange. Simply, the deacon proclaims the invitation, but the priest holds the Chalice since he alone will be administering the sacrament.

---

506 Symeon of Thessaloniki, *On the Sacred Liturgy*, PG 155. Cited in Taft, *Communion*, 716.

507 When few people are expected to receive, the priest places the Amnos and all the particles in the chalice, leaving the discos clean. Then he places the aer with the veils and the asteriskon on the discos. If a deacon is serving, he usually prepares the chalice and the discos.

The **Priest (or deacon)** exits the Holy Doors holding the chalice in both hands and facing the people he says:

With the fear of God, with faith, and with love draw near... Μετὰ φόβου Θεοῦ, πίστεως, καὶ ἀγάπης προσέλθετε...[508]

In the past, the call to Communion included a response by the people, which gradually fell into disuse and was eventually eliminated from Greek texts. The response consisted of two familiar psalm verses: "Amen. Amen. Blessed is he who comes in the name of the Lord. God is the Lord and has appeared to us" (Psalm 117/118:26, 27). The two psalm verses speak of the Lord's appearance or manifestation. Here, it is used to emphasize Christ's appearance – his real presence in the consecrated Gifts.

---

*Having proclaimed the invitation, the **priest(s)** steps down to the solea to administer Communion to the people. If it is more practical, he stands on the lower step. When two or more clerics are administering Communion, they stand at strategic positions to facilitate the orderly distribution of the sacrament.*[509]

Parish Council members should be available to direct the people according to the order established by the parish. It is also prudent for two persons to stand on either side of

---

508 The new, second summons to Communion appeared first in manuscripts of the tenth century. The earliest form contained just one word, "Προσέλθετε ... Approach or Draw Near." By the eleventh century the summons was expanded to say, "Μετὰ φόβου Θεοῦ προσέλθετε ... Approach with the fear of God." Within a short period of time, the words "καὶ πίστεως...and faith" were added to the text. The formula was completed in the twelfth century with the addition of the words, "καὶ ἀγάπης ... and love." Various forms of the formula found their way into later manuscripts. The received formula achieved permanency after the sixteenth century. Echoes of the formula are found in the words of St. John of Damascus (*Exposition of the Orthodox Faith* (Book 4:13) concerning the Mystery of Holy Communion: "The bread and the wine are not merely figures of the body and blood of Christ (God forbid!) but the deified body of the Lord itself.... Wherefore *with all fear and a pure conscience and certain faith let us draw near* and it will assuredly be to us as we believe, doubting nothing."

509 In earlier times, especially in large churches, communion tables or communion *antimensia* were strategically placed in the nave. The Holy Gifts were brought to these tables from which Communion was distributed to the people. These tables served other purposes as well. Auxiliary liturgical tables (*παρατραπέζια*) are common in our churches to this day and are used for a variety of purposes. Every church has at least one such table, which is used to hold various articles, vessels, or implements at baptisms, weddings, memorials, and artoklasia and euchelaion services, etc. See Taft, *Communion*, 257-60.

the priest with the communion cloth to catch any spillage as the priest administers Communion.[510] *According to tradition, after receiving each communicant takes a piece of antidoron from a tray held by an altar server and returns to his/her place.*[511]

The Call to Communion sets before the people three basic conditions or requirements for the reception of the sacred mysteries. First, the call counsels the communicants to approach the Chalice with the fear of God, which is to say with a clean heart and conscience, and an attitude of deep reverence and humility, qualities that are formed in each person through the observance of the Commandments (1 John 5:2-3). Second, the communicants are counselled to approach with faith, that is with the certainty that the Gifts they are about to receive are truly the deified Body and Blood of Christ; and that in the affairs of everyday life they draw from and are guided by the tenets of the Orthodox faith. Third, the communicants are counselled to draw near with love, the specific nature and characteristics of which are enumerated by St. Paul in his First Epistle

---

510 Administering Communion to infants is sometimes difficult, especially when they are uneasy, agitated, or frightened. If the infant strongly resists it is better to wait for another day. Parents should learn to hold the infant in their right hand because it makes it easier for the priest to reach their mouth (unless the priest is left-handed). If a child appears uneasy, the parent or some other person should gently hold the head and/or hands of the child. Needless to say, the priest's demeanor should be welcoming and kind to allay the child's apprehensions and fears. The sexton or some other person(s) should be trained to assist the priest in these situations. Of course, regular church attendance and frequent communion will help infants and little children overcome their anxieties. Particular attention should be paid to children with special needs. The priest should confer with the parents to address and meet the individual needs of the child effectively. I have heard it said that in Russia some clergy use the following practice to commune babies who are fretful. The parent lays the child down in their arms, and the deacon or altar attendant holding the cloth very gently and quickly pinches the baby's nose shut. When the surprised baby automatically opens his mouth to breath, the priest places the drops of Holy Communion on their tongue. It is very discrete and gentle, and according to my informant, is over before the baby can protest.

511 In many parishes the children depart for their Church School class immediately after Communion and are not afforded the opportunity to offer thanks. To meet this need, with proper introductions, catechism classes should start with a post-communion prayer or hymn such as: "May your holy Body, O Lord Jesus Christ, our God, be to me..." (prayer) and/or hymn, "Πληρωθήτω τὸ στόμα ἡμῶν ... Let our mouths be filled with your praise, O Lord..." Reciting the prayer or singing the hymn, or both, will help children appreciate the awesomeness, wonder, and uniqueness of the act of Communion. Because children love to sing, they should be taught at an early age to sing the hymn, "*Plerotheto.*" In fact, it behooves the teacher, from time to time, to speak to the children on the meaning of Holy Communion and how Orthodox Christians should prepare to receive it. The Department of Religious Education (DRE) of the GOA has material available for such a purpose.

to the Corinthians (13:1-8) and are explained by St. John the Evangelist in his First Epistle (4:1-21). Needless to say, the prescribed Eucharistic fast, about which we spoke earlier, is presupposed. Its purpose is to arouse within each communicant the desire for the true and unique Food which will satisfy our innermost hunger and quench our most intense thirst.[512]

The Manner of Receiving. *The people, both adults and children, should be taught to stay focused on the sacred mysteries as they wait their turn in the Communion line. To avoid distractions, one can say a pre-Communion prayer, or sing in a low voice the Communion hymn with the choir, or simply remain silent in prayerful thought. The people should also know how to physically receive the sacrament. They should stand close to the priest and tell him their baptismal name, then tilt their head back and open their mouth wide. Two assistants hold the communion cloth under their chin. After receiving, they also receive (take) a piece of antidoron and return to their place to offer silently their own personal thanksgiving prayer for God's blessings and wait to participate in the post-Communion hymns and prayers.*

---

512 The priest must be prudent in the exercise of his responsibility to protect the Holy Mysteries and at the same time be respectful of the communicants' freedom and conscience. The priest is neither a policeman nor a judge but a caring spiritual parent, a wise teacher, a thoughtful counselor, and a fervent intercessor. He must not place unnecessary, excessive demands on the people but teach them the basic requirements for Communion – not in terms of disciplinary prescriptions, including forced confession as a ticket to Communion. It behooves us to be mindful of St. Paul's words, "let a man examine himself, and so let him eat..." (1 Cor. 11:28). To quote Fr. Alexander Schmemann, "Intercession constitutes the only real preparation for communion ... No one has been worthy to receive communion, no one has been prepared for it. At this point all merits, all righteousness, all devotions disappear and dissolve. Life comes again to us as a Gift, a free divine gift. This is why in the Orthodox Church we call the Eucharistic elements Holy Gifts.... Everything is free, nothing is due and yet all is given. And, therefore, the greatest humility and obedience is to accept the gift, to say yes – in joy and gratitude. There is nothing we can do, yet we become all that God wanted us to be from eternity, when we are eucharistic." In his *For the Life of the World*, 45. See also Fountoulis, Ἀπαντήσεις εἰς Λειτουργικὰς Ἀπορίας, vol. A, 16-21.

Priest

When communicating the people, the priest says to each person:

The servant of God (N) receives the Body and Blood of Christ for forgiveness of sins and eternal life. – Μεταλαμβάνει ὁ δοῦλος (ἡ δούλη) τοῦ Θεοῦ Σῶμα καὶ Αἷμα Χριστοῦ εἰς ἄφεσιν ἁμαρτιῶν καὶ ζωὴν αἰώνιον.[513]

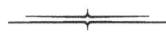

The conferral formula, though brief, points to three things. First, it emphasizes the fact that what is being offered are the deified Body and Blood of Christ. Second, the formula underscores the belief that Holy Communion is a gift, which the Lord offers to his faithful servants by the hand of the priest. And third, it announces the benefits or fruits that are being bestowed upon those who partake of the Gifts in faith: forgiveness of sins (Matt. 26:28) and eternal life (John 6:54).

When all have received, the priest covers the chalice with the cloth.

---

513 The conferral formula in the received text is similar to the one used by the clergy when they commune the Gifts. It emerged gradually when the Eucharistic elements were no longer administered separately but together with a spoon. (See Trembelas, Τρεῖς Λειτουργίαι, 148-9). Interestingly, the *Ieratikon (A)* published by the Monastery of Simonopetra of Mt. Athos (1992) contains a two-part conferral formula. The first part is said for each communicant: Σῶμα καὶ Αἷμα Χριστοῦ. ... *The Body and Blood of Christ.*" The second part is said for all the communicants after the last one receives: "Εἰς ἄφεσιν ἁμαρτιῶν καὶ εἰς ζωὴν αἰώνιον. ... *For the forgiveness of sins and life eternal.*"

What should the priest say when communing infants and little children? Saint John Chrysostom taught that infants and little children are sinless. On the basis of this teaching, it seems appropriate that we omit the phrase "for the forgiveness of sins," when communing infants and little children.

N. POST-COMMUNION RITES

Between Communion and the apolysis the order of the service contains the following elements: a blessing, a hymn, manual acts, showing the Chalice, returning the Holy Gifts to the prothesis, a second hymn, folding the antimension, and a litany and prayer of thanksgiving.

The Blessing

*When all have received, the **priest** covers the chalice with the communion cloth and facing the people he raises the chalice saying,*

Save, O God, your people and bless your inheritance (Ps. 27/28:9).[514]

*He **does not** bless with the chalice; he only raises it.*[515]

*Immediately after, the **priest** enters the sanctuary and places the chalice on the Holy Table.*

Neither the blessing nor the response was part of the original post-Communion rites. They appear in eleventh/twelfth century manuscripts. However, they were not linked together until the twelfth/thirteenth century. Initially, the verse was said in a low voice by the celebrant, an indication that it began as a devotional tradition, as Taft suggests.[516] *By*

---

514 This particular verse is omnipresent. It is found in various prayers, dismissals, and hymns. For example, we find it in the prayer of the second antiphon, the prayer behind the *ambo*, and the *apolytikion* of the feasts of the Holy Cross. On the meaning of the phrase "*God's inheritance*," see Appendix C:12.

515 The rubrics were not always clear on how the blessing was performed. For certain, the chalice was not used for blessing. An eleventh/twelfth century mss, for example, notes that the hierarch gave a blessing with his hand after Communion. The *Diataxis of Philotheos Kokkinos* contains the following rubric. "If there are some communicants, the priest takes the Chalice from the hands of the deacon and communes them. And having thus blessed the people, he returns. If, however, there are none [communicants], he [the priest] blesses the people, while the deacon holds the Holy Chalice, and in addition says silently, "Save, O God…" See Trembelas, Τρεῖς Λειτουργίαι, 14-15. Blessing with the Chalice was unknown before the fifteenth century. It entered the liturgy among the Greeks little by little. The innovation, however, was never universally practiced. In recent years, the practice has come under scrutiny and the clergy are urged to end it. The Slavic tradition, which reflects an older practice, requires the priest to return the Chalice to the Holy Table and then bless the people. In fact, the same rubric is also found in Greek mss. The priest has three options. He can simply raise the chalice as he exclaims the blessing; or he can hold the Chalice in his left hand and bless with his right hand by the side of the Chalice; or he can return the Chalice to the Holy Table and then turn toward the people to bless them.

516 Taft, *Communion*, 468.

the sixteenth century the rule was to recite the words aloud as the priest blessed with his hand.

The verse is meant to remind the people that salvation belongs to God. It is not achieved through human effort but is conferred by God as a gift. God, as the psalmist says, "satisfies the longing soul, and fills the hungry soul with goodness. He brings us out of darkness and the shadow of death…that we would give thanks to the Lord for his goodness and wonderful works" (Ps. 106/107:9, 10, 14-15). What is required of us is an inward faith, an act of personal commitment to Christ, who "bestows his riches upon all who call upon him" (Rom. 10:12).

The Response Hymn[517]

People

Immediately after the blessing, the chanter/choir sings the hymn,

"Εἴδομεν τὸ φῶς τὸ ἀληθινόν…. We have seen the true light…."

This hymn is borrowed from the Vespers of the Feast of Pentecost, one of the stichera troparia. It first appeared in seventeenth-century mss and printed editions. According to Constantinopolitan usage, the hymn is replaced by the apolytikion of the feast on dominical feasts, including their respective apodosis, and on Marian feasts. The same is true for the Third Sunday of Lent and the Saturday of Lazarus. On Holy Thursday we sing, "Τοῦ δείπνου σου…Of your mystical supper…" and on Holy Saturday, "Μνήσθητι εὔσπλαγχνε…Remember us…" From the Sunday of Pascha to the Apodosis, the hymn is replaced by the Paschal Hymn, "Christ is risen from the dead…." From the Feast of the Ascension to its apodosis we sing the apolytikion of the feast. On the Saturday before Pentecost, we sing, "Μνήσθητι εὔσπλαγχνε…" and on the Sunday of Pentecost, the apolytikion of the feast. Starting with the Monday after Pentecost we sing, "We have seen the true light." The Presanctified Liturgy has its own special hymn made up of verses from Psalm 33/34:1, 9: "I will bless the Lord at all times…."[518]

It bears repeating that the prayers and hymns of the Church give expression to what we hope to achieve or what we have already accomplished in worship. As I have noted elsewhere, this hymn describes what happened, what was accomplished, and what we experienced at the Divine Liturgy. It refers to three specific things: "We have seen the true light; we have

---

517 See Taft, *Communion*, 471-3.

518 See Papagiannis, Σύστημα Τυπικοῦ, 92 and Alexopoulos, *Presanctified Liturgy*, 266-7.

received the Heavenly Spirit; we have found the true faith, worshipping the undivided Trinity." The question is: Did the worshipping community and its individual members experience these three things and to what degree did they experience them?[519]

The Manual Acts

While the hymn, "We have seen the true light," is being sung, the priest cleans all the remaining particles on the discos into the chalice. The antimension is also cleaned of any particles that may have dropped on it. As the priest cleans the discos, he recites to himself four Paschal troparia. When he places the particles of the living and the dead into the chalice, he offers a brief prayer on their behalf. Having completed these tasks, he places the folded aer, the two veils, and the asterisk on the discos and covers the chalice with the communion cloth. He censes the gifts three times as he recites a psalm verse. Holding the chalice in his right hand over the discos, which he holds with his left hand, he turns to the people and exclaims, "Now and forever…" and brings the vessels to the prothesis table.

The Paschal Hymns

This set of hymns includes the troparion, "Having beheld the resurrection of Christ," and the three hymns of the ninth ode of the Paschal Orthros, "Shine, shine, O new Jerusalem…" "O divine and beloved and most sweet voice…" and "O great and most sacred Pascha…"

These hymns are not found in any Greek manuscript, or in any early printed editions, or in any of the *Diataxeis*.[520] According to Fountoulis, the hymns found their way into some later editions of the *Ieratikon*. By the early twentieth century most clergy were reciting them silently while cleaning the discos.[521]

As it happens in other parts of the liturgy, so also in this instance. Private extra-liturgical prayers and acts were introduced into the text to accompany manual acts that hitherto were executed in silence. Because the Divine Liturgy is experienced as a paschal feast and the partaking of Communion a participation in the Messianic Banquet, these hymns were deemed appropriate

---

519 Calivas, *Liturgy in Dialogue*, 17.

520 Taft, *Communion*, 475-7. Trembelas, Τρεῖς Λειτουργίαι, 146. The *Great Euchologion* published in 1862, for example, and the *Ieratikon* published by the Monastery of Simonopetra in 1992 make no mention of the hymns. The 2015 bilingual edition of the GOA has them. They are typeset, however, in italics with an explanatory note that the hymns are not found in any codex. An additional rubric reads: "It is customary for the deacon to say the following [hymns] at this time."

521 Fountoulis, Ἀπαντήσεις, vol. 2, 8-11.

to accompany the act. Fountoulis suggests that the troparion, "O great and most sacred Pascha," was perhaps the first of the hymns to be interpolated into the text because it refers to Christ himself as the great and sacred Pascha. He is our paschal Lamb (1 Cor. 5:7). His once-for-all offering of himself is realized continually at every Eucharist. Partaking of him in Communion, we anticipate the age to come when "we shall partake of him fully in the unwaning day of his kingdom."[522] In addition, the hymns accentuate our belief that in Communion we partake of the risen and deified Body and Blood of Christ.

The Prayer "Wash away, Lord…."

Priest

As he places the particles of the living and the dead in the chalice, the priest says:

Wash away, Lord, by your holy Blood, the sins of your servants here remembered through the intercessions of the Theotokos and all your saints. Amen."

The Ieratika always assume the presence of a deacon, who is assigned the task of cleaning the discos. I suspect the transfer of the particles into the chalice at this point served a very practical purpose: the only way that they could be easily consumed. The prayer, "Wash away, Lord…" is also assigned to the deacon.[523] This is highly unusual, since the deacon never offers prayers or blessings that are integral to the liturgy or to any other sacrament. He offers only petitions, exclamations, and biddings and, in some instances, recites extra-liturgical prayers.

The prayer for the living and the dead at this point can only be seen as an extension or continuation of the petitions offered at the proskomide. Here, the prayer is more intense and more striking. The particles are immersed into the consecrated Chalice. And so, the priest or deacon prays that the persons for whom the particles were offered may be cleansed of their sins, "washed away by [the Lord's] Holy Blood."

Saint Symeon of Thessaloniki says the following about this practice: "For the particle offered for someone, lying right next to the holy bread as it is being sacrificed in the sacred rite and becomes the Body of Christ, partakes immediately of his holiness. Placed in the chalice, it is united with his Blood. Therefore, it passes on the grace to the soul for whom it

---

522 From the troparion, "O great and most sacred Pascha," the ninth ode of the canon of Pascha.

523 See, for example, Trembelas, Τρεις Λειτουργιαι, 143; Ιερατικον (Apostolike Diakonia, 2004), 143; *Divine Liturgy* (OCA, 1967), 74; *The Divine Liturgy of our Father Among the Saints John Chrysostom* (Archdiocese of Thyateira and Great Britain, 1997), 47.

was offered. A spiritual communion really takes place. If they are people who strive for piety or those who have sinned and are repenting, the person receives in an unseen manner the communion of the Spirit in the soul, as we said. Often the person obtains physical benefits, as we have learned."[524]

Intercessory prayer is always an act of love (James 5:16). We supplicate God on behalf of all. We pray for those who love us and for those who hate us. Nothing and no one is erased from our memory and our prayers.[525] *Imitating the goodness of our great God and Savior Jesus Christ, who loves the righteous and shows mercy to sinners, we place everyone and most especially our kin into his hands. We ask that he be merciful and compassionate and cleanse them of every defilement of flesh and spirit. We do so in the hope that the spark of divinity is alive and flickering in their soul whether they are on this side of death or the other.*

This prayer first appeared in the service books of the late seventeenth century. Prior to that, the discos was cleaned with little or no fanfare – in silence.[526]

Censing and Showing the Chalice

After the Communion of the people the priest returns the Chalice to the Holy Table. If the particles of the saints and the living and the dead are still on the discos, he disposes of them as described above. Once the discos is clean, he places the aer, the two veils, and the asteriskon on the discos. He leaves the communion spoon in the Chalice, which he covers with the communion cloth. Then he takes the censer from the altar server (or deacon) and censes the sacred vessels three times, repeating each time the psalm verse, "Be exalted, O God…" If a deacon is present, the priest gives him the discos with the covers. The deacon holds the discos at eye level, shows it to the people, and then circles the Holy Table and brings the discos to the prothesis table. If no deacon is serving, after the censing, the priest holds the discos in his left hand and the Chalice in his right above the discos. He turns and shows the Chalice to

---

524 Symeon of Thessaloniki, *Explanation of the Divine Temple,* cited in Taft, *The Communion,* 715

525 On prayers for the dead in private devotions and ecclesial rites see Dumitru Staniloae, *The Fulfillment of Creation* (Brookline, MA 2013), 93-104.

526 Fountoulis, Ἀπαντήσεις, vol, 5, 114-9; 341-4.

the people, exclaiming, "Now and forever...." Then he proceeds directly to the prothesis, where he deposits the vessels. On the way he is preceded by an altar server who censes the Holy Gifts. After depositing the vessels, the priest censes the Gifts three times and returns to the Holy Table to fold the antimension and offer the thanksgiving litany and prayer. Immediately after the showing of the Chalice, the people sing the hymn, Plerotheto... Let our mouths be filled...

Priest

After the vessels have been prepared, the priest censes them three times saying each time in a low voice:

Be exalted, O God, above the heavens, and let your glory be over all the earth – Ὑψώθητι ἐπὶ τοὺς οὐρανούς, ὁ Θεός, καὶ ἐπὶ πᾶσαν τὴν γῆν ἡ δόξα σου.

The censing ritual is not mentioned in the Barberini Codex but appears in mss of the eleventh century. The psalm verse attached to the censing becomes fixed from the twelfth century on. The showing of the Chalice attracted an iconic or symbolic meaning put forward in the Protheoria, which likened the act to the Ascension of Christ who, as he departed from his disciples promised them, "Lo I am with you always, to the close of the age" (Matt.28:20). Even though the Mystery of the Eucharist has been accomplished, the Lord who was invisibly present among his people, does not leave them. He has no need of a vicar because he is always present to his Church, to his people, to his inheritance. To affirm this, the priest exclaims, "Now and forever...."

The verse, "Be exalted, O God...." (Psalm 56/57:5, 11; cf. Ps. 107/108:5) was added to the censing to reinforce the suggested Ascension imagery.527 In fact, some later mss include a second passage, "God has gone up with a shout ... Ἀνέβη ὁ Θεὸς ἐν ἀλαλαγμῷ" (Psalm 46/47:5), which is the entrance hymn (εἰσοδικόν) and the koinonikon of the feast of the Ascension.

---

527 The verse, "Be exalted, O God ... Ὑψώθητι ἐπὶ τοὺς οὐρανούς, ὁ Θεός," is used as the prokeimenon of the Apostolos of the feast of the Ascension.

*The **priest** takes up the discos and the Chalice, as described above, and says to himself, "Blessed is our God." Then turning to the people, he shows the Chalice and says aloud:*

Always, now and forever and to the ages of ages – Πάντοτε, νῦν καὶ ἀεὶ καὶ εἰς τοὺς αἰῶνας τῶν αἰώνων.[528]

The priest turns and proceeds directly to the prothesis, where he deposits the sacred vessels. He censes the Holy Gifts three times and returns to the Holy Table.

The Hymn Πληρήθητω -- Plerotheto

*The **people** sing the hymn:*

Πληρωθήτω τὸ στόμα ἡμῶν αἰνέσεως, Κύριε...

Let our mouth be filled with your praise, O Lord, that we may sing of your glory, because you have made us worthy to partake of your holy Mysteries. Keep us in your holiness, that all the day long we may meditate upon your righteousness. Alleluia.

According to the Chronicon Paschale (Πασχάλιον Χρονικόν),[529] the hymn was introduced into the Divine Liturgy in May of 624 when Sergios was Patriarch of Constantinople: "…it was then first introduced that after all have received the Holy Mysteries, when the clergy are about to return to the skeuophylakion the precious ripidia, chalices, patens and the other sacred vessels; and after the distribution of Communion from the side tables, everything is brought back to the holy altar; and finally, after chanting the final verse of the koinonikon; this troparion be sung, Let our mouth be filled with your praise, O Lord."[530]

---

528 Originally, the "Now and forever" probably concluded the koinonikon, which, as initially noted, was a whole psalm and not just one verse of it. Once the Ascension image was attached to the showing of the Chalice, the "Now and forever," served to enhance the symbolism. It also served a practical purpose, to signal the singing of the plerotheto. As Taft notes, standing by itself the "Now and forever..." is unintelligible. The "Blessed is our God," prefix which is said by the priest inaudibly "is nothing more than one of several later attempts to make sense out of the hanging doxology ending." The prefix began to appear in mss of the eleventh century. In his *Communion*, 482.

529 The *Chronicon Paschale* is the name of a seventh-century Greek Christian chronicle of the world. Its name is derived from its system of chronology based on the paschal cycle.

530 The text is cited in Taft, *Communion*, 479.

The hymn receives its name from its incipit (opening word), Πληρωθήτω – Plerotheto. By the early sixteenth century the hymn fell into disuse among the Greeks, probably because of the decline in frequent Communion. However, in recent years it was restored to the service thanks to the 1985 bilingual Holy Cross faculty edition of the Divine Liturgy. It is contained in the 2015 bilingual edition of the GOA and in the 1992 edition of the Ieratikon of Simonopetra.

Saint Nicholas Cabasilas provides us with a brief but thoughtful reflection on the meaning of this lovely hymn, which the people should learn to sing in unison. He writes:

"The congregation intones the canticle taken from the writings of the psalmist: 'Let my mouth be filled with your praise, O Lord, and with your glory all the day' [Ps. 70/71:8, 15]. We are not worthy, Lord, to offer you a hymn of praise for the benefits you have granted to us, but grant us this also by filling our mouths with praise; and as you have given us the grace of prayer to those who ask for it, that we may know for what, and how to pray, so now give our lips the power to praise you. Then the faithful ask that the sanctification which they have received may remain with them, and that, supported by his hand, they may not lose grace or the gift which has been given them. 'Keep us in your holiness.' By doing what? – for our efforts are also necessary. 'By meditating always on your righteousness.' Righteousness here means the wisdom of God and his love, which we have seen in the Holy Mysteries.... Meditation upon this righteousness has the power to preserve sanctification in us, for it increases our faith in God, enkindles charity, and does not allow the soul to suffer evil."[531]

---

[531] Cabasilas, *Commentary*, 4:41. In some mss the plerotheto is called an apolytikion or dismissal hymn. It links all that we have done and prayed for at the liturgy to the affairs of daily life: "that all the day long we may meditate upon your righteousness."

Thanksgiving Litany and Prayer

*As the people sing the plerotheto, the **priest** folds the antimension. When the plerotheto is finished and/or as he finishes folding the antimension, he intones the thanksgiving litany. If a deacon is present, he says the litany from his familiar place in the solea.*

Priest

Let us be attentive! Having partaken of the divine, holy, immortal, heavenly, life-giving, and awesome mysteries of Christ, let us worthily give thanks to the Lord.

People

Lord, have mercy.

Priest

Help us, save us....

People

Lord, have mercy.

Priest

Having prayed for a perfect, holy....

People

To you, O Lord.

Priest

Offers the prayer of thanksgiving:

We thank you, loving Master, benefactor of our souls, that on this day you have made us worthy once again of your heavenly and immortal Mysteries....

Priest

For you are our sanctification....

People

Amen.

By custom, when intoning the doxology, "For you are our sanctification...," the priest makes the sign of the cross over the folded antimension with the Evangelion, which he then places on the folded antimension. The action is comparable to the one at the beginning of the Divine Liturgy.

The litany and the prayer of thanksgiving are found in the earliest manuscripts, including the Barberini Codex. In later mss, starting with the eleventh century, the prayer was transferred and placed out of sequence, after the Communion of the clergy and read by them inaudibly.[532] This probably happened because of the decline in frequent Communion by the people. Thankfully, in recent years the prayer has been restored to its proper place. Now, the clergy must learn to recite it aloud after the litany for the benefit of all.

The litany is very brief with two petitions, and a bidding. The first petition begins with a call to attention, Ὀρθοί! Stand aright, pay attention, so that we may worthily give thanks to the Lord for the privilege of having partaken of the Mysteries of Christ, which are described, known, and experienced in faith as divine, holy, immortal, heavenly, life-giving, and awesome. The adjectives are powerful. Communion is not an ordinary act of eating and drinking but an encounter with the divine – an event which is simultaneously both awe-inspiring and joyous.

The second petition, "Help us, save us, have mercy on us…." is the familiar ending of all litanies, except for the fervent litany.

The bidding is comprised of the familiar petition of the Completion or Dismissal Litany, "for a perfect, holy…day," and the equally familiar bidding, "let us commend ourselves…." The verb αἰτησώμεθα, however, which ends the petition is changed to a participle, αἰτησάμενοι, linking the petition to the bidding which follows: "Having asked (αἰτησάμενοι) for a perfect, holy, peaceful and sinless day, let us…." The petition acts as a type of summary of what was prayed for at the sacred service. And that which was prayed for can be accomplished only when the bidding is fulfilled according to each person's resolute desire: "Let us commend (commit) ourselves and one another and our whole life to Christ our God."

The Thanksgiving Prayer in CHR combines two themes: thanksgiving for the privilege of receiving the sacred Mysteries of Christ[533] and an entreaty

---

532 See Taft, *Communion*, 492-3.

533 The opening of the Thanksgiving prayer of CHR is similar to those of the Pre-communion prayer and the Prayer of Inclination. The Thanksgiving Prayer draws from the content of those two prayers. The prayer reads in part: "We thank you, loving Master, benefactor of our souls, that on this day you have made us worthy once again of your heavenly and immortal mysteries."

for the needs of everyday life.[534] According to Taft, this prayer was not only a prayer of thanksgiving but also the original dismissal prayer of CHR before the addition of the present blessings and dismissals.[535]

The parallel prayer in BAS is slightly different. The first part of the prayer also contains words of thanksgiving. The second part, however, refers to the benefits or fruits of Communion. The prayer in PRES is similar. It offers thanksgiving for Communion and entreats the Lord for his shelter and for the grace to partake of the Holy Gifts worthily, even to one's last breath, so that the soul may be enlightened and the kingdom may be inherited.[536]

The doxological ending of the prayer, "For you are our sanctification," is the same in all three Liturgies, CHR, BAS, and PRES.

O. THE DISMISSAL RITES – APOLYSIS

The dismissal rites in the present order are the same in all three liturgies, CHR, BAS, and PRES. The elements which comprise the rite of dismissal may be grouped in three strata.

The Present Order

Priest

Exiting from the holy doors, he faces the people and says:

Let us go forth in peace.

People

In the Name of the Lord. *(This response has been omitted in current Greek usage).*

Priest (or Deacon)

Let us pray to the Lord.

People

Lord, have mercy.

Priest

Standing at the center outside the Holy Doors facing the people or facing the icon of Christ, he recites the Prayer behind the Ambon.

---

[534] The second part of the prayer transitions to the cares and concerns of everyday life: "Direct our ways on the right path, establish us firmly in your fear, guard our lives, and make our endeavors safe…" (CHR).

[535] Taft, *Communion*, 490-3.

[536] Alexopoulos, *Presanctified Liturgy*, 269-71.

People

Amen. *Then they sing the psalm verse three times:* Blessed be the name of the Lord, both now and to the ages.

Priest

Re-enters the sanctuary via the Holy Doors, bows before the Holy Table, and proceeds to the prothesis where he reads inaudibly the "Prayer in the Skeuophylakion:" Christ our God, you are the fulfillment of the Law and the Prophets...(CHR).

*When the people have finished singing, the **priest** (or **deacon**) faces the people and says:*

Let us pray to the Lord.

People

Lord, have mercy.

Priest

Standing outside of the Holy Doors and facing the people, he blesses them with his hand in the usual manner saying:

May the blessing of the Lord and his mercy come upon you...

People

Amen.

Priest

Facing the people says:

Glory to you, O God, our hope, glory to you.

Priest

May Christ our true God (who rose from the dead), as a good, merciful, and loving God, have mercy upon us and save us through the intercessions of his most pure and holy Mother....

People

Amen. Τὸν εὐλογοῦντα καὶ ἁγιάζοντα ἡμᾶς ... Lord grant many years to the one who blesses and sanctifies us.

Priest

Δι' εὐχῶν τῶν ἁγίων πατέρων ἡμῶν ... Through the prayers of our holy fathers...

*The **priest** blessing the people says:*

May the Holy Trinity protect all of you.

*Following the dismissal, the **priest** stands in the middle of the solea and distributes the antidoron to the people, saying to each person,*

May the blessing and the mercy of the Lord come upon you ... Εὐλογία Κυρίου καὶ ἔλεος ἔλθοι ἐφ' ὑμᾶς.

The received rite of dismissal developed over a period time. It is not difficult to see that the present rite contains not one but three conclusions to the liturgy. Each stratum has its own final blessing and prayer.[537]

The Earliest Stratum

According to the early sources, the Eucharist ended immediately after the post-communion prayer with a command, a response, and a departing procession or recession. CHR, for example, in the *Barberini Codex* contains this simple order. Following the post-communion prayer, the deacon announces the command, "Let us go forth in peace," to which the people respond, "In the name of the Lord."[538]

In the received tradition, the command to depart is given by the priest. However, in patristic writings, liturgical mss, and diataxeis the deacon is the minister of the dismissal.[539] That the announcement of the dismissal has now fallen on the priest is probably due to the gradual decline of the diaconate.[540] The announcement is a command and not a blessing. This is underscored by the fact that it was originally given by the deacon.

The command addresses everyone, the clergy and the people alike, "Let us [all] go forth." This invitation, however, is accompanied with a phrase, "in peace," which gives the action a special nuance. The short response of the people, "In the name of the Lord," amplifies further the meaning of the departure. It is as if we are saying: Yes, we will go forth and return to the realities of everyday life – with all its burdens, challenges, promises, and opportunities – carrying within our hearts the peace of God and in our minds the memory of Christ, so that all our thoughts and actions will be guided by his truth and his love (Philp.4:4-9). Or, as one ancient writer put it, "The Christian who is always

---

537 See Taft, *Communion*, 565-91.

538 Parenti and Velkovska, *L' Euchologio Barberini gr. 336*, 41.

539 *Ibid.*, 23. See also the *Diataxis* of Philotheos Kokkinos in Trembelas, Τρεῖς Λειτουργίαι, 15.

540 At a hierarchical liturgy the command is given by the hierarch.

engaged in the words, works, and thoughts of the Divine Logos, Christ, who is by nature his Lord, is always living in his days and is constantly observing the Lord's days."

The early dismissal rite included a recessional hymn. As the clergy entered the church with the people at the beginning of the liturgy, they also departed with them at the end of the service. The clergy brought with them the remaining eucharistic elements and the various sacred vessels, which they deposited in the skeuophylakion where they also left their vestments.[541] The procession was probably conducted with song, perhaps in imitation of the happenings at the Last Supper: "And when they had sung a hymn, they went out to the Mount of Olives" (Matt. 26:39; Mark 14:26). The hymn, "Blessed be the name of the Lord..." in the received tradition may be an original recessional hymn. It is the second verse of Psalm 112/113, which in Jewish liturgical tradition was used at Passover and other great festivals. It is a song of joy in praise of the Lord who cares for his people. Perhaps, as in other instances, the entire psalm was sung with the second verse serving as a refrain which the people sang.

The Middle Stratum

By the end of the eighth century two new elements were added to the primitive dismissal rite: *The Prayer Behind the Ambon* (Ὀπισθάμβωνος εὐχή - *Opisthambonos Prayer*) or simply, the *Ambon Prayer* and the *Prayer at the Skeuophylakion*.[542]

The Prayer Behind the Ambon or Ambon Prayer: Each of the three Divine Liturgies of the Byzantine Rite, BAS, CHR, and PRES, has an ambon prayer. BAS and CHR share a common prayer, "Lord, who blesses those who bless you...." In later editions of the Ieratikon, a different prayer, unique to BAS—Ὁ θυσίαν αἰνέσεως καὶ λατρείαν εὐάρεστος ... *O Christ, our God, accept from those who call upon you with all their heart*—is assigned to BAS on January 1, when we celebrate the feast of the Circumcision of the Lord and honor and commemorate St. Basil. In recent years the rubrical directives in the *Epetiris* of the Ecumenical Patriarchate assign the prayer to every celebration of BAS. This practice, however, is not universally practiced.[543] PRES has its own opisthambon prayer,

---

541 For more on the skeuophylakion, the processions, and the recession at Hagia Sophia see Taft, *Communion*, 495-591. See also the relative references in Thomas F. Mathews, *Early Churches of Constantinople*.

542 For the earliest extant collection of these prayers see Parenti and Velkovska, *L' Euchologio Barberini*, 299-310. On the origins, history, and use of the opisthambon see Taft, *Communion*, 592-698. Fountoulis, Ἀπαντήσεις, vol. 2, 147-53; vol. 3, 67-70; and vol. 5, 267-73.

543 The 2004 Ieratikon of the Church of Greece, for example, prefixes the prayer, "Lord, who blesses those who bless you" but also allows for the recitation of the prayer, "O Christ our God" in its place. In the Barberini Codex the prayer, "Lord who blesses those who bless you," is the opisthambon prayer of BAS.

which is appropriate for the period of Lent and Holy Week, when PRES is celebrated on specific weekdays.

The *Barberini Codex* contains several such prayers. One is found in the text of BAS (Εὐχὴ ἐπιστάμβωνος) and nine others in an addendum. Of these prayers, one bears the title, "Ὀπιστάμβωνος τοῦ Χρυσοστόμου."[544] The addendum contains three additional prayers, one of which is attributed to Patriarch Germanos. The addendum also has five ambon prayers for PRES. Notably, most of the ambon prayers bear the title "Ἐπιστάμβωνος." Only two have the title "Ὀπιστάμβωνος." The difference of the two epithets may or may not be significant. One suggests the prayer was recited from or on the ambon (ἐπιστάμβωνος); the other suggests it was said behind the ambon (ὀπισθάμβωνος). The epithets unequivocally define the place where the prayer was recited: the ambon, whether from it or behind it.

In Hagia Sophia and other Constantinopolitan churches the ambon was located a little to the east of the precise center of the nave. It was supported by columns. Its platform was reached by two flights of stairs, one at the east end and the other at the west end. The ambon was connected to the central door (holy door) of the sanctuary by the solea, a path bordered by two waist-high barriers. The sanctuary by custom lay at the eastern end of the building. In some instances, the ambon prayer was read from or on the ambon (ἐπὶ τοῦ ἄμβωνος); in other instances, the recitation took place behind the ambon (ὄπισθεν τοῦ ἄμβωνος), that is at the west end of the ambon. In either case, the prayer was read in the midst of the people who were gathered around the ambon waiting for the clergy to start the recessional.

The ambon prayer was added to the dismissal rite as a final prayer of blessing over the people. In fact, Symeon of Thessaloniki calls it "a prayer on behalf of the people." A tenth century mss of BAS, for example, has the following rubric: "The deacon: Let us go forth in peace. After which the hierarch goes off to behind the ambon. And the deacon says: Let us pray to the Lord. The hierarch: Blessing those who bless you. And the servers respond, Amen. And they go off to the skeuophylakion and take off their sacred [vestments] near the prothesis."[545]

As the liturgical disposition of churches changed and parishes were being served by a single priest, the place from which the prayer was recited also changed. The ambon was no longer situated in the center of the nave. The skeuophylakion as a separate edifice gradually vanished and with it so did the departing procession. The ambon prayer, however, retained its name and place

---

[544] *Barberini Codex*, 299. This prayer may have been original to CHR before it displaced BAS as the chief liturgy of Constantinople.

[545] Cited in Taft, *Communion*, 604.

within the dismissal rites. It also kept its character as a prayer of blessing. Even when the ambon was no longer situated in the middle of the church, the prayer was still recited in the center of the nave among the people. In a later development, it was recited from the Holy Doors of the sanctuary,[546] with the priest facing the people and blessing them as he said the words, "save your people and bless your inheritance."[547]

Following the lead of the deacon, the people listened to the prayer with heads bowed. In fact, in many texts the prayer is preceded by a request of the people, "Lord, have mercy (3). Father bless (us)." The request underscores the nature of the prayer as a blessing. Gradually, additional material was also attached to the dismissal rites, which in turn diminished the original blessing character of the prayer. This was further emphasized by the rubrics in the newer *Ieratika* which instruct the priest to face the icon of Christ when he recites the prayer.[548] Obviously, in this position it is hardly possible for him to offer the traditional blessing. Eventually, the blessing was transferred and attached to one of the newer elements of the dismissal rite, "May the blessing of the Lord and his mercy come upon you...."

The description of the dismissal rites in Cabasilas' *Commentary* (VI. 53) is instructive. In his time (mid-14th century), the ambon prayer was still recited in the middle of the church in the midst of the people but the recession had already disappeared. Instead, the antidoron was distributed immediately after the prayer as the people sang the hymn, "Blessed be the name of the Lord." Also, Psalm 33/34 was chanted until the distribution of the antidoron was complete. This was followed by another prayer of blessing, which we now call the Apolysis, the prelude of which is: "May he who rose from the dead, Christ our true God...." Cabasilas writes:

> After the sacrifice is completed with its concluding doxology...one should note how the priest brings to an end, as it were, his communing with God, and gradually descends from these heights to converse with mankind. He does this as befits a priest, for it is in prayer, and both the

---

546 See Fountoulis, Ἀπαντήσεις, vol. 3, 67-70.

547 In the Slavic tradition, the priest exits the sanctuary through the Holy Doors and recites the ambon prayer at the center of the nave facing the sanctuary. After the prayer, he retraces his steps into the sanctuary and goes to the prothesis, where he recites the Prayer of the skeuophylakion.

548 See Fountoulis, Ἀπαντήσεις, vol. 5, 267-73. Personally, I follow the old tradition and read the prayer facing the people and bless them at the appropriate time. In the same volume, see p. 285-288. In these pages, Fountoulis discusses an interesting philological/theological question regarding the phrase, "Ὅτι πᾶσα δόσις ἀγαθή...For every good gift" which is borrowed from James 1:17. The correct reading in the Greek liturgical text requires placing a comma after the words, "ἄνωθεν ἐστί...is from above."

manner and the place of his prayer symbolize his descent. First of all, within the sanctuary he addresses himself to God and prays secretly on his own behalf. Then he leaves the sanctuary and standing in the midst of the congregation he says aloud, so that everyone can hear,[549] the prayer of common supplication for the Church and for all the faithful. Then the bread which has been offered up, and from which the sacred Lamb was taken, is broken into small pieces and given to the faithful as something which has been hallowed by being dedicated and offered to God. The faithful receive this [antidoron] with all reverence, kissing the hand which has so recently touched the all-holy Body of our Savior Christ.... And so, they glorify him who is the Origin and Dispenser of these blessings which they receive. This doxology is taken from the Scriptures: 'Blessed be the name of the Lord,' and so on. This is proclaimed several times, and then they say a psalm which particularly stresses doxology and thanksgiving. Which is this psalm? It is Ps.33/34, 'I will bless the Lord at all times.' After the distribution of the bread and after the psalm, the priest says the last prayer over the people." This prayer is now called the Apolysis.

Through the centuries, the Constantinopolitan tradition has retained only three ambon prayers, one which is shared by BAS and CHR, another unique to BAS,[550] and a third for PRES. However, in the wider "Byzantine periphery" we find a large number of mss with dozens of ambon prayers for major feast days and other occasions.[551] The ambon prayers in these mss have been studied by a number of scholars from the beginning of the twentieth century to the present time.[552] Their works have appeared in various academic journals.

---

549 Significantly, even though it was common by then to read the prayers of the liturgy inaudibly, the rubrics specifically note that the ambon prayer must be read aloud for all to hear. This clearly supports the idea that it is a prayer of blessing.

550 For more on the prayer Ὁ θυσίαν αἰνέσεως see Fountoulis, Ἀπαντήσεις, vol. 2, 147-51. The prayer is associated exclusively with BAS in a number of manuscripts and printed editions. However, it is not at all clear why and how it came to be linked only with the celebration of BAS on January 1, the feast day of St. Basil, as recorded, for example, in the Typikon of Violakis. In some Ieratika the celebrant is given the option to read one or the other of the two prayers, "Ὁ εὐλογῶν τοὺς εὐλογοῦντάς σε, Κύριε" or "Ὁ θυσίαν αἰνέσεως." Reciting this prayer at every celebration of BAS helps to accentuate the difference between the two Divine Liturgies, BAS and CHR. The reintroduction of special Behind the Ambo Prayers for the Dominical and Marian feasts will help emphasize the meaning of these feasts.

551 For a comprehensive study of the ambon prayers see Taft, Communion, 645-698. Taft defines the Byzantine periphery as the Greek Orthodox Patriarchates of Alexandria, Antioch, and Jerusalem and those areas of Byzantine culture like Greece, Sicily, and Southern Italy. From there, these prayers travelled to the non-Greek areas of Byzantine Orthodoxy (667).

552 See Fountoulis, Ἀπαντήσεις, vol. 2, 151-3.

As a result of these studies, a Greek *Ieratikon* was published in Rome in 1950 with an addendum that contains thirteen ambon prayers for various feasts and occasions. More recently, in 2005 the Greek Orthodox Holy Theotokos Monastery in North Fort Pierce, FL published a collection of ambon prayers, *Prayers Behind the Ambon: for the Divine Liturgy of St. John Chrysostom, St. Basil the Great, and the Presanctified*. Copies of both texts are available in the Archbishop Iakovos Library of Hellenic College and Holy Cross. Perhaps, the Holy Eparchial Synod of the GOA may wish to study the issue and authorize the publication of a collection of ambon prayers with guidelines for their proper use.

Prayer of the Skeuophylakion:[553] As already noted, in earlier times the liturgy ended with the diaconal command, "Let us go forth in peace." At this point, the people exited the church in procession following the clergy and singing a recessional hymn. The people spilled into the courtyard and the clergy proceeded to the skeuophylakion.

At the skeuophylakion the clergy consumed the remaining Holy Gifts, took off their vestments, and read a prayer which bears the title: "Εὐχὴ λεγομένη ἐν τῷ σκευοφυλακίῳ ... A Prayer said in the Skeuophylakion."[554] An alternate title reads: "Εὐχὴ λεγομένη ἐν τῷ συστεῖλαι τὰ ἅγια ἐν τῷ σκευοφυλακίῳ ... A Prayer said at the consumption of the Holy Gifts at the Skeuophylakion." Originally, the prayer was said after the remaining Eucharistic elements were consumed in thanksgiving for the gift of Communion as the clergy prepared to transition from the liturgy to the affairs of everyday life. In other words, the term "skeuophylakion" in the title only indicates the place where the prayer was said. The title has been retained in most *Ieratika* even though the prayer is now recited at the prothesis. The original purpose of the prayer has been eclipsed as new elements were added to the dismissal rite.

When the skeuophylakion ceased to exist, its place, in part, was taken by the prothesis. Originally located within the skeuophylakion, the prothesis eventually was transferred to and situated in the northeast side of the sanctuary in the form of a free-standing adorned table or a decorated shelf within a niche.[555] The essential function of the prothesis has remained the same through the centuries. The eucharistic gifts are prepared at the prothesis and after Communion the remaining elements are returned to it so that they may be consumed according to a specified order about which we will speak below.

---

553 For more on the skeuophylakion, processions, and recession see Taft, *Communion*, 495-591 and 734-49.

554 In some later mss and printed editions the term skeuophylakion is eliminated or replaced by other terms such as prothesis and diakonikon.

555 From the ninth century and thereafter there is evidence that the prothesis was also called skeuophylakion. See Trembelas, Τρεῖς Λειτουργίαι, 156.

The dismissal rites described by Cabasilas in the passage cited above indicate that the recession was no longer practiced in his time. The priest distributed the antidoron immediately after the ambon prayer as the recessional hymn(s) was chanted. This was followed by the apolysis. Meanwhile the deacon(s) or other designated persons consumed the remaining Holy Gifts at the prothesis. With the decline of the diaconate, it fell to the priest(s) to consume the Gifts but after the distribution of the antidoron.

Despite the changes in the dismissal rites, the Prayer of the Skeuophylakion is read in its original order, after the Prayer of the Ambon. In current practice, as the people sing the old recessional hymn, the priest re-enters the sanctuary and proceeds to the prothesis. There he recites the skeuophylakion prayer. When he has finished, he reverences the Holy Gifts by kissing the covered Chalice or he simply bows his head. He returns to the Holy Table to complete the remaining portions of the dismissal rite.

Obviously, the original skeuophylakion prayer was not heard by the people because it was recited at the skeuophylakion. To this day it continues to be said inaudibly and out of the sight of the people at the prothesis. For the edification and benefit of the people, however, the priest may wish to recite the prayer aloud from time to time. The respective prayer in each of the three liturgies, CHR, BAS, and PRES, is brief, distinct, and instructive and fitting to be prayed aloud occasionally for the benefit of the people.

The prayer in CHR is addressed to Christ and reads as follows:

> "Christ our God, you are the fulfillment of the Law and the Prophets. You have fulfilled all the dispensation of the Father (πᾶσαν τὴν πατρικὴν οἰκονομίαν). Fill, our hearts with joy and gladness always, now and forever and to the ages of ages. Amen."

The prayer begins with two creedal statements and ends with a petition. First, Christ is acknowledged as the "fulfillment of the Law and the Prophets." He is, in other words, the Messiah, the Savior of the world, Word and Son of God who became flesh and dwelt among us (John 1:14, 41, 45, 49; 4:42). The phrase, "fulfillment of the Law and the Prophets," also brings to mind the risen Lord's words to the two disciples on the road to Emmaus concerning his person and mission.[556]

---

556 "And beginning with Moses and all the prophets, he interpreted to them in all the scriptures the things concerning himself.... They said to each other, Did not our hearts burn within us while he talked to us on the road, while he opened to us the scriptures?" (Luke 24:27, 32).

Second, we declare and confess that Christ is the One who fulfilled the Father's entire plan of salvation (John 4:34; 17:4-7; Phil. 2:5-11). The Eucharist is not explicitly mentioned in the prayer. However, we believe that at the Divine Liturgy the Church remembers and celebrates in faith the mystery of the Father's dispensation, his economy which was accomplished for the life of the world by his Son (1 John 4:14). Moreover, it is through the liturgy that the faithful become the recipients of the saving, life-giving, and sanctifying grace that flows from the Father's economy, from his plan of salvation.

The prayer ends with a supplication that is direct and brief. Christ is implored to fill the hearts of all with joy and gladness – gifts that come only from above (John 14:11; 16:24; 17:13; Rom. 15:13; James 1:17). Having completed the Eucharist, the priest prays that Christ will fill his heart with joy and gladness as he resumes his daily activities with all their uncertainties. The same holds true for all the faithful who hear or read this prayer.

The prayer in BAS is also addressed to Christ and reads as follows:

> "The mystery of your dispensation, O Christ our God, has been accomplished and perfected as far as it was in our power. We have had the memorial of your death. We have seen the type of your resurrection. We have been filled with your unending life. We have enjoyed your inexhaustible delight which in the world to come be well pleased to give to us all, through the grace of your holy and good and life-giving Spirit, now and forever and to the ages of ages. Amen."

The prayer in BAS focuses directly on the Mystery of the Eucharist. At the outset it underscores a basic sacramental teaching of the Church, that all sacraments are accomplished by Christ through the agency of ordained ministers, sacred rituals, and material elements. The celebrant declares humbly: "The mystery of your dispensation, O Christ our God, has been accomplished and finished/perfected[557] as far as it was in our power." In other words, the priest is declaring: Lord, we accomplished the sacrament of the Eucharist, as far as it was in our power. We did what was entrusted to us to the best of our limited abilities.

---

557 Christ used the same word on the Cross when he breathed his last, τετέλεσται – *it is finished* (John 19:30) – from the verb **τελέω**, which means to finish, complete, fulfill, accomplish, perfect. The first word in the prayer, **ηνυσται**, is from the verb **ἀνύω**, which means to accomplish, complete.

The prayer then lists four basic experiences of the Divine Liturgy. We have been afforded the *remembrance of Christ's death and the type or figure of his resurrection*. We were *filled with his unending life and we enjoyed his inexhaustible delight (τρυφή).*"558

The earliest form of the prayer is found in the *Barberini Codex* 336. There are slight differences between the prayer in the *Codex* and the received text. The four experiences or gifts are listed differently in the *Codex*.559 The verbs in the last two gifts are reversed as is their order in the text.560 The wording and the sequence is as follows: "*We have been filled with your inexhaustible delight (τρυφή). We have enjoyed your unending life.*"

The supplicatory element of the prayer is introduced by the final gift or experience. In the *Barberini* text it is: "We have enjoyed your unending life, which, in the world to come, be well pleased to give to us all through the grace of your holy, good, and life-creating Spirit, now and forever and to the ages of ages. Amen." In the received text we declare and ask for something different: "We have enjoyed your inexhaustible delight, which, in the world to come, be well pleased to give to us all...." In the first instance, the object of our petition is to share in Christ's unending life. In the second instance, the object is the enjoyment of his good pleasure unto the ages.

The prayer in PRES reads as follows:

> Lord our God, you have guided us to these most solemn days and have made us communicants of your awesome Mysteries, join us to your spiritual flock and declare us heirs of your kingdom, now and forever, and to the ages of ages. Amen.

---

558 The word τρυφή is used in Gen. 3:24 for the Garden of Eden (Septuagint): "Καὶ ἐξέβαλε τὸν Ἀδὰμ καὶ κατῴκισεν αὐτόν ἀπέναντι τοῦ *παραδείσου τῆς τρυφῆς* καὶ ἔταξε τὰ Χερουβίμ ... He drove out the man; and at the east of the Garden of Eden he placed the Cherubim." In the Septuagint, the Garden (paradise) is not named after a geographical region, Eden, but with a similar sounding Hebrew word, which means "delight." The Garden is the locale of God, the place of extreme joy and satisfaction. The same prayer with slight differences is found in an eleventh-century *Hagiasmatarion* and *Archieratikon*. Chief among the differences is the word τρυφή. It is replaced with the word τροφή, food. Hence the formula reads, "We have been filled with your inexhaustible food." See, Miguel Arranz, *L'Euchologio Constantinopolitano agli inizi del secolo XI* (Rome 1996), 495-6. The reading τροφη found its way into Slavic texts. Thus, in the Slavic version of the prayer the specific formula reads, "We have enjoyed your inexhaustible food." See, for example, *The Divine Liturgy* (OCA, 1967), 111.

559 See *L'Eucologio Barberini gr. 336*, 24. Brightman, *Eastern Liturgies*, 344.

560 The verb in the first item is also different in the *Barberini Codex*. Instead of the verb ἔσχομεν in the received text, the *Barberini* text has the verb ηὕραμεν, we found. The second item has the same verb but in a different tense, εἴδαμεν instead of εἴδομεν.

The prayer reflects the special time of the year during which PRES is celebrated: the most solemn days of the Great Fast and Holy Week. As worthy partakers of Holy Communion and members of God's holy flock we are graced by God to be inheritors of his kingdom.[561]

The Final Strata

Beginning with the twelfth century a few mss indicate that new material was being appended to the concluding rites thus expanding them further.[562]

The Blessing: One such new element is the blessing formula, *"Εὐλογία Κυρίου καὶ ἔλεος αὐτοῦ ... May the blessing of the Lord and his mercy come upon you...."* The blessing is said by the celebrant, hierarch or priest, while facing the people from the Holy Doors. As he intones the blessing, he makes the sign of the cross over the people in the usual manner. If a priest, he blesses with his hand, if a hierarch, with the blessing cross.

The blessing appears in the *Diataxis of Philotheos Kokkinos* but not in the *editio princeps* of Doukas. By the seventeenth century it had become a permanent part of the dismissal rite.

Interestingly, the same formula, either in the plural or in the singular form, is used by the priest when he gives the antidoron to each congregant. This is probably due to the fact that the term *εὐλογία* – *blessing* is often applied to the gifts one receives from God. The antidoron is such a gift, a concrete, material expression of God's bounties. In days past, the prosphoron was often called an *εὐλογία*, an offering of love.

The diaconal bidding, "Let us pray to the Lord," which precedes the blessing was once attached to the Prayer of the Skeuophylakion. Or, it may have been an invitation to the people to bless God – to praise and thank him – silently in their hearts in preparation for the blessing they were about to receive from the priest, that is the priestly benediction and the antidoron. The opening words of the Ambon Prayer may be construed as suggesting such a possibility: "O Lord, who blesses those who bless you...).

A careful analysis of the several dismissal prayers that form the rite indicates that they are basically forms of blessing. At the conclusion of the service as the people prepare to depart, the priest blesses them, imparting to them the love, mercy, compassion, peace, and joy of Christ.

---

561 See Alexopoulos, *Presanctified Liturgy*, 278-81.

562 See Taft, *Communion*, 750-84.

The Apolysis: The term *apolysis* is used generally for the entire dismissal rites and specifically for the last prayer of intercession and blessing: "*Ὁ ἀναστὰς ἐκ νεκρῶν, Χριστὸς ὁ ἀληθινὸς Θεὸς ἡμῶν … May he who rose from the dead, Christ our true God…*"[563]

The present final blessing (apolysis) was used initially in the services of the daily office. It appeared first in a few texts of the Divine Liturgy in the thirteenth and fourteenth centuries. Cabasilas refers to it in his *Commentary on the Divine Liturgy*, but it is missing from the *Diataxis of Philotheos Kokkinos*. By the end of the sixteenth century it was used widely and gradually came to be regarded as the indispensable dismissal prayer.[564]

The apolysis is both supplicatory and intercessory. In praying the apolysis, we acknowledge and confess that Christ is the true God, and that he is both good (ἀγαθός) and loving (φιλάνθρωπος). Confident, therefore, of his ineffable goodness and steadfast love for humankind, we implore him to show mercy and to save us. To aid our cause, we invoke the help of his Holy Mother, the Theotokos, and of all the saints, that they may intercede on our behalf.

Some editions of the liturgy contain a short form of the apolysis and others a long form. The difference between the two rests in the number of saints invoked and commemorated.[565] The long forms include lengthy lists of saints together with their respective epithets. By contrast, the older, more traditional forms contain only a few names.[566] The most recent *Ieratikon of the Church of*

---

563 As mentioned earlier, this form of the apolysis is used on Sundays and throughout the Paschal season. The apolysis of each dominical feast has its own incipit (opening phrase). On weekdays, the apolysis has no special introductory phrase. We say simply, "May Christ our true God…" For more on the apolysis see the relevant comments in part one of the present study, the Service of Vespers.

564 Fountoulis, Ἀπαντήσεις, vol. 3, 62.

565 The commemorations in the short form include the Theotokos, the Holy Angels, St. John the Baptist, and the Holy Apostles. Also included as a group are the holy, glorious, and triumphant martyrs and the righteous and God-bearing fathers. Also mentioned by name is the saint in whose honor the church is dedicated; the saint whose liturgy has been celebrated; and the saint(s) of the day whose memory we celebrate. Immediately after the Theotokos, the apolysis includes the phrase "(through) the power (δυνάμει) of the precious and life-giving Cross." The commemoration of the Theotokos is preceded by the phrase "through the intercessions (πρεσβείαις) of his all-pure…;" that of the holy Angels, (through) "the protection (προστασίαις) of the honorable…" The commemoration of St. John the Baptist is preceded by the phrase, "(through) the supplications (ἱκεσίαις)," which applies to all the other saints that follow. In effect, we are asking Christ to save us through the intercessions of the Theotokos; the power of his Cross; the protection of the heavenly powers; and the supplications of his saints.

566 Some clergy include their own "favorite" saints in the commemorations. This should be avoided.

Greece and the new bilingual translation of the GOA employ the short form.

The Exclamation: The apolysis is preceded by a short exclamation: "Δόξα σοι, Χριστὲ ὁ Θεός, ἡ ἐλπὶς ἡμῶν, δόξα σοι ... *Glory to you, Christ God, our hope, glory to you.*" The formula is not consistent. In some forms the name of Christ is not mentioned, "Glory to you, O God, our hope....;" in others the last phrase, "glory to you" is dropped. The exclamation first appeared in a few late mss and in the *editio princeps* of Doukas. It gained currency slowly and by the end of the seventeenth century it attained permanency. Some texts include the small doxology, "Glory to the Father...." after the exclamation together with the bidding, "Father, bless."

The "Δι' εὐχῶν": For many people, clergy and laity alike, the saying, "Δι'εὐχῶν τῶν ἁγίων πατέρων ἡμῶν, Κύριε Ἰησοῦ Χριστέ, ὁ Θεὸς ἡμῶν, ἐλέησον ἡμᾶς ... *Through the prayers of our holy fathers, Lord Jesus Christ, our God, have mercy on us,*" is synonymous with completion – the very seal that confirms the end of a service. The saying, however, is not used by all the Orthodox churches but is common in the Greek church and elsewhere.

The saying, Δι' εὐχῶν, like the apolysis, is borrowed from the monastic office of the Hours. It is found in the office of the Intermediary Hours (Μεσώρια), where it is used to signal the end of the service and as a bridge to the service that follows.[567] It is also used in the Great Compline (Apodeipnon). It is recited at the end of each of its three sections, as a bridge or link in the first two instances and as a signal of completion in the last.

The "fathers" mentioned in the saying refers to the members of a given monastic community and not to the Fathers of the Church. For example, at the conclusion of the Great Compline we find the following exchange between the hegoumenos and the monks. "Straightway the presider making a deep prostration, says to the brethren, 'Bless, holy fathers, forgive me the sinner.' And the brethren [say], May God forgive you, holy father."

While the saying has remained unchanged in parish usage, the phrase "holy fathers" is actually irrelevant and inapplicable. To be true to the intent of the saying, the phrase "holy fathers" should be replaced by a suitable phrase that refers to the gathered community, such as, "By the prayers of your faithful people."

We read in the Epistle of James, "pray for one another that you may be healed. The effective fervent prayer of a righteous man avails much" (5:16). As disciples of Christ we are commanded to love and to pray for one another. These virtues must be active and operational in our daily lives and in particular at every communal worship service and in times of personal prayer. Time and again,

---

567 See, for example, the Intermediary First Hour in the *Great Horologion* (1856/1973), 80.

the prayers of the church remind us of our obligation to remember other people – their needs, concerns, challenges, and predicaments – and to pray for their well-being and deliverance from all affliction and distress; and when practicable to translate the words of our prayers into fitting acts of kindness.

It is fitting, therefore, to conclude our prayer services with the **Δι' ευχων**; with the fervent plea to our Lord Jesus Christ to manifest his mercy, goodness, and saving power to all his people through the humble prayers of the worshipping community gathered in his name – a people who are mindful of the power of intercessory prayer – the prayer of faith that saves (James 5:15).

Additional acclamations and greetings: At the conclusion of the apolysis and before the Δι' εὐχῶν, the people sing an acclamation asking the Lord to protect and grant many years to the priest, who "blesses and sanctifies them."[568]

The acclamation is in keeping with true Byzantine etiquette, which requires a person(s) to respond in kind to another's greetings or blessings. In some recent editions of the *Ieratikon*, the priest responds to the people's greeting saying, "Διαφυλάξαι Κύριος ὁ Θεὸς πάντας τοὺς εὐσεβεῖς καὶ ὀρθοδόξους χριστιανούς, τοὺς κατοικοῦντας ἐν τῇ πόλει καὶ ἐνορίᾳ ταύτῃ σὺν γυναιξὶ καὶ τέκνοις αὐτῶν" or more simply, "Διαφυλάξαι Κύριος ὁ Θεὸς πάντας ἡμᾶς." ... "*May the Lord God preserve* [or *watch over*] *all of you.*"

The more traditional greeting or blessing, however, recorded in most, if not all the editions, is: "'Η Ἁγία Τριὰς διαφυλάξαι πάντας ἡμᾶς ... *May the Holy Trinity preserve all of you.*" The blessing is said after the Δι' εὐχῶν. As the priest pronounces the blessing, he makes the usual sign of the cross over the people.

---

568 It is customary in some Orthodox churches to sing an acclamation for newlyweds at the conclusion of the marriage rite. The same is true for the newly baptized. The "Memory Eternal—Αἰωνία ἡ μνήμη" which is sung at funerals and memorial services is an acclamation for the deceased.

P. THE ANTIDORON – ΑΝΤΙΔΩΡΟΝ

When the dismissal rites are ended, the priest stands in the middle of the solea to distribute the antidoron to the people.[569] To preserve proper decorum, parishes should require the people to approach row by row under the guidance of parish council members. According to a long-standing tradition, the chanter or choir sings Psalm 33/34 during the distribution of the antidoron.[570]

Offering the antidoron, the priest says to each person, "Εὐλογία Κυρίου καὶ ἔλεος ἔλθοι ἐφ' ὑμᾶς ... May the blessing and the mercy of the Lord come upon you." When the last person has received the antidoron, the priest says, "Τῇ αὐτοῦ θείᾳ χάριτι καὶ φιλανθρωπίᾳ πάντοτε νῦν καὶ ἀεὶ καὶ εἰς τοὺς αἰῶνας τῶν αἰώνων. Ἀμήν. ... By his divine grace and love always, now and forever and to the ages of ages. Amen."

The antidoron is closely associated with the Prothesis Rite.[571] As the rite expanded during the eleventh and twelfth centuries to include, in addition to the Lamb, particles for the Theotokos and the saints and for the living and the dead, the number of prosphora from which the various particles were extracted increased. These prosphora, having been set apart and sealed with the sign of the cross, were considered blessed. Hence, the question arose what to do with these left-over breads? The answer was to cut them into small pieces

---

569 Should it be necessary, the priest makes all important announcements before the distribution of the antidoron.

570 Because this is not always feasible, some priests use a recording to fulfill the tradition. On major feast days chanters sometimes substitute other material, such as the katavasiai, another suitable psalm, or festal hymns appropriate to the occasion.

571 On the antidoron see Taft, *Communion*, 699-719. Trembelas, *Τρεῖς Λειτουργίαι*, 157-8.

and distribute them to the clergy and the people.⁵⁷² Originally, the distribution took place after the ambon prayer. But with the expansion of the dismissal rites, the antidoron was distributed after the final dismissal, as we do today.

At first, the antidoron was called εὐλογία – *blessing*. This may be the reason for the formula which accompanies its distribution, "May *the blessing* of the Lord and his mercy come upon you." Indeed, every good and perfect gift which comes from above is considered a blessing. Thus, the piece of the unconsecrated bread – the antidoron – is seen as a visible material manifestation of God's plenteous mercy and goodness. Before long, the word εὐλογία was replaced by the term ἀντίδωρον – antidoron, which literally means, "instead of the Gifts." With the decline of frequent Communion, for many people the antidoron became a sort of substitute, "in the place of," the Holy Gifts.

At the end his *Commentary* (VI: 53), St. Nicholas Cabasilas offers a brief reflection on the antidoron. He says, "Then the bread which has been offered up, and from which the Lamb was taken, is broken into small pieces and given to the faithful as something which has been hallowed by being dedicated and offered to God. The faithful receive this with all reverence, kissing the hand which has so recently touched the all-holy Body of the Savior Christ and which, thus sanctified, can communicate this sanctification to those who touch it. And so, they glorify him who is the Origin and Dispenser of these blessings which they receive."

The antidoron is also given to those who receive Communion. Immediately after Holy Communion, each recipient takes a piece of the antidoron and consumes it. The purpose for this is to help purify the mouth of the communicant. By eating the antidoron it is supposed that every last particle of the eucharistic elements are taken up with it.

R. CONSUMING THE GIFTS AT THE PROTHESIS

When the distribution of the antidoron is completed, the priest returns to the sanctuary and proceeds to the prothesis in order to consume the left-over Holy Gifts and purify the chalice.⁵⁷³ He approaches the task reverently. To focus on the task before him, the priest recites the initial, admonitory verses in the extra-liturgical post-Communion Thanksgiving Prayers: "And when you

---

572 In large parishes the left-over breads of the prothesis are not sufficient to meet the needs of the congregation. Hence, additional prosphora are cut and mixed in with the bread(s) of the prothesis. The prosphora are prepared by individual families or by a group of parishioners who bake them weekly, biweekly, or monthly. The sexton sees to it that a sufficient number of prosphora is always available.

573 To make the task easier, the priest may remove the phelonion while consuming the Gifts.

obtain the blessed Communion, of the life-creating mystical Gifts, straightway give praise and great thanks, and fervently from your soul say to God: Glory to you, O God; glory to you, O God; glory to you, O God."[574]

To retain a prayerful atmosphere, the priest may assign an altar server or a congregant(s) to read the Thanksgiving Prayers as he consumes the Holy Gifts.[575] If not, he will read them after the Gifts have been consumed.

The priest crosses himself, uncovers the Chalice, and with the communion spoon begins to consume with care the remaining Eucharistic elements, eating all the particles, even the tiniest morsel, and drinking all that remains in the Cup. After this, he purifies the Chalice.

In most *Ieratika*, the manner by which the chalice is purified is rarely mentioned, except in very general terms. Some mss of the seventeenth and eighteenth centuries, however, contain a specific rubric regarding the purification of the chalice. After the Gifts have been consumed, the deacon or priest is instructed "to wash the holy chalice with wine twice and with water once and with exactness wipe away all the moisture with a sponge ... ἀποπλύνων δε τὸ ἅγιον ποτήριον τῷ οἴνῳ δὶς καὶ τῷ ὕδατι ἅπαξ καὶ ἐκμασσῶν ἀκριβῶς τὴν ὑγρότητα πᾶσαν μετὰ σπόγγου..."[576]

In other words, the priest is instructed to clean the chalice twice with wine, which of course he drinks and then with water, which he also drinks. The use of wine twice is of particular interest. I suspect the wine was used twice for practical reasons. First, it makes it easier to wash away any tiny bread particles that cling to the sides of the chalice. The second use of the wine, I believe, was to sterilize the cup. The water is used to wash away any residue of the wine. (In fact, more than one washing with water may be required).

Having consumed everything in the chalice, the priest pours some wine along the rim into the chalice cleaning the sides with the spoon, if necessary. He drinks what is in the cup and repeats the action once again pouring some wine over the spoon as well. After drinking the wine, he pours some fresh

---

574 These prayers are usually appended to CHR in the *Ieratika* and the various translations. See, for example, the GOA (2015) bilingual translation of CHR, 88-97.

575 In my seminary days as the ecclesiarch, I would often read the set of prayers for the celebrant as he consumed the Holy Gifts. When our beloved professor and chaplain, Fr. Gerasimos Papadopoulos was the celebrant (the revered and blessed elder Bishop Gerasimos of Abydos), he would himself recite the brief prayer, "Τὸ σῶμα σου τὸ ἅγιον, Κύριε Ἰησοῦ Χριστὲ ὁ Θεὸς ἡμῶν ... Lord Jesus Christ, my God, let your sacred Body be unto me...." He taught me to do the same, because as he said, "this prayer is the summary of all the thanksgiving prayers."

576 In Trembelas, Τρεῖς Λειτουργίαι, 158.

water over the spoon into the chalice and wipes the spoon clean with a clean communion cloth and lays it aside. Taking the cruet with the water, or better still using the *zeon*, he pours the water along the rim into the chalice and drinks it. He repeats the action, making certain that the cup is clean. When he is certain the cup is clean, he wipes the inside of the chalice and its rim with a communion cloth. Then he places the sponge into the cup to capture any remaining moisture and covers the chalice with the cloth. He consumes the small portion of the prosphoron left on the prothesis.[577] He may share it, if he wishes, with the person(s) who read the thanksgiving prayers or any other.

When the service of thanksgiving is completed,[578] the priest makes certain the prothesis is left in good order, free of crumbs. He covers the discos and the chalice with the appropriate cloths. Then he removes his priestly vestments and stores them properly. He washes his hands and his lips. He makes certain the Holy Table is in good order. He venerates the Holy Table and Evangelion and places a cloth cover over it. He departs in peace with joy and thanksgiving in his heart.

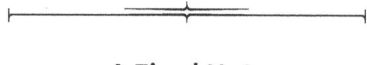

A Final Note

The power for effective ministry, in all its dimensions and expressions, does not rest entirely on the individual cleric but on the grace and love of God which enable him to be "a vessel for honor, sanctified and useful for the Master, prepared for every good work" (2 Tim. 2:21; cf. Heb. 5:1-4). The essential task of every priest is to be worthy of the grace by discharging his responsibilities faithfully, conscientiously, and courageously, mindful that whatever good thing he does, he does by the grace and guidance of the Holy Spirit. A conscientious priest never stops praying, loving, caring, hoping, or learning as he seeks to fulfill his high calling to the fullest of his God-given abilities as a humble celebrant of the divine mysteries, as an effective preacher and teacher of the faith, and as a solicitous, devoted shepherd of souls.

---

577 After consuming the Chalice and before he begins the purification, the priest may wish to eat some of the bread. Being on an empty stomach for many hours, he may need the bread to minimize the effects of the additional wine he is about to drink.

578 The service of thanksgiving is extra-liturgical and of monastic origins. Its purpose is to heighten the sense of gratitude for the gift of Communion and the awareness of the communicant to its many blessings. It opens with the admonitory verses mentioned above. It contains five prayers, one of which is attributed to St. Basil and another to St. Symeon the Translator (Μεταφραστής), the other three are from anonymous authors. The last prayer is addressed to the Theotokos. Following the last prayer, the priest recites the Song of St. Symeon (Luke 2:29-32). This is followed by the Trisagion; the apolytikion of the day; the apolytikion and kontakion of St. John Chrysostom (or of St. Basil the Great); and the apolysis.

The priesthood requires hard work, patience and resolve. It is not an office for the timid, the indifferent, the cynical, the acquisitive, or the indolent but for those who live life humbly, zealously, and fearlessly for God as servants of redemption.[579]

Yet, even the most dedicated priest often feels inadequate and questions his worthiness and abilities. However, the weekly celebration of the Eucharist offers each priest the opportunity to overcome his doubts, heal his wounds, replenish his strength, and, in the words of St. Paul, "rekindle the gift of God that is within [him] through the laying on of hands…for God did not give [him] a spirit of timidity but a spirit of power and love and self-control…not in virtue of [his] works but in virtue of [God's] own purpose and the grace which he gave us in Christ Jesus" (2 Tim. 1:6-7, 9).[580] *Allow me to end this reflection on the Divine Liturgy with the Prayer of the Skeuophylakion in BAS. It summarizes all that the worshipping community—priests and people together—celebrated, accomplished, experienced, and received through the sacred eucharistic rite:*

The mystery of your dispensation, O Christ our God, has been accomplished and perfected as far as it was in our power. We have had the memorial of your death. We have seen the type of your resurrection. We have been filled with your unending life. We have enjoyed your inexhaustible delight which, in the world to come, be well pleased to give to us all, through the grace of your holy and good and life-giving Spirit, now and forever and to the ages of ages. Amen.

---

579 See Calivas, "The Presbyter and the Essential Activities of the Church," in *Church, Clergy, Laity, and the Spiritual Life*, 65-87.

580 These very same sentiments have been incorporated in the anaphora-epiclesis of BAS: "Therefore, most holy Master, we also, your sinful and unworthy servants, whom you have permitted to serve at your holy altar not because of our own righteousness, for we have done nothing good upon the earth, but because of your mercy and compassion which you have so richly poured out on us…"

Appendices

Appendix C:1

A note on the anteri, rason, and kalemaukion

In the extant manuscripts or in the printed editions of the Euchologion, the *anteri*, *rason*, and *kalemaukion* are never mentioned by name in any of the ordination rites as liturgical vestments or even as external attire of the ordained clergy.

These garments, however, are mentioned in the rites for the making of monastics.[581] The word *rason* appears in the title of the service for the making of a novice. The novice is clothed with a tunic (χιτών) and a kalemaukion (head cover/hat). When the novice is deemed worthy and enters the monastic life, he receives the monastic habit which includes a cloak (the anteri), belt, kalemaukion, the pallium (another word for rason), sandals, and a *mandyas* (long enveloping cloak). A monk of the Great Schema receives two additional articles, the *koukoulion* (cowl or hood) and the *analabos*—a long linen cloth decorated with the instruments of Christ's passion. The monastic habit also includes the *epanokalemauhon* or veil, which is draped over the kalemaukion or over a skoufos. The veil is worn by ordained and nonordained monks alike.[582]

---

[581] On clerical attire see Calivas, *Church, Clergy, Laity, and the Spiritual Life*, 89-150. See also Panagiotis Papaevangelou, Ἡ Διαμόρφωσις τῆς ἐξωτερικῆς ἐμφανίσεως τοῦ Ἀνατολικοῦ καὶ ἰδία τοῦ Ἑλληνικοῦ κλήρου (Thessaloniki 1965). Vasilios Thermos, "Ποιμαντικές καὶ Ψυχολογικές Διαστάσης τῆς Ἱερατικῆς Περιβολῆς" in Τὰ ἱερὰ Ἄμφια καὶ η ἐξωτερική περιβολή τοῦ Ὀρθοδόξου Κλήρου — Σειρά Ποιμαντική Βιβλιοθήκη, volume 5 (Athens 2002.

[582] On the monastic habit and the symbolic meaning of its several articles see St. Germanos of Constantinople in his treatise on the Divine Liturgy.

During the latter half of the nineteenth century, for the sake of uniformity, individual metropolitans and hierarchs began to impose the monastic anteri, rason, and kalemaukion on parish clergy. However, it was not until 1931 that the Greek state, with the approval of the Synod of the Church of Greece, established these garments as the official public attire of the Orthodox clergy within the Greek domain.

Through the centuries, the public attire of the clergy was basically simple, modest, and similar to, if not identical with, the garments worn by ordinary people. In fact, until the sixth century there was little to distinguish the clergy from the laypeople by way of outer garments, even at liturgical services. During the sixth century and thereafter civilian dress began to change as clothes became more stylish and ornate. The clergy, however, were slow to follow the new trends. While the styles and cuts of clothing changed periodically, the public attire of both the rich and poor remained basically the same up to modern times – namely, over the undergarments, people wore layers of long and short loose-fitting tunics combined with various forms of cloaks (*phelonia*) and scarves (*loros*) and different designs of trousers, especially for adult males.[583]

The aforementioned decree of 1931 also enumerated the liturgical vestments proper to each order of the sacred priesthood. Significantly, neither the rason nor the kalemaukion were listed among the liturgical vestments.

Nonetheless. long before the established rule, the rason had begun to acquire a semi-liturgical function. It was used both as public attire and as a kind of liturgical garment in monasteries and in parish churches. The double use of the rason came about for practical reasons.

Except for the Divine Liturgy, the clergy began to abandon the use of the complete vesture of their respective office at all other divine services—a long standing tradition. The rason became a convenient replacement for the sticharion. Thus, in the case of deacons, it is used together with the orarion. Priests wear it together with the epitrachilion and phelonion, and in the case of hierarchs in combination with the epitrachilion and omophorion. Only readers and chanters use the rason unaccompanied in liturgical services. The priestly orders, on the other hand, may use the rason as a covering at any time but may not conduct church services with it unaccompanied by their distinctive vestments.

---

583   See A. Calivas, *Church, Clergy, Laity and the Spiritual Life* (Brookline, MA 2013), 90.

In former times, clerics wore the vestments proper to their order at all the sacred services (Divine Liturgy, sacramental and other rites, vespers and orthros). This practice has been retained for the Divine Liturgy and for several other services: the Orthros of Holy Saturday (Epitaphios Service), the Vespers of Pascha Sunday, and the Vespers and Orthros celebrated during Renewal or Bright Week.[584]

Clerical vestments (ἄμφια) have their origins in the secular garments worn by ordinary people and public officials in the ancient Graeco-Roman world, not in the vestments of the Old Testament priesthood as was previously thought.[585] During the first several centuries, clergy probably set aside and used a better set of "ordinary" clothing for the performance of their liturgical functions. Priestly vestments began to appear well after the fourth century. As we learn from the life of St. Marcian the Oeconomos, there was no special liturgical vesture in the early Byzantine tradition.[586]

Eventually, the tunic, for example, became the sticharion, which is common to the three orders of the priesthood, although different in style for each order. The cloak is the basis for the development of the phelonion and the *loros*, a

---

584 Some also include the Vespers of Holy Friday.

585 See Exodus 28 and 29.

586 See Robert Taft, "Byzantine Liturgical Evidence in the Life of St. Marcian the Oeconomos: Concelebration and the Pre-anaphoral Rites," in *OCP* 48 (1982), 159-70. Saint Marcian lived during the reign of Emperor Leo I (457-474) and Patriarch Gennadios (458-471). The *Vita* recounts a miraculous occurrence in the life of St. Marcian which took place on the occasion of the transfer of the holy relics of St. Anastasia (ca. 468-470). Saint Marcian followed the proceedings when he was approached by a beggar. The saint found a quiet place, took off all his clothes, draped himself in a humble cloak, and brought his clothes to the beggar. When the relics were properly deposited in the chapel honoring the saint, the archbishop turned to the saint and invited him "to complete the mystery. He [Marcian] accepting with all zeal, was accomplishing the rite. And at the time of the kiss of peace, washing his hands as is the custom for the priests, he wrapped his *phelonion* [cloak] about himself girding it tightly lest it be seen that he was naked. Now the priests standing by and the archbishop, were surprised to see that he was wearing royal dress under his phelonion. When the prayer of the mystery had been completed and they were partaking of the most pure Communion from his hands, they observed in his hands the apparition of the garments shining through and they did not know what had happened...When the whole service had been completed, and they went to the skeuophylakion, Archbishop Gennadios began to accuse Blessed Marcian saying, "What is this you have done, and gone against the canons? It is not fitting for you to wear the royal attire." But he humbly threw himself down...saying, "Forgive me father, but I did not do any such thing. But he said to him, "all of us saw it, and you deny it?" And he came up and lifted his *phelonion* and found his body to be naked. And thus, discovering by himself the cause, he praised God who shows favor to those who love him and keep his commandments." From this story of the miracle of the clothes, we learn that in the performance of their liturgical duties during the early centuries the clergy did not wear special liturgical vesture.

type of scarf, developed into the deacon's orarion, the priest's epitrachilion, and hierarch's omophorion.[587] Thus, the use of liturgical vesture came to identify particular roles within the worshipping community.

As we shall see, vestments have a symbolic value. They are not meant to create an unbridgeable chasm between the members of the worshipping community. On the contrary, they convey symbolically the nature and purpose of the Christian life and of the priesthood. Though the clergy are set apart from the laity by virtue of their ordination, they are not ontologically different from the people they serve and lead; they do not constitute a separate cast or an isolated entity. They are of the same nature and partake equally of the same salvation wrought by our Lord Jesus Christ. The clergy and the laity together constitute the people of God, the Church.[588]

Vestments define liturgical roles, but they also help the worshipping community discern its high calling. The idea of the sacredness of the liturgy is so ingrained in the Orthodox conscience that no one attends the divine services dressed shabbily or casually, if they can help it.[589] However deep or shallow one's inner awareness or sensitivities may be, everyone senses that you come before God as a new creation clothed appropriately – without frivolity, vanity, or conceit. One's "church clothes," however plain and simple, are perceived as an extension of one's baptismal garment – a vestment or article of clothing that signifies the newness of life in Christ. Modesty, genuineness, and goodness (Phil. 4:5-9) are the hallmark of the Christian life born of faith in the Triune God. These virtues extend to one's physical appearance and behavior inasmuch as they both form and are part of one's identity.

---

587 For a brief account on the development of vestments together with a bibliography see Calivas, *Church, Clergy, Laity, and the Spiritual Life,* 133-135. See also the pertinent articles by Metropolitan Efthimios, Aristides Panotis, Ioannis Fountoulis, and Athanasios Gikas in *Τὰ ἱερά Ἄμφια καὶ ἡ ἐξωτερική περιβολή τοῦ Ὀρθοδήξου Κλήρου,* 25-122.

588 Calivas, *Church, Clergy, Laity, and the Spiritual Life,* 6-10.

589 Cf. Matt. 22: 11-12. The parable of the marriage feast.

Appendix C:2

A Note on the Color of Vestments

Few parishes own vestments. The clergy are expected to make provisions for their own vestments, to purchase them and to take care of them. In time every clergyman will acquire several sets of vestments which they must maintain in good condition.

Besides the sacred vestments proper to each order, every clergyman must have an *exorason* (ἐξώρασον) which is always black in color and a *zostikon* (*anteri* or *esorason*). For public attire the Greek Orthodox Archdiocese of America has designated black or dark suits and clerical shirts with collar.

The Orthodox Church does not adhere to an official color scheme for vestments, except for the ancient practice that they be simple in two basic colors: white and red.[590] Even so, over time several venerable traditions have helped to shape a color scheme for the different liturgical periods of the year and for various feasts. These color schemes are observed today by most clergy, to the degree possible due to financial constraints and other factors.

It is important to note that colors are not neutral. Colors carry meaning and have symbolic value. They influence people's perceptions and create moods. Appropriate colors serve to highlight the distinctive quality of liturgical seasons, feasts, and rites. Colors heighten people's awareness of such things as joy, purity, triumph, glory, sorrow, humility, hope, martyrdom.

The color schemes listed below reflect the usages of two great monastic centers, which are renowned for their rich liturgical traditions and adherence to ancient customs: Mount Athos and the Monastery of St. John the Theologian on the island of Patmos. The listing of colors is for the services of Vespers, Orthros, and the Divine Liturgy. A difference in the color scheme for a given feast or period in the two traditions is noted by the letter **A** (Mt. Athos) and the letter **P** (Patmos).

As I have already noted, inasmuch as the sticharion represents the baptismal garment, it should always be made of a white or a bright colored cloth. In addition, when choosing the material of the vestments, clergy should prefer the beautiful over the gaudy and simplicity over luxuriousness. Costly vestments and accessories are in sharp contrast with the spirit of the priesthood and a source of scandal especially when so many people in the world, even within our own parishes, suffer from want.

---

590 See Konstantinos Kalokyris, *Τὰ Θεαματικὰ Δρώμενα τοῦ Τελετουργικοῦ τῆς Μεγάλης Ἑβδομάδος* (Thessaloniki 2003), 78-96.

Period of the Triodion

a) On the weekdays of Lent, we use vestments whose color is deep reddish purple (mauve), or deep reddish brown, or black.

b) At the service of the Salutations (Χαιρετισμοί), we use red or white (A); or blue (P).

c) On the Saturdays of Lent, we wear red vestments.

d) On the Sundays of Lent, we use white or bright colors (A); or violet or light, bright purple (P).

e) On the Sunday of Orthodoxy, if possible, we wear green (P) vestments.

f) On the Sunday of the Veneration of the Cross, if possible, we wear red velvet or crimson-colored vestments (P).

g) On the Sunday Lenten Vespers, we use the color of vestments noted above in (a).

The Period of Holy Week

a) On the Saturday of Lazarus, we wear white or bright vestments

b) On Palm Sunday, we use white or bright (A) or green (P) vestments.

c) On Holy Monday, Tuesday and Wednesday we wear "Lenten color" vestments.[591]

d) On Holy Thursday (at the Divine Liturgy), we use bright purple or crimson; at the other services purple, mauve, or black.

e) On Holy Friday (at the Great Hours and the Great Vespers), we use purple or black. At the *Epitaphios* service (Orthros of Holy Saturday), we wear bright purple or gold.

f) On Holy Saturday morning (at the Divine Liturgy), we wear white, gold or another bright color.

---

591 Red or purple vestments were used during fast days and Holy Week in the East. In time, the color red which once symbolized the blood of Christ and martyrdom came to be associated with joy. And so purple and mauve became the dominant colors of Holy Week. Black vestments were introduced gradually after the fifteenth century but not universally. The use of black colored vestments originated in the West. The practice was adopted by the Russian Church and by some Greek clergy in lands occupied by the Venetians. See Kalokyris, Τὰ Θεαματικὰ Δρώμενα, 80-2.

The Period of the Pentecostarion

a) For Pascha and all of Renewal Week, we wear white or bright colored vestments (red, gold).

b) For the entire Paschal season, Sundays and weekdays we wear white or a bright color.

c) On the Feast of the Ascension, we wear red or crimson (A).

d) On the Feast of Pentecost, we use white or a bright color (gold, green, red).

The Period of the Octoechos

a) On Sundays and weekdays from Pentecost to September we wear white or bright colors.

b) On Sundays and weekdays from September to the Great Lent we wear chiefly reds (P) or various bright colors (A).

c) On the feasts of saints: red (especially for martyrs) or green (especially for the righteous – ὅσιοι) (A).

c) On Dominical Feasts (Δεσποτικαὶ ἑορταί) we wear white or bright colors (A). On Christmas and the feast of St. Basil we wear gold or another bright color (P). On Theophany and the feast of St. John the Baptist we use blue or green (P).

d) As a general rule on the feasts of the Theotokos (Θεομητορικαὶ ἑορταί) we wear red or blue vestments (A). On the feast of the Entrance (November 21) we use gold or bright color vestments (P).

e) On the feast of the martyrdom of St. John the Baptist (August 29) we wear violet.

Appendix C:3

A Note on the Kingdom of God (Also Called the Kingdom of Heaven):

As Fr. Theodore Stylianopoulos reminds us, God's new and decisive era of salvation broke into the fabric of human history through the ministry of the incarnate Son of God and the gift of the Holy Spirit. "This new reality of salvation and its benefits are expressed in various images and concepts such as "the kingdom of God" in the Synoptic Gospels, or "eternal life" in the Gospel of John, or "justification" and "new creation" in Paul's letters, or "being born anew" in 1 Peter (1:3), or "new covenant" in Hebrews."[592]

We bless and glorify the kingdom of the Triune God – the reality of God's salvation in Christ and the Spirit and its benefits – at the very beginning of the eucharistic celebration because the kingdom of God is made manifest or depicted in the Church and its gifts are shared with and imparted to God's faithful people through the Eucharist in anticipation of the age to come.[593] The kingdom is the locale of God where his uncreated light, his divine energies, shine forth and his righteousness and glory have their dwelling place.

In the Divine Liturgy we experience simultaneously two movements: one from the kingdom, celebrating its presence in worship, and the other toward the kingdom, as we pray, "*Come, Lord Jesus,*" (Rev. 22:20). At the Eucharist, Christ comes to us from the future, from the kingdom: "*Maranatha – Our Lord, come!*" (1 Cor. 16:22). Concurrently, the Church is on its way to the kingdom – on its way to fulfillment and completion, on its way to incorruptibility and deification. The Church lives in active expectation of the Parousia but also in ceaseless remembrance and celebration of the events that brought it into being and that continually form it.

The Church has not yet crossed the ultimate frontier. It is still in the world, gradually reaching completion in accordance with God's plan of salvation. The Church is waiting and preparing for the end time when, at God's command and in an instant, creation as we know it will change; it will pass away only to appear new, transfigured, and imperishable (1 Cor. 15:50-58; 2 Peter 3:10-14).[594] The renewal of creation, however, is not just a future event. It has already begun, realized first in the resurrected, deathless, and glorified body of Christ, of which we partake in Holy Communion at the Eucharist. Indeed, until the end of time, the transformed eucharistic elements – the bread and

---

592 Theodore G. Stylianopoulos, *The Apostolic Gospel* (Brookline, MA 2015), 17; 40-4.

593 For more on the Eucharist and the kingdom see Schmemann, *Eucharist*, 40-8. Also see Philip Zymaris, "The Sacramental Life of the Church: Participation in the Kingdom Here and Now," in *Evangelist, Shepherd, and Teacher*, 353-73.

594 On the image of the world made new see Staniloae, *Fulfillment of Creation*, 149-59

wine changed into the deified Body and Blood of the risen Christ through the prayer of the Church and the action of the Holy Spirit – witness to the coming transfiguration of the cosmos, when, the creative Logos, the Jesus of history, and the Christ of glory will appear as the Lord of the Parousia and of the judgement.[595] The saints are also signs of the coming renewal. Through their saintly lives and deeds, they overcome the temptations and divisive powers of the devil. As instruments of the Spirit, they experience the hidden mysteries of the kingdom in their hearts. Their transformed lives point to the Parousia and the defeat of the devil.

Through the Divine Liturgy the historical community – the Church – is continually actualizing itself, really and effectively, here and now, as the mystical Body of Christ by the power of the Holy Spirit. And where the Holy Spirit is, there is the renewal of creation and the manifestation of that which is to come in power and glory. The Holy Spirit dwells in the Church and in each of its members through his consecrating, sanctifying, and perfecting action. The Holy Spirit is leading the Church and its members toward the heavenly kingdom from which they draw their identity and supplies them with the will and power to shape their personal lives and structure their communal mission and activities accordingly.

From Jesus we learn that the kingdom is a spiritual realm in which we can "enter into" by means of Baptism (John 3:5). The kingdom is not a physical place on earth, or a particular area located somewhere in the sky, but the kingly rule and presence of God encompassing yet transcending the whole universe (John 18:36). The kingdom is beyond time and space; beyond the materiality of the cosmos. Even so, it has appeared on earth in the person of Jesus Christ and made accessible to all who embrace him and his words. "The kingdom of God," Jesus said, "does not come with observation; nor will they say, 'See here!' or 'See there!' For indeed the kingdom of God is within you" (Luke 17:20-21). Or as St. Paul teaches, "the kingdom of God is not food and drink but righteousness and peace and joy in the Holy Spirit" (Rom. 14:17). The kingdom is not a distant place. It is the gracious presence of God within us experienced as a personal new way of being and new manner of relating and doing, as inspired and perfected day by day by the Holy Spirit.

How does one know if the kingdom is within them? Saint Symeon the New Theologian offers the following insight: "As for the signs and proof that [the kingdom] is within anyone they consist in not desiring anything that is visible and subject to corruption, by which I mean the affairs and pleasures of this world...but that one so abstains from all these things that one takes

---

595 See Boris Bobrinskoy, *The Mystery of the Trinity* (Crestwood, NY, 1999), 169.

displeasure at them in soul and will."[596] Saint Symeon also says that the kingdom – the treasure that lies within – can be forfeited and lost through carelessness, idleness, and slackness.[597] In other words, the kingdom is not present in individuals whose heart becomes hard and cold and defiled by vices. The kingdom is present in those who believe and worship rightly; whose heart is aflame with the love of Christ; who conscientiously pursue the moral and ethical demands of the Gospel with humility and joy; who discern right from wrong and bring forth fruits of repentance (Rom. 8:1-13) – each according to their ability.

The kingdom is both a present and a future reality – always present yet always anticipated. It is here now in our midst, as the Scriptures affirm: "The time is fulfilled, and the kingdom of God is at hand. Repent and believe in the gospel" (Mark 1:14; cf. Matt. 10:7-8, 18:20, 28:20). The kingdom burst into the world, inaugurated and established in history through the life, teachings, and mighty acts of the incarnate Son and Word of God, who, by taking on our nature and form, graced humanity and all of creation with supreme worth and value.

The kingdom has not yet come in fullness and glory. "Of that day and hour no one knows, not even the angels, nor the Son, but the Father only... Watch therefore..." (Matt. 24:36, 42). Creation has not yet been delivered from the bondage to decay (Rom. 8:21). The anticipated fullness of the kingdom, while veiled in mystery, is certain to come in glory. "For the Son of Man is to come with his angels in the glory of his Father, and then he will repay every man for what he has done" (Matt. 16:27; cf. Matt. 25:31-32; Rev. 21:1-8). Until then, all we can do is wait in readiness, mindful of the Lord's admonition: "Not everyone who says to me, 'Lord, Lord,' shall enter the kingdom of heaven, but he who does the will of my Father who is in heaven.... Whoever hears these words of mine and does them, I will liken him to a wise man who built his house upon the rock" (Matt. 7:21, 24).

The Gospel of Matthew contains a series of remarkable parables that pertain to the mysteries of the kingdom – God's just rule and reign.[598] The image of the kingdom is startling, unexpected, and even baffling, especially to the indifferent, the proud, the powerful, and the self-righteous of world who are blinded by the lures and false promises spread by the devil, the father of lies. Some, the Lord said, may even draw near to God with their mouth, and honor him with their lips but their heart is far from him and in vain they worship him (Matt. 15:8-9, 19:16-30).

---

596 St. Symeon the New Theologian, *The Discourses*, (II:6), in The Classics of Western Spirituality (Paulist Press, New York 1980), 51. See Matt. 7:19-21.

597 Ibid. IV:15, 87.

598 See, for example, Matt. 13:1-50; 18:21-35; 20:1-16; 21:28-44; 22:1-14, and 25:1-46.

The kingdom of God, Jesus said, belongs not to the haughty and the mighty but to those who have a trusting, loving, and humble heart and love righteousness: "Blessed are the poor in spirit for theirs is the kingdom of heaven" (Matt. 5:3, 10). In another of his sayings, Jesus declared that the kingdom will be shared only with those who are graced with child-like simplicity, guilelessness, and wonder: "Whoever does not receive the kingdom of God like a child shall not enter it" (Luke 18:17). In other words, the kingdom will be inherited by those who, "depend on God as on a father in trustful simplicity." And so, St. Paul, is quick to affirm that whoever is led by the Spirit of God is a child of God and an heir of his glory (Rom. 8:14-17). God's faithful people, his children, experience the kingdom as a gift – a treasury of great blessings which fills life with purpose and meaning.

Jesus also likens the kingdom to a large bountiful and fertile field. Surprisingly, this same field is also filled with thorns, thistles, tares, and weeds (Matt. 13:3-8, 28-30). Similarly, Jesus associates the kingdom with a fishing net that is thrown into the sea and gathers up fish of every kind (Matt. 13:47). What purpose do these images serve? Why the odd mixture of good and bad seeds, of edible and inedible fish? Why does God permit the existence of good and evil together in this age?

Conceivably, because in his lovingkindness God embraces and calls all people to repentance, so that they may experience his unlimited love and forgiveness and come to the knowledge of the truth and be saved (1 Tim. 2:1-4). In other words, everyone is given the chance, if they so desire, as St. Paul teaches, "to work out [their] own salvation with fear and trembling; for God is at work in [them], both to will and to work for his good pleasure" (Phil. 2:12-13). Jesus gives an additional reason. The tares, he said, are sown secretly and deliberately by an enemy of the landowner, in order to destroy the crop of his competitor (Matt. 13:28). Jesus identifies the protagonists in the parable, telling us that the landowner is none other than the Son of Man and the devil is the enemy who plants the tares. He also tells us that the good seed are the sons of the kingdom and the tares the sons of the wicked one (Matt. 13:37-43). The parable suggests the need for awareness! The devil is at work planting weeds trying in vain to subvert and destroy the Church from within by causing scandal, confusion, and division, in order to thwart the mysterious spread and growth of the kingdom.

Before the Second Coming of Christ, the Church, and the kingdom depicted by it, appears in the world as a mixed body. It is both the Church of the redeemed and the Church of wretched sinners – both at once. It is comprised of persons who actively and humbly engage the spiritual warfare and of those other persons who lose their way – the prideful, impervious and unresponsive to the word of God, who trust in themselves that they are righteous and despise others (Luke 18:9-14).

However, at the close of the age, at the Final Judgment, a sorting and sifting by God's agents will take place. (Matt. 13:24-30, 36-43, 47-50). Then the righteous will be separated from the wicked and the impious. The righteous will inherit the kingdom prepared for them from the foundation of the world. The others, the ungodly and ill-prepared who willfully or carelessly give up the fight, will forfeit their place; they will be shut out of the kingdom and cast into the outer darkness, into the everlasting fire prepared for the devil and his angels (Matt. 25:1-46; cf. Rev. 21:1-8).

In this life, Jesus said, no one has the right to usurp divine judgment by condemning others (Matt. 7:1-5). The final judgment belongs to Christ alone because he alone knows the hidden secrets of the mind and heart of every person together with their fatal deficiencies (Luke 16:15; Ps. 7:9). In the time between Christ's two comings, as we await the fullness of the kingdom, God's people fulfill their discipleship best when they show patience and forbearance, prudence in their judgments, are constantly vigilant, perform righteous works of love and mercy, and nurture a humble and welcoming heart.

Equally crucial is an unwavering desire to imitate the limitless goodness and compassion of God who is ready to forgive the debts and sins and transgressions of every repentant sinner. The willingness to both give and accept forgiveness is an indispensable component of discipleship, as Jesus tells us in the parable of the unforgiving servant (Matt. 18:21-35). How can we plead for forgiveness of our sins and transgressions, if we are unwilling or incapable of offering genuine forgiveness to those who trespass against us? Forgiveness, as the parable teaches, is the gateway into the kingdom. The Lord's Prayer is a constant reminder of one's duty to imitate God's boundless compassion by offering forgiveness to others and thereby experience its healing power. "Our Father in heaven... forgive us our debts, as we also have forgiven our debtors; and lead us not into temptation, but deliver us from evil. For yours is the kingdom, and the power, and the glory..." (Matt. 6:9-13).

Jesus also likens the kingdom to a grain of mustard seed and to leaven (Matt. 13:31-33). Just like the tiniest of seeds, the kingdom is unpretentious in its beginnings but destined for enormous and startling growth.[599] And its powers, like leaven, work in a mysterious hidden manner. Again, Jesus likens the kingdom to a hidden treasure and to a pearl of great value (Matt. 7:44-45). Like a powerful irresistible magnet, the kingdom draws to it those who discern, yearn, and struggle hard for spiritual riches, that is, for that which is good,

---

599 See Stylianopoulos, *Apostolic Gospel*, 77-85.

true, honorable, pure, just, and lovely. So great is its appeal, that they struggle valiantly, earnestly, and passionately to acquire it and be worthy of it (Matt. 22:2-14).

Those who belong to Christ behold his glory and are changed into his likeness from one degree of glory to another (2 Cor. 3:18). And apprehending in faith the ineffable mysteries of his kingdom, they are able in the present time to experience what God has prepared for those who love him – that which no eye has seen, nor ear heard, nor the heart of man conceived (1 Cor. 2:9).

In the midst of the anomalies and vagaries of this fallen and broken world, we have been called to seek first God's kingdom and his righteousness (Matt. 6:33; Luke 12:31). The mysteries of the kingdom are central to the Church's faith and worship. They are also the inner motivating power of every devout Christian. And so, we pray daily: "Our Father in heaven, hallowed be Your name. *Your kingdom come*. Your will be done on earth as it is in heaven."

"*Come, Lord Jesus*," bring and grant us your kingdom of light, life, truth, joy, love, goodness, and justice. Amen.

Appendix C:4

What and Where is Heaven?

In the metaphorical language of the Bible and the liturgy, the eternal, uncircumscribed, and infinite God is said to reside in heaven – indeed, in the highest heaven (ἐν τοῖς ὑψίστοις) – where he reigns in unapproachable light and his will is done. In the Divine Liturgy, the word heaven (οὐρανός - οὐρανοί) appears first in the Prayer of Entrance.[600] It will be mentioned several times more but not always with the same meaning. In the Bible, so also in the Divine Liturgy, the word heaven is used to signify one of three things: the physical universe; the dwelling place of God and the angels; and the goal and resting place of the righteous.

In addition to the word heaven, the Divine Liturgy also contains two other related words: ἐπουράνιος – heavenly or celestial, and ὑπερουράνιος – above the heavens. In other liturgical texts we also find the words οὐράνιος – in or of heaven; and οὐρανόθεν – from heaven.[601]

---

600 Earlier, in the second petition of the Great Synapte or Litany, we meet the phrase, "ὑπέρ τῆς ἄνωθεν εἰρήνης – for the peace from above." The adverb ἄνωθεν means from above or from heaven. Similarly, we meet the word τα υψιστα – the highest heaven, as in the angelic hymn: "Δόξα ἐν ὑψίστοις Θεω – Glory to God in the highest..."

601 The angelic host, for example, are called heavenly powers (επουράνιαι δυνάμεις). God is said to rule over the whole of creation, over the celestial and the terrestrial (Σὺ γὰρ μόνος, Κύριε ὁ Θεός ὑμῶν, δεσπόζεις τῶν ἐπουρανίων καὶ τῶν ἐπιγείων). The Holy Mysteries (Holy Communion) are referred to as heavenly Mysteries. We find a similar phrase in the Prayer of the Proskomide in BAS, but with a different meaning. In this instance, the word ουρανια – heavenly refers to the revealed mysteries of the heavenly realms ("You have bestowed on us the revelation of heavenly mysteries – ουρανιων μυστηριων"). The anaphora of BAS also refers to the gifts God bestows as heavenly: "Remember, O Lord, those who bring offerings and do good...and those who remember the poor. Reward them with your rich and heavenly gifts. Grant them in return for earthly things, heavenly gifts; for temporal, eternal; for corruptible, incorruptible." God's holy and mystical altar (τὸ ἅγιον καὶ νοερόν θυσιαστήριον) is also called, ὑπερουράνιον θυσιαστήριον – an altar that is above and beyond the heavens. In the well-known hymn of Pentecost addressed to the Holy Spirit, which doubles as a prayer in the daily office and other services, the Holy Spirit is addressed as, "Heavenly King – Βασιλευ ουρανιε..." In one of the verses of the Great Doxology, God the Father is addressed as "heavenly God – ἐπουράνιε Θεὲ." "Κύριε Βασιλεῦ, ἐπουράνιε Θεὲ, Πάτερ παντοκράτωρ – Lord King, heavenly God, Father almighty..." In the Gospel of John, Jesus proclaims that he is "the living bread which came down from heaven – ἐγώ εἰμι ὁ ἄρτος ὁ ζῶν ὁ ἐκ τοῦ οὐρανοῦ καταβάς" (John 6:51).

In the Prayer of Entrance, the word heaven refers to the abode of the angels, that is, to the kingdom of heaven where the Holy Trinity reigns supreme. In the kingdom the angels are eternally present before God and are bathed in his uncreated light as they behold his divine glory. In this heavenly realm the angelic host hear God's voice, do his will, and bless his holy Name "with unceasing voices and ever resounding praises" (Matt. 18:10; Ps. 102/103:19; Is. 6:3).[602]

In the Symbol of Faith (Creed) – confessed, proclaimed, and prayed reverently at every Divine Liturgy – we find the word heaven three times. It is used in the initial article of the Creed to refer to the cosmos; to the star-filled firmament which appears to the human eye as an immense dome that surrounds the earth. Here, the word heaven (or the heavens) specifies the vast physical universe with its millions of galaxies which God the Father created out of nothing through his Son in the Holy Spirit: "I believe in one God, Father Almighty, Creator of *heaven* and earth, and of all things visible and invisible.... And in one Lord Jesus Christ, the only-begotten Son of God...through whom all things were made.... And in the Holy Spirit, the Lord, the Giver of life..."

The opening words of the Creed remind us of the initial affirmation in the Book of Genesis: "In the beginning God created the *heavens* and the earth" (1:1). Heaven and earth – the cosmos with its myriad wonders and mysteries yet to be fully disclosed – are filled with the glory of God (Trisagion Hymn; cf. Is. 6:1-3). The heavens, as the Psalmist proclaims, "are telling the glory of God; and the firmament proclaims his handiwork" (Ps. 19:1).

---

[602] The anaphora of CHR contains these words: "We thank you also for this liturgy, which you have deigned to receive from our hands, even though thousands of archangels and tens of thousands of angels stand around you, the Cherubim and the Seraphim, six-winged, many eyed, soaring aloft upon their wings, singing the triumphal hymn, exclaiming, proclaiming, and saying, Holy, Holy, Holy, Lord Sabaoth..." BAS contains a longer and more elaborate statement: "Through him {Christ} the Holy Spirit was manifested...through whom every rational and spiritual creature is made capable of worshipping you and giving you eternal glorification, for all things are subject to you. For you are praised by the angels, thrones, dominions, principalities, authorities, powers, and the many-eyed Cherubim. Round about you stand the Seraphim, one with six wings and the other with six winds; with two they cover their faces; with two they cover their feet; with two they fly, crying out to one another with unceasing voices and ever-resounding praises, singing the victory hymn, proclaiming, crying out and saying: Holy, Holy, Holy, Lord Sabaoth..."

The Symbol of Faith also uses the word heaven to denote the dwelling place of God from which the Son and Word of God came down into the world and to which he returned after he fulfilled the Father's divine plan of salvation, having clothed himself with our nature which he mystically deified (John 1:1-18, 6:38-59, 17:1-26).[603] In the Creed we pray and say these words: "For us and for our salvation [the Son of God] came down from *heaven* and was incarnate of the Holy Spirit and the Virgin Mary and became [hu]man...He ascended into *heaven* and is seated at the right hand of the Father." The ascension into heaven is also remembered and proclaimed in the anamnesis of the anaphora of both CHR and BAS. In CHR we read: "Remembering, therefore, this saving command and all that has been done for our sake: the Cross...the Ascension into heaven (τῆς εἰς οὐρανούς ἀναβάσεως), the enthronement at the right hand..."

Here, as in other instances, the word heaven refers to God's holy dwelling place – his kingdom – far above the highest heavens, which is to say beyond the material universe (1 Kings 8:27). The word heaven defines the sacred and transcendent place of the absolutely transcendent and infinite personal God who is above and outside his creation, yet also exists within it through his divine uncreated energies – through his deifying grace and love – so that the world may be saved and transfigured, upbuilding itself in love (John 8:16-25; Ephes. 4:10-16).[604]

St. Paul, who was gifted with a vison of this sacred non-physical place, describes his experience in these terms. "I know a man in Christ who fourteen years ago was caught up to the third heaven – whether in the body or out of the body I do not know, God knows. And I know that this man was caught up into Paradise – whether in the body or out of the body I do not know, God knows – and he heard things that cannot be told, which man may not utter."

---

603 See, for example, the second sticheron of the Vespers of the feast of the Ascension: "God the beginningless, who did exist before all ages and who took man's nature on himself and deified it mystically, was taken up on this day. Hence the angels ran before and did indicate him unto the Apostles as he rose with great glory to heaven's heights. And as they worshipped him, they cried out and said: Glory be to God who was taken up."

He who ascended into heaven is never absent from but always present to his people. At every Divine Liturgy the earthly meet the heavenly. We come before God and he comes to us. It is he who offers us his Holy and Life-giving Gifts, as we affirm in the Communion Prayer: "Lord Jesus Christ, our God, hear us from your holy dwelling place and from the glorious throne of your kingdom. You are enthroned on high with the Father and are also invisibly present among us. Come and sanctify us, and let your pure Body and precious Blood be given to us by your mighty hand and through us to all your people."

604 See Timothy Ware, *The Orthodox Church – New Edition* (Penguin Books, New York and London 1997), 209. Cf. Psalm 138/139:1-18.

Saint Paul had a glimpse of the highest heaven, called Paradise – a place of indescribable blessedness, joy and communion.

The word heaven is also used in the Lord's Prayer twice to denote the immaterial dwelling place of God and to describe the ineffable, awe-inspiring and blessed reality that reigns there.

The Lord's Prayer addresses God as Father, who, as the name implies, is compassionate, merciful, forgiving, gentle, and loving. He is the Father of all and delights in revealing himself to all. He dwells in the highest heaven, in a holy and sacred place of inexpressible beauty, his kingdom. It is a place of light and life. In God's dwelling place, his will is eternally and faithfully accomplished by the angelic host. The frequent recitation of the Lord's Prayer makes us more and more conscious of the realities of God's heavenly kingdom, so that we too may strive to know, conform to and fulfill on earth, both in our personal and communal life, God's will and purposes: "Our Father, in heaven, hallowed be your name. Your kingdom come. Your will be done on earth as it is in heaven…"

However broken and flawed we may be, to fulfill all that is sublime and authentic in our personal embodied existence, we must choose to bear the image of Christ, our archetype and model, our beginning and our end. This process begins with one's conscious, deliberate, and unending effort to conform, by grace, to the will of God: "Your will be done on earth as it is in heaven." By seeking first God's kingdom and his righteousness (Matt. 6:33), we will keep at bay the machinations of the devil and his workers, who prey on us. The clearer the image of Christ is in us, the more aware we become of God's heavenly gifts and perfections in us.

Heaven or Paradise also describes the resting place of the righteous dead (τῶν δικαίων) – their joyful spiritual state in everlasting communion with God. For example, we read in the anaphora of CHR, "You brought us out of nothing into being, and when we had fallen away, you raised us up again. You left nothing undone until you had led us up to heaven and granted us your kingdom, which is to come."

In the ancient prayer for the dead (Ὁ Θεός τῶν πνευμάτων καὶ πάσης σαρκός – O God of spirits and of all flesh) the resting place of the righteous dead is described in vivid language. It is called a bright and shining place – φωτεινόν (a place of light), a verdant place – χλοερόν, and a place of refreshment – ἀνάψυξις, where there is no pain, sorrow, and suffering (cf. Rev. 21:1-4).

Appendix C:5

A word on the Liturgical Homily

Preaching the Word at every Divine Liturgy and sacred service with humility, fervor, conviction, and joy is of paramount importance. Every priest must take to heart St. Paul's admonition to his beloved disciple Timothy: "I charge you in the presence of God and of Christ Jesus who is to judge the living and the dead, and by his appearing and his kingdom: preach the word, be urgent in season and out of season, convince, rebuke, and exhort, be unfailing in patience and in teaching.... Always be steady, endure suffering, do the work of an evangelist, fulfill your ministry" (2 Tim. 4:1-2, 5; cf. 2 Peter 1:12-13).

The natural and most favorable time to offer the sermon is immediately after the readings when the people are mentally, psychologically, spiritually, and even physically open, ready, and eager to hear a meaningful, challenging, persuasive, and edifying message. The people deserve to hear a homily that mines and explains the inexhaustible riches of the Scripture and the doctrines of the faith. A homily also helps the people apply the teachings of the Church to the circumstances of everyday life, thereby helping them to count their blessings and the joys of life. The homily may aid others to build upon and strengthen their faith; and others to overcome their doubts and the hidden fears and anxieties that burden their souls.

Preaching is not an option but an obligation. It is an essential act to be performed with dedication, due care, eagerness, and a joyous, humble heart. The good tidings of salvation must be proclaimed and shared. Saint Paul tells us that "faith comes from hearing, and what is heard comes by the preaching of Christ" (Rom. 10:17). Every sermon is an act of evangelism, a reaching out to those of faith who have need of further assurances, encouragement, and comfort. It is also a reaching out to those who have heard the words of life but have forgotten them but also to those who have never heard them and need to hear them. No opportunity should be lost to tell the story of God's goodness and to recount his manifold blessings and providential love for the world. The heart of the priest should overflow with a godly theme – λόγον ἀγαθόν (Ps. 44/45:1) because of the liberating, transforming and sanctifying power that flows from the Word of God.

As with the prophets of old and the apostles, the clergy are envoys of God, those who have been charged to proclaim the wonders of the Most High; called to be the signs of his presence among his people through the words they speak and the deeds they practice. Though different in temperament and talents, every clergyman must be guided by a common awareness and purpose: to preach the word of God with conviction through words that are their own and yet not their own since what they proclaim are not their thoughts but the truths recorded in the Scriptures and promulgated through the dogmas of the Church, which is "the pillar and bulwark of the truth" (1 Tim. 3:15).

In most churches today the sermon is delayed, placed well after the readings, in order to accommodate the "late comers." However, this only perpetuates bad habits. The priest should encourage the people to be on time to hear the Scriptures. The reason for attending the liturgy on time transcends mere formalities.

The two parts of the Divine Liturgy – Word and Eucharist – were linked together from the start (cf. Luke 24:13-35) because both constitute an act of communion. The bond between Word and Eucharist is indissoluble as the words of the Lord recorded in the Gospel of John (15:3) declare: "*You are already made clean by the word which I have spoken to you. Abide in me, and I in you.*" The word of God penetrates the soul to cleanse it of its impurities making possible our union with Christ, a union which is fully realized in the reception of Holy Communion. God's word has the power to judge, cleanse, liberate, vivify, comfort, encourage, and sanctify.[605]

As St. Paul tells us, "The word of God is living and powerful, and sharper than any two-edged sword, piercing even to the division of soul and spirit, and of joints and of marrow, and is a discerner of thoughts and intents of the heart" (Heb. 4:12). The first part of the Divine Liturgy, the Liturgy of the Word, the proanaphora, is a call to repentance and a cleansing of the soul through the conversion of the heart. It is a preparation for the Eucharist, the Mystery of Holy Communion, "*He who eats my flesh and drinks my blood abides in me and I in him*" (John 6:56).

If, for some good reason, the sermon cannot be delivered after the readings, the priest must find another suitable time, preferably before the distribution of Holy Communion, perhaps after the blessing, "And the mercies of our great God and Savior…"[606] Preaching after the apolysis should be avoided. The sermon is not an independent, extraneous act apart from the liturgy but an integral part of it. The sermon should not be detached from the Divine Liturgy.

---

605 See, for example, Gerasimos Papadopoulos (Bishop of Abydos), *The Gospel of John: A Commentary*, Peter Chamberas, trans. (Brookline, MA 2010), 103-7; 248-50.

606 In many places in Greece, for example, the sermon is delivered just before the people are called to Communion while the clergy are partaking of the Holy Gifts in the sanctuary. However, this practice or one similar to it becomes a distraction for both the clergy and the people. It interrupts the natural flow of the service and interferes with the mental processes of those who are preparing to receive Communion. Others preach after Communion and before the Apolysis. In truth, the most appropriate time for the homily is after the Scripture readings. We should make every effort to maintain this tradition and practice. At every mass, Roman Catholic priests preach after the readings. Can we not do the same?

If the arrangement of the liturgical space allows it, the priest should consider preaching from the ambo or pulpit. The ambo (or ambon) has long been considered a symbol associated with the stone which was rolled away from Christ's tomb on which the angel sat and proclaimed the resurrection to the myrrhbearing women. Preaching from the pulpit serves two purposes. It reminds the priest of his duty to imitate the angel, that is, to be an ardent evangelizer, an inspired herald of the good tidings of salvation. Preaching from the pulpit also underscores the two distinct but inseparable foci of the Divine Liturgy: The Word proclaimed from the ambon and the Holy Eucharist celebrated and received at the Holy Table.

Appendix C:6

On the Catechumenate

In current practice the petitions and prayer for the catechumens are usually said inaudibly by the priest. Most clergy eliminate them altogether because, they argue, the ancient order of the catechumenate has disappeared and there are no catechumens in their parish, except on rare occasions. Hence if no catechumens are present, for whom is the community praying and who is being dismissed from the assembly? In its present form the litany is viewed by some as anachronistic, mere ritual formalism. However, we must not be quick to reject this unit of the service completely. After all, our services are replete with intercessory prayers for various categories of absent members of the community, including the sick, the exiled, and travelers, among others.

Retaining prayers for the catechumens is important for several reasons. First and foremost, prayers for catechumens help highlight an essential activity of the Church, namely, evangelization: "Go into all the world and preach the gospel to the whole creation" (Mark 16:15). Until the Parousia, the Church is always a *church-in-mission*, a spiritual force for renewal and change forming people and their cultures in the direction of God's kingdom, bearing witness to Christ, and engaging all people with the truths and values of the Orthodox faith. Praying for catechumens also helps energize the local parish's interest in and support of the Church's programs on home and foreign missions.

While the Order of the Catechumenate disappeared centuries ago, individual and small groups of catechumens exist all over the world. There are still many people who are being prepared for baptism and admittance into the Church. There are also two other categories of people who are not catechumens in the strict sense of the word but are also hearers of the faith: the converts from other Christian communities and the children of our parishes who have been baptized but who are now being instructed in the faith. Do not all these people deserve the intercessory prayers of the worshipping community, if not every Sunday at least periodically and certainly on major feasts?

With the approval of church authorities, the present anachronistic form of the petitions can be altered to reflect current realities. A version of a new set of petitions may read as follows:

Priest

Let us the faithful, pray for the catechumens who live among us and in other parts of the world. May the Lord have mercy on them; teach them the word of truth; reveal to them the gospel of righteousness; and unite them to his holy, catholic, and apostolic church.

People

Lord, have mercy.

Priest

Let us also pray for our separated brethren, who here and everywhere earnestly seek and desire to be united to the Orthodox Church. May the Lord send forth his Spirit upon them to guide them to the knowledge of the truth; grant that they may truly accept and confess the Orthodox faith and fulfill its precepts joyfully; and number them with God's chosen flock that they may be counted worthy to partake of the holy mysteries.

People

Lord, have mercy.

Priest

Let us also pray for the children of this and every parish who in infancy received the gift of Holy Baptism and are now being taught the truths of our holy faith. May they be diligent in studying God's law and in doing such things as are pleasing to him. May they increase the measure of grace entrusted to them and grow up in every way into Christ our Lord.

People

Lord, have mercy.

Priest

Lord our God, the creator of all, the source of light, and the fountain of wisdom, look upon your servants the catechumens and make them worthy of the laver of regeneration. Be mindful also of your servants, our separated brethren who seek the fullness of your truth, and join them to your holy, catholic, and apostolic Church. Gracious and merciful Lord, who said, "Let the little children come to me, for of such is the kingdom of heaven," we implore you nourish the infants and instruct the young, guarding their hearts and minds. For to you are due all honor and worship, to the Father and the Son, and the Holy Spirit, now and forever and to the ages of ages.

People

Amen.

Appendix C:7

The Eiliton and Antimension

The terms *eiliton* and *antimension* have become synonymous. Originally, the eiliton was a plain linen cloth that was spread on the Holy Table in preparation for the Eucharist.[607] Theodore of Mopsuestia (+428) was the first to attest to its existence and use. He informs us that, in addition to the eucharistic elements, a linen cloth, called the eiliton, was brought and spread on the Holy Table.[608] Before long, the cloth came to symbolize the shroud (burial cloth) in which the crucified dead body of Christ was wrapped (Mark 15:45-46). The eiliton became the forerunner of the *aer* and *epitaphios*, about which we will speak below.

The word *antimension* is derived from the Greek word ἀντί (instead of) and the Latin word *mensa* (table) and means "*in place of the table.*" Originally, the antimension was used as a portable Holy Table or altar. It was made of wood or cloth in the shape of a rectangular parallelogram – a quadrilateral with opposite sides parallel and equal. For practical reasons, the cloth antimensia eventually prevailed over the wooden. Antimensia are known to have existed as early as the eighth century and used in places where there was no church or altar such as army camps and ships and in churches with an unconsecrated Holy Table. Antimensia proved especially useful during the iconoclastic persecutions when the Orthodox had difficulties maintaining secure houses of worship.[609]

---

607 The eiliton is like the Roman Catholic corporal, the linen cloth on which the Gifts are placed.

608 In time, the Holy Table came to be adorned with two cloths: the *katasarkion* (κατασάρκιον) and the *endyte* (ἐνδύτη). The katasarkion is a plain linen cloth. It is fastened permanently to the tablet (slab) of the Holy Table during the consecration ceremonies. Like the eiliton, it symbolizes the shroud of Christ. The *endyte*, on the other hand, is a decorative colored cloth. Each church has several of these cloths in different colors. It is changed periodically to reflect the nature and character of the liturgical season. The Holy Table also has a third cloth, the *antimension* or *eiliton* which is unfolded only when the Divine Liturgy is celebrated. In addition, the Holy Table is adorned with the epitaphios which rests on top of the endyte from the end of the Orthros of Holy and Great Saturday until and including the feast of the Apodosis of Pascha. For more on altar vestments see A. Soteriou, "Τὰ Λειτουργικὰ Ἄμφια τῆς Ὀρθοδόξου Ἐκκλησίας," in Θεολογία, vol. 20 (1949), 603-14. P. Johnstone, *The Byzantine Tradition in Church Embroidery* (London, 1967).

609 On the antimension see the classic work of Januarius M. Izzo, *The Antimension in the Liturgical and Canonical Tradition of the Byzantine and Latin Churches* (Rome 1975). Also see Deacon-Monk Nilos, "Antimension" in *Simonopetra Mount Athos* (ETBA Hellenic Industrial Development Bank SA, 1991), 248-50. Nicon D. Patrinacos, *A Dictionary of Greek Orthodoxy* (New York 1984), 31.

Gradually, antimensia came to be used even on consecrated Holy Tables replacing the eiliton, as is the practice in our own times.[610] Besides its symbolic significance, the antimension serves a practical purpose as well. Particles from the discos are sometimes inadvertently spilled and fall on the antimension from which they can be easily retrieved without loss. The spilled particles are properly collected by the priest and placed in the chalice to be consumed at the prothesis with the remaining portions of the Holy Gifts. The priest should make every effort to keep the antimension free of such particles.

Antimensia are consecrated only by a hierarch, usually when the consecration of a church takes place. After the Holy Table has been ritually washed, it is anointed with the Holy Myrrh or Chrism. The unconsecrated antimensia are spread on the Holy Table to absorb the Holy Chrism and are so consecrated. In times past, a tiny portion of a relic of a saint was also sown into antimensia in imitation of the ancient practice that required the placing relics in a consecrated Holy Table.[611] The practice of placing relics in antimensia is not universally observed today. Antimensia may also be consecrated by a hierarch, as the need arises, with a special service bearing the title, "*Τάξις Γινομένη ἐπὶ Καθιερώσει Ἀντιμινσίων – Order for the Consecration of Antimensia*," which is contained in the *Great Euchologion* Usually, consecrated antimensia bear the name and signature of the consecrating hierarch and the name and place of the church at which they were consecrated to validate their authenticity.

In addition to various inscriptions, antimensia also contain iconographic material which developed over many centuries. Initially, the decorative material, drawn in black ink, was simple.[612] A cross on a stand was placed at the center with the instruments of Christ's Passion on either side (reed with sponge and lance – Matt. 27:48 and John 19:34). Also, the names of the Four Evangelists were written on the four corners.[613]

In time, the iconographic material became more elaborate. The cross retained its central position but remained in the background, incorporated in both of

---

610 To protect the antimension from wear and tear, many priests enclose it within another simple cloth.

611 The placement of relics in Holy Tables came about from the practice of the early church to celebrate the Divine Liturgy over the tomb of martyrs on the anniversary of their martyrdom.

612 In fact, through the centuries, the iconographic material and inscriptions on antimensia have been drawn in black ink with few exceptions. This tradition was broken in recent years with the appearance of antimensia drawn and engraved in colored inks.

613 In rare instances, instead of the names of the Four Evangelists, the words from the Apocalypse (Revelation), "singing, proclaiming, crying out, and saying" were inscribed. See Nilos, "Antimensia," 249. These very same words are said by the priest at the Anaphora when he speaks of the heavenly host singing the Thrice-holy Hymn, "Holy, holy, holy, Lord Sabaoth..."

the two icons which began to appear on antimensia. The first of these icons was the Extreme Humility (Ἄκρα Ταπείνωσις);[614] the other, in a variety of forms, depicted the recumbent dead body of Christ laid out for burial covered with a loincloth, known as the *Epitaphios* (Ἐπιτάφιος).[615] The instruments of the Passion were also included. However, instead of the names of the Evangelists, images of the four living creatures mentioned in Revelations 4:6-8 were drawn on the corners of antimensia. These creatures are associated traditionally with the four Evangelists: angel (Matthew), lion (Mark), ox (Luke), and eagle (John).

From the early eighteenth century, a new icon began to appear on the antimensia: the Ἐπιτάφιος Θρῆνος - *The Epitaphios Lamentation*, which has lasted to our day. The icon depicts the dead body of Christ after the Deposition lying on a draped bier and wearing a loincloth. The earliest versions of the icon include two angels (dressed as deacons) in the background holding *ripidia* or *exapteryga* (liturgical fans). Standing over the figure of Christ lamenting his death, are the Theotokos, St. Mary Magdalene, St. Joseph of Arimathea and St. Nikodemos.[616] Later depictions of the lamentation include additional figures of the Myrrhbearers. The instruments of the Passion were also increased and included the crown of thorns, the cock, and others. The icons of the Four Evangelists replaced the figures of the four living creatures on the corners. Sometimes the evangelists are depicted together with their respective symbolic figure. The creators and engravers of antimensia have, through the years, added various secondary iconographic material and symbolic items to the antimensia. The central icon, however, the *Epitaphios Threnos*, remains intact.

Around the outer border of the antimensia is an inscription, the form of which varies but reads essentially the same: "A divine and sacred altar for the celebration of the Divine Liturgy." The antimension also includes in tiny letters the name of the iconographer and engraver and in larger letters the name of the benefactor who provides and distributes the antimension.[617] In our case, as an Eparchy of the Ecumenical Patriarchate, the Greek Orthodox Archdiocese of America receives its antimensia directly from the Ecumenical Patriarch. The antimensia sent by the patriarchate are unconsecrated. They

---

614 The icon depicts the crucified body of Christ in a vertical position in an open sarcophagus with head bowed and hands folded and the Cross, the instrument of his Passion, in the background.

615 The word *Epitaphios* is from the Greek ἐπιτάφιος (ἐπί + τάφος = on or over a tomb): "Ὁ ἐπὶ τοῦ τάφου Χριστός" or "Ὁ Ἐπιτάφιος Χριστός" – "Christ on the Tomb." In antiquity the word epitaphios was also used to denote a funeral oration.

616 On the burial of Christ see Matt. 27:57-61; Mark 15:42-47; Luke 23:50-56; and John 19:38-42.

617 Since the early nineteenth century, if not earlier, Mount Athos has been an important center for the production of antimensia created by noted iconographers and engravers.

are consecrated by the local hierarch when a church is consecrated. Today, most antimensia in the United States carry the name of Patriarch Bartholomew who was elected and enthroned in 1991. Still in existence and in use are older antimensia that bear the name of his predecessor, Patriarch Demetrios (enthroned in 1973) and, in rare instances, the name of Patriarch Athenagoras (enthroned in 1948).[618]

Every antimension (linen cloth) is encased within another cloth made of silk or some other fabric to protect it from wear and tear. This outer cloth is usually crimson or blue in color. As already noted, the antimension is unfolded only when the Divine Liturgy is celebrated. At all other times it remains folded under the Evangelion at the approximate center of the Holy Table.[619]

---

618 Perhaps, among the liturgical heirlooms of some older parishes one may find an antimension with the name of an earlier patriarch.

619 When refolding an open antimension, the priest first folds the lower part so that it touches directly on the linen cloth. Some antimensia have two folds on the upper part. In this case, first we fold the upper part with one section facing down and the other up. Then we fold the lower part. The right and left sections are folded last.

Appendix C:8

Regarding the command, "The doors, the doors"

In the course of time, as changes occurred in the liturgy and in the composition of the congregation, the original intent and understanding of this and other diaconal commands also changed. Eventually, through monastic influence, the doors of the sanctuary and not the church doors became the object of the command. In Syria during the late fourth century, the sanctuary area began to be concealed, covered by a veil during the celebration of the Eucharist proper.[620] The concealed sanctuary was meant to signify mystery and awe. The Syrian practice gradually spread to other areas and was readily adopted in monastic communities.[621] Eventually, the practice led to the development of the solid iconostasis. To this day, in most, if not all, monasteries and some local churches the Holy Doors are shut after the Great Entrance and often remain closed until the call to Communion.[622]

In effect, the concealed sanctuary in combination with the inaudible recitation of the priestly prayers increasingly modified the role of the laity. From active participants in the service they slowly became bystanders and observers. Happily, however, the practice of the Greek Church has insisted on an open, visible sanctuary – a custom that was established early on at the cathedral

---

620 See Dix, *Shape of the Liturgy*, 480-5. In addition to a veiled sanctuary the Syrian architectural plan included an *exedra* or raised rectangular enclosure in the middle of the nave reserved for the hierarch and the priests and served the same purpose as the synthronon which was located in the apse of the sanctuary in the Constantinopolitan plan. See, Richard Krautheimer, *Early Christian and Byzantine Architecture* (Baltimore, MD 1965), 110. Today, when several hierarchs concelebrate at a Divine Liturgy, chairs are placed in a semicircle in the middle of the nave, one for each hierarch. At the center facing the sanctuary sits the senior hierarch with the others on either side of him according to seniority.

621 The closing of curtains immediately after the Creed in the Byzantine liturgy is first mentioned by Nicholas of Andida (1054-67). He writes, "The shutting of the doors and the closing of the curtain over them, *as they are accustomed to do in monasteries*, and the covering over of the gifts with the so-called aer signifies, I believe, the night on which took place the betrayal of the disciple, the bringing [of Christ] before Caiaphas, the arraignment before Annas, the false testimonies, the mockery, the blows, and the rest…. But when the aer is taken away and the curtain drawn back, and the doors opened, this signifies the dawn on which they led him away and handed him over to Pontius Pilate, the governor." Cited in Thomas Mathews, *The Early Churches of Constantinople: Architecture and Liturgy* (University Park and London 1977), 171. Without doubt, the commentary of Nicholas, an invention of a vivid imagination, is an example of exaggerated, forced forms of liturgical allegory and symbolism which distract the worshipper from what is real.

622 In some Greek churches the Holy Doors are shut only when the clergy receive Holy Communion. This is done mostly for practical reasons, because the preacher is tasked – unfortunately – to deliver the sermon at this time.

church of Hagia Sophia.[623] The solid templon or iconostasis is a strictly medieval development. According to the practice of the GOA, the Holy Doors remain open throughout the entire Divine Liturgy so that the Holy Table and the sanctuary are visible to the people.[624]

Toward the end of the Byzantine era the diaconal command, "The doors...," came to be associated symbolically with the Creed. Let me explain. In places where the closing of the Holy Doors after the Great Entrance took root, a new practice was gradually introduced. The closed doors were opened just before the Creed, in order to signify the people's readiness to receive and confess the Creed. The original command directing that the doors be shut was now reversed to mean that they should be opened.[625] Now, the object of the command had less to do with physical doors and more to do with the "doors" of the human body – namely, the mouth, eyes and ears of the faithful. Called to proclaim the Creed with their mouth and to hear it in the deepest recesses of their minds, the opening of the Holy Doors of the sanctuary supposedly served to remind the people to open the doors of their heart and mind to the fundamental tenets of the faith. It was like saying, "People, open your hearts and minds to the truths of the faith, so that you may increasingly comprehend and live by them."

In his *Commentary*, St. Nicholas Cabasilas adopted this new approach and interpretation of the command, "The doors!" He writes: "Now the priest commands the congregation to proclaim that which they have learned and

---

623 See Mathews, *Early Churches of Constantinople*, 168-9. Mathews makes the following important observation. "References to veils enclosing the sanctuary are numerous in Egypt, Syria, and Pontus from an early date, but in Constantinople not a single mention has been found.... Paul the Silentiary [a court official and author under Justinian I] describes the construction of the *templon* of Hagia Sophia, the number of columns and doors, the parapet slabs of silver, the architrave with its medallions of saints, and the cluster of lamps above; but he does not mention curtains. His description of the sanctuary and its coverings, moreover, implies that it was quite visible to those who stood outside the chancel barrier.... Procopius [a sixth-century court historian] refers to sanctuaries in a number of the churches of Constantinople, but never mentions separating curtains; the characteristic of the sanctuary, according to him, is that it should be inviolable (ἀβέβηλος), or a place which may not be entered. It does not occur to him that it should be unseen (ἀόρατος) or concealed." See also, Rowland J. Mainstone, *Hagia Sophia: Architecture, Structure and Liturgy of Justinian's Great Church* (New York, 1988), 219-22. He also notes: "There is no reason to believe that any veils hung between the arches to hide the altar, so that whatever took place there would have remained fully visible to anyone in the congregation whose view was not otherwise obstructed" (222).

624 In fact, according to an old tradition, the Holy Doors and the north and south doors of the iconostasis are kept open throughout Renewal or Bright Week even when services are not being performed. As already noted above, the same holds true for the Holy Doors during the entire Paschal season.

625 See Taft, *Great Entrance*, 410.

which they believe concerning God…It is in this wisdom that the priest asks us *to open all the doors – that is, our mouths and ears.* Open the doors in this wisdom, proclaiming and listening to these high teachings constantly; not inattentively but eagerly, devoting your minds to it. Then the faithful recite aloud the whole profession of faith, the creed."[626]

Once again, allegorical and symbolic interpretations are at work so that an obsolete, vestigial practice may be salvaged. The command, "The doors…," is reinterpreted in order to maintain its existence in the service. However, the success of symbolic meanings depends largely on the degree to which they are intuitively understood by the people. Forced meanings, however clever they may be, are rarely grasped immediately.

---

626 Cabasilas, *Commentary on the Divine Liturgy*, 26.

Appendix C:9

The Phrase, "Κατὰ πάντα καὶ διὰ πάντα" – What Does it Mean?

What does the phrase «κατὰ πάντα καὶ διὰ πάντα» really mean? Various interpretations, each with a corresponding English translation, have been offered to explain the neuter accusative plural, πάντα–*all*, the object of both prepositions κατά and διά.

As I have noted elsewhere,[627] the first part of the phrase, *"Τὰ σὰ ἐκ τῶν σῶν – Your own of your own"* is taken from 1 Chronicles 29:14.[628] The second part, however, is not sufficiently clear in the Greek original to warrant a definitive translation. As a result, for now at least, the Orthodox Churches in the English-speaking world have yet to settle on a common authoritative translation of the phrase "κατὰ πάντα καὶ διὰ πάντα." The following are some of the translations currently in use or which have been put forth for consideration: "In all and for all;" "In all places and for all that you have done for us;" "In (or On) behalf of all and for all;" "According to all and for all;" "In all things and for all things;" "At all times and in all places;" "In all places and at all times;" "Always and everywhere;" and "Always and for all."[629]

The translations which relate the offering of the Eucharist to time and place are based chiefly on three texts, the prophecy of Malachi 1:11; the Didache 14:2 and 1 Tim. 2:8. In Malachi we read, "*In all places* incense is offered in his name, and a pure offering." Early Christian writers connected these words to the eucharistic sacrifice or the sacrifice of the cross. The *Didache* contains these words, "For it was of this sacrifice [the Eucharist] that the Lord said, '*In all places and all times* they will offer me a pure sacrifice." We meet similar phraseology in 1 Timothy 2:8. "I desire then that *in every place* the men should pray, lifting holy hands without anger or quarreling." The reference to time and place as it relates to the Eucharist is also emphasized in the first Prayer of the Faithful in CHR: "By the power of your Holy Spirit, make us...able to call upon you *at every time and place (ἐν παντὶ καιρῷ καὶ τόπῳ)*, so that, hearing us, you may be merciful to us in the abundance of your goodness."

However, despite the evidence contained in these sources, the problem remains unresolved. In each of the four texts we find the preposition *ἐν (in)*, while the liturgical text has two different prepositions, *κατά* and *διά*. Despite this difference, the phrase, "At all times and in all places" or its equivalent, may yet be the preferred translation. Unlike the sacrifices of the Old Testament

---

627 See Calivas, *Aspects of Orthodox Worship* 218-22.

628 In the Septuagint: *Παραλειπομένων Α΄, 29:14: "Ὅτι σὰ τὰ πάντα, καὶ ἐκ τῶν σῶν δεδώκαμέν σοι."*

629 *Ibid.* 281-2: notes 418-24.

that were localized in one place, the temple in Jerusalem, the Christian eucharistic sacrifice is offered everywhere, in all places. And the reality which the sacrament renders present is the same every time.

From another perspective, it can be shown that the phrase *"κατὰ πάντα καὶ διὰ πάντα,"* was connected originally to the sacrifice of praise *(Σὲ ὑμνοῦμεν)* and not to the preceding pronouncement *(Τὰ σὰ ἐκ τῶν σῶν)*. This being the case, the prayer would read as follows: "Remembering, therefore, this saving commandment and all that has been done for our sake: the cross, the tomb, the resurrection on the third day, the ascension into heaven, the enthronement at the right hand, and the second and glorious coming, and offering to you your own of your own, *always and everywhere* we praise you, we bless you, we give thanks to you, and we pray to you, Lord our God... Send down your Holy Spirit upon us and upon the Gifts here presented..."

Appendix C:10

The meaning of sacrifice

The Church has a radically new and different understanding of sacrifice. The initiative for sacrifice is not with us but with God who continually offers himself to us. At the Eucharist we commune the Gift of the Father, his incarnate Word and Son, who, through the cross, "gave himself as a ransom to death, in which we were held captive, sold under sin" (BAS). This does not suggest that the Eucharist attempts to reclaim past events; it does not repeat what is unique and unrepeatable. Christ is not slain anew and repeatedly at every Eucharist, for he died *once for all* – ἐφάπαξ (Heb. 7:27; 9:24-28; 10:12). Ours is a spiritual worship without the shedding of blood.

At each Eucharist the Holy Spirit changes the offering of the Church, the bread and wine, into a reality that remains constant, the Body of Christ that was sacrificed once for all and now lives in glory. The Eucharist is neither a mere representation nor a simple memorial of the sacrifice of the Cross. The eucharistic elements are changed concretely and really into the Body and Blood of the Lamb of God, the crucified and risen Christ, who freely sacrificed himself for our sake.

At the Eucharist we come to recognize that what we offer is not something of ours at all, but that which is the Father's already: the *kenosis* or sacrifice of his Only-begotten Son. In the Eucharist we experience the eternal priesthood of Christ, the God-Man (Θεάνθρωπος), whose sacrifice is being eternally celebrated upon the altar in heaven (Rev. 5:6-14). As the great High Priest and Intercessor, Christ, the God-Man, continues in a state of sacrifice before the Father, making intercession on our behalf and uniting our prayers within his (Heb. 7:24-25; 9:24). But Christ who is enthroned on high with the Father is also invisibly present with us at every Eucharist that he may share his life with us – to abide in us and we in him by partaking of his Body and Blood (John 6:56-57). The consecrated Gifts are indeed his own risen and glorified Body which died once for our sake and now lives and reigns (Heb 10:12; Rev. 1:18). At the Eucharist we come to realize that the altar of God is always a table of communion and life (cf. Exodus 24:8-11).[630]

Saint Symeon the New Theologian expresses this truth in dramatic fashion saying: "How do you deem worthy to be seen and to let me behold you; to allow yourself to be held in my hands, you who hold all things, you whom all the hosts of heaven cannot contemplate, inaccessible even to Moses, the first of the prophets. For he was not found worthy to see your face, nor was

---

[630] Note the words in the Prayer of the Cherubic Hymn common to both Divine Liturgies: "For you, Christ our God, are the Offerer and the Offered, the One who receives and is distributed…"

any other man, lest he should die. How am I judged worthy to hold you, to love you, to see and to eat you, to have you in my heart, O Christ? You are the only incomprehensible, the only inexpressible, the One no one can contain, inaccessible to all. Why am I not consumed? Torn as I am between joy and fear, why do I sing your immense love for man, O Christ?"[631]

In response to Christ's unique offering, the Church also offers a sacrifice. First, the sacrifice we offer is not an act of appeasement, but an *offering given in return*, an *antiprosphora* – ἀντιπροσφορά on account of God's great goodness and mercy. In the final analysis, our offering in return can only be Christ himself, whose saving work remains constant and immediate for every generation in every place, until he comes again.

Second, our sacrifice is an offering of praise and thanksgiving: *"We praise you, we bless you, we give thanks to you…"* In BAS, for example, we pray the words: "By the power of your Holy Spirit enable us also to perform this service; so that standing blamelessly before your holy glory, we may offer you a sacrifice of praise…. May our sacrifice be acceptable and well-pleasing in your sight, O Lord, for our sins and the errors of all your people" (Second Prayer of the Faithful).

Third, the Eucharist brings us before the unutterable mystery of the Father's inscrutable initiative and love: the offering of his Son in the Holy Spirit for the salvation and life of the world. (John 3:16). In the Eucharist we experience and enact for ourselves the mystery of Christ's *kenosis* (Phil. 2:5-11). Hence, at its deepest level our *antiprosphora*, our offering in return, is an act of *kenosis*, a willingness to lose our life in order to gain it (Luke 9:23-24). Through this self-emptying or self-offering, we acknowledge our complete dependence on God, *"Your own of your own."* We come to realize that nothing of ours is our own, even life itself, considering that God alone has life in himself. Through the bread and wine – the unique human food – the appropriate symbols of our mortal life, we offer up our life in exchange for Christ's life, which is granted to us in and through the consecrated eucharistic elements.

---

631 St. Symeon the New Theologian, *Hymn 19*: 21-32, in Archbishop Basil Krivocheine, *In the Light of Christ: St. Symeon the New Theologian* (Crestwood, NY 1986), 123. In chapter VII of this volume, the author sets forth the teachings of St. Symeon on the Holy Eucharist, 103-23.

Appendix C:11

A Note on the Common Communion Spoon:[632]

Liturgical spoons have existed from at least the sixth-seventh century.[633] But this does not mean that they were used for Communion. In fact, canon 101 of the *Penthekte* Synod (691-692) prohibits the use of any receptacle for the reception of the consecrated Bread other than the human hand.[634] The canon reads: "So that if anyone should wish to partake of the pure Body during the time of the *synaxis*...let him form his hands into the shape of a cross, and thus approaching, let him receive the communion of grace.... For we nowise welcome those men who make certain receptacles out of gold or any other material to serve instead of their hands for the reception of the divine gift."[635]

Before the eleventh/twelfth century everyone, clergy and people alike, received the Holy Gifts separately, in the manner the clergy do to this day. When the people approached, they extended their hands, right over left with palms open, on which the priest placed a portion of the Holy Bread. After consuming the Bread, the communicants were offered the Chalice by the deacon.[636]

---

632 This note, written in a period of historical importance, appeared in the *Orthodox Observer* and in *Orthodoxia.info* on May 25, 2020. It is also included in the volume, *The Church in a Period of Pandemic: Can the Present Pandemic Crisis Become a Meaningful Storm for Renewal in our Churches?* Petros Vassiliadis and George Demacopoulos, eds., (Thessaloniki 2020), chapter 9.

633 The early communion spoons (λαβίς or κοχλιάριον) were larger and deeper than those we use today. On the history of the communion spoon see Robert F. Taft, "Byzantine Communion Spoons: A Review of the Evidence," in *Dumbarton Oaks Papers* (*DOP*), vol. 50 (1996), 209-38; and Taft, *Communion,* 266-306. Also see, Panagiotis Skaltsis, "'Ο Τρόπος Κοινωνίας" in www.Orthodoxia.info (June 14, 2020) and Nicholas Dassouras, "From One Spoon to Many," in *Public Orthodoxy*, the online publication of the Orthodox Christian Studies Center of Fordham University (August 4, 2020).

634 On the Penthekte Synod and liturgical reforms see Calivas, *Aspects of Orthodox* Worship, 227-34.

635 *Pedalion/Rudder*, 408

636 See, for example, the description in Cyril of Jerusalem, *Mystagogical Catechesis*, V: 21, 22.

The first clear evidence for the use of communion spoons appeared in the eleventh and twelfth centuries. As we learn from the noted canonist Theodore Balsamon (+ca. 1195), the common spoon had become the established norm in many places by the mid-twelfth century. Commenting on Canon 101 of the *Penthekte* Synod, he complained that the traditional way of distributing communion was being abandoned in some areas.[637]

Centuries later, in a comment on the same canon, St. Nikodemos (+1809) suggests that the introduction of the communion spoon came about as a result of the scarcity of deacons. By the late twelfth century many churches were served by a single priest, which made the administration of the eucharistic elements separately both awkward and difficult. The problem was solved with the introduction of the spoon. The priest was now able to offer the eucharistic elements together in a spoon. In addition, St. Nikodemos tells us that the placement of the Holy Gifts directly into the mouth of communicants helped to curb abuses and avoid spillage when drinking from the Chalice. Evidently, some people were careless and dropped particles of the Holy Bread. Others hid it and "used it for wicked purposes."[638]

The use of the communion spoon was not enacted by a synod, ecumenical or local. Its use came about gradually. Initially, the spoon may have been used to commune children, the sick and the dying. At first, as one would expect, its use in the liturgy met with some resistance, as any significant liturgical innovation would. Replacing the centuries-old manner of receiving the consecrated Holy Gifts separately, based on the biblical model, was not easy. However, new pastoral needs made the use of the spoon inevitable. In the final analysis, the spoon was accepted, even reluctantly, because it did not violate, contradict, or compromise any doctrinal teachings.

---

637 See Rallis and Potlis, *Οἱ Θεῖοι κὰι Ἱεροὶ Κανόνες*, vol. 2, 548. Earlier, Cardinal Humbert of Silva Candida, the papal legate and leading figure in the azyme controversy which lead to the Schism of 1054, accused the Eastern Church of innovation: "Next, what are you representing where, by custom, you take up with a spoon the holy bread of life eternal that has been in the cup?" (PL 143: 951A), cited in Mahlon H. Smith, *And Taking Bread...Cerularius and the Azyme Controversy of 1054* (Paris, 1978), 150, (note 230)

638 *Pedalion/Rudder*, 410.

The method by which communion is administered is purely functional. It serves a practical purpose. Thus, as warranted by needs and circumstances, a local Church in its collective wisdom and authority is free to adapt, modify, and manage the method by which Holy Communion is distributed. Whatever method a Church chooses, the single most important concern is that it does not violate any dogmas and that it is appropriate; that it upholds and maintains the dignity of the sacred act of communing.

We learn from St. Nikodemos that during plagues priests were known to use arbitrary methods to administer communion to the sick and dying.[639] In a comment on Canon 28 of the *Penthekte* Synod, he chides the clergy for using unsuitable methods to deliver Communion to the sick. He recommends a more appropriate method. He writes: "Hence, both priests and prelates must employ some shift in time of a plague to enable them to administer Communion to the sick without violating this canon; not, however, by placing the Holy Bread in currants, but in some sacred vessel, so that the dying and the sick may take it thence with tongs or the like. The vessel and the tongs are to be placed in vinegar, and the vinegar is to be poured into a funnel, or in any other manner that they can that is safer and canonical."[640]

Saint Nikodemos' brief note is significant in two ways. First, he insists the vessels used for Communion be sterilized with vinegar, a popular disinfectant from ancient times. This is an acknowledgment that the vessels or instruments used for communing could be contaminated by dangerous parasitic microbes. Second, he insists that the instrument be fitting for the purpose.

---

639 To my knowledge, no one has yet undertaken a thorough examination of the historical record to ascertain how the Church handled various pastoral needs – especially the distribution of Communion – in times of major epidemics and other crises which effected societal and ecclesial norms. In such instances, did the long-standing custom of infrequent Communion play a role? Was it a mitigating factor? The lengthy burial services in the *Great Euchologion* were being abbreviated in Constantinople and other large cities during the mid-seventeenth century because of the great number of deaths due to epidemics. See Fountoulis, Τελετουργικὰ Θέματα, 157-60. What other changes and concessions has the Church made in times of crises?

640 *Pedalion/Rudder*, 322 (note). The note may well be the work of an annotator. Nonetheless, the fact that the Holy Synod of the Ecumenical Patriarchate officially recognized the canonical authority of the *Pedalion/Rudder* gives the note as much weight as if it were written by St. Nikodemos himself. We know that Dorotheos Voulismas, an ardent conservative eighteenth-century churchman, was appointed by the Synod of the Ecumenical Patriarchate to review and examine critically a copy of the manuscript of the *Pedalion/Rudder* submitted to the patriarchate to secure its approval for publication.

In the past forty years several worldwide deadly epidemics, AIDS, SARS, Ebola, and MERS provoked fear among the people. Presently (2020), the world is experiencing another more frightening global threat: the pandemic coronavirus or COVID-19, a contagion with lethal force which has upended all social, economic, political, cultural, and religious norms. People are justly apprehensive and frightened. The disease has already infected millions of people and claimed the lives of thousands globally. As with the preceding epidemics, the highly contagious coronavirus has many people wondering and questioning the continued use of a common spoon for Communion.

The real fears, reservations, and apprehensions of the people should not be dismissed with an air of superiority or a call to greater faith, as if the act of communing is void of human considerations and the limitations of the created order. People want to feel safe, listened to, and protected by their Church. They do not want to be exposed to unnecessary risks, nor should they be.

Statements like, "the Eucharist is the Body and Blood of Christ, and the medicine of immortality," or "the Eucharist is a divine remedy, a divine medicine," may be true. But they are not sufficient to calm the fears and concerns of the faithful. People are not questioning the sacred character and identity of the Holy Gifts but the reliability of the instrument by which they are offered to them.

In my sixty-four years in the priesthood, I have consumed the chalice thousands of times after countless Divine Liturgies without fear or hesitation, as every priest does. I am not certain, however, that every faithful parishioner would do the same, if they were asked. My point is this. Holy Communion should be a source of joy, hope and strength for everyone and not a test or measure of one's faith in God's providential care (cf. Matt. 4:5-7). Saint Paul reminds us that the love of Christ requires that we care for all persons, whatever their situation and be sensitive and responsive to their just needs and concerns for the sake of the Gospel (1 Cor. 9: 19-23).

Orthodox sacramental theology, distinguishes between what is mystical and what is physical. The divine realities in each sacrament are distinct from the material elements by which they are mediated. We believe and confess that the Eucharistic Gifts – the bread and wine – are changed into the Body and Blood of Christ through the prayer of the Church and the power and operation of the Holy Spirit. The change, however, is mystical and not physical. The bread and wine preserve their natural properties and qualities and are bound to the natural laws of their kind.⁶⁴¹ The mode by which the transformation of the Gifts takes place remains a profound mystery. But we know by faith that the change occurs so that Christ may become our food in order to impart his life to us (John 6:56).

The communion spoon is an imperfect material instrument. It does not share in the incorruptibility of the risen and deified Body of Christ which is really present to us through the eucharistic elements. On its own, the spoon is simply a spoon, a utensil. Its dignity is derived from its use as the instrument by which the Body and Blood of Christ is offered to his people. Long ago it replaced another venerable form of communing. It was itself an innovation.

The very thought of replacing the common spoon has caused great anxiety in some circles. There are those among the clergy and the laity who see the replacement of the common spoon or any other kind of departure from the current practice as a repudiation of the doctrine of the real presence of Christ in the Eucharist. Of course, this is not true.

---

641 This is in keeping with the dogmatic definition of the Fourth Ecumenical Synod of Chalcedon: "Therefore, following the holy fathers, all of us teach unanimously that everyone must confess that our Lord Jesus Christ is one single and same Son, who is perfect according to divinity and perfect according to humanity, truly God and truly man...consubstantial with the Father according to divinity and consubstantial with us according to humanity, completely like us except for sin; He was begotten by the Father before all ages according to his divinity and, in these latter days, He was born for us and our salvation of Mary the Virgin, the Theotokos according to His humanity; one single and same Christ, Son, Lord, only begotten, known in two natures, without confusion, without change, without, division, without separation (ἀσυγχύτως, ἀτρέπτως, ἀδιαιρέτως, ἀχωρίστως); the difference of nature is in no way suppressed by their union, but rather the properties of each are retained and united in one single person (πρόσωπον) and single hypostasis (ὑπόστασις)..." In Archbishop Peter L'Huillier, *The Church of the Ancient Councils* (Crestwood, NY 1996), 194.

Two examples will illustrate that the natural properties of the bread and wine are retained. Persons who suffer from a severe form of celiac disease, an auto-immune disorder, react badly when they ingest gluten, a protein in wheat, barley, rye and other grains, from which most prosphora are made. These persons often request that they be give the tiniest morsel of the consecrated Bread for fear of a bad reaction. Newly-ordained clergy, who are not used to drinking alcoholic beverages, often have difficulty consuming and purifying the Chalice after the Divine Liturgy on an empty stomach. Even more to the point, the Reserved Sacrament which is traditionally prepared and consecrated every Holy Thursday is handled in a special way. After it has dried thoroughly, it is separated into small pieces and placed under or over fire (heat). This is done to help preserve it.

In response to the present deadly pandemic, three local Churches have instituted changes in the manner by which Holy Communion is distributed.[642] Circumstances require that every local Church study the issue carefully taking into consideration the cultural and hygienic sensibilities of the people and the sanitary measures and protocols of their respective nations.

The Church of Russia has introduced a small but significant change in the traditional manner of administering Communion, which appears to be based on the model suggested by St. Nikodemos. The common communion spoon is dipped in alcohol and wiped clean after each communicant. The Church of Romania has considered, among other possibilities, allowing people to bring their own spoon from home. In Ukraine, Communion is distributed via intinction – a portion of the Bread is dipped in the chalice and placed by the priest in the hand of the communicant.

In addition to these, several other models have been proposed. Some who wish to retain the common spoon believe it is sufficient to teach the communicants to tilt their head back and open their mouth wide, so that the priest may drop or pour the sacred elements into the mouth of the recipient. The aim of this method is to avoid touching the communicant's mouth and lips. However, this model is not fail-safe; it does not guarantee the desired outcome. Another suggestion, close to the Romanian model, allows each family to bring its own "family communion spoon" which will be used to commune family members only. This model, however, runs counter to the spirit of Canon 101 of the *Penthekte* Synod which prohibits the use of private vessels for fear that they would lead to social distinctions and the like. Communion, as has been already noted, is both a personal and a communal act. "Unite us all to one another who become partakers of the one Bread and the Cup" (BAS). The Ukrainian model, Communion by intinction, has found support in some quarters. It is a version of the ancient practice. However, it is difficult to manage on several counts, the most obvious being communing the elderly, disabled, and children.

Another model calls for the replacement of the common spoon with multiple individual spoons; spoons made with common material and of equal value, which each local parish provides. According to this model, each parish will obtain (perhaps from a common source) a sufficient number of disposable spoons made of plastic or wood. Once used, each spoon would be collected

---

[642] See the important article by Nicholas Denysenko, "Do Sacraments Prevent Illness?" in *Public Orthodoxy* (March 19, 2020).

and properly discarded (burned or buried) after each liturgy.

Or, each parish procures a sufficient number of reusable metal spoons (stainless steel) from a common source. The used spoons are collected and properly sterilized after each Liturgy and are reused multiple times.

Each of these methods shares a common goal: to administer Communion in the safest, most practical, and most dignified way possible. Whatever the model, the fundamental intent is the same: to mitigate the transmission of dangerous parasitic microbes. Of the several methods, the use of multiple metal reusable spoons seems to be the safest and more practical, and the one closest to the received tradition.

Also, of concern is the common communion cloth, which many people use to wipe their mouth after communing. This practice is problematic and must end. The common cloth should serve only one purpose, to catch any accidental spillage when administering Communion. A group of people, altar servers and regular church goers, should be trained to hold the cloth properly as each communicant approaches. The use of personal disposable paper napkins has also been suggested. The napkin is placed in a special basket after each use, and then burned. This may not be as simple as it appears.

On June 25, 2020 the Ecumenical Patriarchate issued the following statement on the mode of distribution of Holy Communion.

> The Mystery of the Divine Eucharist is non-negotiable, because we believe that through it the Body and Blood of the Savior Christ is transmitted to the faithful "unto the remission of sins and life eternal" and it is impossible that through this Mystery of Mysteries any disease might be communicated to those who partake. For this reason, the Church remains steadfast and immovable in its teaching towards the essence of the Mystery of Christ. As to the mode of distributing the ineffable Mystery to the faithful, the Church, respecting Holy Tradition that is interwoven inextricably with the daily ecclesial practice and kenotic experience, and as the guardian and vigilant watchman of those traditions handed down from the Holy Fathers, finds no need for change of this mode, especially under pressure from external factors. At the same time, the Mother Church, mindful of the special needs of her children in the diaspora, urges the Chief Shepherds who serve in the diaspora that with a pastoral sensitivity, responsibility, and consciousness, to temporarily make by *economia*, accommodations to problematic situations that arise from local laws of the state for the greater spiritual benefit of the Christian people, always in coordination with the sacred center of the Phanar.

No one knows what the future will bring. Even now, in the United States as the churches are being re-opened according to strict protocols and guidelines the "traditional mode of communing" has in many places been modified. Communicants are told to tilt their heads back and open their mouths wide so that the priest may drop the Holy Gifts into their mouth using the common spoon. They are not to touch the spoon or wipe their mouth on the communion cloth; and the antidoron after Communion is no longer available or is distributed with a tong by a server wearing gloves. In most instances, the priest who is communing the people wears a mask. A change in the manner by which Communion is distributed will be coming, perhaps not now but at some point, in the foreseeable future. It is important, therefore, that everyone – clergy and people alike – are properly prepared.

Appendix C:12

What does God's Inheritance—Κληρονομία mean?

The verse "God's inheritance" reminds us that we are God's possession, his own people. Cabasilas explains the mystery like this. "Now, inheritance is a far closer relationship than creation. The Son, in inheriting us, possess us far more highly and excellently than he did by creating us. Through creation, he had dominion over man's nature; through inheritance he has become Lord of our minds and wills, and that is true dominion.... But how did he, by inheritance become the Lord of our minds and wills? In this way: we subjected them to him who came down on earth, who was crucified and rose from the dead; we submitted our minds in recognizing him as true God and sovereign Lord of every creature; we submitted our wills in giving him our love, accepting his rule, and taking his yoke upon our shoulders with joy. That is how God took perfect possession of humankind and truly acquired us; it was this possession that the Prophet Isaiah desired so long ago when he said, 'O Lord our God, possess us' (26:13). This is the inheritance which the Scriptures tell us that the Only-Begotten received from his Father, and which we recall in this prayer."[643]

This lovely passage indicates clearly that Christ possess no one by force (Mark 8:34), but by the power of his love, the might of his truth, and the attractiveness of his beauty. He possesses us only because we freely submit our minds and wills to him in response to his call. We choose to come under his rule. We accept his yoke gladly and give him our love and devotion.

Father Georges Florovsky explains this truth as follows. "The first followers of Jesus in the "days of his flesh," were not isolated individuals engaged in their private quest for truth. They were Israelites, regular members of an established and instituted community of the "chosen people" of God.... A church already existed when Jesus began his ministry. It was Israel, the People of the Covenant.... The community which Jesus had gathered around himself was, in fact, the faithful *"Remnant"* of Israel, a reconstituted People of God. Each person had to respond individually by an act of personal faith This personal commitment of faith incorporated the believer into the community. And this remained forever the pattern of Christian existence: one should believe and confess, and then he is baptized into the Body."[644]

In the Old Testament we read that out of all the peoples of the earth, God set his heart on Israel (Deut. 7:6). To the angels God delegated authority to

---

643 Cabasilas, *Commentary*, 4:40.

644 Georges Florovsky, "Worship and Everyday Life: An Eastern Orthodox View," in *Studia Patristica*, vol. 2 (1963), 266. The article was later reproduced and circulated in pamphlet form with the same title.

rule other nations. But Israel became his portion, his allotted heritage, his chosen people, whom "he found in a desert land…and encircled him and cared for him and kept him as the apple of his eye" (Deut. 32:8-10). With Israel he established a covenantal relationship (Deut. 5:20, 31), which Christ fulfilled through his saving work.

The Church is the New Israel and her faithful members are God's people. Those who live by the Spirit are the inheritance, "chosen by God and precious" (John 17:1-26; 1 Peter 2:1-9). The Church is the eternal witness of the Triune God and the sacrament of his love; the sign and herald of his kingdom in the midst of the contradictions and anomalies of the fallen world. The Church is the house of all, the universal community where the people of the earth find salvation. And so, the Church, Christ's Mystical Body, is the continuation and fulfillment of the covenant and the inheritance of God.

The exclamation, "Save, O God, your people and bless your inheritance," invites us to ponder humbly the magnitude and the splendor of God's love for the Church and for every one of its faithful members. We must ponder the awesome gift God has bestowed upon us and be joyful. We are God's people, his inheritance, the apple of his eye, the object of his love.

Think of the tremendous responsibility we have, both as persons and as community, to be faithful stewards of the precious and wondrous gift we have received, but also willing, able, and committed to sharing this treasured gift with others. Father George Papademetriou expresses this mission of the Church and her faithful members in these words: "The understanding of the [Church] as God's people does not mean a naturalistic particularism…. The Scriptures do not intend to promote a racist view of the people of God, but rather, to draw attention to the universal mission of the [Church] as the people called by God to promote holiness and show forth the way by which salvation might be found."[645]

---

[645] George C. Papademetriou, *Orthodox Christian Views of Other Religions* (Boston, 2019), 66-7. On the relationship between Biblical Israel and the Church see Demetrios E. Tonias, "Fulfillment in Continuity: The Orthodox Christian Theology of Biblical Israel," in *Review of Ecumenical Studies*, vol. 11 (2/2019), 209-36. For more on the Church in the public sphere, ecumenical relations, human rights, and its engagement with the world see the recently published pioneering document, *For the Life of the World: Toward a Social Ethos of the Orthodox Church*, David Bentley Hart and John Chryssavgis, editors (Brookline, MA 2020).

www.ingramcontent.com/pod-product-compliance
Lightning Source LLC
Chambersburg PA
CBHW080955130426
PP18130700002B/12